3rd edition

Marketing Theory

a student text

edited by

MICHAEL J. BAKER &
MICHAEL SAREN

Los Angeles | London | New Delhi
Singapore | Washington DC | Melbourne

Los Angeles | London | New Delhi
Singapore | Washington DC | Melbourne

SAGE Publications Ltd
1 Oliver's Yard
55 City Road
London EC1Y 1SP

SAGE Publications Inc.
2455 Teller Road
Thousand Oaks, California 91320

SAGE Publications India Pvt Ltd
B 1/I 1 Mohan Cooperative Industrial Area
Mathura Road
New Delhi 110 044

SAGE Publications Asia-Pacific Pte Ltd
3 Church Street
#10-04 Samsung Hub
Singapore 049483

Editor: Matthew Waters
Editorial assistant: Lyndsay Aitken
Production editor: Sarah Cooke
Copyeditor: Jane Fricker
Proofreader: Lynda Watson
Indexer: Elizabeth Ball
Marketing manager: Alison Borg
Cover design: Francis Kenney
Typeset by: C&M Digitals (P) Ltd, Chennai, India
Printed and bound in Great Britain
by Ashford Colour Press Ltd

© Michael J. Baker and Michael Saren 2016

First edition published by Cengage in 2000
Second edition published by SAGE in 2010
Reprinted in 2013
This third edition published 2016

Preface and editorial arrangement © Michael J. Baker and Michael Saren 2016 Chapter 1 © Michael J. Baker 2016 Chapter 2 © Michael Saren 2016 Chapter 3 © D.G. Brian Jones and Mark Tadajewski 2016 Chapter 4 © Patrick E. Murphy and Kelly D. Martin 2016 Chapter 5 © Richard J. Varey 2016 Chapter 6 © Allan J. Kimmel 2010 Chapter 7 © Kjell Grønhaug and Ingeborg Astrid Kleppe 2016 Chapter 8 © Kam-hon Lee and Cass Shum 2010 Chapter 9 © Walter van Waterschoot, Thomas Foscht, Marion Brandstaetter and Andreas B. Eisingerich 2016 Chapter 10 © Robin Wensley 2010 Chapter 11 © Sally Dibb and Lyndon Simkin 2016 Chapter 12 © Margaret K. Hogg and Rob Lawson 2016 Chapter 13 © Julia Wolny 2016 Chapter 14 © Mark S. Glynn and Roderick J. Brodie 2016 Chapter 15 © Susan Hart 2016 Chapter 16 © Kristian Möller 2016 Chapter 17 © Christopher Moore and Stephen Doyle 2016 Chapter 18 © Evert Gummesson 2016 Chapter 19 © Stephen L. Vargo, Robert F. Lusch and Kaisa Koskela-Huotari 2016 Chapter 20 © Sharyn Rundle-Thiele 2016 Chapter 21 © William E. Kilbourne and Anastasia Thyroff 2016

Library of Congress Control Number: 2015955645

British Library Cataloguing in Publication data

A catalogue record for this book is available from the British Library

ISBN 978-1-47390-400-2
ISBN 978-1-47390-401-9 (pbk)

At SAGE we take sustainability seriously. Most of our products are printed in the UK using FSC papers and boards. When we print overseas we ensure sustainable papers are used as measured by the PREPS grading system. We undertake an annual audit to monitor our sustainability.

Contents

List of Contributors   viii

Preface   xviii

PART ONE: OVERVIEW OF MARKETING THEORY   **1**

1   Marketing: Philosophy or Function?   3
Michael J. Baker

2   Marketing Theory   31
Michael Saren

3   A History of Historical Research in Marketing   60
D.G. Brian Jones and Mark Tadajewski

4   Marketing Ethics   90
Patrick E. Murphy and Kelly D. Martin

**PART TWO: DISCIPLINARY UNDERPINNINGS OF
MARKETING THEORY**   **109**

5   The Economics Basis of Marketing   111
Richard J. Varey

6   The Psychological Basis of Marketing   137
    Allan J. Kimmel

7   The Sociological Basis of Marketing   160
    Kjell Grønhaug and Ingeborg Astrid Kleppe

8   Cultural Aspects of Marketing   180
    Kam-hon Lee and Cass Shum

**PART THREE: THEORIES OF MARKETING MANAGEMENT
  AND STRATEGY**   **197**

9   The Marketing Mix – A Helicopter View   199
    *Walter van Waterschoot, Thomas Foscht, Marion Brandstaetter
    and Andreas B. Eisingerich*

10 Marketing Strategy   224
    Robin Wensley

11 Market Segmentation and Segment Strategy   251
    Sally Dibb and Lyndon Simkin

PART FOUR: THEORETICAL SUB-AREAS OF MARKETING   **283**

12 Consumer Behaviour   285
    Margaret K. Hogg and Rob Lawson

13 Marketing Communications in a Digital World   318
    Julia Wolny

14 Theories of Value and Brand Equity   344
    Mark S. Glynn and Roderick J. Brodie

15 Innovation and New Product Development   361
    Susan Hart

16 Relationships and Networks   387
    Kristian Möller

17 Theories of Retailing   415
    Christopher Moore and Stephen Doyle

PART FIVE: THEORIES OF SERVICE IN MARKETING   **433**

18 The New Service Marketing   435
    Evert Gummesson

19 Service-Dominant Logic   458
    Stephen L. Vargo, Robert F. Lusch and Kaisa Koskela-Huotari

**PART SIX: MARKETING THEORY, SOCIETY AND
    THE ENVIRONMENT**   **477**

20 Social Marketing Theory   479
    Sharyn Rundle-Thiele

21 Sustainable Marketing   492
    William E. Kilbourne and Anastasia Thyroff

Index   509

List of Contributors

Michael J. Baker is Emeritus Professor of Marketing, Strathclyde Business School where he founded the Department of Marketing in 1971, serving as Dean 1978–84, and Deputy Principal 1984–1992. He is past National Chairman of the Institute of Marketing and the founding Dean of its Senate. He was Chair of the Marketing Education Group (Academy of Marketing) 1972–86, and its President between 1986 and 2005. Professor Baker is the author/editor of over 50 books and 150 academic papers and was founding editor of the *Journal of Marketing Management*, *Journal of Customer Behaviour* and *Social Business*.

Marion Brandstaetter studied business administration at the Karl-Franzens-University Graz, Austria, where she also earned her PhD. She was a Research Associate at the Department of Marketing at the Karl-Franzens-University Graz, Austria, and currently, she is an Assistant Professor in the aforementioned department. Her research interests include consumer behaviour and brand management.

Roderick J. Brodie is Professor in the Department of Marketing at the University of Auckland, New Zealand. His 200 plus research outputs include over 90 articles many of which have appeared in the leading international journals. He is in the top 1% of marketing academics worldwide based on citations. He is an Associate Editor for *Marketing Theory* and the *Journal of Service Research* and has served on several editorial boards including the *Journal of Marketing*, the *International Journal of Research in Marketing* and the *Journal of Academy of Marketing Science*. In 1998 he was the founding President of ANZMAC and in 2004 he was made one of the founding Fellows. In 2011 he was made a Fellow of EMAC.

Sally Dibb is Professor of Marketing at the Open University Business School and Director of the Institute for Social Marketing (ISM-Open). She served on the Higher Education Funding Council for the UK REF 2014 panel for Business and Management. Sally's research focuses on consumer behaviour change, market segmentation, and social marketing, with recent projects funded by the ESRC, Leverhulme, FP7, and InnovateUK. Sally is Chair of the Academy of Marketing's *Segmentation and Targeting Strategy* special interest group, and a Fellow of the Chartered Institute of Marketing. She has authored eleven books including *The Market Segmentation Workbook* and *Market Segmentation Success!* and over 90 articles in European and US academic journals. Sally is a trustee and board member of the charity *Alcohol Research UK*, appointed by the Secretary of State.

Stephen A. Doyle is a Senior Lecturer in Fashion Marketing and Sustainability Lead in the School of Materials, University of Manchester. He is a graduate of the universities of Stirling and Strathclyde. His research interests are located primarily in the fashion and luxury sectors and have addressed themes such as design and design management, retailer internationalization and brand strategy. His research has resulted in invitations to deliver lectures to a number of European, American and Chinese institutions.

Andreas B. Eisingerich is Professor of Marketing at Imperial College Business School, Imperial College London. He earned his PhD at the University of Cambridge, and worked at the Center for Global Innovation at the University of Southern California, Marshall School of Business. He has published on customer–brand relationships, customer engagement and service management in the *Journal of Consumer Psychology*, *Journal of Marketing*, *Journal of Service Research*, *Journal of Business Research*, *Harvard Business Review* and *MIT Sloan Management Review*, among others.

Thomas Foscht earned his PhD and his habilitation degree at Karl-Franzens-University Graz, Austria. He was an Assistant and Associate Professor of Marketing at this university before he became Full Professor of Marketing at California State University, East Bay (San Francisco), USA. Currently he is a Full Professor of Marketing and Dean of the School of Business, Economics and Social Sciences at Karl-Franzens-University Graz, Austria. He co-authored a textbook on consumer behaviour, a text book on retail management and also the book *Reverse Psychology Marketing*, which has been published in English, Spanish and Korean. His papers have been published in leading international academic journals like *Long Range Planning*, *International Journal of Retail & Distribution Management*, *Journal of Retailing and Consumer Services*, *International Journal of Bank Marketing* and *Journal of Product & Brand Management*.

Mark S. Glynn is an Associate Professor in the Faculty of Business and Law at the Auckland University of Technology, Auckland, New Zealand. He has a PhD in marketing from the University of Auckland and won an Emerald/EFMD Best Thesis Award for outstanding doctoral research in marketing strategy. His research areas include branding, business-to-business marketing, private labels and buyer–seller relationships. Mark's research has been published in many international journals including the *European Journal of Marketing, Industrial Marketing Management, Journal of Business Research, Journal of Business & Industrial Marketing* and *Marketing Theory*. He recently co-edited a special issue on resource management for the *Australasian Marketing Journal*.

Kjell Grønhaug is Professor Emeritus at NHH-Norwegian School of Economics, Bergen, Norway. He holds an MBA and a PhD in marketing from the School, an MS in sociology from the University of Bergen, and did his postgraduate studies with emphasis on quantitative methods at the University of Washington. He has been Visiting Professor at the universities of Pittsburgh, Illinois at Urbana-Champaign, California, Irvine, Kiel and Innsbruck and several other European institutions. He has also been Adjunct Professor at the Helsinki School of Economics and associated (Professor II) at the University of Tromsø, Bodø Graduate School of Business and the University of Stavanger as well at the Institute of Fishery Research and Rogaland Research. He is honorary doctor at Turku School of Economics and Business Administration, Stockholm School of Economics and University of Gothenburg. Grønhaug has been recognized for several of his research contributions, including being the recipient of the prize for excellence in research at his own institution awarded every fifth year. Over the years he has been involved in a number of research projects related to a variety of marketing-related problems, corporate strategy, industry studies and multiple evaluation studies. His publications include 18 authored or co-authored books, numerous articles in leading American and European journals and multiple contributions to many international conference proceedings. His present research interests relate to creation and use of knowledge, cognitive aspects of strategy, marketing strategies in novel high-tech markets and methodological issues.

Evert Gummesson (PhD, DHc) is Emeritus Professor of Marketing at the Stockholm Business School, Stockholm University, Sweden. His research interests are marketing as relationships, networks and interaction; service systems; and research methodology. He has 256 publications registered, including articles, books and book chapters. His book *Total Relationship Marketing* will shortly be published in its 4th revised edition. The Chartered Institute of Marketing (CIM) has listed him as one of the 50 most important contributors to marketing; he has received two awards from the American Marketing Association (AMA); and was the first recipient of the Service-Dominant (S-D) Logic Award and the Grönroos Award for Excellence in Service Research. His is a co-founder and co-chair of the biennial conference series Naples Forum on Service. He also has 25 years of experience as a business practitioner.

Susan Hart is currently Dean of Durham University Business School from July 2016, formerly Associate Deputy and Business School Dean at the University of Strathclyde. Her research areas of interest include innovation and product-service development, marketing and competitive success and marketing performance measurement. She has been awarded research grants by the Leverhulme Trust, Economic and Social Research Council, Science and Engineering Research Council, Design Council Scotland and the Chartered Institute of Management Accountants, Scottish Enterprise. She has written more than 100 articles and papers, as well as writing and editing numerous books and publications. Susan Hart is a member of the Board of Directors of AACSB, also the European Advisory Committee and Accreditation Panel for AACSB, a fellow of the Marketing Society, the Royal Society of Edinburgh and the Leadership Trust Foundation. She is an Associate Director of Quality Services at the European Foundation of Management Development and an Advisory Board member of: Ecole de Management, Paris, Kemmy Business School, University of Limerick, Wirtschaft Universiteit, ESSCA and the Universiti Putra, Malaysia. She is also a Director of Yorkhill Children's Charity.

Margaret K. Hogg holds the Chair of Consumer Behaviour and Marketing in the Department of Marketing at Lancaster University Management School, UK. Before joining Lancaster University in May 2004, she was Reader in Consumer Behaviour at Manchester School of Management, UMIST. She read Politics and Modern History at Edinburgh University, followed by postgraduate studies in history at the Vrije Universiteit, Amsterdam and then by an MA in Business Analysis at Lancaster University. She spent six years working in marketing with K Shoes, Kendal. She completed her part-time PhD at Manchester Business School in Consumer Behaviour and Retailing. Her principal research interests lie in the relationship between identity, self and consumption particularly in relation to transitions and women's changing experiences of motherhood and family work (e.g. empty nest women, new mothers). She is Associate Editor (Buyer Behaviour) for the *Journal of Business Research*. She is a regular attendee at US and European conferences of the Association of Consumer Research (ACR) and Consumer Culture Theory (CCT). Her work has appeared in refereed journals including the *Journal of Advertising, Journal of Business Research, Consumption, Markets & Culture, Journal of Marketing Management, Journal of Services Marketing*, the *European Journal of Marketing* and the *International Journal of Advertising*. She edited six volumes of papers on Consumer Behaviour in the Sage Major Works series (2005 and 2006), and along with Michael Solomon, Gary Bamossy and Soren Askegaard she is one of the co-authors of the 6th European edition of *Consumer Behaviour: A European Perspective* (2016, Pearson forthcoming). She is a co-editor (along with Stephanie O'Donohoe, Pauline Maclaran, Lydia Martens and Lorna Stevens) of *Motherhoods, Markets and Consumption: The Making of Mothers in Contemporary Western Cultures* (Routledge, 2014).

D.G. Brian Jones is Professor of Marketing at Quinnipiac University. He is the current and founding Editor of the *Journal of Historical Research in Marketing* and co-editor of the Routledge Studies in the History of Marketing. His research focuses on the history of marketing ideas and has been published in the *Journal of Marketing, Journal of the Academy of Marketing Science, Journal of Marketing Management, European Journal of Marketing, Journal of Macromarketing, Marketing Theory, Psychology & Marketing, Journal of Historical Research in Marketing*, and other publications. He is the author of (2012) *Pioneers in Marketing*, and co-editor, with Mark Tadajewski of the (2008) three-volume set of readings titled *The History of Marketing Thought*.

William Kilbourne received his Ph.D. from the University of Houston in 1973. He is currently a Professor Emeritus of Marketing and Trevillian Distinguished Professor at Clemson University,

USA. His research interests are in the areas of macromarketing issues in globalization and the environment and the general area of marketing and society. Most recently, his attention has been directed to developing, both theoretically and empirically, the role of a society's Dominant Social Paradigm in environmentally relevant consumption behavior and in materialistic values, quality of life, and happiness studies. His publications have appeared in the *Journal of Business Research, Journal of Macromarketing, Journal of Economic Psychology*, the *Journal of Advertising, Environment and Behavior, European Journal of Marketing, Marketing Theory*, the *Journal of Marketing Management*, the *Journal of the Academy of Marketing Science, Psychology & Marketing*, and the *Journal of Marketing Research*.

Allan J. Kimmel is Professor of Marketing at ESCP Europe in Paris, France. He holds MA and PhD degrees in social psychology from Temple University (USA). He has filled visiting professor positions at Université Paris IX-Dauphine (Paris) and ESSEC Business School (Cergy-Pontoise, France), and has served as a visiting lecturer at TEC de Monterrey (Mexico), Universidad de San Andrés (Buenos Aires, Argentina), Turku School of Economics (Finland), the University of Vaasa (Finland) and Lehigh University (USA). His research and writing interests focus on consumer behaviour, marketing and research ethics, deception, word of mouth and commercial rumours, consumers' relationship to products, and connected marketing. He has published articles in the *Journal of Consumer Psychology, Psychology & Marketing, Journal of Marketing Communications, Ethics & Behavior* and *American Psychologist*, among others. His most recent books are *People and Products: Consumer Behavior and Product Design* (Routledge, 2015), *Psychological Foundations of Marketing* (Routledge, 2012) and *Connecting with Consumers: Marketing for New Marketplace Realities* (Oxford University Press, 2010).

Ingeborg Astrid Kleppe is Professor of Marketing at the NHH-Norwegian School of Economics, Bergen, Norway. She holds an MBA and a PhD in marketing from the School, and an MS in sociology from the University of Bergen. Kleppe has extensive international experience from universities in the USA, Sweden and Australia. In her current research she collaborates with researchers from the School of Economics, University of Gothenburg; the University of Sydney; the Schülich School of Business York University, Toronto; and Leeds University Business School. She has also worked in the World Bank doing poverty research in sub-Saharan Africa. Kleppe has taken her interdisciplinary and international experience into her research on different topics in consumer behaviour. Currently she is doing research on consumer communities in the social media and consumers' adoption of public health interventions in developing countries. Kleppe has also published on country-of-origin and national images in tourism and international marketing journals.

Kaisa Koskela-Huotari is a PhD student in CTF, Service Research Centre at Karlstad University, Sweden and a research scientist at VTT Technical Research Centre of Finland. Her research interests lie at the intersection of service-dominant logic, institutional theory and systems thinking.

Rob Lawson is Professor of Marketing at the University of Otago, New Zealand, where he has worked since 1987. Rob's education and early career were at the universities of Newcastle and Sheffield in the UK and, though he has published over 160 papers across a wide range of topics in marketing, his main area of interest is consumer behaviour. Much of his current work looks at household energy behaviours and understanding the adoption of energy efficient practices and technologies. He has received competitive funding for a seven-year research programme in this area which has a strong applied focus and close collaborations with industry, local and national government. Most of Rob's teaching is now at graduate level, including extensive PhD supervision. He is a past-president of ANZMAC and was granted Distinguished Membership of the Academy in 2007. He has also worked as Research Dean at the University of Otago and was a member of the PBRF Business and Economics assessment panel for research quality New Zealand in both 2003 and 2006.

Professor Kam-hon Lee is Emeritus Professor of Marketing at The Chinese University of Hong Kong (CUHK). He became an Honorary Fellow of CUHK in 2013. His research areas include business negotiation, cross-cultural marketing, marketing ethics, social marketing and tourism marketing. He obtained his Bachelor of Commerce in 1967 and Master of Commerce in 1969 at CUHK and his Ph.D. in Marketing in 1975 at Northwestern University in Evanston, Illinois, USA. Professor Lee has published in *Journal of Marketing, Journal of International Business Studies, Journal of International Marketing, Journal of Business Ethics, Cornell HRA Quarterly* and other refereed journals. Professor Lee has rendered consulting services to different institutions including the World Bank, Procter & Gamble (Guangzhou), and Hong Kong Travel Industry Council.

Robert F. Lusch is Professor of Marketing and the Muzzy Chair in Entrepreneurship at the University of Arizona where he also holds appointments in Philosophy and Sociology. Professor Lusch is an active scholar in the field of marketing strategy, services marketing and marketing theory. He is a past editor of the *Journal of Marketing* and the past chairperson of the American Marketing Association. In 2013 the AMA awarded him with its most prestigious award for marketing scholars: the AMA/Irwin Distinguished Educator Award. Previously the Academy of Marketing Science awarded him their Distinguished Marketing Educator Award (1997). His current research is focused on service-dominant logic and service ecosystems. Cambridge University Press recently published his book (with Steve Vargo), *Service-Dominant Logic: Premises, Prospects and Promises*, in 2014.

Kelly D. Martin is Associate Professor of Marketing, Monfort Professor (2014-2016), and FirstBank Faculty Fellow at Colorado State University. Her research interests involve the intersection of marketing and society—especially in the areas of strategy and ethics, and customer well-being. Her work has appeared in journals such as the *Academy of Management Journal, Journal of Consumer Research, Journal of the Academy of Marketing Science, Journal of Public Policy & Marketing*, and *Business Ethics Quarterly*, among other academic journals. Kelly was awarded the inaugural AMA Marketing and Society Emerging Scholar Award for early career research contributions. She serves on the editorial boards of *Journal of the Academy of Marketing Science, Business Ethics Quarterly*, and the *Journal of Public Policy & Marketing*.

Kristian Möller is an Emeritus Professor of Marketing at the Aalto University School of Business (former Helsinki School of Economics). Formerly the President of the European Marketing Academy and the Head of the Marketing and Management Department of the HSE, Dr Möller is an active member of the international research network. He has been a visiting scholar at PennState, Aston Business School, University of Bath, the European Institute for Advanced Studies in Management and the Haas School of Business at the University of Berkeley. His current research is focused on business and innovation networks, competence-based marketing and business performance, and on marketing theory. His articles have been published in *California Management Review, European Journal of Marketing, Industrial Marketing Management, Journal of Business Research, Journal of Business-to-Business Marketing, Journal of Management Studies, Journal of Marketing Management* and *Marketing Theory*.

Christopher M Moore is Assistant Vice Principal of Glasgow Caledonian University and is the Director of the British School of Fashion. With a PhD in international marketing, his research outputs have been published in the leading academic business journals in the area of retailer brand globalisation. Professor Moore has held Visiting Professorships in a number of Universities in the UK, Europe, Japan and the USA. An expert in global fashion brand building, he currently provides Director-level support and advice to leading fashion and department store businesses. As Founding Director of the British School of Fashion, he oversees the activities of the School at GCU London. The British School of Fashion founding patron is Don McCarthy and the School's London campus is home to the Marks and Spencer Studio.

Patrick E. Murphy is Professor of Marketing in the Mendoza College of Business at the University of Notre Dame. He is a past chair of the Department of Marketing and was a Fulbright Scholar at University College Cork in Ireland and University of Lille 2 in France. He specializes in business and marketing ethics. His work has appeared in leading ethics and marketing journals. His articles have won awards from three academic journals. In 2011, he received the Lifetime Achievement Award from the Marketing and Society Special Interest Group of the American Marketing Association. Professor Murphy holds a BBA from Notre Dame, an MBA from Bradley University and a PhD from the University of Houston.

Sharyn Rundle-Thiele leads Social Marketing @ Griffith (www.griffith.edu.au/social-marketing) and is Editor of the *Journal of Social Marketing*. Sharyn's research focuses on behaviour change. She has published and presented over 80 books, journal papers and book chapters. She currently serves as an advisor on a diverse range of social marketing projects. Her current projects include changing adolescent attitudes towards drinking alcohol (see http://gameon.rcs.griffith.edu.au/) and increasing healthy eating and physical activity to combat obesity. Research partners include VicHealth, SA Health, Department of Health and Aging, Siggins Miller Consulting, Defence Science and Technology Organization, Queensland Catholic Education Commission and Mater Health Services.

Michael Saren is Professor of Marketing at the University of Leicester, UK. He previously held chairs in marketing at the universities of Stirling and Strathclyde and is an honorary fellow and lifetime member of the UK Academy of Marketing. He holds a PhD from the University of Bath and an honorary professorship at St Andrews University. He was a founding editor of the journal *Marketing Theory* (SAGE Publishing) and co-editor of *Rethinking Marketing* (Brownlie et al, 1999, Sage). His introductory text is *Marketing Graffiti: The Writing on the Wall* (Routledge).

Dr. Cass Shum is Assistant Professor in Hospitality Organizational Behavior at William F. Harrah College of Hotel Administration, University of Nevada, Las Vegas (UNLV). She received her Ph.D. in Management from Hong Kong University of Science and Technology. Prior to joining UNLV, Dr. Shum worked in Chinese University of Hong Kong as research assistant and stayed in University of Florida as visiting scholar. Her research focuses on interpersonal relationship and behaviors at work including abusive supervision, coworker support and influence, and employee's ethical behaviors. Dr. Shum's works can be found in *Organizational Science, International Journal of Hospitality Management*, and other peer-reviewed journals.

Lyndon Simkin is Executive Director of the Centre for Business in Society at Coventry University, before which he was Professor of Strategic Marketing at Henley Business School at the University of Reading. Lyndon is Associate Editor of the Journal of Marketing Management, a member of the Academy of Marketing's Research Committee and he co-chairs two of the Academy's special interest groups: Segmentation and Targeting Strategy and CRM and Services. Lyndon has published widely and authored numerous books, including *Marketing: Concepts and Strategies, Marketing Planning, Market Segmentation Success, The Marketing Casebook, Marketing Briefs* and *The Dark Side of CRM*. Lyndon advises many blue chip companies and mentors CEOs in strategy development and execution.

Mark Tadajewski is Professor of Marketing at Durham University. He is the co-editor of the *Journal of Marketing Management*, an Associate Editor of the *Journal of Historical Research in Marketing*, the co-editor of the Routledge Studies in Critical Marketing monograph series, co-editor of the Routledge Studies in the History of Marketing, and author of numerous books and articles. He also serves on the editorial and policy boards of the *Journal of Macromarketing*, the editorial board of *Marketing Theory*, the Board of Directors of the Conference on Historical Analysis and Research in Marketing (CHARM), and on the Academy of Marketing Research Committee.

Anastasia Thyroff, Assistant Professor of Marketing at Clemson University, received her MMR from the University of Georgia and PhD from the University of Arkansas. Dr Thyroff's research interests are in consumer culture theory, market system dynamics, sociology based macromarketing and critical theory. Some of the contexts that she has focused on include: technology, generosity and sustainability. Her research has appeared in outlets including the *Journal of Business Research, Journal of Interactive Marketing* and the *Journal of Consumer Affairs*. Some of her recent awards include: the SMA Paper in Conference Award (2013), the SMA Solomon

Best Paper in Buyer Behavior Track (2012), Outstanding Graduate Student Teaching Award (2012) and the *Journal of Consumer Affairs* Best Article Award (2011).

Walter van Waterschoot was a doctoral student at the Catholic University of Leuven and served as assistant in the European Marketing Programme of Insead/Cedep before earning his PhD at Saint-Ignatius University (Antwerp). Before he retired he was a Professor of Marketing and Channel Management at the University of Antwerp. He was a vested author of marketing textbooks written in Dutch. The general marketing management textbook he co-authored achieved its 12th edition. He has also contributed numerous chapters in international monographs, including the *Oxford Textbook of Marketing* (2000). He prepared entries for several encyclopaedias, including the *International Encyclopedia of Marketing* (2000). He published papers in leading academic journals including the *Journal of Marketing*, the *Journal of Retailing*, the *Journal of Retailing and Consumer Services*, the *International Journal of Research in Marketing* and *Health Marketing Quarterly*. His paper on the classification of the marketing mix ('The 4P classification of the marketing mix revisited' with Christophe van den Bulte, *Journal of Marketing* 46(4)) was included in the compilation of the most influential articles in the history of marketing published by Routledge (2000). Walter van Waterschoot unexpectedly passed away in 2012.

Richard J. Varey is Visiting Professor in Marketing at the University of Otago, New Zealand. He was formerly Professor of Marketing and Chair of Department at the Waikato Management School, Reader and Director of the BNFL Corporate Communications Research Unit at the University of Salford, and Senior Lecturer at the Sheffield Business School, UK. Richard completed his MSc Management Sciences and PhD in Marketing at Manchester School of Management. His award-winning scholarship has been published widely – on marketing theory, relationship marketing, marketing communication, social responsibility and sustainable business, and the future of marketing. Richard is a reviewer for several journals, including *Marketing Theory*, *Journal of Marketing Management*, *Social Business*, *Journal of Customer Behaviour* and *Journal of Macromarketing*. He was born in East Yorkshire, England, and emigrated with his family to New Zealand in 2003.

Stephen L. Vargo is a Shidler Distinguished Professor and Professor of Marketing at the University of Hawai'i at Manoa. He has held visiting positions at the Judge Business School at the University of Cambridge, the University of Warwick, Karlstad University, the University of Maryland, Collage Park, and other major universities. He has articles published in the *Journal of Marketing*, the *Journal of the Academy of Marketing Science*, the *Journal of Service Research*, and other major journals and has been awarded the Harold H. Maynard Award and the AMA/Sheth Foundation Award for his contributions to marketing theory. Thomson-Reuters recently identified him as one of the *World's Most Influential Scientific Minds* in economics and business.

Robin Wensley is Emeritus Professor of Policy and Marketing at Warwick University and Professor of Strategic Marketing at the Open University. He was Director the ESRC/EPSRC funded AIM Research initiative from 2004 to 2011 and Deputy Dean at Warwick Business School from 2000 to 2004. He was Chair of the School from 1989 to 1994 and Chair of the Faculty of Social Studies from 1997 to 1999. He was previously with RHM Foods, Tube Investments and London Business School, and was Visiting Professor twice at UCLA and once at the University of Florida. He was a Council member of the ESRC from 2000 to 2003, having been a member of the Research Grants Board from 1991 to 1995. He was also Chair of the Council of the Tavistock Institute of Human Relations from 1998 to 2003. His research interests include the long-term evolution of competitive markets and structures, the process of strategic decision making, the nature of sustainable advantages, and issues of choice in public policy and he has published a number of books, most recently *Effective Management in Practice: Analytical Insights and Critical Questions,* and articles in the *Harvard Business Review*, the *Journal of Marketing* and the *Strategic Management Journal*, and has worked closely with other academics both in Europe and the USA. He was joint editor of the *Journal of Management Studies* from 1998 to 2002. In 2012 he was recipient of the British Academy of Management's Richard Whipp Lifetime Achievement Award and he has twice won the annual Alpha Kappa Psi Award for the most influential article in the US *Journal of Marketing*, as well as the *Journal of Marketing Management* Millennium Article award.

Julia Wolny is an industry-focused academic and Chair of the e-Marketing Subject Interest Group (SIG) at the Academy of Marketing UK, which brings together academics and organizations in digital and omnichannel marketing research and education. She is currently Principal Fellow in Marketing at the University of Southampton, UK and sits on the Executive Editorial Board of the *Journal of Direct, Data and Digital Marketing Practice*. Her main areas of expertise are multichannel consumer behaviour, digital/augmented experience design and marketing in the creative industries. Findings from her own and collaborative research have been shared at over 50 international academic and practitioner conferences over the last 15 years, including at Google and IBM. Previously she was the Director of Fashion Business Resource Studio at London College of Fashion and continues to work with innovative brands to enhance the effectiveness of their marketing practice.

Preface

The first edition of *Marketing Theory: A Student Text* was published in 2000 in order to fulfil the need for an advanced marketing text which focused on theory. At the time this was a novel approach distinct from many of the principles and practices of marketing texts which elicited theoretical aspects as adjunct to a managerial or functionalist approach to the subject. In contrast, *Marketing Theory: A Student Text* provided an overview of the theoretical foundations and current status of thinking on topics central to the marketing discipline. Because marketing does not depend on a 'pure' or single disciplinary base we believe that in order to be qualified to practise the profession of marketing one should know and understand the sources of the original ideas and theories on which it is founded. This third edition of the successful 2000 and 2010 texts is designed to fulfil this need.

While many of its key ideas and core concepts remain unchanged, the discipline of marketing has continued to evolve and for this reason we have produced another new, revised, updated and extended edition. The aim of this new edition is to provide an up-to-date and well-structured introduction to the major areas of theory in marketing from an academic perspective. As the subtitle suggests, like previous editions it is directly aimed at students, both undergraduate and postgraduate, in order to introduce and explain the role of theory in marketing, which is often challenging for students, in a readable and clear style. Each chapter is supported by extensive references enabling in-depth research into the subject matter of the individual chapters.

This edition has been substantially updated with new versions of many of the original chapters along with new contributions in specific theoretical areas including completely new chapters on Service-Dominant Logic, Social Marketing Theory, Consumer Behaviour, Social

Media and Virtual Marketing. Both new and original chapter authors have been selected by the editors as before on the basis of their academic leadership and authority in the topic, experience with theoretical aspects of their subject and ability to explain theoretical concepts in a clear and concise manner. The contributors have added more discussion of emerging and future theoretical developments in their areas of the discipline, as the editors have more generally in the first two chapters.

With several reprints it is clear that this book fills a need for more advanced students of marketing looking for a clear description and analysis of the theoretical foundations of the discipline. For PhD students it brings together in a single text a comprehensive review of the major sub-fields of the discipline which otherwise could only be found by specific reference to the literature of those sub-fields involving considerable effort and expense. This text also provides a key resource for students on the final year of undergraduate programmes, taking a specialist Marketing Theory module, or those following taught programmes such as MBA or MSc in Marketing. In addition, many of the chapters will be particularly useful as methodological and research design preparation for students embarking on marketing-based dissertations or extended projects involving marketing.

Michael J. Baker and Michael Saren

Part One

Overview of Marketing Theory

Part I Contents

1   Marketing: Philosophy or Function?   3

2   Marketing Theory   31

3   A History of Historical Research in Marketing   60

4   Marketing Ethics   90

Marketing: Philosophy or Function?

Michael J. Baker

1

Chapter Topics

Overview	3
Introduction	4
Exchange and economic growth	5
The rediscovery of marketing	9
The marketing management school	13
The European perspective	14
So what is marketing?	18
Marketing's mid-life crisis	20
A new marketing paradigm?	23
Déjà vu?	26
Summary	28

Overview

This opening chapter seeks to define what might be considered the true essence of marketing: that it is the establishment of mutually satisfying exchange relationships. The modern marketing concept would appear to have undergone at least three major phases of evolution – the emergence of the mass market, the articulation of the modern marketing concept, and the transition from an emphasis upon the transaction to the relationship. Also, arising from the stress upon relationships, the interaction between seller and buyer has become prominent as the basis for the co-creation of 'value'. Because of the distinguishing attributes of services – intangibility, etc. – interaction assumes greater importance and has become the focus of what Vargo and Lusch (2004) have defined as the service-dominant logic. In parallel with these changes, the practice of marketing has been seen as having increased relevance in promoting behavioural change in both the commercial and non-commercial context.

Next, I review a number of specific definitions of marketing to document how these have changed over time and speculate as to the possible nature and direction of future change in addressing the question, what is marketing?

In conclusion, I look briefly at the relationship between theory and practice which is the subject matter of the book as a whole and identify the existence of a 'gap' between the two. Some reasons for this are identified and are touched on in many of the chapters that follow.

Introduction

On first introduction to a subject it is understandable that one should seek a clear and concise definition of it. If nothing else this definition should enable one to distinguish the domain of that subject from others while also giving an indication of its scope and nature. Of course, none of us expect that a short definition will be able to encompass the complexity of a subject as extensive as marketing. That said, it does seem reasonable that persons who profess or claim expertise on the subject should be able to define it.

In this introductory chapter it will become clear that there is no scarcity of definitions of marketing and I will review a number of them. In doing so it will also become clear that views as to the scope of the subject tend to polarize in the manner implied by the title between those who perceive marketing as a philosophy of business, or state of mind, and those who regard it as a managerial function responsible for particular activities in much the same way as production, finance or human resource management.

To throw light on this dichotomy it will be helpful first to review what is seen to be the true essence of marketing – mutually satisfying exchange relationships – and its evolution over time in parallel with stages of economic growth and development. On the basis of this review it will be argued that marketing has always been an intrinsic element of the commercial exchange process but that its importance has waxed and waned with shifts in the balance between supply and demand. Without anticipating unduly Brian Jones's discussion of historical research in marketing it will be suggested that we can detect at least three major phases in the evolution of the modern marketing concept – the emergence of the mass market circa 1850, the articulation of the modern marketing concept circa 1960, and the transition from an emphasis upon the transaction to the relationship circa 1990. In conclusion I review specific definitions of marketing to document how these have changed over time and speculate as to the possible nature and direction of future change in order to answer my opening question, marketing – philosophy or function?

Exchange and economic growth

Since time immemorial humans have had to live with scarcity in one form or another. In its most acute form scarcity threatens the very existence of life itself but, even in the most affluent and advanced post-industrial societies, its existence is still apparent in the plight of the homeless and the poor. Indeed, in some senses it is doubtful whether humankind will ever overcome scarcity, if for no other reason than that there appears to be no upper limit to human wants.

The use of the noun 'wants' is deliberate for early on in any study of marketing it is important to distinguish clearly between 'needs' and 'wants'. Needs have been classified as existing at five levels by Abraham Maslow (1943) and his Hierarchy of Human Needs (Figure 1.1) is a useful starting point for discussion of the nature of marketing. As can be seen in Figure 1.1, Maslow's hierarchy conceives of human needs as resting on a foundation of physiological needs, essential to existence, and ascending through a series of levels – safety, love and esteem – to a state of self-actualization in which the individual's specification of a need is entirely self-determined. According to this conceptualization one can only ascend to a higher level once one has satisfied the needs of a lower level, and the inference may be drawn that scarcity would only cease to exist once every individual has attained the highest level of self-actualization.

From this description it is clear that 'needs' are broadly based and defined and act as a summary statement for a whole cluster of much more precisely defined wants which reflect the exact desires of individuals. In a state of hunger the Westerner may want bread or potatoes but the Easterner is more likely to want rice. Both of these wants are fairly basic. While they have the ability to satisfy the need 'hunger', they offer little by way of variety. The desire for variety, or choice, is another intrinsic element of human nature and much of human development and

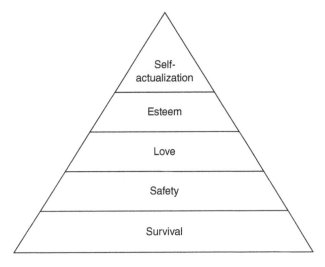

Figure 1.1   Maslow's Hierarchy of Human Needs.

Source: Maslow (1943).

progress may be attributed to a quest for variety – of new ways of satisfying basic needs. Indeed, the process appears to be self-sustaining, which prompted me to propose that a maxim of marketing is that 'the act of consumption changes the consumer' (Baker, 1980). In other words, each new experience increases and extends the consumer's expectations and creates an opportunity for a new supplier to win their patronage by developing something new and better than existing solutions to the consumer's need.

Faced with an apparent infinity of wants the challenge to be faced is in determining what selection of goods and services will give the greatest satisfaction to the greatest number at any particular point in time. Indeed, the purpose of economic organization has been defined as 'maximising satisfaction through the utilisation of scarce resources' (Baker, 2001: 13). Marketing is a function which facilitates achievement of this goal. To understand how it does this, it will be helpful to review the process of economic development. Rostow's (1962) Stages of Economic Growth model provides an excellent basis for such a review.

Rostow's model is shown in Figure 1.2 and proposes that human societies progress from the lowest level of subsistence or survival in a series of clearly identified stages until they achieve the sophistication and affluence of the modern post-industrial state. In grossly simplified terms certain key events appear to be associated with the transition from one stage to the next.

At the lowest level of all is the subsistence economy based upon hunting, gathering and collecting. Such economies are nomadic and entirely dependent upon nature for their survival. While members of such nomadic tribes may share food and shelter, and band together for safety, they are societies which are devoid of any recognizable form of commercial exchange.

With the domestication of animals and the development of primitive agriculture humans begin to exercise a degree of control over their environment. At the same time new activities

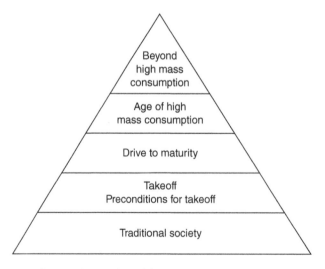

Figure 1.2   Rostow's Stages of Economic Growth model.

Source: Rostow (1962).

create new roles and the potential for the first step towards increased productivity and economic progress – task specialization. Once it becomes recognized that some people are better suited to some tasks than others then the potential for task specialization exists. For it to be realized, however, an agreed system of exchange must be developed. Indeed, it seems likely that the creation of a system of exchange was a necessary prerequisite for task specialization to flourish.

A fundamental law of economics is that beyond a certain point each additional unit of any good or service becomes worth progressively less and less to its owner (the law of diminishing marginal utility). Given a surplus of any specific good the owner will be able to increase their overall satisfaction by exchanging units of their surplus for another good which they want. Thus hunters can exchange meat for vegetables with farmers to their mutual and enhanced satisfaction.

For an exchange to occur there must be at least two persons, each with a surplus of one good which is desired by the other. Once contact has been established between the two persons they can then negotiate an exchange which will increase their overall satisfaction by swapping units until the marginal utility of the two goods is equal (i.e. one would receive less satisfaction by acquiring one additional unit of the other person's surplus than by retaining a unit of one's own output). While this concept is easy to understand in principle, especially when discussing only one exchange, its implementation in practice poses numerous problems. To reduce these problems three additional developments are called for.

First, in order that those with services to exchange can be brought together it will be helpful to set aside a specific place for the purpose – a market. Second, one needs an accepted store of value that will act as a universal medium of exchange – money. Third, because marketing is a separate task from production it will further increase productivity and add value if specialist intermediaries – merchants and retailers – come into existence to perform these functions. Clearly, markets, money and intermediaries have existed since the earliest civilizations. Indeed, it would be no exaggeration to claim that the development of formal commercial exchange relationships was the foundation for civilization as we know it today. It would seem that marketing is perhaps not such a recent phenomenon as many believe it to be!

The creation of markets and the development of exchange provides preconditions for takeoff. For takeoff to occur task specialization has to be taken a stage further to what economists call the division of labour. One of the earliest and best known examples of the division of labour is provided by Adam Smith's description of the pin making industry.

> To take an example, therefore, from a very trifling manufacture; but one in which the division of labour has been very often taken notice of, the trade of the pin maker; a workman not educated to this business (which the division of labour has rendered a distinct trade), nor acquainted with the use of the machinery employed in it (to the invention of which the same division of labour has probably given occasion), could scarce, perhaps, with his utmost industry, make one pin in a day, and certainly could not make 20. But in the way in which this business is now carried on, not only the whole work is a peculiar trade, but it is divided into a number of branches, of which the greatest part are likewise a peculiar trade. One man draws out the wire, another straights it, a third cuts it, a fourth points it, the fifth grinds it at the top receiving the head; to make the head requires three distinct operations; to put it on is a peculiar business, to whiten the pins is another; it is even

a trade by itself to put them into the paper; and the important business of making a pin is, in this manner, divided into about 18 distinct operations, which, in some manufactures, are all performed by distinct hands, though in others the same man will sometimes perform two or three of them. I have seen a small manufactury of this kind where 10 men only were employed and where some of them consequently performed two or three distinct operations. But though they were very poor, and therefore but indifferently accommodated with the necessary machinery, they could, when they exerted themselves, make among them about 12 pounds of pins in the day. There are in a pound upwards of 4000 pins of the middling size. These 10 persons therefore, could make among them upwards of 48,000 pins in the day. Each person, therefore making 1/10 part of 48,000 pins, might be considered as making 4800 pins in a day. But if they had all wrought separately and independently, and without any of them having been educated to this peculiar business, they could certainly not each of them have made 20, perhaps not one pin in a day; that is, certainly, not the 240th, perhaps not the 4800th part of what they are at present capable of performing, in conseçquence of a proper division and combination of their different operations. (Smith, 1970 [1776]: Book 1, Ch. 1, para 3)

It seems reasonable to assume that under conditions of craft industry, where each craftsman was responsible for all the tasks associated with the production of a particular good, the number of craftsmen in a community would be approximately sufficient to satisfy the demands of that community. Indeed, the medieval craft guilds (and, more recently, trade unions) strictly controlled the number of apprentices that could be trained in a craft to ensure that a satisfactory balance between supply and demand be maintained. Clearly, the enormous increase in productivity associated with the division of labour destroyed this conçtrol and flooded the market with the product in question, driving the price down and making many craftsmen redundant. One new pin factory employing 10 pin makers could match the output of 240 craftsmen and so service the needs of 240 times as many customers. As a result, production became concentrated in locations possessing natural advantages associated with the product – sources of power and raw material, labour, good channels of communication – and it became necessary to employ salespersons to help sell the output in a greatly enlarged market.

Because of the enormous increase in output associated with factory production, standards of living improved substantially with a consequential increase in life expectancy and the numçbers of children surviving infancy. As the size of the market is determined ultimately by the size of the population, an expanding population represented an expanding market and further fuelled the rapid economic growth associated with takeoff. This growth was to receive an even greater impetus with the spate of scientific and technological innovation of the 18th century, which gave birth to what has become known as the Industrial Revolution and forms the founçdation for Rostow's fourth stage of economic growth – the age of high mass consumption.

In his original conceptualization, Rostow (1962) perceived that some of the more advanced and affluent industrialized economies were approaching the limits of mass conçsumption. While population growth had slowed to a near steady-state further improvements in productivity had created saturated markets and the potential for excess supply. John Kenneth Galbraith (1958) designated this post-industrial society while Rostow merely termed it the age beyond high mass consumption. Eight years later, in 1970, Rostow revised his model and designated the final stage the search for quality – the inference being that if a static population could not physically consume more then the only way growth could be sustained would be to consume 'better'.

Elsewhere (Baker, 1994b) I have discussed the way in which the stages in Maslow's needs hierarchy correspond closely to the stages in Rostow's economic stages model, e.g. subsistence economies are concerned primarily with physiological needs; the search for quality with self-actualization, etc. Clearly, human needs (demand) motivate supply creation and the matching of supply and demand is achieved through a process of exchange and marketing. It is also clear that these processes have existed for a very long time indeed, so why is marketing often represented as a 20th-century phenomenon? I turn to this question in the next section, but, before doing so, will summarize some of the key points that have emerged from a greatly simplified account of economic development.

First, exchange adds value and increases satisfaction. It also encourages variety and improves choice. Second, the parties to a commercial exchange are free agents so that for an exchange to occur both parties must feel that they are benefiting from that exchange. It is from these observations that we derive our basic definition of marketing as being concerned with mutually satisfying exchange relationships. Third, task specialization and the division of labour greatly increase productivity and increase the volume of goods available for consumption. In turn, this increased supply results in an improved standard of living and an increase in the population thereby increasing demand and stimulating further efforts to increase supply. Fourth, the concentration of production and the growing size and dispersion of the market increase the need for specialized channels of distribution and other intermediaries to service and manage them. Fifth, improved standards of living in the advanced industrialized economies lead to a stabilization of population growth and absolute market size (demand) but accelerating technological innovation continues to enhance our ability to increase supply. It was this which was to lead to the 'rediscovery' of marketing.

The rediscovery of marketing

As we have seen, markets and marketing are as old as exchange itself yet many people regard marketing as a phenomenon which emerged in the second half of the 20th century – to be precise about 1960 when Professor Ted Levitt published an article entitled 'Marketing myopia' in the *Harvard Business Review* in which he addressed the fundamental question of why do firms, and indeed whole industries, grow to a position of great power and influence and then decline. Taking the American railroad industry as his main example, Levitt showed that this industry displaced other forms of overland transportation during the 19th century because it was more efficient and effective than the alternatives it displaced. By the beginning of the 20th century, however, development of the internal combustion engine, and the building of cars and trucks, had provided an alternative to the railroads for both personal and bulk transportation. In the early years this challenge was limited because of the high cost of the substitute product, its lack of sophistication and reliability and low availability. However, its potential was clear to see – if you owned a car or truck you had complete personal control over your transportation needs and could travel from door to door at your own convenience. Henry Ford perceived this market opportunity, invented the concept of mass assembly and began to produce a reliable, low-cost motorcar in constantly increasing numbers. From this time on the fortunes of the railroads began to decline so that, by the 1950s, this once great industry appeared to be in terminal decline.

What went wrong? Levitt's thesis is that those responsible for the management of the railroads were too preoccupied with their product to the neglect of the need that it served, which was transportation. Because of their myopia, or 'production orientation', they lost sight of the fact that the railroad product had been a substitute for earlier, less attractive products so that, offered a choice, consumers had switched from the old to the new to increase their personal satisfaction. It should have been obvious, therefore, that if a new, more convenient mode of transportation was developed then consumers would switch to it too. Thus, if the railroad management had concentrated on the need transportation served rather than their product they might have been able to join the infant automobile industry and develop a truly integrated transportation system. In other words, the railroads failed because they were lacking in marketing orientation.

At almost the same time as the appearance of Levitt's seminal paper, Robert Keith (1960) published an article in which he described the evolution of marketing in the Pillsbury Company in which he worked. In Keith's view the company's current marketing approach was a direct descendant of two earlier approaches or eras, which he termed production and sales. This three eras or stages model – production, sales, marketing – was widely adopted by what has come to be known as the marketing management school whose ideas dominated the theory and practice of marketing for 30 years or more.

The essence of the production orientation – a preoccupation with the product and the company – and the marketing orientation – a focus on the consumer's needs and the best way to serve them – have already been touched on in reviewing Levitt's 'Marketing myopia'. Keith's contribution then was to propose an intermediate or transitional phase he termed the sales era. In the sales era firms were still largely production orientated but as demand stabilized supply continued to grow, resulting in fierce competition between suppliers. One aspect of this was that producers committed more effort to selling their products with an emphasis on personal selling, advertising and sales promotion – hence the 'sales orientation'.

Chronologically, the production era was dated from the mid-1850s and lasted until around the late 1920s, which saw the birth of the sales era that lasted to around the mid-1950s, when the marketing era commenced. This conceptualization is now seen to be seriously flawed in terms of its historical accuracy but nonetheless remains a useful pedagogical device for reasons I will return to. First, however, it will be helpful to set the record straight.

As I have noted on several occasions there has been a tendency to date the emergence of marketing to the late 1950s and early 1960s. In an article entitled 'How modern is modern marketing?', Fullerton (1988) provides a rigorous analysis based on historical research.

At the outset it will be helpful to summarize the three key facets of the historical approach. First, there is a 'philosophical belief that historical phenomena such as markets are intrinsically rich and complex; efforts to simplify or assume away aspects of such phenomena are deeply distrusted' (Fullerton, 1988: 109). Second, the historical research tradition emphasizes 'systematic and critical evaluation of historical evidence of accuracy, bias, implicit messages, and now extinct meanings' (Fullerton, 1988: 109). The third facet of historical research is the process itself through which the researcher seeks to synthesize and recreate what actually happened in the past.

While there is considerable evidence that supports the existence of a production era there are also strong arguments to support a contrary view. Fullerton summarizes these as follows:

1. It ignores a well-established historical fact about business conditions – competition was intense in most businesses, there was overproduction and demand was frequently uncertain.
2. It totally misses the presence and vital importance of conscious demand stimulation in developing the advanced modern economies. Without such stimulation the revolution in production would have been stillborn.
3. It does not account for the varied and vigorous marketing efforts made by numerous manufacturers and other producers.
4. It ignores the dynamic growth of new marketing institutions outside the manufacturing firm. (Fullerton, 1988: 111)

Each of these arguments is examined in detail and substantial evidence is marshalled to support them. A particularly telling point concerns the need for active demand stimulation and the need for production and marketing to work in tandem.

Some of the famous pioneers of production such as Matthew Boulton and Josiah Wedgwood were also pioneers of modern marketing, cultivating large-scale demand for their revolutionary inexpensive products with techniques usually considered to have been post-1950 American innovations: market segmentation, product differentiation, prestige pricing, style obsolescence, saturation advertising, direct mail campaigns, reference group appeals and testimonials, among others (Fullerton, 1988: 112).

In Fullerton's view, 'demand enhancing marketing' spread from Britain to Germany and the USA. In the USA it was adopted with enthusiasm and Americans came to be seen as 'the supreme masters of aggressive demand stimulation', a fact frequently referred to in contemporary marketing texts of the early 1990s. Numerous examples support Fullerton's contention that producers of the so-called production era made extensive use of marketing tools and techniques as well as integrating forward to ensure their products were brought to the attention of their intended customers in the most effective way. That said, the examples provided (with one or two possible exceptions) do not, in my opinion, invalidate the classification of the period as the 'production era' in the sense that it was the producer who took the initiative and differentiated their product to meet the assumed needs of different consumer groups based on economic as opposed to sociological and psychological factors. In other words, producers inferred the consumer's behaviour but they had not yet developed techniques or procedures which would enable them to define latent wants and design, produce and market products and services to satisfy them.

Similarly, while the period from 1870 to 1930 saw the emergence and development of important marketing institutions in terms of physical distribution, retailing, advertising and marketing education, which are still important today, it does not seem unreasonable to argue that all these institutions were designed to sell more of what was being produced. This is not to deny the 'rich marketing heritage' documented by Fullerton but to reinforce the point that the transition to a 'marketing era' was marked by a major change in business philosophy from a producer-led interpretation of consumer needs to a consumer-driven approach to production.

As to the existence of a sales era (rejected by Fullerton) this seems as convenient a label as any to give to the transitional period between a production and marketing orientation. In addition to the reality of a depressed world economy in the 1930s, which required large-scale producers to sell more aggressively to maintain economies of scale, the period saw the migration of many behavioural sciences from a politically unstable Europe to the safety of the USA. In retrospect, it appears that it was this migration that led to the more rigorous analysis of consumer behaviour which was to underpin the emergence of a new 'marketing era'.

Combined with a greater insight into consumer behaviour was a period of great economic growth and prosperity following the Second World War, together with a major increase in the birth rate, which was to result in a new generation of consumers brought up in a period of material affluence (the baby boomers). It was this generation which sought to reassert consumer sovereignty and so initiated the change in the balance of power between producer and consumer which heralded the 'marketing era'.

Fullerton's argument that the production–sales–marketing era framework is a 'catastrophic model' 'in which major developments take place suddenly, with few antecedents' (1988: 121) is not without merit. Certainly, it could and has had the effect of disguising the evolutionary nature of marketing thought and practice. In place of a catastrophic model, or indeed, a continuity model which tends to observe differences over time, Fullerton suggests a 'complex flux model'. Such a complex flux model has the ability to incorporate dramatic changes but it also 'stresses that even dramatic change is based on and linked to past phenomena' (Fullerton, 1988: 121). It is also neutral in the sense that it does not automatically equate development or evolution with 'improvement', leaving such judgements for others to make.

Fullerton's complex flux model embraces four eras:

1. *Setting the stage: the era of antecedents.* A long gestational period beginning around 1500 in Britain and Germany, and the 1600s in North America. This was a period of low levels of consumption in which '75–90% of the populace were self-sufficient, rural and viscerally opposed to change' (1988: 122). Commerce was generally discredited but its standing improved as the benefits of trade became apparent.
2. *Modern marketing begins: the era of origins.* Britain in 1759; Germany and the USA circa 1830. 'This period marked the beginning of *pervasive* attention to stimulating and meeting demand among *nearly all of society*' (1988: 122, emphasis in original). Precipitated by the Industrial Revolution, and the mass migration from the countryside to an urban environment, potential markets had to be created through marketing techniques and activities.

3. *Building a superstructure: the era of institutional development.* Britain in 1850; Germany and the USA circa 1870 until 1919. 'During this period most of the major institutions and many of the practices of modern marketing first appeared' (1988: 122).
4. *Testing, turbulence, and growth: era of refinement and formalization.* From 1930 to the present day. 'The era's most distinguishing characteristic, however, has been a further development, refinement, and formalisation of institutions and practices that were developed earlier' (1988: 122).

Fullerton's analysis reflects a growing interest in the history of marketing thought and confirms that 'modern marketing has a rich heritage worthy of our attention' (1988: 123). Whether one should substitute his conceptualization as contained in his complex flux model for the widely accepted production–sales–marketing eras model is not seen as an either/or choice. Indeed, Fullerton's emphasis on the origins and evolution of marketing thought and practice reflects the historical research approach and merits attention in its own right. By contrast the 'eras model' is seen, at least by this author, as serving a different purpose in that it seeks to distinguish between marketing as a practice clearly present in both the production and sales eras, and marketing as a philosophy of business which shifts the emphasis from the producer's pursuit of profit as the primary objective to the achievement of customer satisfaction, which, in the long run, is likely to achieve the same financial reward.

In other words the three eras model provides a convenient framework for summarizing changes in the dominant orientation of business management. Thus it is a useful, albeit oversimplified model of the evolution of modern marketing or what I prefer to designate 'the rediscovery of marketing' (Baker, 1976). In truth, marketing has been around since the very first commercial exchange but there can be little doubt that until comparatively recently it has been of secondary or even tertiary importance to other more pressing imperatives in terms of increasing supply to meet the needs and wants of a rapidly expanding population. The objective of authors and teachers in using the three-stage evolutionary model has been to highlight the major changes in the dominant orientation of business rather than to analyse in detail the much more complex processes which underlay and resulted in these changes. What is beyond doubt is the fact that from around 1960 onwards marketing thinking and practice have been dominated by the marketing management school of thought.

The marketing management school

The marketing management school which evolved in the late 1950s and early 1960s is inextricably linked with the concept of the marketing mix and an analytical approach to marketing management following the positivist sequence of analysis, planning, control. As with most major paradigm shifts, no single author/researcher can claim sole credit for the new phenomenon. Among those who contributed significantly to the new school of thought were Joel Dean, Peter Drucker, Ted Levitt, E. Jerome McCarthy, Neil Borden and Philip Kotler. Dean and Drucker writing in the early 1950s pave the way but it was McCarthy's *Basic Marketing* (1960) which first promoted what came to be known as the 4 Ps of marketing – the idea that the marketing manager's task was to develop unique solutions to competitive marketing problems by manipulating the four major marketing factors – product, price, place and promotion. This idea of a 'marketing mix' (4 Ps) was elaborated by Neil Borden (1965) building on an earlier idea of James Culliton (1948), and confirmed by the appearance in 1967 of the first edition of Philip Kotler's bestselling *Marketing Management: Analysis, Planning and Control.* Levitt's contribution in distinguishing the essence of the marketing orientation/concept – a focus on customer needs – has already been referred to.

An authoritative view of the marketing management school is to be found in Frederick E. Webster Junior's 1992 article in the *Journal of Marketing* ('The changing role of marketing in the corporation'). In his own words, 'the purpose of this article is to outline both the intellectual and the pragmatic roots of changes that are occurring in marketing, especially marketing management, as a body of knowledge, theory, and practice and to suggest the need for a new paradigm of the marketing function within the firm' (Webster, 1992: 1).

While Webster's article recognized the need for 'a new paradigm of the marketing function within the firm', in the opinion of many European scholars a much more radical reappraisal was called for which challenged the very roots of the marketing management school.

The European perspective

One of the leading critics of the marketing management school was French professor Giles Marion. Marion's views are contained in a paper 'The marketing management discourse: what's new since the 1960s?' (1993), which is 'an attempt to describe the formalisation of ideas which make up marketing management as a school of thought' (1993: 143), based upon the content of the most popular marketing textbooks (American and European).

Marion argues that 'marketing as a discipline, should show greater humility by presenting its prescriptions in a more prudent manner, and by describing more systematically the interaction between supply and demand and the organisational consequences that follow' (1993: 166). In conclusion he expresses the view that, while the normative theory of marketing management may well have had a useful impact on managerial thinking and practice, 'there has been nothing new since the 1960s or even well before' (1993: 166).

While Marion's critique struck at the very heart of the marketing management school promoted by Americans it was comparatively mild compared with the trenchant criticism expressed by Evert Gummesson, a leading member of the Scandinavian School. In Gummesson's view, 'the traditional textbooks do not satisfactorily reflect reality' and he proposed six objections to support his thesis (1993):

1. Textbook presentations of marketing are based on limited real-world data – specifically, they are largely concerned with mass marketed, packaged consumer goods.
2. Goods account for a minor part of all marketing, but the textbook presentations are focused on goods; services are treated as a special case.

3. Marketing to consumers dominates textbooks, while industrial/business marketing is treated as a special case.
4. The textbook presentations are a patchwork; new knowledge is piled on top of existing knowledge, but not integrated with it.
5. The textbooks have a clever pedagogical design; the form is better than the content.
6. The Europeans surrendered to the USA and its marketing gurus and do not adequately promote their own original contributions.

In sum, Gummesson argues that US textbooks represent the colonization of thought and that this thought excludes or ignores much of the development in marketing thinking which had occurred in the fields of industrial and services marketing in Europe during the 1970s and 1980s and even before. To some extent the blame must rest with the Europeans for failing to promote their ideas in the USA, but the dismissive, not invented here attitudes of American academics who act as gatekeepers to US-based publications must also bear some of the blame.

Many of the views expressed by Marion and Gummesson are echoed in the works of Christian Grönroos (another leading member of the Scandinavian School). In Grönroos's view (1994) the majority of marketing academics and textbooks treat marketing as a subject which emerged in the 1960s and is founded upon the concept of the marketing mix and the 4 Ps of product, price, place and promotion (McCarthy, 1960) which comprised it. As a consequence, 'empirical studies of what the key marketing variables are, and how they are perceived in use by marketing managers have been neglected. Moreover structure has been vastly favoured over process considerations' (Kent, 1986: 347–8).

While McCarthy's simplification of Borden's original conceptualization of the marketing mix has obvious pedagogical attractions, its application appears best suited to mass markets for consumer packaged goods underpinned by sophisticated distribution channels and commercial mass media. Indeed, this is the context or setting of many marketing courses and texts, but it is clearly representative of a limited aspect of the domain and process of marketing.

However, the concept of the marketing mix is more seriously flawed. To begin with the paradigm is a production-oriented definition in the sense that its approach is that customers are persons to whom something is done rather than persons for whom something is done (see Dixon and Blois, 1983; Grönroos, 1989, 1990). A second deficiency is that while McCarthy recognizes the interactive nature of the 4 Ps 'the model itself does not explicitly include any interactive elements. Furthermore, it does not indicate the nature and scope of such interactions' (Grönroos, 1994: 351).

However, perhaps the major deficiency of the 4 Ps approach is that it defines marketing as a functional activity in its own right and so creates the potential for conflict with other functional areas, discourages persons from becoming involved in marketing because it is the preserve of the marketing department and, as a result, can frustrate or compromise the adoption of the marketing concept.

Grönroos sees the 4 Ps as a direct development from the microeconomic theory of imperfect competition developed by Robinson and Chamberlin in the 1930s, but argues that the separation of the 4 Ps model from its theoretical foundations left it without roots. Indeed, Grönroos goes even further and argues that 'the introduction of the four Ps of the marketing mix with their simplistic view of reality can be characterised as a step back to the level of, in a sense equally simplistic, microeconomic theory of the 1930s' (1994: 351). This observation is largely prompted by the apparent failure of marketing academics in the USA to detect the evolution of the Copenhagen School's parameter theory. Building upon the work of Frisch (1933), von Stackelberg (1939), Kjaer-Hansen (1945) and Rasmussen (1955), Gösta Mickwitz observed:

> When empirically based works on marketing mechanisms show that the enterprise uses a number of different parameters markedly distinct from each other, the theory of the behaviour of the enterprise in the market will be very unrealistic if it is content to deal only with ... [few] ... of them. We have therefore tried throughout to pay attention to the presence of a number of different methods which firms employ to increase their sales. (Mickwitz, 1959: 217)

Grönroos (1994: 351) explains further: 'The interactive nature of the marketing variables was explicitly recognised and accounted for in parameter theory by means of varying market elasticities of the parameters over the life of the product life cycle.'

At the same time that the 4 Ps was becoming the established 'theory' or normative approach to marketing in the USA, and many other countries, new theories and models were emerging in Europe – specifically, the interaction/network approach to industrial marketing and the marketing of services (1960s) and more recently, the concept of relationship marketing.

The interaction/network approach originated in Uppsala University in Sweden during the 1960s and was subsequently taken up in many countries following the establishment of the IMP (Industrial Marketing and Purchasing) group. As Grönroos explains:

> Between the parties in a network various interactions take place, where exchanges and adaptation to each other occur. The flow of goods and information as well as financial and social exchanges takes place in the network. (See, for example, Håkansson 1982, Johanson and Mattson 1985, and Kock 1991). In such a network the role and forms of marketing are not very clear. All exchanges, all sorts of interactions have an impact on the position of the parties in the network. The interactions are not necessarily initiated by the seller – the market according to the marketing mix paradigm – and they may continue over a long period of time, for example, for several years. (1994: 352)

The interaction/network model recognizes that exchanges are not the exclusive preserve of professional marketers and may, indeed, involve numerous other members of the interacting organizations, some of whom may well have more influence and impact on the relationship than the functional specialists.

In the 1970s interest in the marketing of services developed simultaneously in the USA and Europe. But, while the 4 Ps framework continued to prevail in the USA, in Scandinavia and Finland the Scandinavian School of Services saw the marketing of services as an integral element of overall management. Grönroos and Gummesson have been strong proponents of the school and have written extensively on the subject.

The interaction and network approach to industrial marketing and modern service marketing approaches 'clearly views marketing as an interactive process in a social context where *relationship building* is a vital cornerstone' (Grönroos, 1994: 353). He argues that this approach is similar to the system-based approaches to marketing of the 1950s (e.g. Alderson, 1957) and contrasts strongly with the clinical approach of the 4 Ps paradigm which makes sellers active and buyers passive. As noted earlier, the latter emphasis tends to put exchange relationships into the hands of professional marketers which may psychologically alienate other members of an organization from becoming involved. This is a far cry from Drucker's (1954) observation that the sole purpose of the business is to create customers!

As a consequence of rapid advances in both manufacturing (flexible manufacturing, CAD, CAM) and information technology, the mass consumer markets suited to the 4 Ps approach have become fragmented and call for flexible and adaptable marketing approaches. In the 1980s the response to this need was the emergence of *relationship marketing*. Grönroos refers to his own (1990) definition of relationship marketing: 'Marketing is to establish, maintain and enhance relationships with customers and other partners, at a profit, so that the objectives of the parties involved are met. This is achieved by mutual exchange and fulfilment of promises' (1994: 355). While more extended and explicit, this definition is essentially similar to that proposed by Baker (1976: 4) a number of years earlier: 'Marketing is concerned with mutually satisfying exchange relationships.' Similarly, Baker (and other authors) have argued consistently for the need to regard marketing both as a philosophy of business and a business function. As a business function responsible for coordinating and executing the implementation of a marketing plan, marketing is likely to continue to find the marketing mix model a useful one, albeit that the 4 Ps is an oversimplified version of the original concept. It is, of course, important to emphasize that continuing to use such an organizational and planning framework is in no way inimical to the emphasis on relationship marketing as contrasted to the prior emphasis on a transactional model.

Today, relationship marketing is widely accepted as reflecting the essence of the marketing concept. In reality, this has always been the case in the majority of buyer–seller interactions since commercial exchanges were first initiated. Buyers have always looked for reliable sources of supply at a fair price as this reduces the dissonance and uncertainty of having to consider every single transaction as an entirely new decision. Similarly, sellers recognize that there are increased opportunities for long-term survival and profit if they can establish a customer franchise and repeat purchasing behaviour. That said, there can be no doubt that there are radically different interpretations of capitalism and the market economy, one of which emphasizes long-term relationships, the other a one-off transaction.

It was perhaps only with the collapse of the centrally planned and controlled command economies of Eastern Europe and the Soviet Union that the existence of two models of capitalism came into sharper relief and focus. Based on a book by Michel Albert (1991), Christian Dussart (1994) highlighted the differences between the Anglo-Saxon model of capitalism, as practised in the UK and USA, which is essentially short-term and transactionally based, and the

Alpine/Germanic model, which also embraces Scandinavia (and Japan), and which emphasizes long-term relationships as a source of buyer satisfaction and seller profitability.

So what is marketing?

At the 1993 UK Marketing Education Group conference a group of researchers from the Henley Management College (Gibson et al., 1993) presented their findings of a content and correspondence analysis of approximately 100 definitions of marketing in an attempt to answer the question 'What is marketing?' Specifically, the authors set out to 'shed some light on the nature of the process of defining marketing, to identify strong and emerging themes, and to develop a map of the territory' (1993: 383). By using content analysis to evaluate the definitions collected, and using these findings as an input to a correspondence analysis, the authors provided both a qualitative and quantitative analysis of how scholars had defined marketing over the years and up to that time.

To begin with, a collection of approximately 100 explicit marketing definitions were collected from textbooks, journals and institutes/association publications which spanned the 20th century. The majority of these definitions were academic and originated in the USA, UK and Europe. Themes were selected as the unit of assessment and five clusters were established as:

1. object of marketing
2. nature of the relationship
3. outcomes
4. application
5. philosophy or (versus) function.

The authors describe in some detail how each of these themes was derived and how definitions falling within them have changed in approach and emphasis over time. However, 'in order to simplify the definitions of various authors, and give more relevance to the five themes identified earlier, some of the definitions gathered and analysed for content were subjected to a process of correspondence analysis' (Gibson et al., 1993: 383). In essence, correspondence analysis is a graphic technique which enables one to develop a two-dimensional plot indicating the degree of similarity or correspondence between rows or columns of data which have similar patterns. Using the authors as rows and their perspectives on the themes as columns the map reproduced here as Figure 1.3 was produced.

They explain:

> ... the authors' perspective on the original themes were constructed as dichotomies and include, first 'profit and non-profit', which related to the outcomes and application themes; secondly, 'micro and macro', which translated across to philosophy or function; thirdly, 'static and dynamic' and 'open and closed' which referred to the relationship theme and to some extent provided some insight into the content and nature of the whole definition; and finally, two additional dichotomies were included, 'positive and normative' namely, whether the definitions described what exists or prescribed what 'ought' to happen, and whether the definition was 'explicit or implicit'. (Gibson et al., 1993: 383)

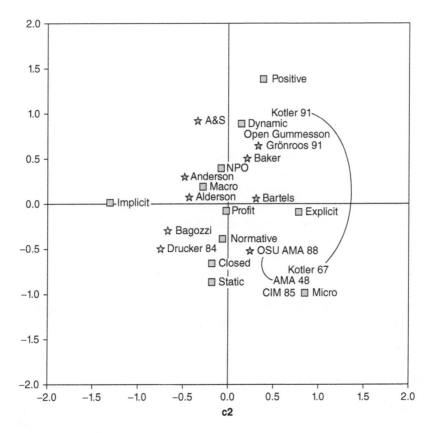

Figure 1.3 Marketing definitions: a map of the territory.

(Gibson et al., 1993). Used with permission

Based upon both qualitative and quantitative analyses certain conclusions were derived.

1. Changes have occurred across all five content themes indicating significant evolution in the concept of marketing since its earliest definition.
2. The greatest change has occurred in the 'nature of the relationship' (i.e. between provider and user), from one-way narrow, discrete transactions to the recognition and positioning of relationships as a key strategy resource. This change is also reflected in the other themes, particularly 'philosophy or function', and marks the moderation of economic explanations of consumption behaviour through the admission of concepts derived from psychology and sociology.
3. Changes in the marketing environment have resulted in a broadening and softening of the original concept and its transfer to other domains – services, not-for-profit, etc.
4. 'Marketing' has shown itself to be adaptable, flexible, international and open. But Gibson et al. warn that 'this latitude has allowed ambiguity to creep into its definition and cause confusion. Definitional clarity is essential in the future.'

In conclusion, Gibson et al. offered three further points prompted by their analysis:

1. Marketing and its guardians continue to foster its open and innovative culture.
2. A single definition is not aimed for as its existence would probably discourage future development of the subject.
3. Nonetheless, greater rigour should be given to the formulation of definitions in future.

Now, more than two decades later, it is believed that a similar study would result in much the same conclusions and recommendations. Views on the nature and scope of the marketing concept continue to evolve and there is widespread agreement that mutually satisfying relationships are the essence of a marketing orientation and marketing practice. In parallel with this evolution it has become accepted that the cocreation of value, as perceived by the parties to a relationship, lies at the very heart of both marketing theory and practice and this notion has spread beyond simple commercial exchange to infuse all manner of human interactions. As a result, insights into the nature of 'value', choice behaviour and change developed by marketers have been adopted by policy makers, NGOs and not-for-profit organizations.

At the time, however, in the turbulent and recessionary environment which characterized the early 1990s, Webster's call for a new approach to the practice of marketing cited earlier was widely echoed, particularly in practitioner publications.

Marketing's mid-life crisis

Among the more influential of these was McKinsey's (1993) observation that marketing was experiencing a 'mid-life crisis' (Brady and Davis, 1993). In simplified terms the argument ran that if exchange was concerned with relationships between individuals and organizations then marketing must be everybody's business and not the preserve of a privileged few to be found within a formal marketing department. This perception was probably magnified by the fact that several important developments in managerial thinking such as benchmarking, total quality management, strategic alliances, globalization and strategic thinking might properly be considered the primary concern of marketers. These fields had been pre-empted by others.

In the new millennium marketers appear to have recovered some of their confidence and are able to take a more balanced view of their discipline. It is now generally accepted that the relationship marketing approach has effectively extended the marketing concept into areas such as services and business-to-business marketing, which were poorly served by the marketing management model based as it was upon concepts of mass production, mass distribution and mass marketing essentially of packaged consumer goods. At the same time, it has also been appreciated that many marketing exchanges are based upon low involvement and transactions and that the two distinct approaches can coexist together. Simultaneously, a clearer distinction is being drawn between the philosophy of marketing which is encapsulated in a marketing orientation that can be held by everybody, both internal and external to an organization, and the market-oriented organization which is customer oriented and market driven.

The former marketing-orientated organization is committed to the philosophy of mutually satisfying exchange relationships while the latter market-oriented company is focused on how to achieve this through the professional practice and management of the marketing function.

In 2004 the *Journal of Marketing* published an article by Stephen Vargo and Robert Lusch that has prompted extensive debate about the need for a new model, or paradigm, of the domain of marketing. The article that precipitated this debate is entitled 'Evolving to a new dominant logic of marketing'. In the abstract the authors write:

> The purpose of this article is to illuminate the evolution of *marketing* thought toward a new dominant logic. ... Briefly, *marketing* has moved from a goods-dominant view, in which tangible output and discrete transactions were central, to a service-dominant view, in which interchangeability, exchange processes, and relationships are central. (2004: 2)

The authors then stress that their interpretation of 'service-centred' should not be equated with current conceptualizations of services as a residual, i.e. not a tangible good, or something to add value to a good – value-added services – or service industries like healthcare and education. They state:

> Rather, we define services as the application of specialised competences (knowledge and skills) through deeds, processes, and performances to the benefit of another entity or the entity itself. ... Thus, the service-centred dominant logic represents a reoriented philosophy that is applicable to all *marketing* offerings, including those that involve tangible output (goods) in the process of service provision. (2004: 2)

In effect Vargo and Lusch are arguing that we move away from a model of exchange inherited from economics with a focus on 'goods' in which intangible services are treated as a residual or special case. One consequence of the economic model is its emphasis upon the management and allocation of scarce resources. This, in turn, results in a focus on the supply side and the marketing management model which is concerned with advising suppliers how to manipulate demand in order to dispose of the supply which they have created. This is not to say that suppliers do not take into account the needs and wants of customers in determining what goods and services to create, but rather that their interpretation could be much improved through closer collaboration with their intended customers.

While some would point to the emergence of customer relationship management as recognition by the supply side of a need to engage more closely with the customer, my own, more cynical view, is that this is paying lip service to the notion of 'relationships'. Relationships are interactions that have to be worked at by both parties; as soon as one party believes that they can 'manage' or manipulate the relationship to their advantage – the objective of most customer relation management (CRM) schemes I have come across – then it would seem to be doomed to failure.

At the heart of Vargo and Lusch's argument is the distinction between what they term operand and operant resources. Operand resources are those on which some actual operation has to be performed to produce an effect, while operant resources are those that produce effects.

Put another way, operand resources are equivalent to the economist's 'scarce resources' while operant resources may be equated with the actions that transform these into goods and services. Clearly it is decisions with regard to the latter which are the more important and I agree with Vargo and Lusch when they claim:

> Operant resources are often invisible and intangible; often they are core competences or organisational processes. They are likely to be dynamic and infinite and not static and finite, as is usually the case with operand resources. Because operant resources produce effects, they enable humans both to multiply the value of natural resources and to create additional operant skills. (2004: 3)

In light of this it is then argued that a 'service-centred logic' is necessary to reflect this change of emphasis. This proposal is based on the view that traditional marketing is seen as focusing on operand resources, is goods centred and concerned with the notion of utility(ies). By contrast, service-centred marketing is grounded in and largely consistent with resource advantage theory and is customer centric and market driven.

In the original article (it has been revisited by the authors and many others since) Vargo and Lusch develop their arguments through a comparison between traditional and service-centred marketing and conclude that the latter is the model to be followed in future. For my part I tend to agree with Evert Gummesson (2007: 114), that 'Their logic opened up an international dialogue on the output of marketing as value propositions rather than as goods or services.' He goes on to say:

> The *service-dominant logic* suggests *service* (in the singular) as the core concept replacing both goods and services. A supplier offers a *value proposition*, but *value actualisation* occurs in the usage and consumption process. Thus value is the outcome of *co-creation* between suppliers and customers. (2007: 117)

However, the debate initiated by Vargo and Lusch has prompted a radical reappraisal of the nature of marketing and its theory. While all marketing academics would not subscribe to the proposition that service-dominant (S-D) logic has displaced or superseded alternative theorizations, there can be little doubt that it has become a major focus of attention. And, in this edition, we are fortunate to include a new chapter written by Vargo and Lusch, who are recognized as the founding fathers of S-D logic.

It is my view that an emphasis on value as opposed to 'service' is more consistent with the original conceptualization of marketing as a philosophy of exchange focused upon 'mutually satisfying relationships'. This view is supported by a subsequent (2006) definition offered by Lusch and Vargo to the effect that 'marketing is the process in society and organisations that facilitates voluntary exchange through collaborative relationships that create reciprocal value through the application of complementary resources'. Somewhat lengthier, but very much in the spirit of my own 1976 definition.

By contrast, stressing 'service' may merely prolong the goods versus services debate; but the reader will need to consult current marketing journals to determine how this debate is developing. What is clear to my mind is that the concept or 'philosophy' of marketing remains the same – it is the implementation of the function through marketing practice that continues to evolve to better achieve the intention and objectives of the philosophy.

However, the notion that interactions between seller and buyer result in the cocreation of value has resulted in much greater attention being given to what constitutes the nature of 'value'? In his seminal work *The Wealth of Nations* (1776), Adam Smith saw it as axiomatic that 'Consumption is the sole end and purpose of production.' For him this was a self-evident truth which needed no restatement and the remainder of his work is focused on the creation of products and services for sale. The corollary of this is that if the thing produced is not consumed then it has no value. So, while producers may impute value to their inventories of stock the reality is that until they are sold they record past expenditures where the imperative is to convert these into revenues to enable the organization to continue in business.

Looked at this way it becomes obvious why sellers should become concerned with what represents 'value' for potential customers. In turn, this results in concentration upon the basic principle underpinning the marketing concept – the identification of precise customer wants and the production of goods/services that will meet these at an acceptable (profitable) expenditure by the producer. By establishing what represents 'value' for the customer the supplier has a target or benchmark to determine whether they can satisfy this at a cost plus margin that will be mutually satisfying to them.

A new marketing paradigm?

In parallel with revising this chapter I was also engaged with a revision of a chapter entitled 'What is marketing?' for a new 7th edition of *The Marketing Book*. Originally published in 1987 by the Institute of Marketing in collaboration with Butterworth-Heinemann, the objective was to compile an authoritative handbook for students and practitioners written by experts and covering the main topics of the marketing discipline. The purpose of *Marketing Theory* is more focused in that it is written specifically for persons who have studied the subject of marketing in some depth with an explicit interest in the principal ideas, concepts and theories that underpin the marketing discipline. Inevitably, however, there is a considerable overlap in the content relevant to these for both audiences, which creates something of a dilemma for me. Plagiarism, which involves the passing off of another's work as one's own, is in Wikipedia's words 'considered academic dishonesty and a breach of journalistic ethics. It is subject to sanctions like penalties, suspension, and even expulsion' (see http://en.wikipedia.org/wiki/Plagiarism). But, what about self-plagiarism which involves citation of one's own prior work? Personally, I take the view that provided one clearly identifies the other source then it is both a permissible and sensible practice and cite in my defence Pamela Samuelson's (1994: 25) justification that 'I said it so well the first time that it makes no sense to say it differently a second time.' I also hope that this self-reference will encourage you to consult Chapter 1 in *The Marketing Book* which also contains my personal views on how the marketing discipline may develop in future.

Writing in the *Journal of the Academy of Marketing Science* (2012: 35–52), Ravi Achrol and Philip Kotler proposed 'a three-tiered explanation of the emerging field of marketing – its sub phenomena (consumer experiences and sensory systems), its phenomena (marketing networks), and its super phenomena (sustainability and development)'.

To begin with it is stressed that the focus is upon the future and the emerging paradigms of marketing. However, to do so, it is necessary to summarize the assumptions of both the received and emergent marketing paradigms as perceived by the authors, and these have been summarized in Table 1.1. Effectively, this is presented as a three-tiered framework comprising consumption experiences, marketing networks and sustainability.

The first three assumptions all relate to aspects of what are described as 'sub phenomena' relating to consumer behaviour. These are elaborated on as covering: Marketing and the human senses; Neurophysiology and marketing; and Marketing and nanotechnology. The next four assumptions define what are described as 'phenomena' and deal with 'mid-range theories that have predictive power' and are concerned with relational concepts that are bringing *production and consumption* closer together'. The topics explored here include: The evolution of production and innovation networks; Distributed production–consumption networks; Consumption networks. And, finally, four assumptions identified as 'super phenomena' of which two, *'sustainability and poverty'*, are selected for detailed discussion. Topics covered include: The sustainable marketing concept and Base of the pyramid marketing.

Table 1.1   Key issues and assumptions underpinning the current and future marketing paradigm.

PARADIGM STATUS/ISSUE	CURRENT	FUTURE
A SUB-PHENOMENAL: CONSUMER BEHAVIOUR	Need satisfaction	Sense-making
	Cognitive psychology	Neurophysiology
1. Experience 2. Disciplinary focus 3. Sensory focus	Objective	Subjective
B PHENOMENAL: RELATIONAL CONCEPTS	Mass production	Cocreation. One-to-One
4. Supply orientation 5. Dominant technology 6. Managerial orientation 7. Source of competitive advantage	Computer based	Bio and nanotechnology
	Internally focused	Externally directed
	Distinctive competence	Leadership in production and consumption networks
C SUPER PHENOMENAL	Growth emphasis on customers with discretionary purchasing power	Circular economy and sustainability
8. Strategic management priorities 9. Unit of analysis 10. Strategic emphasis 11. Public policy	Anthropocentric	Bio-centric
	Buyer-seller	Society
	Corporate social responsibility	Human welfare
	Laissez-faire	Regulated social business

Adapted from: Achrol and Kotler (2012).

Based on this initial conceptualization, the authors set out to make its complexity more tractable by analysing 'it in three dimensions – marketing's substructure, its structure and its superstructure'.

In this way we can span:

1. the theoretically more tractable domain of the marketing microcosm, its sub phenomena;

2. its phenomenal realm (including the managerial realm) with its mid-range theories that have predictive power even if their putative mechanisms are less than rigorously explicated, and

3. super phenomenal realm of marketing and society, that are largely a descriptive field of analysis. (Achrol and Kotler, 2012: 36)

Each of these is described and evaluated in some detail and provide important pointers to the potential and likely future development of the marketing discipline. Of particular relevance is the discussion of the 'sustainable marketing concept' in which 'market capacity' and 'resource capacity' are brought into equilibrium. For this to occur overconsumption must be abandoned, 'whether it is oversold currencies, financial instruments, real estate, business opportunities or dreams' (Achrol and Kotler, 2012: 44).

Managerial marketing is clearly associated with excessive consumption and Achrol and Kotler 'emphasise a new philosophy for firms to proactively':

1. Communicate the harmful side-effects of wasteful consumption;

2. Grow the segments of environmentally conscious consumers, by developing superior products at standard market prices; and

3. Demarket/countermarket certain products, technologies, and marginal consumer segments (e.g. consumers who cannot afford expensive homes). (2012: 45)

As confirmed and endorsed by numerous authors and theorists, the marketing paradigm has evolved from a focus on marketing as a *function*, through marketing as a *managerial practice* to marketing as *exchange*. While credit for this evolution is largely attributed to the work of American scholars it is felt that this largely overlooks the contributions of numerous European and other scholars whose work, chronologically, preceded recognition of marketing as mutual. Based upon this perception the IMP group focused upon the interaction between parties to an exchange and the relationships in the networks formed between them. In parallel, the role of service and services was given explicit recognition. It is significant that apart from Gummesson (1998), himself writing in an American journal, none of this research is cited by Achrol and Kotler. Indeed, virtually all their sources are American based. On these grounds I consider it wrong to attribute the view that we are now 'at the threshold of the *network* paradigm' to an earlier paper by the authors in 1999.

In making this observation I fully acknowledge that both authors, and especially Philip Kotler, have made very important contributions to the evolution of marketing thought and theory. Indeed, many developments like the transfer of the marketing concept to a non-commercial context (social marketing) are founded on insights first promoted by Kotler and Kotler and Levy. Nonetheless, the failure to consider the publication of research findings in non-American journals constitutes a form of 'research myopia' that I referred to directly in an address to the American Marketing Association's Winter Educators (1994) meeting.

To avoid a similar oversight it is important that one does not confine one's research solely to papers published in leading American journals.

This advice is confirmed by Volume 6 in the *Legends in Marketing* series, edited by Roderick Brodie (Brookes and Little, 2013), which is concerned with Marketing Theory and chronicles the published work of Finnish scholar Christian Grönroos. The volume contains 13 papers written by Grönroos together with commentaries by Brodie and four other contributors including myself. In the absence of any contact between me and Richard Brookes and Victoria Little, who contributed Chapter 14, 'What really is marketing?', it was reassuring to find a high level of agreement in our answers to the question that is the subject of this chapter.

Brookes and Little identify three overriding themes in Grönroos's work:

1. critique of the mainstream American Marketing Association (AMA) approach
2. a customer management/marketing practice perspective
3. a business marketing, service and relationship lens.

Their commentary concludes with an observation which is an appropriate introduction to this book:

> However, clearly, we are still looking for the answers to that basic question: '*What really is marketing?*' We have seen that it can be a philosophy, a toolkit, process, a set of practices and, in large organisations, a dedicated but somewhat constrained function. Christian has long argued that perhaps we need a new word for what has been labelled marketing. It would need to be a word which connotes what the combined part-time and full-time 'marketers' really do to gain, keep, and grow their customers. (Brookes and Little, 2013)

Déjà vu?

As noted earlier, in 1992 Fred Webster published a seminal and highly influential paper in the *Journal of Marketing* concerned with the 'The changing role of marketing in the corporation' and this is a theme that he returned to 20 years later in collaboration with Bob Lusch. In 'Elevating marketing: Marketing is dead! Long live marketing! (2013), they observe: 'If marketing is to survive as a business function and academic discipline and be seen as a legitimate institution in society, it must be elevated to a higher level in the consciousness of managers, the consuming public, and public policy makers.' And, in order to do this, it needs to reflect on fundamental changes in the environment, the economy, society and politics and rethink the dominant paradigm that has governed its evolution since the early 1960s. To accomplish this the authors 'propose a shift from a narrow focus on *customers* to a broader concern for *citizen-consumers*. The objective is to recommit marketing to the fundamental purpose of improving the standard of living for all citizens not only as consumers and producers but also as actors in relationships with multiple partners in the co-creation of value at all levels within the social economic system' (2013: 390).

In other words, marketing needs to switch its focus from the individual, self-interested consumer to consumers as members of a global society who are willing to reflect upon the impact of their behaviour on others and, as exhorted by the Golden Rule, 'Do unto others as you would have them do unto you'. To do so calls for transformative marketing (Mick et al., 2012) and an approach to what I have termed 'social business', which is a much broader conceptualization than that proposed by Muhammad Yunus, which is primarily focused on the use of microfinance to facilitate social entrepreneurship.

Webster and Lusch comment on the development of marketing as an academic discipline since the 1960s and see it as having been driven by three main factors: an emphasis on methodology and data-driven analysis, a narrow microeconomic paradigm and a myopic focus on the firm. In other words, what is generally referred to as the marketing management school of thought. The result has been 'Little interest developed in the overall welfare of the field of marketing as academic theory, business practice, and societal institution. Rigor triumphed over relevance. In the unrelenting pursuit of rigor, relatively unimportant simple issues tended to move attention away from larger, less well-defined complex problems facing business and society' (2013: 390).

Unfortunately, there is more than a little irony in the authors' reference to a myopic focus. Myopia was the theme of what is probably the most widely read and best known paper written on the subject of marketing (Levitt, 1960), yet it is a deficiency that still bedevils American marketing scholars who remain singularly ill-informed of developments in marketing thought that have occurred in other countries and publicized in their own 'domestic' journals. That is, of course, until they are belatedly rediscovered and brought to our attention through publication in the leading American journals.

As is apparent from my earlier discussion of the 'European perspective', to state that the distinction between customers and consumers has been ignored in the marketing literature is to completely overlook the IMP group of European scholars (which included the Americans Wilson and Woodside) who focused on industrial or business-to-business marketing from the mid-1970s onwards and identified clearly the importance of interaction, networks and relationships. And, closely associated with their emphasis on relationship marketing, anticipated much of the literature on what was to become known as services marketing.

In making this comment my intention is to reinforce the point that in order to understand the evolution of marketing thought it is necessary to look beyond what is claimed to be the dominant paradigm by any special interest group and think critically about alternative explanations and hypotheses. That said, the Webster and Lusch paper makes an important contribution in both pulling together and reinforcing arguments that the philosophy of marketing has always been concerned with increasing customer/consumer welfare to the mutual benefit of both seller and buyer. It also spells out a number of specific research topics deserving of attention and very likely to influence the future agenda in years to come.

Summary

In this chapter I have endeavoured to shed some light on the nature and scope of 'marketing'. As we have seen, marketing is a large and complex subject which covers a multitude of economic and social activities. Many of these are described in some detail in the chapters which follow. That said, the practice of marketing is founded on a very simple philosophy, that of 'mutually satisfying (commercial) exchange relationships'.

In the 1990s relationship marketing became the dominant theme almost everywhere, despite its somewhat belated recognition in the USA. As my review has attempted to show it was ever so but, depending upon the existing balance between supply and demand at any point in time, one or other of the parties to an exchange is likely to exercise more control over the relationship than the other. If this is the producer/seller it does not necessarily mean that they are production or sales oriented and insensitive to customer needs. Indeed, it is a truism that all successful businesses are marketing orientated – if they were not meeting and satisfying customers' needs profitably they would not be successful. What matters is the state of mind of the producers/sellers – their philosophy of business. If this philosophy includes a concern for the customer's needs and wants, and appreciation of the benefits and satisfactions which are looked for, a genuine effort to establish a dialogue and build a long-term relationship then this is the marketing philosophy irrespective of whether or not the organization possesses any personnel or function designated as 'marketing'.

In the chapters which follow many facets and aspects of the subject are examined and explored by internationally recognized experts. Taken together these provide an extensive overview and introduction to the underlying theories and principles which underpin both the theory and practice. While personal perspectives may vary, the core proposition remains – marketing is concerned with the identification, creation and maintenance of mutually satisfying exchange relationships.

Recommended further reading

Readers are strongly recommended to read the *Journal of Marketing Management* 30th Anniversary Special Issue: Pushing the Boundaries, Sketching the Future (Vol. 30, Nos 11–12, September 2014), which contains seven articles by leading authorities documenting past research into important areas of marketing theory together with comment on the likely future developments.

References

Achrol, R.S. and Kotler, P. (2012) 'Frontiers of the marketing paradigm in the third millennium', *Journal of the Academy of Marketing Science* 40(1): 35–52.

Albert, M. (1991) *Capitalisme contre capitalisme*. Paris: Seuil, L'Histoire Immédiate.

Alderson, W. (1957) *Marketing Behavior and Executive Action*. Homewood, IL: Irwin.

Baker, M.J. (1976) 'Evolution of the marketing concept', in M.J. Baker (ed.) *Marketing Theory and Practice*. London: Macmillan.

Baker, M.J. (1980) 'Marketing maxims', *Advertising* 66 (Winter).

Baker, M.J. (1994a) 'Research myopia: recency, relevance, reinvention and renaissance (the 4 R's of marketing)', Working paper series, Department of Marketing, University of Strathclyde.

Baker, M.J. (ed.) (1994b) *The Marketing Book*, 3rd edn. Oxford: Butterworth-Heinemann.

Baker, M.J. (ed.) (2001) *Marketing: Critical Perspectives on Business and Management,* 5 Volumes, Introduction Book 1. Routledge: London.

Borden, N.H. (1965) 'The concept of the marketing mix', in G. Schwartz (ed.) *Science in Marketing*. Chichester: John Wiley, pp. 286ff.

Brady, J. and Davis, I. (1993) *The McKinsey Quarterly* 2 (Spring).

Brookes, R.W. and Little, V.J. (2013) 'What really is marketing?', in R.P. Brodie (ed.) *Legends in Marketing. Volume 6: Marketing Theory*. New Delhi: Sage.

Chamberlin, E.J. (1933) *The Theory of Monopolistic Competition*. Cambridge, MA: Harvard University Press.

Culliton, J.W. (1948) *The Management of Marketing Costs*. Andover, MA: The Andover Press.

Dean, J. (1951) *Managerial Economics*. Englewood Cliffs, NJ: Prentice-Hall.

Dixon, D.F. and Blois, K.J. (1983) 'Some limitations of the 4 Ps as a paradigm for marketing', Proceedings, Marketing Education Group Conference, Cranfield.

Drucker, P. (1954) *The Practice of Management*. New York: Harper & Row.

Dussart, C. (1994) 'Capitalism versus capitalism', in M.J. Baker (ed.) *Perspectives on Marketing Management*, Vol. 4. Chichester: John Wiley.

Frisch, R. (1933) 'Monopole-Polypole-la notion de la force dans l'économie', *Nationalokonomisk Tidskrift*, Denmark.

Fullerton, R.A. (1988) 'How modern is modern marketing? Marketing's evolution and the myth of the production era', *Journal of Marketing* 52 (January): 108–25.

Galbraith, J.K. (1958) *The Affluent Society*. Harmondsworth: Penguin.

Gibson, H., Tynan, C. and Pitt, L. (1993) 'What is marketing? A qualitative and quantitative analysis of marketing decisions', Proceedings, Marketing Education Group Conference, Loughborough.

Grönroos, C. (1989) 'Defining marketing: a market-oriented approach', *European Journal of Marketing* 23: 52–60.

Grönroos, C. (1990) *Service Management and Marketing: Managing the Moments of Truth in Service Competition*. Lexington, MA: The Free Press/Lexington Books.

Grönroos, C. (1994) 'Quo vadis marketing? Toward a relationship marketing paradigm', *Journal of Marketing Management* 10(5): 347–60.

Gummesson, E. (1993) 'Broadening and specifying relationship marketing', invited paper, Monash Colloquium on Relationship Marketing, Monash University, Melbourne, Australia, 1–4 August 1993.

Gummesson, E. (1998) 'Implementation requires a relationship marketing paradigm', *Journal of the Academy of Marketing Science* 26(3): 242–9.

Gummesson, E. (2007) 'Exit *services* marketing – enter *service* marketing', *Journal of Customer Behaviour* 6(2): 113–41.

Håkansson, H. (ed.) (1982) *International Marketing and Purchasing of Industrial Goods*. New York: John Wiley.

Johanson, J. and Mattson, L.-G. (1985) 'Marketing investments and market investments in industrial networks', *International Journal of Research in Marketing* 2(3): 185–95.

Keith, R.J. (1960) 'The marketing revolution', *Journal of Marketing* 24(3): 35–8.

Kent, R.A. (1986) 'Faith in 4 Ps: an alternative', *Journal of Marketing Management* 2(2): 145–54.

Kjaer-Hansen, M. (1945) *Afsaetningsokonomi* [Marketing]. Copenhagen: Erhvervsokonomisk Forlag.

Kock, S. (1991) *A Strategic Process for Gaining External Resources through Long-lasting Relationships*. Helsingfors/Vara, Finland: Swedish School of Economics and Business Administration.

Kotler, P. (1967) *Marketing Management: Analysis, Planning and Control*. Englewood Cliffs, NJ: Prentice-Hall.

Levitt, T. (1960) 'Marketing myopia', *Harvard Business Review* July–August: 24–47.

Lusch, R.F. and Vargo, S.L. (eds) (2006) *Toward a Service-dominant Logic of Marketing: Dialog, Debate, and Directions*. New York: M.E. Sharpe, pp. xvii–xviii.

McCarthy, E.J. (1960) *Basic Marketing: A Managerial Approach*. Homewood, IL: Irwin.

Marion, G. (1993) 'The marketing management discourse: what's new since the 1960s?', in M.J. Baker (ed.) *Perspectives on Marketing Management*, Vol. 3. Chichester: John Wiley.

Maslow, A.H. (1943) 'A theory of human motivation', *Psychological Review* July: 370–96.

Mick, D.G., Pettigrew, S., Pechman, C. and Ozanne, J.L. (eds) (2012) *Transformative Consumer Research*. New York: Routledge.

Mickwitz, G. (1959) *Marketing and Competition*. Helsingfors, Finland: Societas Scientarium Fennica.

Rasmussen, A. (1955) *Pristeori eller parameterteori-studier ombring virksombedens afsaetning*. Copenhagen: Erhvervsokonomisk Forlag.

Robinson, J. (1933) *The Economics of Imperfect Competition*. London: Macmillan.

Rostow, W.W. (1962) *The Process of Economic Growth*, 2nd edn. New York: W.W. Norton.

Samuelson, P. (1994) 'Self-plagiarism or fair use?', *Communications of the ACM* 37(8): 21–5.

Smith, A. (1970 [1776]) *The Wealth of Nations*, ed. A. Skinner. Harmondsworth: Pelican Books.

Vargo, S.L. and Lusch, R.F. (2004) 'Evolving to a new dominant logic for marketing', *Journal of Marketing* 68(1): 1–17.

von Stackelberg, H. (1939) 'Theorie der Vertreibspolitik and der Qualitatsvariation', *Schmollers Jahrbuck* 63/1.8

Webster, F.E. Jr (1992) 'The changing role of marketing in the corporation', *Journal of Marketing* 56(4): 1–17.

Webster, F.E. Jr and Lusch, R.F. (2013) 'Elevating marketing: Marketing is dead! Long live marketing!', *Journal of the Academy of Marketing Science* 41(4): 389–99.

Marketing Theory

Michael Saren

Chapter Topics

Overview – Why we need theory in marketing   31
Historical evolution of theory in marketing   33
Is marketing a science or an art?   35
What form should marketing theory take?   36
Problems with marketing theory   41
Where to now?   47

Overview – Why we need theory in marketing

Reviewing the state of the marketing discipline at the end of the 20th century, Day and Montgomery (1999) noted that a major weakness was the lack of a connection between the process of theory formulation and verification. They recognized the need to rethink the role of theory as one of three key challenges for academic research in marketing. The evolution of theory is essential for any discipline. This assertion is taken for granted in the natural sciences but has to be re-emphasized in an applied social science like marketing. All academic disciplines build their own bodies of theory and apply their own unique lens to particular phenomena. In this way marketing is a bit like a magpie in that it takes many of its theories from other disciplines, such as psychology, sociology and economics (Baker, 1995a). The challenge for marketing as a relatively young discipline is to build its own distinct body of theory (Murray et al., 1997).

In this chapter we can summarize the arguments put forward for the need for theory in marketing under four main headings – practical, knowledge, and academic and intellectual.

1. *Practical value.* Better theories will improve managerial decision making and problem solving.
2. *Knowledge creation.* Theory provides direction and structure to academic enquiry and helps 'make sense of facts'.
3. *Academic status.* Marketing as an academic discipline requires its own theory. It cannot rely on borrowing from other disciplines.
4. *Intellectual curiosity.* Only theory can provide the basis for understanding how the marketing system works and explaining the underlying foundations and forces.

One of the main reasons why marketing scholars cannot agree on a common definition for theory is because, depending on philosophical orientation, scholars will have different views of what constitutes theory. The term theory is sometimes used to refer to a set of propositions or an abstract conceptualization of the relationship between entities. At other times, it can be a general principle that is used to explain or predict facts or events. Often 'theory' conveys verification of facts, systems of organization, lawlike generalizations and tested hypotheses. Consequently, it is frequently associated with the production of scientific knowledge and the notion of an objective, explanatory lens upon the world.

Hunt (1991) states that the purpose of theory, more broadly, is to increase scientific understanding through a systematized structure capable of both explaining and predicting phenomena. If we look to the role of theory in the management literature, Bacharach (1989: 496) defines theory as 'a statement of relations among concepts within a set of boundary assumptions and constraints'. He goes further to argue that theory is no more than a linguistic device used to organize a complex empirical world. Van de Ven (1989) maintains that it is the use of theory that matters. As Kurt Lewin is reputed to have put it: 'nothing is so practical as a good theory'. Llewelyn (2003) argues that the value of qualitative empirical research lies in its 'conceptual framing' of organizational actions, events, processes and structures, and the possibilities for conceptual framing extend beyond the highly abstract schema generally considered as 'theories' by academics.

There is common agreement from all sides, however, that theory offers explanations of the physical and social worlds around us that can reveal deeper understandings of how and why things happen. Essentially, theory is really an organized way to think about a topic. The various views above also illustrate that theory is by no means value free. For example, some marketing theorizing implicitly adopts a machine metaphor to characterize human behaviour that is also inherently gendered in its assumptions. This metaphor has for a long time privileged the mind and cognitive activity (assumed male) over the (female) body and emotions (Campbell et al., 2009). Many other types of power relationships, such as those implicated in the 1960s Space

Race and the Cold War, have also influenced the development of marketing theory (Schwarzkopf, 2015; Wooliscroft, 2011). As Maclaran et al. (2009) argue, this is why we also need to be suspicious of theory. Just like the use of metaphor, theory can both broaden our minds and tie us into particular ways of thinking, skewing our perspectives in ways that often go unquestioned and unrecognized.

An essential aspect in developing marketing theory is the understanding of its historical evolution, the current knowledge base, its relative strengths and weaknesses, potential dangers and future direction. Providing an introduction and review of these topics is the objective of this chapter.

Historical evolution of theory in marketing

Debates around the best way of seeking knowledge about marketing phenomena are long-standing. These can be traced all the way back to the philosophy of science debates that began at the turn of the 20th century between the laissez-faire oriented scholars versus their German historical counterparts (Jones and Monieson, 1990). Serious discussion of the scientific nature of marketing began to appear in late 1940s (Alderson and Cox, 1948; Bartels, 1951; Converse, 1945; Kelley, 1956). The reasons for the emergence of this interest in theory at that time were explained by Alderson and Cox (1948) as partly intellectual curiosity and partly 'follow-the-leader': 'When some people become avidly and outspokenly interested in anything, others will take a look and see what is going on' (1948: 138). More fundamentally, they argue that the underlying foundations of this interest in theory consisted of two core elements: (1) students of marketing, for all their efforts, have produced very few accurate, comprehensive and significant generalizations, principles or theories; and (2) the belief that they have achieved little, even in setting themselves fundamental problems, and less still in developing procedures for solving such problems. The authors complain, 'the multitude of facts thus far assembled seems to add up to very little' (Alderson and Cox, 1948: 138). A sound theory is needed, not simply to produce immediate generalizations, but because it helps marketers to better initiate and direct their enquiries.

Alderson and Cox's fundamental rationale for their call in 1948 for better theory was that it would help identify salient problems to be solved and thus direct the researcher to understand which facts to assemble and how to analyse them. 'Only a sound theory of marketing can raise the analysis of such problems above the level of an empirical art and establish truly scientific criteria for setting up hypotheses and selecting the facts by means of which to test them' (1948: 139). This reasoning was subsequently endorsed by Baumol (1957: 160), who stated succinctly that 'facts are silent' and therefore theory is needed to describe and explain the workings of facts.

The Marketing Science Institute (MSI) was founded in 1961 to 'create knowledge that will improve business performance' (Lehman and Jocz, 1997: 141). The Institute established four 'position studies', which went some way to setting out the 'fundamental problems' that Alderson and Cox cited, and one of these was to conduct long-term research on marketing theory and its application in order to provide the 'concepts, methods and opportunities for more creative and imaginative solutions for more difficult and important problems' (Lehman and Jocz, 1997: xiv). Several reasons for the importance of this effort to improve the theory were presented in the 1965 report by Michael Halbert, as follows:

1. Theoretical rules are a prerequisite for learning. 'It is said that we learn by experience, but we really learn only by the analysis of experience. ... But without a theoretical base, we cannot analyse, for the rules of proper analysis are theoretical rules; we cannot be selective about which experiences are relevant, for the criteria of relevance are theoretical criteria' (1965: xiv). There are a great deal of data and knowledge available about the operation of the marketing system but theory is needed to provide a formal structure for organizing, analysing and evaluating this knowledge. Adequate theories would also help present a much more 'coherent, understandable and useful picture' of the entire marketing process.
2. Practitioners need theory in order to make better decisions. As well as facts, the executive's informational needs also include marketing theory 'because it can reduce the cost and uncertainty of decision making while increasing the productivity and assurance of decision makers' (Halbert, 1965: xxii). Examples given here are theory concerning how pricing affects distribution and what happens if advertising spend doubles.
3. Marketing cannot rely on borrowing from other disciplines. Not all borrowing is bad, but one must distinguish between three classes of borrowing: (i) of content, which presents few problems; (ii) the adaptation of techniques and methods from other subjects, which is acceptable if properly applied; and (iii) the borrowing of theories and concepts from other disciplines, which is 'dangerous at best and larceny at worst ... often semantic similarity is mistaken for formal appropriateness' (Halbert, 1965: xxvi). It is seldom that a theoretical structure from one area is directly applicable to another and the many problems associated with marketing's reliance at that time on borrowing particularly from economics, behavioural sciences and law are examined in the report.

The need for marketing theory is now largely accepted and a successful academic journal devoted to its generation, analysis and development is well established (*Marketing Theory*, published by Sage). In his influential text *Marketing: Theory and Practice* (1995b) Michael Baker devotes a whole chapter to 'The need for theory in marketing'. Taking a marketing-as-exchange position along with Bagozzi (1978), he presents the core reason as 'the recognition and acceptance of the need to improve our understanding of the manner in which the [marketing] system works which underlies the need to develop a workable theory of exchange' (Baker, 1995b: 20). The benefits resulting from this he agrees with Halbert (1965) will be: (1) the satisfaction of intellectual curiosity; and (2) improved operational performance. By solving immediate operating problems, the latter would permit marketing academics to concentrate on the more fundamental problems underlying them. This would also liberate marketing practitioners from 'fire-fighting' activities in order to concentrate on anticipating and avoiding marketing problems in an increasingly complex business world.

In true demand–pull fashion, the early identification of a need for theory stimulated its development by academics such as Alderson himself (1957), McGary (1953) (both functionalist), Bartels (1968) (general theory) and McInnes (1964) (systems model), which, as we shall see in the next sections, spawned over 50 years of debate as to what marketing theory should be like and, indeed, whether it is possible at all.

Is marketing a science or an art?

Marketing would appear to be primarily an area for application of findings from the sciences (primarily the behavioural sciences) and not a science in itself. Should then the attempt to make it a science be abandoned as a wild-goose chase? (Buzzell, 1963: 34)

Robert Buzzell in his 1963 *Harvard Business Review* article, 'Is marketing a science?', expressed the question over which marketing theorists have been locked in debate (in one form or another) ever since Alderson and Cox made their 'call to arms' nearly 70 years ago. Indeed, only six months after their article appeared Roland Vaile published a direct commentary on it in the *Journal of Marketing*, in which he took the contrary view that 'marketing will remain an art' (1949: 522). Thus began the 'marketing as science versus art' controversy that filled the journals up to the mid-1960s and still reverberates today. Those who began the need for theory tended to recommend a scientific approach to its development and evaluation, at least along the positive lines of the social sciences, if not akin to the physical sciences (Alderson and Cox, 1948; Bartels, 1951). Those who responded from the managerial, normative perspective regarded marketing as a vocation, an application of scientific principles, like engineering or medicine (Vaile, 1949). Managers certainly do not regard marketing as scientific: 'The businessman's practical wisdom is of a completely different character than scientific knowledge. While it does not ignore generalities, it recognizes the low probability that given combinations of phenomena can or will be repeated. … In place of scientific knowledge, then, the businessman collects lore' (Ramond, 1962, quoted in Buzzell, 1963: 34).

Few would disagree with this today, especially given the recent anthropological attention to management behaviour, but adducing the paucity of managers' use of marketing models and theories is not sufficient to refute the possibility of the development of scientific theories in marketing. To do so requires detailed attention to exactly what constitutes a theory. Vaile (1949) raised this issue initially in his critique of Alderson and Cox (1948), who proposed that a systematic theory of marketing can and should be developed and that it may become scientific. 'Useful discussion of the propositions just stated requires definition of the term "theory". This the authors do not undertake' (Vaile, 1949: 521). Vaile suggests a dictionary definition of theory as 'a coherent group of general propositions used as principles of explanation for a class of phenomena' (1949: 521). Marketing theory cannot exist, he argues, because (1) marketing has many, not one, coherent groups of propositions; and (2) marketing must do more than explain, it also must make judgements about marketing policies.

Buzzell (1963) also argued that marketing is not a science because it does not meet his definition. In order to qualify as a distinct science in its own right, marketing will have to meet some rather stringent requirements. For example, it is generally agreed that a science is:

> ... a classified and systematized body of knowledge, organized around one or more central theories and a number of general principles, usually expressed in quantitative terms, knowledge which permits the prediction and, under some circumstances, the control of future events. Few believe that marketing now meets these criteria. (Buzzell, 1963: 33)

Shelby Hunt, the leading proponent of the 'marketing-is-science' school, argued that these definitions are overly restrictive, and, following Rudner (1966), proposed that: 'Theories are systematically related sets of statements, including some law-like generalizations, that are empirically testable. The purpose of theory is to increase scientific understanding through a systematized structure capable of both explaining and predicting phenomena' (Hunt, 1971: 65). This avoids the central theory requirement, which, even today, for marketing is clearly untenable, and by 1983 Hunt was able to assert that 'both philosophers of science and marketing theorists agree on the nature of theory' (p. 10). He cited the definitions adopted by many of the marketing-is/not-science writers such as Alderson (1957), Zaltman et al. (1973), Bagozzi (1980), Ryan and O'Shaunessy (1980) and even Keat and Urry (1975), to demonstrate that both advocates and critics 'basically concur as to the general characteristics of theory' (Hunt, 1983: 10).

In reviewing the *Journal of Marketing*'s 60-year pursuit of the 'ideal' of advancement of science and practice in marketing, Roger Kerin argues that by 1965 marketing literature had become more scientific, particularly in terms of quantitative analysis being an integral element. 'Marketing phenomena, originally addressed by intuition and judgement, were increasingly studied with fundamental tenets of the scientific method' (Kerin, 1996: 5)

The debate about whether it is possible to have scientific theories in marketing then moved on from the 'definition' issue to the question of what marketing theory should be like.

What form should marketing theory take?

The fall 1983 issue of the *Journal of Marketing* began the next 'round' in the contest about the nature of marketing theory (Kavanagh [1994] likens the debate to a boxing match). In that edition Paul Anderson questions particularly Hunt's positivistic concept of the scientific method: 'Despite its prevalence in marketing, positivism has been abandoned by these disciplines [philosophy and sociology of science] over the last two decades in the face of overwhelming historical and logical arguments that have been raised against it' (1983: 25). Thus, the debate moved from whether marketing can have scientific theory to what form of scientific theory is appropriate. It is argued that there is no longer one 'correct' method for evaluating theory and different research disciplines will adopt different methodologies, ontologies and epistemologies. These marketing theorists draw on Kuhn's (1962) revolutionary view of scientific progress in terms of competing paradigms (see Dholakia and Arndt, 1985), which within any discipline are 'incommensurable' – that is scientists of each persuasion have different 'world-views' and are unable to agree on salient problems, theories or terminologies to be employed, and thus could never agree on any 'experiments' or data that would resolve their differences. In marketing, Anderson (1983) cites theory of consumer behaviour and theory of the firm as incommensurable. With no agreed or agreeable 'demarcation criterion' between theory and non-theory, or even science and non-science, in marketing, Anderson concludes that a relativistic approach is the only viable one.

As Kavanagh (1994) notes, Hunt (1984) was quick to counter-attack Anderson's naive relativist advocacy, which can easily be forced to its (il)logical conclusion of nihilism, ontological solipsism (death of the *object*) and epistemological anarchy (cannot know anything or can know everything). Interestingly, both Hunt and Anderson shifted their positions somewhat after each other's attack in this 'round' in order to defend their 'weak flanks'. Hunt moved from logical empiricism to scientific realism, in which he accepts a critical realist position that some of our perceptions may be illusions and certainly some are more accurate than others (thus moderating pure empiricism). Therefore the job of science is to develop theories that have 'long-run predictive success' (Hunt, 1991) in explaining behaviour, 'even if we cannot finally "know" whether the entities and structure postulated by the theory actually exists' (McMullin, 1984: 26).

Anderson meanwhile was adopting critical relativism, which accepts the possibility of a single pre-existing 'reality' but rejects the notion that it can be discovered via the scientific method (1986: 157). So, it seemed for a while that boxing had brought them closer together. This debate between realism and relativism in marketing theory mirrors debate which had been going on in the social sciences (see Burrell and Morgan, 1979) about how we can *know* the world; is reality out there or a product of one's mind? As Kavanagh rightly observes, epistemology and ontology tend to be conflated in all these debates – that is, 'being is reduced to knowledge and knowledge is reduced to being' (1994: 31). Although this certainly all follows from the Cartesian dictum *cogito ergo sum*, the question for marketing theory is that one needs to be able to know more about reality beyond one's own existence.

Hunt (1976) refutes all forms of relativism, arguing that the knowledge claims of any theory must be *objective*, in the sense that 'its truth content must be intersubjectively certifiable' and that 'requiring that theories, laws and explanations be empirically testable ensures that they will be intersubjectively certifiable since different (but reasonably competent) investigators with differing attitudes, opinions and beliefs will be able to make observations and conduct experiments to ascertain their truth content' (Hunt, 1976: 27). He challenges all those academics in what he calls marketing's 'crisis literature' who have questioned the very possibility of objective marketing research, for example, 'Objectivity is an illusion' (Peter, 1992: 77), 'objectivity is impossible' (Mick, 1986: 207), 'Researcher objectivity and intersubjective certifiability are chimeras – they cannot be achieved' (Fullerton, 1986: 433). Hunt categorizes and articulates the five 'primary arguments' which marketing writers have employed 'ostensibly implying the impossibility of objective marketing research' (1993: 80). He summarizes these as follows:

Table 2.1   Arguments against objectivity.

1. Objectivity is impossible because the language of a culture determines the reality that members of that culture see.
2. Objectivity is impossible because the paradigms that researchers hold are incommensurable.
3. Objectivity is impossible because theories are undermined by facts.
4. Objectivity is impossible because the psychology of perception informs us that a theory-free observation language is impossible.
5. Objectivity is impossible because all epistemically significant observations are theory-laden.

Hunt then refutes each argument from a scientific realist perspective, often asserting that the marketing authors have misconstrued, misunderstood or misapplied the ideas from the philosophy of science literature.

Following the discussion above of the influence on marketing theory of Kuhnian ideas about the progress of science (see also Dholakia and Arndt, 1985), take, for example, Hunt's refutation of argument 2 in Table 2.1, which had been used by Anderson inter alia, that 'objectivity is impossible because the paradigms that researchers hold are incommensurable'. Countering it Hunt (1993: 82) makes two points: first, that it is 'simply incoherent' to compare and contrast different paradigms in marketing and then to claim that they are incommensurable because they are 'non-comparable'; and second, that for incommensurability to bar objective choice between two paradigms implies that they are *rival,* but most of the so-called paradigms identified by marketers are simply *different*, not necessarily putting forward conflicting knowledge claims. Going on to counter all five arguments, Hunt concludes that 'there is nothing, absolutely nothing, in modern philosophy of science or psychology that makes objectivity either impossible or undesirable' (1993: 87).

Whether Hunt is correct or not about 'rival' or 'different' paradigms in marketing there certainly are a lot of them. Carmen (1980) identifies six (microeconomic, persuasion/attitude change, conflict resolution, generalist system, functionalist and social exchange paradigms). Fisk and Meyers (1982) classify another six (network flow, market scarcity, competitive marketing management, evolutionary systems change, general systems and dissipative structures paradigms). Sheth and Gardener (1988) list 12 'schools of thought' in marketing (commodity, functional, functionalist, regional, institutional, managerial, buyer behaviour, activist, macromarketing, organizational dynamics and social exchange schools). Kerin (1996) chooses six 'metaphors' which characterized marketing science and practice in each of the six decades since the launch of the *Journal of Marketing* in 1936 – marketing as applied economics, a managerial activity, a quantitative science, a behavioural science, a decision science and an integrative science. Wilkie and Moore (2003) identify 'four eras' of thought development, which are: 1900–20, 'Founding the Field'; 1920–50, 'Formalizing the Field'; 1950–80, 'A Paradigm Shift – Marketing, Management, and the Sciences'; 1980–present, 'The Shift Intensifies – A Fragmentation of the Mainstream'.

Of course, taking Hunt's point about interpreting Kuhn's ideas correctly, many of the above are not strictly 'paradigms' and it can be seen that they are by no means all posited as such. Indeed, as so often happens with even the supposedly technical language of science (cf. argument 1 in

Table 2.1 above), a term loses its 'original' meaning in the noise of academic discourse. The 'paradigm' is (adopting the vernacular) an excellent paradigm of this phenomenon. Even those who take an 'alternative paradigm' approach to marketing theory recognize this. 'It is commonly agreed that the paradigm concept itself remains somewhat vague and unclear. This is partly because [it] has taken on different meanings over time' (Arndt, 1985: 19). Even in its original formulation the notion was ambiguous and Kuhn has been accused of using the paradigm notion in many different ways (Morgan, 1980).

Arndt (1985) attempts to make sense of the concept for use in marketing theory by adapting Morgan's (1980) hierarchy, which distinguishes paradigms (alternative realities or world-views) at the second level from *orientations* (perspective of the researcher relating to the role of data, theory and values) above it at level 1 with *metaphors* (basis for schools of thought) at level 3 and *puzzle-solving* (based on specific tools or procedures) at level 4. Using Morgan's framework, Arndt analyses and categorizes the different paradigms and metaphors in marketing theory, identifying four main paradigms based on different (and indeed one would have to say *conflicting*) worldviews. These contain 'different metatheoretical assumptions about the nature of science, the subjective–objective dimension and the explicitness of long-term conflicts in society. There are also assumptions about the nature of the marketing discipline and the study of marketing phenomena' (Arndt, 1985: 15). He thus classifies four paradigms in marketing along these dimensions: (1) logical empiricist; (2) socio-political; (3) subjective world; and (4) liberating paradigms.

The *logical empiricist paradigm* emphasizes measurability and intersubjective certification. It takes a mechanistic approach, assuming that marketing relations have a real existence independent of the observer and a systematic character resulting in regularities in marketing behaviour and equilibrium-seeking marketing systems. Neoclassical economics provides the basis for many of its typical metaphors such as *instrumental man* with rational decision making and the *organism metaphor* for the organized behaviour and environmental learning of the marketing system.

The *socio-political paradigm* is similarly based on the assumption of a real and measurable world of marketing phenomena and predictable uniformities in marketing behaviour. Unlike the value-free and equilibrium assumptions of logical empirical theories however, this paradigm explicitly recognizes conflicts of interests, resources and relations in marketing exchanges and systems. The metaphors of this paradigm constitute the *political markets and economies* and even spaceship *Earth*, the global, ecological approach of much of what would nowadays be called green marketing.

The *subjective world paradigm* rejects the existence of social reality in any verifiable or concrete sense. It is the product of the subjective experiences and inter-experiences of individuals and therefore marketing phenomena cannot be understood from the perspective of an external observer, but must be studied from the viewpoint of the participant. It thus incorporates the interpretive and social constructionist approaches and adopts the motivational and psychology-based metaphor of *irrational man*, the phenomenological metaphor of *experiencing man*, with an existential and semiological basis, and the *language and text* metaphor for understanding the behaviour of marketing actors from stories, myths, rhetoric and discourse.

The *liberating paradigm* also takes a social constructionist perspective regarding the onto-logical status of reality but focuses on the social, economic and technological processes that constrain and control human beings in the marketing system. The role of theoretical enquiry is to identify and analyse the conflicts and contradictions in the system and point the way to emancipation. Critical theory adherents within this paradigm often take *alienation* and *victimi-zation* as metaphors for the oppressed groups in modern mass consumer society.

A strong case is made by Arndt (1985) that marketing has been dominated by one paradigm – that is, logical empiricism:

> Even a cursory perusal of scholarly articles in marketing journals is bound to confirm the dominant status of logical empiricism. The principles of empiricism appear to be treated synonymously with the scientific method as such. … The control technology and instrumentalist of the logical empiricist paradigm may well be compatible with the problem solving needs and pragmatism of marketing practitioners. (Arndt, 1985: 19)

This is directly opposed by Hunt's contention that to even ask the question 'what philosophy dominates marketing?' *presumes* that marketing is *dominated* (which carries pejorative over-tones) by one view or another and that in any case, on the contrary, the marketing discipline has been amazingly eclectic and the most accurate answer is: No single philosophy dominates marketing (Hunt, 1991: 398).

Arndt makes a strong case for pluralism in orientations and paradigms for the develop-ment of marketing theory: 'by limiting itself to the empiricist orientation and logical empiricist paradigms such as instrumental man, marketing has remained essentially a one-dimensional science concerned with technology and problem solving' (Arndt, 1985: 21). Adopting other paradigms and metaphors will result in the asking of quite different research questions. 'The *notion* of paradigms should be viewed as an argument for paradigmatic tolerance and plural-ism' (Arndt, 1985: 21). Perhaps this explains one reason why Hunt goes to such great effort to reject the notion itself for marketing theory.

Despite the length and intensity of the debate regarding the appropriate characteristics of and scientific underpinning for the development of marketing theories, and despite the coales-cence of key positions around the two poles of relativism and realism, there is no consensus as to what marketing theory should be like. We do have several competing schools of thought, if not exactly 'paradigms'. Attempts at constructing 'general/generic' theories of marketing (Alderson, 1957; Bartels, 1968) have not led to any shared, let alone agreed theoretical basis for the discipline. Worse still, whether it is because of overemphasis on empirical research at the expense of theory generation by positivists (Deshpande, 1983; Peter, 1992) or because of the advocacy of loosely thought out epistemological 'anarchy' by relativists (Hunt, 1994), the one thing that most authors on both sides agree about is that, since Alderson and Cox's call nearly 70 years ago, marketing theory has not advanced as well as it should have done – or even satisfactorily. The next question then is: 'What's gone wrong?'

The American Marketing Association (AMA) set up a task force in 1984 to investigate the development of marketing thought. Its report (AMA, 1988) recognized that 'the marketing discipline has come a long way since 1959. Nevertheless the task force believes that our self-evaluation of how marketing develops, disseminates and utilizes marketing knowledge indicates that, as a discipline, we still have a long way to go' (AMA, 1988: 24). An earlier commission set up under the auspices of the AMA and the MSI to assess the effectiveness of research and development for marketing management had concluded that marketing research 'has had relatively little impact on improving marketing management practice' (Myers et al., 1980: 280). The AMA task force identified six principle barriers:

1. Insufficient resources devoted to marketing knowledge and development;
2. Too few people generating and disseminating knowledge;
3. The premature end to too many research careers at pre-tenure and post-tenure stages;
4. Senior faculty do not devote sufficient time to knowledge generation;
5. Restrictions against practical, innovative and long-term projects and reports by journals and doctoral programmes;
6. Extremely limited dissemination of knowledge.

Since this report many other problems for the marketing discipline have been identified and discussed in the literature, all of which point to underlying failings in the development of theory.

Problems with marketing theory

It has been observed that theory takes on the character of its subject; i.e. theory in history is old and grand, in physics theory is material and infinite and theory in philosophy is conceptual and abstract. Similarly theory in marketing reflects its subject – fast-moving, fashionable, numbers-focused and attention-seeking. These characteristics, to some extent, explain the problems with marketing theory. Another glaring, long-standing issue is the gap between marketing theory and practice.

Fast-moving current generalizations

One criticism of marketing practice is that it tends to focus on the short-term. Product life-cycles (PLCs) are shortening, products have built in obsolescence, managers aim for the quick-fix, sales targets are quarterly or even monthly. Similarly, it can be argued that marketing theories tend to have short life-spans, high turnover, theories that provide current general explanations, not long-lasting conceptual foundations for the discipline. At any point in time leading researchers are competing to have their latest theories accepted, or even just debated, by the academic community. If noticed at all, most marketing theories have currency for a few years before being superseded by the next latest thing.

This short-term, fast-moving character may be one explanation for the lack of attention to history of which marketing theorists have been accused.

Michael Baker notes that 'what is regarded as history by a new generation was an important element in the education and experience of the old' (Baker, 1995a: 1004). This carries with it,

Baker cautions, a grave danger for the new generation of marketing scholars in their rush to make their own impact that they may overlook or, even worse, ignore the lessons of the past. 'Will our concern for recency blur our vision of what is relevant? In ignoring the past will we reinvent what is already known?' (Baker, 1995a: 1004).

According to Savitt (1980), this may be one reason for the subject's lack of progress in developing marketing theory. He argued for more attention to, and awareness of, marketing's history and theoretical foundations in order for marketing scholars to gain a better under-standing of the discipline's origins and patterns of change. Cunningham and Sheth similarly argued that:

> Much research in marketing fails because its hypotheses are not well founded in theory. This inevitably leads to ill-defined research and excessively narrow research ideas. ... An effective theory paper begins with an exhaustive and critical historical review of past work. Marketing theory is made up of a set of building blocks. Readers of a theoretical paper should be able to see how the new theory builds on past theoretical work. (1982: 11)

Since these criticisms were made, more recently there has been much more attention devoted to historical research in marketing (e.g. Brown et al., 2001; Shaw and Jones, 2005; Wilkie and Moore, 2003), which is reviewed in Chapter 3. The application of the historical approach has made some significant shifts in academic thinking about the framework of evolution marketing (notably Fullerton's [1988] reassessment of the 'marketing era'). It has also provided an alternative technique for the analysis of practice and potentially for the development of theory. Nevett (1991) emphasizes the advantages of the historical approach to establishing facts, relevance and causality, which is more impressionistic and intuitive than positivist 'scientific' analysis.

Despite more attention to the history of marketing theory, there remains a high turnover in marketing theories. As Brown (1999) has noted this may be an inevitable feature of each generation of marketing scholars seeking to supplant the old theories with their latest ones. This may account for the fast-moving short-termism in marketing theorizing, but it does not explain Baker's (1995b) observation that the preference for recency leads new scholars to *ignore* theories which precede them in their enthusiasm to establish their latest ideas. Marketing researchers are now presented with a rapidly changing selection of new theories from which they can choose, just like the fast-moving consumer goods offered to customers on supermarket shelves. The difference is that academics are often offering short-term theories which are more like fast-moving current generalizations. A related problem is that marketing theory has become a slave to fashion.

Theory is a slave to fashion

Historical analyses of the antecedents and development of the western market-based economies post the Second World War show that the mass consumer society in the 1950s did not develop in a vacuum, but emerged from changing societal and industrial requirements and the growth in production capabilities that were an outcome of the Second World War itself (Strasser, 1989). In the same way that mass manufacturing techniques were applied to the production of consumer goods after the war, marketing incorporated all the pre-war techniques of propaganda, persuasion and control which had been refined and applied to political warfare (Schwarzkopf, 2011).

Similarly, marketing theory is not immune from the spirit of the times. On the positive side its fast-moving tendencies discussed above enable it to develop new ones quickly and adapt more easily to changes in the economic and social environment. On the other hand, it is arguable that this tendency has encouraged marketing theorists to follow the latest trends sometimes uncritically in topics like celebrity culture, virtual technology and neuropsychology, where the theoretical implications may be less profound than their current emphasis in the business, media or social arenas. This might not be a problem if it only leads to a few false avenues for theory to pursue. As we have seen earlier however, attention to theory is very limited in marketing and there is a finite amount of research resources to devote to it, therefore there are opportunity costs to consider in following fashion. Most obviously the danger is that theorists are constantly changing their focus of attention and too little theory remains to be developed and nurtured within the discipline.

Looking at the recent history of marketing theories we can see how they are developed, enhanced and superseded sometimes in fairly short order according to the dictates of the latest intellectual fashion. Industrial marketing became B2B; B2C separates managerial aspects from consumer research; now both are superseded by C2C and P2P (peer to peer) marketing. Even the 4 Ps did not remain four for long, expanding quickly to 5, 7 or 9 Ps. Bagozzi' s (1978) emphasis on social and economic theories of exchange as central to marketing discipline has gone out of fashion as the attention of marketing researchers has shifted to theories of networks, value creation, relationships, marketplace institutions, sustainability and consumer culture.

Reibstein et al. (2009) argue that in recent years the domain of academic marketing has been shrinking. This is often due to marketing frameworks, concepts and methods being pre-empted by other academic disciplines, usually where the topic overlaps with other areas and marketers' lack of progress in researching these topics and developing theory when they fell out of fashion or were superseded by new issues. Reibstein et al. cite the example of the strategy field, which has incorporated key marketing concepts such as product-market selection, segmentation, positioning, innovation, diffusion processes and value propositions (e.g. Christensen and Raynor, 2003; Kim and Mauborgne, 2005; Porter, 1985). Sometimes academic marketing has left voids that other management disciplines have filled, such as work on product quality and variety, product design and integrated customer solutions which is now predominantly in the operations management area (e.g. Ulrich and Eppinger, 2007).

Too much focus on numbers

It is perhaps understandable that marketing managers are focused on the metrics of marketing operations. Quantitative measures are nowadays the accepted basis of evaluation for business performance, accounting standards, managers' remuneration, shareholders' return and company value, which go way beyond the marketing discipline. What is more surprising however is that marketing research and theory development display such overwhelming reliance on quantitative methods. J.M. Anderson (1994) considered that progress has been impeded by the marketing discipline's 'quantitative bias'. The analytical and empirical 'toolkit' has become ever more sophisticated with far less attention to techniques of theory development. 'Academic research in marketing has been more technique- than theory-driven' (Anderson, 1994: 11). Venkatesh (1985) argued that one reason for the disappointing development of marketing theory in traditional university marketing departments is 'the emphasis on empirical research, data analysis, and quantitative modelling. These areas offer little potential for theory generation' (Venkatesh, 1985: 62).

Deshpande (1983) recommends the use of qualitative methods to generate new theory and furthermore advocates them for triangulation in theory testing as well as quantitative methods. In consumer behaviour, Belk (1986) shows how art can be used, in particular, to suggest and inspire hypotheses and theories.

Even Shelby Hunt, the renowned advocate of rigour in marketing, laments the paucity of qualitative research publications:

> Numerous marketers have pointed out over the last decade that research using qualitative methods could usefully complement our quantitative analyses. I have never heard anyone dispute the potential value of qualitative research – but qualitative works in marketing are few. Why are our major journals almost exclusively devoted to studies using quantitative methods? (Hunt, 1994: 13)

Following his familiar modus operandi, Hunt proceeds to answer his own question by constructing a step-by-step refutation of the arguments of relativists, constructionists and subjectivists who, according to him, proffer their standard (and to Hunt totally false) reasoning as a basis for advocating the use of qualitative methods. 'Is it any wonder then', he concludes, 'that mainstream marketers have been reluctant to accept qualitative methods when their advocates have explicitly grounded them in relativism, constructionism and subjectivism? How could marketers trust the output of such research methods?' (Hunt, 1994: 21).

There is, then, little disagreement about the *need* for increased and appropriate application of qualitative, as opposed to quantitative techniques for research leading to theory generation in marketing. But despite more use of qualitative methods in areas like consumer behaviour, little has changed since Hunt made these comments in terms of the overwhelming dominance of quantitative methods in marketing research.

Making theory attention-seeking and memorable

In marketing communications and branding, practitioners emphasize the desirability of creating consumer awareness by communicating easily recognizable and memorable images or messages. One means of achieving this is through simplification and repetition of a catchy, ideally unforgettable name, image, slogan, logo, phrase, video, blog name, hashtag or 'brand'.

The basis of these methods can be traced back to the techniques of propaganda developed in the 1930s by Bernays, Dichter and others (Baines and O'Shaughnessy, 2013; Schwarzkopf, 2015). Marketing academics manifest similar behaviour in the propagation of their theories, often adopting shortened mnemonics, acronyms or catch phrases which capture the essence of their theoretical 'message': PLC, S-D logic, CCT, NPD, value chain, segmentation, consumer cocreation.

Similarly, it has been argued that the language chosen by marketing academics to explicate their theoretical findings reveals similar characteristics of simplification, labelling and ordering of their concepts and ideas (Brown, 1999; Stern, 1989, 1990), One possible reason for the pressure on theorists to devote such efforts to advertising and marketing theories is the lack of attention to the theorizing process in the marketing discipline. In particular, it is argued that there is a disconnection between the development of sophisticated research techniques for gathering empirical data and the relative lack of attention to the methods for using empirical evidence to inform theoretical development.

One solution to the inherent difficulty of creating a better connection between empirical research and the development of generalizable theory is the development of so-called bridging theories (Brodie et al., 2011). Some researchers are exploring the use of developments such as 'middle-range theory' which has received attention in other management disciplines, including organizational studies and strategic management. This potentially offers an intermediary body of theory which builds a bridge between general theory and empirical findings. The creation of intermediate bridging theories with clearer links to supporting empirical evidence might potentially reduce the perceived need for marketing academics to market their theories in oversimplified, repetitive and memorable terms.

Lack of impact on practice

A related and arguably even more important disconnection in marketing theory is that all the marketing discipline's efforts at knowledge development, model building and theorizing have had little impact on the practice of marketing. As Myers et al. (1979: 28) put it, 'there isn't a single problem area with regard to the practice of marketing and management that marketing research or the world of technology and concepts has mastered'. Three types of explanation for this state of affairs have been put forward:

1. Marketing theories reflect the realities of the builder, not the user. Managers do have principles and theories that they have acquired over time and use when approaching marketing decisions. They are guided by their own theories-in-use. The trouble is that many of the academic theories do not reflect managers' language or their business realities.
2. Marketing theory provides complex answers to marketing problems. On the contrary, managers want complex problems to be solved as simplified representations and with clarity. 'Why have concepts like the product life cycle and the product portfolio matrix been adopted so quickly? Primarily because they are simple representations of marketing phenomena that can affect their decisions' (Heffring, 1985: 107).

3. Marketing theories may be logically correct but practically incorrect. Managers have several problems with this: (i) many theories focus on strategy not tactics and do not give guidance for their implementation; (ii) theory is judged by academics by process not relevance of the content; (iii) theory focuses on problem formulation whereas mangers are concerned with problem solving; and (iv) pro-theory bias. It is assumed that theory is good, that it improves managers' decision making and that to have any theory is better than to have none at all. Managers in fact are often confused by theories that they find difficult to interpret.

Other authors have blamed the academic system for its lack of impact on practice, because of its emphasis on research and publication regardless of their significance for managers. Venkatesh (1985: 63) describes this as the 'crisis of relevance' and considers that theories of researchers are not perceived as useful because practitioners want their everyday problems solved and marketing academics *cannot* perform this function.

These problems do not appear to have been overcome. In the July 2009 volume of the *Journal of Marketing*, Reibstein et al., in a question remarkably reminiscent of the AMA task force, ask: 'Why do marketing academics have little to say about critical strategic marketing issues and emerging issues … ?' They point to broader concerns regarding wider management education.

> Criticisms are being levelled at the dominant MBA focus on narrow analytical and cognitive skills, stylized treatment of complex issues by teachers with no direct business experience, self-centred careerism and the declining recognition that management is as much a clinical art as a science. It is further charged that the prevailing paradigm of reductionist, narrowly specified and fragmented research … cannot address the multi-functional and interconnected problems for managers. Although these concerns loom large for management education in general, *the dilemma is magnified in marketing* – a field that is supposed to be concerned about the connection of the firm with its customers and other stakeholders. (Reibstein et al., 2009: 1, emphasis added)

In another *Journal of Marketing* commentary, entitled 'When executives speak, we should listen and act differently', Brown (2005) notes that:

> Several of the essays in this issue note the weak linkage between marketing scholarship and marketing practice. Further contributing to this scholarship–practice gap is the diminished role and influence of marketing in companies. Sheth and Sisodia indicate (p. 11) that 'many strategically important aspects of marketing … are being taken away by other functions in the organisation.' The authors also note that at many companies, marketing has become a form of sales support. (Brown, 2005: 3)

These comments come from authors who are senior established figures in the marketing discipline, not the 'usual suspects' from marketing's perpetual so-called 'crisis literature'. Perhaps more surprisingly, some maintain that this lack of connection between academic theory and managerial practice is not really a problem. Holbrook (1989) argues that basic or pure research is best carried out by the curiosity-driven and self-directed academic, free from the constraints of relevance.

The development of theory is necessarily basic and creative in nature, rather than applied research, and therefore the conditions best suited to theory development are those of 'pure' academic freedom. Furthermore, academic theory does not normally produce immediate impact and what 'relevance' means in this context is itself a problematic construct (Wensley, 1995).

There is, nevertheless, a serious issue for marketing theory in this regard and for the academy's understanding of its role. In the recent debate about the 'gap' between the approach and concerns of marketing practitioners and academics, between theory and practice, it is perhaps not surprising that the two 'worlds' are regarded as 'separate'. But the paradox is, that 'the criteria for relevance are theoretical criteria' (Halbert, 1965: 48). If we all, academics and managers, need theory (or at least if it is *implicit*, if not explicit) in order to distinguish salient facts and to learn from experience, then what exactly are the reasons for the long-term continuance of this vast gap between the two 'worldviews'? The answer may be that it has been constructed and maintained by the marketing academy itself (Brownlie and Saren, 1996; Zwick and Cayla, 2011).

One avenue with potential to address this issue is the application to marketing of 'practice theory'. Practice theory tries to explain the way phenomena occur in practice and also attempts to bridge the perceived theory/practice divide. In particular it focuses on the practices – i.e. routinized types of behaviour that include both doing and saying – around which individuals express and share meanings in their personal activities and identity construction. Practice theory looks at how meanings are produced and reproduced in an evolving dialectic between everyday life and wider cultural forces. Svenssen (2007) argues that it is important to explore the human side of marketing in order to eventually move to higher level theories on the nature of marketing work that will counter mainstream marketing management applications and better match theory with the 'lifeworlds' of marketing practitioners.

Where to now?

It was concluded in the first part of this chapter that despite earlier debates the need for marketing theory is now well accepted (Kerin, 1996; Maclaren et al., 2010). As we have seen, however, it has largely failed to live up to its potential to the satisfaction of either academics or practitioners. The need for theory may be even more important today than it was at the time of Alderson and Cox (1948) for two reasons.

First, there has been more emphasis and awareness of 'the power effects of knowledge' (Morgan, 1992: 151), that is, what knowledge *does*. The synonymity of knowledge and power (Foucault, 1980) implies that 'doing-in-the-world' (after Heidegger, 1962) is inexorably intertwined and embedded in 'knowing-the-world' in a particular way. If theory helps create knowledge, as most marketing academics now accept, then theory also helps create power. This underlies and reinforces both mangers' and academics' need for marketing theory in order to increase their relative *professional power* over competitors (and colleagues!).

Second, in an increasingly information-saturated world, knowledge needs to be firmly rooted in order to be distinctive and meaningful. It has been argued that information is now packaged, mediated and re-presented in various forms and that marketing knowledge has become a 'commodity' to be shaped, packaged, distributed and marketed like any other (Brownlie and Saren, 1995). Academics are now not only producers of marketing knowledge, but also merchandisers, retailers and consumers of it as authors, researchers, teachers and consultants. One effect of this process is that the product life-cycle of marketing knowledge is shortening, and thus its velocity of circulation is accelerating. The capital value of marketing knowledge has a shorter shelf life. Under these conditions the need for theory is now even greater in order to provide an anchor and a referent for marketing information and knowledge and to differentiate it and set it in context.

But where are the advances in marketing theory going to come from in the future? There are a number of possibilities.

Service-dominant logic

A distinct service marketing sub-discipline has developed along with the rise of service-based economies and markets over the past 50 years or so. Vargo and Lusch (2004, 2008) challenged this view of the key differentiators of services versus goods and proposed a new 'service-dominant logic' (S-D) for *all* marketing that constitutes a general theory of marketing. As a new contender for dominance in marketing theory, in a short time S-D logic has stimulated much renewed interest and discussion about theory development in marketing (Lusch and Vargo, 2006). The focus of S-D logic is on marketing as a value cocreation process that is service-based. Marketers can only provide value propositions, embedded in offerings, and their value depends entirely on the experiential evaluation of customers. Service, not goods, is the fundamental basis of exchange and goods are merely 'distribution mechanisms for service provision'. Another key aspect is the role of know-how, capabilities and competencies, which are the key 'operant resources' for both creating value propositions and extracting value from them as the primary source of competitive advantage. The corollary is that the role of tangible, finite 'operand resources' is to provide the raw material inputs.

Central to S-D logic is its distinction from that approach referred to by Vargo and Lusch as the historical and still prevailing, goods-dominant logic (G-D), based on tangible goods and the activities associated with their delivery. The G-D logic approach is presented as an antithesis to S-D, which provides a '*shift in thinking*'. Vargo and Lusch advocate that S-D logic should form the basis of a unified theory of marketing. It can be seen more critically, however, in terms of an orientation – that is, a perspective providing guidelines on how certain existing schools of marketing should be utilized in normative fashion in value creation. Further, Schembri (2006) highlights the limitations of S-D logic and challenges its key foundational premises. She argues that while the service-dominant logic recognizes the emergent service orientation, Vargo and Lusch's analysis of its implications for marketing continues to be founded on the same rationalistic assumptions as the traditional goods-centred logic. Marketers and researchers need to question their underlying assumptions and seek to understand services as constituted in the customer's experience, as opposed to rationalizing the phenomena in terms of a foundational 'logic'.

Networks and relationships

The traditional view of the firm and how managers conduct marketing activities has evolved significantly over the past 40 years or so. The theoretical basis has shifted from the biological analogy of the autonomous organism operating in a changing business environment towards an overlapping network of market actors operating in more or less contingent or strategic modes. In 1982 a research project reported how it had developed an approach that challenged traditional ways of examining industrial marketing and purchasing. In business-to-business settings this Industrial Marketing and Purchasing (IMP) study showed that companies were dominated by long-term business relationships with a limited number of counterparts, within which both marketing and purchasing of industrial goods were seen as 'interaction processes' between the two parties (see Ford, 1990; Håkansson, 1982; Mattsson, 1985). These researchers also observed that interaction in itself included an important content of its own. This concept of interaction in networks challenged the prevailing conceptualizations in B2B marketing in four major respects. First, IMP challenged the narrow analysis of single discrete purchases and emphasized the importance of business relationships. Second, the view of industrial marketing as manipulation of marketing-mix variables in relation to a passive market was challenged. The third aspect concerned the assumption of an atomistic market structure where buyers and sellers can easily switch business partners. Fourth, IMP challenged the separation of theoretical and empirical analysis into either the process of purchasing or the process of marketing.

A range of alternative, broader perspectives of organizations' approach to markets have emerged, which have important implications for the theories regarding firms' relations with markets. Greater emphasis is now placed on marketing organizations' processes, relationships with customers and networks with stakeholders. Reviewing the research undertaken by the Contemporary Marketing Practice (CMP) group, Brodie et al. (2008) develop the case for a multi-theory perspective of the marketing organization. They examine the conceptual foundations of the CMP research and how it evolved to encompass a multi-theory approach. Brodie et al. (2008) also point to the positioning of most marketing theories towards the level of middle-range theory (Merton, 1948; Saren and Pels, 2008).

These approaches all provide potential for the development of a unified general theory of marketing beyond the marketing-as-exchange view (Bagozzi, 1978). In contrast to traditional marketing's microeconomic base, the relational approach emphasizes long-term collaboration as opposed to competition between market and social actors (Webster, 1992). Conceivably all marketing activities, problems, systems and behaviour can be conceptualized and researched taking the unit of analysis as the relationships in which they occur. At the micro-level, dyadic relational theory is being developed from social psychology and human relations literature. At the macro-relational level, social network theory has been well applied and refined towards a theory of industrial marketing by the IMP group. Relationships and networks may not yet be a new general marketing theory, but as an expanding area of knowledge within the discipline it has considerable potential for providing the basis for a new theory of marketing.

Marketing as practice

The term 'marketing as practice' encompasses a number of approaches which explicitly focus on the role of wider cultural practices, including marketing activities and processes, in the construction of markets. Araujo et al. (2008) argue that marketing practice and practices influence the operation of markets. They show that the particular definition and understanding of the market that managers adopt affect their operations and the outcomes in their chosen, 'enacted marketplace'. As Araujo (2007) neatly explains, these reject the assumptions inherent in most economics and marketing theories where markets appear as 'a natural given', as exemplified by Williamson's (1975: 20) dictum: 'In the beginning there were markets'. On the contrary, Araujo addresses the role of marketing in the construction and operation of markets by taking a perspective based on recent contributions in economic sociology that had previously been largely ignored in marketing academics' conceptualization of the exchange process.

The marketing-as-practice approach is influenced by the work of Callon (1998) and others to focus on the calculating agencies that enable the creation and operation of markets. Rather than regarding marketing practices as operating within predefined markets, Araujo argues that marketing practices have *a performative role* in helping to create the market and consumption phenomena they describe. The central notion of 'performativity' goes beyond issues such as how theoretical frameworks permeate market participants' language and behavioural assumptions to the relationship between theories and practice in general.

Kjellberg and Helgesson (2006) develop a practice-based framework that comprises multiple theoretical influences that can play a part in the shaping of markets. They apply a broad definition of performativity to take account of these multiple theoretical influences and they conjecture that the issues facing market actors are likely to be dynamic and multiple in character rather than static and dualist. They approach this issue by examining the practices that constitute markets and how theories shape such practices, e.g. through being embedded in mundane tools that assist in regulating exchanges or in producing images of markets. The multitude of practices that constitute markets suggests the simultaneous presence of many efforts to shape markets.

New consumer theories

Perhaps consumer behaviour can provide the basis for a new general theory since it occupies a unique position in marketing theory development, with the consumer positioned at the centre of the marketing concept, according to Zaltman et al. (1973). They argued that, as opposed to the conflicting and partial explanations of theories in marketing as a whole, the field of consumer behaviour alone contains several grand theories claiming to hold the key to explaining consumer behaviour. The situation today is, if anything, that these approaches are now even more divergent in their methodologies and research orientations, making agreement about theories or even core problems less likely. More recently though there has been a movement in consumer behaviour away from an information-processing view of the consumer. This has involved more theoretical work from an interdisciplinary perspective based on interpretivist, ethnographic and semiotic methods, which adopt more macro, cultural perspectives to studying the consumer.

For example, Warde (2005) notes that the wider practices in which the consumption process is integrated have often been ignored by consumer researchers. This is an important omission, he argues, because people consume to support the particular conventions of the practice in which they are engaged such as eating, skiing, motoring, etc. The similarities and differences between people in terms of their possessions can then be seen less as an outcome of personal choice, and more as an outcome of the way in which the practice is organized.

Cova and Cova (2012) use this approach to examine how marketing discourses help shape consumers. They employ a performative or practice-based approach to examine and critique the notion of the so-called 'new consumer', who is supposed to be 'active, knowledgeable, demanding, channel-hopping and, above all, experience seeking' (Stuart-Menteth et al., 2006: 415). Far from possessing such agency they find that there is a role for marketing ideas that perform, shape and format the structure of consumer competencies. The paper concludes that marketing discourse comprises a governmental process that pressurizes citizens to see themselves primarily as consumers.

Another approach is encompassed in the framework of consumer culture theory (CCT) as developed by Arnould and Thompson (2005), which maps out the conceptual domain and the theoretical advances in this field. CCT adopts an integrative process by combining findings and theories from various disciplines, such as economics, political theory, consumer culture, anthropology, sociology and psychology, thus producing a general framework for theory that is inherently interdisciplinary in nature.

In a 10-year retrospective review of CCT research, Arnould and Thompson (2015) defend their attempt to distil and integrate these cultural oriented strands of consumer research under one 'umbrella theory'. Among other criticisms (e.g. Cova et al., 2013) several commentators have suggested that CCT is not sufficiently theoretical to be labelled a theory (e.g. Moisander et al., 2009). Arnould and Thompson reflect on their contribution as follows:

> Our original text referred to consumer culture theory, and did so for the very specific reason of moving towards recognition of the articulating role of consumption in later capitalist market mediated societies, and further towards insistence upon the globalizing, but also the simultaneously particularizing and reflexive localizing dimensions of this consumer culture. Our 2005 conceptualization built upon Don Slater's definition (1997, 8) of consumer culture as a social arrangement in which the relations between lived culture and social resources, and between meaningful ways of life and the symbolic and material resources on which they depend, are mediated through markets. We further emphasized the importance of market-made commodities, market-mediated social relationships and identity projects, and desire-inducing marketing symbols in the socio-cultural and ideological operations of consumer culture. And consumer culture also encompasses an interconnected system of commercially produced images, texts, and objects that groups use – through the construction of overlapping and even conflicting practices, identities, and meanings – to make collective sense of their environments and to orient their members' experiences and lives.

Taking a completely different perspective on future developments in consumer theory, Wind (2006) argues that the conceptual separation of consumer marketing from other aspects, notably business and industrial marketing, is no longer valid. He recognizes the advantages of specialization and depth of focus that follow from focusing on either business or consumer markets, but the separate fields have now matured, he suggests, and the environment has changed so dramatically that we cannot continue with this separation. The distinct lines between what have come to be labelled B2B and B2C are blurring in five key respects:

1. Convergence of B2B and B2C markets, driven by the development of the internet and the rise of small businesses;
2. Blurring of value chains through outsourcing and other relationships that allow networks of firms to do what was once done within the firm;
3. Blurring of relationships with customers, as customers are invited to participate with companies in the design and delivery processes;
4. Blurring of functions within the firm as marketing and other functions are more integrated through EDI (electronic data interchange) and other systems; and
5. Blurring of products, services and customer experience, moving from an 'industrial' base to a knowledge-based society.

On these bases Wind outlines the case for rethinking the separate approaches to business and industrial marketing which have dominated the theoretical and conceptual underpinnings of theory in both consumer and business marketing sub-disciplines.

Alternative approaches

Theory building is a crucial part of the struggle for academic credibility as well as the basic building blocks for knowledge development. Today, however, the domain of the marketing discipline remains as complex and as contested as ever. There have been several examples of new theories and models that have had the effect of altering the field of possibilities of what marketing phenomena are and what marketing is about (e.g. relationships, services, culture). Most theorists would accept that marketing is a complex, multilayered, and dynamic social phenomenon. With so many different philosophies, methods and theories in the discipline and yet with so little agreement about marketing research in the academy, it may be that 'better theory' in the subject will inevitably be partial.

In the UK and Europe there were attempts to take a more critical approach to the subject in the 1990s through publications such as Brownlie et al.'s *Rethinking Marketing: Towards Critical Marketing Accountings*. Through an edited collection of contributions from leading and emerging new scholars it aimed to offer 'a bigger picture of the social space which marketing occupies and the taken-for-granted ideas which occupy it' (Brownlie et al., 1999: 15). The radical philosophies and methodologies which they discussed were presented under the portmanteau label as 'critical' in marketing, but the approaches which this comprised did not always sit comfortably together; for example postmodernism and critical theory. What these all have in common however is that they embraced distinctly alternative objectives in their analysis and critique of marketing theory and practice.

Other marketing academics have responded to these concerns about the state of the discipline by seeking to find out what knowledge is useful, relevant and valid for marketing today and developing new tools, different approaches and alternative perspectives that offer new insights to particular or general issues. Each of these offers a different way to look at and understand marketing phenomena from alternative methodological and theoretical perspectives with different underlying assumptions. Möller et al. (2010) observe this transition as follows:

> From a fairly monolithic theoretical position in the 1960's we have traveled to a world of differentiated and specialised research scenes involving metatheoretically disparate research traditions. From an initial functional view of marketing our focus has extended in various directions including the aspects of services marketing, political dimensions of channel management, and interaction in business networks, relationship marketing, and a service-logic informed theory development. As marketing academics we should not mind this, the current flux is an indication of the progress of the discipline. (Möller et al., 2010: 151)

The editors of the 30th Anniversary edition of the *Journal of Marketing Management* selected papers which reflected their vision of 'Pushing the boundaries, sketching the future' of marketing knowledge (Hewer and Tadajewski, 2014). These cover the following areas, all of which comprise later chapters in this edition:

- Behavioural psychology
- Consumer theory
- Digital consumption
- Social marketing
- Sustainability
- Relational marketing
- Historical research in marketing theory.

In Chapter 1 of this book, Michael Baker strongly recommends these articles contained in the anniversary edition of *JMM* as core reading to supplement his chapter and as commentaries on future directions of marketing theory. One direction which Baker highlights as critical to all our futures is meeting the challenge of achieving a sustainable form of economic development (Baker, 2014: 525). He believes that the marketing discipline can make a major contribution towards *transformational* change to achieve sustainable development in the global market system while maximizing satisfaction from consumption of scarce resources.

The variety of new approaches reflects this recognition that marketing is no longer, if it ever was, a homogeneous 'universally applicable concept, transcending cultures' and contexts (Cannon, 1980: 35). This is caused in part by the dramatic wide-ranging shifts in the work in which marketing occurs, such as globalization, technology, migration, digital economy, virtuality, market deregulation, climate change, consumerism, and many others of which marketing is part.

This presents a continual challenge for academics in an applied discipline like marketing operating in a fast-moving world because existing models and theories may tie them into particular ways of thinking, skewing their perspectives in ways that often go unquestioned and unrecognized. The building blocks of theory are its underlying concepts and definitions, the unstated assumptions that are often normative and shared among a particular group of individuals. That is why we also need academics who are able and willing to question, interrogate and when necessary overthrow existing theory (Maclaran et al., 2009).

Recommended further reading

Arnould, E.J. and Thompson, C.J. (2005) 'Consumer culture theory (CCT): twenty years of research', *Journal of Consumer Research* 31 (March): 868–82.

Arnould, E.J. and Thompson, C.J. (2015) 'CCT: ten years gone (and beyond)', in A. Thyroff, J.B. Murray and R.W. Belk (eds) *Research in Consumer Behavior*, Vol. 17. Bingley: Emerald Group, forthcoming.

Brownlie, D., Saren, M., Wensley, R. and Whittington, R. (eds) (1999) *Rethinking Marketing: Towards Critical Marketing Accountings*. London: Sage.

Coviello, N.E., Brodie, R.J., Danaher, P.J. and Johnston, W.J. (2002) 'How firms relate to their markets: an empirical examination of contemporary marketing practice', *Journal of Marketing* 66(8): 33–46.

Day, G.S. and Wensley, R. (1983) 'Marketing theory with a strategic orientation', *Journal of Marketing* 47 (Fall): 79–89.

Dholakia, N. and Arndt, J. (eds) (1985) *Changing the Course of Marketing: Alternative Paradigms for Widening Marketing Theory* (Research in Marketing Supplement 2). Greenwich, CT: JAI Press.

Hunt, S.D. (1991) *Marketing Theory: Conceptual Foundations of Research in Marketing*. Homewood, IL: Irwin.

Kelley, W.T. (1956) 'The development of early thought in marketing and promotion', *Journal of Marketing* 21 (July): 62–7.

Kjellberg, H. and Helgesson, C. (2007) 'On the nature of markets and their practices', *Marketing Theory* 7(2): 137–62.

Lusch, R. and Vargo, S. (2006) *The Service Dominant Logic of Marketing: Dialog, Debate and Directions*. New York: M.E. Sharpe.

Maclaran, P., Saren, M. and Tadajewski, M. (eds) (2008) *Marketing Theory*, Vols I, II and III, Sage Library in Marketing Series. London: Sage.

Sheth, J.M., Gardner, D.M. and Garrett, D.E. (1988) *Marketing Theory: Evolution and Evaluation*. New York: John Wiley.

Zaltman, G., LeMasters, K. and Heffring, M. (1982) *Theory Construction in Marketing*. New York: John Wiley.

References

Alderson, W. (1957) *Marketing Behaviour and Executive Action*. Homewood, IL: Irwin.

Alderson, W. and Cox, R. (1948) 'Towards a theory of marketing', *Journal of Marketing* 13 (October): 137–52.

AMA (American Marketing Association) (1988) 'Task force on the development of marketing thought: developing, disseminating and utilizing marketing knowledge', *Journal of Marketing* 52 (Fall): 1–25.

Anderson, J.M. (1994) 'Marketing science: where's the beef?', *Business Horizons* January–February: 8–16.

Anderson, P.F. (1983) 'Marketing, scientific progress and scientific method', *Journal of Marketing* 47 (Fall): 18–31.

Anderson, P.F. (1986) 'On method in consumer research: a critical relativist perspective', *Journal of Consumer Research* 13 (September): 155–73.

Araujo, L. (2007) 'Markets, market-making and marketing', *Marketing Theory* 7(3): 211–26.

Araujo, L., Kjellberg, H. and Spencer, R. (2008) 'Market practices and forms: introduction to the special issue', *Marketing Theory* 8(1): 5–14.

Arndt, J. (1985) 'On making marketing science more scientific: role of orientations, paradigms, metaphors, and puzzle solving', *Journal of Marketing* 49(3): 11–23.

Arnould, E.J. and Thompson, C.J. (2005) 'Consumer culture theory (CCT): twenty years of research', *Journal of Consumer Research* 31(4): 868–82.

Arnould, E.J. and Thompson, C.J. (2015) 'CCT: ten years gone (and beyond)', in A. Thyroff, J.B. Murray and R.W. Belk (eds) *Research in Consumer Behavior*, Vol. 17. Bingley: Emerald Group, forthcoming.

Bacharach, S.B. (1989) 'Organizational theories: some criteria for evaluation', *Academy of Management Review* 14(4): 496–515.

Bagozzi, R.P. (1978) 'Marketing as exchange: a theory of transactions in the marketplace', *American Behavioral Scientist* 21 (March/April): 535–56.

Bagozzi, R.P. (1980) *Causal Models in Marketing*. New York: John Wiley.

Baines, P. and O'Shaughnessy (eds) (2013) *Propaganda*, Vols. I–IV. London: Sage.

Baker, M.J. (1995a) *Companion Encyclopaedia of Marketing*. London: Routledge.

Baker, M.J. (1995b) *Marketing: Theory and Practice*. London: Macmillan.

Baker, M.J. (2014) *Marketing Strategy and Management*. London: Palgrave.

Bartels, R. (1951) 'Can marketing be a science?', *Journal of Marketing* January: 319–28.

Bartels, R. (1968) 'The general theory of marketing', *Journal of Marketing* 32 (January): 29–33.

Baumol, W. (1957) 'On the role of marketing theory', *Journal of Marketing* April: 413–8.

Belk, R.W. (1986) 'Art versus science as ways of generating knowledge about materialism', in D. Brinberg and R.J. Lutz (eds) *Perspectives on Methodology in Consumer Research*. New York: Springer-Verlag, pp. 3–17.

Brodie, R.J., Coviello, N.E. and Winklhofer, H. (2008) 'Investigating contemporary marketing practices: a review of the first decade of the CMP research program', *Journal of Business & Industrial Marketing* 23(2): 84–94.

Brodie, R., Saren, M. and Pels, J. (2011) 'Theorizing about the service dominant logic: the bridging role of middle range theory', *Marketing Theory* 11(1): 75–91.

Brown, S. (1999) 'Marketing and literature: the anxiety of academic influence', *Journal of Marketing* 63 (January): 1–15.

Brown, S.W. (2005) 'When executives speak, we should listen and act differently', *Journal of Marketing* 69 (October): 2–4.

Brown, S., Hirschman, E.C. and Maclaren, P. (2001) 'Always historicize! Researching marketing history in a post-historical epoch', *Marketing Theory* 1(1): 49–89.

Brownlie, D. and Saren, M. (1995) 'On the commodification of marketing knowledge', *Journal of Marketing Management* 11(7): 619–28.

Brownlie, D. and Saren, M. (1996) 'Beyond the one-dimensional marketing manager: the discourse of theory, practice and relevance', *International Journal of Research in Marketing* 14(2): 147–61.

Brownlie, D., Saren, M., Wensley, R. and Whittington, R. (eds) (1999) *Rethinking Marketing: Towards Critical Marketing Accountings*. London: Sage.

Burrell, G. and Morgan, G. (1979) *Sociological Paradigms and Organisational Analysis*. London: Heinemann.

Buzzell, R. (1963) 'Is marketing a science?', *Harvard Business Review* January–February: 32–48.

Callon, M. (ed.) (1998) *The Laws of the Market*. Oxford: Basil Blackwell.

Campbell, N., O'Driscoll, A. and Saren, M. (2009) 'The posthuman: the end and the beginning of the human', EIASM Workshop on Interpretive Methods in Consumer Research, Milan, April.

Cannon, T. (1980) 'Managing international and export marketing', *European Journal of Marketing* 14(1): 34–49.

Carmen, J.M. (1980) 'Paradigms for marketing theory', in J.N. Sheth (ed.) *Research in Marketing*, Vol. 3. Greenwich, CT: JAI Press.

Christensen, C.M. and Raynor, M.E. (2003) *The Innovator's Solution: Creating and Sustaining Successful Growth*. Boston, MA: Harvard Business School Press.

Converse, P.D. (1945) 'The development of the science of marketing – an exploratory survey', *Journal of Marketing* 10 (July): 14–23.

Cova, B. and Cova, V. (2012) 'On the road to prosumption: marketing discourse and the development of consumer competencies', *Consumption, Markets & Culture* 15(2): 149–68.

Cova, B., Maclaran, P. and Bradshaw, A. (2013) 'Rethinking consumer culture theory from the postmodern to the communist horizon', *Marketing Theory* 13(2): 213–25.

Cunningham, W. and Sheth, J.N. (1982) 'From the editor', *Journal of Marketing* Spring: 11–12.

Day, G. and Montgomery, D. (1999) 'Charting new directions for marketing', *Journal of Marketing* 63: 3–13.

Deshpande, R. (1983) 'Paradigms lost: on theory and method in research in marketing', *Journal of Marketing* 47(4): 101–10.

Dholakia, N. and Arndt, J. (eds) (1985) *Changing the Course of Marketing: Alternative Paradigms for Widening Marketing Theory* (Research in Marketing Supplement 2). Greenwich, CT: JAI Press.

Fisk, G. and Meyers, P. (1982) 'Macromarketers' guide to paradigm', in R. Bush and S.D. Hunt (eds) *Marketing Theory: Philosophy of Science Perspectives*. Chicago, IL: AMA.

Ford, I.D. (ed.) (1990) *Understanding Business Markets: Interaction, Relationships and Networks*. New York: Academic Press.

Foucault, M. (1980) *Power/Knowledge: Selected Interviews and Other Writings*, ed. C. Gordon. New York: Pantheon Books.

Fullerton, R. (1986) 'Historicism: what it is and what it means for consumer research', in M. Wallendorf and P. Anderson (eds) *Advances in Consumer Research 14*. Provo, UT: Association for Consumer Research, pp. 431–4.

Fullerton, R. (1988) 'How modern is modern marketing? Marketing's evolution and the myth of the production era', *Journal of Marketing* 52 (January): 108–25.

Håkansson, H. (ed.) (1982) *International Marketing and Purchasing of Industrial Goods – An Interaction Approach*. New York: John Wiley.

Halbert, M. (1965) *The Meaning and Sources of Marketing Theory*. New York: McGraw-Hill.

Heffring, M. (1985) 'A theory-in-use approach to developing marketing theories', in N. Dholakia and J. Arndt (eds) *Changing the Course of Marketing: Alternative Paradigms for Widening Marketing Theory* (Research in Marketing Supplement 2). Greenwich, CT: JAI Press.

Heidegger, M. (1962) *Being and Time*, trans. J. McQuarrie and E. Robison. New York: Harper Row.

Hewer, P. and Tadajewski, M. (2014) 'Pushing the boundaries, sketching the future', *Journal of Marketing Management* 30th Anniversary Special Issue 30(11–12): 1083–5.

Holbrook, M. (1989) 'Aftermath of the task force: dogmatism and catastrophe in marketing thought', *ACR Newsletter*, President's column, September: 1–11.

Hunt, S.D. (1971) 'The morphology of theory and the general theory of marketing', *Journal of Marketing* 35 (April): 65–8.

Hunt, S.D. (1976) 'The nature and scope of marketing', *Journal of Marketing* 40 (July): 17–28.

Hunt, S.D. (1983) 'General theories and the fundamental explananda of marketing', *Journal of Marketing* 47(4): 9–17.

Hunt, S.D. (1984) 'Should marketers adopt relativism?', in P.F. Anderson and M.J. Ryan (eds) *Scientific Method in Marketing: AMA Winter Educators Conference Proceedings*. Chicago, IL: AMA, pp. 30–4.

Hunt, S.D. (1991) *Marketing Theory: Conceptual Foundations of Research in Marketing*. Homewood, IL: Irwin.

Hunt, S.D. (1993) 'Objectivity in marketing theory and research', *Journal of Marketing* 57 (April): 76–91.

Hunt, S. (1994) 'On rethinking marketing: our discipline, our practice, our methods', *European Journal of Marketing* 28(3): 13–25.

Jones, D.G.B. and Monieson, D.D. (1990) 'Early development in the philosophy of marketing thought', *Journal of Marketing* 54(1): 102–13.

Kavanagh, D. (1994) 'Hunt versus Anderson: round 16', *European Journal of Marketing* 28(3): 26–41.

Keat, R. and Urry, J. (1975) *Social Theory as Science*. London: Routledge and Kegan Paul.

Kelley, W.T. (1956) 'The development of early thought in marketing and promotion', *Journal of Marketing* 21 (July): 62–7.

Kerin, R. (1996) 'In pursuit of an ideal: the editorial and literary history of the *Journal of Marketing*', *Journal of Marketing* 60(1): 1–13.

Kim, W.C. and Mauborgne, R. (2005) *Blue Ocean Strategy: How to Create Uncontested Market Space and Make the Competition Irrelevant*. Boston, MA: Harvard Business School Press.

Kjellberg, H. and Helgesson, C. (2006) 'Multiple versions of markets: multiplicity and performativity in market practice', *Industrial Marketing Management* 35(7): 839–55.

Kuhn, T. (1962) *The Structure of Scientific Revolutions*. Chicago, IL: University of Chicago Press.

Lehman, D.R. and Jocz, K.E. (1997) *Reflections on the Futures of Marketing: Practice and Education*. Cambridge, MA: Marketing Science Institute.

Llewelyn, S. (2003) 'What counts as "theory" in qualitative management and accounting research? Introducing five levels of theorizing', *Accounting, Auditing & Accountability Journal* 16(4): 662–708.

Lusch, R. and Vargo, S. (2006) *The Service Dominant Logic of Marketing: Dialog, Debate and Directions*. New York: M.E. Sharpe.

Maclaran, P., Saren, M., Goulding, C. and Stevens, L. (2009) 'Rethinking theory building and theorizing in marketing', 38th European Marketing Academy Conference, University of Nantes, France, May 2009.

Maclaran, P., Saren, M., Stern, B. and Tadajewski, M. (2010) *The Sage Handbook of Marketing Theory*. London: Sage.

McGary, E.D. (1953) 'Some new viewpoints in marketing', *Journal of Marketing* XVIII(1): 33–40.

McInnes, W.C. (1964) 'A conceptual approach to marketing', in R. Cox, W. Alderson and S. Shapiro (eds) *Theory in Marketing* (2nd Series). Homewood, IL: Irwin.

McMullin, E. (1984) 'A case for scientific realism', in J. Leplin (ed.) *Scientific Realism*. Berkeley: University of California Press.

Mattsson, L.G. (1985) 'An application of the network approach to marketing', in N. Dholakia and J. Arndt (eds) *Changing the Course of Marketing: Alternative Paradigms for Widening Marketing Theory*. Greenwich, CT: JAI Press.

Merton, R.K. (1948) 'Discussion', *American Sociological Review* 13: 164–8.

Mick, D.G. (1986) 'Consumer research and semiotics: exploring the morphology of signs, symbols and significance', *Journal of Consumer Research* 13(2): 196–213.

Moisander, J., Valtonen, A. and Histo, H. (2009) 'Personal interviews in cultural consumer research', *Consumption, Markets & Culture* 12(4): 329–48.

Möller, K., Pels, J. and Saren, M. (2010) 'The marketing theory or theories into marketing? Plurality of research traditions and paradigms', in P. Maclaran, M. Saren, B. Stern and M. Tadajewski (eds) *The Sage Handbook of Marketing Theory*. London: Sage, pp. 151–73.

Morgan, G. (1980) 'Paradigms, metaphors and puzzle-solving in organisation theory', *Administrative Science Quarterly* 25 (December): 605–22.

Morgan, G. (1992) 'Marketing discourse and practice', in M. Alvesson and H. Willmott (eds) *Critical Management Studies*. London: Sage.

Murray, J.B., Evers, D.J. and Janda, S. (1997) 'Marketing, theory borrowing and critical reflection', *Journal of Macromarketing* 15(2): 92–106.

Myers, J.G., Greyser, S. and Massey, W. (1979) 'The effectiveness of marketing's R & D for marketing management: an assessment', *Journal of Marketing* 43(1): 17–29.

Myers, J.G., Massey, W. and Greyser, S. (1980) *Marketing Research and Knowledge Development: An Assessment for Marketing Management*. Englewood Cliffs, NJ: Prentice-Hall.

Nevett, T. (1991) 'Historical investigation and the practice of marketing', *Journal of Marketing* 55 (July): 13–23.

Peter, P.J. (1992) 'Realism or relativism for marketing theory research: a comment on Hunt's "scientific realism" ', *Journal of Marketing* 56(2): 72–9.

Porter, M.E. (1985) *Competitive Advantage: Creating and Sustaining Superior Performance*. New York: The Free Press.

Reibstein, D.J., Day, G. and Wind, J. (2009) 'Is marketing academia losing its way?', *Journal of Marketing* 73 (July): 1–3.

Rudner, R. (1966) *Philosophy of Social Science*. Englewood Cliffs, NJ: Prentice-Hall.

Ryan, M. and O'Shaunessy, J. (1980) 'Theory development: the need to distinguish the levels of abstraction', in C. Lamb and P. Dunne (eds) *Theoretical Developments in Marketing*. Chicago, IL: AMA.

Saren, M. and Pels, J. (2008) 'A comment on paradox and middle-range theory', *Journal of Business & Industrial Marketing* 23(2): 105–7.

Savitt, R. (1980) 'Historical research in marketing', *Journal of Marketing* 44 (Fall): 52–8.

Schembri, S. (2006) 'Rationalizing service logic, or understanding services as experience?', *Marketing Theory* 6(3): 281–8.

Schwarzkopf, S. (2011) 'The consumer as "voter," "judge," and "jury": historical origins and political consequences of a marketing myth', *Journal of Macromarketing* 31(1): 8–18.

Schwarzkopf, S. (2015) 'Mobilizing the depths of the market: motivation research and the making of the disembedded consumer', *Marketing Theory* 15(1): 39–57.

Shaw, E.H. and Jones, D.G.B. (2005) 'A history of schools of marketing thought', *Marketing Theory* 5(3): 239–81.

Sheth, J.N. and Gardener, D.M. (1988) 'History of marketing thought: an update', in R. Bush and S.D. Hunt (eds) *Marketing Theory: Philosophy of Science Perspectives*. Chicago, IL: AMA.

Slater, D. (1997) *Consumer Culture and Modernity*. Cambridge: Polity Press.

Stern, B.B. (1989) 'Literary criticism and consumer research: overview and illustrative analysis', *Journal of Consumer Research* 16(3): 322–34.

Stern, B.B. (1990) 'Literary criticism and the history of marketing thought: a new perspective on "reading" marketing theory', *Journal of the Academy of Marketing Science* 18(4): 329–36.

Strasser, S. (1989) *Satisfaction Guaranteed: The Making of the American Mass Market*. New York: Pantheon Books.

Stuart-Menteth, H., Wilson, H. and Baker, S. (2006) 'Escaping the channel silo: researching the new consumer', *International Journal of Market Research* 48(4): 415–37.

Svenssen, P. (2007) 'Producing marketing: towards a social-phenomenology of marketing work', *Marketing Theory* 7(3): 271–90.

Ulrich, K.T. and Eppinger, S.D. (2007) *Product Design and Development*. New York: McGraw-Hill.

Vaile, R. (1949) 'Towards a theory of marketing – a comment', *Journal of Marketing* 14 (April): 520–2.

van de Ven, A.H. (1989) 'Nothing is quite so practical as a good theory', *Academy of Management Review* 14(4): 486–90.

Vargo, S.L. and Lusch, R.F (2004) 'Evolving to a new dominant logic for marketing', *Journal of Marketing* 68(1): 1–17.

Vargo, S.L. and Lusch, R.F. (2008) 'Service dominant logic: continuing the evolution', *Journal of the Academy of Marketing Science* 36(1): 1–10.

Venkatesh, A. (1985) 'Is marketing ready for Kuhn?', in N. Dholakia and J. Arndt (eds) *Changing the Course of Marketing: Alternative Paradigms for Widening Marketing Theory* (Research in Marketing Supplement 2). Greenwich, CT: JAI Press.

Warde, A. (2005) 'Consumption and theories of practice', *Journal of Consumer Culture* 5(2): 131–53.

Webster, F.E. Jr (1992) 'The changing role of marketing in the corporation', *Journal of Marketing* 56(1): 1–17.

Wensley, R. (1995) 'A critical review of research in marketing', *British Journal of Management* 6: S63–S82.

Wilkie, W.L. and Moore, E.S. (2003) 'Scholarly research in marketing: exploring the "4 Eras" of thought development', *Journal of Public Policy and Marketing* 22(2): 16–46.

Williamson, O.E. (1975) *Markets and Hierarchies: Analysis and Antitrust Implications*. New York: The Free Press.

Wind, Y. (2006) 'Blurring the lines: is there a need to rethink industrial marketing?', *Journal of Business & Industrial Marketing* 21(7): 474–81.

Wooliscroft, B. (2011) 'Marketing theory as history', *Marketing Theory* 11(4): 499–501.

Zaltman, G., Pinson, C. and Angelmar, R. (1973) *Metatheory and Consumer Research*. New York: Holt Rinehart and Winston.

Zwick, D. and Cayla, J. (2011) *Inside Marketing: Practices, Ideologies, Devices*. Oxford: Oxford University Press.

A History of Historical Research in Marketing

D.G. Brian Jones and
Mark Tadajewski

3

Chapter Topics

Introduction	60
Recording the facts: 1930–59	63
Foundations of the new marketing history: 1960–79	65
The new marketing history: 1980–2009	66
The emerging discipline: Today and tomorrow	75
Post-script	77

Introduction

The purpose of this chapter is to review historical research in marketing. Because of space limitations, this review is more a chronicle of what has been published about historical research in marketing than a critical historical analysis, hopefully providing the reader with a roadmap to further reading on historical topics of interest. Scholars in a wide range of disciplines have published historical research about marketing and have done so in various publications, many outside what would be considered the 'marketing literature'. Except for some overall frequencies of publications reported in this introduction, this review has focused mostly on historical research published in marketing periodicals and in books.

The discipline of marketing emerged early in the 20th century as a branch of applied economics strongly influenced by the German Historical School and its offspring, the American Institutional School (Jones and Monieson, 1990). Thus, from its beginnings the academic study of marketing was influenced by an historical perspective. However, for economists studying marketing at the turn of the 20th century, history was a means to an end rather than an end in itself. Marketing economists during that era studied the histories of marketing practices carried out in industries and by firms in order to discover marketing functions and principles.

The earliest university courses in marketing in North America were taught in 1902/3 when the universities of Illinois, Michigan and California offered the first courses in what was then called distribution (Bartels, 1962). The term 'marketing' was used by economists in a manner consistent with current practice as early as 1897 (Bussiere, 2000) and gradually replaced 'distribution'. A handful of general marketing texts was published by 1920 (Converse, 1933) and the first scholarly journals on the subject appeared in the mid-1930s merging to form the *Journal of Marketing* in 1936 (Witkowski, 2010). Their sponsoring associations, the American Marketing Society and the National Association of Marketing Teachers, also merged to form the American Marketing Association on 1 January 1937. As the marketing discipline crystallized in the 1930s, scholars began to reflect on their heritage and published what today is considered some of the earliest historical research in marketing.

With some exceptions, historical research about marketing and marketing-related subjects is conducted by two relatively distinct groups of scholars – marketing professors working in business schools, and business history professors, who, for the most part, work in history departments. Again, with some exceptions, these two groups tend to present their work at different academic conferences and publish in different journals. Throughout this chapter we will focus mostly, but not exclusively, on the work of marketing historians publishing in marketing periodicals as well as books.

Marketing historians usually recognize two overlapping, but relatively distinct, general fields within historical research in marketing – 'marketing history' and the 'history of marketing thought'. Marketing history includes, but is not limited to, the histories of advertising, retailing, channels of distribution, product design and branding, pricing strategies and consumption behaviour – all studied from the perspective of companies, industries, or even whole economies. The history of marketing thought examines marketing ideas, concepts, theories and schools of marketing thought including the lives and times of marketing thinkers. This includes biographical studies as well as histories of institutions and associations involved in the development of the marketing discipline. These two fields or categories of historical research provide one of the two main organizing themes for this chapter. The other theme, of course, is chronological. The history of historical research in marketing is divided here into three eras: (1) 1930–59; (2) 1960–79; (3) 1980–present. Periodization in this case is driven by turning points in the material being reviewed (Hollander et al., 2005), developments that occurred during the early 1960s and early 1980s.

As detailed below, marketing history as History began to be published during the early 1930s. The 1960s saw a decline of interest in historical research by marketing scholars, probably driven by an increasing pragmatism in business education during that time. Nevertheless, the scope and rigour of individual works published after 1960 were improved considerably over earlier research. During the early 1980s, a number of specialized conferences, collections of readings and special issues of periodicals fuelled a dramatic growth of interest in historical research in marketing. This growth of interest is illustrated in Table 3.1, which shows the cumulative number of publications on historical research in marketing by decade since 1930 as listed in the Google Scholar database. That database includes peer-reviewed papers, theses, books, abstracts and articles from academic publishers, professional societies, reprint repositories, universities and other scholarly organizations. Using the search phrases indicated in Table 3.1 yielded a cumulative 6,566 entries for historical research in marketing from 1930 through to May 2012. These searches undoubtedly understate the actual amount of research activity since some authors do not use those particular phrases in their publications. For example, during the 1930s and 1940s there were numerous studies published in the *Journal of Marketing* about the origins of the discipline that are not registered in searches of the Google Scholar database.

The growth in historical research since the 1980s stimulated the publication of occasional overviews of this literature. For instance, most publications prior to 1980 are covered in this chapter. Jones et al. (2009) presented a content analysis of the 445 papers presented at CHARM conferences from 1983 to 2007 and traced the impact of CHARM on publishing activity in marketing history more generally. Jones and Shaw (2006) reviewed the strong record of the *Journal of Macromarketing* in publishing historical research from its inception in 1981 through to 2006. While these studies offer intellectual substance, each deals with selected

Table 3.1 Cumulative volume of historical research in marketing.

Ending date	Marketing History[a]	Retailing History[b]	Advertising History[c]	Combined history of marketing[d]	History of thought[e]	Total
1940	7	0	2	9	0	9
1950	17	3	12	32	0	32
1960	29	4	30	63	0	63
1970	40	19	66	125	0	125
1980	89	27	141	257	7	264
1990	244	68	356	668	52	720
2000	680	188	1,014	1,882	165	2,047
2010	2,021	705	3,070	5,796	614	6,410
2012	2,082	716	3,130	5,928	638	6,566

Source: Google Scholar database accessed 25 May 2013. Includes peer-reviewed papers, theses, books, abstracts and articles from academic publishers, professional societies, reprint repositories, universities and other scholarly organizations. The search phrases used here capture the major categories of historical research in marketing.

[a] Using the search phrases 'marketing history' and 'history of marketing', with 'history of marketing thought' excluded to avoid double counting.

[b] Using the search phrases 'retail history', 'retailing history' and 'history of retailing', with 'marketing history' excluded to avoid double counting.

[c] Using the search phrases 'advertising history' and 'history of advertising', with 'marketing history' excluded to avoid double counting.

[d] Total of marketing history, retailing history and advertising history.

[e] Using the search phrase 'history of marketing thought'.

subsets of publication sources and, at the same time, with broader historical terrain than marketing management.

Of course, not all of the publications counted in Table 3.1 were reviewed for this chapter. The relatively smaller number of publications through the 1970s was manageable. However, as Table 3.1 indicates, since 1980 and especially during the past decade there has been dramatic growth of publication activity in this field. For that more recent period this review is more selective, focusing on major publications in the marketing periodical literature as well as the most relevant books. Also note the post-script that is included at the end of this chapter. That section briefly summarizes a significant and more recent review (Tadajewski and Jones, 2014) that nicely complements this chapter.

Recording the facts: 1930-59

The first scholarly marketing journals, *The Journal of Retailing*, *The American Marketing Journal* and *The National Marketing Review*, began publication in 1925, 1934 and 1935 respectively, with the latter two merging in 1936 to form the *Journal of Marketing*. The sponsoring organizations for the two parent journals, the American Marketing Society and National Association of Marketing Teachers, also merged in 1937 to form the American Marketing Association. These developments provided an important impetus for historical work as they naturally led to reflection about the origins and development of the marketing discipline. At the same time, the *Journal of Marketing* provided a specialized outlet for the publication of such historical reflection. Thus, beginning in the early 1930s there were a number of attempts to put things on the record.

History of marketing thought

From the early 1930s to late 1950s historical research in marketing was dominated by the study of marketing thought. During this period, attention was focused on tracing the earliest literature (Applebaum, 1947, 1952; Bartels, 1951; Converse, 1933, 1945; Coolsen, 1947; Maynard, 1951) and marketing courses taught in American universities (Bartels, 1951; Hagerty, 1936; Hardy, 1954; Litman, 1950; Maynard, 1941; Weld, 1941). The earliest historical study included in this review was Converse's (1933) 'The first decade of marketing literature' published in the *NATMA Bulletin*. Converse's article was typical in its attempt to identify historically significant events. In his opinion the first modern books on marketing were Nystrom's (1915) *Economics of Retailing* and A.W. Shaw's (1915) *Some Problems in Market Distribution*.

Other early historical studies focused on the individuals and organizations that pioneered the development of the discipline (Agnew, 1941; Bartels, 1951; Converse, 1959b). A series of 23 biographical sketches published in the *Journal of Marketing* between 1956 and 1962 was later reprinted as a collection edited by Wright and Dimsdale (1974) and subsequently reprinted along with other, more recent biographies of other pioneer marketing scholars in Tadajewski and Jones (2008). Bartels' (1951) article titled 'Influences on the development of marketing thought, 1900–1923' was seminal in its attempt to go beyond a simple chronicle of 'firsts'. It drew upon numerous interviews of pioneer scholars in order to examine some of the sources of early marketing ideas. Bartels' article was also the most ambitious historical analysis at that time as it was based on his (1941) doctoral dissertation at Ohio State University, the first such work known.

During the 1950s a trend began towards focusing on the history of marketing concepts (Breen, 1959; Kelley, 1956), theories (McGarry, 1953) and schools of thought (Brown, 1951). Cassels (1936) had earlier examined the influence of significant schools of economic thought on marketing, but it was not until the 1950s that marketing *ideas* or *concepts* were developed enough to warrant a retrospective. An important collection of such articles was published in 1951 under the title *Changing Perspectives in Marketing*. It claimed to be 'one of the few, if not the only one, in which a series of papers has been compiled to give historical treatment and perspective to the development of marketing [thought]' (Wales, 1951: v). This included topics such as retailing, sales management, marketing research and marketing theory. Its contributors were eminent scholars in marketing. Most had been recipients of the American Marketing Association's prestigious Paul D. Converse Award.

Marketing history

There was less research done during this early period on marketing history, most of which focused on the history of retailing and wholesaling (Barger, 1955; Emmet and Jeuck, 1950; Jones, 1936; Kirkwood, 1960; Marburg, 1951; Nystrom, 1951; Phillips, 1935). Barger's (1955) book, entitled *Distribution's Place in the American Economy Since 1869*, examined the changing role of wholesale and retail sectors in the American economy from 1869 to 1950. It was a unique study of the cost and output of distribution, and of the relative importance of wholesale and retail sectors as measured by the proportion of the labour force engaged in each. Early books on retailing history included Hower's (1946) history of the R.H. Macy department store; the well-known classic history of mail-order house Sears, Roebuck and Company by Emmet and Jeuck (1950); and histories of the F.W. Woolworth chain store by Phillips (1935) and Kirkwood (1960).

A more general history of marketing, distinctive both for its scope of subject matter and for its breadth of historical perspective, was Hotchkiss's (1938) *Milestones of Marketing*. Using the American Marketing Association's definition of marketing to guide his choice of topics, Hotchkiss traced what he believed to be the most important steps in the evolution of marketing back to ancient Rome and Greece through medieval England to modern North American practices focusing on retailing, advertising and merchandising.

Another marketing history which complemented the Hotchkiss book in time period covered by focusing on marketing practices of the early 20th century was Converse's (1959a) *Fifty Years of Marketing in Retrospect*. This was written as a companion to his (1959b) study of the beginnings of marketing thought cited earlier. Converse described his marketing history book as 'the story of business and particularly of market distribution as I have seen it and as I have studied it' (1959a: vi). In addition to marketing practices such as advertising and promotion, pricing and merchandising, Converse described the changing economic conditions and technological developments during the early 20th century that influenced such practices.

Throughout this early period, historical research was relatively descriptive as marketers focused on recording the facts of marketing history and the history of marketing thought. The most prolific and perhaps most important contributor during this era was Paul D. Converse, whose two monographs published in 1959 are typical of historical research in marketing to that point in time.

Foundations of the new marketing history: 1960–79

The 1960s was a transition period with fewer, but more ambitious studies of marketing history and the history of marketing thought. A number of significant works and events laid the foundation for the growth of interest in historical research evident today. For example, during the early 1960s successive conferences of the American Marketing Association featured tracks on historical research (Greyser, 1963; Smith, 1964). Most of the papers presented at those sessions called for more historical research and offered justifications for doing such work and, in that way, helped to legitimate subsequent historical research. Although there was a notable decline in the number of publications in the periodical literature (Grether, 1976), there were several important books published. Four books in rapid succession were published on the history of marketing thought (Bartels, 1962; Converse, 1959b; Coolsen, 1960; Schwartz, 1963). A wide-ranging collection of work on 17th-, 18th- and 19th-century marketing practices was also published (Shapiro and Doody, 1968). And finally, a carefully researched, well-documented study of changes in American distribution channels during the 19th century provided some foundation for later studies of retailing history (Porter and Livesay, 1971).

History of marketing thought

Converse's (1959b) *The Beginnings of Marketing Thought in the United States* served as a transition, both in time and in depth of analysis, in the study of the history of marketing thought. One of Converse's students, Frank Coolsen, followed with a dissertation on the marketing ideas of four 19th-century liberal economists (Edward Atkinson, David Wells, Arthur Farquhar and Henry Farquhar) which was published in 1960 under the title *Marketing Thought in the United States in the Late Nineteenth Century*. According to Coolsen, the writings of those four economists presented a fairly comprehensive view of the scope and importance of marketing in the late 19th century. However, their work did not have much influence on the early 20th-century development of the marketing discipline (Jones and Shaw, 2002).

Two other books on the history of marketing thought which complemented each other were Bartels' (1962) *The Development of Marketing Thought* and Schwartz's (1963) *Development of Marketing Theory*. Bartels' book was essentially a chronology of published literature, university courses and events that had played a role in the development of marketing thought since 1900. Schwartz was more concerned with specific theories in marketing.

His was a more concentrated and rigorous follow-up to the 1951 collection edited by Hugh Wales (cited above). In addition to examining the development of well-recognized marketing theories such as retail gravitation, regional theory, marketing functions and Alderson's functionalist theory, Schwartz included chapters examining the potential contribution of fields such as social physics and game theory. That may explain why it has been largely ignored by students of the history of marketing thought. Bartels' book (1962), on the other hand, was twice updated (1976, 1988) and became a staple reading for many doctoral courses in North America. In addition to those general works, there were a few studies of specific concepts and theories during the 1960s. Examples included Hollander's historical analysis of retailing institutions (1960, 1963a, 1966), and historical examinations of marketing management by Keith (1960), Lazer (1965) and LaLonde and Morrison (1967).

During the 1960s some researchers began to integrate marketing history with the history of marketing thought. Such work went beyond the narrower approach of earlier writings by using the history of marketing practice to interpret the development of marketing thought. A good example of this was Hollander's work cited above, and more recently his re-examination of the origins of the marketing concept (1986). Hollander's distinctive approach to historical research was deconstructed by Rassuli (1988).

Marketing history

As the marketing discipline moved away from the traditional institutional and commodity schools of thought and began to popularize marketing functions through the managerial approach, research into marketing history during the 1960s reflected that trend. This included historical research in advertising and promotion (McKendrick, 1960), product innovation (Silk and Stern, 1963) and personal selling (Hollander, 1963b, 1964). A broad range of marketing history, especially in economic development, regulation, institutions and advertising, was covered in Shapiro and Doody's (1968) *Readings in the History of American Marketing: Settlement to Civil War*. As editors of that extensive collection, Shapiro and Doody stated that their objective was to 'awaken the interest of students of marketing in history and historical analysis' (1968: 12). Their book of readings and Bartels' (1962) *Development of Marketing Thought* were probably the most important publications during the 1960s. In both of those books the scope of coverage was unprecedented.

However, as the 1960s drew to a close there seemed to be a decline of interest in historical research in marketing. After the publication of the Gordon and Howell (1959) report, the marketing discipline moved during the 1960s in a more quantitative, scientific direction and historical research may have seemed less rigorous and less relevant.

The new marketing history: 1980–2009

Returning to Table 3.1, the increase in number of publications since 1980 is dramatic. During the 1980s, a number of specialized conferences, collections of readings and special issues of periodicals fuelled the tremendous growth of interest in historical research in marketing. Perhaps most important was the organization of the biennial North American marketing history conference. In 1983 the first North American Workshop on Historical Research in Marketing was held at Michigan State University. That conference, now known as the Conference on Historical Analysis and Research in Marketing (CHARM), has been held biennially ever since. The entire collection of papers is available online at the CHARM website, www.charmassociation.org. A history of the CHARM conference and content analysis of the first 13 conference proceedings is provided by Jones et al. (2009).

In the early 1990s, CHARM became a major contributor of content for the *Journal of Macromarketing* (see Jones and Shaw [2006] for a review of that body of work). From 1994 through 2008 historical research accounted for 72 of the 196 full articles published in *JMM* representing fully 37% of that journal's content. Most of those articles were first presented at a CHARM conference. More recently, the CHARM Association was the driving force behind the new *Journal of Historical Research in Marketing* which began publication in March 2009.

In 1985 and 1988 the Association for Consumer Research and American Marketing Association respectively held conferences that included a major focus on historical research in marketing. In 1990 the *Journal of the Academy of Marketing Science* published a special issue on the history of marketing thought. Most of those articles were originally papers presented at CHARM. Other journals to feature special issues on historical research in marketing included *Psychology & Marketing* in 1998 and *Marketing Theory* in 2005 and again in 2008. Since its inception in 2000, *Marketing Theory* has regularly published articles dealing with the history of marketing thought. In the UK, the University of Reading hosted conferences in 1991 and again in 1993 on historical research in marketing that resulted in the 1993 publication *The Rise and Fall of Mass Marketing* (Richard Tedlow and Geoffrey Jones, 1993) which includes an interesting selection of papers about British marketing history. Strong interest in historical research in marketing in the UK is further evident by the formation in 1998 of the Centre for the History of Retailing and Distribution (CHORD) at the University of Wolverhampton, which hosts annual workshops and seminars. Beyond these specialized marketing conferences and periodicals, there is a growing interest in marketing-related history by business historians which is represented by the Business History Conference and in periodicals such as *Enterprise & Society*, the *Business History Review*, *Economic History Review* and others.

Reflecting on the increased volume, changing focus and rigour of historical research in marketing since the early 1980s, Hollander and Rassuli described it as the 'new marketing history' (1993: xv). In addition to research on marketing history and history of marketing thought, one of the important developments in historical research in marketing since 1980 is a growing discussion about the use of historical research methods in marketing.

Historical research methods and historical research in marketing

If one were looking for a single publication that signalled the emergence (or rather, the revival) of history as a 'legitimate' field within the marketing discipline, it might be Savitt's (1980)

'Historical research in marketing' published in the *Journal of Marketing*. In substance it was a statement of the rationale and method for historical research, although in the latter, only one of a range of possible approaches. In spirit Savitt's article was both a symbol of the legitimacy of doing historical research by marketing scholars, and a challenge to them to do so. As a statement on method, Savitt's article initiated a much needed discussion in the marketing literature about the theory and methods of historical scholarship.

'Historical research in marketing' thus represented an early attempt to articulate some of the methodological issues faced by marketing scholars interested in doing historical research, as well as a rallying cry for more historical research by marketing scholars, and, as such, it created a bridge to the mainstream marketing journals. More recently, Savitt (2009) used the format of a memoir to describe what he has learned about doing historical research over the last 30 years, how he learned, and how those lessons can be applied to historical research and teaching in marketing. Admitting that his earlier discussion of historical method was an over-simplified extension of logical positivism, Savitt's more recent work suggests a more interpretive approach to historical research in marketing. As Savitt (2009: 198) concludes, 'Good marketing history ... recognizes (1) historical events are in the past and cannot be known as contemporary events are known; (2) historical events are unique and unclassifiable; (3) history is about actions, statements, and the thoughts of human beings; and (4) historical events have irreducible richness and complexity.'

It is important to recognize that history is a discipline or subject, not a singular research method or methodology. There is a wide range of methodological approaches to studying history from positivistic (e.g. Hempel, 1959) to hermeneutic (e.g. Collingwood, 1974) or from scientific to traditional (Jones, 1993). Like marketing, history is viewed by some as a social science (Golder, 2000; Kumcu, 1987; Savitt, 1980; Smith and Lux, 1993) capable of producing scientific knowledge, and by others as an art or as one of the humanities (Fullerton, 1987; Jones, 1998; Nevett, 1991; Savitt, 2009; Stern, 1990; Witkowski and Jones, 2006). History as social science tends to rely on formal hypothesis testing, development and testing of theory, classification and quantification of data, statistical analysis and generalization. History as art relies more on unique, qualitative evidence, creative interpretation and descriptive narrative sometimes described as story-telling. Both of these methodological approaches are used in historical research in marketing, yet even such pluralism is considered inadequate by Brown et al.'s (2001) postmodern critique of historical research methods in marketing.

Fullerton (1987) and Jones (1993) distinguish between the philosophy of history, which is concerned with epistemological and ontological issues, and historical method, the techniques of data collection, analysis and reporting that follow from the philosophy of history in which one believes. While the philosophical assumptions of most marketing historians may be evident from their work, they are seldom made explicit. Published work rarely includes discussion of research method beyond a description of source materials, if that. And while some of the contributors to this historiographic discussion in marketing acknowledge different points of views (Golder, 2000; Smith and Lux, 1993; Witkowski and Jones, 2008), there is to date no complete discussion of the range of possible methodological approaches to historical research in marketing. However, a special issue of the *Journal of Historical Research in Marketing* published in 2011 (vol 3, no 4) includes a useful introduction to historical methods in marketing as well as articles discussing historiography, oral history, biographical method, the use of ephemera and collecting, and methodological issues in critical studies of marketing.

In the echoes of discussions about the philosophy and method of marketing history, there have also been voices calling for more historical research (Fullerton, 1987; Savitt, 1980, 1982), and providing rationales for using marketing history in teaching (Nevett, 1989; Witkowski, 1989). Nevett (1991) described how historical method relates to marketing decision making and offered recommendations for applying historical thinking to marketing practice. As well, there are various descriptions of source materials for historical research in marketing (Jones, 1998; Pollay, 1979, 1988a; Rassuli and Hollander, 1986a; Witkowski, 1994) and a discussion of various strategies for periodizing marketing history (Hollander et al., 2005).

Marketing history

Until the 1980s, historical research in marketing was dominated by interest in the history of marketing thought. That emphasis has since changed with most research now focusing on marketing history. Of the 487 papers presented at CHARM conferences from 1983 through 2009, 318 focused on marketing history (see Jones et al. [2009] for a content analysis of that body of work), the most popular topics being histories of industry/firm marketing strategies (94 papers), advertising history (74), macro-level consumption behaviour history (67) and the history of retailing and distribution channels (52). From 1981 through 2005, the 75 historical articles published in the *Journal of Macromarketing* included 47 that focused on marketing history (see Jones and Shaw [2006] for an historical review of that literature) with histories of marketing strategies leading in popularity followed by marketing regulation, retailing and channels, macro-level consumption behaviour and marketing systems.

The interest in histories of various aspects of marketing strategy, cited above, was also generally evident in periodicals and books that focused on advertising and promotion history (Beard, 2005; Branchik, 2007; Davis, 2007; De Iulio and Vinti, 2009; Fox, 1984; Gross and Sheth, 1989; Hawkins, 2009; Johnston, 2001; Jones et al., 2000; Kopp and Taylor, 1994; Laird, 1998; Lears, 1994; Marchand, 1985; Meyer, 1994; Mishra, 2009; Nevett, 1982; Pollay, 1984a, 1984b, 1985, 1988a, 1988b, 1994; Pollay and Lysonski, 1990; Pope, 1983; Robinson, 2004; Schudson, 1984; Sivulka, 1998; Stern, 1988; Witkowski, 2003), personal selling (Friedman, 2004), product simplification strategy (Hollander, 1984), product innovation (Keehn, 1994), channel management (Hull, 2008; Marx, 1985), segmentation strategy (Fullerton, 1985; Hollander and Germain, 1992; Tedlow, 1990), branding (Bakker, 2001; Church and Clark, 2001; Duguid, 2003; Golder, 2000; Koehn, 2001; Low and Fullerton, 1994), market research (Fullerton, 1990; Germain, 1994; Ward, 2009), retailing (Benson, 1986; Bevan, 2001; Dixon, 1994; Howard, 2008; Monod, 1996; Stanger, 2008; Witkowski, 2009), and marketing strategies in industries such as the public library system (Kleindle, 2007) and specific companies such as Nestlé (Kose, 2007) and Singer (Godley, 2006). It would seem that no matter what your interest in marketing, there is now historical research about it in print.

As evident in Table 3.1, advertising and retailing are two major topics of interest within marketing history. In advertising history, the work of two marketing scholars is noteworthy. One of these was Terence Nevett, who published extensively on the history of British advertising (1982, 1985, 1988a, 1988c, 1988d). Much of Nevett's work was comparative and cross-cultural, for example, his study with Fullerton of societal perceptions of advertising in Britain and Germany (Fullerton and Nevett, 1986), and of American influences on British advertising (Nevett, 1988a), as well as British influences on American advertising (1988c). At times his work has taken on a macromarketing perspective (Fullerton and Nevett, 1986; Nevett, 1985, 1988b) by looking at the impact of advertising on society. Others have also contributed to the study of British advertising history, focusing on specific companies (Ferrier, 1986; Seaton, 1986), professional sales promotion organizations (Leigh, 1986) and self-regulation in the advertising industry (Miracle and Nevett, 1988).

A second marketing scholar whose work on advertising history has been prominent is Richard Pollay. During the late 1970s Pollay observed that there were very few significant sources of advertising history (1979: 8) and those had been written outside the marketing discipline. To address that situation, he outlined an ambitious research programme for advertising history, including the justification, research method and data sources required for such work (Pollay, 1977, 1978, 1979). Having identified and developed important archival sources (Pollay, 1979, 1988a), Pollay conducted a rigorous content analysis of 20th-century American print advertising in order to identify the portrayed values (Belk and Pollay, 1985; Pollay, 1984a, 1988b), the extent of informativeness (1984b) and the creative aspects of advertising strategy (1985). Later on his work, like Nevett's, took on a macromarketing perspective (Pollay and Lysonski, 1990), specifically his work on the history of cigarette advertising and its impact on society. That interest in the history of cigarette advertising is shared by others such as Wilcox (1991), who examined the correlation between advertising and cigarette consumption for the period from 1949 to 1985, and Beard and Klyueva (2010), who provide a detailed account of one of the most controversial advertising campaigns of all time – the 'Reach for a Lucky Instead of a Sweet' cigarette campaign.

A wide range of methodological approaches to historical research is evident in advertising history. Pollay's use of quantification, content analysis and hypothesis testing is representative of the social scientific approach to historical research. In a similar fashion, Gross and Sheth (1989) performed content analysis of advertisements spanning 100 years in the *Ladies Home Journal* to investigate the use of time-oriented appeals. On the other hand, Stern (1988) has used literary criticism to examine the medieval tradition of allegory in relation to the development of contemporary advertising strategies. Nevett also used biographical data and a qualitative interpretation of advertisements to examine the development of British advertising (1988d).

There is an impressive collection of books about advertising history that have been published since the early 1980s, written by business historians (Fox, 1984; Johnston, 2001; Laird, 1998; Lears, 1994; Marchand, 1985; Norris, 1990; Pope, 1983; Robinson, 2004; Schudson, 1984; Sivulka, 1998). Laird's work is particularly valuable for marketing scholars because of its relatively broad scope in relating changes in advertising during the period from the late 19th century through early 20th century to changes in business culture and consumer marketing practice, and for its relevance to marketing strategy more generally.

Two of the more wide-ranging studies of marketing history focusing on marketing strategy more broadly were Tedlow's (1990) *New and Improved: The Story of Mass Marketing in America* and Strasser's (1989) *Satisfaction Guaranteed: The Making of the American Mass Market*. These are the two assigned readings in the undergraduate course I teach in marketing history at Quinnipiac University. Tedlow's book describes how some of America's most important corporations of the 20th century, including Coca-Cola and Pepsi, Ford and General Motors, A&P and Sears and Montgomery Ward, battled for dominance in key consumer product markets during the past hundred years. An emergent theme in Tedlow's work is the evolution of market structure in America from a fragmented market in the 19th century, to a mass market, and then to market segmentation. For example, with respect to the soft drink industry Tedlow concludes, 'there was no such thing as the Pepsi Generation until Pepsi created it' (1990: 372). It is that statement which is turned around in the title of Hollander and Germain's (1992) in-depth examination of the history of segmentation practices. Hollander and Germain disagreed with Tedlow's three-phase theory and provided detailed evidence of earlier segmentation practices as well as conceptualizations of segmentation by early marketing scholars.

Like Tedlow, Strasser (1989) covers a wide range of marketing strategies including branding, channel strategy, product development, market research, advertising and promotion, as well as retailing. Both Tedlow and Strasser make extensive use of archival materials, trade periodicals, ephemera and available company histories. Both clearly demonstrate that modern, sophisticated marketing practices were in place by the early 20th century. One of the key differences between these two important studies of marketing history is the class of firm studied: Tedlow clearly focused on large corporations, Strasser on small-scale independent retailers. Another key difference between these two histories is the time period covered, with Strasser's more focused on the late 19th and early 20th centuries, while Tedlow covers most of the 20th century.

Other sub-categories of marketing history, more macro in orientation, have attracted considerable attention. First, corporate and industry marketing history has emerged as a popular topic of study (Carlos and Lewis, 2002; Godley, 2006; Hawkins, 2009). Second, the study of the history of marketing systems – whole economies or systems of marketing – also emerged during the 1980s as a significant topic for historical research (Corley, 1987; Fisk, 1988; Fullerton, 1988b; Kaufman, 1987; Kitchell, 1992; Pirog, 1991; Speece, 1990). This is undoubtedly related to the important role played by historical research in the *Journal of Macromarketing*, cited earlier. Pirog's (1991) study of changes in the structure and output of the US distribution system builds on Barger's (1955) seminal work mentioned earlier in this review. Of course, a key issue in the study of marketing systems is the relationship between marketing and economic development (Dixon, 1981; McCarthy, 1988; Savitt, 1988), and that critical role for marketing history has been used as a justification for more historical research in marketing since the late 1950s (Myers and Smalley, 1959).

One other major field of interest that has emerged since the early 1980s is the history of consumption. Some of this work has been carried out by marketing scholars interested in consumer behaviour (Belk, 1992; Belk and Pollay, 1985; Friedman, 1985; Witkowski, 1989, 1998, 2004). However, there is a growing body of literature on the history of the 'consumer society' written by business historians (Blaszczyk, 2009; Cohen, 2003; Cross, 2000; Fox and Lears, 1983; McKendrick et al., 1982). The ideology behind much of this work, like that by other business historians writing about advertising history, is more liberal and more critical of marketing's impact on consumer welfare than typical of marketing scholars studying marketing history.

History of marketing thought

Earlier research on the history of marketing thought focused on identifying the first textbooks, university courses and pioneer teachers. During the 1960s some work began to trace the development of key marketing concepts and theory. During the 1980s and since, there have been much more sophisticated historical studies of influences on the development of marketing thought, of the evolution of schools of marketing thought and examinations of important theoretical developments over time. As well, there has been renewed interest in biographical research. While the relative volume of work on the history of marketing thought has declined (compared with marketing history) since the early 1980s, there has been important work published including the final edition of Bartels' seminal book (1988), a survey of schools of marketing thought (Sheth et al., 1988), edited collections of readings (Baker, 2001; Hollander and Rassuli, 1993; Tadajewski and Jones, 2008; Wooliscroft et al., 2006) and book-length studies of the history of marketing management (Usui, 2008) and advertising education (Ross and Richards, 2008). There have also been broader studies of the development of the marketing discipline that complement Bartels' earlier work (Jones and Shaw, 2002; Wilkie and Moore, 2003) as well as historical studies of schools of marketing thought (Shaw and Jones, 2005; Sheth et al., 1988).

Since the early 1980s, there has been less research on the history of the marketing literature. Grether's (1976) 40-year review of the *Journal of Marketing* (*JM*) was followed by a 60-year retrospective of *JM* by Kerin (1996) and there is a related, detailed study of the founding of *JM* by Witkowski (2007). There have been retrospectives of other major journals in the field of marketing (Berkman, 1992; Muncy, 1991) and, while somewhat dated now, McCracken's (1987) is a very good review of the consumption history literature. More recently, there has also been less research about the history of marketing teaching (Lazer and Shaw, 1988; Schultz, 1982) but some on the teaching of marketing history (Witkowski, 1989). There remains a need, however, to examine such developments that occurred outside the United States, such as in Jones's (1992) study of early marketing courses in Canada and Jonsson's (2009) history of early marketing education in Sweden.

There is renewed interest in biographical research (Bourassa et al., 2007; Green, 2001; Harris, 2007; Hollander, 2009; Jones, 1994, 1998, 2004, 2007; Kreshel, 1990; Nason, 2009; Shaw and Tamilia, 2001; Wittink, 2004; Wooliscroft et al., 2006; Wright, 1989), which had dropped from the historical agenda after the early 1960s. In that connection, the third edition of Bartels' (1988) *History of Marketing Thought* is notable for its addition of biographical information about important scholars of the 1960s, 1970s and 1980s. Some 35 short biographies of marketing pioneers are included in a recent three-volume collection of readings on the history of marketing thought (Tadajewski and Jones, 2008) including many from the original *Journal of Marketing* series published between 1956 and 1962 as well as more recent biographical sketches. Stephen Brown has added an interesting dimension to this biographical work by analysing the writing styles of several pioneer marketing scholars including Theodore Levitt (Brown, 2004), Stanley Hollander (Brown, 2009) and Wroe Alderson (Brown, 2002).

Biographical work is featured in a noteworthy collection of work examining the life and career of Wroe Alderson, considered by many to be the greatest marketing theorist of the

20th century, in *A Twenty-First Century Guide to Aldersonian Marketing Thought* (Wooliscroft et al., 2006). This encyclopaedic historical study of Alderson and his work is divided into six parts including a biographical sketch of Alderson, selected writings by Alderson about his theory of market behaviour and about marketing management practice, commentaries about Alderson's thinking by other well-known scholars, some fascinating biographical commentaries from other scholars about Alderson, and finally exhaustive bibliographies of Alderson's published work. As one reviewer described it, this collection of readings is 'a fitting tribute to the life, writings, and intellectual legacy of Wroe Alderson ... and a reference work of the first magnitude' (Shaw, 2007: 197). Shortly following the publication of this collection of readings, the *European Business Review* (2007, Vol. 19, No. 6) published a special issue about Alderson, adding to the body of work about this pioneer marketing scholar. And finally, Tadajewski (2009d) documented Alderson's trip to Russia as part of a Quaker-organized visit to comment on US foreign policy. The latter work adds an interesting detail to our knowledge about Alderson.

Alderson was best known as a marketing theorist and the history of ideas and theory in marketing now attracts considerable attention. This work includes historical studies of Reilly's retail gravitation theory (Brown, 1994), spatial theory in retailing (Babin et al., 1994), motivation research (McLeod, 2009; Tadajewski, 2006), service marketing (Vargo and Lusch, 2004; Vargo and Morgan, 2005), channels theory (Wilkinson, 2001), the four utilities concept (Shaw, 1994) and marketing productivity. Both Shaw (1987, 1990) and Dixon (1990, 1991) have done extensive work on the historical development of the concept and measurement of marketing productivity. Shaw's historical review of empirical studies concludes that marketing productivity in the USA during the past century has increased, but he points to the continuing lack of clear concepts and measures of marketing costs and effectiveness (1990: 290).

One theory, in particular, has generated much controversy and considerable interest for marketing historians. It is, in fact, an historical stage theory of marketing's development – the so-called four eras of marketing, first proposed by Keith in 1960. The essential historical question here is when the 'marketing concept' and its closely related notion of relationship marketing emerged, and not just the practice but the articulation of this concept as well. Hollander (1986), Fullerton (1988a), Gilbert and Bailey (1990), Jones and Richardson (2007) and Tadajewski (2009b, 2010) have all published detailed, critical historical accounts of the development of the marketing concept and Church (1999) provides an overview of related historical work. A parallel line of research by Tadajewski examines the history of relationship marketing (Tadajewski, 2008, 2009a, 2009c; Tadajewski and Saren, 2008) building on similar work by Keep et al. (1998). As a body of work, these studies all concluded that serious and sophisticated marketing activities driven by a customer orientation have been practised much longer than conventional wisdom suggests, and that marketers have used a customer or marketing orientation at least since the 19th century. With some measure of poetic justice, Tadajewski (2010) uses FBI files to test Keith's own (1960) claims regarding the marketing practices adopted at Pillsbury during the so-called 'marketing' and 'marketing control' eras. Tadajewski documents the participation of Pillsbury in anti-competitive practices beginning in 1958 and continuing through the mid-1960s, resulting in Pillsbury being charged and fined for their involvement in a price-fixing cartel, behaviour that is hardly consistent with a consumer-friendly, relationship-building 'marketing orientation'.

Taken together, these studies point to the value, and in some cases the necessity, of historical research in evaluating existing theory, *especially, of course, historical theory*. More importantly perhaps, they have contributed to a more critical perspective and to a rewriting of the history of marketing thought presented by Bartels and other mid-20th-century marketing historians. This includes an extensive re-evaluation of the schools of thought from which marketing emerged as a discipline (Jones and Monieson, 1990), an extension of our historical perspective beyond the 20th century (Dixon, 1978, 1979, 1981, 1982) and studies of the development of marketing thought outside of North America (Ingebrigtsen, 1981; Jones, 1992; Jones and Monieson, 1990; Jonsson, 2009; Usui, 2000). Ironically, a Japanese scholar has recently taken a much more detailed look at the emergence of marketing management in America between 1910 and 1940 (Usui, 2008). That work is distinctive for its focus on the connections between scientific management and the early development of marketing management ideas.

Schools of marketing thought have attracted increasing attention from marketing historians. Discussions of the so-called traditional schools – institutional (Hollander, 1989), functional (Hunt and Goolsby, 1988) and commodity (Zinn and Johnson, 1990) – have been complemented by studies of more contemporary schools of thought including consumer behaviour (Kassarjian, 1994; Mittelstaedt, 1990; Sheth and Gross, 1988), macromarketing (Layton and Grossbart, 2006; Savitt, 1990) and others (Shaw and Jones, 2005; Sheth et al., 1988). In *Marketing Theory: Evolution and Evaluation* (1988), Sheth et al. identified, classified and evaluated 12 schools of marketing thought including commodity, functional, regional, institutional, functionalist, managerial, buyer behaviour, activist, macromarketing, organizational dynamics, systems and social exchange schools. The classification and meta-theoretical 'evaluation' by Sheth et al. could easily be debated, but are not essential to the historical theme which provides the bulk of the presentation. Using the Sheth et al. work as a point of departure, Shaw and Jones (2005) identified and chronicled 10 schools of marketing thought beginning with the traditional functional, commodities, and institutional schools; adding the interregional school; and followed by more modern schools of marketing management, marketing systems, consumer behaviour, macromarketing, exchange and even marketing history. The theme that emerges from the latter work is a lament over the growing loss of identity, vagueness of subject matter and lack of disciplinary boundaries in marketing. Much of that theme overlaps with Wilkie and Moore's (2003) study, which divided the development of the marketing discipline into four eras: (1) founding the field of marketing (1900–20), (2) formalizing the field (1920–50), (3) a paradigm shift to more managerial and scientific perspectives (1950–80) and (4) fragmentation of the mainstream into specialized interest areas (1980–present).

If the Sheth et al. (1988) book replaced Bartels' (1962, 1976, 1988) classic as the staple reading material for doctoral courses during the late 1980s and into the early 1990s, it too was eventually replaced by a two-volume set of readings by Hollander and Rassuli (1993). Hollander was an outspoken critic of Bartels' work on the history of marketing thought and for the doctoral course Hollander taught at Michigan State University (Jones and Keep, 2009) he developed a comprehensive set of readings on both marketing history and the history of marketing thought (Hollander and Rassuli, 1993), a collection that in several ways suggested a new approach to teaching the history of marketing thought to graduate students of marketing. Hollander believed that one could not understand the history of marketing thought without a parallel understanding of marketing history, and included both fields in this two-volume collection. The readings also included discussions of a wide range of macromarketing issues, marketing research and consumer behaviour in addition to the more obvious material about the history of various aspects of marketing strategy. The collection also included several selections about historical methods in marketing.

Fourteen important readings about the history of marketing thought are included in Baker's (2001) multi-volume collection on critical perspectives in marketing. The historical work there includes some older, seminal works that are difficult to access. Another distinctive feature of this collection is the inclusion of European authors, for example Gilbert and Bailey (1990) and Vink (1992), whose work is often overlooked.

A more recent, three-volume collection of readings, edited by Tadajewski and Jones (2008), is respectfully titled *The History of Marketing Thought*. (That was the same title used by Bartels for his seminal work in this area.) Like the Hollander and Rassuli collection of readings, this more recent offering takes a much broader approach than that by Bartels and earlier historians. At the same time, the Tadajewski and Jones collection is more focused than the Hollander and Rassuli collection or the Baker collection, including only articles on the history of marketing thought, and more depth in that area blending vintage historical scholarship with much of the more recent contemporary work. The Tadajewski and Jones collection begins by examining historical research about pre-20th-century marketing thought, segues into several key readings about the early development of the marketing discipline, and includes considerable coverage of the schools of marketing thought. The collection features 35 biographical sketches of marketing pioneers, including recent work on Robert Bartels, Stanley Hollander and Sidney Levy. This extensive collection of biographical sketches provides details about the intellectual backgrounds and political context of key marketing thinkers and in that way is intended to connect theoretical debates in marketing with wider socio-political changes. A final section of the readings in this collection continues that ideal by focusing on more macro, contextualizing influences on marketing thought.

The emerging discipline: Today and tomorrow

History adds perspective, richness and context to the study of marketing. More practically speaking, history provides a framework for building and integrating knowledge. We must know where we have been in order to understand where we are, to know what questions have already been answered and which ones still need further study. The history of marketing and marketing ideas has not always been a popular or rewarding field of study. That has clearly changed. Yet, ironically, there was also a time when the study of the history of marketing thought was required in many, if not most, doctoral programmes in marketing. Sadly, that no longer seems to be the case. So while more scholars are doing more and better historical research in marketing, fewer marketing students are being educated about marketing history and the history of marketing thought.

Historical research in marketing has developed over time, naturally enough, from recording the facts about the founding of the discipline to studies of marketing practices and the ideas about those practices, to schools of thought and eras of study. Over time marketing historians have extended the scope of history beyond the turn of the 20th century, beyond the core elements of marketing strategy, and have broadened their toolkit of historical methods of research. We have used history to situate the current status of the marketing discipline and have critically evaluated conventional wisdom about how and when key marketing practices and concepts emerged. There has long been a place for marketing history as a component in the work done by business historians, but more business historians are specializing in marketing history, especially in advertising history, retailing history and the history of consumption. That is also broadening the study of marketing history in some valuable ways.

Over the past 30 years there has been a dramatic growth of interest and activity in marketing history and the history of marketing thought. Specialized academic associations have been formed that sponsor conferences on historical research in marketing. Historical research is now explicitly included in statements of scope and content for several marketing periodicals and we can celebrate the launch of a new academic quarterly dedicated to publishing historical research in marketing. There is a bounded body of knowledge about marketing history and the history of marketing thought and a critical mass of academics that self-identify as marketing historians. In some ways, marketing history (more broadly defined) might qualify as a discipline according to the criteria used by Richardson in his recent study of the development of accounting history (Richardson, 2008; Witkowski and Jones, 2008).

What are some of the priorities for future historical research in marketing? There needs to be greater synthesis and contextualization of marketing history and the history of marketing thought. Too many studies have focused on marketing practices or marketing ideas in isolation without considering the social, economic and political conditions of the time period being studied. Further in that connection, we need to acknowledge that practice is not entirely thoughtless and that thought, especially in a discipline that has relied so much on inductive reasoning, is driven by practice. In other words, marketing history and the history of marketing thought must be integrated. This was the foundation of Stanley Hollander's thinking about historical research in marketing (1989). However, as a 'discipline', marketing history still has not made much progress in that direction.

Most of the historical research about marketing and marketing thought is done by marketing scholars trained in social science research methods and can be, therefore, naive about even the most basic historiographic issues such as the differences between primary and secondary source material. There is a need for more discussion of the broad range of historical research methods, illustrated with examples from historical research in marketing. Finally, marketing historians need to make their work more relevant to marketing education. Marketing history and the history of marketing thought must be integrated into graduate, certainly, and even undergraduate curricula. As Richardson (2008: 268) notes in his history of accounting history, 'the ultimate test of an academic discipline is its ability to offer courses in its own area'. I hope the student text you are reading now will help in that connection.

Post-script

The chapter above was written for the second edition of this book, which was published in 2010. As indicated in the introduction and in Table 3.1 herein, there has been recent and dramatic growth in interest and publication of work on historical research in marketing and that growth has continued since this chapter was first published. Quite recently, an exhaustive review of historical research on marketing was published (Tadajewski and Jones, 2014) ranging across the humanities and social sciences – as well as in the narrower marketing periodical literature covered in this chapter. That review, 'Historical research in marketing theory and practice: a review essay' published in the *Journal of Marketing Management* (*JMM*) for its 30th Anniversary issue, provides a complementary resource for this chapter and, hence, is strongly recommended as further reading to accompany this chapter.

The *JMM* article reviews the past 30 years of published interdisciplinary research on marketing history and the history of marketing thought. It focuses on topics central to marketing management including the history of marketing management more broadly, as well as histories of product management, market research, market segmentation, retailing and channels, advertising and promotion, and the history of marketing thought. It also incorporates discussion of related issues which fall under the scope of marketing's effects on wider society by engaging with the relationship between marketing and the management of subjectivity. Further, it explores the growing calls for historical research to form an influential component of interpretive, consumer culture theoretical and critical marketing research. Thus, in many ways it includes sources and topics not covered in this chapter.

Noteworthy in the *JMM* article is the discussion of the history of market research, which until very recently had received very little attention and has been the subject of some outstanding work, especially in the area of motivation research. More biographical research has also been published on subjects active in market research. Another characteristic of this recent work on the history of market research as well as other fields within marketing history has been the focus on contributions outside of America. Thus, studies have been published about market research practices in Canada, Australia, practices in the British motion picture industry, French real estate, as well as market research in various other European countries. Recently, there has been lively debate about the origins of market segmentation. Thus, the history of segmentation practices has been documented for a wide range of products and industries as far back as the 18th century. In what is likely to be a seminal publication on this topic, Fullerton describes the sophisticated and aggressive market segmentation and targeting practices used in the German book trade during the 19th century (Fullerton, 2016). Branding history has quite recently and rapidly become the most popular topic within the broader area of product management history. The golden era of branding is generally believed to be from the late 19th to early 20th centuries. Most of the recent published work consists of historical case studies of branding practices in specific industries or companies, some in specific countries. Retailing and advertising have long been the most popular topics within the broader field of marketing history and some excellent recent reviews of that work are discussed in the *JMM* article – a sort of meta-analysis if you will.

More recent research on the history of marketing thought has gone beyond the earlier work that rewrote the histories of key concepts such as the marketing concept and relationship marketing, although the latter has remained popular with historians. Issues of power relations have been studied with attempts to revise the history of marketing thought that reveals both indications of practitioner enlightenment – ethical orientations for instance – as well as problematic assumptions and practices brought into play at the same time. There has also been great interest in charting the impact of key institutions on the development of marketing theory, thought, pedagogy and practice. That has included an outpouring of biographical reflection as well as the study of non-university forms of education in marketing such as correspondence schools.

We believe that being historically minded is central to good academic practice. Indeed, history and the development of marketing theory go hand in hand. As Witkowski (1989: 55) reminds us,

> The study of history will contribute much to the developing managerial skills and judgment of marketing students. Learning from the lessons of the past will help students avoid the naïve perceptions and statements and, instead, learn from the lessons of the past. Historical knowledge provides a much needed reference point.

Again, we hope that this chapter, augmented by the *JMM* anniversary review article, will provide a starting point for that historical knowledge.

Recommended further reading

Journal of Historical Research in Marketing.
Bartels, R. (1988) *The History of Marketing Thought*, 3rd edn. Columbus, OH: Publishing Horizons.
Hollander, S.C. and Rassuli, K. (eds) (1993) *Marketing*, 2 vols. Brookfield, VT: Edward Elgar.
Jones, D.G.B. and Shaw, E. (2006) 'Historical research in the Journal of Macromarketing: 1981–2005', *Journal of Macromarketing* December: 178–92.
Jones, D.G.B. and Tadajewski, M. (eds) (2016) *The Routledge Companion to Marketing History*. London: Routledge.
Tadajewski, M. and Jones, D.G.B. (2014) 'Historical research in marketing theory and practice: a review essay', *Journal of Marketing Management* 30(11–12): 1239–91.
Tadajewski, M. and Jones, D.G.B. (eds) (2008) *The History of Marketing Thought*, 3 vols. London: Sage.

References

Agnew, H.E. (1941) 'The history of the American Marketing Association', *Journal of Marketing* 5(4): 374–79.
Applebaum, W. (1947) 'The *Journal of Marketing*: the first ten years', *Journal of Marketing* 11(4): 355–63.

Applebaum, W. (1952) 'The *Journal of Marketing*: post war', *Journal of Marketing* 16(3): 294–300.

Babin, B., Boles, J. and Babin, L. (1994) 'The development of spatial theory in retailing and its contribution to marketing thought and marketing science', in J. Sheth and R.A. Fullerton (eds) *Research in Marketing: Explorations in the History of Marketing*. Greenwich, CT: JAI Press, pp. 103–16.

Baker, M.J. (ed.) (2001) *Marketing: Critical Perspectives in Business and Management*, Vol. II, Part 1. London: Routledge.

Bakker, G. (2001) 'Stars and stories: how films became branded products', *Enterprise & Society, The International Journal of Business History* 2(3): 461–502.

Barger, H. (1955) *Distribution's Place in the American Economy Since 1869*. Princeton, NJ: Princeton University Press.

Bartels, R. (1941) 'Marketing literature: development and appraisal', unpublished doctoral dissertation, Ohio State University, Columbus, OH.

Bartels, R. (1951) 'Influences on the development of marketing thought, 1900–1923', *Journal of Marketing* 16 (July): 1–17.

Bartels, R. (1962) *The Development of Marketing Thought*. Homewood, IL: Irwin.

Bartels, R. (1976) *The History of Marketing Thought*, 2nd edn. Columbus, OH: Grid.

Bartels, R. (1988) *The History of Marketing Thought*, 3rd edn. Columbus, OH: Publishing Horizons.

Beard, F. (2005) 'One hundred years of humor in American advertising', *Journal of Macromarketing* 25(1): 54–65.

Beard, F. and Klyueva, A. (2010) 'George Washington Hill and the "Reach for a Lucky…" campaign', *Journal of Historical Research in Marketing* 2(2): 148–65.

Belk, R.W. (1992) 'Moving possessions: an analysis based on personal documents from the 1847–1869 Mormon migration', *Journal of Consumer Research* 19 (December): 339–61.

Belk, R.W. and Pollay, R.W. (1985) 'Images of ourselves: the good life in twentieth century advertising', *Journal of Consumer Research* 11 (March): 887–97.

Benson, S.P. (1986) *Counter Cultures: Saleswomen, Managers, and Customers in American Department Stores, 1890–1940*. Urbana, IL: University of Illinois Press.

Berkman, H.W. (1992) 'Twenty years of the journal', *Journal of the Academy of Marketing Science* 20(4): 299–300.

Bevan, J. (2001) *The Rise and Fall of Marks and Spencer*. London: Profile Books.

Blaszczyk, R. (2009) *American Consumer Society 1865–2005: From Hearth to HDTV*. Wheeling, IL: Harlan Davidson.

Bourassa, M., Cunningham, P. and Handelman, J. (2007) 'How Philip Kotler has helped to shape the field of marketing', *European Business Review* 19(2): 174–92.

Branchik, B. (2007) 'Pansies to parents: gay male images in American print advertising', *Journal of Macromarketing* 27 (March): 38–50.

Breen, J. (1959) 'History of the marketing management concept', in L. Stockman (ed.) *Advancing Marketing Efficiency*. Chicago, IL: AMA, pp. 458–61.

Brown, G.H. (1951) 'What economists should know about marketing', *Journal of Marketing* 16(1): 60–6.

Brown, S. (1994) 'Reilly's Law of Retail Gravitation: what goes around, comes around', in J. Sheth and R.A. Fullerton (eds) *Research in Marketing: Explorations in the History of Marketing*. Greenwich, CT: JAI Press, pp. 117–50.

Brown, S. (2002) 'Reading Wroe: on the biopoetics of Alderson's functionalism', *Marketing Theory* 2(3): 243–71.

Brown, S. (2004) 'Theodore Levitt: the ultimate writing machine', *Marketing Theory* 4(3): 209–38.

Brown, S. (2009) 'A litotes of what you fancy: some thoughts on Stanley Hollander's writing style', *Journal of Historical Research in Marketing* 1 (March): 74–92.

Brown, S., Hirschman, E. and Maclaran, P. (2001) 'Always historicize! Researching marketing history in a post-historical epoch', *Marketing Theory* 1(1): 49–89.

Bussiere, D. (2000) 'Evidence of a marketing periodic literature within the American Economic Association: 1895–1936', *Journal of Macromarketing* 20(2): 137–43.

Carlos, A.M. and Lewis, F.D (2002) 'Marketing in the land of Hudson Bay: Indian consumers and the Hudson's Bay Company, 1670–1770', *Enterprise & Society, The International Journal of Business History* 3 (June): 285–317.

Cassels, J.M. (1936) 'The significance of early economic thought on marketing', *Journal of Marketing* 1 (October): 129–33.

Church, R. (1999) 'New perspectives on the history of products, firms, marketing, and consumers in Britain and the United States since the mid-nineteenth century', *Economic History Review* 52(3): 405–35.

Church, R. and Clark, C. (2001) 'Product development of branded, packaged household goods in Britain, 1870-1914: Colman's, Reckitt's, and Lever Brothers', *Enterprise & Society, The International Journal of Business History* 2 (September): 503–42.

Cohen, L. (2003) *A Consumers' Republic: The Politics of Mass Consumption in Postwar America*. New York: Vintage Books.

Collingwood, R.G. (1974) 'Human nature and human history', in P. Gardiner (ed.) *The Philosophy of History*. London: Oxford University Press, pp. 17–40.

Converse, P.D. (1933) 'The first decade of marketing literature', *NATMA Bulletin Supplement* November: 1–4.

Converse, P.D. (1945) 'The development of the science of marketing – an exploratory survey', *Journal of Marketing* 10 (July): 14–23.

Converse, P.D. (1959a) *Fifty Years of Marketing in Retrospect*. Austin, TX: Bureau of Business Research, University of Texas.

Converse, P.D. (1959b) *The Beginnings of Marketing Thought in the United States*. Austin, TX: Bureau of Business Research, University of Texas.

Coolsen, F. (1947) 'Pioneers in the development of advertising', *Journal of Marketing* 12 (July): 80–6.

Coolsen, F. (1960) *Marketing Thought in the United States in the Late Nineteenth Century*. Lubbock, TX: Texas Technical Press.

Corley, T.A.B. (1987) 'Consumer marketing in Britain, 1914–1960', *Business History* 29 (October): 65–83.

Cross, G. (2000) *An All-Consuming Century: Why Commercialism Won in Modern America*. New York: Columbia University Press.

Davis, J.F. (2007) ' "Aunt Jemima is alive and cookin"? An advertiser's dilemma of competing collective memories', *Journal of Macromarketing* 27 (March): 25–37.

De Iulio, S. and Vinti, C. (2009) 'The Americanization of Italian advertising during the 1950s and 1960s: mediations, conflicts, and appropriations', *Journal of Historical Research in Marketing* 1 (July): 230–40.

Dixon, D.F. (1978) 'The origins of macro-marketing thought', in G. Fisk and R.W. Nason (eds) *Macromarketing: New Steps on the Learning Curve*. Boulder, CO: University of Colorado, Business Research Division, pp. 9–28.

Dixon, D.F. (1979) 'Medieval macromarketing thought', in G. Fisk and P. White (eds) *Macromarketing: Evolution of Thought*. Boulder, CO: University of Colorado, Business Research Division, pp. 59–69.

Dixon, D.F. (1981) 'The role of marketing in early theories of economic development', *Journal of Macromarketing* 1 (Fall): 19–27.

Dixon, D.F. (1982) 'The ethical component of marketing: an eighteenth century view', *Journal of Macromarketing* 2 (Spring): 38–46.

Dixon, D.F. (1990) 'Marketing as production: the development of a concept', *Journal of the Academy of Marketing Science* 18 (Fall): 337–44.

Dixon, D.F. (1991) 'Marketing structure and the theory of economic interdependence: early analytical developments', *Journal of Macromarketing* 11 (Fall): 5–18.

Dixon, D.F. (1994) 'A day's shopping in thirteenth-century Paris', in J. Sheth and R.A. Fullerton (eds) *Research in Marketing: Explorations in the History of Marketing*. Greenwich, CT: JAI Press, pp. 13–24.

Duguid, P. (2003) 'Developing the brand: the case of alcohol, 1800–1880', *Enterprise & Society, The International Journal of Business History* 4 (September): 405–41.

Emmet, B. and Jeuck, J.E. (1950) *Catalogues and Counters: A History of Sears, Roebuck and Company.* Chicago, IL: University of Chicago Press.

Ferrier, R.W. (1986) 'Petroleum advertising in the twenties and thirties: the case of the British Petroleum Company', *European Journal of Marketing* 20(5): 29–51.

Fisk, G. (1988) 'Interactive systems frameworks for analyzing spacetime changes in marketing organization and processes', in T. Nevett and R. Fullerton (eds) *Historical Perspectives in Marketing: Essays in Honor of Stanley C. Hollander*. Lexington, MA: Lexington Books, pp. 55–70.

Fox, R. and Lears, T.J.J. (1983) *The Culture of Consumption: Critical Essays in American History, 1880–1980*. New York: Pantheon Books.

Fox, S. (1984) *The Mirror Makers: A History of American Advertising and its Creators*. New York: William Morrow.

Friedman, H.H. (1985) 'Ancient marketing practices: the view from Talmudic times', *Journal of Public Policy and Marketing* 3 (Spring): 194–204.

Friedman, W.A. (2004) *Birth of a Salesman: The Transformation of Selling in America*. Cambridge, MA: Harvard University Press.

Fullerton, R.A. (1985) 'Segmentation strategies and practices in the 19th century German book trade: a case study in the development of a major marketing technique', in C.T. Tan and Jagdish N. Sheth (eds) *Historical Perspective in Consumer Research: National and International Perspectives*. Provo, UT: Association for Consumer Research, pp. 135–9.

Fullerton, R.A. (1987) 'The poverty of ahistorical analysis: present weakness and future cure in U.S. marketing thought', in F. Firat, N. Dholakia and R.P. Bagozzi (eds) *Philosophical and Radical Thought in Marketing*. Lexington, MA: Lexington Books, pp. 97–116.

Fullerton, R.A. (1988a) 'How modern is modern marketing? Marketing's evolution and the myth of the production era', *Journal of Marketing* 52 (January): 108–25.

Fullerton, R.A. (1988b) 'Modern western marketing as a historical phenomenon: theory and illustration', in T. Nevett and R. Fullerton (eds) *Historical Perspectives in Marketing: Essays in Honor of Stanley C. Hollander*. Lexington, MA: Lexington Books, pp. 71–89.

Fullerton, R.A. (1990) 'The art of marketing research: selections from Paul F. Lazarsfeld's "Shoe Buying in Zurich" (1933)', *Journal of the Academy of Marketing Science* 18(4): 319–27.

Fullerton, R.A. (2016) *Foundations of Marketing Practice: A History of Book Marketing in Germany*. New York: Routledge.

Fullerton, R.A. and Nevett, T.R. (1986) 'Advertising and society: a comparative analysis of the roots of distrust in Germany and Great Britain', *International Journal of Marketing* 5(3): 225–41.

Germain, R. (1994) 'The adoption of statistical methods in market research: the early twentieth century', in J. Sheth and R.A. Fullerton (eds) *Research in Marketing: Explorations in the History of Marketing*. Greenwich, CT: JAI Press, pp. 87–102.

Gilbert, D. and Bailey, N. (1990) 'The development of marketing – a compendium of approaches', *Quarterly Review of Marketing* 15(2): 6–13.

Godley, A. (2006) 'Selling the sewing machine around the world: Singer's international marketing strategies, 1850–1920', *Enterprise & Society, The International Journal of Business History* 7 (June): 266–314.

Golder, P. (2000) 'Historical method in marketing research with new evidence on long-term market share stability', *Journal of Marketing Research* 37 (May): 156–72.

Gordon, R.A. and Howell, J.E. (1959) *Higher Education for Business*. New York: Columbia University Press.

Green, P.E. (2001) 'The vagaries of becoming (and remaining) a marketing research methodologist', *Journal of Marketing* 65(3): 104–8.

Grether, E.T. (1976) 'The first forty years', *Journal of Marketing* 40 (July): 63–9.

Greyser, S. (ed.) (1963) *Toward Scientific Marketing*. American Marketing Association Proceedings Series. Chicago, IL: AMA.

Gross, B.L. and Sheth, J.N. (1989) 'Time oriented advertising: a content analysis of United States magazine advertising, 1890–1988', *Journal of Marketing* 53(4): 76–83.

Hagerty, J.E. (1936) 'Experiences of an early marketing teacher', *Journal of Marketing* 1(1): 20–7.

Hardy, H. (1954) 'Collegiate marketing education since 1930', *Journal of Marketing* 19(2): 325–30.

Harris, G. (2007) 'Sidney Levy: challenging the philosophical assumptions of marketing', *Journal of Macromarketing* 27(1): 7–14.

Hawkins, R.A. (2009) 'Advertising and the Hawaiian pineapple canning industry, 1929–39', *Journal of Macromarketing* 29 (June): 172–92.

Hempel, C.G. (1959) 'The function of general laws in history', in P. Gardiner (ed.) *Theories of History*. Glencoe, IL: The Free Press, pp. 344–55.

Hollander, S.C. (1960) 'The Wheel of Retailing', *Journal of Marketing* 25 (July): 37–42.

Hollander, S.C. (1963a) 'A note on fashion leadership', *Business History Review* (Winter): 448–51.

Hollander, S.C. (1963b) 'Anti-salesman ordinances of the mid-nineteenth century', in S. Greyser (ed.) *Toward Scientific Marketing*. Chicago, IL: AMA, pp. 344–51.

Hollander, S.C. (1964) 'Nineteenth century anti-drummer legislation in the United States', *Business History Review* 38 (Winter): 479–500.

Hollander, S.C. (1966) 'Notes on the retail accordion', *Journal of Retailing* 42 (Summer): 29–40.

Hollander, S.C. (1984) 'Herbert Hoover, Professor Levitt, simplification and the marketing concept', in P. Anderson and M. Ryan (eds) *Scientific Method in Marketing*. Chicago, IL: AMA, pp. 260–3.

Hollander, S.C. (1986) 'The marketing concept: a deja-vu', in G. Fisk (ed.) *Marketing Management Technology as a Social Process*. New York: Praeger, pp. 3–28.

Hollander, S.C. (1989) 'Introduction', in T. Nevett, K. Whitney and S. Hollander (eds) *Marketing History: The Emerging Discipline*. Lansing, MI: Michigan State University Press, pp. xix–xx.

Hollander, S.C. (2009) 'My life on Mt Olympus', *Journal of Historical Research in Marketing* 1 (March): 10–33.

Hollander, S.C. and Germain, R. (1992) *Was There a Pepsi Generation Before Pepsi Discovered It?* Lincolnwood, IL: NCT Business Books.

Hollander, S.C. and Rassuli, K. (1993) *Marketing*, 2 vols. Brookfield, VT: Edward Elgar.

Hollander, S.C., Jones, D.G.B., Rassuli, K. and Dix, L. (2005) 'Periodization in marketing history', *Journal of Macromarketing* 25(1): 32–41.

Hotchkiss, G.B. (1938) *Milestones of Marketing*. New York: Macmillan.

Howard, V. (2008) ' "The biggest small-town store in America": Independent retailers and the rise of consumer culture', *Enterprise & Society, The International Journal of Business History* 9 (September): 457–86.

Hower, R.M. (1946) *History of Macy's of New York, 1858–1919*. Cambridge, MA: Harvard University Press.

Hull, B. (2008) 'Frankincense, myrrh, and spices: the oldest global supply chain?', *Journal of Macromarketing* 28 (September): 275–88.

Hunt, S.D. and Goolsby, J. (1988) 'The rise and fall of the functional approach to marketing: a paradigm displacement perspective', in T. Nevett and R. Fullerton (eds) *Historical Perspectives in Marketing: Essays in Honor of Stanley C. Hollander*. Lexington, MA: Lexington Books, pp. 35–52.

Ingebrigtsen, S. (ed.) (1981) *Reflections on Danish Theory of Marketing*. Copenhagen: Ehrvervsokomisk Forlag.

Johnston, R. (2001) *Selling Themselves: The Emergence of Canadian Advertising*. Toronto: University of Toronto Press.

Jones, D.G.B. (1992) 'Early development of marketing thought in Canada', *Canadian Journal of Administrative Science* 9(2): 126–33.

Jones, D.G.B. (1993) 'Historiographic paradigms in marketing', in S. Hollander and K. Rassuli (eds) *Marketing*, Vol. 1. Brookfield, VT: Edward Elgar.

Jones, D.G.B. (1994) 'Biography and the history of marketing thought: Henry Charles Taylor and Edward David Jones', in R. Fullerton (ed.) *Research in Marketing: Explorations in the History of Marketing*. Greenwich, CT: JAI Press, pp. 67–85.

Jones, D.G.B. (1998) 'Biography as a methodology for studying the history of marketing ideas', *Psychology & Marketing* 15 (March): 161–74.

Jones, D.G.B. (2004) 'Simon Litman (1873–1965): pioneer marketing scholar', *Marketing Theory* 4 (December): 343–61.

Jones, D.G.B. (2007) 'Theodore N. Beckman (1895–1973): external manifestations of the man', *European Business Review* 19(2): 129–41.

Jones, D.G.B. and Keep, W. (2009) 'Hollander's doctoral seminar in the history of marketing thought', *Journal of Historical Research in Marketing* 1 (March): 151–64.

Jones, D.G.B. and Monieson, D.D. (1990) 'Early development of the philosophy of marketing thought', *Journal of Marketing* 54(1): 102–13.

Jones, D.G.B. and Richardson, A. (2007) 'The myth of the marketing revolution', *Journal of Macromarketing* 27 (March): 15–24.

Jones, D.G.B. and Shaw, E. (2002) 'A history of marketing thought', in R. Wensley and B. Weitz (eds) *Handbook of Marketing*. London: Sage, pp. 39–65.

Jones, D.G.B. and Shaw, E. (2006) 'Historical research in the *Journal of Macromarketing*: 1981–2005', *Journal of Macromarketing* 26(2): 178–92.

Jones, D.G.B., Richardson, A. and Shearer, T. (2000) 'Truth and the evolution of the professions: a comparative study of "truth in advertising" and "true and fair" financial statements in North America during the progressive era', *Journal of Macromarketing* 20(1): 23–35.

Jones, D.G.B., Shaw, E. and Goldring, D. (2009) 'Stanley C. Hollander and the conferences on historical analysis and research in marketing', *Journal of Historical Research in Marketing* 1 (March): 55–73.

Jones, F. (1936) 'Retail stores in the United States, 1800–1860', *Journal of Marketing* 1 (October): 135–40.

Jonsson, P. (2009) 'Marketing innovations and the Swedish consumer cooperative movement, 1904–1930', in R. Hawkins (ed.) *Marketing History: Strengthening, Straightening, and Extending: Proceedings of the 14th Biennial Conference on Historical Analysis & Research in Marketing (CHARM)*. Leicester: University of Leicester, pp. 130–43.

Kassarjian, H.H. (1994) 'Scholarly traditions and European Roots of American consumer research', in G. Laurent, G. Lillien and B. Pras (eds) *Research Traditions in Marketing*. Boston, MA: Kluwer Academic Publishers, pp. 265–79.

Kaufman, C.J. (1987) 'The evaluation of marketing in a society: The Han Dynasty of Ancient China', *Journal of Macromarketing* 7(2): 52–64.

Keehn, R.H. (1994) 'Jockey international: a brief history of marketing innovation', in J. Sheth and R.A. Fullerton (eds) *Research in Marketing: Explorations in the History of Marketing*, Greenwich, CT: JAI Press, pp. 183–204.

Keep, W., Hollander, S.C. and Dickinson, R. (1998) 'Forces impinging on long-term business-to-business relationships in the United States: an historical perspective', *Journal of Marketing* 62 (April): 31–45.

Keith, R.J. (1960) 'The marketing revolution', *Journal of Marketing* 4 (January): 35–8.

Kelley, W.T. (1956) 'The development of early thought in marketing and promotion', *Journal of Marketing* 21 (July): 62–76.

Kerin, R. (1996) 'In pursuit of an ideal: the editorial and literary history of the *Journal of Marketing*', *Journal of Marketing* 60 (January): 1–13.

Kirkwood, R.C. (1960) *The Woolworth Story at Home and Abroad*. New York: Newcomen Society.

Kitchell, S. (1992) 'Foundation of the Japanese distribution system: historical determinants in the Tokugawa period (1603–1868)', in C. Duhaime (ed.) *Marketing Proceedings*, Administrative Sciences Association of Canada Conference. Windsor, ON: Administrative Sciences Association of Canada, pp. 108–16.

Kleindle, B. (2007) 'Marketing practices used by the emerging American public library system from inception to 1930', *Journal of Macromarketing* 27 (March): 65–73.

Koehn, N.F. (2001) *Brand New: How Entrepreneurs Earned Consumers' Trust from Wedgwood to Dell*. Boston, MA: Harvard Business School Press.

Kopp, S.W. and Taylor, C.R. (1994) 'Games, contests, sweepstakes, and lotteries: prize promotion and public policy', in J. Sheth and R.A. Fullerton (eds) *Research in Marketing: Explorations in the History of Marketing*. Greenwich, CT: JAI Press, pp. 151–66.

Kose, Y. (2007) 'Nestlé: a brief history of the marketing strategies of the first multinational company in the Ottoman empire', *Journal of Macromarketing* 27 (March): 74–85.

Kreshel, P.J. (1990) 'John B. Watson at J. Walter Thompson: the legitimation of "science" in advertising', *Journal of Advertising* 19(2): 49–59.

Kumcu, E. (1987) 'Historical method: toward a relevant analysis of marketing systems', in F. Firat, N. Dholakia and R.P. Bagozzi (eds) *Philosophical and Radical Thought in Marketing*. Lexington, MA: Lexington Books, pp. 117–33.

Laird, P.W. (1998) *Advertising Progress: American Business and the Rise of Consumer Marketing*. Baltimore, MD: Johns Hopkins University Press.

LaLonde, B.J. and Morrison, E.J. (1967) 'Marketing management concepts, yesterday and today', *Journal of Marketing* 31(1): 9–13.

Layton, R. and Grossbart, S. (2006) 'Macromarketing: past, present, and possible future', *Journal of Macromarketing* 26 (December): 193–213.

Lazer, W. (1965) 'Marketing theory and the marketing literature', in M. Halburt (ed.) *The Meaning and Sources of Marketing Theory*. New York: McGraw-Hill, pp. 58–94.

Lazer, W. and Shaw, E. (1988) 'The development of collegiate business and marketing education in America: historical perspectives', in S. Shapiro and A.H. Walle (eds) *Marketing: A Return to the Broader Dimensions, Proceedings of the Winter Educators' Conference*. Chicago, IL: AMA, pp. 147–52.

Lears, J. (1994) *Fables of Abundance: A Cultural History of Advertising in America*. New York: Basic Books.

Leigh, F. (1986) 'Half a century of professional bodies in sales promotions', *European Journal of Marketing* 20(9): 27–40.

Litman, S. (1950) 'The beginnings of teaching marketing in American universities', *Journal of Marketing* 15 (October): 220–3.

Low, G.S. and Fullerton, R.A. (1994) 'Brands, brand management, and the brand management system: a critical-historical evaluation', *Journal of Marketing Research* 31 (May): 173–90.

McCarthy, E.J. (1988) 'Marketing orientedness and economic development', in T. Nevett and R. Fullerton (eds) *Historical Perspectives in Marketing: Essays in Honor of Stanley C. Hollander*. Lexington, MA: Lexington Books, pp. 133–46.

McCracken, G. (1987) 'The history of consumption: a literature review and consumer guide', *Journal of Consumer Policy* 10 (June): 139–66.

McGarry, E.D. (1953) 'Some new viewpoints in marketing', *Journal of Marketing* 18(1): 33–40.

McKendrick, N. (1960) 'Josiah Wedgwood: an eighteenth century entrepreneur in salesmanship and marketing techniques', *Economic History Review* 12(3): 408–31.

McKendrick, N., Brewer, J. and Plumb, J.H. (1982) *Birth of a Consumer Society: The Commercialization of Eighteenth Century England*. Bloomington, IN: Indiana University Press.

McLeod, A. (2009) 'Pseudo scientific hokus pokus: motivational research's Australian application', *Journal of Historical Research in Marketing* 1 (July): 211–20.

Marburg, T. (1951) 'Domestic trade and marketing', in H.F. Williamson (ed.) *The Growth of the American Economy*. New York: Prentice-Hall, pp. 551–3.

Marchand, R. (1985) *Advertising the American Dream: Making Way for Modernity, 1920 – 1940*. Berkeley, CA: University of California Press.

Marx, T.G. (1985) 'The development of the franchise distributive system in the United States auto industry', *British History Review* 59 (August): 465–74.

Maynard, H.H. (1941) 'Marketing courses prior to 1910', *Journal of Marketing* 5 (April): 382–4.

Maynard, H.H. (1951) 'Developments of science in selling and sales management', in H.G. Wales (ed.) *Changing Perspectives in Marketing*. Urbana, IL: University of Illinois Press, pp. 169–84.

Meyer, T.P. (1994) 'Tobacco advertising on trial: an assessment of recent attempts to reconstruct the past and an agenda to improve the quality of evidence presented', in J. Sheth and R.A. Fullerton (eds) *Research in Marketing: Explorations in the History of Marketing*. Greenwich, CT: JAI Press, pp. 205–20.

Miracle, G.E. and Nevett, T. (1988) 'A comparative history of advertising self-regulation in the United Kingdom and the United States', *European Journal of Marketing* 22(4): 7–23.

Mishra, K. (2009) 'J. Walter Thompson: building trust in troubled times', *Journal of Historical Research in Marketing* 1 (July): 221–30.

Mittelstaedt, R. (1990) 'Economics, psychology, and the literature of the subdiscipline of consumer behavior', *Journal of the Academy of Marketing Science* 18 (Fall): 303–12.

Monod, D. (1996) *Store Wars: Shopkeepers and the Culture of Mass Marketing, 1890–1939*. Toronto: University of Toronto Press.

Muncy, J.A. (1991) 'The journal of advertising: a twenty year appraisal', *Journal of Advertising* 20 (December): 1–12.

Myers, K. and Smalley, D. (1959) 'Marketing history and economic development', *Business History Review* 33 (Autumn): 387–401.

Nason, R. (2009) 'An uncommon scholar', *Journal of Historical Research in Marketing* 1 (March): 34–54.

Nevett, T. (1982) *Advertising in Britain, A History*. London: Heinemann.

Nevett, T. (1985) 'The ethics of advertising, F.P. Bishop reconsidered', *International Journal of Advertising* 4(4): 297–304.

Nevett, T. (1988a) 'American influences in British advertising before 1920', in T. Nevett and R. Fullerton (eds) *Historical Perspectives in Marketing: Essays in Honor of Stanley C. Hollander*. Lexington, MA: Lexington Books, pp. 223–40.

Nevett, T. (1988b) 'Reform in Great Britain – The Scapa Society', in S. Shapiro and A.H. Walle (eds) *Marketing: A Return to the Broader Dimensions*. Chicago, IL: AMA, pp. 120–4.

Nevett, T. (1988c) 'The early development of marketing thought: some contributions from British advertising', in S. Shapiro and A.H. Walle (eds) *Marketing: A Return to the Broader Dimensions*. Chicago, IL: AMA, pp. 137–41.

Nevett, T. (1988d) 'Thomas Barratt and the development of British advertising', *International Journal of Advertising* 7(3): 267–76.

Nevett, T. (1989) 'The uses of history in marketing education', *Journal of Marketing Education* 11(2): 48–53.

Nevett, T. (1991) 'Historical investigation and the practice of marketing', *Journal of Marketing* 55 (July): 13–23.

Norris, J.D. (1990) *Advertising and the Transformation of American Society, 1865–1920*. New York: Greenwood Press.

Nystrom, P.H. (1915) *The Economics of Retailing*. New York: Ronald Press.

Nystrom, P.H. (1951) 'Retailing in retrospect and prospect', in H.G. Wales (ed.) *Changing Perspectives in Marketing*. Urbana, IL: University of Illinois Press, pp. 117–38.

Phillips, C.F. (1935) 'A history of the F.W. Woolworth Company', *Harvard Business Review* 13: 225–36.

Pirog, S.F. (1991) 'Changes in U.S. distribution output, 1947–1977: the effects of changes in structure and final demand', *Journal of Macromarketing* 11 (Fall): 29–41.

Pollay, R.W. (1977) 'The importance, and the problems, of writing the history of advertising', *Journal of Advertising History* 1(1): 3–5.

Pollay, R.W. (1978) 'Maintaining archives for the history of advertising', *Special Libraries* 69(4): 145–54.

Pollay, R.W. (1979) *Information Sources in Advertising History*. Riverside, CT: Greenwood Press.

Pollay, R.W. (1984a) 'The identification and distribution of values manifest in print advertising 1900–1980', in E. Pitts Jr and A. Woodside (eds) *Personal Values and Consumer Behavior*. Lexington, MA: Lexington Press, pp. 111–35.

Pollay, R.W. (1984b) 'Twentieth century magazine advertising: determinants of informativeness', *Written Communication* 1(1): 56–77.

Pollay, R.W. (1985) 'The subsiding sizzle: a descriptive history of print advertising, 1900–1980', *Journal of Marketing* 49 (Summer): 24–37.

Pollay, R.W. (1988a) 'Current events that are making advertising history', in T. Nevett and R. Fullerton (eds) *Historical Perspectives in Marketing: Essays in Honor of Stanley C. Hollander*. Lexington, MA: Lexington Books, pp. 195–222.

Pollay, R.W. (1988b) 'Keeping advertising from going down in history – unfairly', *Journal of Advertising History* 1 (Autumn): 21–32.

Pollay, R.W. (1994) 'Thank the editors for the buy-ological urge! American magazines, advertising, and the promotion of the consumer culture, 1920–1980', in J. Sheth and R.A. Fullerton (eds) *Research in Marketing: Explorations in the History of Marketing*. Greenwich, CT: JAI Press, pp. 221–36.

Pollay, R.W. and Lysonski, S. (1990) 'Advertising sexism is forgiven, but not forgotten: historical, cross cultural and individual differences in criticism and purchase boycott intentions', *International Journal of Advertising* 9(4): 317–29.

Pope, D. (1983) *The Making of Modern Advertising*. New York: Basic Books.

Porter, G. and Livesay, H. (1971) *Merchants and Manufacturers: Studies in the Changing Structure of Nineteenth Century Marketing*. Baltimore, MD: Johns Hopkins University Press.

Rassuli, K.M. (1988) 'Evidence of marketing strategy in the early printed book trade: an application of Hollander's historical approach', in T. Nevett and R. Fullerton (eds) *Historical Perspectives in Marketing: Essays in Honor of Stanley C. Hollander*. Lexington, MA: Lexington Books, pp. 91–108.

Rassuli, K.M. and Hollander, S.C. (1986a) 'Comparative history as a research tool in consumer behaviour', in M. Wallendorf and P. Anderson (eds) *Advances in Consumer Research 14*. Provo, UT: Association for Consumer Research, pp. 442–6.

Richardson, A. (2008) 'Strategies in the development of accounting history as an academic discipline', *Accounting History* 13(3): 247–80.

Robinson, D. (2004) 'Marketing gum, making meanings: Wrigley in North America, 1890–1930', *Enterprise & Society, The International Journal of Business History* 5 (March): 4–44.

Ross, B. and Richards, J. (2008) *A Century of Advertising Education*. American Academy of Advertising.

Savitt, R. (1980) 'Historical research in marketing', *Journal of Marketing* 44 (Fall): 52–8.

Savitt, R. (1982) 'A historical approach to comparative retailing', *Management Decision* 20(4): 16–23.

Savitt, R. (1988) 'A personal view of historical explanation in marketing and economic development', in T. Nevett and R. Fullerton (eds) *Historical Perspectives in Marketing: Essays in Honor of Stanley C. Hollander*. Lexington, MA: Lexington Books, pp. 113–32.

Savitt, R. (1990) 'Pre-Aldersonian antecedents to macromarketing: insights from the textual literature', *Journal of the Academy of Marketing Science* 18 (Fall): 293–302.

Savitt, R. (2009) 'Teaching and studying marketing history: a personal journey', *Journal of Historical Research in Marketing* 1 (July): 189–99.

Schudson, M. (1984) *Advertising, the Uneasy Persuasion: Its Dubious Impact on American Society*. New York: Basic Books.

Schultz, Q.J. (1982) 'An honourable place: the quest for professional advertising education 1900–1917', *Business History Review* 56(1): 16–32.

Schwartz, G. (1963) *Development of Marketing Theory*. Cincinnati, OH: South-Western Publishing.

Seaton, A.V. (1986) 'Cope's and the promotion of tobacco in Victorian England', *European Journal of Marketing* 20(9): 5–26.

Shapiro, S. and Doody, A.F. (eds) (1968) *Readings in the History of American Marketing: Settlement to Civil War*. Homewood, IL: Irwin.

Shaw, A.W. (1915) *Some Problems in Market Distribution*. Cambridge, MA: Harvard University Press.

Shaw, E. (1987) 'Marketing efficiency and performance: an historical analysis', in T. Nevett and S. Hollander (eds) *Marketing in Three Eras*. Lansing, MI: Michigan State University Press, pp. 181–200.

Shaw, E. (1990) 'A review of empirical studies of aggregate marketing costs and productivity in the United States', *Journal of the Academy of Marketing Science* 18 (Fall): 285–92.

Shaw, E. (1994) 'The utility of the four utilities concept', in J. Sheth and R.A. Fullerton (eds) *Research in Marketing: Explorations in the History of Marketing*. Greenwich, CT: JAI Press, pp. 47–66.

Shaw, E. (2007) 'A twenty-first century guide to Aldersonian marketing thought', *Journal of Macromarketing* 27 (June): 193–6.

Shaw, E. and Jones, D.G.B. (2005) 'A history of schools of marketing thought', *Marketing Theory* 5(3): 239–82.

Shaw, E. and Tamilia, R. (2001) 'Robert Bartels and the history of marketing thought', *Journal of Macromarketing* 21(2): 156–63.

Sheth, J.N. and Gross, B.L. (1988) 'Parallel development of marketing and consumer behaviour: a historical perspective', in T. Nevett and R. Fullerton (eds) *Historical Perspectives in Marketing: Essays in Honor of Stanley C. Hollander*. Lexington, MA: Lexington Books, pp. 9–34.

Sheth, J.N., Gardner, D.M. and Garrett, D. (1988) *Marketing Theory: Evolution and Evaluation*. New York: John Wiley.

Silk, A. and Stern, L. (1963) 'The changing nature of innovation in marketing: a study of selected business leaders, 1852–1958', *Business History Review* 37(3): 182–99.

Sivulka, J. (1998) *Soap, Sex, and Cigarettes: A Cultural History of American Advertising*. Belmont, CA: Wadsworth.

Smith, G.L. (ed.) (1964) *Reflections on Progress in Marketing*, Proceedings Series. Chicago, IL: AMA.

Smith, R.A. and Lux, D.S. (1993) 'Historical method in consumer research: developing causal explanations of change', *Journal of Consumer Research* 19 (March): 595–610.

Speece, M. (1990) 'Evolution of ethnodominated marketing channels: evidence from Oman and Sudan', *Journal of Macromarketing* 10 (Fall): 78–93.

Stanger, H. (2008) 'The Larkin Clubs of Ten: consumer buying clubs and mail-order commerce, 1890–1940', *Enterprise & Society, The International Journal of Business History* 9 (March): 125–64.

Stern, B.B. (1988) 'Medieval allegory: roots of advertising strategy for the mass market', *Journal of Marketing* 52 (July): 84–94.

Stern, B.B. (1990) 'Literary criticism and the history of marketing thought: a new perspective on "reading" marketing theory', *Journal of the Academy of Marketing Science* 18 (Fall): 329–36.

Strasser, S. (1989) *Satisfaction Guaranteed: The Making of the American Mass Market*. Washington, DC: Smithsonian Books.

Tadajewski, M. (2006) 'Remembering motivation research: toward an alternative genealogy of interpretive consumer research', *Marketing Theory* 6(4): 429–66.

Tadajewski, M. (2008) 'Relationship marketing at Wanamaker's in the 19th and early 20th centuries', *Journal of Macromarketing* 28(2): 169–82.

Tadajewski, M. (2009a) 'The foundations of relationship marketing: reciprocity and trade relations', *Marketing Theory* 9(1): 11–40.

Tadajewski, M. (2009b) 'Eventalizing the marketing concept', *Journal of Marketing Management* 25(1): 191–217.

Tadajewski, M. (2009c) 'Competition, cooperation and open price associations: relationship marketing and Arthur Jerome Eddy (1859–1920)', *Journal of Historical Research in Marketing* 1(1): 122–43.

Tadajewski, M. (2009d) 'Russian travels, fellow traveller? Wroe Alderson's visit to Russia during the Cold War', *Journal of Macromarketing* 29(3): 303–24.

Tadajewski, M. (2010) 'Reading "the marketing revolution" through the prism of the FBI', *Journal of Marketing Management* 26(1–2): 90–107.

Tadajewski, M. and Jones, D.G.B. (eds) (2008) *The History of Marketing Thought*, 3 vols. London: Sage.

Tadajewski, M. and Jones, D.G.B. (2014) 'Historical research in marketing theory and practice: a review essay', *Journal of Marketing Management* 30(11–12): 1239–91.

Tadajewski, M. and Saren, M. (2008) 'The past is a foreign country: amnesia and marketing theory', *Marketing Theory* 8(4): 323–38.

Tedlow, R. (1990) *New and Improved: The Story of Mass Marketing in America*. New York: Basic Books.

Tedlow, R. and Jones, G. (eds) (1993) *The Rise and Fall of Mass Marketing*. London: Routledge.

Usui, K. (2000) 'The interpretation of Arch Wilkinson Shaw's thought by Japanese scholars', *Journal of Macromarketing* 20(2): 128–36.

Usui, K. (2008) *The Development of Marketing Management: The Case of the USA c. 1910–1940*. Aldershot: Ashgate.

Vargo, S. and Lusch, R. (2004) 'Evolving to a new dominant logic for marketing', *Journal of Marketing* 68(1): 1–17.

Vargo, S. and Morgan, F.W. (2005) 'Services in society and academic thought: an historical analysis', *Journal of Macromarketing* 68 (June): 42–53.

Vink, N. (1992) 'Historical perspective in marketing management, explicating experience', *Journal of Marketing Management* 8(3): 219–37.

Wales, H. (ed.) (1951) *Changing Perspectives in Marketing*. Urbana, IL: University of Illinois Press.

Ward, D. (2009) 'Capitalism, market research, and the creation of the American consumer', *Journal of Historical Research in Marketing* 1 (July): 200–10.

Weld, L.D.H. (1941) 'Early experience in teaching courses in marketing', *Journal of Marketing* 5 (April): 380–1.

Wilcox, G.B. (1991) 'Cigarette brand advertising and consumption in the United States: 1949–1985', *Journal of Advertising Research* 31(4): 61–7.

Wilkie, W.L. and Moore, E. (2003) 'Scholarly research in marketing: exploring the "4 Eras" of thought development', *Journal of Public Policy & Marketing* 22 (Fall): 116–46.

Wilkinson, I. (2001) 'A history of network and channels thinking in marketing in the 20th century', *Australasian Marketing Journal* 9(2): 23–52.

Witkowski, T.H. (1989) 'History's place in the marketing curriculum', *Journal of Marketing Education* 11(2): 54–7.

Witkowski, T.H. (1994) 'Data sources for American consumption history: an introduction, analysis, and application', in J. Sheth and R.A. Fullerton (eds) *Research in Marketing: Explorations in the History of Marketing*. Greenwich, CT: JAI Press, pp. 167–82.

Witkowski, T.H. (1998) 'The early American style: a history of marketing and consumer values', *Psychology & Marketing* 15 (March): 125–43.

Witkowski, T.H. (2003) 'World War II poster campaigns: preaching frugality to American consumers', *Journal of Advertising* 32 (Spring): 69–82.

Witkowski, T.H. (2004) 'Re-gendering consumer agency in mid-nineteenth century America: a visual understanding', *Consumption, Markets & Culture* 7 (September): 261–83.

Witkowski, T.H. (2009) 'General Book Store in Chicago, 1938–1947: linking neighborhood to nation', *Journal of Historical Research in Marketing* 1 (March): 93–121.

Witkowski, T.H. (2010) 'The Marketing discipline comes of age, 1934–1936', *Journal of Historical Research in Marketing* 2(4): 370–98.

Witkowski, T.H. and Jones, D.G.B. (2006) 'Qualitative historical research in marketing', in R.W. Belk (ed.) *Handbook of Qualitative Research Methods in Marketing*. Cheltenham: Edward Elgar, pp. 131–57.

Witkowski, T.H. and Jones, D.G.B. (2008) 'Historiography in marketing: its growth, structure of inquiry, and disciplinary status', *Business and Economic History On-Line* 6 (June): 1–18.

Wittink, D.R. (2004) 'An accidental venture into academics', *Journal of Marketing* 68(3): 124–32.

Wooliscroft, B., Tamilia, R. and Shapiro, S. (eds) (2006) *A Twenty-First Century Guide to Aldersonian Marketing Thought*. Boston, MA: Kluwer.

Wright, J.S. (1989) 'Return biography to the "Journal of Marketing": A polemic', in T. Nevett, K. Whitney and S.C. Hollander (eds) *Marketing History: The Emerging Discipline*. Lansing, MI: Michigan State University Press, pp. 132–48.

Wright, J.S. and Dimsdale, P.B. (eds) (1974) *Pioneers in Marketing*. Atlanta, GA: Georgia State University Press.

Zinn, W. and Johnson, S.D. (1990) 'The commodity approach in marketing research: is it really obsolete?', *Journal of the Academy of Marketing Science* 18 (Fall): 345–54.

Marketing Ethics

Patrick E. Murphy and Kelly D. Martin

4

Chapter Topics

Introduction	90
Theoretical focus in marketing ethics	92
Empirical research in marketing ethics theory	98
Future research directions	99
Suggestions for conducting research on marketing ethics	102
Conclusion	103

Introduction

The field of marketing ethics has matured in recent years. If one were to apply the product life-cycle concept to it, the introductory stage would be the 1960s and 1970s, while the growth period occurred during the 1980s and 1990s (as will be noted later, the most articles on this topic were published in the 1990s), and the time since the turn of the century could be labelled as the maturity stage. The earliest work appeared in the 1960s and was mostly published in the *Journal of Marketing*. The 1970s and 1980s saw marketing ethics topics beginning to be published with some regularity in other academic journals. According to

Murphy (2002: 166), 'marketing ethics came of age in the 1990s'. At that time, substantial attention was devoted to it in the academic and business press. Marketing ethics, then, moved from being called an 'oxymoron' to a subject of academic legitimacy. Since the turn of the century, more scholarship has been devoted to this topic but most of it is now being published in specialty journals rather than ones that most marketing academics would consider as top tier.

At the outset, it is important to characterize the field of marketing ethics and its theoretical underpinnings. The definition that will be used here is: 'Marketing ethics is the systematic study of how moral standards are applied to marketing decisions, behaviors and institutions' (Laczniak and Murphy, 1993: x). Many observers view marketing ethics as a sub-field within business ethics, much like ethics in finance, accounting, human resources and quantitative analysis. Business ethics is also considered to be an 'applied' area similar to legal or medical ethics. The theoretical foundation is often viewed as coming primarily from moral philosophy, but other disciplines associated with ethics are law, psychology and theology.

One barometer that a field is maturing and gaining a substantial literature base is the publication of review articles on the topic. During approximately the last 35 years, a number of such articles have been written on marketing ethics. The first was Murphy and Laczniak's review piece (1981) where they characterized this area at that time as being mostly comprised of philosophical essays. Another review article focusing on marketing ethics was published in the *Journal of Business Ethics* a few years later (Tsalikis and Fritzsche, 1989). Since 2000, three such efforts have been undertaken, with Whysall (2000) focusing primarily on work in Europe, and Nill and Schibrowsky (2007) emphasizing some of the more recent research in the field. A wide-ranging literature review that traces marketing ethics back to its roots in the 1960s is the most extensive such review (Schlegelmilch and Öberseder, 2009). The authors categorize almost 550 articles on marketing ethics according to 18 areas and draw several conclusions about the state of the field.

Another indicator that any sub-field has standing within the overall discipline is articles appearing in major research anthologies on a topic. In recent years, marketing ethics, societal marketing and corporate social responsibility have chapters devoted to them in several important handbooks including Bloom and Gundlach (2001), Gundlach et al. (2007), Katobe and Helsen (2009), Hill and Langan (2014) and Nill (2015). The most extensive anthology of marketing ethics articles was edited by Smith and Murphy (2012). This set of 90 previously-published articles is organized into five volumes: Foundations of Marketing Ethics; Positive Marketing Ethics; Normative Marketing Ethics; Ethical Issues in Marketing; and New and Emerging Ethical Issues in Marketing. Most recently, Murphy and Sherry (2014) edited a book featuring a number of societal concerns in marketing, including sustainability, public policy questions as well as several ethical issues.

Still another factor is the publication of textbooks on a particular subject. Seven texts (excluding anthologies or casebooks) have been published to date on marketing ethics. The first two appeared in 1993 (Laczniak and Murphy, 1993; Smith and Quelch, 1993). Two more followed in that decade (Chonko, 1995; Schlegelmilch, 1998). (For a brief description of these four books, see Murphy, 2002.) Since 2000, only three new books have been published. Murphy et al. (2005) introduced an updated version of the Laczniak and Murphy book and changed the title to *Ethical Marketing* to reflect a more positive approach to the subject. The emphasis in this book was on ethical, rather than unethical, marketing practices. Brenkert (2008) wrote a new text on marketing ethics from a more philosophical perspective. Furthermore, Murphy et al. (2012) included two theory chapters in their new casebook. The fact that none of these books has been revised signals that few courses on marketing ethics are offered in business curricula throughout North America and Europe. The thrust of current macro-oriented marketing courses seems to focus on sustainability and corporate social responsibility.

Although 58 journals (Schlegelmilch and Öberseder, 2009) have been identified as publishing articles in marketing ethics, the vast majority of work in this area appears in a handful of them. The dominant outlet is the *Journal of Business Ethics*, which has featured nearly 30% of all articles over the years and has a dedicated section editor for marketing ethics. Marketing ethics has been the focus of several special issues of *JBE* (for a synopsis, see Murphy, 2002). Other academic journals that have published several marketing ethics articles in the last two decades include *European Journal of Marketing*, *International Marketing Review*, *Journal of the Academy of Marketing Science*, *Journal of Advertising*, *Journal of Public Policy & Marketing* and *Marketing Education Review*. Two other major business ethics journals, *Business Ethics Quarterly* and *Business Ethics: A European Review*, have only sporadically included marketing ethics articles.

Theoretical focus in marketing ethics

As noted above, the theoretical foundation of all ethics is moral philosophy and several other disciplines. Marketing ethics too draws from these areas. However, substantial efforts have been made by a number of scholars to build a theoretical basis for the field that extends its social science roots. Table 4.1 summarizes 23 different articles published in academic journals that have contributed to the growing theoretical basis for marketing ethics. In this section several of them will be discussed in detail.

Table 4.1   Frameworks for ethical decision making in marketing.

Article	Level/focus	Orientation	Normative approach(es)	Use of detailed examples
Abela and Murphy (2008)	Individual and corporate managers	Normative	Service-dominant logic and the separation thesis	Multiple success metrics and cash flow
Dunfee, Smith and Ross (1999)	Individual marketers and society	Normative	Integrative social contracts	Bribery
Ferrell and Gresham (1985)	Individual marketers	Descriptive (framework)	Dependent on decision maker	None
Ferrell et al. (2013)	Marketing decision makers	Normative/ historical	Multiple moral perspectives	None

Article	Level/focus	Orientation	Normative approach(es)	Use of detailed examples
Hunt (2013)	Marketing managers	Normative	Inductive realistic model of theory generation	None
Hunt and Vitell (1986)	Individual marketers	Descriptive (model of decision making)	Deontological/teleological	Two short scenarios (gifts, auto safety)
Laczniak (1983)	Marketing decision makers	Normative	Non-teleological (Ross, Rawls and Garrett)	Six short scenarios
Laczniak (1999)	Individual and corporate managers	Normative	Catholic social thought	Vulnerable consumers
Laczniak and Murphy (2006)	Individual, corporate and societal responsibility of managers	Normative	Duty and virtue-based ethics	AMA norms and values
Laczniak and Murphy (2008)	Marketing managers	Normative	Rawls	Vulnerable consumers
Laczniak and Murphy (2012)	Marketing managers and policy makers	Normative	Stakeholder theory	BP, J&J, Toyota
Mascarenhas (1995)	Marketing decision makers	Instrumental/ diagnostic	Pluralistic	Breast implants, consumer use profiles
Murphy, Laczniak and Wood (2007)	Individual and marketers	Normative	Virtue ethics	Lego, UPS, Harley-Davidson
Murphy, Oberseder and Laczniak (2013)	Corporate marketers and society	Normative	Institutional theory, ISCT, stakeholder, theory, virtue theory	Natura, multinational marketers
Nantel and Weeks (1996)	Individual marketers	Normative	Deontology	None
Nill and Shultz (1997)	Individual marketers	Normative	Dialogic ethics	None
Nill (2003)	Individual marketers	Normative	Communicative ethics	AIDS drugs, WTO
Robin and Reidenbach (1987)	Multilevel (societal/ organizational/ individual)	Normative	Descriptive (contextual, bounded relativism)	None
Santos and Laczniak (2009)	Multinational marketing managers	Normative	Integrative justice model	Marketing to the poor
Smith (2001)	Individual marketer	Normative	Multiple theories	None
Thompson (1995)	Individual marketer	Instrumental/ normative	Ethics of care/ethical relativism	None
Vitell, King and Singh (2013)	Consumer decision making	Normative	Emotions	None
Williams and Murphy (1990)	Multilevel (individual, organization)	Normative	Ethics of virtue	Johnson & Johnson, Nestlé

Source: partially adapted from Dunfee et al. (1999: 15).

The first article that could be considered a major theoretical contribution was Laczniak (1983) on frameworks for normative ethics in marketing, which he presented as a series of questions based on non-teleological works by leading 20th-century philosophers. Ferrell and Gresham's (1985) *Journal of Marketing* article was the second contribution of this type to appear in the literature. They examined a contingency framework for ethical decision making in marketing and drew from several different literatures in developing their model. While they did not explicitly apply the usual background theories in the article, they stated: 'marketers develop guidelines and rules for ethical behavior based on moral philosophy' (1985: 88). Probably the most widely cited and applied theory in marketing ethics was published a year later by Hunt and Vitell (1986). They called theirs a 'general theory' of marketing ethics and, as indicated in Table 4.1, both deontological (duty-based) and teleological (consequences-based) arguments were used to ground their theory. As will be noted in the next section, many articles have subsequently appeared, testing aspects of this model. Robin and Reidenbach (1987) posited a framework for integrating social responsibility and ethics into the strategic marketing planning process.

As shown in Table 4.1, the decade of the 1990s was a fruitful time for the scholarly efforts on ethical theory in marketing. It seems noteworthy that the authors of these works are all different with one exception from those discussed above. Thus, one can conclude that theory development in marketing ethics was not at this time the province of just a few marketing scholars. Williams and Murphy (1990) introduced the ethics of virtue into the discussion as a foundation for marketing ethics. This article was partially in response to Robin and Reidenbach (1987), who did not utilize virtue theory in their analysis. Three articles appeared in 1995 and all were published in different journals. Smith (1995) formulated a test of consumer sovereignty that requires marketers to establish that consumers can exercise informed choice. Mascarenhas (1995) proposed a diagnostic framework for assessing the individual responsibilities of marketing executives for the consequences of their unethical actions. Thompson (1995) used a contextualist, rather than a normative, approach to conceptualizing and studying marketing ethics. Nantel and Weeks (1996) argued for the superiority of duty-based thinking over utilitarian guidelines for making ethical marketing decisions. Drawing on the European tradition of dialogic idealism, Nill and Shultz (1997) contend that solving ethical issues in marketing is related not so much to opportunity as will. Dunfee et al. (1999) proposed that integrative social contracts theory (ISCT) was a useful theory to apply to ethical questions in marketing. They advanced the ISCT decision process (1999: 21) which is predicated on multiple communities and multiple competing norms. Laczniak (1999) introduced the notion of Catholic social thought as another important foundation for marketing ethics. He noted that principles such as the dignity of the person, stewardship and the importance of treating vulnerable markets fairly can be applied to many issues facing marketing ethics.

Table 4.1 depicts a different picture for the early years of the 21st century. Most of the theoretical work that has been undertaken in marketing ethics during this century can be attributed to Laczniak and Murphy and their co-authors. Eleven articles have appeared since 2000, and they have been involved in all but four of them. In a response to an article that called into question the field of marketing ethics (Gaski, 1999), Smith (2001) proposed that normative ideas are central to the development and application of marketing ethics. The Abela and Murphy (2008) article shows how marketing ethics and integrity are integral to the application of the service-dominant logic paradigm. They identify seven tensions that exist between current marketing theory and ethics. In their groundbreaking work on a new dominant logic for marketing, Vargo and Lusch (2004) have challenged the marketing profession to look at marketing as having services, not tangible goods, as the central organizing framework for the field. These services are cocreated by the marketer and consumer.

Laczniak and Murphy (2008), in an introduction to a special issue of the *Journal of Macromarketing*, stated that one of the overarching issues with assessing distributive justice in marketing are the questions: What is fair? Or, whose conception of fairness should be used to settle competing marketing claims? They invoked Rawls's (1999) notion of fairness and his powerful notions of the original position, veil of ignorance and difference principle (Laczniak and Murphy, 2008: 8). Santos and Laczniak (2009) developed a new normative framework for marketing to the poor. It is called the 'integrative justice model' and is built on seven important elements. This marketing to impoverished segments integrated several concepts that are widely used in the ethics and corporate social responsibility literature: a stakeholder perspective; the triple bottom-line approach; socially responsible investing; and the sustainability perspective (Santos and Laczniak, 2009: 10–11).

Two articles discussed here have both been recognized with 'best paper' awards from the journals that published them and have had an impact on marketing scholarship more widely since these works were selected from a competitive set that included articles on many other marketing topics. The Laczniak and Murphy (2006) article was entitled 'Normative perspectives for ethical and socially responsible marketing'. Thus, the focus was decidedly normative and the seven 'basic perspectives' (BPs) were advanced. Figure 4.1 shows the seven essential BPs and how they fit together. Each builds on the next and BP1 notes that ethical marketing puts people (customers, employees, managers, etc.) first or at the centre, as is shown in the figure. BP2 focuses on legal and ethical questions and basically says that ethics creates a higher standard for managers than the law does. There are three central elements (intent, means and ends) to BP3, four types of managers (i.e. egoist, legalist, moral strivers and principled) in BP4. There are five points related to BP5, six stakeholders are identified in BP6 and a seven-step model for making ethical decisions in BP7. In addition to extensive discussion of each of the seven BPs, Laczniak and Murphy draw ethical lessons from this set and provide implications for researchers, managers and educators. The authors conclude with the following synopsis:

> This article presents a comprehensive, normative examination of ethical marketing practice. Our approach is firmly grounded in the centrality of exchange to marketing and the inherent role of societal outcomes attributable to the marketing system. Seven BPs are advanced, and each builds on the preceding ones. Furthermore, the sophistication of ethical analysis that is required by the marketing manager escalates as one internalizes these perspectives *because they are integrative*. (Laczniak and Murphy, 2006: 173, emphasis in original)

The Murphy et al. (2007) article appeared in the *European Journal of Marketing*. It presented a normative approach to relationship marketing. The ethical theory that served as the foundation

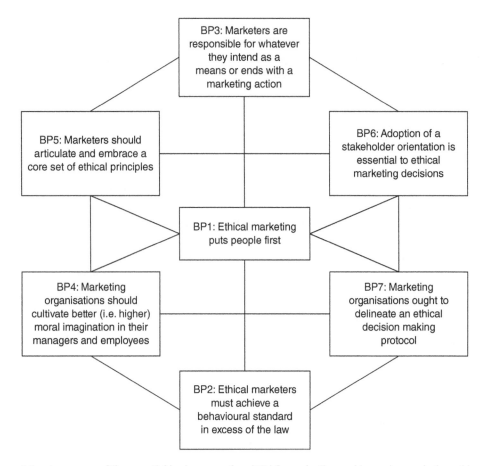

Figure 4.1   A summary of the essential basic perspectives (BPs) for evaluating and improving marketing ethics.

Source: Laczniak and Murphy (2006: 157).

for this work was virtue ethics. Figure 4.2 shows the model that was formulated in the paper. The middle of the diagram depicts the three stages of relationship marketing: establishing, sustaining and reinforcing. Paired with these three stages are three central virtues that should be associated with the stages. In other words, trust is essential if one is to establish a relationship with another person or organization. Commitment is necessary if one wants to maintain such a relationship. Finally, diligence is needed if the relationship is to be maintained or reinforced. Surrounding these stages are four facilitating or supporting virtues. Integrity is a hallmark virtue of all professions, including marketing. It has been labelled a 'supervirtue' by the late Robert Solomon (1992). The second critical virtue to enhancing relationship marketing is fairness. This notion of fairness ties in with the recent work of Santos and Laczniak (2009). Respect is another virtue that is increasingly important in the multicultural world of this century. It has been recognized that one can 'respectfully disagree' with the point of others in a marketing context

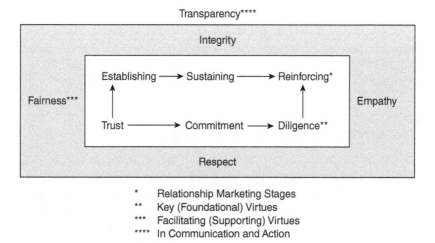

Figure 4.2   Ethical bases of relationship marketing.

Source: Murphy et al. (2007: 44).

(Murphy, 1999). Empathy is the final facilitating variable and has resonance with the Golden Rule and the ethic of care. Marketers who are successful in a relationship setting seem to know the importance of and practise this virtue. Transparency surrounds the other virtues and is needed in communication and action.

Two additional normatively oriented articles have been written by Laczniak and Murphy (see Table 4.1) in recent years. The first focused on stakeholder theory and marketing (Laczniak and Murphy, 2012) and argued that the view of stakeholders advanced by many marketing scholars is pragmatic and firm-centric. They advance a 'hard form' of stakeholder theory that is more normative, macro/societal and network-oriented. The authors contend that 'marketing managers must realize that serving stakeholders sometimes requires sacrificing maximum profits to mitigate outcomes that would inflict major damage on other stakeholders, especially society' (2012: 284). Taking a similar 'societal' perspective, Murphy et al. (2013) developed a new theory of corporate social/societal responsibility in marketing that was normatively based. This conceptualization draws from a number of theoretical perspectives. Four foundational perspectives for responsible marketing are proposed: an ethical foundation, a multi-stage stakeholder process, ethical leadership in the supply chain and an integrity-based marketing strategy.

In the same issue of the *AMS Review* as the Murphy et al. work, three other articles appeared that also advanced theoretical arguments relating to marketing ethics. Ferrell et al. (2013) took an historical perspective towards the field. They discussed both normative and descriptive approaches to marketing ethics research. For the future, they advocated institutional, resource-advantage and value chain research as foundations for research into ethical decision making in marketing. Hunt (2013) proposed an inductive realist model of theory generation in marketing ethics. He incorporates recent works in philosophy of science and uses them to decompose the process through which the Hunt–Vitell theory of ethics was developed. In his closing comments,

Hunt encourages marketing scholars to continue to generate marketing ethics theory. He also conveys his hopes that by illuminating the inductive realist model of theory generation, the theory development process might seem more accessible. Vitell et al. (2013) contrast the dominant cognitive and rational processes for ethical decision making with emotional approaches. The article concludes with a theoretical model and testable hypotheses.

Empirical research in marketing ethics theory

In addition to the substantial theoretical literature in marketing ethics examined above, a number of theory-based empirical studies have been conducted. While the list is long, only those projects which have been undertaken as tests of theories are reviewed here. Goolsby and Hunt (1992) undertook a study of cognitive moral development in marketing and found this theory helps to explain the ethical views of consumers. Another of Hunt's graduate students, John Sparks (Sparks and Hunt, 1998), examined the concept of ethical sensitivity in the context of the marketing research profession and found that awareness of norms is an influence on ethical sensitivity. Smith and Cooper-Martin (1997) also undertook an empirical study and developed a typology based on product harm and consumer vulnerability.

As noted above, the most extensive theory testing has occurred with the Hunt–Vitell theory of marketing ethics. Scott Vitell, Anusorn Singhapakdi and various co-authors have undertaken numerous tests of some aspects of the Hunt–Vitell model. Some of the applications have focused on sales professionals (Singhapakdi and Vitell, 1991), marketing managers (Singhapakdi et al., 1996), international managers (Singhapakdi et al., 1994) and organizational culture (Vitell et al., 1993). Furthermore, Vitell has also used the Hunt–Vitell theory to evaluate the ethics of consumers (Vitell and Muncy, 1992). The topic of consumer ethics is receiving more attention, especially by European scholars (see Brunk, 2010). A more extensive discussion of the empirical work in marketing ethics up to this point in time is contained in Schlegelmilch and Öberseder (2009).

Two additional streams of empirical research have advanced marketing ethics theory in the past decade. The first has focused on ethical consumption. Work in this domain has led to important breakthroughs about consumers' interpretation of green product claims, as well as the tradeoffs consumers perceive in making ethical purchase decisions. For example, using consumer decision theory and, more specifically, theory of managing negative emotions, Ehrich and Irwin (2005) found that consumers sometimes practise wilful ignorance, or avoid potentially ethically inconsistent information, when it comes to ethical product claims. They conclude their series of experiments with the question, 'Do consumers actually have moral values?' (2005: 276), and suggest that yes, in spite of conditions where wilful ignorance did occur, consumers' conjoint weighting of preferences reflected the importance of ethical attributes to them.

Ethical attributes are product features associated with moral principles. Luchs et al. (2010) found that products with ethical attributes could sometimes be perceived by consumers as being less effective on performance dimensions. However, in their experiments, marketers could explicitly make performance benefits claims to soften the sustainability liability to which this study refers. Relatedly, using self-accountability theory, Peloza et al. (2013) found that priming consumers' self-accountability led to greater preference for products with ethical attributes. Moreover, in the field study conducted as part of their research programme, they found that consumers selected the ethical option when others were around to view their choice behaviour.

A second stream of empirical research in marketing ethics attempts to link ethical marketing initiatives to firm performance. Spurred in large part by greater focus on marketing's contribution to the firm (e.g. see the special issue of the *Journal of Marketing* [2004] on 'Linking Marketing to Financial Performance and Firm Value'), studies began to purposefully examine how corporate social responsibility initiatives or cause-related marketing directly influence the firm's bottom line. For example, in two studies using firm financial data, Luo and Bhattacharya found that these initiatives can, indeed, positively influence performance for firms in certain situations (2006), while simultaneously reducing harmful firm-idiosyncratic risk (2009). Robinson et al. (2012) found that cause-related marketing has positive firm benefits when consumers can exercise some choice over the cause, and when there is perceived fit between the company's core competencies and the nature of the cause.

Future research directions

Marketing ethics is not a static field. In fact, the conception of ethical marketing practise has taken on greater meaning in the wake of the global financial meltdown. Subprime mortgages, which were at least partially responsible for the collapse of financial institutions across the globe, have long been understood in the context of marketing ethics as unfair to many consumers (Courchane et al., 2004) and irresponsibly utilized by some financial institutions. This issue was folded into the indictment of finance but it is very much a marketing ethics problem since over-selling and marketing contributed to this dire situation.

Given the dynamic and unpredictable way in which ethical crises reveal themselves, it is hard to predict which issues within marketing will be hot topics in the future. The first author identified several areas in an earlier work (Murphy, 2002) and they will not be repeated here. Likewise, the second author proposed several categories of unexplored research questions that might enlarge marketing's more traditional frames to include a broader scope of ethical issues (Hill and Martin, 2014). Hill and Martin proposed three categories of marketing research challenges that were comprised of unexplored, or underexplored, research domains. These included marketplace challenges aimed at broadening consumer research, marketer challenges aimed at broadening firm-level or marketing strategy research, and paradigm challenges calling for broadened marketing theory to better understand marketing systems. In addition to these categories, we focus on the three topical domains below that suggest fruitful and important future research directions in marketing ethics. Specifically, we consider sustainable marketing, health and safety issues and base of the pyramid consumption as critical topics likely to be investigated using marketing theories for the foreseeable future.

Sustainable marketing

Environmental issues in marketing were studied in some depth during the 1970s and 1980s. However, until the last few years, minimal attention has been devoted to these issues. Although the Bruntland Commission (1987) developed the most commonly used definition of sustainability – meeting the needs of the present without compromising the ability of future generations to meet their own needs – some time ago, efforts to examine sustainable marketing did not 'take off' until the early 2000s. Terms such as green marketing and environmental marketing have been supplanted with the new terminology of sustainability.

Global issues such as climate change, energy use and water shortages have brought renewed attention to this area. In response, marketing scholars have redoubled their efforts in focusing on overall environmental issues (Belz and Peattie, 2009; Grant, 2007), as well as specific ones like energy (Press and Arnould, 2009). One more general evaluation of sustainable marketing (Murphy, 2005) proposed several ethical bases for sustainable marketing, including the precautionary principle, ethic of the mean/balance, power and responsibility equilibrium, the environment as a stakeholder and planetary ethics. In addition to these, the notion of stewardship proposed earlier by Laczniak (1999) provides some needed theoretical foundation for future work in this area.

Since 2010, much more academic research in marketing has focused on sustainability topics. Kotler (2011) proposes 'reinventing' marketing to respond to the environmental imperative. In the introduction to a special issue on the subject, McDonagh and Prothero (2014) discuss the nine articles that appeared in the *Journal of Macromarketing*. Even the top tier marketing journals are publishing occasional articles on green or sustainable marketing (e.g. Gershoff and Frels, 2015; Luchs et al., 2010).

Health and safety issues

The selling of toys in 2007 tainted with lead-based paint was a major blemish on toy makers, retailers and, of course, the Chinese production facilities that produced them. This incident has caused all members of the supply chain for these products to be more vigilant. While now reaching international proportions, problems with tainted meat, peanut butter and produce that causes illness and sometimes death, have also focused attention on food marketing in a new way. Although Martin and Johnson (2010) provided a look at marketing ethics decisions in an information asymmetric, upstream supplier context, clearly additional scholarship is needed to 'sort out' these emerging supply chain safety issues, as well as the multifaceted effects on stakeholders. Both conceptual and empirical work is necessary to gain a more complete understanding of how product safety is understood by consumers and marketers in the 21st century.

A major health issue that continues to capture the public attention in recent years is obesity, both of the population in general and in children especially. More academic study of this topic has occurred and is serving as one input to regulatory bodies in their assessment of how best to move forward in mitigating these serious health issues. Unfortunately, obesity leads to a host of medical maladies that plague some consumers throughout their lives.

In an introduction to a special issue of the *Journal of Public Policy & Marketing,* Moore (2007) detailed the magnitude of the problem by stating that childhood obesity has become an increasingly serious health problem in the United States, and around the world. Obesity among pre-school and school-aged children in the US has increased almost three-fold since the late 1970s, with 14% of two- to five-year-olds and 19% of six- to eleven-year-olds now characterized as overweight. The role of marketing in contributing to this issue is receiving attention. Serious questions are being asked about the impacts of food marketing in both public and private sectors. Two comprehensive research reviews have been published, one by the Food Standards Agency in the UK (Hastings et al., 2003) and the other in response to a Congressional directive by the Institute of Medicine (2006). Moore concludes her essay by stating that childhood obesity has become an epidemic in our nation and around the world (World Health Organization, 2003); the associated risks to children's health and well-being are substantial. In a recent book chapter, Moore (2014) updated her views on this important topic and highlighted the vulnerability of children as consumers. Marketing's role as both a contributor to the problem and as a force in its alleviation is a complex one; many significant questions are yet to be addressed.

Finally, with the 2010 passage of the Patient Protection and Affordable Care Act, many Americans debated health insurance and medical care like never before. Likewise, influential marketing scholars have advanced thoughtful overviews of the relevant issues demanding research attention (e.g. Scammon et al., 2011). No doubt, marketing ethics scholarship can contribute to this important conversation in areas of consumer well-being, the ethics of preventive care and the marketing of proactive health behaviours, the collection, use and protection of consumer health data, and ethical marketing of health exchange programmes, to name just a few. Given the controversial nature of this health policy, marketing ethics scholars have great potential to be a positive force in this dialogue.

Base of the pyramid

As we have seen, the ethical treatment of consumers at the 'base of the pyramid' – those individuals at the lowest socio-economic level of the financial pyramid (Prahalad, 2005) – continues to capture scholarly attention. As noted above, Santos and Laczniak (2009) have outlined a new conceptual approach to dealing with the impoverished market, and have extended that thinking to consider transformative justice for base of pyramid populations (Santos et al., 2015) and advanced specific cases illustrating marketing to this segment (Santos and Laczniak, 2012). Furthermore, Vachani and Smith (2008) have identified several precepts that should exist in 'socially responsible distribution' by studying an innovative company, an education-based NGO and the government run postal service in India. The lessons they identify focus both on improving the financial and educational position of those at the base of the pyramid as well as the ways socially responsible distribution can enhance the workings of the market.

In Prahalad's (2005) influential book, he identifies a number of organizations that he sees as succeeding in serving this market. One firm profiled is Casas Bahia, based in Brazil. It is a large retailer selling mostly clothing and household and durable goods to the middle and lower classes, usually on an extended payment plan. Although Prahalad shows the impressive growth the company has experienced, he does not discuss the fact that the firm forces consumers to make their payment in the store, and they tend to buy other products (sometimes unneeded ones) on these trips to the store. This situation was developed into a case and was published in a marketing ethics casebook (Murphy et al., 2012). The point in raising this example is that academics in marketing ethics should be alert to seemingly successful strategies aimed at this vulnerable market and discuss them with students and colleagues to raise awareness of the quality of the products they are offered, the level of fairness in pricing these products, and the most viable distribution channels that need to exist in these emerging markets.

In the spirit of the Santos and Laczniak (2009) and Santos et al. (2015) articles and their prescriptions for fairly serving the poor, Madhu Viswanathan and colleagues have helped create the Subsistence Marketplaces movement and the Marketplace Literacy Project that have resulted in journal special issues and an annual conference. These initiatives, coupled with Viswanathan's impressive stream of research (see Viswanathan et al., 2005 and 2010 for examples), have created an action-based approach to serving some of the world's most vulnerable populations in fair, ethical and transformative ways. As this collective work highlights, however, we are only beginning to understand fair, just and ethical ways of serving these vulnerable populations across the vast contexts of global poverty.

Suggestions for conducting research on marketing ethics

In examining this significant literature base in marketing ethics theory, several suggestions come to mind on how best to undertake research in this field. Before moving to the positive developments, a number of trends that one of the authors has identified earlier (Murphy, 2002) as being 'not so positive' should be addressed. One troubling trend in empirical research on marketing ethics is the continued and even growing use of student samples. Ethical decisions are made in companies and in the transaction situation (whether online or in the physical store). Thus, sole reliance on students as surrogate consumers or managers seems misguided. For studies (not only in ethics but also in the wider field of academic marketing research) that employ student samples as part of their research programme, we strongly recommend additional research using non-student subjects in as externally valid conditions as possible. Of course, an exception is executive MBA students who are usually practising managers during the time of their programme. We also advocate ethics-based cross-cultural investigations where researchers have strong theoretical reasons for administering the same instrument to respondents in multiple countries. For those research efforts that do employ such techniques, and especially those that rely on secondary data programmes, rigorous evidence of cross-national comparability and measurement invariance is a must. Likewise, the situation is compounded if student samples are used in multiple countries. Ethics-based empirical research has long relied on the use of a variety of scenarios to put respondents in an ethical decision making frame of mind. The criticism here is not with the technique, but that we often see scenarios that are too many (one study had 20 scenarios) or too few (one or two) or too old (scenarios developed 10 or 20 years ago). If the researcher uses scenarios in an experimental fashion, valuable and generalizable information can be gained. Such experimentation might study recent ethical issues like online selling, privacy on the web and online surveys. A final area of concern is the testing of narrow theoretical propositions. In the 1990s, much empirical research was undertaken to test various aspects of the Hunt and Vitell (1986) model. Some of this research focused too narrowly on a single aspect of that or other models. The assessment made several years ago bears repeating here:

> While it is quite difficult to operationalize generalized theories and models, some marketing scholars have been content to investigate such narrow propositions and theories that the outcome of their work is marginalized. The field of marketing ethics seems increasingly to be using the same narrow lens that has characterized much of the consumer behavior research over a prolonged period. ...The work of marketing ethics can impact the practice of marketing if researchers keep in mind that they are not engaged in just a narrow academic exercise. (Murphy, 2002: 171)

The quote above leads to the type of research that these authors believe is most effective. First, the impressive list of articles shown in Table 4.1 confirms that it is possible to publish important theoretical and conceptual articles on marketing ethics. Future researchers are encouraged to not be intimidated by this somewhat daunting task of contributing to the theoretical base of this field. Second, theory testing is needed especially for the new more global theories of marketing ethics depicted in Figures 4.1 and 4.2. As noted in the quote above, the task of operationalizing the BPs or virtues will likely take a significant investment in scale construction and validation. Furthermore, a sample of managers would most likely need to be studied in order to draw conclusions about which aspects of these models are most applicable to marketing practice. Third, in-depth interviews of managers are one (but certainly not the only) method to study marketing practitioners. Some of the insights gained by the consumer culture theory (CCT) researchers may be valuable for those interested in studying both consumer and marketer behaviour. The first author has been involved with two projects in marketing ethics where in-depth interviews were conducted (Drumwright and Murphy, 2004, 2009) and though the process of interviewing executives is arduous, the insights gained are valuable. Fourth, a thrust of current ethics research, especially in Europe, appears to be on consumer ethics and responsible consumption (Brinkmann, 2004; Brunk, 2010). Several of the caveats mentioned above regarding avoiding student samples and narrow cross-cultural studies should be heeded here as well. The notion of responsible consumption is important from a marketing, sustainability and societal perspective, but the projects that will make the greatest contribution will likely be those that are the hardest to carry out. Another fruitful area is to examine marketing ethics from the standpoint of another foundational discipline. The highly cited Gundlach and Murphy (1993) article is an illustration of this type of endeavour. Certainly, dissertations are not meant to be a life work, but slicing the project 'too thin' means that the future impact of the work will be affected.

Conclusion

This chapter has provided an historical discussion of theoretical research in marketing ethics as well as a brief analysis of some of the empirical work in this field. Three emerging areas in marketing ethics – sustainable marketing, health and safety issues and the base of the pyramid – were proposed as potential areas for future research. A number of challenges and opportunities for conducting research on marketing ethics were outlined. Hopefully, future scholars will build on this substantial body of knowledge in marketing ethics.

Recommended further reading

Dunfee, T., Smith, N.C. and Ross, W. (1999) 'Social contracts and marketing ethics', *Journal of Marketing* 63(2): 14–32.

Goolsby, J.R. and Hunt, S.D. (1992) 'Cognitive moral development and marketing', *Journal of Marketing* 56(1): 55–68.

Gundlach, G.T. and Murphy, P.E. (1993) 'Ethical and legal foundations of relational marketing exchanges', *Journal of Marketing* 57(4): 35–46.

Hill, R.P. and Martin, K.D. (2014) 'Broadening the paradigm of marketing as exchange: a public policy and marketing perspective', *Journal of Public Policy & Marketing* 33(1): 17–33.

Hunt, S. and Vitell, S. (1986) 'A general theory of marketing ethics', *Journal of Macromarketing* 6(1): 6–15.

Laczniak, G.R. (1983) 'Frameworks for analyzing marketing ethics', *Journal of Macromarketing* 3(1): 7–18.

Laczniak, G.R. and Murphy, P.E. (2006) 'Normative perspectives for ethical and socially responsible marketing', *Journal of Macromarketing* 26(2): 154–77.

Laczniak, G.R. and Murphy, P.E. (2012) 'Stakeholder theory and marketing: moving from a firm-centric to a societal perspective', *Journal of Public Policy & Marketing* 31(2): 284–92.

Murphy, P.E., Laczniak, G.R. and Wood, G. (2007) 'An ethical basis for relationship marketing: a virtue ethics perspective', *European Journal of Marketing* 41(1 and 2): 37–57.

Nill, A. (2003) 'Global marketing ethics: a communicative approach', *Journal of Macromarketing* 23(2): 90–104.

Smith, N.C. (2001) 'Ethical guidelines for marketing practice: a reply to Gaski and some observations on the role of normative marketing ethics', *Journal of Business Ethics* 32(1): 3–18.

Williams, O.F. and Murphy, P.E. (1990) 'The ethics of virtue: a moral theory for marketing', *Journal of Macromarketing* 10(1): 19–29.

References

Abela, A.V. and Murphy, P.E. (2008) 'Marketing with integrity: ethics and the service-dominant logic for marketing', *Journal of the Academy of Marketing Science* 36(1): 39–53.

Belz, F.-M. and Peattie, K. (2009) *Sustainability Marketing: A Global Perspective*. London: John Wiley.

Bloom, P.N. and Gundlach, G.T. (eds) (2001) *Handbook of Marketing and Society*. Thousand Oaks, CA: Sage.

Brenkert, G. (2008) *Marketing Ethics*. Cambridge, MA: Blackwell.

Brinkmann, J. (2004) 'Looking at consumer behavior in a moral perspective', *Journal of Business Ethics* 51(2): 129–41.

Brunk, K.H. (2010) 'Exploring origins of ethical company/brand perceptions – a consumer perspective of corporate ethics', *Journal of Business Research* 63(3): 255–62.

Bruntland Report (1987) *Our Common Future*. Report of the World Commission on Environment and Development. Oxford: Oxford University Press.

Chonko, L.B. (1995) *Ethical Decision Making in Marketing*. Thousand Oaks, CA: Sage.

Courchane, M.J., Surette, B.J. and Zorn, P.M. (2004) 'Subprime borrowers: mortgage transitions and outcomes', *Journal of Real Estate Finance and Economics* 29(4): 365–92.

Drumwright, M.E. and Murphy, P.E. (2004) 'How advertising practitioners view ethics: moral muteness, moral myopia and moral imagination', *Journal of Advertising* 33(2): 7–24.

Drumwright, M.E. and Murphy, P.E. (2009) 'The current state of advertising ethics: industry and academic perspectives', *Journal of Advertising* 38(1): 83–107.

Dunfee, T., Smith, N.C. and Ross, W. (1999) 'Social contracts and marketing ethics', *Journal of Marketing* 63(2): 14–32.

Ehrich, K.R. and Irwin, J.R. (2005) 'Willful ignorance in the request for product attribute information', *Journal of Marketing Research* 42 (August): 266–77.

Ferrell, O.C. and Gresham, L. (1985) 'A contingency framework for understanding ethical decision making in marketing', *Journal of Marketing* 49(3): 87–96.

Ferrell, O.C., Crittenden, V.L., Ferrell, L. and Crittenden, W.F. (2013) 'Theoretical development in ethical marketing decision making', *AMS Review* 3(2): 51–60.

Gaski, J.F. (1999) 'Does marketing ethics really have anything to say? – a critical commentary of the literature', *Journal of Business Ethics* 18 (February): 315–34.

Gershoff, A.D. and Frels, J.K. (2015) 'What makes it green? The role of centrality of green attributes in evaluations of the greenness of products', *Journal of Marketing* 79(1): 97–110.

Goolsby, J.R. and Hunt, S.D. (1992) 'Cognitive moral development and marketing', *Journal of Marketing* 56(1): 55–68.

Grant, J. (2007) *The Green Marketing Manifesto*. Chichester: John Wiley.

Gundlach, G.T. and Murphy, P.E. (1993) 'Ethical and legal foundations of relational marketing exchanges', *Journal of Marketing* 57(4): 35–46.

Gundlach, G.T., Block, L. and Wilkie, W.L. (eds) (2007) *Explorations of Marketing and Society*. Cincinnati, OH: Thomson Southwestern.

Hastings, G., Stead, M., McDermott, L., Forsyth, A., MacKintosh, A.M., Rayner, M., Godfrey, C., Caraher, M. and Angus, K. (2003) *Review of Research on the Effects of Food Promotion to Children*, Report to the Food Standards Agency. Glasgow: Centre for Social Marketing, University of Strathclyde.

Hill, R.P. and Langan, R. (eds) (2014) *Handbook of Research on Marketing and Corporate Social Responsibility*. Northampton, MA: Edward Elgar.

Hill, R.P. and Martin, K.D. (2014) 'Broadening the paradigm of marketing as exchange: a public policy and marketing perspective', *Journal of Public Policy & Marketing* 33(1): 17–33.

Hunt, S.D. (2013) 'The inductive realist model of theory generation: explaining the development of a theory of marketing ethics', *AMS Review* 3(2): 61–73.

Hunt, S. and Vitell, S. (1986) 'A general theory of marketing ethics', *Journal of Macromarketing* 6(1): 6–15.

Institute of Medicine (2006) *Food Marketing to Children and Youth: Threat or Opportunity?* Washington, DC: National Academies Press.

Katobe, M. and Helsen, K. (2009) *The Sage Handbook of International Marketing*. Los Angeles, CA: Sage.

Kotler, P. (2011) 'Reinventing marketing to manage the environmental imperative', *Journal of Marketing* 75 (July): 132–5.

Laczniak, G.R. (1983) 'Frameworks for analyzing marketing ethics', *Journal of Macromarketing* 3(1): 7–18.

Laczniak, G.R. (1999) 'Distributive justice, Catholic social teaching, and the moral responsibility of marketing', *Journal of Public Policy & Marketing* 18(1): 125–9.

Laczniak, G.R. and Murphy, P.E. (1993) *Ethical Marketing Decisions: The Higher Road*. Needham Heights, MA: Allyn & Bacon.

Laczniak, G.R. and Murphy, P.E. (2006) 'Normative perspectives for ethical and socially responsible marketing', *Journal of Macromarketing* 26(2): 154–77.

Laczniak, G.R. and Murphy, P.E. (2008) 'Distributive justice: pressing questions, emerging directions and the promise of a Rawlsian analysis', *Journal of Macromarketing* 18 (March): 5–11.

Laczniak, G.R. and Murphy, P.E. (2012) 'Stakeholder theory and marketing: moving from a firm-centric to a societal perspective', *Journal of Public Policy & Marketing* 31(2): 284–92.

Luchs, M.G., Naylor, R.W., Irwin, J.R. and Raghunathan, R. (2010) 'The sustainability liability: potential negative effects of ethicality on product preference', *Journal of Marketing* 74 (September): 18–31.

Luo, X. and Bhattacharya, C.B. (2006) 'Corporate social responsibility, customer satisfaction, and market value', *Journal of Marketing* 70 (October): 1–18.

Luo, X. and Bhattacharya, C.B. (2009) 'The debate over doing good: corporate social performance, strategic marketing levers, and firm-idiosyncratic risk', *Journal of Marketing* 73 (November): 198–213.

McDonagh, P. and Prothero, A. (2014) 'Introduction to the special issue: sustainability as a megatrend I', *Journal of Macromarketing* 34(3): 248–52.

Martin, K.D. and Johnson, J.L. (2010) 'Ethical beliefs and information asymmetries in supplier relationships', *Journal of Public Policy & Marketing* 29(1): 38–51.

Mascarenhas, O.A.J. (1995) 'Exonerating unethical marketing behaviors: a diagnostic framework', *Journal of Marketing* 59(2): 43–57.

Moore, E. (2007) 'Perspectives on food marketing and childhood obesity: introduction to the special section', *Journal of Public Policy & Marketing* 26(2): 157–61.

Moore, E. (2014) 'Should marketers be persuading our children? A controversial question', in P.E. Murphy and J.F. Sherry Jr (eds) *Marketing and the Common Good: Essays from Notre Dame on Societal Impact.* New York: Routledge, pp. 191–211.

Murphy, P.E. (1999) 'Character and virtue ethics in international marketing: an agenda for managers, educators, and researchers', *Journal of Business Ethics* 18(1): 107–24.

Murphy, P.E. (2002) 'Marketing ethics at the millennium: review, reflections, and recommendations', in N.E. Bowie (ed.) *The Blackwell Guide to Business Ethics.* Cambridge, MA: Blackwell, pp. 165–85.

Murphy, P.E. (2005) 'Sustainable marketing', *Business & Professional Ethics Journal* 24(1&2): 171–98.

Murphy, P.E. and Laczniak, G.R. (1981) ' "Marketing ethics": a review with implications for managers, educators and researchers', in B.M. Enis and K.J. Roering (eds) *Review of Marketing.* Chicago, IL: American Marketing Association, pp. 107–24.

Murphy, P.E. and Sherry, J.F. Jr (eds) (2014) *Marketing and the Common Good: Essays from Notre Dame on Societal Impact.* New York: Routledge.

Murphy, PE., Laczniak, G.R., Bowie, N.E. and Klein, T. (2005) *Ethical Marketing.* Upper Saddle River, NJ: Pearson Education.

Murphy, P.E., Laczniak, G.R. and Wood, G. (2007) 'An ethical basis for relationship marketing: a virtue ethics perspective', *European Journal of Marketing* 41 (1&2): 37–57.

Murphy, P.E., Laczniak, G. and Prothero, A. (2012) *Ethics in Marketing: International Cases and Perspectives.* New York: Routledge.

Murphy, P.E., Öberseder, M. and Laczniak, G.R. (2013) 'Corporate societal responsibility in marketing: normatively broadening the concept', *AMS Review* 3(2): 86–102.

Nantel, J. and Weeks, W. (1996) 'Marketing ethics: is there more to it than the utilitarian approach?', *European Journal of Marketing* 30(5): 9–19.

Nill, A. (2003) 'Global marketing ethics: a communicative approach', *Journal of Macromarketing* 23(2): 90–104.

Nill, A. (ed.) (2015) *Handbook on Ethics and Marketing.* Northampton, MA: Edward Elgar.

Nill, A. and Schibrowsky, J.A. (2007) 'Research on marketing ethics: a systematic review of the literature', *Journal of Macromarketing* 27(3): 256–73.

Nill, A. and Shultz, C. (1997) 'Cross cultural marketing ethics and the emergence of dialogic idealism as a decision marketing model', *Journal of Macromarketing* 17(1): 4–19.

Peloza, J., White, K. and Shang, J. (2013) 'Good and guilt-free: the role of self-accountability in influencing preferences for products with ethical attributes', *Journal of Marketing* 77 (January): 104–19.

Prahalad, C.K. (2005) *The Fortune at the Bottom of the Pyramid*. Upper Saddle River, NJ: Wharton School Publishing.

Press, M. and Arnould, E.J. (2009) 'Constraints on sustainable energy consumption: market system and public policy challenges and opportunities', *Journal of Public Policy & Marketing* 28(1): 102–13.

Rawls, J. (1999) *A Theory of Justice*, revised edn. Cambridge, MA: Harvard University Press.

Robin, D.P. and Reidenbach, E.R. (1987) 'Social responsibility, ethics and marketing strategy: closing the gap between concept and application', *Journal of Marketing* 51(1): 44–58.

Robinson, S.R., Irmak, C. and Jayachandran, S. (2012) 'Choice of cause in cause-related marketing', *Journal of Marketing* 76 (July): 126–39.

Santos, N.J.C. and Laczniak, G.R. (2009) 'Marketing to the poor: an integrative justice model for engaging impoverished market segments', *Journal of Public Policy & Marketing* 28(1): 3–15.

Santos, N.J.C. and Laczniak, G.R. (2012) 'Marketing to the base of the pyramid: a corporate responsibility approach with case-inspired strategies', *Business & Politics* 14(1): 1–39.

Santos, N.J.C., Laczniak, G.R. and Facca-Miess, T.M. (2015) 'The "integrative justice model" as transformative justice for base-of-the-pyramid marketing', *Journal of Business Ethics* 126(9): 697–737.

Scammon, D.L., Keller, P.A., Albinsson, P.A., Bahl, S., Catlin, J.R., Haws, K.L., Kees, J., King, T., Gelfand Miller, E., Mirabito, A.M., Peter, P.C. and Schindler, R.M. (2011) 'Transforming consumer health', *Journal of Public Policy & Marketing* 30(1): 14–22.

Schlegelmilch, B. (1998) *Marketing Ethics: An International Perspective*. London: International Thomson Business Press.

Schlegelmilch, B. and Öberseder, M. (2009) 'Half a century of marketing ethics: shifting perspectives and emerging trends', *Journal of Business Ethics* 93(1): 1–19.

Singhapakdi, A. and Vitell, S. (1991) 'Analysing the ethical decision making of sales professionals', *Journal of Personal Selling & Sales Management* 11(1): 1–12.

Singhapakdi, A., Vitell, S. and Leelakulthanit, C. (1994) 'A cross cultural study of moral philosophies, ethical perceptions and judgments: a comparison of American and Thai marketers', *International Marketing Review* 21(4): 65–78.

Singhapakdi, A., Vitell, S. and Kraft, K. (1996) 'Moral intensity and ethical decision making of marketing professionals', *Journal of Business Research* 36(3): 245–55.

Smith, N.C. (1995) 'Marketing strategies for the ethics era', *Sloan Management Review* 36 (Summer): 85–97.

Smith, N.C. (2001) 'Ethical guidelines for marketing practice: a reply to Gaski and some observations on the role of normative marketing ethics', *Journal of Business Ethics* 32(1): 3–18.

Smith, N.C. and Cooper-Martin, E. (1997) 'Ethics and target marketing: the role of product harm and consumer vulnerability', *Journal of Marketing* 35 (July): 3–12.

Smith, N.C. and Murphy, P.E. (eds) (2012) *Marketing Ethics*, Vols I–V. London: Sage.

Smith, N.C. and Quelch, J.A. (1993) *Ethics in Marketing*. Homewood, IL: Irwin.

Solomon, R. (1992) *Ethics and Excellence: Cooperation and Integrity in Business*. Oxford: Oxford University Press.

Sparks, J.R. and Hunt, S.D. (1998) 'Marketing researcher ethical sensitivity: conceptualization, measurement, and exploratory investigation', *Journal of Marketing* 62 (April): 92–109.

Thompson, C.T. (1995) 'A contextualist proposal for the conceptualization and study on marketing ethics', *Journal of Public Policy & Marketing* 14(1): 177–91.

Tsalikis, J. and Fritzsche, D.J. (1989) 'Business ethics: a literature review with a focus on marketing ethics', *Journal of Business Ethics* 8(9): 695–743.

Vachani, S. and Smith, N.C. (2008) 'Socially responsible distribution: distribution strategies for reaching the bottom of the pyramid', *California Management Review* 50(2): 52–84.

Vargo, S.L. and Lusch, R.F. (2004) 'Evolving a new dominant logic for marketing', *Journal of Marketing* 68 (Spring): 1–17.

Viswanathan, M., Rosa, J.A. and Harris, J.E. (2005) 'Decision making and coping of functionally illiterate consumers and some implications for marketing management', *Journal of Marketing* 69 (January): 15–31.

Viswanathan, M., Rosa, J.A. and Ruth, J.A. (2010) 'Exchanges in marketing systems: the case of subsistence consumer-merchants in Chennai, India', *Journal of Marketing* 74 (May): 1–17.

Vitell, S. and Muncy, J. (1992) 'Consumer ethics: an empirical investigation of the factors influencing ethical judgements of the final consumer', *Journal of Business Ethics* 11(8): 585–97.

Vitell, S., Rallapalli, K. and Singhapakdi, A. (1993) 'Marketing norms: the influences of personal moral philosophies and organizational ethical culture', *Journal of the Academy of Marketing Science* 21(4): 331–7.

Vitell, S.J., King, R.A. and Singh, J.J. (2013) 'A special emphasis and look at the emotional side of ethical decision-making', *AMS Review* 3(2): 74–85.

Whysall, P. (2000) 'Marketing ethics – an overview', *Marketing Review* 1(2): 175–95.

Williams, O.F. and Murphy, P.E. (1990) 'The ethics of virtue: a moral theory for marketing', *Journal of Macromarketing* 10(1): 19–29.

World Health Organization (2003) 'Obesity and overweight', Global Strategy on Diet, Physical Activity and Health. Available at: http://www.who.int/dietphysicalactivity/publications/facts/obesity/en/ (accessed 12 July 2007).

Part Two

Part

Disciplinary Underpinnings of Marketing Theory

Part II Contents

5 The Economics Basis of Marketing 111

6 The Psychological Basis of Marketing 137

7 The Sociological Basis of Marketing 160

8 Cultural Aspects of Marketing 180

The Economics Basis of Marketing

Richard J. Varey

5

Chapter Topics

Forethoughts	111
Economics	113
The evolution of economics and the adoption of neoclassical thought	117
Recent challenges to economic thought and implications for future 'marketing thinking'	124
Reflections	130

Forethoughts

The marketing discipline strives to understand the economic behaviour of persons, groups and communities, and thereby influence the purchase and use of production outputs and service (the term 'individual' is not used at this point as it implies that each human operates independently in a social system, although we will see that it is universally adopted in basic microeconomics). In beginning a discussion of the economic thinking that has become common marketing thinking, it is important to distinguish that part of the marketing field concerned with managerial control of markets and that which is a science of markets. Marketing thus sits in a commercial exchange economy between producers and consumers, as well as between economics and managerial practices. If we understand how 'the market' operates as an alternative to state authority, then we can see what marketing is supposed to do before focusing on how to do marketing. To do this it is better to investigate economics from beyond the confines of the typical marketing or introductory economics textbook.

Marketing, when seen at the macro level, is a process for maximizing society's overall satisfaction – of economic enrichment – from the consumption of scarce resources. When seen at the micro-level, it appears much more like a process for inter-firm competition that manipulates consumer preferences. Marketing operates in and on the *market*. Since the 18th century, this has meant the society-wide space (institution) in which prices communicate preferences to producers of goods and services, so not any longer the public meeting place of earlier times, but, in the neoclassical tradition, an abstract supra-individual equilibrium mechanism, which stands as the bold alternative to tradition and central planning.

The notion of a competitive market is attractive to liberal sensibilities, since it implies shared meanings and fairness, social interdependence and equal human dignity in transactions, contracts, promises, as well as the sanctity of contractual obligations. It aligns with conservative thought in offering a self-regulating alternative to state authority. Yet, the marketplace is recognizably fraught with opportunities for fraudulent behaviour as rational human beings compete independently of each other in society.

The philosophic origins of marketing are largely founded on the liberal neoclassical economic thinking that has dominated the academic economics profession since the middle of the 20th century – Hayek and Friedman are notable representatives. J.K. Galbraith calls this the 'central tradition' (Galbraith, 1970). This modern liberal tradition has been concerned with tempering the neoclassical economic analysis and advocating government intervention to correct market imperfections and failures. There are reservations about laissez-faire policies, and the power of large corporations is recognized as working against the perfect market competition assumption. The social desirability and consumption of some commodities are recognized as part of society's general well-being, even though private capitalists would not make a profit from their production. Externalities are recognized as the cause of divergent private costs and social costs. The solution for all of these market imperfections is government intervention in the economy, rather than any extreme or perfect laissez-faire.

Some economists do not take marketing very seriously, and consider the research and theory development to be facile. We will see that this is an interesting stance to take, given the status of economics. Those who study market efficiency within the structure–conduct–performance paradigm see little significance in the practice of marketing. Others are looking to marketing to provide explanations of real market behaviour. For example, a major role of marketing is to present buyers with rules for making choices[1] and connections between products, vendors and lifestyles, and with cases for adopting these rules in their consumption decisions.

The purpose of this chapter is not to make economics experts out of marketing students, but rather to highlight key origins, understandings and assumptions by which marketing thought is apparently supported. The chapter will explore the important consumer theory and producer theory concepts that we think we are familiar with from our marketing principles textbooks and lectures. The historical perspective, well beyond the current crop of introductory textbooks, reveals some intriguing insights and quite a few issues. It may be that many marketing students – and their lecturers – are not at all clear about the diversity of approaches to explaining market behaviour. An understanding of classical, neoclassical, behavioural and institutional perspectives can raise insights that are not evident when a single perspective is (perhaps unwittingly) taken. It is widely believed that economics began with one of Adam Smith's books, *Wealth of Nations*, published in 1776. Economics then progressed with the work of Jevons and Menger in 1871, adding marginal utility in the founding of the Austrian School of thinking. For others, modern economics came about in Hicks's 1936 formalization of the modelling approach (the neoclassical synthesis). A rather more diligent enquiry reveals important developments dating from 1570 and 1660, and an historical exploration of ideas, people and circumstances is both intriguing and revealing. 'History of economics' texts are plentiful and rewarding reading (Canterbery, 1987; Guillet De Monthoux, 1993; Hunt, 2002; Roll, 1992; Routh, 1989). In the context of marketing, we consider what are the important concepts, interpretations, issues? What misconceptions and vagueness in use are evident, and what is the essential nature of marketing when seen from the economics point of view?

Why have certain central concepts (exchange, value, etc.) become so prominent in everyday talk? Why did 'consumer behaviour' develop as a parallel field of study along with managerial marketing? We look below the surface appearances to understand the consequences and implications of adopting certain ideas and assumptions as the basis for the logic of marketing. In doing so, we are concerned that there seems to be an over-dependence on a misguided, even incomplete, orthodoxy in our undergraduate (and much of our postgraduate) marketing education. We can summarize this by observing that for most students of marketing, the subject of economics is synonymous with neoclassical (general equilibrium) thinking, and with the central assumption that growth is good (more is better). The mantra of 'marketing principles' is (almost entirely without reflection), 'wealth creation through competition and choice'.

As we will see, there is so much strong criticism and opposition to neoclassical economic thinking, that it seems prudent to disregard it as a satisfactory basis for understanding 21st-century marketing. Whereas Adam Smith is held up as the hero and founder of economics, and thus as a guide to the market and market control (marketing), that version of economics might be best disregarded. How can this be?

Economics

This discussion is about economy, and the field that studies human activity in the dynamic (changing) markets of economies is economics. Although 'the market' is rarely studied by marketing specialists, it is the raison d'être of the practices of marketing, and of the logic of economics, or rather marketing is the managerial technology for ensuring that the 'perfect' market is not allowed to operate. The proactive form of managed marketing distorts the market for its own interests. Pretty much all of the economic theory that underlies orthodox marketing theory (Jones and Monieson, 1990) is of a neoclassical market model[2] that is widely adopted as a guide to practice. This is a problem because the model is largely a rhetorical tool. It purports to be descriptive, but that is only of an abstract theoretical institution, and presents difficulties when applied to practical business problems, and worse, it is also used prescriptively on that basis. Further, it does not represent actual market behaviour very well at all (Carrier, 1997)! The model is a simplification of a complex whole, yet it is common for people to simplistically invoke the 'laws of the market' in planning to persuade people to think and act in certain ways. The neoclassical economics framework is useful within limits, given its extreme assumptions about human behaviour, social structure and the nature of the biosphere (Ekins and Max-Neef, 1992; Stokes, 1992), yet is used well beyond situations for which the assumptions can be held valid.

In Western/Northern states, societies are market-directed as the primary basis for economic choices. That is the most convenient way of organizing economic aspects of life, especially when markets are not dominated by a few large corporations. The market logic has become firmly embedded in the modern mind, in both the private and public spheres, although most of us are peripherally aware that centrally planned (authoritative) and tradition-directed (historically determined) economies have existed and do operate, even as the market mechanism predominates. Citizens of democratic societies tend to equate market choice with freedom (or liberty, both narrowly defined) and the right to be individuals.

The dominant capitalist *provisioning system* (taking Applbaum's [2004] extension beyond mere exchange and sales) is the shared, sometimes cooperative, process in which producers and consumers act to satisfy needs through the production and distribution of objects and the enactment of services. In this, the market and therefore marketing are central ideas. This capitalism, as we now understand it, has certain institutional and behavioural arrangements (Hunt, 2002): market-oriented commodity production; privately owned means of production; a majority of the population earning buying power by selling labour in the employment market; ruggedly individualistic, acquisitive, utility-maximizing private enterprise behaviour by most individuals. The products have physical features that make them useable – they have use-value. Further, they are valued because they can be sold for money in the market – they have exchange-value. There is no direct connection between a person's productive capacity (to work) and their consumption, so exchange in the market mediates. Further, a person has no direct relationship with the producers of what they consume. Again, the market is a mediator since there is physical and psychological distance of producers from consumers.

> In a social economy, where the maker of economic goods does not use them and the provider of economic services does not benefit from them, there is a real separation between producers and consumers. But while they are separated, they are also necessarily related. Hence, the separation is accompanied by an interdependence which is very real. ... There is a natural, necessary attraction between the parties. Another name for this real, interdependent relationship between producer and consumer is a market. The market is the gap which separates producer and consumer. As the separation of producer and consumer grows greater under an expanding division of labor and increasingly differentiated consumer wants, the relationship becomes no less real but only more complex. (McInnes, 1964: 56)

Economics can be thought of as a 'derived' normative 'social science' that deals with what ought to be done to organize for economic tasks that maximize accomplished objectives (ends) with the allocation of scarce resources (means) through decision-making processes. Although economists have long strived to claim economics as a science, it is not now, and never has been, value free. Robert Clower recalled that Swedish economist Johan Wicksell once said that it should not be the job of economists to make commonsense difficult (Colander and Coats, 1989: 26).

Economics is limited (inexact) as a science because it is simplified and abstracted. Salient properties are selected from the multitude of variables that bear on the complex real-world economy, in intellectual experiments in the laboratory of the imagination, for the purpose of problem solving. It is thus an endeavour for understanding problems, as well as providing a basic language, and a common metaphor in 'the market'. It has provided concepts (tenets) for the marketing discipline, so we trace the sources of the foundational economic theories. In so doing, we get a picture of the current status, and a look towards the future of marketing. The dominant paradigm that persists was established in the 17th century during the Scientific Revolution and prior to the Industrial Revolution. Marketing's quest for scientific status is rather shakily, in the minds of many, built on the presumption that economics is an established science, although this is seemingly wrong!

The basic concepts of economics are a price economy, household and individual decision-making units, competitive business firms, a system of competitive pricing and economic power to interfere with (manipulate) the supply–demand–price adjustment process. The market system produces order out of the decentralized decision making of buyers and consumers, reconciling many conflicting interests, and solving the problems of economic choice. The complex of social and economic relationships of the market appears to each person as just so many impersonal relationships among things, and each person depends on the impersonal forces of buying (demand) and selling (supply) for the satisfaction of their needs.

Fundamental to the idea of the market, modern social conventions and pervading attitudes see the market as the source of satisfaction of subjectively recognized needs and of happiness, if only one can buy more things. This 'more is better' thinking is right to a point, yet extensive research shows that once a threshold of wealth is achieved, then diminishing returns set in and the more one gets the more needy one feels (see, for example, various discussions of consumerism: De Graaf et al., 2002; Hamilton and Denniss, 2005; James, 2006, 2007; Lane, 2000, 1991). Economic growth is not creating high levels of life satisfaction, genuine well-being and true happiness for society (Myers, 2000; Speth, 2008).

We can think of economics as the social 'science' that analyses decisions about the allocation of scarce resources among alternative uses by individuals, companies and states to satisfy wants – what to produce, how to produce and how to distribute to society, and the consumption of exchangeable personal property ('goods[3] and services'). This is mostly about how markets are organized, participants and their behaviour, and the effects of patterns of behaviour on social welfare. Marketers are interested in the (assumed) rationality of buying behaviour, which is the behaviour of individuals in markets when faced with a choice. The challenge is to understand why people behave as they do in economic situations. If marketing is the answer, what (from an economics point of view) are the questions? How the market operates? How decision-making units behave in and out of the market?

Whereas microanalysis deals with how individual buyers interact through the market with sellers in terms of prices, income, preferences and so on, macroanalysis attends to the economy as a whole. Microeconomics has a role in relation to management that is akin to the role that macroeconomics plays in politics (Kay, 1996). Importantly, we should note the distinction between thinking of a society as an economy and thinking of a society as having an economy, and understand economy as an autonomous sphere of trading activity that impresses rules on everything else. Increasingly, society is governed by the rules of the market as the commercial ethos takes root (see for example, *In Praise of Commercial Culture* [Cowen, 1998]). 'The whole society is in one sense part of the economy, in that all of its units, individual and collective, participate in the economy. Thus households, universities, hospitals, units of government, churches etc. are in the economy. But no concrete unit is "purely economic" ' (Parsons and Smelser, 1956: 14).

Knowledge of marketing in a range of fields attempts to understand human organization and behaviour and modification for human ends. In this multitude of perspectives, economics seems to be the natural integrative discipline of management science. Significantly, it explains, but also influences market behaviour.

All societies produce, distribute and consume things. It is only in modern societies that such 'goods' and their prices, and the conditions of ownership and work, are determined by 'laws' of economic efficiency (note, not equality) in pursuit of material wealth accumulation (Sachs, 1992).

Sociology examines the internal structure of marketing groups and their interaction, while *political science* considers legislation, regulation and the judiciary that determine market structure and behaviour. *Psychology* studies manifestations of personal behaviour in market activity, examining unobservable attitudes, learning, motivation and personality to explain the observable behaviour.

Social psychology, on the other hand, examines marketing activities as the behaviour of socialized individuals. *Anthropology* is concerned with physical, social and cultural origins of market relationships. Importantly, these perspectives deal with understanding relations of meaning rather than explaining cause and effect relations. The *ecology* perspective seeks to understand the relationship of market participants and their environment.

Although marketing is usually learned as a managerial technology, it has considerable scope beyond. Indeed, 12 schools of thought covering economic and non-economic purposes, and interactive and non-interactive forms, of which managerial marketing is just one possibility, can be discerned (Sheth et al., 1988).

Economics is the study of market organization and the behaviour and interaction of producers and consumers, and the effects on resource use and allocation. The subject is people contemplating the money they earn and the money they need for consumption (Galbraith and Salinger, 1978). This perspective presupposes dominance of an economic enrichment motive, and the natural environment as a set of resources for this purpose.

The economic, social and ethical are inextricably intertwined – any 'pure' economics is simplified and abstracted from reality and is of limited use. The world cannot be represented completely from a single point of view, nor intelligibly if represented with all! The non-economic – moral, social and political – are important aspects of our lives, so it is better to view from many points of view sequentially, thus being aware of particular prejudices of specific views.

In considering the economics basis for marketing, we are interested in appreciating what to understand in economics in order to understand marketing's purpose and practices, so it is easy to think of marketing as just applied economics. Partly this involves the mastering of the language of economists who are concerned with explaining and predicting the satisfaction of wants through the supply of industrial and consumer goods and services and the achievement of economic exchange relationships played out in the buying and selling activities in which assets are exchanged by two parties, each motivated by the desire for gain.

Economics emerged at the end of the 19th century out of the political economy[4] of Adam Smith and later early thinkers, just as the discipline of marketing was also emerging formally. This narrowed the field of enquiry, assuming that government was outside the market in which producers and consumers came together. All important needs would be supplied by the market, the all-powerful regulatory force in society. Galbraith observes that economics was political economy 'cleansed of politics' (Galbraith and Salinger, 1978: 5). As we will see later in this discussion, some economists are arguing for a return to political economy these days.

Marketing is an economic activity, for sure, but it is important to recognize that economic tools can be used to accomplish economic as well as other objectives. Further, knowledge beyond economics may be required for the effective use of economic resources. This highlights the social nature of marketing (Douglas, 1975). Indeed, well before the emergence of relationship marketing, the scope of marketing was recognized. Bartels proposed two ways to understand marketing, as a managerial technology and as a social process. As a technology of things, marketing is an impersonal act for the achievement of self-determined corporate goals, drawing on economic concepts, space–time, processes, intangibles, objects. Alternatively, marketing is a process of social interaction, a system of role relationships and a type of management responsibility. In this view, the process of marketing is social, in which society fulfils personal and institutional needs for goods and services, in the action and interaction of *people*. Thus, marketing is understood as the sets of relationships which arise in the performance of the process of economic want-satisfaction, and is behaviour in relationships (Bartels, 1970). This highlights the coordinating function of the discipline of marketing, as a social system for organizing.

The evolution of economics and the adoption of neoclassical thought

Economics provides analytical tools for the interpretation of recorded history. Facts never tell their own story, so theorizing is necessary in applying the humanities and sciences in the political economy of life. Logical reasoning is fundamental in making all economics useful in describing, analysing and explaining, and at the higher levels of economic theory, mathematics is also necessary for modelling and correlation in a systematic pattern. So what did the emerging field of economics assume about the individual and their fate in a commercial society?

Economics has its Western foundations in the thinking of a number of important figures who contributed to the discipline leading up to and during the 18th-century Scottish Enlightenment, in the outpouring of the assertion of reason above authority and the 'science of man'. Most of these people were British (and men). Then, during the birth of the discipline of marketing at the beginning of the 20th century, the men who established the first university departments in the USA had mostly studied in the Austrian School.[5] Their perspective emphasizes the spontaneous organizing power of the price mechanism, holds that the complexity of subjective human choices makes mathematical modelling of the evolving market extremely difficult (or impossible) and therefore advocates a laissez-faire approach to the economy – focusing on the entrepreneur as the matcher of capabilities and wants. They are the founding figures who influenced early foundational marketing thinking. Economists' ideas cannot be dissociated from their personal situations and the prevailing social conditions of their time, and so an historical perspective is important. The early economists mostly had little influence during their lifetimes and not until several generations later did their thinking impact on ideas about social betterment, now deeply embedded in the institutions we live by, including our notions of social justice. These people made the history – they shaped our modern minds on what we still regard as the idea of market economy.

Critique of mainstream 'neoclassical marketing': The economic functions of markets and marketing

> Economics is the study of how people and society end up choosing, with or without the use of money, to employ scarce productive resources that could have alternative uses, to produce various commodities and distribute them for consumption, now or in the future, among various persons and groups in society. It analyzes the costs and benefits of improving patterns of resource allocation. (Samuelson, 1976: 3)

There is a rich tradition around the birth of formalized marketing in the early 1900s. Some would argue that marketing emerged as a sub-discipline of economics, while others would suggest that marketing is a branch of applied economics, with its origins in economics as a foundation, plus a strong emphasis on the seller's viewpoint. Marketing has evolved considerably, taking in non-economic explanations of seller and buyer behaviour, and increasingly emphasizing the viewpoint of the buyer (Sheth et al., 1988). Marketing has had a highly focused, but rather narrow, explanation of marketplace behaviour, assuming economic values as drivers of actor behaviour. The purpose of the marketing system is seen as the fulfilment of individual consumer needs, seeking efficiency in their actions to maximize profits. Critical economic variables are production and distribution efficiency, prices and outputs and consumer income levels. The underlying condition is the use of finite incomes to satisfy unlimited wants. Non-economic factors would be the domain of the psychologist, sociologist and anthropologist, and would increasingly come into marketing thinking in the 20th century. The economic perspective applies certain values, orientation and 'basic' philosophies to the problem of market operation.

Orthodox economists see the market automatically adjusting supply and demand. Heterodox economists (e.g. Williamson, 1985) and sociologists (e.g. Simon, 1957) see managerial practices shaping the market, and see choice objectives other than utility maximization. Thus, in this view, marketing *performs* the market, it does not just react to it. Interestingly, it can be observed that while economics has been the inspiring discipline for marketing, it has not directly provided useful frameworks (Cochoy, 1998).

Political economy, or the classical school, originated in moral philosophy and came to be the study of production and buying and selling, in relation to custom, law and government. This field flourished from about 1700 to almost the end of the 19th century, just prior to the establishment of the institution of marketing in the early 20th century. Reference to the *Oxford English Dictionary*, however, shows that a system of provisioning had been developing since the 16th century, long before a marketing discipline was formalized (in theory or in practice).

By about 1870, the term 'economics' had been adopted for the neoclassical school of thought, following Alfred Marshall. Whereas the classical school studied factors of long-run growth and change in the then emerging capitalist economy, the neoclassical focus was on the way that resources are allocated to meet the wants of the population of the state. The market was seen as the mechanism that could harmoniously reconcile the differing interests of producer and consumer and of employees and employers. A market model and theory of individual choice were developed to explain individual decision making towards profit maximization by the firm and utility (happiness) maximization by each individual consumer. Economics became the study of market actor behaviour and material decisions.

It is vital to realize that the market is not what people do and think, and how they interact when they buy and sell, give and take. It is a conception of an idealized form of buying and selling – a culturally determined construct, an idea of a sphere of life. The evolving marketing logic largely adopted the early economists' constructions of market system and market actors.

The market model is a representation of a mechanism for generating personal sustenance and prosperity (looking to the future). It was considered natural – as evolving – what people would do spontaneously if not constrained. Economies exist because people trade, and not the other way around. Thus, wealth was created because of the division of labour through the increased efficiency of specialization and consequent technical progress. This mechanism was capable of producing greater utility and satisfaction than by other means through efficiency in resource allocation. Thus a rational motor for growth was identified that could provide the greatest net human welfare.

In adopting neoclassical thinking, a number of significant *assumptions* are made about people and their conditions, with departures from the ideal having been considered sinful or negligent or incompetent – such has been the power of this rationality. These theories to which undergraduates are subjected instil misconceptions, and it is helpful to recognize that the orthodox market model is too unrealistic to be generally acceptable, yet, this is just how it is passed on as established 'common knowledge'. We will now reflect on some key assumptions that make the model unlike anything real.

First, choice is taken, axiomatically, to be the *essence* of the economy. In 'economic choice making' it is most rational to maximize utility, but the model did not account for individual behaviour but rather average behaviour of a system of the economy. In this view, we live in an atomistic world of individuals, each with an individual identity and autonomy. Market actors are and must be autonomous, so the market is a means of communication between consumers and producers. This plays out secular, acquisitive individualism. The basic goal of the individual is to satisfy their own materialistic wants, in pursuit of self-centred, hedonistic tastes ordered in a pattern of desire, a pre-existing and unchanging set of preferences. In this economic (instrumental) rationality of marginality, we always want more for less. Because ends are infinite, in the rational calculating spirit of capitalism individuals choose the best action according to stable preference functions and constraints facing them. This is a world of asocial buyers and sellers focused on self-interest in interaction, wielding dispassionate judgement in their calculation of gain, dealing with each other from a distance, in conflict because each wants more for less. There is displayed in this thinking a belief that the exchange process monitors individual values ('laws of the market' and 'the invisible hand of the market'). This equates market prices and social values. In earlier thinking, a civilizing and pacifying influence and moralizing agency was ascribed to the market in the 18th century, in which exchange would create prosperity by dealing with mutual interests, thus inhibiting aggression.

Hirschman examines the notion of 'interest' and the rather narrow meaning that is adopted in marketing as the drive for material economic advantage. This motivation for rational instrumental action was assumed in the 18th century and is still regarded by some as a 'law' of human motivation, obviously preferable to 'destructive passions'. Hirschman elaborates this view well, that interest is 'the construct of the self-interested, isolated individual who chooses freely and rationally between alternative courses of action after computing their prospective costs and benefits to him or herself, that is while ignoring costs and benefits to other people and to society at large' (Hirschman, 1986: 36). This is a person who is self-centred in 'minding their own business'. Since Adam Smith (1776), who saw growth as an inherent characteristic of capitalism, there has been a belief that the pursuit of private gain indirectly serves the public interest. The Scottish satirical writer, essayist, historian and social commentator Thomas Carlyle (1795–1881) observed this shift from medieval values of glory and chivalry to the calculation of 'a profit and loss philosophy'. Some argue that commerce produces civilized society, while others see civilized society as the basis for commerce.

This worldview further presumes that buyer choice is a moral good, entailing competition among sellers,[6] who will thus innovate, extending choice and increasing efficiency. The producing firm is a 'black box', and people are selfish individuals who will act deviously if the price is right in one-off encounters around price. Enlightened self-interest is a sense of the necessity to 'give up something to not lose everything'.

All moral rights are taken to lie in the individual, who is the legitimate decision maker. Thus, 'consumer sovereignty' implies and accepts that attempts to modify tastes are inappropriate. The market comprises many price-taking anonymous buyers and many sellers supplied with perfect information to support the most efficient decisions. This perfect competition is the regulator impersonally setting prices, and beyond the power of any individual. At the point of equilibrium, when supply and demand naturally balance, there appears to actors to be no other price deal that would improve their allocation of resource. This is a natural mechanism, and as such requires little government intervention to ensure 'free trade'.

The abstract modelling, positivistic science of neoclassical economics provides a convenient simplified explanation of the world which is purely competitive, with perfect information, moving towards general equilibrium of supply and demand, in which buyers are indifferent to rival suppliers of identical product characteristics. Real-world ambiguities are assumed away in explaining society as a 'price system'. This was to be expected in the emergent modernism, which emphasizes the institutions of science (mechanistic causality), state (bureaucratic rationality) and market (law of supply and demand). This is, of course, a limited culture-specific logic, not generally applicable as it appears.

The neoclassical synthesis approach as we now know it was developed in the 1930s (Hicks, 1946; Hicks and Allen, 1934). It is *deductive*, in that axioms are assembled to build rigorous models of consumer behaviour, each with its own simplifying assumptions: well-defined preferences and constraints, equilibrium states, constrained optimization. In this paradigm, it is presumed that we 'know' that demand, supply and price are co-determined and tend to equilibrium. It is assumed that all that is necessary to be known is known. This global rationality comes about because of the bounded rationality of the neoclassical economist. For past decades, economists have had a predilection for deductive reasoning, rather than empirical investigation (Eichner, 1983).

In Routh's view, the standard economics textbooks (especially those of Samuelson and Lipsey) are 'powerful instruments of disorientation; for confusing the mind and preparing it for the acceptance of myths of growing complexity and unreality' (Routh, 1989: 339). Notable exceptions are Robinson and Eatwell (1973), Koutsoyiannis (1975) and Heilbroner and Thurow (1982).

The 'economistic fallacy' identifies the abstract model with reality, thus considering real behaviour only to the extent that it corresponds to the model, and moving to policy conclusions from a highly abstract basis. It universalizes the nature of economic activity of a particular place and time, and assumes that as the essence of economic activity at all times and places (it is radically ethnocentric). The economics focus is economizing behaviour that pursues optimal resource allocation. Alternative 'heterodox' approaches, however, study the ways in which different societies provide for their material needs, and the various ways they solve their economic problems. The *institutionalist* approach, thus, is concerned with social rather than market values (Stanfield, 1983).

Heterodox analysis does not assume full rationality – psychological factors are accounted for. By the 1950s, a more *inductive* approach was developing, in which actual decision-making problems were examined to generate generally applicable theory (Simon, 1957, 1959). In this view, choice is an ongoing problem-solving process during which consumer viewpoints, aspirations, habits, beliefs and wants evolve through a decision cycle. A burgeoning consumer behaviour field has been developed on this basis (Blackwell et al., 1969, 2005). Herbert Simon argued that all decisions are made within bounded rationality: 'The capacity of the human mind for formulating and solving complex problems is very small compared to the size of the problems whose solution is required for objectively rational behavior in the real world' (1957: 198). The market model simply was too simple! *Behavioural* economics integrates insights from neoclassical economics and psychology to take account of cognitive and emotional factors in better understanding economic decisions, thus challenging assumptions of rational behaviour. Importantly, Adam Smith (1776) had described psychological aspects of individual behaviour, and Jeremy Bentham's work on utility (1793) considered psychological factors extensively. Gary Becker's 'theory of crime' (1968) is considered a seminal work on psychological elements of economic decision making.

By the 1980s, marketers and economists had differing perspectives! Whereas as the neoclassical perspective saw selling costs as wasteful and pernicious, and product differentiation as no more than trickery, marketers had qualifying assumptions within the emerging thinking about the firm's competitive strategies (Earle, 1995).

The operation of the economy and behaviour of its actors can best be understood as part of the wider reality. The simplified modelling removes the extensive richness of non-equilibrium conditions. For example, much of the controversy over perfect and imperfect competition analysis of pricing behaviour and supply and demand theory seems to have passed by the world of the marketing student and their lecturers. As early as the 1950s, imperfect competition became the normal assumption (Chamberlin, 1933; Robinson, 1933, 1953). It is also revealing to note that, among others, Nicholas Kaldor, a market equilibrium fan in 1934, then thought it irrelevant by 1972 (Kaldor, 1934, 1972). Also, notable is Hicks's 1979 comment: 'As economics pushes on beyond "statics", it becomes less like science and more like history' (Hicks, 1979: xi). Other critics have seen that a static equilibrium can never, and never should, exist, and the continuing belief in this idea as a 'major ill' in (especially American) economics. The mechanistic view cannot deal adequately with the dynamic, interactive complexity of society.

Given the assumptions outlined earlier, it remains to be asked whether the market mechanism as the basis for society produces social integration (Durkheim, 1964 [1893]; Simmel, 1955 [1922]) or corrosive atomism (Horkheimer, 1974; Schumpeter, 1954)? The assumption of autonomous individuals each with a freely chosen different identity denies sociality, morality and cultural values. Bagozzi has recently propounded a corrective (Bagozzi, 2005), because the neoclassical *homo economicus* does not account for altruism, commitment to ethical values, concern for the group and the public interest, and a variety of non-instrumental behaviour.

Heterogeneity of interests is assumed away, and reasons for desires are considered irrelevant in that world of 'if you want it, you can have it all – if you can pay for it'. Rationality assumes that each individual can foresee the consequences of their actions and the actions of others, as well as everyone's abilities and intentions. Yet, in practice there are highly significant information imperfections. There is ignorance and incomplete information on both the supply side and among buyers (actual and potential customers).

In theory, of the neoclassical kind, sovereign consumers influence what should be produced through continuing marginal adjustments. But this is not how consumers really behave. The information needed to construct a market demand curve, which is purported to show what demand would be at various prices, is never known before the fact of actual market outcomes. Such a simple analysis also assumes that expectations are realized. This raises another issue with the role of utility. This is an abstract concept denoting subjective pleasure, usefulness, or derived satisfaction. But in market activity, consumers may also be disappointed in their expectations. They may also be cheated, misled, or otherwise suffer, resulting in remorse instead of enjoyment of utility.

Nor does the market model very accurately represent the actual behaviour of firms – it is common that firms that deal with each other over an extended period seek stability in the face of uncertainty (the future and the behaviour of others), and establish relatively durable relations with a clear moral aspect. These marketing relationships are regulated by criteria of fairness and strong expectations of trust and abstention from opportunism. These firms abandon autonomy and competition for the possibility of certainty. There is a considerable recent literature on marketing relationships and so-called 'contracting' (see Block, 1990; Dore, 1983; Foxall, 1999; Granovetter, 1985; Macauley, 1963).

Nor is competition perfect in that the reality is an oligopoly. There is a concentration of market power (to set prices and other terms) when there are a few large corporations (20% of marketers win 80% of the business), then the market model mechanism will not operate as an impersonal competitive market. Each powerful actor has market power to set prices for itself. Even without this problem, there are logical difficulties with the notion of a supply curve – who sets the price if all producers are price-takers (Arrow, 1959)?

Other issues that make the market model untenable include: the prevalence of non-price aspects of competition, the interdependence of cost and revenue functions, the dynamic changing nature of the market, innovation and new product launch ('creative destruction') in which buyer and seller both learn (Schumpeter, 1991), competitors who respond to market devices (dynamic competition), uneven distribution of power among sellers and buyers, and identical product offerings that do not lead to pro-rata market share. Because the 'no information problem' assumption is invalid, and consumers do not choose randomly among identical offers, increased goodwill leads to increased market share, and word-of-mouth effects and trust-based relationships are effective.

Nor does the model account for moral commitments. It is easily observed that our normative and affective values and emotions heavily influence our choices, social groups and communities are often the context for decisions, and normative rules apply for commitment to fairness in competition and trust that this is the commitment of others. Social bonds reflect the reality that competition thrives in social communities where they are strong enough to sustain 'natural' trust and low transaction costs, but not so strong as to suppress exchange. This is not so in impersonal calculative systems of independent actors unbounded by social relations. It is important to understand that firms exist to modify market relationships by introducing mutuality, thereby turning them into marketing relationships (Foxall, 1999). The neoclassical paradigm underemphasizes the significance of ethical judgements in accounting for market behaviour and policy making.

For example, economist Gary Becker appears to treat children as 'durable consumer goods' that can be traded off for other goods (a new car, for example) (Becker, 1976). This calculative mentality debases moral values, secularizing cost-benefit calculations in the otherwise sacred, for example legitimizing the selling of rights to pollute.

Finally, the term 'free market' imputes a pejorative feel to the notion of government intervention, yet there are no examples of workable intervention-free economies.

It is peculiar that only one view of economics is adopted, especially since that is invariably neoclassical economics with its limited practical application! This way of thinking is ill-suited to framing business and public policy problems. Perhaps this is all that textbook authors were taught in business school. This approach circumscribes possibilities of recognizing implications of the particular way of thinking.

Then again, why should we expect a way of thinking that was crafted before the dawn of large corporations and our age of affluence, that we now take for granted – especially the Generation X – to remain eternally relevant and helpful? We still expect the economic basis of marketing to be the neoclassical (equilibrium market) logic, but it should by now be behavioural (consumer choice) and institutional (firms) economics to which we turn for analytical support to our problem solving – to understand people in pursuit of profit for a purpose. 'Betterment' was the term used by Adam Smith in the language of the 18th century, but see also Kenneth Boulding on *welfare* economics more recently (Boulding, 1984).

So what form of economic analysis is more useful for understanding and shaping the form and purpose of marketing? The 'invisible hand' of the market is a far too well-entrenched idea, and even economists doubt its usefulness: 'Is it true that the pursuit of private interests produces not chaos but coherence, and if so, how is it done?' (Hahn, 1970: 1).

There has been extensive *reformation* of the market model. The *institutional* view extends the traditional view, by asking questions the neoclassical approach claimed not to address. For example, social institutions are considered as existing prior to, and thus conditioning, individual behaviour. Markets are considered to be the result of the complex interactions of a range of institutions with diverging interests. Key figures include Thorstein Veblen, John R. Commons (Commons, 1924, 1934), Adolf Berle (1895–1971) and John Kenneth Galbraith. Institutional analysis defines the economy differently, adopts a different method of enquiry, and applies alternative values in constructing meaning from its enquiry.

Transaction cost economics deals with the reality of a lack of knowledge and less than perfectly rational decision making (Williamson, 1975, 1985). However, it is important to realize that Williamson adheres to the neoclassical assumption that people are selfish individuals who will act deviously if the price is right – he considers only the opportunism scenario. Information economics deals with the lack of information, often asymmetric, and thus the inevitability of information costs, divergence of interests and the firm as the nexus of contracts in various forms.

Markets are seen as partly mechanisms that facilitate contractual agreements and the exchange of property rights by supporting consensus on prices and communicating information about products, prices, quantities, potential buyers and potential sellers. Thus, the market can be defined as 'a set of social institutions in which a large number of commodity exchanges of a specific type regularly take place, and to some extent are facilitated and structured by those institutions' (Hodgson, 1988: 174).

Economic sociology focuses on how market exchange arises from social relations, shifting attention from exchange as events in pre-existing markets, to understanding markets as social institutions. It is argued that marketing brings about markets – marketing is a market-making activity (Araujo, 2007; Callon, 1998; Callon et al., 2007).

Recent challenges to economic thought and implications for future 'marketing thinking'

Since writing this chapter in 2009, some very significant developments and issues have been surfacing, and more so in the mainstream media than in the professional journals. The following is a brief selection of issues that raise questions about adoption and adaption of economic thinking into the marketing discipline, especially when ideas are partially selected, erroneous and/or naively transplanted. We should consider these in terms of *society*, then economics, and then *marketing*.

As we have already recognized, marketing is a process by which needs and wants are satisfied with goods and services. Increasingly, this is problematic since 'consumption' uses up what may be finite resources and the processes of production generate waste and pollution that damage our habitat. How can necessary and desirable provisioning of needs and wants be *sustainable?* The problem has become critical, in part due to humanity's growth in number of people and compounded by a dramatic rise in personal demands for goods and services. The resulting accelerated energy needs during the 'baby boomer' generation (just 60 years), particularly fed by an economic system that demands increasing levels of consumption and inputs of natural resources, are rapidly driving planetary systems towards their breaking point (see recent research from the Planetary Boundaries 2.0, Stockholm Resilience Centre, Stockholm University). In a single lifetime humanity has become a geological force at the planetary scale – our actions are changing the very place we inhabit and our life support systems. The world's dominant economic model – a globalized form of neoliberal capitalism, largely based on international trade and fuelled by extracting and consuming natural resources – is the driving force behind planetary destruction. Material consumption patterns in the 'Anthropocene Era' do not fall equally on the human population, and the economic system which is underpinning planetary destruction is rife with inequality, in which certain populations consume at vastly higher levels than others, and destruction, waste and pollution are largely 'not in my backyard' for the affluent and rich. In 2010 the OECD countries accounted for about 74% of global GDP but only 18% of the world population. 'It's clear the economic system is driving us towards an unsustainable future and people of my daughter's generation will find it increasingly hard to survive. History has shown that civilizations have risen, stuck to their core values and then collapsed because they didn't change. That's where we are today.' So says Alex Steffen, co-author of the Planetary Boundaries report, in a recent interview article entitled 'Rate of environmental degradation puts life on Earth at risk, say scientists' (*The Guardian*, 15 January 2015).

The most recent report of the Club of Rome (Korten, 2015) explains how we live by stories and shows that the stories that today govern our society are taking us down a path to certain self-destruction. Future development expert David Korten points to the story we have adopted that tells us that money is the measure of all worth and the source of all happiness. Earth is simply a source of raw materials. Inequality and environmental destruction are unfortunate but unavoidable. Although many of us recognize that this story promotes bad ethics, bad science and bad economics, it will remain our guiding story until we replace it with one that aligns with our deepest understanding of our place in and our relationship with our habitat home. To guide our path to a viable human future, Korten offers an alternative story that is grounded in a holistic understanding that affirms that we are living beings whose health and well-being depend on an economy that works in partnership with the processes by which Earth's community of life maintains the conditions of its own existence.

A new capitalism is being proposed that addresses the problem that our established capitalism does not benefit everyone to the extent it should. The reason capitalism is only marginally the best economic system, even when running at peak performance, is that unchaste materialism costs us some part of our habitat. Further, since at the core of capitalism is competition, there is always a cost as the process requires a loser for every winner. Several variants of a new value set and way of doing business can be found in conscious capitalism (Aburdene, 2007; Schwerin, 1998; Sisodia et al., 2007), mindful business (Benett and O'Reilly, 2010; Magnuson, 2008) and humanistic business (Brockway, 2001; Lutz and Lux, 1979; Spitzeck et al., 2009; Varey and Pirson, 2014). There are growing calls for a revolution against orthodox capitalism that will bring positive transformation in society, to harness the goods of capitalism and rid society of the evils no longer seen as 'necessary'. Respect and dignity in our dealings with each other are at the heart of such 'new economics'.

There are a number of forces driving a movement towards *rethinking economics in society*. People are expressing doubts about the scientific reputation of economics, ranking it well below established scientific fields such as physics or biology, and even below sociology. It is not the statistical models used by economists that is the problem, but the rejection of qualitative methods, other fields and other viewpoints. People are speaking out about the devastating consequences of placing too much authority in the ideas and policies of economists. For example, in June 2009, the National Bureau of Economic Research declared that the United States was no longer in a recession, in stark contrast with the felt, economic experience of the vast majority of Americans in the following year. Nowhere is the discipline's failure more apparent than in the area of development economics. Only recently have economists come to accept the primacy of institutions in explaining and promoting economic growth, a position long held by sociologists and political scientists.

The tales of mainstream economists do not ring true. Yet they govern us. Environmental scientist David Suzuki refers to conventional economics as a form of brain damage as it leads us into wrong thinking about resource use and our relationship with our habitat. Others have used the term psychopathy in explaining that meritocratic neoliberalism favours some personality traits and penalizes others, thus bringing out the bad in us and suppressing the good. The advent of a consumer society has changed our norms and values. In recent years, a campaign called Kick it Over has been active – one of a growing body of social movements. The aim is to combat what its members describe as 'the fantasy world of neoclassical economics – a faithbased religion of perfect markets, enlightened consumers and infinite growth that shapes the fates of billions'. The group is connected with the anti-consumerist magazine *Adbusters* in promoting alternative economics.

So what does the economics establishment tell us that is so wrong? Economic orthodoxy says we are selfish, rational, individual utility maximizers. Indeed, many people trained in marketing have a very cynical view of human nature (assuming that most, if not all, others are greedy, gullible, lazy, selfish, adversarial accumulators of wealth-as-money-and-possessions). Everyday experience, and the whole of the arts, as well as much empirical science, all testify that this mischaracterizes most humans. The phenomenon of individualism is an anomaly introduced into studies as a sampling error from almost entirely Western, educated, industrialized, rich, democratic populations. Most cultures – and so most people living on the planet – remain socio-centric. And even so-called individualists have measurable mixed motivations: some are 'individualists' who seek absolute gain, maybe not in all situations; some of us are 'cooperators' in search of joint gains; and a few are outright 'competitors' hunting for relative payoffs.

A 'naturalistic' economics must incorporate our evident behavioural heterogeneity – and address the empirically observable emotions that writers know drive the logic of our actions. No realistic account of human behaviour can ignore multiple motives, including 'self-regarding' motives such as greed, and 'other-regarding' motives including sympathy.

Reducing human motivation to 'utility' is a gross and aggressive oversimplification and self-fulfilling assumption. We survive and prosper socially and cooperatively, but economists typically ignore the mechanisms that evolved to solve the central challenges of team survival – the social and moral emotions that shape 'relational rationality'. The rational-for-self-only character in economics can promote excessive individualism, which undermines the logic of group survival. Cultures that do not balance self-only-interest with group cooperation do not thrive.

Homo economicus, the rationally acting egoist who populates economists' models, is being removed from discussion, because all too often s/he does not represent the real behaviour of persons. 'Neoliberalism' has become a term of derision for many because it has come to be viewed as a doctrine of deregulation and pure laissez-faire ('leave well alone'; 'the market is the cure for the ill of want and need'). But in Europe, at least, neoliberalism has a very different meaning. The term was coined by Alexander Rüstow in 1932 when he proclaimed the end of old liberalism and called for a new liberalism featuring a strong state that lays down a solid legal framework within which firms operate.

For some critics, the persistence of the orthodoxy carries a threat to society's advance because of an unhealthy knowledge base. A recent study entitled *The Superiority of Economics* (Fourcade et al., 2014) concluded that, compared to other social scientists, economists consider themselves elite, smarter than others, not needing to explore outside their discipline, and to be listened to first when problems are to be solved. The researchers also found that this view may actually be accepted by those other social scientists who place themselves and their disciplines at the fringe of a 'superior discipline' looking in. Other findings suggest that a dominant view is more widely shared within economics than in other social sciences, and that it is enforced by a stricter hierarchy and by a narrower control group, associated with elite institutions. Thus, prestige and compensation may confirm an economist's standing in the profession as much as competence or demonstrable results. This prevents cross-disciplinary connections to other social sciences and stifles debate within the profession itself (Francis, 2015). Unsurprisingly, the study traces this decline to the marginalization of Marxian and Keynesian thought by the mainstream during the neoclassical and neoliberal counter-revolution of the 1970s. That resistance to humility and reflexive critical thought is an endemic trait within the world of mainstream economics should ring alarm bells and even suggest opportunities for advancement in other fields.

Earlier we introduced some examples of alternative forms of economic thought such as welfare, institutional, conscious and so on. In some respects this is reflective of a return to basics – economics as careful use of available resources – but is also part of a movement towards transdisciplinary understanding of complex problems. For us, economics is not merely a component of the study of marketing, along with communication and design. We can widen our viewpoint to see different kinds of economies in society. We are experiencing a transitional phase in society expressed by concerns for corporate social responsibility, consumer protection, anti-consumption and sustainability. In the creative economy, there is no separation and functional opposition of producing and consuming. Value is not all monetizable, and valuation includes the non-monetary, including reciprocal obligations. It is recognized that contemporaneous *public*, *gift* and *contribution* economies operate as economies of existence, as well as the *market* economy of exchange for subsistence. Marketing is presented as a corporate tool, but the process is social and markets come into existence for economic and social reasons. One change that recognizes a much broader (and deeper) conception of marketing is the *feminization of economics*. Our economics gives us an almost exclusively male understanding of the social world – so this reinforces a conservative patriarchy, and the possibility of an emancipatory science is lost. The feminization of economics has, seemingly, been a long time coming. Unorthodox economist Charlotte Perkins Gilman published her book *Women and Economics* in 1898. Her groundbreaking contributions were picked up by Thorstein Veblen, only to be forgotten by his followers. Veblen is known today as the father of evolutionary economics. John Stuart Mill's work was inspired by the works of his wife Harriet Taylor Mill. Even Gary Becker, as leader of the New Home Economics research programme in the 1960s, found himself relying on the previous works of three economists: Elizabeth Hoyt, Hazel Kyrk and Margaret Reid. This body of 'feminist' work, spanning 50 years, includes major contributions by Joan Robinson (who appears elsewhere in this chapter), acknowledged by the Library of Economics and Liberty as 'arguably the only woman born before 1930 who can be considered a great economist'. She was a student of Keynes, as well as a colleague of and professor to Amartya Sen and Joseph Stiglitz! To date since the award was established in 1968, only one of 79 Laureates of the Sveriges Riksbank Prize in Economic Sciences in Memory of Alfred Nobel is a woman (Elinor Ostrom, in 2009). Some 39 (50%) recipients of the award are US citizens, but not all Laureates are economists by education or profession. There remains a 'glass ceiling' impediment to women entering and succeeding in the academy and profession of economics.

Even with this rather concise and highly selective review of revised economic thinking, it is easy to realize that a *new curriculum* for studying economics and marketing is indicated. Most students of economics (still referred to as the dismal science – perhaps more so now that we have living memory of financial crises that have affected almost everyone) are faced with a core of basic material that has not changed much for decades. As we have seen, mainstream economics does not do a good enough job incorporating perspectives on gender and class – and according to Joseph Stiglitz, economics has to come to terms with wealth and income inequality. In the way that economics is taught, there is an unstated value judgement. All else is denied or ignored – yet we are clear that there is fundamental divergence of ideologies around the distinct ideas of money and wealth and how to create the latter, and the conception and operation of 'free markets'.

Groups such as 'Rethinking Economics', a London-based network of student reformers, have emerged in recent years to challenge the conventional wisdom of the classroom. At Manchester

University, a student revolt led to plummeting student satisfaction scores, driving the economics course down the league table. Teachers are responding with a new curriculum for a more robust, pluralist economics education – one that offers the breadth of theoretical perspectives and methodologies needed to tackle the great crises of the 21st century. There is a recognizable need to wake up the profession from its decades long neoclassical coma. 'Rethinking Economics' wants curricula to cover heterodox schools of thought. For example, mainstream economic models rely heavily on the concept of equilibrium – a state in which nobody has an incentive to change their behaviour. Critics say this is never reached in the real world, so is a flawed starting point. They want more philosophical discussion about how best to approach economics. Two rather different questions have been posed about economics education. One asks whether courses do a good job of equipping students with the most important insights from mainstream academic research. The other asks whether young economists should learn more than just today's favoured approach. It would be odd if curricula departed radically from the academic consensus. But perhaps mainstream theory must catch up with its students.

Another question concerns the focus of economic, and thus marketing, thinking. Are goods more important than people and is consumption more important than creative activity? The answers lead to very different courses of study. 'Work and leisure are complementary parts of the same living process and cannot be separated without destroying the joy of work and the bliss of leisure', says E.F. Schumacher in his landmark 'alternative' economics book, a collection of essays at the intersection of economics, ethics and environmental awareness, published in 1973 (p. 45).

Even our *language* is changing, perhaps with a surprising effect on our thinking. The term 'consumers' is routinely used in place of 'people' and 'citizens'. Most people (consumers?) do not notice or care much about the terms being used interchangeably, but there are those who resent being labelled as 'consumers', as if their sole purpose and reason for existence on this planet is to consume and keep the economy turning (and growing?). A recent psychological study (Bauer et al., 2012) shows that it may be in everyone's interest if we stop referring to (disrespecting?) persons as only consumers. When participants in the study were labelled as 'consumers' they were more likely to selfishly focus on their own individual consumption. It has become commonplace to use *consumer* as a generic term for people, said Bodenhausen, but a subtle difference activates different psychological concerns depending on whether 'consumer' is used, as opposed to the more neutral terms 'Americans', 'citizens', or 'people'. When we view ourselves and each other first and foremost as materialistic 'consumers', according to this research, the results are a more depressed, anxious population and a more antisocial, isolated society. Do you want to live with everyday *people*, or be surrounded by desperate, ultra-selfish *consumers* who are all battling it out over precious resources in some ugly post-apocalyptic world that resembles Black Friday at the mall? Is marketing more than managing (i.e. controlling, manipulating) consumers as a way to make money?

So, there are implications for the next generation of marketing education and its textbooks. To date, have marketing students read an overly narrow economics curriculum? Are too many marketing students being hardened with mathematics, when understanding human thought and action and social processes is the real need? The marketing field is increasingly recognizing the biases and limitations of economics, and thus is drawing on a more holistic body of knowledge across the social sciences (and, in some cases, the humanities). The marketing mix is a partial and managerialistic vision steeped in orthodox ideas and so is outmoded and counterproductive for society because it costs everyone too much for some people to realize benefits. Conventional economics is proving to be a durable (stubborn) and tenacious obstacle to moving forward with transforming to a sustainable society. Marketing applies economic and other thinking about human behaviour to efficiently match service and production with demand to provide for needs of the person, group and community. Economics is part of the foundation of marketing, and is transforming, as are other contributing fields of knowledge.

Reflections

We should be careful to not ask what economics is, but rather what it has been, how it got to be what it is now, and what it can be? It is a developing discipline, which corrects its mistakes and omissions. The value of a knowledge of economics to a prospective marketing executive is in understanding the market metaphor and thus the purpose of marketing. But there is a social responsibility to not limit understanding to 'market' and 'exchange', in the pursuit merely of how to do better marketing. It raises the possibility of answering what can marketing be and for what purpose?

Economics has always been focused on human action, with the goal of predicting and explaining the behaviour of people in social groups, distinct from that of the individual. Yet, studies of 'rational economic man' are blind to social organization. As one of the humanities, economics enquiry can provide understanding, which in turn drives the very social system it studies. 'Modern' economists have formulated economic 'laws' as if they are immutable 'laws of nature', yet economics must deal with people. It has to deal with the social and political if it is to be truly helpful outside the academic discipline (Canterbery, 1987). Too much modern economics supposes that people behave like inanimate particles in a clock-like mechanism. Microeconomic analysis explained decision making by individual buyers, who maximized satisfaction by choosing among assortments of goods and services, and individual sellers, whose manipulation of marketing variables contributed to social welfare. However, market behaviour could not be studied in isolation if the market was understood as a social institution. Macroeconomic thinking was necessary to an understanding of the interactions between the market and other social institutions (Dixon, 2002).

The study of marketing can be for the accumulation of market intelligence, but also for understanding the possibilities for social betterment. In this regard, we can ask whether scholars of marketing need to treat consumers like fish in the way that fishermen study them, or in the way that marine biologists study them (Tuck, 1976)?

It is hard to separate attitude to market form and function from political views. The market seems attractive from the marketing point of view. However, the market, according to the economist, controls income as well as spending power since most consumers are also earners. So, for the individual the market is a discipline that many would prefer to escape. In returning to the political economy of the moral philosophers, it would seem that re-humanizing our provisioning needs is a reorientation to a greater focus on people and a lesser emphasis on things. A balance of natural, economic and social systems for sufficiency in a resource-light economy focuses on whether less emphasis on economic expansion can enhance the quality of civilization by asking 'how much is enough?' (Diener and Seligman, 2004; Durning, 1992).

The blindness of the market to any claim on society's output except wealth and income creates very serious problems (Heilbroner and Thurow, 1982). In redefining wealth we might observe that the 'faster, further, more' mentality may be counter-productive. Even as wants (ends) seem infinite and mostly unmet, creating a sense of scarcity of means, there is a simultaneous assumption of abundance of sources and sinks for the production and waste of material output that is to supply satisfactions, and thus presumed to be the source of wealth and well-being. This presumption, since the 19th century, of continuously expanding wants of course renders any and all means insufficient. Well-being has been understood as 'well-having', that welfare depends on material output. Production growth has been taken for granted, so the solution to resource limits has been to improve efficiency of means.

In conditions of abundance, product utility is taken for granted, so experiences and identity, i.e. the symbolic value of goods and services, become paramount. By labelling nature as 'resource', as useful inputs to industry, we have removed limits on exploitation. In industrial society's consumption of nature – by producers, and thus consumers – we have become 'cheerful enemies of nature' (Sachs, 1999) in our ever-expanding commodification.

The problem facing economics today is not the efficient allocation of resources, but how society should live, or what, how much and in what way it should produce and consume – this focuses on values and institutional patterns (qualities) rather than energy–material processes (quantities). Indeed, lower levels of production may enhance well-being. Opportunities abound in the search for a society that is able to not want what it would be capable of providing. Self-restraint and intermediate performance, within forms of prosperity that do not require permanent growth, will require a suitable form of marketing: 'the productivity of a sustainable society will be measured not by the eco-efficiency of an ever expanding number of technologies, but by the quality of the civilization it creates out of limited means' (Sachs, 1999: 182).

So, my final thought is what if the economics basis of marketing was less tautological, more empirical, and non-axiomatic and non-atomistic? Typical teaching does not recognize the effects of the loss of historical connections in the field of economics. The problem addressed in the neoclassical foundation, especially in the basic maximizing model, is not of the real world of actual buyers and sellers interacting, but of the abstracted models in the mental operations of theorists. Much of the work is the outcrop of a mere fascination with the problems of optimal resource allocation, and many of the key propositions cannot be empirically demonstrated. The 'introductory principles of economics' are useful as a beginner's toolkit, but are grossly overextended when applied to real management problems. Neoclassical economics, especially of the mathematical formalist, aims to explain all of reality without even looking at it (Mini, 1974). There is little real relevance to everyday life!

In accepting, even seeking, an economic basis for marketing, we need to also deal with the problems of adopting, uncritically, the orthodoxy. There remain serious concerns about assuming a stable, stationary equilibrium as the foundation for marketing principles. The resulting convenient analyses are practically meaningless, and worse, misleading. What of a marketing that has a more realistic basis? This is already the case, well beyond the 'useful myth' of the 'self-regulating' market mechanism.

Acknowledgements

The author gratefully acknowledges the generously extensive recommendations for fruitful readings that Associate Professor Peter E. Earle provided, and recognizes the substantial influence this collegial attitude has had on the writing of this chapter.

Notes

1. A choice requires the relinquishment of desirable alternatives.
2. For the typical economist, a 'model' is a small system of equations to describe some or all of an entire economy in terms of a few aggregative variables, often without recourse to actual data.
3. What is the origin of referring to exchangeable objects as 'goods', given that this sounds like a generally applicable positive evaluation?
4. This name was current before it became fashionable to treat economics as a science, then for the purpose of gaining respectability. Clearly it is not since the economist's subject 'is flooded by the human powers of discovery and imagination' (Shackle, 1973: 122). In other words, the market, in this view, is not a 'mechanism' since individual action is subjective.
5. Emphasizes the market as a discovery process, naturally and spontaneously evolving out of human interdependence and interaction. See, for example, Hayek (1978).
6. Adam Smith observed many small firms in increasingly intense competition as the Industrial Revolution emerged in England, following the Scientific Revolution in Europe. Much of his thinking is still applied today, even though we experience quite different circumstances, and his assumptions drawn from his religious beliefs and naive natural science no longer fit.

Recommended further reading

Applbaum, K. (2004) *The Marketing Era: From Professional Practice to Global Provisioning*. London: Routledge.

Bakan, J. (2004) *The Corporation: The Pathological Pursuit of Profit and Power*. New York: The Free Press.

Dixon, D.F. (1999) 'Some late nineteenth-century antecedents of marketing theory', *Journal of Macromarketing* 19(2): 115–25.

Dixon, D.F. (2002) 'Emerging macromarketing concepts: from Socrates to Alfred Marshall', *Journal of Business Research* 55(9): 737–45.

Earle, P.E. (1995) *Microeconomics for Business and Marketing*. Cheltenham: Edward Elgar.

Galbraith, J.K. (1970) *The Affluent Society*, 2nd revised edn. London: Pelican Books.

Guillet De Monthoux, P. (1993) *The Moral Philosophy of Management: From Quesnay to Keynes*. Armonk, NY: M.E. Sharpe.

Heilbroner, R.L. (1961) *The Worldly Philosophers: The Lives, Times, and Ideas of the Great Economic Thinkers*, revised edn. New York: Time Inc. Book Division.

Hirschman, A.O. (1970) *Exit, Voice and Loyalty: Responses to Decline in Firms, Organizations, and States.* Cambridge, MA: Harvard University Press.

Jones, D.G.B. and Shaw, E.H. (2006) 'A history of marketing thought', in B. Weitz and R. Wensley (eds) *Handbook of Marketing.* London: Sage, pp. 39–65.

Lindblom, C.E. (2001) *The Market System: What It Is, How It Works, and What to Make of It.* New Haven, CT: Yale University Press.

Marshall, A. (1890) *Principles of Economics,* 1st edn. London: Macmillan – any edition will prove illuminating.

Muller, J.Z. (2002) *The Mind and the Market: Capitalism in Modern European Thought.* New York: Alfred A. Knopf.

Wilkie, W.L. and Moore, E.S. (2003) 'Scholarly research in marketing: exploring the "4 eras" of thought development', *Journal of Public Policy & Marketing* 22(2): 116–46.

References

Aburdene, P. (2007) *Megatrends 2010: The Rise of Conscious Capitalism.* Charlottesville, VA: Hampton Roads Publishing.

Applbaum, K. (2004) *The Marketing Era: From Professional Practice to Global Provisioning.* London: Routledge.

Araujo, L. (2007) 'Markets, market-making and marketing', *Marketing Theory* 7(3): 211–26.

Arrow, K.J. (1959) 'Towards a theory of price adjustment', in M. Abramowitz et al. (eds) *The Allocation of Economic Resources: Essays in Honor of Bernard Francis Haley.* Stanford, CA: Stanford University Press.

Bagozzi, R.P. (2005) 'Socializing marketing', *Marketing – Journal of Research and Management* 2: 101–10.

Bartels, R. (1970) *Marketing Theory and Metatheory.* Homewood, IL: Irwin.

Bauer, M.A., Wilkie, J.E.B., Kim, J.K. and Bodenhausen, G.V. (2012) 'Cuing consumerism: situational materialism undermines personal and social well-being', *Psychological Science* 23(5): 517–23.

Becker, G.S. (1968) 'Crime and punishment: an economic approach', *Journal of Political Economy* 76: 169–217.

Becker, G.S. (1976) *The Economic Approach to Human Behavior.* Chicago, IL: University of Chicago Press.

Benett, A. and O'Reilly, A. (2010) *Consumed: Rethinking Business in the Era of Mindful Spending.* Basingstoke: Palgrave Macmillan.

Blackwell, R.D., Engel, J.F. and Kollat, D.J. (1969) *Cases in Consumer Behavior.* Fort Worth, TX: The Dryden Press.

Blackwell, R.D., Miniard, P.W. and Engel, J.F. (2005) *Consumer Behavior,* 10th edn. Boston, MA: South-Western College Publishing.

Block, F. (1990) *Postindustrial Possibilities: A Critique of Economic Discourse.* Berkeley, CA: University of California Press.

Boulding, K.E (ed.) (1984) *The Economics of Human Betterment.* Albany, NY: State University of New York Press.

Brockway, G.P. (2001) *The End of Economic Man: An Introduction to Humanistic Economics.* New York: W.W. Norton.

Callon, M. (ed.) (1998) *The Laws of the Market.* Oxford: Blackwell.

Callon, M., Millo, Y. and Muniesa, F. (eds) (2007) *Market Devices.* London: Wiley-Blackwell.

Canterbery, E.R. (1987) *The Making of Economics,* 3rd edn. Belmont, CA: Wadsworth.

Carrier, J.G. (ed.) (1997) *Meanings of the Market: The Free Market in Western Culture.* Oxford: Berg.

Chamberlin, E.H. (1933) *The Theory of Monopolistic Competition*. Cambridge, MA: Harvard University Press.

Cochoy, F. (1998) 'Another discipline for the market economy: marketing as a performative knowledge and know-how for capitalism', in M. Callon (ed.) *The Laws of the Markets*. Oxford: Blackwell.

Colander, D.C. and Coats, A.W. (eds) (1989) *The Spread of Economic Ideas*. Cambridge: Cambridge University Press.

Commons, J.R. (1924) *The Legal Foundations of Capitalism*. Clifton, NJ: Augustus M. Kelley.

Commons, J.R. (1934) *Institutional Economics*. New York: Macmillan.

Cowen, T. (1998) *In Praise of Commercial Culture*. Cambridge, MA: Harvard University Press.

De Graaf, J., Wann, D. and Naylor, T.H. (2002) *Affluenza: The All-Consuming Epidemic*. San Francisco, CA: Berrett-Koehler.

Diener, E. and Seligman, M. (2004) 'Beyond money: toward an economy of well-being', *Psychological Science in the Public Interest* 5(1): 1–31.

Dixon, D.F (2002) 'Emerging macromarketing concepts: from Socrates to Alfred Marshall', *Journal of Business Research* 55(2): 87–95.

Dore, R. (1983) 'Goodwill and the spirit of market capitalism', *British Journal of Sociology* 34(4): 459–82.

Douglas, E. (1975) *Economics of Marketing*. New York: Harper & Row.

Durkheim, E. (1964 [1893]) *The Division of Labor in Society*, trans. G. Simpson. New York: The Free Press.

Durning, A.T. (1992) *How Much is Enough? The Consumer Society and the Future of the Earth*. New York: W.W. Norton/WorldWatch Institute.

Earle, P.E. (1995) *Microeconomics for Business and Marketing: Lectures, Cases and Worked Essays*. Cheltenham: Edward Elgar.

Eichner, A.S. (ed.) (1983) *Why Economics Is Not Yet a Science*. London: Macmillan Press.

Ekins, P. and Max-Neef, M. (eds) (1992) *Real-Life Economics: Understanding Wealth Creation*. London: Routledge.

Fourcade, M., Ollion, E. and Algan, Y. (2014) 'The superiority of economists', MaxPo Discussion Paper 14/3, Max Planck Sciences Po Centre on Coping with Instability in Market Societies, Paris, November.

Foxall, G.R. (1999) 'The marketing firm', *Journal of Economic Psychology* 20: 207–34.

Francis, J. (2015) 'The rise and fall of debate in economics'. Available at: http://www.joefrancis.info/economics-debate/ (accessed January 2015).

Galbraith, J.K. (1970) *The Affluent Society*, 2nd revised edn. London: Pelican Books.

Galbraith, J.K. and Salinger, N. (1978) *Almost Everyone's Guide to Economics*. London: Andre Deutsch.

Granovetter, M. (1985) 'Economic action and social structure: the problem of embeddedness', *American Journal of Sociology* 91(3): 481–510.

Guillet De Monthoux, P. (1993) *The Moral Philosophy of Management: From Quesnay to Keynes*. Armonk, NY: M.E. Sharpe.

Hahn, F.H. (1970) 'Some adjustment problems', *Econometrica* 38: 1–17.

Hamilton, C. and Denniss, R. (2005) *Affluenza: When Too Much is Never Enough*. Sydney, NSW: Allen & Unwin.

Hayek, F.A. (1978) *New Studies in Philosophy, Politics, Economics and the History of Ideas*. London: Routledge and Kegan Paul.

Heilbroner, R.L. and Thurow, L. (1982) *Economics Explained*. Englewood Cliffs, NJ: Prentice-Hall.

Hicks, J.R. (1946) *Value and Capital*, 2nd edn. London: Macmillan.

Hicks, J.R. (1979) *Causality in Economics*. Oxford: Basil Blackwell.

Hicks, J.R. and Allen, R.G.D. (1934) 'A reconsideration of the theory of value: parts I and II', *Economica* 1: 52–76.

Hirschman, A.O. (1986) *Rival Views of Market Society and Other Recent Essays*. Cambridge, MA: Harvard University Press.

Hodgson, G.M. (1988) *Economics and Institutions: A Manifesto for a Modern Institutional Economics*. Cambridge: Polity Press.

Horkheimer, M. (1974) *Critique of Instrumental Reason*. New York: Seabury.

Hunt, E.K. (2002) *History of Economic Thought: A Critical Perspective*, 2nd edn. Armonk, NY: M.E. Sharpe.

James, O. (2006) *Affluenza*. London: Vermilion/Random House.

James, O. (2007) *The Selfish Capitalist: The Origins of Affluenza*. London: Vermilion/Random House.

Jones, D.G.B. and Monieson, D.D. (1990) 'Early development of the philosophy of marketing thought', *Journal of Marketing* 54: 102–13.

Kaldor, N. (1934) 'The equilibrium of the firm', *Economic Journal* 44: 60–76.

Kaldor, N. (1972) 'The irrelevance of equilibrium economics', *Economic Journal* 82: 1237–55.

Kay, J. (1996) *The Business of Economics*. Oxford: Oxford University Press.

Korten, D. (2015) *Change the Story, Change the Future – A Living Economy for a Living Earth*. San Francisco, CA: Berrett-Koehler.

Koutsoyiannis, A. (1975) *Modern Microeconomics*. London: Macmillan.

Lane, R.E. (1991) *The Market Experience*. New York: Cambridge University Press.

Lane, R.E. (2000) *The Loss of Happiness in Market Democracies*. New Haven, CT: Yale University Press.

Lutz, M.A. and Lux, K. (1979) *The Challenge of Humanistic Economics*. San Francisco, CA: Benjamin Cummings.

Macauley, S. (1963) 'Non-contractual relations in business: a preliminary study', *American Sociological Review* 28(1): 55–67.

McInnes, W. (1964) 'A conceptual approach to marketing', in R. Cox, W. Alderson and S.J. Shapiro (eds) *Theory in Marketing*. Homewood, IL: Irwin.

Magnuson, J. (2008) *Mindful Economics: How the US Economy Works, Why it Matters, and How it Could be Different*. New York: Seven Stories Press.

Mini, P.V. (1974) *Philosophy and Economics*. Gainesville, FL: University Press of Florida.

Myers, D.G. (2000) *The American Paradox: Spiritual Hunger in an Age of Plenty*. New Haven, CT: Yale University Press.

Parsons, T. and Smelser, N. (1956) *Economy and Society: A Study in the Integration of Economic and Social Theory*. London: Routledge & Kegan Paul.

Robinson, J.V. (1933) *The Economics of Imperfect Competition*. London: Macmillan.

Robinson, J.V. (1953) 'Imperfect competition revisited', *Economic Journal* 63: 579–93.

Robinson, J.V. and Eatwell, J.L. (1973) *An Introduction to Modern Economics*. Maidenhead: McGraw-Hill.

Roll, E. (1992) *A History of Economic Thought*, 5th edn. London: Faber & Faber.

Routh, G. (1989) *The Origin of Economic Ideas*, 2nd edn. London: Macmillan.

Sachs, W. (1992) 'The economist's prejudice', in P. Ekins and M. Max-Neef (eds) *Real-Life Economics: Understanding Wealth Creation*. London: Routledge.

Sachs, W. (1999) *Planet Dialectics: Explorations in Environment and Development*. London: Zed Books.

Samuelson, P.A. (1976) *Economics*, 10th edn. New York: McGraw-Hill.

Schumacher, E.F. (1973) *Small is Beautiful: A Study of Economics as if People Mattered*. London: Abacus/Sphere Books.

Schumpeter, J.A. (1954) *History of Economic Analysis*. New York: Oxford University Press.

Schumpeter, J.A. (1991) *The Economics and Sociology of Capitalism*. Princeton, NJ: Princeton University Press.

Schwerin, D.A. (1998) *Conscious Capitalism: Principles for Prosperity*. Oxford: Butterworth-Heinemann.

Shackle, G.L.S. (1973) *An Economic Querist*. Cambridge: Cambridge University Press.

Sheth, J.N., Gardner, D.M. and Garrett, D.E. (1988) *Marketing Theory: Evolution and Evaluation*. Chichester: John Wiley.

Simmel, G. (1955 [1922]) *Conflict and the Web of Group Affiliations*, trans. K.H. Wolff. Glencoe, IL: The Free Press.

Simon, H.A. (1957) *Models of Man*. New York: John Wiley.

Simon, H.A. (1959) 'Theories of decision-making in economics and behavioral sciences', *The American Economic Review* 49: 253–83.

Sisodia, R.S., Wolfe, D.B. and Sheth, J.N. (2007) *Firms of Endearment: How World-Class Companies Profit from Passion and Purpose*. Upper Saddle River, NJ: Prentice-Hall.

Speth, J.G. (2008) *The Bridge at the Edge of the World: Capitalism, the Environment, and Crossing from Crisis to Sustainability*. New Haven, CT: Yale University Press.

Spitzeck, H., Pirson, M., Amann, W., Khan, S. and von Kimakowitz, E. (2009) *Humanism in Business*. New York: Cambridge University Press.

Stanfield, J.R. (1983) 'Institutional analysis: toward progress in economic science', in A.S. Eichner (ed.) *Why Economics Is Not Yet a Science*. London: Macmillan Press.

Stokes, K.M. (1992) *Man and the Biosphere: Toward a Coevolutionary Political Economy*. Armonk, NY: M.E. Sharpe.

Tuck, M. (1976) *How Do We Choose?* London: Methuen.

Varey, R.J. and Pirson, M. (2014) *Humanistic Marketing*. Basingstoke: Palgrave Macmillan.

Williamson, O.E. (1975) *Markets and Hierarchies: Analysis and Anti-Trust Implications, a Study in the Economics of Internal Organization*. New York: The Free Press.

Williamson, O.E. (1985) *The Economic Institutions of Capitalism: Firms, Markets, and History*. Cambridge: Cambridge University Press.

The Psychological Basis of Marketing

Allan J. Kimmel

6

Chapter Topics

Introduction	137
Psychology as a discipline	138
A survey of the psychological foundations of marketing	140
Motivation	140
Perception	143
Decision making	145
Attitudes	149
Persuasion	154
Conclusion	156

Introduction

Whether one considers marketing as a managerial process or as a formalized field of enquiry, it is clear that it is interdisciplinary in nature, spanning a variety of academic fields, including the behavioural and social sciences, communications and economics. These disciplinary links serve to enrich the marketing enterprise, providing it with empirically grounded theories and concepts that lie at the heart of the pluralistic perspective typically employed by marketers to ply their trade. The purpose of this chapter is to focus on the psychological foundations of marketing – a daunting task in light of the breadth of contributions of psychology to the marketing discipline, but one that nonetheless is essential to carry out in order to gain a fuller understanding of what marketing is and how the marketing process functions. Psychology's contributions to marketing are perhaps most evident in the study of consumer behaviour, which serves as the focus of Chapter 12; however, a broader perspective reveals psychology's relevance to each of marketing's various activities, including product design, promotion, pricing and the like.

Psychology as a discipline

Psychology encompasses the scientific study of behaviour and mental processes. Like marketing, the discipline of psychology has strong connections to other fields of enquiry, including philosophy, biology, evolution and the social sciences. It also similarly is comprised of numerous sub-fields, such as: experimental psychology (e.g. the rules governing how people perceive, learn and remember); cognitive psychology (e.g. the mental mechanisms that underlie how people make judgements and decisions); personality psychology (e.g. the measurement, origins and influence of personality differences); social psychology (e.g. how individuals' attitudes, thoughts, emotions and behaviours affect and are affected by other people and the social environment); industrial-organizational psychology (e.g. the factors that influence job motivation and satisfaction); clinical, counselling and community psychology (e.g. how behaviour and mental processes become disordered, and how they can be treated or prevented); and developmental psychology (e.g. changes in thinking, social skills and personality that occur throughout the lifespan). This is but a small sampling of psychology's sub-fields and their corresponding topical areas and issues; in fact, the American Psychological Association formally recognizes 54 specific divisions of the discipline. These areas are dominated by a core set of psychological constructs (see Table 6.1); that is, explanatory concepts that conceptualize intangible elements of the domain studied within a particular science.

Table 6.1 Psychological constructs and some associated marketing areas.

Construct	Marketing areas
Learning	Brand recall, loyalty
Motivation	Consumer needs, choice conflicts
Perception	Product packaging, advertising content
Decision making	Brand selection, consumer involvement, post-purchase evaluation
Attitudes	Customer satisfaction, trust, ad influence
Personality	Consumer segmentation, materialism, addictions

Psychological constructs are essential to fields like psychology because they help explain how and why people think and behave the way they do within their physical and social contexts. For example, learning is a construct that helps explain observable changes in behaviour that come about from experience, as when a consumer develops a loyalty to a particular brand that has proven to have high quality across previous usage situations. The utility of psychological constructs is not limited to the discipline of psychology; as will become evident in this chapter, they are essential to understanding the marketing process. Nonetheless, for a construct to be of any value, it first must meet certain criteria: it must be precisely and unambiguously defined, including specification of its domain and clarification as to its distinctiveness relative to similar other constructs, and it must be capable of being measured (Churchill, 1979). Marketers have adopted many of the measurement and observation techniques developed and honed over the years by psychologists, including a wide range of self-report measurement tools (such as opinion surveys, attitude scales, personality scales), projective techniques (such as the interpretation of ambiguous illustrations) and interview approaches (such as in-depth interviews and personal journals or diaries). Consider, for example, the need for cognition, which falls within the domain of the psychological construct of personality. This trait, which reflects the chronic tendency to engage in purposive thinking and to enjoy problem solving, is measured by a series of statements (e.g. 'I really enjoy a task that involves coming up with solutions to problems') that comprise the need for cognition scale (Cacioppo and Petty, 1982). When employed in advertising research, the scale revealed interesting differences between high and low need for cognition consumers. Compared with low scorers, high need for cognition consumers processed advertising information more thoroughly, had superior recall for brands and brand claims, and relied more heavily on print sources than television for news information. Consistent with elaboration likelihood theory (see 'Persuasion' below), high need for cognition consumers are apt to base their attitudes on message arguments and brand features, whereas lows use peripheral cues such as music and emotional elements to guide their attitudes (Haugtvedt et al., 1992). The insight provided by such measurement approaches can prove invaluable to advertisers in the design of message content and the selection of channels of message delivery.

The application of knowledge derived from systematic research in psychology and other disciplines is crucial to the ongoing evolution of the hybrid field of marketing. For example, psychologist George Katona pioneered the use of survey methodologies in order to assess consumer expectations and attitudes. His work resulted in effective predictors of purchasing behaviour which ultimately were incorporated into the index of consumer sentiment, a leading economic indicator (Friestad, 2001). The applied tradition in psychology also in part can be traced back to the work of social psychologist Kurt Lewin, who, in his often quoted comment that 'there is nothing as practical as a good theory', implied that once we have obtained scientific understanding of some aspect of behaviour, it should be possible to put that knowledge to practical use. During the Second World War, in a series of experiments, Lewin set out to determine the most effective persuasive techniques for convincing women to contribute to the war effort by changing their families' dietary habits. The goal was to influence the women to change their meat consumption patterns to less desirable, but cheaper and still nutritious meats, to buy more milk in order to protect the health of family members, and to safeguard the well-being of their babies by feeding them cod liver oil and orange juice. Lewin compared the effectiveness of two kinds of persuasive appeals by randomly assigning housewives to an experimental condition involving either a lecture or group discussion on the recommended changes. The results of the research revealed that actively discussing ways to achieve good nutrition resulted in greater changes towards healthier eating habits than passively listening to lectures. Lewin explained the findings by suggesting that group processes had come into play to reinforce the desired normative behaviour for those individuals who had participated in the discussions. To some extent, contemporary support groups, such as Alcoholics Anonymous and Weight Watchers, can be seen as part of the legacy of Lewin's wartime research (Brehm and Kassin, 1993).

A survey of the psychological foundations of marketing

It has been suggested that one way of defining marketing is to consider it as psychology applied to business. Although an overly simplistic definition given the evolving complexity and breadth of the marketing discipline, the definition fits perfectly with the key objective of this chapter, which is to describe the various ways that the discipline of marketing is psychological in nature. To satisfy that objective, the remainder of this chapter surveys five essential topical areas that exemplify the ways that psychology provides insight into customer behaviour and can be incorporated within formulations for marketing actions and marketing management decision making. In turn, the following areas are covered: (1) motivation; (2) perception; (3) decision making; (4) attitudes; and (5) persuasion.

Motivation

A good starting point for surveying the psychological underpinnings of marketing is by considering some basic notions related to motivation. Indeed, the essence of marketing, as clarified by the well-known marketing concept, is firmly rooted within the context of motivational needs. The marketing concept presumes that the various aspirations and objectives of marketing practitioners are oriented to beneficial outcomes for all of the stakeholders involved in a marketing exchange. Primarily, marketing is held to play a useful role in helping consumers satisfy their needs and thereby enables the smooth operation of the exchange relationship between consumers and organizations. This is done through the development of needed products and services that are priced so as to give good value to buyers, while providing profit to the product producer, service provider and other intermediaries. Thus, marketers are beholden to identify the physiological and psychological needs that motivate consumers and the means through which those needs can be satisfied through the development and provision of appropriate marketplace offerings.

Derived from the Latin term *movere* ('to move'), motivation is a psychological construct that encompasses a range of processes that energize, direct and sustain goal-directed behaviour.

It is widely understood that consumer behaviour typically is stimulated by an internal defi-ciency that results in an imbalance or disequilibrium attributed to a discrepancy between the present condition and some ideal state. The resulting state of tension tied to the unfilled need gives rise to a drive – an internal psychological force that impels a person to engage in an action designed to satisfy the need. Such behaviour is goal directed, that is, it is not randomly selected, but chosen on the basis of learning (e.g. the outcomes of previous experiences) and cognitive processes (e.g. expectations of future outcomes). Motivated behaviour is directed towards certain end states or outcomes (typically referred to as 'goal objects' or 'incentives') that the individual anticipates will satisfy extant needs, reduce the inner state of tension and thereby restore the system to a state of balance.

Consumers play an active role in selecting their goals, and products and services represent means by which they can satisfy their various needs. Goal objects that attract the behaviour of consumers (so-called 'positively-valent' objects) reflect consumer wants or desires and, in that sense, represent external manifestations of consumer needs. By contrast, undesired goal objects (so-called 'negatively-valent' objects) repel behaviour, as would be the case when a consumer avoids a brand of soap that is thought to cause drying of the skin. A person's needs are strongly interrelated, and, as a result, needs can operate simultaneously on behaviour. An expensive fur coat can satisfy certain practical or utilitarian needs (e.g. to be warm during the winter) as well as more emotional or experiential needs (e.g. the excitement associated with wearing the coat in public) and status needs (e.g. the personal satisfaction that comes from being envied by others). Divergent forces can place consumers in a state of motivation conflict, as when the attracting forces of the expensive fur coat are opposed by the need to maintain one's budget or the desire to protect the rights of endangered animals. In such cases, marketers can assist consumers in overcoming such 'approach-avoidance' conflicts by designing appeals that emphasize the desirable aspects of the product and downplay the negative (e.g. by offer-ing a suitable financing arrangement for the purchase). Many marketing messages are designed specifically to make consumers aware of the needs that can be satisfied through the purchase or use of certain products or services. Thus, an Ericsson advertisement heralded the GH388 cellphone as the one 'made to match the needs of the international traveller' and a Barney's of New York advertisement claimed that the shopper 'will have no difficulty finding anything you need' at the retail clothing store.

It is important to note that both physiological needs (e.g. hunger, thirst, pain avoidance, security, maintenance of body temperature) and psychogenic needs (e.g. achievement, affili-ation, status, approval, power) motivate consumer behaviour. For example, conspicuous con-sumption, a concept that can be traced back to the work of economist Thorstein Veblen (1899) to explain 'the waste of money and/or resources by people to display a higher status than others', is clearly linked to the psychological ego-related needs for status, approval and self-confidence, although it may be influenced in part by extrinsic factors, such as social norms and cultural values. The lavish expenditure of money that is primarily guided by a desire to display one's wealth and success can be seen in the purchase of luxury brand prod-ucts (e.g. a 20,000 euro Patek Philippe watch). This motive can operate at an unconscious level, such that consumers may not be consciously aware of the actual forces that have guided their purchasing behaviour. Projective research techniques are often utilized by marketing researchers to gain insight into the unconscious motives that explain the root causes of unconsciously motivated behaviour (Kassarjian, 1974; Rook, 2006).

Certain needs may become more or less compelling for the consumer as circumstances change. A consumer predilection towards conspicuous consumption is likely to be offset when the satisfaction of certain basic needs is threatened. This was evidenced during the global financial crisis which began in 2008, a period during which consumers grew increasingly responsive to marketers' sales promotions, such as money-off offers. During the fourth quarter of 2008, coupon distribution in the US rose 7.5% and redemptions rose 15% relative to the preceding year, and online searches reflected consumers' concerns about their economic well-being. Searches of value-related words such as 'coupons' rose 161% to 19.9 million compared with 2007 and 'discount' rose 26% to 7.9 million (Howard, 2009). This shift from higher- to lower-order needs is consistent with early conceptualizations of human motivation, such as Maslow's (1943) hierarchy of needs and Herzberg's (1959) motivation-hygiene theory. The fact that the economic recession also reportedly spawned a significant increase in the volume of candy consumed (Haughney, 2009) suggests that transformational needs, as expressed by a desire for sensory gratification, may also influence consumers at the same time they strive to overcome problems or satisfy basic needs (Rossiter et al., 1991).

A good example of how psychological principles of motivation conceptually clarify the effectiveness of promotional marketing messages is illustrated by Rogers' (1983) protection motivation theory, which illuminates the circumstances by which fear appeals have persuasive effects on audiences. In this view, the effectiveness of messages that demonstrate the negative aspects or physical dangers associated with a particular behaviour (e.g. smoking cigarettes, drug abuse, spousal abuse) or improper product usage (e.g. drinking and driving) is less a matter of the degree of fear the messages induce, but rather the extent to which they motivate people to protect themselves from the negative consequences and take steps to deal with the danger. Accordingly, a fear appeal must contain four components if it is to succeed in changing attitudes or behaviour; it must: (1) clearly specify how unpleasant the consequences will be if the recommended actions are not followed; (2) communicate the likelihood or probability of those negative consequences; (3) indicate how the negative consequences can be avoided if the recommendations are followed; and (4) explain that the targeted individuals are capable of performing the recommended action. According to their ordered protection motivation model, Arthur and Quester (2004) propose that the first two components, severity of threat and probability of occurrence, comprise a threat appraisal dimension (i.e. they arouse fear), whereas the last two components, response efficacy and self-efficacy, comprise a coping appraisal dimension (i.e. they compel a person to behaviour). Evidence suggests that both dimensions must be considered when creating fear appeals (e.g. Eppright et al., 1994).

Other recent marketing applications of motivational concepts can be seen in research on consumer self-control (Vohs and Faber, 2007), response to marketing scams (Langenderfer and Shimp, 2001), dietary behaviours (Bock et al., 1998) and product usage and abandonment (Wansink et al., 2000).

Perception

Perception refers to a set of psychological processes that enable individuals to experience and make sense of their surrounding environment through the active cognitive processes of selection, organization and interpretation. Unprocessed sensory information received via the sensory systems that enable vision, hearing, taste and touch is rendered meaningful on the basis of innate human abilities, prior learning and past experiences. For example, seeing a red can on the table might be perceived as a Coca-Cola soft drink, without any apparent indication of the brand name. Marketers must be attentive to perceptual principles because it is the consumer's subjective experience or personal construction of objective reality that determines his or her reactions to marketing phenomena. Many difficult lessons have been learned when marketing decisions have been made without a concern for consumer perception, including new product launches, promotional campaigns and pricing considerations. For example, Starbucks was forced to pull from stores its 'Collapse into Cool' promotional posters for the popular coffee chain's new Tazo citrus drinks when consumers complained that the poster's imagery (flying insects surrounding two tall iced beverages) was too reminiscent of the September 11 attacks on New York's Twin Towers. Although the ad had nothing to do with the event, the combination of the term 'collapse' and the unfortunate choice of illustration was perceived by some consumers as insensitive on the part of the company and a malicious attempt to capitalize on the misfortunes of others (Roeper, 2002).

The perceptual process can be understood as comprised of a chain of events that begins with sensorial input (i.e. the immediate response of our sensory receptors to basic stimuli like light, sound and texture) and ends with the conscious recognition (i.e. a meaningful perception) of an external event (e.g. 'Aha, there's a Coke on the table'). In other words, perception is not a single, discrete experience, but rather the conscious determination of a sequence of non-conscious processes. This point helps us understand why certain stimuli may not be noticed by individuals even after exposure to the stimulus has occurred (e.g. 'I didn't even see the can on the table because I was concentrating on the song that was playing in the background'). As the initial stage of the perceptual process, exposure tends to be influenced by stimulus factors (colour, size, position, novelty, contrast) and personal factors (past experience, expectations, motives, needs, mood). Thus, some stimuli are more likely to capture our attention (e.g. those that are unexpected, unique, or in direct contrast to their surroundings) than are others (non-changing, repetitive and similar to background stimuli), because the former are more utile in overcoming the tendency for *sensory adaptation*, the process whereby responsiveness to an unchanging stimulus decreases over time. Perceptual vigilance describes the tendency for people to have a heightened sensitivity to stimuli that are capable of satisfying their motives (e.g. 'I noticed that Coke right away because I was so thirsty'), whereas perceptual defence pertains to the tendency for people to screen out stimuli that are too threatening, even though exposure may have occurred (e.g. 'I probably didn't see the soft drink because I'm trying to stick to my diet').

The relevance of these perceptual notions to marketing should be apparent. Marketers and advertisers clearly want consumers to perceive their offerings and messages (i.e. to select them), but must counter consumers' tendency to screen out marketing-related stimuli, whether it be an advertisement in a magazine, a package on a store shelf, an email that announces a promotion, and so on. The problem of capturing consumer attention has increased in recent decades as the number of offerings and marketing communications to promote those offerings have steadily proliferated. Indeed, the excessive bombardment of promotional messages has led to *advertising clutter*, the 'proliferation of advertising that produces excessive competition for viewer attention, to the point that individual messages lose impact and viewers abandon the ads (via fast-forwarding, changing channels, quitting viewing, etc.)' (Lowrey et al., 2005: 121). Beyond the most obvious case of television advertising, the problem of clutter also characterizes consumers' rising aversion to other marketing formats, including outdoor signage, email spamming, internet pop-up messages and SMS messaging. Clutter is likely to impede message recall, especially when one considers that a majority of consumers engage in multitasking, such as using their PC or mobile phone while watching television (Greenspan, 2004).

The ability for any one promotional message to break through marketing clutter in order to capture attention, arouse interest and have its intended effects has become exceedingly difficult. Marketing research must be carried out to determine the appropriate strategies for capturing attention and enhancing recall; for example, by developing messages that are at odds with commonly held beliefs, including a lot of white space or vivid colours in print ads, incorporating humour or allusions to sexuality in the message content, presenting incomplete stimuli that stimulate audience involvement in the message, and so on. In retail settings, where the number of stock-keeping units (SKUs) continues to rise – the average number of products carried by a typical supermarket has more than tripled since 1980, from 15,000 to 50,000 (Nestle, 2002) – effective product packaging and display are required in order to be noticed and selected by shoppers. As a result, many consumer goods companies now view product packages not only as containers for shipping and storing products, but as three-dimensional ads for grabbing shopper attention (Story, 2007). This is seen in Pepsi's striking bottle designs for its Mountain Dew soft drink, Evian's luxurious glass container for a line of bottled water, rounded Kleenex packages bearing artistic imagery and NXT's men's products bearing light-emitting diodes that light up the product every 15 seconds to illuminate air bubbles suspended in the clear gel.

Beyond considerations related to stimulus exposure and attention, psychological principles of perception also explain how stimuli are organized and interpreted. The groundbreaking work on perceptual organization was carried out by a group of German psychologists during the early 20th century, who suggested that people tend to organize their perceptions according to certain innate tendencies, such as closure (the tendency to derive meaning from incomplete stimuli by forming a complete perception), figure/ground (the tendency to designate part of the perceptual field as a figure and the rest as background) and grouping (the tendency to group stimuli automatically according to proximity, similarity, or continuity so they form a unified and meaningful impression) (Sternberg, 2008). These principles help explain how the overall unity of perception or 'Gestalt' (i.e. organized form or total configuration) is greater than or fundamentally different from the sum of its individual sensations. Applications of Gestalt principles are apparent in a variety of marketing activities, such as the development of promotional messages (e.g. advertisements that are purposely left incomplete or interrupted before their expected finish in order to involve the perceiver more actively in the message itself and enhance recall), the presentation of goods in the retail setting (e.g. private label brands packaged to look like market leaders and shelved next to them in order to appear to have comparable quality) and pricing (e.g. partitioning the base price and the surcharge so that consumers perceive the total price as cheaper than if the all-inclusive price had been given).

Another basic notion of perception that underlies marketing practice has to do with the fact that there are limits in human sensory reception. The point at which individuals are incapable of detecting weak stimulation is referred to as the absolute threshold, whereas the differential threshold demarcates the point below which people are incapable of noticing changes in a stimulus or differences between similar stimuli (the so-called 'just noticeable difference' or JND). Research has shown that the JND for two stimuli is not equal to an absolute amount, but an amount that is relative to the intensity of the initial stimulus, a proportionate relationship that is described by Weber's law. Briefly, Weber's law suggests that the greater the initial intensity of a stimulus, the more the stimulus must be changed in order to be detected by the perceiver. This relationship is utilized by marketers in determination of changes that are not intended to exceed the JND and be noticed (e.g. decreases in product size or reductions in product quality attributed to the rising costs of ingredients) or changes that are intended to exceed the JND while keeping costs to a necessary minimum (e.g. product improvements, price reductions).

Other recent applications of perception in marketing are apparent in ongoing research on eating behaviour. In addition to identifying the motivational forces that spark a rise in obesity levels, marketing researchers are actively engaged in studies intended to illuminate how diet is influenced by perceptual factors. Research has shown that low-fat labels increase snack-food consumption for normal-weight and overweight consumers, who are apt to misperceive 'low-fat' foods as lower in calories and to overestimate appropriate serving size (Wansink and Chandon, 2006). Consumers also tend to underestimate the caloric content of main dishes, leading them to choose higher calorie side dishes, drinks or desserts (Chandon and Wansink, 2007).

For a discussion of the critical role of perception in the marketing of brands, see Batey (2008).

Decision making

A fundamental focus of psychological research and theory is that of human decision making; specifically, the cognitive processes by which people make judgements. These processes provide significant insight into our understanding of human consumption, which can be conceptualized as a sequence of decision-making stages, ranging from the decision to consume (whether to spend or save, timing of the consumption, amount of goods to consume), product category spending (the category of goods or services to consume), brand selection (choice of benefits, role of reputation and status, loyalty and preference, brand image and positioning), buying behaviour (how and where to shop and pay, whether to comparison shop, frequency of shopping and product acquisition), to product usage and disposition (nature of product usage, how to dispose of products, environmental concerns).

Decision making typically begins with problem recognition; that is, the individual perceives a discrepancy between a current state of his or her condition and a desired state. As suggested by motivation theory, the imbalance arouses tension that in turn provokes behaviour. This initial decision-making stage may be attributed to changes in one's actual condition (e.g. depletion of stock, dissatisfaction with current products, changes in one's finances) or ideal state (e.g. new need or want circumstances, recent purchases that create a need for other product add-ons, new product opportunities). In most cases, the imbalance between these states will be perceived as a problem that must be eliminated (such as the depletion of breakfast cereal that requires replenishment), although in other cases, a perceived opportunity will stimulate action (as when an increase in one's finances motivates one to spend).

Problem recognition is likely to be followed by information search, such that one considers the various alternatives available for solving or eliminating the problem. Information search may be comprised of two steps, an internal search, which involves scanning one's memory for previous experiences that recall the current situation, and an external search, which involves the search for relevant information from a variety of alternative sources, including social relations (e.g. friends, family members), public sources (e.g. news channels, independent product-rating organizations, online forums) and marketing-dominated sources (e.g. advertising, company websites, salespersons). The degree to which such searches are carried out by the individual will depend upon that person's involvement in the problem or the focal concern of the problem. Psychologists conceptualize *involvement* as a construct related to self-relevance; specifically, the term has been defined as 'a motivational state induced by an association between an activated attitude and some aspect of the self-concept' (Johnson and Eagly, 1989: 293). Depending upon the psychological theory, this definition has varying interpretations, suggesting three types of involvement (Verplanken and Svenson, 1997). *Ego-relevant involvement*, derived from social judgement theory (e.g. Sherif and Hovland, 1961), refers to the psychological state resulting from the activation of enduring attitudes (i.e. evaluative reactions to some stimulus or situation; see 'Attitudes' below) that define a person. According to this perspective, attitudes are comprised of so-called 'latitudes of acceptance' (a range of positions one finds acceptable), 'latitudes of rejection' (a range of positions one finds unacceptable) and 'non-commitment' (positions towards which one is indifferent). Because high ego involvement attitudes are less easily influenced, high ego involvement tends to enhance latitudes of rejection, thereby inhibiting persuasion (Johnson and Eagly, 1989).

Impression-relevant involvement, a concept which stems from dissonance theory, refers to self-presentation motives that are activated in situations in which someone expresses an attitude. This type of involvement pertains to the concern one has with defending a position, and thus increases when an individual believes that the expression of an attitude will have an impact on the impression others form of him or her (Leippe and Elkin, 1987; Zimbardo, 1960). Finally, *outcome-relevant involvement*, which stems from dual-process persuasion theory (Chaiken, 1987; Petty and Cacioppo, 1986), has to do with the degree to which situations or issues are linked to the attainment of desirable outcomes. This type of involvement is assumed to be associated with message-relevant thinking, such that high involvement in a message is likely to result in careful scrutiny of the merits of the arguments that comprise a persuasive message. By contrast, argument strength is less likely to influence the attitudes of persons with low involvement in the message (see 'Persuasion' below).

Aspects of each of these psychological conceptualizations of involvement are reflected in marketing applications of the involvement construct and its role in the information search and evaluation of alternative stages of consumer decision making (Andrews et al., 1990). From a marketing perspective, *consumer involvement* has been defined as the motivation to process product-related information (Solomon, 2008). Implicit in this definition is the understanding that involvement relates to the importance or relevance of a product/service or its purchase and the perceived risks involved in the purchase, elements that maintain the self-relevance notion rooted in the psychological conceptualizations.

During the information search stage of the decision-making process, consumers are likely to be motivated to engage in an extensive external search to the extent that a purchase is high in relevance and perceived risks (i.e. perceived negative consequences, which may be functional, financial, social or personal in nature). Products that evoke high involvement processes tend to elicit high levels of perceived risk, given that they are infrequently purchased, higher in cost, complex, personally relevant and publicly visible to others (e.g. a new car, home, computer, expensive suit). The high involvement decision-making process involves extensive problem solving; that is, considerable time and effort are devoted to an external search for information and the subsequent evaluation of alternatives. The abundant information, gathered from a wide array of external sources, is likely to be applied to an evaluation of alternatives through a compensatory approach, which implies that an offer or brand will be selected through a determination of the preponderance of desired product attributes (i.e. characteristics or features that come to mind when considering a product category), weighted according to personal preference (the so-called 'weighted-additive rule'). Because the decision is based on a careful, rational scrutiny and comparison of all the facts, an alternative may be selected even though it has certain weaknesses or drawbacks, so long as they are compensated by important, personally relevant strengths. For example, after careful evaluation, a new car buyer may opt for the Toyota Camry, despite its high cost (a key drawback), because its higher ratings on specific features (e.g. performance, safety, comfort) result in an overall evaluation that surpasses that of the considered alternatives. Further, preferences are likely to be shaped during the analysis of alternatives, such that a favourable attitude towards one alternative will precede its selection (i.e. preference precedes trial).

By contrast, products that evoke low involvement processes are associated with low levels of perceived risks – they are frequently purchased, inexpensive and low in personal relevance (e.g. household cleaning products, soft drinks, candy). Such purchase situations are unlikely to motivate the consumer to devote much time or effort to the information search; rather, the problem-solving approach utilized is often limited to a minimal external search or internal search of stored memories pertaining to the various alternatives. For example, when choosing from among the soft drink beverages in a supermarket, a consumer may select Pepsi Max as a result of a point of purchase display that stimulates recall of the slogan 'Max your Life', which had been stored in memory during exposure to ads associated with the launch of the brand.

Because the consumer lacks the motivation to engage in extensive information search for such a low involvement product, a distinct preference is unlikely to be developed until after the choice is made and the product is consumed.

Consumers are apt to apply non-compensatory decision-making rules or other heuristics when evaluating low involvement alternatives; in essence, these are approaches that provide shortcuts for a relatively effortless and speedy decision. One example of a non-compensatory strategy, 'satisficing', involves the selection of the first adequate option, without the consumer exploring or giving consideration to the entire set of options. A similar strategy is to apply the lexicographic rule, which consists of selecting an alternative among those to be considered that receives the highest evaluation on the most important or salient attribute; in the case that a choice is not clear, the remaining brands are compared on the second most important attribute, and so on until one alternative remains. With such approaches, alternatives that excel on other features will not be selected; that is, a tradeoff of the benefits of some attributes against the deficits of others will not occur. Satisficing and the lexicographic rule represent examples of *heuristics*, which are simple rules of thumb, educated guesses, or intuitive judgements that simplify the decision-making process, leading to outcomes that often result in satisfactory, albeit sub-optimal, outcomes. In the marketing context, consumers may approach complex choices by simply concluding that the most expensive brand has the highest quality, or simply select a brand which offers the most extra features because it is thought that one will probably wish to have those features later. The nature of heuristics and their potential pitfalls (see Table 6.2) have been experimentally studied and elaborated on by cognitive psychologists Daniel Kahneman and Amos Tversky (Kahneman and Tversky, 2000; Kahneman et al., 1982).

Table 6.2 Examples of heuristic biases and marketing examples.

Bias	Description	Marketing example
Affect heuristic	Hastily judging objects or people by an immediate feeling of 'goodness' or 'badness'	Overly trusting a friendly seller; exaggerating the performance quality of a product due to its external appeal (e.g. a freshly painted used car)
Availability heuristic	Salient memories override normative reasoning	A consumer rejects all Sony products because of an early bad experience with one cheap Sony product
Confirmation bias	The tendency to seek out opinions and facts that support one's own beliefs and hypotheses	Tendency to take into account product reviews that laud an item you want to purchase, while ignoring negative reviews
False consensus effect	Inclination to assume that one's beliefs are more widely held than they actually are	Assuming that others will be satisfied with the same brands and service providers that you prefer
Gambler's fallacy	Pervasive false beliefs about the nature of random sequences	Lottery players who play the same numbers every time, assuming the number is 'due' to win
Planning fallacy	People consistently underestimate the amount of time and effort it will take for them to accomplish a given task	A consumer waits until the last minute to shop for presents; people underestimating the time and effort required to assemble a newly purchased item
Representativeness heuristic	The tendency to blindly classify objects based on surface similarity; 'like goes with like'	Assuming that the quality of a cheaper brand is equal to that of a brand leader due to similar packaging

Adapted from: Anissimov (2004). Reprinted with kind permission.

Although beyond the scope of the present chapter, it should be noted that psychologists have identified a number of additional factors that are likely to influence decision making, including personality (e.g. some consumers are more likely to seek variety than others, or are more receptive to new and innovative options), lifestyles and values (e.g. consumption decisions are influenced by one's personal priorities and characteristic way of living), learning (e.g. consumers are likely to be influenced by previous decisions and experiences), social influences (e.g. word-of-mouth recommendations from friends can have a significant influence on a person's choices) and situational forces (e.g. store atmospherics can enhance the shopping experience and influence choices). Finally, psychological insight into the decision-making process has been applied by marketers in the design of advertising and other types of promotions (see Mehta, 1994; Rossiter et al., 1991).

Attitudes

The topic of attitudes has been the focus of an enormous amount of research attention in psychology, although interest in the construct dates back to the turn of the 20th century (Kraus, 1995; Rajecki, 1990). One reason for the intense scrutiny of attitudes has to do with their pervasiveness in everyday life. Any time people make evaluations of something in their social world, or react positively or negatively to the things they encounter, in essence, they are revealing their attitudes. Thus, whenever marketers or researchers ask consumers what they think or how they feel about something in the marketplace – a product, brand, price, service, store, advertisement and so on – their effort is oriented towards the assessment of attitudes. A common assumption is that attitudes influence how people react in a behavioural sense, that is, that attitudes precede and influence behaviour. Although once the subject of contentious debate, the causal link between attitudes and behaviour in certain specified circumstances (assuming appropriate measurement approaches are utilized) is indisputable (Kraus, 1995). These points help us understand why the attitudes of the various stakeholders in the marketing process are so compelling to marketers, and why the measurement of attitudes is considered so important to researchers. If accurate measures of consumer attitudes can be obtained, then it should be possible to predict behaviour with a certain degree of accuracy.

A common view of the attitude construct is that it represents a person's tendency to respond favourably or unfavourably to the object of the attitude, which may be a concrete entity (such as a product), something more abstract (such as quality of service), other persons, or ideas. According to Eagly and Chaiken (1998: 269), *attitude* is defined as 'a psychological tendency that is expressed by evaluating an entity with a certain degree of favor or disfavor'. One view of the attitude construct conceptualizes it as a relatively enduring organization of three interrelated psychological dimensions: (1) cognitive, which is comprised of beliefs about the attitude object; (2) affective, which consists of feelings towards the object; and (3) conative, which refers to intentions leading to behaving in a certain way towards the object. This so-called tricomponent theory emphasizes the ABC of attitudes (affect, behaviour and cognition) (Rajecki, 1990).

It has long been held that attitudes are capable of serving four useful functions for the individual: (1) utilitarian (i.e. attitudes guide behaviour in order to maximize rewards and minimize punishments administered by others; (2) ego-defensive (i.e. attitudes serve as a defence mechanism that can protect the individual from personally threatening realities); (3) knowledge (i.e. attitudes provide order and structure to one's social world); and (4) value-expressive (i.e. attitudes assist the individual in expressing his or her values to others) (Katz, 1960; McGuire, 1969). Each of these functions can readily be applied to understand various aspects of consumer behaviour, including brand preferences, customer loyalty and reactions to promotional efforts (Solomon, 2008). A straightforward example of the utilitarian function is evident in situations in which consumers develop positive attitudes towards products that bring pleasure and negative attitudes towards products that make them feel bad. Advertisements are often designed to express the utilitarian benefits that can be accrued from the consumption of a product or brand (e.g. Diet Coke, 'Just for the Taste of It').

The power of attitudes in the marketing sphere is especially apparent in the context of customer loyalty to a brand. Brand loyalty is conceptualized as a pattern of repeat product purchasing, accompanied by an underlying positive attitude towards the brand. This suggests that there are two key components that comprise loyalty, one of which is behavioural (the purchasing support that comes from buying a particular brand repeatedly) and the other of which is attitudinal (brand commitment attributed to a strong positive attitude or liking for the brand). In what Knox and Walker (2001) deem the 'brand loyalty matrix', considering both of these components together as either high or low suggests different kinds of brand consumers (see Figure 6.1). When both commitment and purchasing support are low for a brand, consumers fall into the 'switchers' category; that is, they show no loyalty towards any one brand but rather switch from brand to brand, assuming they are all essentially alike and the one selected should be that which offers the most savings. 'Habituals' are high on purchasing support, but low on commitment. Such consumers regularly purchase the same brand repeatedly, not out of any true loyalty towards the brand, but more out of habit (or so-called *inertia*, i.e. they lack the motivation to put forth the effort to evaluate and compare specific brands). 'Variety seekers' tend to have a strong brand preference (i.e. high commitment), but like to play the field and thus show low purchasing support. Such consumers are apt to try out alternative brands, even though they have a preferred brand that they ultimately will return to, because they like to experiment, especially for different use situations (e.g. buying an imported brand to share with guests during a party).

'Loyals' are those consumers who score high on both purchasing support and commitment. These are persons who are truly committed to a brand, take pride in using it, recommend it to others, and view the brand as important to their self-concept. The commitment to the brand is likely to be reflective of an underlying attitude that serves the utilitarian function (i.e. the consumer has a strong liking for the brand because it is viewed as highest in quality and therefore is rewarding) as well as the value-expressive function (i.e. true brand loyals define themselves, in part, through their commitment to the brand and can project this sense of self to others through an association with the brand). Personality psychologists suggest that the *self-concept*, defined as one's perceptions of or feelings about oneself, can be extended or

		Brand Commitment	
		High	Low
Brand Support	High	**LOYALS** Active decision making, based on product features and quality High perceived risk in changing Small portfolios	**HABITUALS** Passive decision making based on simplification Will readily change if first brand is unavailable Small portfolios
	Low	**VARIETY SEEKERS** Multi-brand buying Active search based on quality Large portfolios Seek variety for own sake or alternative use occasions	**SWITCHERS** Sensitive to price and promotion Large and varied portfolios Low perceived risk in changing

Figure 6.1   Brand loyalty matrix and characteristics of loyalty types.

Source: Knox and Walker (2001) .

modified by the possessions that one owns and uses. In essence, consumers can create them-selves and allow themselves to be created by the products, services and experiences they consume, and this is especially likely to be the case for brand loyals, some of whom have such admiration for a brand that they will tattoo themselves with the brand logo. Thus, some per-sons may define their rebellious and free-spirited self-concept by owning a Harley-Davidson motorcycle, others exhibit their conscientious and caring nature by purchasing Body Shop products, and others demonstrate their environmental sensitivities by driving a Toyota Prius (Maynard, 2007).

Consistent with the increasing difficulties in reaching consumers through traditional media channels and the growing trend towards consumer-to-consumer influence via social network-ing, blogging, brand communities and other forms of social connectedness, marketing strate-gists have begun to seek out new approaches for engaging customers and converting their loyalty into advocacy. Brand advocates are consumers who appreciate a product or brand so much that they are willing to serve as ambassadors for the offering, enthusiastically recom-mending it to others. One approach is simply to offer consumers a monetary incentive for each brand referral that leads to a purchase (Ryu and Feick, 2007), a strategy that was utilized by Procter & Gamble during the successful launch of Whitestrips, a leading brand of teeth whiten-ing strips. Another approach is the icecard process, which enables brand adorers (i.e. current buyers especially satisfied with the brand and who have a strong connection and loyalty to it) to order free sets of branded contact cards ('icecards') featuring brand artwork on one side and their own personal details on the other. Hugely popular among young brand loyals, research has revealed that a majority of cards (78%) are distributed to friends and acquaintances, and in 65% of the cases, distribution triggers a brand conversation (Rusticus, 2006). Such approaches can be seen as a form of push marketing in which companies encourage customers with favourable attitudes towards certain offerings to spread the word to others; that is, in each case, the goal is to convert attitudes into behaviours above and beyond a purchase.

Efforts to convert brand loyals into advocates inevitably leads us back to a consideration of the extent to which behaviours can be accurately predicted from measurements of attitudes. In efforts to assess the causal link between attitudes and behaviour, consumer researchers have utilized the self-report research approach pioneered by such psychologists as Louis Thurstone (1928) and Rensis Likert (1932). Measures are obtained by having people describe their own behaviour or state of mind through the use of direct interviews, questionnaires, diaries and the like. Researchers have found that attitudes are good predictors of behaviour when the following conditions are met: (a) there is a correspondence between the attitude and behavioural measures (i.e. specific attitudes predict specific behaviours); (b) a correspondence exists between attitudinal and behavioural objects, such that the attitude target (i.e. the object of the attitude) matches the behavioural target (i.e. the object towards which behaviour is directed) and the attitude action (i.e. what one would like to do with the object) matches the behavioural action (i.e. the activity that comprises the behaviour); (c) measures of attitudes and behaviours are obtained from the same people; and (d) other factors that influence the attitude–behaviour relationship are considered (e.g. situational variables, other competing attitudes, attitude strength and attitude accessibility) (see Fazio, 1986; Kraus, 1995).

Several of these insights into the attitude–behaviour relationship were taken into account in the development of the behavioural intentions model by social psychologists Fishbein and Ajzen (Ajzen and Fishbein, 1980; Fishbein and Ajzen, 1975). Consistent with their theory of reasoned action (now revised as the theory of planned behaviour), they contend that behaviour can most accurately be predicted from a consideration of an individual's *intention* to perform or not perform the behaviour, where intention is defined as the subjective estimate of the probability that one will behave in a certain way towards an attitude object. According to Ajzen's revised model (see Figure 6.2), intention is shaped by one's attitude towards the behaviour (i.e. beliefs about the anticipated consequences of the behaviour under consideration and one's evaluations of those consequences) and by subjective norms (i.e. the extent to which one's behaviour is influenced by beliefs about what others prefer and one's motivation to comply with their wishes). The relative importance of these two sets of intention-influencing factors will determine the nature of a person's intention, assuming the person holds a sufficient degree of perceived control over performing the behaviour, and intention should serve as an efficient guide as to how likely a person is to perform or not perform the behaviour.

As an example applied to the marketing context, consider the case of a young student who has been saving to purchase her first car. If we wanted to predict the likelihood of her purchasing a sports car that aroused her interest at a local dealership, we might first try to gauge her attitude towards purchasing it. Through appropriate questioning – Fishbein and Ajzen utilized written questionnaires with closed-ended rating scales for this purpose – we might learn that,

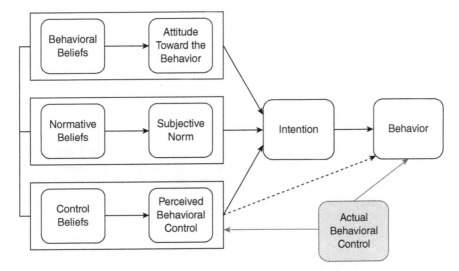

Figure 6.2 Behavioural intentions model based on theory of planned behaviour/reasoned action.

Source: Reprinted from Ajzen (1991). Copyright 1991, with permission from Elsevier.

for the most part, she believes the purchase will have positive consequences (e.g. the car will impress others, she will feel good about herself by driving such a cool car, parking will be easier with a small car, the car will require few repairs), albeit with a couple of potential negative outcomes as well (e.g. she may have to borrow a small sum of money from her parents to make the purchase, car parts may be difficult to locate). Overall, however, the preponderance of positive outcomes is likely to result in a strong positive attitude towards purchasing the sports car. In terms of subjective norms, the story might be quite different. When considering the student's perceptions about the beliefs of important others, we may learn that, overall, the people she cares about do not think the purchase is a good idea (e.g. her parents think the sports car is too extravagant and unsafe, her boyfriend thinks the car is too expensive and he would be a bit jealous). On the other hand, she believes the dealer thinks the sports car was 'made for her' and that she would be unwise to forego such a great deal. Because the seller's reactions are less important to the student than those of her parents and boyfriend, it is likely that a strong negative subjective norm will be working against her intention to purchase the sports car. Finally, our prediction must take into account the student's beliefs about the presence of factors that may facilitate or impede her purchase (e.g. a friend knows the dealer and may be able to encourage him to offer an attractive financing arrangement). If the balance of these three sets of forces – attitude towards the behaviour, subjective norms and perceived control – results in a relatively high intention to buy the car, it is likely that we will be correct in predicting that she will buy it, assuming the measures are obtained within a reasonably close temporal proximity to when the behaviour is likely to occur.

The behavioural intentions model is an example of a psychological framework that has been borrowed and applied by researchers and practitioners in a variety of other disciplines, and marketing is no exception. The model has successfully predicted purchases for a wide variety of product and service categories (e.g. toothpastes, automobiles, laundry detergents, clothing, medical therapies, weight control drugs) and other consumption activities (e.g. dieting, exercising, use of money-saving coupons, donating blood) (see Ajzen, 2008; Sheppard et al., 1988).

Persuasion

Another reason that researchers and practitioners have devoted such formidable attention to the attitude construct has to do with the interest in attitude change, commonly referred to as 'persuasion'. Attitude change is related to the assumption that attitudes and behaviour are causally linked; in short, if attitudes influence behaviour, then it should be possible to have an impact on behaviour by first changing the attitudes that give rise to the behaviour. The ability to change or somehow influence consumer preferences, their likes and dislikes, and their loyalties to companies or brands is of fundamental interest to marketers. For example, if a competitor's brand is preferred over that offered by another company, resulting in higher market share for the former, then the latter company could attempt to modify how customers feel about the respective brands in order to have an impact on their buying behaviour. The means by which such attitude change can be accomplished have been the focus of an enormous amount of research over the years by social psychologists and communication researchers (Gilbert et al., 1998; Hovland et al., 1953). One of the pioneers in persuasion research, social psychologist Carl I. Hovland, borrowed as the guiding focus for this research the didactic statement attributed to communication theorist Harold Laswell, 'who says what to whom with what effect'. Each element of the statement has served as the focus of research programmes since the Second World War, the results of which have been utilized by marketers in the design of marketing messages (e.g. one-sided vs two-sided messages; order of arguments), determination of message source (e.g. celebrity endorsements; salesperson characteristics), audience variables (e.g. utilized in segmentation and targeting considerations), development of social marketing programmes (e.g. safe driving campaigns), among a broad array of other applications.

In one widely applied approach for understanding and implementing persuasive interventions, social psychologists Petty and Cacioppo (1986) incorporated notions related to involvement theory in the development of their elaboration likelihood model (ELM). In their view, there are two possible paths or 'routes' to persuasion, a central route and a peripheral route. The route taken depends on one's motivation and ability to process information presented in the message; that is, to think about and carefully scrutinize arguments in the persuasive communication. When the central route is followed, the receiver is thought to be very active and involved, as in situations where persuasive messages deal with issues that are important and personally relevant. In contrast, the peripheral path is likely to be taken when messages deal with issues that are uninvolving or unimportant for the recipient.

In order to better distinguish between the two explanations for how attitude change can be effected, imagine the case in which you are actively shopping for a new car. Because a new car purchase is something very important to you – that is, it is high in risk, an expensive purchase, and a choice that entails complex consideration – your head will be spinning with questions as you contemplate the arguments being presented to you by a salesperson who is attempting to convince you to purchase a car that you had expressed interest in. Are you better off with an earlier offer? Will you be able to keep up with the payments? Is this really the right car for you? In other words, when confronted with a personally significant message, we do more than simply listen for the sake of acquiring information, we think about the message, its arguments and their implications. This process is what Petty and Cacioppo refer to as 'high elaboration', which consists of evaluating the strength or rationality of a persuasive message, considering whether the message contents agree or disagree with one's current belief system, and weighing the personal implications of the message points and arguments.

Now imagine that you are not interested at all in buying a car. However, while in the cinema awaiting the start of a movie, a 30-second advertisement for a new Chevrolet car model is shown that captures your attention. It begins by showing the popular singer Bruce Springsteen and his band performing the song 'Born in the USA'. The music continues as the Chevrolet appears, transporting an attractive young couple through the idyllic landscape of the American West. Copy text describing various features of the car is eventually superimposed on this scene, and the advertisement ends with the car eventually disappearing over the horizon. Chances are, because of your lack of involvement in a car purchase and your lack of interest in cars in general, you paid little attention to the message arguments (i.e. the car's features), and no doubt would be unable to recall them even immediately after the ad was aired. Because your motivation was low to process the brief message, message elaboration did not occur; rather, your attention was placed on so-called 'peripheral (or persuasion) cues' – features of the communication that were incidental to message content, such as characteristics of the message source (Bruce Springsteen) and the style or form of the message (the music and compelling images, the attractive couple inside the car).

Attitude change might be accomplished in both of the scenarios described above, but in different ways. At the car dealership, the quality and strength of the message arguments presented by the salesperson would determine the ability of his or her communication to influence your attitudes towards the car being considered. This is because when people are motivated to consider a message carefully, their reaction to it depends on its content. If the arguments are strong and they stimulate favourable evaluation, the message will be persuasive. In the second case, you may leave the cinema with a more favourable attitude towards the Chevrolet depicted in the ad, but for reasons unrelated to message arguments. When you think of the car, it might remind you of Bruce Springsteen, or the song, or of images of the American West, and those thoughts may enhance your feelings about the product.

The ELM model helps to clarify some of the research findings accrued through experimental research on persuasion. For example, it has been found that strong arguments result in more post-communication attitude change than weak arguments, but mostly for research participants who are highly involved in the communication. On the other hand, a message delivered by an expert source (e.g. an endorsement of a new medication by a noted doctor) results in more post-communication attitude change, but mostly for research participants who are not very involved in the message. In the first case, message strength had an impact on highly involved persons who followed the central route to persuasion, whereas in the second case, a characteristic of the source (degree of expertise) had an impact on low involved persons who followed a peripheral course to persuasion (White and Harkins, 1994).

The implications of the ELM model for marketing strategy are relatively straightforward: strategy should be based on the level of cognitive processing the target audience is expected to engage in and the route they are likely to follow to attitude change. If the processing level is low, due to low motivation and involvement, the peripheral route should dominate, and emphasis will need to be placed on the way messages are executed and on the emotions of the target audience. If the central route is anticipated, then the content of the messages should be dominant – messages will need to be informative and the executional aspects need only be adequate (to maintain attention) (see Mehta, 1994; Petty and Wegener, 1998).

Conclusion

This chapter has provided an overview of the psychological basis of marketing through a focus on five topical areas of the behavioural sciences. Other areas that were only briefly alluded to here due to space constraints, but which have significant implications for marketers, include learning, personality, social behaviour and developmental psychology (see Chapter 12). Because the marketing enterprise is comprised of exchange activities that involve people, it is not an exaggeration to suggest that psychological principles and concepts permeate every marketing action in one sense or another. As the examples presented in this chapter attest, much can be gained when marketing activities are planned and implemented with an eye towards psychology's role in the process.

The future holds great promise for further applications of psychology in marketing as our understanding of human behaviour and mental processes continues to evolve. For example, new technologies are making it possible to track what happens in buyers' brains as they consider difficult choices. In one recent study (Hedgcock and Rao, 2009), volunteers' brains were scanned as they pondered a choice between sets of equally appealing options. When the choice set also included a third, less attractive option, the choice between the preferred options became easier and relatively more pleasurable, as indicated by decreased activity in an area of the brain associated with negative emotions. By contrast, the brain scans for persons choosing between only two equally preferred options revealed irritation attributed to the difficulty of the choice process. Apparently, the participants were using heuristics when evaluating three-item choice sets rather than a more complex evaluation process.

It is important to add that although this chapter concerns the impact of psychology on marketing, the discipline of psychology in turn has drawn from the marketing process. For example, marketing tactics are utilized by psychologists to seek coveted research funds for scientific and therapeutic programmes, as well as for influencing public policy and obtaining government support for public interventions (e.g. in efforts to control obesity and other eating disorders and programmes to control domestic abuse and other forms of violence). Mutual sharing and exchange between the disciplines is likely to continue through the 21st century, resulting in further benefits for both marketing and psychology.

Recommended further reading

East, R., Wright, M. and Vanhuele, M. (2013) *Consumer Behaviour: Applications in Marketing*, 2nd edn. Newbury Park, CA: Sage.

Haugtvedt, C.P., Herr, P.M. and Herr, P.M. (eds) (2008) *The Handbook of Consumer Psychology*. New York: Taylor & Francis.

Kimmel, A.J. (2012) *Psychological Foundations of Marketing*. London: Routledge.

MacInnis, D.J. and Folkes, V.S. (2010) 'The disciplinary status of consumer behavior: a sociology of science perspective on key controversies', *Journal of Consumer Research* 36: 899–914.

Solomon, M., Bamossy, G., Askegaard, S. and Hogg, M.K. (2013) *Consumer Behavior: A European Edition*, 5th edn. London: Prentice-Hall Europe.

References

Ajzen, I. (1991) 'The theory of planned behavior', *Organizational Behavior and Human Decision Processes* 50: 179–211.

Ajzen, I. (2008) 'Consumer attitudes and behaviour', in C.P. Haugtvedt, P.M. Herr and F.R. Cardes (eds) *Handbook of Consumer Psychology*. New York: Lawrence Erlbaum Associates, pp. 525–48.

Ajzen, I. and Fishbein, M. (1980) *Understanding Attitudes and Predicting Social Behavior*. Englewood Cliffs, NJ: Prentice-Hall.

Andrews, J.C., Durvasula, S. and Akhter, S.H. (1990) 'A framework for conceptualizing and measuring the involvement construct in advertising research', *Journal of Advertising* 19: 17–40.

Anissimov, M. (2004) 'A concise introduction to heuristics and biases', June. Available at: http://www.acceleratingfuture.com.

Arthur, D. and Quester, P. (2004) 'Who's afraid of that ad? Applying segmentation to the protection motivation model', *Psychology & Marketing* 21: 671–96.

Batey, M. (2008) *Brand Meaning*. New York: Routledge.

Bock, B.C., Marcus, B.H., Rossi, J.S. and Redding, C.A. (1998) 'Motivational readiness for change: diet, exercise, and smoking', *American Journal of Health Behavior* 22: 248–58.

Brehm, S.S. and Kassin, S.M. (1993) *Social Psychology*, 2nd edn. Boston, MA: Houghton Mifflin.

Cacioppo, J.T. and Petty, R.E. (1982) 'The need for cognition', *Journal of Personality and Social Psychology* 42: 116–31.

Chaiken, S. (1987) 'The heuristic model of persuasion', in M.P. Zanna, J.M. Olson and C.P. Herman (eds) *Social Influence: The Ontario Symposium, Vol. 5*. Hillsdale, NJ: Erlbaum, pp. 3–39.

Chandon, P. and Wansink, B. (2007) 'The biasing health halos of fast-food restaurant health claims: lower calorie estimates and higher side-dish consumption intentions', *Journal of Consumer Research* 34: 301–14.

Churchill, G.A. Jr (1979) 'A paradigm for developing better measures of marketing constructs', *Journal of Marketing Research* 16: 64–73.

Eagly, A.H. and Chaiken, S. (1998) 'Attitude structure and function', in D.T. Gilbert and S.T. Fiske (eds) *The Handbook of Social Psychology*. Boston, MA: McGraw-Hill, pp. 269–322.

Eppright, D.R., Tanner, J. and Hunt, J.B. (1994) 'Knowledge and the ordered protection motivation model: tools for preventing AIDS', *Journal of Business Research* 30: 13–24.

Fazio, R.H. (1986) 'How do attitudes guide behavior?', in R.M. Sorrentino and E.T. Higgins (eds) *Handbook of Motivation and Cognition*. New York: Guilford Press, pp. 204–43.

Fishbein, M. and Ajzen, I. (1975) *Belief, Attitude, Intention, and Behaviour: An Introduction to Theory and Research*. Reading, MA: Addison-Wesley.

Friestad, M. (2001) 'What is consumer psychology?', *Eye on Psi Chi* 6: 28–9.

Gilbert, D.T., Fiske, S.T. and Lindzey, G. (1998) *The Handbook of Social Psychology*. New York: Oxford University Press.

Greenspan, R. (2004) 'Media multitaskers may miss messages', 2 April. Available at: http://www.clickz.com.

Haughney, C. (2009) 'When economy sours Tootsie Rolls soothe souls', *The New York Times*, 23 March. Available at: http://www.nytimes.com.

Haugtvedt, C.P., Petty, R.E. and Cacioppo, J.T. (1992) 'Need for cognition and advertising: understanding the role of personality variables in consumer behaviour', *Journal of Consumer Psychology* 1: 239–60.

Hedgcock, W. and Rao, A.R. (2009) 'Trade-off aversion as an explanation for the attraction effect: a functional magnetic resonance imaging study', *Journal of Marketing Research* 46: 1–13.

Herzberg, F. (1959) *The Motivation to Work*. New York: John Wiley.

Hovland, C.I., Janis, I.L. and Kelley, H.H. (1953) *Communication and Persuasion*. New Haven, CT: Yale University Press.

Howard, T. (2009) 'Coupon search clicks: sweet sound for web marketers', *USA Today*, 10 March. Available at: http://www.usatoday.com.

Johnson, B.T. and Eagly, A.H. (1989) 'Effects of involvement on persuasion: a meta-analysis', *Psychological Bulletin* 106: 290–314.

Kahneman, D. and Tversky, A. (eds) (2000) *Choices, Values and Frames*. Cambridge: Cambridge University Press.

Kahneman, D., Slovic, P. and Tversky, A. (eds) (1982) *Judgement under Uncertainty: Heuristics and Biases*. Cambridge: Cambridge University Press.

Kassarjian, H.H. (1974) 'Projective methods', in R. Ferber (ed.) *Handbook of Marketing Research*. New York: McGraw-Hill, pp. 2–87.

Katz, D. (1960) 'The functional approach to the study of attitudes', *Public Opinion Quarterly* 24: 163–204.

Knox, S. and Walker, D. (2001) 'Managing and measuring brand loyalty', *Journal of Strategic Marketing* 9: 111–28.

Kraus, S.J. (1995) 'Attitudes and the prediction of behaviour: a meta-analysis of the empirical literature', *Personality and Social Psychology Bulletin* 21: 58–75.

Langenderfer, J. and Shimp, T.A. (2001) 'Consumer vulnerability to scams, swindles, and fraud: a new theory of visceral influences on persuasion', *Psychology & Marketing* 18: 763–84.

Leippe, M.R. and Elkin, R.A. (1987) 'When motives clash: issue involvement and response involvement as determinants of persuasion', *Journal of Personality and Social Psychology* 52: 269–78.

Likert, R. (1932) 'A technique for the measurement of attitudes', *Archives of Psychology* 140: 44–53.

Lowrey, T.M., Shrum, L.J. and McCarty, J.A. (2005) 'The future of television advertising', in A.J. Kimmel (ed.) *Marketing Communication: New Approaches, Technologies, and Styles*. Oxford: Oxford University Press, pp. 113–32.

McGuire, W.J. (1969) 'The nature of attitudes and attitude change', in G. Lindzey and E. Aronson (eds) *The Handbook of Social Psychology*, 2nd edn, Vol. 3. Reading, MA: Addison Wesley, pp. 136–314.

Maslow, A.H. (1943) 'A theory of human motivation', *Psychological Review* 50: 370–96.

Maynard, M. (2007) 'Toyota hybrid makes a statement, and that sells', *The New York Times*, 4 July. Available at: http://query.nytimes.com.

Mehta, A. (1994) 'How advertising response modeling (ARM) can increase ad effectiveness', *Journal of Advertising Research* 34: 62–74.

Nestle, M. (2002) 'The soft sell: how the food industry shapes our diets', *Nutrition Action Healthletter*, September.

Petty, R.E. and Cacioppo, J.T. (1986) *Communication and Persuasion: Central and Peripheral Routes to Attitude Change*. New York: Springer-Verlag.

Petty, R.E. and Wegener, D.T. (1998) 'Attitude change', in D. Gilbert, S.T. Fiske and G. Lindzey (eds) *The Handbook of Social Psychology*, 4th edn. New York: Oxford University Press.

Rajecki, D.W. (1990) *Attitudes*, 2nd edn. Sunderland, MA: Sinauer Associates.

Rogers, R.W. (1983) 'Cognitive and physiological processes in fear appeals and attitude change: a revised theory of protection motivation', in J. Cacioppo and R. Petty (eds) *Social Psychophysiology*. New York: Guilford Press.

Roeper, R. (2002) 'Starbucks buckles under to 9/11 hypersensitivity', *Chicago Sun-Times*, 10 July.

Rook, D.W. (2006) 'Let's pretend: projective methods reconsidered', in R. Belk (ed.) *Handbook of Qualitative Research Methods in Marketing*. Cheltenham: Edward Elgar, pp. 143–55.

Rossiter, J.R., Percy, L. and Donovan, R.J. (1991) 'A better advertising planning grid', *Journal of Advertising Research* 31: 11–21.

Rusticus, S. (2006) 'Creating brand advocates', in J. Kirby and P. Marsden (eds) *Connected Marketing: The Viral, Buzz and Word of Mouth Revolution*. Oxford: Butterworth-Heinemann, pp. 47–58.

Ryu, G. and Feick, L. (2007) 'A penny for your thoughts: referral reward programs and referral likelihood', *Journal of Marketing* 71: 84–94.

Sheppard, B.H., Hartwick, J. and Warshaw, P.R. (1988) 'The theory of reasoned action: a meta-analysis of past research with recommendations for modifications and future research', *Journal of Consumer Research* 15: 325–43.

Sherif, M. and Hovland, C.I. (1961) *Social Judgement: Assimilation and Contrast Effects in Communication and Attitude Change*. New Haven, CT: Yale University Press.

Solomon, M.R. (2008) *Consumer Behavior: Buying, Having, Being*, 8th edn. Englewood Cliffs, NJ: Prentice-Hall.

Sternberg, R.J. (2008) *Cognitive Psychology*, 5th edn. Belmont, CA: Wadsworth.

Story, L. (2007) 'Product packages now shout to get your attention', *The New York Times*, 10 August. Available at: http://www.nytimes.com.

Thurstone, L. (1928) 'Attitudes can be measured', *American Journal of Psychology* 33: 529–54.

Veblen, T. (1899) *Theory of the Leisure Class: An Economic Study in the Evolution of Institutions*. New York: Macmillan.

Verplanken, B. and Svenson, O. (1997) 'Personal involvement in human decision making: conceptualisations and effects on decision processes', in W.R. Crozier, R. Ranyard and O. Svenson (eds) *Decision Making: Cognitive Models and Explanations*. London: Routledge, pp. 40–57.

Vohs, K.D. and Faber, R.J. (2007) 'Spent resources: self-regulatory resource availability affects impulse buying', *Journal of Consumer Research* 33: 537–47.

Wansink, B. and Chandon, P. (2006) 'Can "low-fat" nutrition labels lead to obesity?', *Journal of Marketing Research* 43: 605–17.

Wansink, B., Brasel, S.A. and Amjad, S. (2000) 'The mystery of the cabinet castaway: why we buy products we never use', *Journal of Family and Consumer Science* 92: 104–8.

White, P.H. and Harkins, S.G. (1994) 'Race of source effects in the elaboration likelihood model', *Journal of Personality and Social Psychology* 67: 790–808.

Zimbardo, P.O. (1960) 'Involvement and communication discrepancy as determinants of opinion conformity', *Journal of Abnormal and Social Psychology* 60: 86–94.

The Sociological Basis of Marketing

Kjell Grønhaug and Ingeborg Astrid Kleppe

7

Chapter Topics

Overview	160
Introduction	161
Marketing and sociology	162
Marketing focus and scientific borrowing	164
Concepts and ideas	166
Individuals, groups and the larger society	166
Relationships, power and conflict	172
Learning and change	174
Summary and future outlook	175

Overview

This chapter claims that marketing is a basic social activity, and shows how the discipline of marketing has borrowed from and been influenced by sociology. Also, the sociological influence on marketing has probably been more profound in Europe than in the USA.

The similarities between the basic characteristics of marketing and sociology are illustrated and it is demonstrated that marketing is essentially a societal activity which has borrowed significantly from sociological thinking. Marketing demands that consumers are considered not only as individuals, but also in terms of the groups in which they exist – for example families, social classes, and indeed the wider society around them – taking into account their status, lifestyle, culture and so on. Then marketing must look at relationships within these groups: networking, conflict and power all have a bearing on the marketing approach to be adopted. Furthermore, sociology can be drawn upon to enlighten the marketer on socialization and learned behaviour. Consideration is also given to how a sociological approach might influence the marketing of the future.

Introduction

Marketing has long been recognized as a 'borrowing' discipline, in particular from the social sciences (Cox, 1964), and is itself claimed to be a social science discipline (Hunt, 1991). The historical roots of marketing are embedded in classical economics. Citation analysis to determine the influences of other disciplines on marketing also shows extensive borrowing from (among others) sociology (Goldman, 1979). An interesting observation is that there has been a considerable mutual influence between economics and sociology as reflected in the sub-discipline of economic sociology (for excellent overviews, see Smelser [1963] and Granovetter and Swedberg [1992]). However, so far marketing has only had a modest influence on sociology. The borrowing consists of concepts, theories and models, and methods and techniques for doing research. Particularly important is the conceptual borrowing. Concepts are the building blocks of any theory, model or hypothesis. The concepts and how they are used (and related) guide and direct. They give focus and largely determine what is captured.

As will be demonstrated in the following, the borrowing from sociology has had – and still has – a considerable influence on marketing thinking; there are also marketing journals with a primarily sociological approach, such as *Consumption, Markets & Culture* and *Journal of Public Policy*. The emphasis here is primarily on the concepts (and perspectives) borrowed from sociology and how they have influenced marketing thinking as reflected in major marketing textbooks. The main reason for using marketing textbooks as a mirror of the sociological influences is that textbooks reflect what is taught and disseminated, and thus capture important aspects of the sociological impact on marketing thinking (and practice). Marketing – as other disciplines – has changed and developed over the years. This is also reflected in changes in the borrowing from other disciplines (e.g. sociology) over time. This is primarily reflected in the literature on business-to-business markets, distribution channels and parts of the literature on consumers and consumption.

The chapter proceeds as follows: first, characteristics of marketing and the discipline of sociology are emphasized. In this section it is also demonstrated that marketing is a societal activity. Similarities in marketing and sociological reasoning are also discussed. Then the dominant focus in marketing thinking and practice, and how this has influenced conceptual borrowing and use, is discussed. Next, specific concepts and ideas borrowed from sociology are emphasized. A distinction is made between concepts and ideas primarily used to characterize individuals, groups and the larger society, and contributions taking relationships between social actors directly into account, as well as contributions focusing on change. Finally, characteristics of the borrowing from and influences of sociology on marketing are summarized and future influences from this discipline (sociology) on marketing are indicated.

Marketing and sociology

Marketing activities have a long history. For thousands of years, humans have transacted goods to satisfy needs and enhance standards of living. As a scientific discipline, however, marketing is young with its origins at the turn of the 20th century.

Marketing as exchange

Marketing takes place in a societal context. The core of marketing as a scientific discipline relates to exchange between social actors, e.g. individuals, groups or organizations, or as claimed by Hunt (1983: 13): 'marketing (science) is the behavioural science which seeks to explain exchange relationships'.

(Social) exchange requires:

- the presence of (at least) two parties;
- that each party has something to offer that might be of value to the other party;
- each party is capable of communicating and delivering;
- each party is free to accept or reject an offer;
- each party believes it is appropriate or desirable to deal with the other party (Kotler, 1984: 8).

Exchange as a phenomenon is, however, a huge area of enquiry, and has been extensively dealt with in sociology and other disciplines. Exchange theory consists not just of one, but several theories. A distinction is often made between individualistic and collective approaches to the study of exchange. Different modes of exchange have been identified as well, such as the market mode (i.e. exchange through markets), the reciprocal exchange mode (which can be thought of as gift exchange between members of a network with reciprocal obligations) and the redistributive mode of exchange (i.e. exchange based on some principle of sharing, e.g. blood donations [Polanyi, 1944]). More lately there has been an emphasis on value creation (see e.g. the definition of marketing by the American Marketing Association from 2004). However, exchange between actors is seen as a prerequisite for value creation.

For a long time, marketing has primarily been associated with the market mode of exchange, where the market is often thought of, in a neoclassical sense, as a large number of exchange partners, and where market prices yield the necessary information and incentives. This view of markets differs greatly from how markets are viewed in sociology. For example, in the literature on the sociology of markets, markets are seen as socially constructed, highly influenced by human beings, their interactions and opportunities (for an excellent overview see Fligstein and Dauter, 2007). The idealized market mode of exchange is considered impersonal (as reflected in neoclassical economics), or, as emphasized by Polanyi, 'it is important to emphasize the abstract and impersonal nature of market exchange' (Polanyi, 1944: 5). In modern societies, reciprocal and redistributive exchanges are also taking place. Forty years ago Codere even claimed that the proportion of market exchanges to all exchanges taking place is declining (Codere, 1968).

Marketers have devoted substantial effort to studying and understanding exchanges. One of the first marketing scholars to recognize the limitations of 'faceless' transactions (i.e. exchange outcomes) in understanding markets and marketing was Wroe Alderson, recognized for his influential contributions to marketing thinking. He introduced the notion of the 'organized behavior system' (Alderson, 1950) to capture the fact that the various actors operating in the market are more or less connected (as reflected in the recent emphasis on 'relationship' marketing). Alderson thus recognized the benefit of sociology, and claimed: 'The initial plunge into sociology is only the beginning since the marketing man must go considerably further in examining the functions and structures of organized behaviour systems' (Alderson, 1957: 12). Benefits from sociology for marketing were also pointed at in an early contribution by Jonassen (1955).

Sociology

Sociology is one of the major social sciences. The term 'sociology' was invented by Auguste Comte, and first published in the fourth volume of his *Cours de philosophie positive* in 1838, even though the ancient roots of the discipline can be traced back to, among others, Plato and Aristotle. The term (sociology) has two stems, the Latin *socius* ('companion') and the Greek *logos* ('study of'), and literally means the study of the processes of companionship. The term 'sociology' can be (and has been) defined in various ways, for example as proposed by Giddens, 'sociology is the study of human life, groups and societies' (Giddens, 1993: 4).

A key point in the sociological perspective is that humans do not operate in a vacuum, but are embedded in their surrounding social context. The individual forms and holds expectations about others, and because he or she is assumed to behave purposefully, expectations about others are taken into account. This basic point of departure has a distinct parallel in marketing. Marketing activities take place in a societal context. Exchange requires the presence of and access to others. Since humankind started transacting goods and services thousands of years ago, the importance of 'others' has been recognized. Sellers have tried to identify potential buyers, their needs and how they make evaluations. Buyers learn about sellers and their product offerings. Through word of mouth, their own experiences and other sources of information, buyers' expectations towards sellers are shaped and influence their behaviour as well.

The individual-in-context is a human being interacting with her or his social environment. The sociological perspective tries to encompass the acting person and the acting group. The acting person is a specific human being who pursues goals, interprets experiences, responds to opportunities and confronts difficulties. As an individual-in-action he or she does not necessarily stay within neat boundaries of specialized activity, nor does he or she always conform to conventional expectations. For example, the seller may cheat, the buyer shoplift, and the marketing entrepreneur may 'break the rules', change the 'social game' – and become successful.

Social organization

To capture the social influences in a society, sociologists study how it is organized. In doing so they often make use of the general term *social system*, emphasizing the interdependencies and interactions among social actors. The same underlying idea can easily be traced in marketing, e.g. as reflected in 'distribution systems', 'system sales', 'relationships' and 'networks'.

In their study of social organizations sociologists also distinguish between different levels, for example micro-level (individual and group) and macro-level or social order. Concepts used and phenomena focused on vary across levels (Collins, 1981). There are, however, interactions and interdependencies between the various levels. Changes at the macro-level may influence expectations and behaviour at the micro-level and vice versa. For example, the automobile has dramatically changed the mobility of the individual (consumer), which has influenced shopping behaviour – and the structure of the distribution system, as reflected in the dramatic changes in the retail trade. A drop in individual fertility, for example influenced by a pessimistic outlook for the future, may add up to dramatic changes in demand for specific goods or services. Such demographic changes are (among others) studied by sociologists – and experienced by marketers. Markets have also been an arena for sociological enquiry, generating substantial insights which in turn have also been of importance for the marketing discipline (for an overview, see Fligstein and Dauter, 2007; Lie, 1997).

Our examples so far show that there are close parallels between sociology and marketing unrecognized in most contemporary marketing textbooks. In what follows the focus will be on the main concepts borrowed from sociology, how they are used and why they are used that way.

Marketing focus and scientific borrowing

The present writers view the borrowing from other disciplines as purposeful behaviour, that is the borrowing is done to obtain something, for example to understand the functioning of markets and/or to improve marketing practices. On the other hand, what is borrowed and how the borrowings are used are heavily influenced by the dominant focus of the borrowing discipline, in this case marketing.

The term 'marketing' has been used with at least three different meanings (Arndt, 1980):

- marketing as a management orientation or discipline;
- marketing as a science;
- marketing as an ideology.

According to the stated purpose, that is to capture the influence of sociology on marketing thinking, as reflected in major textbooks, primarily the first meaning of the term (marketing), but also the second meaning will be emphasized.

As a management orientation or discipline, marketing can be – and has been until now – primarily considered a *business* discipline. In spite of efforts to apply marketing thinking to the public sector, and in non-business and non-profit settings, there is little doubt that most marketing thinking and activities relate to business firms – even though other aspects such as consumers and public policy are becoming more emphasized.

Any business firm specializes and offers a more or less limited set of products (services). The firm is dependent on its surrounding environments, in particular on its market(s), that is on actual and potential customers. For the firm to survive and prosper a sufficient number of customers must be willing to buy its products (services) at prices which at least cover costs. Even though a business firm can survive some losses, in the long run costs must be covered in order to stay in business. Surplus profit which will create optimism, attract admiration and allow for investments, and so on, is – of course – considered advantageous.

The number of buyers and sellers varies across markets, and the products and services offered are multiple. Modern marketing as reflected in the majority of (American) textbooks primarily deals with *mass marketing*. Most textbooks are influenced by the underlying (but implicit) perspective that the market frequently exhibits a situation where a few firms sell their products and services to many customers (primarily individuals and households as reflected in cell (c) in Figure 7.1).

In such markets with a great many customers, there is little room to pay attention to the individual buyer. This is particularly so for low-priced items, where the contribution from the individual buyer is lowest and allows for modest individual attention only. In such cases the market is often considered an 'aggregate' of individual customers to which the firm tries to offer its products (or services). This, however, is in contrast to how such markets are seen by sociologists with their focus on contact and relationships. Deighton (1996), however, argues that advances in modern information technologies enhance processes of individualization and heterogeneity (Alderson, 1957) of consumer preferences in mass markets (in contrast to homogeneous preferences as assumed in neoclassical economics). Marketing situations as reflected in the other cells are also taking place. An important point, however, is that the situation as depicted in cell (c) reflects – until recently – the dominant perspective on marketing thinking and influenced the borrowing from other disciplines.

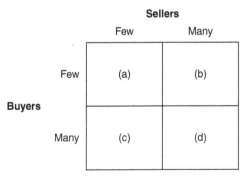

Figure 7.1 Number of sellers and buyers.

Cell (a) in Figure 7.1 reflects the prototypical 'small numbers' market. In such markets the numbers of sellers and buyers are few. The actors are highly visible, and each customer really counts. The emphasis on relationships and networks primarily relates to small numbers and industrial markets, even though such approaches are highly relevant in consumer markets. When the focus is on relationships and networks the presence of others is also directly brought into account, and thus the social aspect of marketing. The growing emphasis on relationships and networks has also contributed to a growing emphasis on sociological aspects by marketers.

Due to the firm's dependence on its market(s) it is of crucial importance for the marketing manager to identify and understand actual and potential customers as the basis for designing and implementing successful marketing strategies. This need to identify, understand, and thus in mass markets, to 'profile' customers in order to become effective can be traced in marketing's borrowing from sociology as reflected in most marketing (and consumer behaviour) textbooks.

Concepts and ideas

The following sections focus on the main concepts and ideas borrowed from sociology. First, concepts and ideas to capture the characteristics of individuals, groups and larger social segments are described. Contributions focusing respectively on relationships between actors, and contributions directed towards change are then discussed.

Individuals, groups and the larger society

Role

An important sociological concept is (social) 'role', which can be conceived as 'the bundles of socially defined attributes and expectations associated with social positions' (Abercombie et al., 1988: 180). For example, the role of 'mother' carries with it certain expected behaviours irrespective of the woman's feeling at any one time. Therefore it is possible to generalize about role behaviour regardless of the individual characteristics of the people who occupy these roles. The concept of role is sociologically important because it reflects how individual activity is socially influenced and thus follows regular patterns. It should also be noted that sociologists employ roles as 'building blocks' to study various social institutions, for example families and organizations (to be discussed later on).

In social life an individual may occupy several roles, for example the role of mother or father, university professor or marketing manager. The number of roles occupied may vary considerably between people. The number of roles occupied by an individual need not be static, as the individual may acquire new roles (and leave others). An individual may also perceive two or more roles to be in conflict. For example, the role of employee, perhaps requiring frequent and lengthy travel, can come in conflict with the parental role of father, associated with expectations of spending time with his child(ren).

The concept of role is a true sociological concept as it implies social relationships. For example, the role of 'husband' is primarily relevant in a household setting, in the presence of a 'wife'. The role concept has been used and has influenced marketing in various ways. The prototypical expectations associated with various roles, for example 'mother' and 'working woman', have been used to identify and profile target groups as the basis for designing appropriate marketing approaches. The frequently quoted roles of 'influencer', 'decider', 'user' and 'gatekeeper' in the organizational (industrial) buying literature have been used in a similar way as the basis for who (and how) to target, as has the focus on 'husband' and 'wife' in the study of family (households). This is a somewhat 'one-eyed' perspective on how the concept of role has been translated into marketing as relationships between actors (e.g. between sellers and buyers), which are crucial in marketing. Some researchers have, however, looked outside the narrow role of the individual as buyer and consumer and addressed consumers as 'real people' who must balance simultaneously multiple role demands, which has contributed to a deeper understanding of consumption in everyday life. This is a central theme in some of the consumer behaviour theory, especially in the literature on consumer culture. In this literature it is also shown how consumers may negotiate their roles and how they adapt to new requirements and situations in a marketing context.

Status

In any social system (e.g. group, organization or society) one may distinguish between different social positions (compare the discussion of social roles). Such positions can also be rank-ordered, implying that positions may be lower, higher or equal in status. Sociologists have long studied how status is achieved. Often a distinction is made between ascribed (e.g. by heritage) and achieved attributes as a basis for status (e.g. education or sports performance). The concept of status has directly (and indirectly) influenced marketing thinking. For example, the observation that things (and behaviours) may symbolize status has been extensively used to develop, introduce and communicate products. In other words, marketers have exploited sociological insights by relating status to consumption alternatives, as reflected in Levy's seminal article 'Symbols for sale' (1959), as well as designing strategies to get access to new markets.

Norm

The term 'norm' refers to social expectations about correct or proper behaviour. Thus norms imply the presence of legitimacy, consent and prescription. When norms are *internalized* they are learnt and accepted as binding the social values and guidelines of conduct relevant to the individual, or her or his group, or wider society. Internalized norms are central for social order. Deviations from norms are punished by sanctions.

The sources of norms can be found in established values, law, expectations and accepted behaviours. Often (in most cases) norms are not written, but are learnt through socialization. Norms may also be more or less specific. For example, specific norms may prevail with regard to specific role behaviours.

For marketers it is important to know the norms in the marketplace in order to behave appropriately. In marketing the concept and knowledge of norms are extensively used as input in market research to get adequate information about target groups. For example, prevailing norms may be barriers to the acceptance of new products. By knowing the norms the marketer may adjust to, or even contribute to, a change of norms. Mason Haire's (1950) well-known 'shopping list' study is an example. When instant coffee was introduced several decades ago, the acceptance rate of the new product was modest. The shopping list study exposed a sample of housewives to one of two shopping lists. The shopping lists were identical, but for one item, coffee. One list contained 'instant coffee', while the other contained the brand name of a well-known regular coffee. The respondents were asked to describe the shopping person. Housewives (who were in the majority at that time) tended to describe the shopper behind the list containing instant coffee as 'lazy', 'not a good housewife', while women working out-side the home described the shopping person as 'smart', 'modern', 'effective' and so on. Apparently the new product was conceived to be in conflict with existing norms of being a good housewife. This knowledge was successfully used in designing marketing strategies to alter this aspect of the prevailing 'housewife norm'. As norms may vary across societies (and social segments), an understanding of prevailing norms represents a true challenge when expanding internationally. More recently marketers have also studied how norms may influence the governance of seller–buyer relationships.

Groups

Social groups are collectives of individuals who interact and form social relationships. A distinction is often made between *primary* and *secondary* groups. The former are small groups, defined by face-to-face interaction. The household (nuclear family) and the clique may serve as examples. Secondary groups are usually larger in number, and each member does not necessarily directly interact with every other member. Examples are unions and associations where the members (at best) interact only with a subset of other members, and where most of the communication is formalized, for example through newsletters. Sociological insights regarding groups have influenced marketing thinking. For example, the family (household) can be conceived as a primary group, and plays an important role in marketing thinking, primarily as a buying and consuming unit. A common observation is that firms' (organizations') buying is usually made by a group, rather than a single individual. This has led to the notion of 'the buying group' or 'buying centre', heavily influenced by sociological group insights. The focus among marketers has been on the role (position) of the buying group, identification (or prediction) of who is included, their tasks and activities, and on their relative influence in purchasing situations, as a basis for designing effective marketing strategies.

A third form of groups is *reference groups*. In forming their attitudes and beliefs, and in performing their actions, people will compare or identify themselves with other people, or other groups of people (reference groups). People can make references both to membership and non-membership groups. Reference group knowledge has influenced marketing thinking. In particular these insights have been applied to relate products or brands to groups to whom it is assumed they will appear attractive. Research findings have demonstrated that reference group influence can be made both at the product category level (particularly for expensive goods) as well as at the brand level. For example, brands of perfume, clothes and equipment are often associated with (distant) attractive reference groups (e.g. movie stars or sports idols). Specific information about the actual reference group(s) of the target group is needed when designing marketing strategies.

Family (household)

The notion of family (household) is extensively used by marketers. In most cases marketers use the notions of 'family' and 'household' interchangeably, indicating the Western perspective that family of a kind (i.e. the nuclear family) often coincides with households (i.e. the unit of dwelling). The family (household) is often considered as an important primary group. The family (household) can also be considered as an important social *institution*. The term (social institutions) refers to established patterns of behaviour, or as defined by Nicosia and Mayer, 'a set of specific activities performed by specific people in specific places through time' (1976: 67). Sociological insights regarding families (households) have in particular been used by marketers to study the relative influence of spouses (and also children) in buying decisions, but also as a basis for studying buying decision processes and how households (families) allocate their scarce economic resources and time.

Family life-cycle

The sociological term 'life-cycle' is used primarily to describe the development of a person through childhood, adolescence, mid-life, old age and death. The concept does not refer to purely biological processes of maturation, but to the transition of an individual through socially constructed categories of age and to the variations in social experiences of ageing. Even though life-cycle is a dynamic concept, the main focus in marketing has been to classify people according to *stages* in the life-cycle, and – in particular – to characterize buying and consumption at the various stages. Such insights have been used to profile target groups and predict future market developments.

Community

Communities or communes come in many forms, for example villages, sections of cities or other groups with something in common (e.g. the domestic lifestyle in the kibbutz). Traditionally communities are located in a discrete geographical area. However, more recently, since the internet has grown in importance, marketing has borrowed the concept (idea) of community and transferred it to a space where actors interact electronically. Examples are online consumer and brand communities. A brand community is 'a specialized, non-geographically bound community, based on a set of structural social relations among addressees of a brand' (Muniz and O'Guinn, 2001: 415). Thus a brand community shares characteristics with traditional communalities, that is consciousness of kind (shared identity), shared traditions and rituals and moral responsibility.

Social class and lifestyle

In most (all?) societies individuals are ranked hierarchically along some dimension, for example wealth, education, prestige, age, or some other characteristics (see discussion of status above). Such rank-ordering is the basis of social class, referring to strata of that rank-ordering, for example the 'upper', 'upper-middle', 'lower-middle' classes and so on. In Western societies wealth, education and prestige (among other things) are important characteristics to determine social class membership. In particular Bourdieu's work related to social class and lifestyle has had and still has a profound impact on marketing thinking (Bourdieu, 1984). Extensive research has shown that members of the various strata or social classes tend to have common characteristics, for example similar consumption patterns and values. For instance, research findings demonstrate that the middle classes spend more on housing and the home, they save more, spend substantially more on education, books and the arts than do the lower classes. (For a detailed description of findings regarding class differences, see Berelson and Steiner, 1964.) Marketers have primarily used such insights to characterize consumption patterns across social classes in order to identify and characterize target groups and segment markets.

The way people live, their consumption patterns and values vary across social strata (and groups). Such differences in lifestyle are *visible* indicators of class position. In sociological research the lifestyle concept has been related to broad classes, for example to distinguish between rural and urban, and urban and suburban forms of social life, as well as age segments and specific interest groups. In marketing, the lifestyle concept has a more psychological orientation, with an emphasis on identifying specific lifestyles based on detailed mapping of consumption activities, media habits, attitudes and opinions.

Culture

Culture has for long been intensively studied by anthropologists and sociologists. Culture is a multidimensional and complex phenomenon, and for decades there has been an ongoing debate about what is meant by the concept; for example, in 1952 Kroeber and Kluckhon reviewed 164 definitions of culture. It is commonly assumed that culture includes patterns of behaviours and values, that culture is learned and shared with other people, and influences not only how one behaves, but also how one expects others to behave. How culture can be best understood and how to explain the functioning of culture have, however, changed over the years. For example, many anthropologists now prefer the term 'enacted' (instead of learned), which recognizes that people do not just passively accept culture, they actively create it. Swidler (1986) in her penetrating analysis sees culture as shaping a repertoire, creating a 'tool kit' of habits, skills and styles from which people construct 'strategies of action' (1986: 273). The acquisition of a repertoire of skills, habits and styles reflects that how to behave in a deliberately rational (goal-directed) fashion can be learned and that this knowledge is context bound, with the cultural context influencing what is conceived as relevant.

Marketing has for long recognized the importance of culture and has extensively borrowed research findings from anthropology and sociology. For example, culture can be characterized according to its *context of communication*, often dichotomized as 'high' versus 'low' (Hall, 1976). Many foreign cultures are characterized as 'high cultural contexts', exhibiting a dependence on non-verbal, 'hidden' insights of communication in contrast to low cultural contexts, relying more on explicit verbal communications and symbols. Such insights have been used to explain market failures and to prepare the marketer when crossing borders. Another finding from cultural research is that the cultural *distance* may vary considerably in importance for marketers when considering new markets to enter. Other aspects from cultural research adopted and used by marketers are differences in media structure and use, the importance of language and symbols, and variations in specific cultural values and the culture associated with consumption. Cultural knowledge has been used to characterize and choose markets, design adequate marketing strategies and to understand and improve international negotiations. Also, the culture of consumers related to the consumption of market-made commodities and marketing activities has attracted substantial interest, as reflected in the article by Arnould and Thompson (2005), which still is debated.

Sub-culture

This term refers to a system of values, attitudes, behaviours and lifestyles of a social group which is distinct from, but related to, the dominant culture of a society. In sociology the concept has been of most use in the study of youth and deviancy. In marketing the concept has primarily been adopted and used to study the buying and consumption activities and lifestyles of specific social groups, for example teenagers. Such insights have primarily been used as the basis for target group descriptions and thus to improve marketing activities and performance.

The idea of sub-culture has also been applied to understanding consumption, defined as a distinct sub-group of society that self-selects on the basis of a shared commitment to a particular product class, brand, or form of consumption. An example is the study of the specific culture among owners of Harley-Davidson motorcycles by Shouten and Alexander (1995). In such a study the unit of analysis is changed from the individual acting unit to the relationship between actors.

As noted above, many sociological concepts (and elements of theories) have been borrowed, primarily as tools to identify and characterize target groups in the effort to improve marketing performance. Thus, even though the concepts are borrowed from a discipline concerned with social relationships, the unit of analysis in the marketing use of these concepts in marketing textbooks has been on the individual acting unit.

Marketing has also borrowed and applied sociological concepts which in a true sense capture aspects of social relationships. This has in particular been the case in situations other than mass marketing, for example in industrial markets where the numbers of buyers are often limited (cf. cells (a) and (b) in Figure 7.1).

Relationships, power and conflict

Relationships

A relationship takes place between (at least) two actors, and the *dyad* is frequently used as the unit of analysis. To be a relationship it has to last (at least for some minimum time). A purposeful relationship assumes some flow of activities. The relationships can be of various kinds and focus on exchange of goods, information, money and so on.

The importance of relationships has for long been recognized in disciplines like sociology and anthropology and business, and now also in the marketing literature. Labels like 'relationship marketing' indicate the attributed importance of relationships. An interesting observation is the rather late interest in relationships and networks in American marketing thinking, in spite of the fact that such ideas have been dealt with by European marketing scholars, and in particular marketing scholars from the Nordic countries (see Ekstrøm, 2010), for more than four decades.

A common observation in industrial marketing is that buyers and sellers tend to enter into rather long-term relationships, that is they tend to transact not only once, but perform recurring transactions. There are several reasons for doing so. For example, it takes time, skill and economic resources to identify, negotiate with and adjust to exchange partners. Such efforts can be conceived as (partly) transaction-specific investments easing future transactions. Relationships between exchange partners ease interaction and flow of information, thereby reducing transaction costs and thus explaining why they (relationships) last. Relationships may, in addition to economics, convey and be influenced by social values and concerns, as reflected in the notion of 'embeddedness' (Granovetter, 1985). The role and functioning of relationships have escalated in marketing over the years.

Any transaction or relationship is guided by a *contract*, either explicitly or implicitly. There is a vast literature on contracts by researchers from several disciplines. Sociologists have primarily been preoccupied with the importance of 'social contracts', which can deviate from legal contracts. Marketers now focus to an increasing degree on various types of contracts, in particular with the purpose of structuring and monitoring relationships (Macneil, 1980).

Relationships vary in strength. Strong relationships are valuable and give access to various resources, for example support. However, weak relationships more easily allow for new information of importance for innovations (Granovetter, 1973).

Network

The notion of 'network', often used to describe systems of relationships between actors, has a long tradition in sociology and anthropology. The last decades have seen an increasing use of the network approach to understand the functioning of markets, and how – through their networking activities – firms may acquire resources and competence, gain access to technologies and achieve competitive advantages. The role of modern information and communication technologies and how these manifest in the social media influence theorising on social networks.

For example the concept of 'electronic tribes', their functioning and how they can be studied (see e.g. Kozinets, 2010). It is claimed that the internet is a new social room where 'weak ties' of importance for diffusion of ideas, opinion and meanings are established. Marketing, to an increasing degree, adopts sociological concepts to capture the new reality created through the internet, which also influences marketing practices.

Relationships and networks imply reciprocity, that is the implicit norm to do things for each other. A central premise is that relationships and networks may be valuable, as reflected in the term *social capital*. Coleman (1988) in his penetrating analysis has shown the use of social capital, that is that the value embedded in relationships and networks may give rise to human capital. The idea of social capital has been borrowed and exploited by marketers and applied to activities that enhance the success rate in new product development.

Conflict and cooperation

When social actors exhibit purposeful behaviour, for example to gain market share or to make money, the interests of social actors may come into conflict. For instance, competition can be seen as conflict over the resources or advantages desired by others. Insights regarding the causes of conflicts, and factors and mechanisms influencing conflict development and solution are important for marketers and have been applied in several ways, for example to understand and solve conflicts between marketing and other functions, and conflicts between members of the distribution channel (for an interesting discussion, see Levy and Zaltman, 1975).

Conflict is closely related to *competition* addressed both in sociology and marketing. However, both sociology and marketing address *cooperation*, implying that potentially conflicting interests are turned into mutual ones. The potential benefits from cooperation have been studied intensively. In marketing, cooperation has been related to cooperation in new product development, brand alliances, new market entrance and more. A related phenomenon *co-opetition*, that is how actors simultaneously handle conflicting and mutual interests, has for long been addressed in sociology. The idea of co-opetition has more recently been adopted by marketers, in particular how actors can simultaneously do business and be friends.

Power

The study of power has a long tradition in sociology, and the concept of power has for long been used by marketers, in particular in the literature on distribution channels. There are several distinct perspectives of power, and the concept has been defined in many ways, for example 'the probability that a person in a social relationship will be able to carry out his or her own will in the pursuit of goals of action, regardless of resistance' (Weber, 1946: 180).

The above definition implies that power is exercised by social actors, and involves agency and choice. Power is exercised over others and may involve resistance and conflict. Insights from sociological studies of power (and conflict) have, for example, been applied to understanding and improving the functioning of distribution systems. An interesting phenomenon is how social media allows multiple consumers to interact, exchange experiences and meanings and form joint opinions. This has allowed the many formerly independent consumers in a weak position to change their power vis-a-vis producers, as reflected in the report 'Power at last. How the internet means the consumer really is king' (*The Economist*, 2005). Thus, social media allows consumers to interact and become a countervailing power, which may suggest a change in market situation from cell (c) to cell (a) (see Figure 7.1).

Learning and change

Socialization

This term is used to describe the process whereby people learn to conform to social norms, a process that makes possible an enduring society and the transmission of its culture between generations. Socialization has been extensively focused on in sociological research. In marketing – so far – the focus has primarily been on how children are socialized as consumers. However, the recent focus on phenomena such as consumer communities and brand communities has directed the attention to socializing activities.

Social change

Sociologists have extensively studied how social systems (e.g. societies) change. This has important implications for marketing. The introduction of marketing thinking and practices to newly developing countries is, for example, assumed to enhance standards of living. A successful introduction of marketing thinking and practice will probably also imply dramatic social changes. Societal characteristics may hamper and/or alter the intended changes as well.

Even though marketing activities are conducted to bring about changes in a societal context, relatively few marketing studies have addressed the problem of social change (Levy and Zaltman, 1975). This is, however, changing. Marketers now to an increasing extent address how attitudes towards stigmatized groups may be altered, how marketing can be applied to change unhealthy behaviour (e.g. smoking) and to change eating habits to fight obesity, and more.

Diffusion of innovations relates to how innovations (e.g. new ideas, practices or products) are spread within social systems. This subject has been intensively studied by researchers from many disciplines, with a great impact from sociology (see Rogers [2003] for an overview). The diffusion of innovation literature has had a profound impact on marketing thinking, and researchers from the (marketing) discipline have contributed to this field as well. When studying diffusion of innovations, the innovation (e.g. a new product) represents something new to the potential adopter, but need not be a novelty in an absolute sense. For example, studies have demonstrated that some technologies take decades to be adopted. Diffusion of innovation is a true social phenomenon as it takes the social context directly into account. This becomes clear when looking at the elements in a diffusion process, that is: (1) the innovation, and (2) its communication (3) from one individual (social actor) to another, (4) within a social system (e.g. a society) (5) over time.

More than 30,000 studies related to diffusion of innovations have been conducted (Rogers, 2003). Research findings show that characteristics of the innovation influence both the extent to which and how fast an innovation is diffused. For example, the perceived relative advantage has been demonstrated to have a profound effect on the propensity to adopt an innovation. This very robust finding is, of course, of prime interest for marketers, and gives direction for marketing activities, for example, new product development.

A large number of studies demonstrate that the number of adopters over time follows an S-shaped curve. The time dimension for the total adoption process may, however, vary tremendously across innovations. Based on this observed pattern, adopters can be grouped according to when they adopt an innovation. Those adopting at an early point in time, 'innovators' (or 'pioneers') and 'early adopters', have been found to differ in characteristics and use of information sources compared to later adopters. For example, those adopting at an early stage tend to be more interested in and know more about the actual innovation, and tend to be more willing to try something new compared to later adopters and non-adopters. Such findings are of prime importance for marketers when defining target groups and designing effective marketing strategies. An important finding from diffusion of innovation research is that later adopters tend to seek earlier adopters' advice, and that mass media information is diffused into the society via personal communication. Those adopting early and/or those who play a key role in personal communication of mass media information are frequently termed *opinion-leaders*.

Findings from research on diffusion of innovation have influenced marketing in many ways, for example in marketers' search for, development and evaluation of new products, marketing research and the profiling of target groups, design of marketing communication strategies, positioning of products and the 'stretching' of the products' life-cycles.

Summary and future outlook

Marketing has borrowed extensively from sociology. A large proportion of this borrowing used to be done in a mass marketing context with the prime purpose of profiling target groups as a basis for designing more effective (mass) marketing. By now the borrowing relationships focus more on aspects related to networks and interactions between social actors.

An interesting observation is the rather modest borrowing from sociology to study change. This is surprising as marketing is primarily a dynamic phenomenon taking place in ever-changing social contexts; in fact a prime purpose of marketing is to bring about changes. However, this is now changing.

An additional observation is that the marketing discipline has primarily been preoccupied with transactions and exchanges falling within socially accepted norms, or even more restrictive, visible, socially accepted market transactions (Grønhaug and Dholokia, 1987). In most societies many (legal) exchanges are taken out of the visible, legal market, for example an exchange of services between neighbours. In addition, illegal exchanges occur. In several countries the 'black economy' booms and is estimated to constitute something in the range of 20–40% of the gross national product. The distribution and marketing of illegal drugs and the selling of stolen goods are examples of deviant behaviours, but so far – in spite of their importance – they have received rather scant attention from marketers. As noted by Zaltman and Wallendorf (1977), there are reasons to believe that the study of illegal exchanges can improve our understanding of marketing and its potential influence within legal and accepted social settings.

To summarize:

- Much of the borrowing from sociology was earlier primarily used as a basis for character-izing and profiling consumers and target groups, that is the use of the concepts has been 'one-sided', overlooking their social relational intentions as reflected in the mother discipline.
- The borrowing from sociology has primarily been applied to legal, visible exchanges, that is only a subset of all marketing exchanges taking place. The extensive work in sociology on deviant behaviour has so far been almost neglected, but this is now changing.
- The borrowed concepts and ideas have mainly been used as static descriptors and only to a modest extent utilized to capture the dynamics of and understand societal changes. This is also seen in scholarly empirical marketing research. In spite of the dynamic character of marketing – which involves time – the majority of empirical research is still based on cross-sectional research designs, or on experiments which capture only a limited time period between pre- and post-tests. However, the dynamics of markets and marketing are becom-ing more emphasized.
- However, to capture, adjust to and benefit from the 'new social reality' in social media, marketing applies sociological concepts and thinking extensively. An interesting and important aspect is that ICT and access to a multitude of relationships and networks pri-marily relates to weak relationships or ties which ease access to novel information.

Developments and changes in marketing perspectives indicate that more focus will be placed on social aspects, emphasizing relationships between social actors. The influence of sociology on marketing thinking will very likely increase in the years to come, and probably be mani-fested in the following ways:

- Previously borrowed concepts, for example 'role', 'status' and 'group', will be applied to capture social dimensions as they were created to do, that is to capture aspects of relationships.
- The borrowing of concepts and ideas to understand relationships and networks, their ini-tiation, changes, duration and termination, will increase dramatically in the years to come.
- The importance of the social context, and how it influences relationships and exchanges, will be more emphasized in future marketing thinking and research.
- It is also believed that dynamics and change as emphasized in much of sociology will have a greater impact on thinking and research in marketing in the years to come.

Recommended further reading

Arnould, E.J. and Thompson, C.J. (2005) 'Consumer culture theory (CCT): twenty years of research', *Journal of Consumer Research* 31 (March): 868–82.

Blau, P.M. (1964) *Exchange and Power in Social Life*. New York: John Wiley. This book represents a penetrating analysis of various forms of social exchanges and offers important insights into marketing phenomena.

Coleman, J.S. (1988) 'Social capital in the creation of human capital', *American Journal of Sociology* 94: S95–S120. A penetrating analysis of how relationships between social actors as such represent value and function.

Emerson, R.M. (1962) 'Power-dependence relations', *American Sociological Review* 27(1): 31–41. An important and very influential article, often quoted by marketers, which deserves to be read.

Granovetter, M. (1985) 'Economic action and social structure: the problem of embeddedness', *American Journal of Sociology* 91(3): 481–570. An important contribution to understanding the importance and disciplining effect of the social context on relationships and transactions.

Grayson, K. (2007) 'Friendship versus business in marketing relationships', *Journal of Marketing* 71(4): 121–39.

Haire, M. (1950) 'Projective techniques in marketing research', *Journal of Marketing* 14 (April): 649–56.

Heide, J. and John, G. (1992) 'Do norms matter in marketing relationships?', *Journal of Marketing* 56(2): 32–44. One of the few empirical marketing contributions on the importance of norms relationships.

Katz, E. and Lazarsfeld, P. (1955) *Personal Influence*. New York: The Free Press. An important study which shows the importance of social networks and of personal interactions. An important contribution to the 'two-step-flow of information' hypothesis.

Levy, S.J. and Zaltman, G. (1975) *Marketing Society and Conflict*. Englewood Cliffs, NJ: Prentice-Hall. Considers marketing from a social system perspective, and focuses in a useful way on marketing as a cause of consequences of change, and inherent conflict.

Rauch, J.E. and Castella, A. (eds) (2001) *Networks and Markets*. New York: Russell Sage Foundation.

Swidler, A. (1986) 'Culture in action: symbols and strategies', *American Sociological Review* 51(2): 273–86. This is a very thought-provoking book on the functioning of culture and its importance for marketers.

Thompson, C.J. (1996) 'Caring consumers: gendered consumption meanings and the juggling lifestyle', *Journal of Consumer Research* 22 (March): 388–407. A useful contribution regarding the potential of applying the role concept to marketing problems.

Zaltman, G. and Wallendorf, M. (1977) 'Sociology: the missing chunk or how we've missed the boat', in B.A. Greenberg and D.N. Bellinger (eds) *Contemporary Marketing Thought 1977: Educators' Proceedings*. Chicago, IL: AMA, pp. 235–8. This paper identifies important topics neglected by marketers, and discusses how sociology can be useful.

References

Abercombie, N., Hill, S. and Turner, B.S. (eds) (1988) *Dictionary of Sociology*, 2nd edn. London: Penguin Books.

Alderson, W. (1950) 'The analytical framework for marketing', in D.J. Duncan (ed.) *Proceedings: Conference of Marketing Teachers from the West*. Berkeley, CA: School of Business Administration, University of California.

Alderson, W. (1957) *Marketing Behavior and Executive Action: A Functionalist Approach to Marketing Theory*. Homewood, IL: Irwin.

American Marketing Association (2004) Available at: https://www.marketingpower.com/Pages/default. aspx.

Arndt, J. (1980) 'Perspectives for a theory of marketing', *Journal of Business Research* 8: 389–402.

Arnould, E.J. and Thompson, C.J. (2005) 'Consumer culture theory (CCT): twenty years of research', *Journal of Consumer Research* 31 (March): 868–82.

Berelson, B. and Steiner, G.A. (1964) *Human Behavior: An Inventory of Scientific Findings.* New York: Harcourt, Brace and World, Inc.

Bourdieu, P. (1984) *Distinction: A Social Critique of the Judgement of Taste.* Cambridge, MA: Harvard University Press.

Codere, H. (1968) 'Social exchange', in D.H. Sills (ed.) *International Encyclopedia of the Social Sciences,* Vol. 5. New York: Macmillan and the Free Press, pp. 238–344.

Coleman, J.S. (1988) 'Social capital in the creation of human capital', *American Journal of Sociology* 94: S95–S120.

Collins, R. (1981) 'On the microfoundations of macrosociology', *American Journal of Sociology* 86: 984–1014.

Cox, R. (1964) 'Introduction', in R. Cox, W. Anderson and S.J. Shapiro (eds) *Theory in Marketing.* Homewood, IL: Irwin.

Deighton, J. (1996) 'The future of interactive marketing', *Harvard Business Review,* November–December: 151–62.

Ekstrøm, K. (2010) *Consumer Behavior – A Nordic Perspective.* Stockholm: Stockholm Universitetsforlaget.

Fligstein, N. and Dauter, L. (2007) 'The sociology of markets', *Annual Review of Sociology* 33: 6.1–6.26.

Giddens, A. (1993) *Sociology,* 2nd edn. London: Polity Press.

Goldman, A. (1979) 'Publishing activity in marketing as an indicator of its structure and disciplinary boundaries', *Journal of Marketing Research* 16: 485–94.

Granovetter, M. (1973) 'The strength of weak ties', *American Journal of Sociology* 78: 1360–80.

Granovetter, M. (1985) 'Economic action and social structure: the problem of embeddedness', *American Journal of Sociology* 91: 481–570.

Granovetter, M. and Swedberg, R. (eds) (1992) *The Sociology of Economic Life.* Boulder, CO: Westview Press.

Grønhaug, K. and Dholokia, N. (1987) 'Consumer, markets and supply systems: a perspective on marketization and its effects', in A.F. Firat, N. Dholokia and R.P. Bagozzi (eds) *Philosophical and Radical Thoughts in Marketing.* Lexington, MA: Lexington Books.

Haire, M. (1950) 'Projective techniques in marketing research', *Journal of Marketing* 14 (April): 649–56.

Hall, E.T. (1976) *Beyond Culture.* Garden City, NY: Anchor Press/Doubleday.

Hunt, S.D. (1983) 'General theories and the fundamental explanda of marketing', *Journal of Marketing* 47: 9–17.

Hunt, S.D. (1991) *Modern Marketing Theory: Critical Issues in the Philosophy of Marketing Science.* Cincinnati, OH: South-Western Publishing.

Jonassen, C.T. (1955) 'Contribution of sociology to marketing', *Journal of Marketing* 24(2): 29–35.

Kotler, P. (1984) *Marketing Management, Analysis, Planning and Control,* 4th edn. Englewood Cliffs, NJ: Prentice-Hall.

Kozinets, R.V. (2010) *Netnografi.* Thousand Oaks, CA: Sage.

Kroeber, A.L. and Kluckhon, C. (1952) 'Culture: a critical review of concepts and definitions', *Papers of Peabody Museum* 47: No. 1A.

Levy, S.J. (1959) 'Symbols for sale', *Harvard Business Review* 37: 117–24.

Levy, S.J. and Zaltman, G. (1975) *Marketing, Society, and Conflict.* Englewood Cliffs, NJ: Prentice-Hall.

Lie, J. (1997) 'Sociology of markets', *Annual Review of Sociology* 23: 341–60.

Macneil, I.R. (1980) *The New Social Contract: An Inquiry into Modern Contractual Relations*. New Haven, CT: Yale University Press.

Muniz, A.M. and O'Guinn, T.C. (2001) 'Brand community', *Journal of Consumer Research* 27: 412–32.

Nicosia, F.M. and Mayer, R.N. (1976) 'Toward a sociology of consumption', *Journal of Consumer Research* 3: 65–75.

Polanyi, K. (1944) *The Great Transformation*. Boston, MA: Beacon Press.

Rogers, E.M. (2003) *Diffusion of Innovations*, 5th edn. New York: The Free Press.

Shouten, J.W. and Alexander, J.H. (1995) 'Subcultures of consumption: an ethnography of bikers', *Journal of Consumer Research* 20 (June): 43–61.

Smelser, N.J. (1963) *The Sociology of Economic Life*. Englewood Cliffs, NJ: Prentice-Hall.

Swidler, A. (1986) 'Culture in action: symbols and strategies', *American Sociological Review* 51: 273–86.

The Economist (2005) 'Crowned at last: a survey of consumer power', in *The Economist*, 'Power at last. How the internet means the consumer really is king (and queen)', 2 April. Available at: http://www.economist.com/node/3785166.

Weber, M. (1946) 'Class, status, party', in H.H. Gerth and C. Wright Mills (eds) *From Max Weber: Essays in Sociology*. New York: Oxford University Press.

Zaltman, G. and Wallendorf, M. (1977) 'Sociology: the missing chunk or how we've missed the boat', in B.A. Greenberg and D.N. Bellinger (eds) *Contemporary Marketing Thought 1977: Educators' Proceedings*. Chicago, IL: AMA, pp. 235–8.

Cultural Aspects of Marketing

Kam-hon Lee and Cass Shum

8

Chapter Topics

Overview	180
Culture can pose marketing problems	182
Marketing efforts can overcome cultural problems	183
Marketing power should respect culture	185
Marketing campaigns can utilize cultural features	187
Culture and the globalization of markets	189
Balance between localization and standardization strategy	191
Learning from different cultures	192
Dynamic culture and dynamic marketplace	193
Conclusion	194

Overview

According to Hatch (1989), culture is:

> ... the way of life of people. It consists of conventional patterns of thought and behavior, including values, beliefs, rules of conduct, political organization, economic activity, and the like, which are passed on from one generation to the next by learning – and not by biological inheritance. (1989: 178–9)

Also, culture is 'governed by its own principles and not by the raw intellect, and the differences among people do not reflect differences in levels of intelligence' (Hatch, 1989: 178–9). As such, there are many cultures in the world. In a way, there can be many cultures in a nation (Swanson, 1989). It is widely recognized that theories in management and marketing are culture bound (Hofstede, 1993; Tse et al., 1988). Marketing in one culture can be very different from marketing in a number of other cultures. A marketing campaign created in developed countries may or may not be transferable to developing countries. International marketers may need to modify the marketing activities generated in one culture and to consider cultural factors when launching marketing activities in another culture. It becomes important to understand various issues related to launching marketing activities in a different culture.

The heart of the matter in marketing is to form a market and strike a business deal, which will bring benefits to all parties involved in the transaction. 'The marketing concept', the fundamental concept in marketing, refers to a philosophical conviction that customer satisfaction is the key to achieving organizational goals. Whether the customer is an individual or an organization, and whether the customer is nearby or in a foreign country, the challenge to the marketer is the same. Thus, the mission of marketing is to facilitate exchange and form a win–win relationship with other parties. This is no easy task when the marketer and the other parties share the same culture. It becomes even more difficult to accomplish when the marketer and the other parties do not share the same culture. What makes things even worse is that within the same nation or ethnicity, people are culturally differentiated. One good example is the Hispanic market in the United States. There is cultural difference between Hispanics and non-Hispanics. There are also cultural variances among all segments of the Hispanic market. For example, while Mexicans and most Central and South Americans are soccer fans, Cubans and Caribbean Hispanics enjoy baseball. Using only one sport in advertisements would result in only partial success in the Hispanic market. An AT&T advertisement was a failure when portraying a wife asking her husband to call a friend to say that they would be late. Although AT&T employed Puerto Rican actors, AT&T failed to notice that in Latin America, it is a norm to be half an hour late and no one phones to warn their friends about this. Also, no Latin American wives dare order their husbands around (Herbig, 1998: 117).

People in different cultures do not just speak different languages. With different values and norms, they have different needs and different attitudes towards advertisements and brands. Customers would not be satisfied if marketers failed to notice the cultural differences both within the same culture and between different cultures.

This chapter will specifically examine three related issues on marketing in a different culture. First, can a marketing success in one culture be reproduced in another culture? If not, why not? If so, what are the conditions of success? Second, should a marketing success in one culture be reproduced in another culture? This is a more basic question than the first one. It examines the ethical foundation of marketing activities. Last, but not least, will cultures eventually converge? This is even more fundamental than the first two questions. When there is only one culture in the whole world, there is no need to study the cultural aspects of marketing.

Culture can pose marketing problems

First, can a marketing success be reproduced in another culture? Marketing people are supposed to be very sensitive to the changing needs of customers. Marketers know that they have to study customers' needs carefully, and deliver products which can meet those needs. When customers have different needs, marketers have to come up with different product offerings. Since customers in different cultures have minds which are programmed quite differently, it becomes important to differentiate their needs and to try to meet those needs differentially. However, other cultural moderating factors are not so obvious. Even world-class marketers may not be sensitive enough to detect the differences in different cultures all the time.

Procter & Gamble (P&G) is an American giant, a company widely known to practise the marketing concept. Procter & Gamble meets basic consumer needs with a strong research commitment to create products that are demonstrably better than the competition when compared in blind tests. They use brand and category management systems and value market research highly, believing that it can enable the company to identify a new trend early on and take the lead in it.

Based on new liquid detergent technology and after extensive blind tests and market tests, P&G launched a new clothing detergent brand named Vizir in the early 1980s in Germany and Europe. Vizir was positioned as a complete main wash product, having superior performance in removing tough, greasy stains even in low temperature washing (Bartlett, 1983).

Vizir got off to a good start all over Europe, and quickly became number one in the heavy-duty detergent category. However, in 1983, business began to weaken and the Vizir brand eventually lost about 15% of its sales volume that year. In 1984, there was an additional 15% sales decline. What P&G had failed to take into account was that European washing machines were at that time equipped to accept powder detergents but not liquids. When liquid detergent was added to a powder dispenser, as much as 20% of the liquid was lost to a collecting point at the bottom of the machine. Thus, the product was not meeting customers' performance expectation.

Procter & Gamble changed the packaging to explain better to consumers how to use Vizir, but research showed that this would not work. Subsequently, P&G managed to convince washing machine manufacturers in Europe to design liquid dispensers, but this had little impact on a market where, on average, a washing machine was replaced only once every 15 years. The next P&G attempt was to develop a retrofit system – a plastic device that fitted into existing powder dispensers and kept the liquid from leaking, while dispensing it at the same time. Procter & Gamble would mail the device to consumers, free of charge, immediately after housewives told them the model number of their washing machines. However, most European machines were bolted to the wall, and the housewives were unable to see the model number; they did not know and they could not tell.

Finally, one technician in a French P&G product development laboratory invented a unique solution – a 'dosing ball' that P&G called a Vizirette. The consumer could fill the porous Vizirette 'dosing ball', place it in the washdrum on top of the clothes, and start the machine. The Vizirette would gradually dispense the detergent, with no waste. Vizir and Vizirette were subsequently introduced as a system (Editors of *Advertising Age*, 1989).

Customers in different cultures may have different needs. This, in turn, determines whether a marketing success can or cannot be reproduced in another culture. Marketers, at all times, should be sensitive to the changing needs of their customers. This is especially important for international marketers when they launch marketing activities in a different culture. They should understand that when customers' needs change, marketing activities should change accordingly to meet these different needs.

Furthermore, as the world becomes more globalized, there will be more international business negotiations. However, the cultural differences remain and inter-cultural negotiations exhibit extra sources of tension on negotiators. America has been the engine for world economic growth. China is the most important emerging economy. Let us review the negotiation challenge between American and Chinese business executives. For the Chinese, greater levels of tension led to an increased likelihood of agreement, but also led to lower levels of interpersonal attraction and in turn lower trust for their American counterparts. For the Americans, greater levels of tension decreased the likelihood of an agreement, did not affect interpersonal attraction, but did have a direct negative effect on trust (Lee et al., 2006). We can see that culture not only affects marketing activities like product design and promotion, but also pre-marketing activities like negotiations.

Marketing efforts can overcome cultural problems

Procter & Gamble entered the Japanese market first in 1972–3. The consumer mindset in Japan was quite unique. The primary buyer of packaged goods was the housewife. In Japan at least half the adult women were employed, but almost no Japanese mothers worked outside the home. Child-rearing was the first priority for a Japanese woman. The average family home was 50 square metres. Lack of storage necessitated several shopping trips per week and affected the structure of the distribution outlets, the market information the housewife commanded and the relationship between shopkeeper and housewife. Thus, the market structure was quite indirect and long. Specialty and small retail stores constituted the bulk of retail outlets, commanding 72.3% in 1982. There was also a close interpersonal relationship between the neighbourhood shopkeeper and the housewife. The typical Japanese customer for branded packaged goods was highly uncompromising, demanding superior quality and defining value more in terms of product performance, quality and reliability, rather than price. This attitude was even more pronounced in the area of personal hygiene. Thus, in Japan virtually all companies manufactured products to a standard of zero defects.

Procter & Gamble entered Japan through a joint venture with Nippon Sunhome. They picked Cheer laundry detergent powder as a wedge to open the Japanese market for other major brands to follow. Procter & Gamble followed their 'successful' formula in the USA to position and advertise Cheer as an all-temperature laundry detergent powder in 1973, featuring price promotions to support the advertising campaign, and went directly to the major retail chains to promote and distribute it. Cheer gained a substantial market share and managed to capture up to 12.6% in the laundry detergents market in 1979. However, Cheer did not bring in profits. Also, when the featured pricing stopped in 1979 Cheer kept losing market share to different competitive brands (Kao's Wonderful, New Beads, Zab Total and Lion's Top Powder). Upon closer examination, it became clear that the three-temperature washing concept was not relevant to Japanese laundry habits. Women typically washed clothes in tap-water and occasionally the recycled family bath-water in the winter. The aggressive pricing practice only forced all players in the industry to incur substantial losses together. For example, P&G's all-temperature Cheer had been selling at 555 yens for two boxes against a suggested retail price of 800–850 yens for one box. Kao's New Beads large box had been selling at 400 yens against a previous retail price of 700–750 yens. This aggressive pricing practice antagonized all the competitors. In addition, the distribution policy through the major retail chains alienated the wholesalers and the small retailers, who were the gatekeepers of mass distribution in Japan.

Practically all other P&G brands either failed in the test market or were pre-empted by competition due to a competitor's national launch of a copycat brand prior to the conclusion of P&G's 24-month test market period. The only exception was Pampers, which was launched in 1981 and immediately captured 85% of the disposable diaper market. However, even Pampers was not completely successful. Unicharm, a relatively unknown company in Japan, introduced Moony in 1982, which was sold at a 40% price premium to Pampers and managed to capture 40% of the market share in 1983. In the meantime, Pampers dropped from its 1981 high of 90% to its 1985 low of 6%. It was quite clear that P&G could afford no more illusions. They had underestimated the sophistication level of Japanese consumers. They had also under-estimated the competitive strength of the Japanese companies. The operation in Japan was a total disaster (Yoshino and Stoneham, 1990a).

It became clear to P&G in 1983 that what was best in the USA might not be good enough in Japan. This was at least true in the consumer packaged goods industry. Procter & Gamble could join other well-respected packaged goods companies such as General Foods, General Mills and Colgate, who had all failed in Japan and retreated. However, P&G was convinced that Japan was a leading-edge country in the consumer goods industry, and the world leader had to be successful there. There was no other choice. If P&G could not compete with the Japanese companies in Japan, they would eventually have to compete with them in the USA. This conviction led to P&G's subsequent success in Japan, which managed to show that marketing efforts could overcome cultural problems (Yoshino and Stoneham, 1990b).

The changing mentality at P&G started with the changing belief in research and development. By that time P&G believed that while American and European trends were helpful, the worldwide centre of innovation should be focused on Japan and Japanese competition. Thus, the R&D team in Japan was trying to develop products that would meet the needs of Japanese consumers. While there were only 60 people in the P&G R&D group in Osaka, in comparison with Kao's 2,000 in Japan, P&G could depend on the unreserved support from the R&D group in Cincinnati. The race in R&D in the diaper product industry was instructive. Procter & Gamble, Kao and Unicharm took turns to leapfrog one another in product upgrades, rendering the latest generation of diapers obsolete within six months. Eventually, P&G's R&D groups in Osaka and Cincinnati jointly developed the world's thinnest and most absorbent diaper, which became a clear winner over both Unicharm's Moony and Kao's Merries.

The biggest marketing challenge for P&G was to determine what advertising would work. It became clear to P&G that there was a virtual absence of side-by-side comparisons in Japanese advertising because of the indirectness of communication and the importance of harmony in Japanese culture. The tone of advertising was always friendly and never aggressive. Commercials often used background music and well-known celebrities. The first author (Lee) reviewed the P&G commercials used in Japan in the late 1970s and those of the early 1990s. The improvement was obvious. For example, previously Pampers commercials featured an unhappy baby in an unhappy situation, while later commercials featured happy babies in happy situations. To promote Cheer detergent originally, P&G had merely applied the American copy to Japan, although Japanese housewives had no problems with water temperature. Later commercials focused on the primary product benefits of dirt and odour removal.

There were commensurate changes in the distribution, manufacturing and organization areas. The whole package of changes showed that P&G was willing to take the other culture seriously, and make a commitment to investing resources to meet customers' needs. While noticing cultural differences is important, it is even more important to develop culture-specific marketing activities to meet local customers' needs. Where there is a will, there is a way, and marketing efforts can overcome cultural problems.

Procter & Gamble invested US$10 million in China in 1998 and set up an R&D centre in Beijing. The centre, located next to Tsinghua University, had a two-fold mission. It enabled P&G to adapt products to local conditions and it also enabled P&G to take advantage of local ideas in improving products around the world (Walsh, 2001). One can see in China the shadow of the earlier hard won successful experience in Japan.

Marketing power should respect culture

The examination of the ethical foundation of marketing in a different culture is equally if not more important. Should a marketing success be reproduced in another culture? Although marketing power is formidable, there should also be a limit. The limitation need not come from customers' resistance, which in fact is important in the marketplace to differentiate the capable from the less capable marketers. Such limitation is part of the reality in marketing interaction. However, there is another kind of limitation. It comes from company efforts to restrain the marketing power when it is necessary for the company to do so. When customers are able to choose what would be best for themselves, consumer sovereignty can be assumed, and companies are free to exercise their marketing power to overcome the resistance and eventually manage to meet the customers' needs and conclude the deals. On the other hand, when customers are not able to choose what would be best for themselves, consumer sovereignty does not exist and it becomes the responsibility of the company to restrain the marketing power for the sake of the public. One notable example is the case of infant formula selling in the Third World (Lee, 1987).

Infant formula was developed by leading food giants in developed countries. The product was initially sold in developed countries as a substitute for breast milk. The case for infant formula is that it is available when breast milk is not (a less than 10% chance), and when properly used it is an excellent alternative among all existing alternatives. In the developed and rich countries like the USA, mothers can usually afford to buy infant formula and know how to use it in hygienic conditions. Their education level is high and consumer sovereignty can be assumed. It would be enough to promote breast milk as the best choice while providing mothers a choice of settling with the 'second best' – the infant formula.

However, while infant formula is not defective in itself, it is demanding. When risk conditions are present, it can be harmful to users. This became a serious issue in 1970 when the infant formula manufacturers adopted aggressive marketing efforts in developing nations (Post, 1986). The problem became obvious when infant formula manufacturers promoted heavily in a much less developed and poor country like Zambia. There are two real dangers. First, through poverty, compounded by ignorance, mothers tend drastically to dilute the infant formula in order to make it last. As a result, infants starve and die. Second, poor hygiene causes serious troubles. Nestlé and other companies in the industry repeatedly claimed that they had no desire or intention to see unqualified consumers using their formula products. However, in 1978 at the US Senate hearings, when representatives from these companies were asked whether they had conducted any post-marketing research studies to determine who actually used their products, all representatives answered that their companies did no such research and did not know who actually used the products.

It becomes clear that the companies should be responsible for their marketing efforts. In order to guarantee that the users of infant formula products have proper information on their safe use and can make intelligent consumer choices, the companies may want to withdraw the marketing efforts or even the products from those countries. Mass marketing would certainly not be appropriate in view of the consumers' culture in such countries. If the product supply is meant to be helpful, it may be wise to do the promotion through the medical and healthcare system. Professionals there can exercise their judgement and make recommendations to mothers. Nestlé's infant formula should not be regarded as an isolated case. Rather it should be seen as an illustrative case for all kinds of First World products being sold in the Third World. There should be a similar level of sensitivity in reviewing the situation. It is important for marketing power to respect culture.

Another example illustrating that marketing power should respect culture is the sustainable development of ecotourism. If managed properly, ecotourism can benefit both tourists and the local community. Tourists can learn more about the local cultures and environment. Through education programmes, tourists can also understand the importance of preserving the local culture and environment. Their spending provides extra sources of funding for environmental protection projects. The local community can enjoy increased income and better quality of life. However, when the marketing activities and development are out of control, the local community, the environment and the customers will all suffer. The case of Zhangjiajie is a good example of this.

Zhangjiajie National Forest Park is the first national park in mainland China. Also, it is the main component of the Wulinyuan Scenic Area, a UNESCO World Natural Heritage Site. The government noticed its potential as a world-class ecotourism site in 1982 and began to promote and develop the destination heavily. Due to its rich cultural resources and beautiful scenery, Zhangjiajie became very popular in a few years. The annual average arrivals increased from around 88,000 visitors in the early 1980s to more than 720,000 visitors in the early 1990s. However, as the marketing campaigns and site development were not managed properly, tourism development impacted on the quality of the park. Tourism activities reduced the biodiversity in the area. As some tourists damaged the trees and threw rubbish in the park, air and water became heavily polluted. The environment suffered seriously. In 1998, experts from the UNESCO committee visited Zhangjiajie and warned that the Zhangjiajie area had been largely transformed. If Zhangjiajie continued to be mismanaged, it would be placed on the UNESCO World Heritage in Danger List. Furthermore, in order to develop the area, some local residents had been relocated. At the same time, more immigrants migrated to the area for better jobs. The local cultural traditions cannot be easily retained under these circumstances. Tourists' experiences were negatively influenced by the environmental and socio-cultural changes. In the visitor survey by Zhong et al. (2008), over 85% of respondents reported that they did not feel a strong ethnic ambience during their stay in the park. Local residents' friendliness towards tourists also faded over time. The area became very commercialized and disappointed tourists (Deng et al., 2003; Zhong et al., 2008).

Marketing campaigns can utilize cultural features

The above discussion may leave readers with the impression that marketing is the conqueror and culture is always trying to defend itself. This need not be the case. As a matter of fact, marketing campaigns can make use of the unique cultural features of the customers and the company to make a lasting impact. When a marketing programme is deeply rooted in a particular culture, the programme can easily enjoy sustainable competitive advantages. In some situations, a company may 'discover' such a 'different' and perfectly compatible culture at home. The turnaround of Harley-Davidson in the American motorcycle industry is one of the most celebrated examples.

Before 1960 the motorcycle market in the USA had been mainly served by the American Harley-Davidson, BSA, Triumph and Norton of the UK and Moto-Guzzi of Italy. Harley-Davidson was the market leader in 1959. However, in that year Honda and Yamaha entered the American market. The Japanese motorcycle industry had expanded rapidly after the Second World War to meet the need for cheap transportation in Japan, and in 1959 the major Japanese producers, Honda, Yamaha, Suzuki and Kawasaki, together produced some 450,000 motorcycles, which was 10 times more than retail sales in the USA. Honda was already the world's largest motorcycle producer. These Japanese producers approached the American market in a systematic way. They started by penetrating the low end, lightweight market niche. They all placed an emphasis on market share and sales volume. To realize their growth goals, the Japanese producers constantly updated or redesigned products to meet the needs of American customers; set prices at levels designed to achieve market share goals; reduced prices further when necessary; appointed full-time dealers to set up an effective distribution and maintenance network; and launched well-planned and heavy advertising campaigns. Because of scale economy and long-term strategic planning, by 1966 Honda, Yamaha and Suzuki together had 85% of the US market. By 1974 Harley-Davidson was virtually the only non-Japanese company left in the market, keeping a mere 6% market share (Buzzell and Purkayastha, 1978).

The only option left for Harley-Davidson was to adopt niche marketing in a matured market. Harley-Davidson just concentrated on the super-heavyweight motorcycle market. However, because of the aggressive Japanese marketing efforts, their market share in that niche had fallen from 75% in 1973 to less than 25% in 1980. At that time the parent company AMF was losing interest in Harley-Davidson. Early in 1981 Vaughn Beals and 12 other Harley executives wanted to take over the company through a leveraged buyout arrangement. They thought that they could do a better job and rescue the company. Subsequently, Harley-Davidson made several strategic moves that eventually led to the celebrated turnaround. In April 1983, President Reagan approved a recommendation by the International Trade Commission (ITC), raising the tariff on 'heavyweight' motorcycles (with engine displacements over 700 cc) from 4.4% to 49.4% for four years. The ITC's recommendation was to protect the domestic industry, and essentially the Harley-Davidson operation. Harley-Davidson made tremendous efforts to renovate the production process. They learned just-in-time manufacturing systems from the Japanese companies and adopted measures to encourage employee involvement. Production cost and product reliability were significantly improved. However, the major change and the secret of their success was on the marketing side.

Harley-Davidson formed the Harley Owners' Group in 1983. The acronym HOG is the affectionate name given by Harley riders to their motorcycles. Since motorcycles are often an impulse purchase, one of Harley's biggest challenges is to hold its new customers after they have bought a bike. The Harley Owners' Group gives the new rider instant companionship through organized rides, rallies and charity runs. In 1991, with more than 155,000 members in 700 chapters worldwide, HOG had become the motorcycle industry's largest company-sponsored enthusiast organization. Club members enjoy such features as a bi-monthly newsletter (*HOG Tales*), an automobile-club-type travel centre and reimbursement for motorcycle safety courses. The major attraction has been that at state, regional, national and international rallies, thousands of HOG members unite with company employees for a weekend of fun, entertainment, motorcycle demo rides and camaraderie in an atmosphere that clearly defines the 'Harley-Davidson lifestyle experience'. The rallies also give Harley executives a chance to find out what is on customers' minds.

When management celebrated Harley's 85th birthday in 1988, they arranged a party which reflected their unique way of getting close to customers. Motorcyclists were invited to participate in the event. All they had to do was to contribute US$10 to Harley-Davidson's favourite philanthropic organization, the Muscular Dystrophy Association. Starting from as far away as San Francisco and Orlando, Florida, groups of cyclists headed for Milwaukee. Each group was led by a Harley-Davidson executive, including the board chairman Vaughn Beals, and chief executive officer Rich Teerlink. Thousands of Harleys, many flying American flags, rumbled into Milwaukee on 18 June, shaking the air with the sound of their engines. Some riders had dogs, others their children. Riders wore different kinds of clothing, and they were all ages. The celebrants spent the day participating in such activities as slow races. Beals and Teerlink, among other executives, submitted themselves to the celebrity dunk tank, where they were dumped into a tank of water by on-target baseball throwers. Music resounded all the time. At the final ceremonies, 24,000 bikers watched videotapes of their ride to Milwaukee projected onto two giant screens. As riders saw their own groups, they would shout. Thousands of Harley owners rose to their feet and burst into an unrivalled demonstration of product loyalty.

In 1989 Harley-Davidson had managed to capture close to 60% of the super-heavyweight motorcycle market in the USA (Rose, 1990). The momentum has continued since and Harley-Davidson has become an exemplar of the 'marketing community' concept. The charity events and public-spirited programmes, such as company reimbursement for Harley owners who took rider education classes, helped a great deal in promoting the company image. The HOG and cross-country motorcycle treks come from the roots of American culture. Only Harley-Davidson can utilize these cultural features and promote nationalism in a natural way. Honda tried to form a similar group to HOG, which quite expectedly soon faded away (*Fortune*, 1989). The case of Harley-Davidson demonstrates that utilizing cultural features can make a marketing campaign more effective.

Brand community has become a powerful concept to advocate brand loyalty (McAlexander et al., 2002; Muniz and O'Guinn, 2001; Thompson and Sinha, 2008). Harley-Davidson and HOG became an exemplar of understanding the concept of brand community (Bagozzi and Dholakia, 2006; McAlexander et al., 2002). A brand community rooted in culture is a brand built on rock.

Culture and the globalization of markets

It would not be appropriate to discuss the cultural aspects of marketing without mentioning Levitt's widely cited article on the globalization of markets (1983). In this powerful article, Levitt asserted that well-managed companies had moved from an emphasis on customizing items to offering globally standardized products that are advanced, functional, reliable and low priced. Will cultures eventually converge? If so, it will no longer be necessary to examine the cultural aspects of marketing. Levitt's thesis was derived from his observation of a power-ful force – technology – which was driving the world towards a converging commonality. High-tech products were standardized. High-touch products like Coca-Cola, Levi jeans and Revlon cosmetics would be the same. According to Levitt, 'everywhere everything gets more and more like everything else as the world's preference structure is relentlessly homoge-nized' (1983: 93). Levitt predicted that the global corporation will know everything about one great thing. The corporation will know about the absolute need to be competitive on a worldwide basis as well as nationally and seek constantly to drive down prices by standard-izing what it sells and how it operates. Its mission is modernity and its mode, price competition, even when the corporation sells top-of-the-line, high-end products. What all markets have in common is an overwhelming desire for dependable, world-standard moder-nity in all things, at aggressively low prices. Later, in 1988, in one of the editorials he wrote for the *Harvard Business Review*, Levitt created a concept called 'the pluralization of con-sumption' to supplement his theory of global homogenization. According to his prediction, the whole world is made up of one market segment, which consists of people with plural preferences – the new world of the heteroconsumer.

While we enjoy reading all Levitt's writings and accept the points he made in most of his articles, we must challenge his contention. If world-class marketers like P&G encountered clear cultural problems in Europe and Japan, it is quite obvious that the market is not homogenized even among the most developed countries. The case of Nestlé's infant formula is even more convincing. The economic gap between the North (those who have) and the South (those who have not) is highly conspicuous. It is not possible to assume that people in the Third World should be approached in the same way as people in the First World. If this is still not enough, the case of Harley-Davidson shows us clearly that even in the most developed marketplace in the world, the USA, culture and its consequences play a key role in marketing. Harley-Davidson depends on cultural features to guard its market niche. No Japanese company can reproduce the same cultural impact on American consumers. The foundation of Hofstede's (1984) seminal studies on culture is the nation. As long as national boundaries exist, and as long as there are reasons for nations to reinforce the differences between nations, the impact of culture will be here to stay.

Coca-Cola is probably the best known brand name in the world. If there is a universal standard product in the world, Coca-Cola is very likely to be one of the best, if not the best, contender. However, when the Coca-Cola company began to sell their products aggressively in China, it was clear that the reception there was atypical. Contrary to expectation, Sprite (the number two brand from the Coca-Cola company) was selling much better than Coca-Cola (the flagship in China). Also, it was quite clear that the universal advertising copy was not at all well received in China. This led to a special advertising production for China. The company gave local managers in mainland China control over advertisement operation. In the new advertising commercial that was launched in 1992, one could see the favourite Chinese images such as family ties, wedding ceremonies, Chinese New Year and the Great Earth. These cultural themes were clearly unique to China and the Chinese. A pop singer from Taiwan, who was well received on the mainland, was commissioned to compose and sing the theme song for that advertising commercial. In addition to localized advertisement operation, Coca-Cola changed its usual distribution strategies when they operated in China. When Coca-Cola first started its operation in China, its direct-to-retail distribution strategy, which was successful in developed countries like the USA, only accounted for a minority of the company's unit sales. In mainland China, around 75% of Coke products went through independent wholesalers. These independent wholesalers might be large state-owned enterprises, private companies, or most often, family business. To handle distribution and sales to these wholesalers, Coca-Cola operated at least one sales centre, which also served as warehouses, in most Chinese cities with a population above 1 million. Coca-Cola also provided training and management assistance to these independent wholesalers through a programme called 'Partnership 101'. This unique distribution strategy allowed Coca-Cola to reach more customers through its giant distribution network, with about 215,000 active retail outlets in 2001. Coca-Cola's 'think local, act local' approach made Coca-Cola the most recognized soft drink brand in mainland China for six consecutive years from 1995 to 2001 (Clifford and Harris, 1996; Weisert, 2001). This is clear evidence that consumers are not homogenized. The impact of culture is here to stay.

Balance between localization and standardization strategy

The above discussion may leave readers with the impression that marketing in different cultures should adopt the local culture or fail. However, the choice between standardization and localization is not an either/or decision. Instead, marketers should balance the two approaches so that they can maximize the benefit from their marketing campaigns. While localization allows marketers to develop marketing campaigns relevant to the local customers' needs, standardization allows marketers to enjoy economies of scale and deliver a consistent branding message (Ferle et al., 2008).

Operating in more than 100 countries, McDonald's is probably the most iconic fast-food chain in the world. For years, McDonald's has used the famous Golden Arches as its logo with red and yellow as the major branding colours. It operates everywhere with the same principle of providing customers with efficient fast-food in a clean environment. However, since the 1990s, McDonald's marketing message has fallen flat. In 2002, the world's largest restaurant chain's stock price dropped to a seven-year low due to decreasing earnings (ElBoghdady, 2002). It was clear that its attempts in creating an emotional connection with its customers were not working and its advertisements were notorious for lacking focus and being out of touch with the culture (Arndorfer, 2005). Even though advertisements were made by local agents, they were given small budgets and worked on similar projects, focusing on price reduction and product attributes (Fowler, 2005). Standardization did not help McDonald's stand out from its rivals. Moreover, selling the Big Mac, the brand-famous product, is not possible in many countries like India where no pork or beef are allowed in the diet. In Israel, the chain has to sell 100% Kosher beef, processed in accordance with Jewish rites. They cannot sell any dairy product or operate on the Sabbath or on any religious holidays. A total standardization is impossible.

In 2003, McDonald's executives were convinced that the traditional one-size-fits-all approach could not cater to the different needs of customers in different cultures. They understood that no one message could tell the whole brand story. However, they also saw a totally localized approach as being too risky and creating confusion. In order to address both local relevance and message consistency, they adopted a new approach – 'brand journalism', which recognized the multidimensional nature of a brand. In the 'brand journalism' approach, McDonald's marketers reach its customers in different cultures with different relevant concepts under the same theme. In other words, creative themes are developed on a global basis. However, local marketers may tailor the theme in locally relevant ways (Cardona, 2004). Accordingly, they launched a series of marketing campaigns all around the world under a unified theme called 'I'm Lovin' It'. The theme connected McDonald's with its customers in a highly relevant and culturally significant way. Local marketers were allowed to use locally relevant advertising channels, tailor-make advertising context and develop new products to suit the needs of local customers. At the same time, through its promotions, media planning, new product developments, merchandising and internal marketing, a single brand message was sent to employees and customers in over 100 countries expressing the 'Forever Young' positioning. It provided message consistency while capturing the spirit, music and flavour of each local country (*PR Newswire*, 2003). This approach allowed McDonald's to sell one facet of the brand in a culturally relevant way and resulted in 86% advertising awareness in its top 10 markets. Sales increased. At the same time, customers and employees were excited about the 'new' brand (Cardona, 2004).

In different cultures, advertisements under the McDonald's 'I'm Lovin' It' theme told different real stories about what their customers like, and how McDonald's relates to them. McDonald's experiences in Asia demonstrate how successful the new strategy is. Like other countries, McDonald's Asian advertisements were made under the 'I'm Lovin' It' theme. The 2009 Hong Kong Chinese New Year prosperity campaign was no exception. However, it was tailored to suit local customers' needs. In terms of product, they developed the Mala Grilled Pork Burger, the Mala Grilled Chicken Burger and Mala McNuggets. As local customers preferred pork and chicken to beef, these Sichuan-style products were relevant to local tastes. In terms of the advertisement, it featured Hong Kong slang, pandas and Chinese traditional lanterns. It also employed SoftHard, a local band popular among the youth, as actors. Furthermore, customers could purchase SoftHard Rangers, a set of 12 Chinese animal zodiac dolls. More importantly, the whole marketing campaigns sent consistent brand messages to its customers under the 'I'm Lovin' It' theme. The marketing success was reflected in its 10.2% monthly sales increase in the Asia Pacific, Middle East and Africa region (*PR Newswire*, 2009). McDonald's demonstrated how marketers can balance standardization and localization and become successful.

Learning from different cultures

When operating in a global environment, it becomes important to understand and learn from different cultures. Executives from a 'strong' business culture should always be sensitive to the opportunity to learn from executives from a seemingly 'weak' business culture. One good example comes from the experience of Sino-US business. After 1993, many more American multinational companies took business in China seriously. There was a renewed interest in studying the Chinese business negotiating style (e.g. Fang, 1997), trying to re-examine what was known in the early days (e.g. Pye, 1982). While this whole research area is still quite unclear, American executives have already discovered that they have at least one important lesson to learn from Chinese executives in negotiating more effectively (Intercultural Training Resources, Inc., 1995). American executives usually arrange negotiation items one by one and prioritize the issues. They would try to negotiate and settle first the most important issue, and then move on to the next one. If there is no settlement for the first issue, they would hesitate to move on. At the same time, once the first issue is settled, they would hesitate to open up the discussion again when they have already moved on and discussed the second issue (sequential approach). Chinese executives are just the opposite. If they cannot come to an agreement on the most important issue, they are willing to put that aside for the time being and move on to discuss the next issue. In addition, even if they have already reached an agreement on the first issue, they are willing to open up the discussion again on the first issue when they are discussing the second issue (holistic approach). Theoretically, the Chinese holistic approach would enhance significantly the chances for both parties to create more value from the business deal.

Dynamic culture and dynamic marketplace

While it is unlikely and undesirable that cultures will converge and form one world culture in the foreseeable future, this does not mean that cultures are stagnant. The impact of culture is here to stay, but culture itself is dynamic and changing. When the culture of a particular economy is changing, more often than not there should be commensurate changes of marketing efforts in order to enable the company and the brand to ride together with the tide. The case of Hong Kong should be instructive since it has gone through significant changes in the past several decades.

Hong Kong had been a British colony for more than 90 years. Culturally, Hong Kong has always been a Chinese society. When the Communist Party was about to take power in mainland China, many Chinese industrialists in the textile industry came to Hong Kong. They brought with them their best technicians and operators, together with money and their best equipment. In the 1950s and the 1960s Hong Kong became a rapidly growing manufacturing centre with a firm base in textiles and clothing. The typical work ethic at that time was diligent and frugal, carried over from the previous agricultural society. Because of continued growth and prosperity, Hong Kong became quite affluent in the 1970s and well into the 1980s. In the meantime, Hong Kong people began to work more shrewdly rather than harder. They no longer felt that they were poor and even if they actually were they felt that they could become rich if they do it right tomorrow. The issue of the end of colonization in 1997 was much felt in Hong Kong, beginning in late 1982, and remains a part of daily news. Hong Kong people have been forced to reflect on their own identities. Before the issue of 1997 became real, Hong Kong people had refused to think about it, and regarded themselves as Chinese. When the changes in 1997 became a reality, Hong Kong people began to see that there is a difference between the identity of a Hong Kong person and the identity of a Chinese person. Although Hong Kong people are also Chinese, they are not Chinese in the same way as those from the mainland or Taiwan. This development is gradual but real and carries implications for marketing campaigns. It may be instructive to review the development of advertising themes for a popular soft drink in Hong Kong, since the soft drink industry may best reflect the preference of the mass society. It is about the story of Vitasoy, a soya bean milk developed in Hong Kong (Lai, 1991).

The Vitasoy story began with a big idea and a little bean. Vitasoy was a milk substitute made from soya beans ground with water and sugar. It was launched as 'the poor people's milk' in the 1940s. Its major principle was to deliver adequate nutrition at low cost. The company promised that people would become taller, stronger and healthier. Vitasoy had always been sold at about two-thirds of the price level of leading soft drinks such as Coca-Cola. Vitasoy met two kinds of needs. People took Vitasoy because it was thirst quenching and at the same time good for body strength. It also appealed to people who were poor and frugal. This product position continued to function well in the 1950s and 1960s. However, in the 1970s this advertising theme became ineffective. Hong Kong people no longer thought of themselves as poor and malnourished. In 1974 Vitasoy decided to make a drastic change and reposition the product. They used Tetra Brik Asceptic packaging to present a new image and to make the product available in supermarkets, which had started to become a more important retail outlet than grocery stores.

They raised the product price level to the ordinary price level for prestigious soft drinks, since price was no longer a concern among customers. The incremental margin would enable the company to put up more aggressive marketing campaigns. The advertising theme was changed to 'More Than a Simple Soft Drink'. The new theme created a 'fun' image and at the same time preserved the 'nutritious/healthy' image, which was still helpful to differentiate Vitasoy from other soft drinks. This advertising theme went well for more than a decade, and then ran out of steam. In 1988 they adopted another new theme, 'You Must Have Been a Beautiful Baby'. This theme reinforced the Hong Kong identity and also enabled Vitasoy to differentiate itself from all other soft drinks which were from different countries. Since Hong Kong people at that time had begun to have confidence in their own identity, this advertising theme was timely and effective. In the 2000s, Hong Kong people were able to identify the dual identity of Hong Kong people in relation to China (Brewer, 1999). The new Vitasoy's advertising theme was 'One Small Step, One Leap Forward'. It featured a son gaining support from his traditional father by showing a childhood drawing of Vitasoy. This advertisement made use of the father–son relationship to portray the relationship between Hong Kong and mainland China. It became quite effective. Vitasoy has been continuously successful and the advertising themes adopted over the years have kept pace with the changing culture in Hong Kong. This is strong evidence that culture and marketing go together in a dynamic fashion. There will be no effective marketing if full attention is not paid to its cultural aspects.

Conclusion

Marketing theories are culture bound. Marketing success is also culture bound. When a company has developed a successful marketing formula in one culture, it is justified to try to enjoy the benefits of scale economy and apply it in another culture. However, it is important to take heed and make sure that the conditions exist there to reproduce the same marketing success. Otherwise, the marketing failure can be very costly. The story of the P&G launch of Vizir is very instructive. On the other hand, the eventual success of P&G in Japan is reassuring. McDonald's 'I'm Lovin' It' marketing campaign further demonstrates how to balance the decision between localization and standardization. Good marketing efforts, even in a different culture, will pay off.

Marketing is not just profit making. When a company launches a marketing programme in a different culture, the first question that should be asked is whether the company respects the host culture. In some special situations, as demonstrated in Nestlé's infant formula case and in the Third World and Zhangjiajie ecotourism development, it may even be appropriate to adopt various demarketing measures at the expense of 'marketing success'. When a company learns to respect culture, the efforts will pay off. When the marketing programme and the culture are joined together, sustainable competitive advantages are guaranteed. The rebirth of Harley-Davidson celebrates this truth.

Although there are merits in Levitt's vision of a convergent world culture (1983, 1988), it is unlikely that that vision will become a reality in the foreseeable future. Coca-Cola's 'think local, act local' marketing activities and the differentiated cultural effects on tension felt during negotiation demonstrated that. In view of the fact that people can learn even from a seemingly 'weak' culture, it becomes desirable to preserve cultural diversity so that marketers can learn more effectively. Thus, it will continue to be important to examine the cultural aspects of marketing – Levitt's thesis, in a way, reinforces the conviction that culture is developing and changing. It becomes important for the marketer to continue to study the cultural aspects of marketing, even when the company is operating in the same place as before. Since culture is constantly developing and changing, even the home culture can become very different in the course of time. It becomes imperative to examine the cultural aspects of marketing whether one is operating at home or abroad.

Recommended further reading

Cateora, Philip R., Gilly, Mary C., and Graham, John L. (2011) *International Marketing*, New York: McGraw-Hill/Irwin.

Hofstede, Geert H. (2001). *Culture's Consequences: comparing values, behaviors, institutions and organizations across nations*, Thousand Oaks, Calif.: Sage Publications.

Jordon, Ann T. (2003) *Business Anthropology*, Prospect Height, Illinois: Waveland.

Levy, Sidney J. (1999) *Brands, Consumers, Symbols and Research: Sidney J. Levy on Marketing, compiled by Dennis W. Rook*, Thousand Oaks, Calif.: Sage Publications.

Zaltman, Gerald, and Zlatman, Lindsay H. (2008) *Marketing Metaphoria: what deep metaphors reveal about the minds of consumers*, Boston, Mass: Harvard Business School Press.

References

Arndorfer, J.B. (2005) 'McDonald's lovin' its new model', *TelevisionWeek* 24: 17.

Bagozzi, R.P. and Dholakia, U.M. (2006) 'Antecedents and purchase consequences of customer participation in small group brand communities', *International Journal of Research in Marketing* 23(1): 45–61.

Bartlett, C.A. (1983) *Procter & Gamble Europe: Vizir Launch*. Boston, MA: Harvard Business School.

Brewer, M.B. (1999) 'Multiple identities and identity transition: implications for Hong Kong', *International Journal of Intercultural Relations* 23: 187–97.

Buzzell, R.D. and Purkayastha, D. (1978) *Note on the Motorcycle Industry – 1975*. Boston, MA: Harvard Business School.

Cardona, M.M. (2004) 'Mass marketing meets its maker', *Advertising Age* 75: 1–2.

Clifford, M.L. and Harris, N. (1996) 'Coke pours into Asia', *Business Week* 3499: 72.

Deng, J., Qiang, S., Walker, G.J. and Zhang, Y. (2003) 'Assessment on and perception of visitors' environmental impacts of nature tourism: a case study of Zhangjiajie National Forest Park, China', *Journal of Sustainable Tourism* 11: 529–48.

Editors of *Advertising Age* (1989) *Procter & Gamble, How P&G became America's Leading Marketer*. Lincolnwood, IL: NTC Business Books.

ElBoghdady, D. (2002) 'At McDonald's, supersize problems', *The Washington Post*, 18 September.

Fang, T. (1997) *Chinese Business Negotiating Style*. Linkoping: Linkoping University Press.

Ferle, C.L., Edwards, S.M. and Lee, W.-N. (2008) 'Culture, attitudes, and media patterns in China, Taiwan, and the U.S.: balancing standardization and localization decisions', *Journal of Global Marketing* 21: 191–205.

Fortune (1989) 'How Harley beat back the Japanese', *Fortune* 25: 93–6.

Fowler, G.A. (2005) 'McDonald's Asian marketing takes on a regional approach', *Wall Street Journal*, 26 January.

Hatch, E. (1989) 'Culture', in A. Kuper and J. Kuper (eds) *The Social Science Encyclopedia*. London: Routledge.

Herbig, P.A. (1998) *Handbook of Cross-Cultural Marketing*. Binghamton, NY: The International Business Press.

Hofstede, G. (1984) *Culture's Consequences, International Differences in Work-related Values*. Beverly Hills, CA: Sage.

Hofstede, G. (1993) 'Cultural constraints in management theories', *Academy of Management Executive* 7: 81–94.

Intercultural Training Resources, Inc. (1995) *Working with China Series*. San Francisco, CA: Intercultural Training Resources, Inc.

Lai, L. (1991) 'Fortune built on a bean', *Hong Kong, Inc.* 18: 26–47.

Lee, K.-h. (1987) 'The informative and persuasive functions of advertising: a moral appraisal – a further comment', *Journal of Business Ethics* 6: 55–7.

Lee, K.-h., Yang, G. and Graham, J.L. (2006) 'Tension and trust in international business negotiations: American executives negotiating with Chinese executives', *Journal of International Business Studies* 31: 623–41.

Levitt, T. (1983) 'The globalization of markets', *Harvard Business Review* 61: 92–102.

Levitt, T. (1988) 'The pluralization of consumption', *Harvard Business Review* 66: 7–8.

McAlexander, J.H., Schouten, J.W. and Koenig, H.F. (2002) 'Building brand community', *Journal of Marketing* 66: 38–54.

Muniz, A.M. Jr and O'Guinn, T.C. (2001) 'Brand community', *Journal of Consumer Research* 27: 412–32.

Post, J.E. (1986) 'Ethical dilemmas of multinational enterprises: an analysis of Nestlé's traumatic experience with the infant formula controversy', in W.M. Hoffman, A.E. Lange and D.A. Fedo (eds) *Ethics and the Multinational Enterprise*. Lanham, MD: University Press of America.

PR Newswire (2003) 'McDonald's® unveils "I'm lovin' it™" worldwide brand campaign', *PR Newswire*, 2 September.

PR Newswire (2009) 'McDonald's reports global comparable sales up 7.1% in January', *PR Newswire*, 9 February.

Pye, L.W. (1982) *Chinese Commercial Negotiating Style*. Cambridge: Oelgeschlager, Gunn & Hain.

Rose, R.L. (1990) 'Harley regains lead in big bike market', *Asian Wall Street Journal*, 7–8 September.

Swanson, L.A. (1989) 'The twelve "nations" of China', *Journal of International Consumer Marketing* 2: 83–105.

Thompson, S.A. and Sinha, R.K. (2008) 'Brand communities and new product adoption: the influence and limits of oppositional loyalty', *Journal of Marketing* 72: 65–80.

Tse, D.K., Lee, K.-h., Vertinsky, I. and Wehrung, D.A. (1988) 'Does culture matter? A cross-cultural study of executives' choice, decisiveness, and risk adjustment in international marketing', *Journal of Marketing* 52: 81–95.

Walsh, D. (2001) 'P&G China lab has global role', *Research Technology Management* 44: 4–5.

Weisert, D. (2001) 'Coca-Cola in China: quenching the thirst of a billion', *The China Business Review* 28: 52–5.

Yoshino, M. and Stoneham, P.H. (1990a) *Procter & Gamble Japan (A)*. Boston, MA: Harvard Business School.

Yoshino, M. and Stoneham, P.H. (1990b) *Procter & Gamble Japan (C)*. Boston, MA: Harvard Business School.

Zhong, L., Deng, J. and Xiang, B. (2008) 'Tourism development and the tourism area life-cycle model: a case study of Zhangjiajie National Forest Park, China', *Tourism Management* 29: 841–56.

Part Three

Theories of Marketing Management and Strategy

Part III Contents

9 The Marketing Mix – A Helicopter View   199

10 Marketing Strategy   224

11 Market Segmentation and Segment Strategy   251

The Marketing Mix – A Helicopter View

Walter van Waterschoot, Thomas Foscht, Marion Brandstaetter and Andreas B. Eisingerich

9

Chapter Topics

Marketing mix origin and background   199
The nature and scope of the marketing mix metaphor and concept   202
Marketing mix functions, instruments and effects   205
Pragmatic, mnemonic and pedagogical mix classifications   210
A functional classification of the marketing mix   214
Criticism of the marketing mix metaphor and concept   215
Conclusion   220

Marketing mix origin and background

The marketing mix concept has been said to follow directly from the very nature of marketing and has been accepted for many decades now. Some go even so far as to say that the mix concept is quintessential to marketing and indeed what marketing is (van Waterschoot and De Haes, 2008: 42). The concept is inherent to many marketing situations – even if this is more obvious in some situations than others. It is, therefore, not surprising that the origin and traces of the concept are intertwined with those of the marketing discipline. The antecedents of marketing practice go a long way back into the histories of many economies, even if their individual histories show different time patterns (Fullerton, 1988). Historical study reveals that managerial marketing practice and corresponding conceptual thinking as a distinct discipline (Bartels, 1962) resulted from dramatically changing market circumstances in the Western world, predominantly taking place around the end of the 19th and during the first half of the 20th centuries. An increasing divide between production and consumption contributed to the structural presence of substantial supply and demand potential in diverse product and service areas (Bernays, 1928). Over the years both supply and demand potential tended to become increasingly substantial as well as heterogeneous, and as a result became also more or less non-transparent. Importantly also, even if potential demand typically increased, for example as a consequence of rising incomes, potential supply expanded or increased even more so, for example as a result of innovations (Schumpeter, 1942). The rise of these buyers' markets forced or allowed marketers to carry through all sorts of marketing efforts to attract the attention, interest and preference of potential customers (van Waterschoot and De Haes, 2008).

The outcome of the aforementioned developments was the rise of a basically new exchange model different from the one traditionally assumed by economists (see Figure 9.1). The new model generically synthesizes the essential forces and properties of any marketing situation as opposed to other types of exchange situations. As such it summarizes the basics of both marketing theory and practice. Their subject matter concentrates on particular types of exchanges, the core conditions of which were generically defined by Philip Kotler (1972). For marketing exchanges to occur, the following conditions are necessary:

(1) [the presence of] two or more parties believing that it is appropriate or desirable to deal with one another; (2) a scarcity of goods [in the generic sense of the latter term]; (3) concept of private property which allows to make, accept or reject an offer; (4) each of the parties must possess

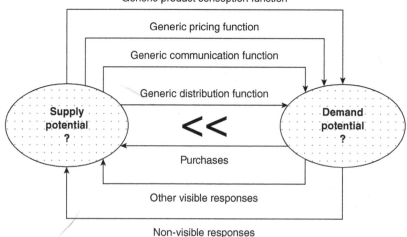

Figure 9.1 The new exchange model.

Source: van Waterschoot et al. (2006)

something that might be of value to the other; (5) the 'wanting' party must be able to offer some kind of payment for it; and (6) the 'owning' party must be willing to forego the object or service for the payment. (Kotler, 1972: 47)

On top of these structural exchange conditions there are some typical properties explaining the distinct character of the new exchange model: heterogeneity and non-transparency of demand and supply as well as the prevalence of buyers' markets (represented in Figure 9.1 by dots, question marks and inequality signs, respectively) (Levitt, 1980; van Waterschoot and De Haes, 2008). A major distinctive idea of the new model as opposed to the traditional microeconomic model is (are) the implied type(s) of buyer response(s). The outcomes of the new model are far more differentiated than the sole key question in the traditional economic models, which is 'to buy or not to buy'. Additional types of visible responses become important like, for example, store visits, active information gathering or the relationship that consumers build with a business or a brand (Grönroos, 1994; Park et al., 2013). On the other hand, non-visible reactions like brand learning as well as delayed reactions, like possibly consumer satisfaction and trust, are considered (Tax and Brown, 1998). Consequently, and importantly, the new exchange model allows the integration of subjective and even non-rational behaviour (Bagozzi, 1975).

This new exchange model structurally implies four unavoidable and therefore generic marketing exchange functions. These are in spectacular contrast with the absence of those functions in the traditional models of microeconomics during the birth era of the new marketing discipline, which were focusing mainly on pure, transparent markets ruled by rationality (van Waterschoot, 2000; van Waterschoot and De Haes, 2008; van Waterschoot and van den Bulte, 1992; van Waterschoot et al., 2006). In Figure 9.1 these four generic marketing exchange functions are represented by arrows originating from the marketer(s) towards the market(s). In 'reciprocal marketing' they go both ways (van Waterschoot and De Haes, 2008).

- *A generic product conception function.* In the era of the emergence of the new exchange model products and services are increasingly becoming heterogeneous, implying a passive or active product conception by marketers. This is in sharp contrast with homogeneous markets, which do not pose any significant strategic choice in terms of product composition. Now, a choice needs to be made anyway – actively or passively – between the many imaginable alternative product concepts to determine which specific product composition(s) would be marketed. So, a first vital, unavoidable exchange function consists of configuring something that would be valued by the prospective exchange party.
- *A generic pricing function.* Market participants enjoy more or less price freedom compared to the harsh reality of solely having to take or leave a market price. Now, they have the opportunity to – again actively or passively – follow a pricing strategy. In fact, in many cases marketers are even forced to. So, a second unavoidable exchange function consists of determining the compensation and sacrifices to be brought by the prospective exchange parties.
- *A generic communication function.* The previous two functions would not allow any exchange if no communication could take place. In the described setting, communication with an eye on information and persuasion has become inevitable as well. The respective

parties need to be informed about one another's existence, intentions and requirements and perhaps be persuaded about the attractiveness of the other party's offering, or even about entering into such an exchange relationship at all. This third fundamental exchange function therefore consists of bringing the offer to the attention of the prospective exchange party and influencing its feelings and preferences about it.

- *A generic distribution function.* In the described setting, production and consumption are separated by different types of gaps – geographic, choice, time and amount (Bucklin, 1966, 1972) – which market participants have to bridge in order to make their products or services available for acquisition. No exchange would come about if the respective parties were actually unable to deliver the object or service that is exchanged for some higher valued object or service. Here arises a fourth fundamental exchange function of placing the offer at the disposal of the prospective exchange party.

The marketing discipline considers these four functions as generic, in the sense that they have to be fulfilled for exchange to come about. This necessity follows from the marketing discipline's realistic market assumptions, which would be called impure by economists because of the supposed lack of instantaneous transactions and perfect knowledge (Houston and Gassenheimer, 1987: 15). Consequently, poor execution of any of these functions would bring about poor exchange results or worse results than those that could potentially have taken place. However, if any of these generic functions were not carried out at all, no exchange could take place, no demand could be created, fulfilled or maintained (van Waterschoot and van den Bulte, 1992).

The nature and scope of the marketing mix metaphor and concept

In view of the properties of the new exchange model, the four generic exchange functions are needed to influence demand to a greater or lesser extent. These functions, however, cannot possibly be instrumental in themselves. In fact, they materialize via actual choices in terms of demand-impinging instruments, namely controllable elements affecting demand like, for example, all sorts of product and/or service attributes, product and/or service ranges, price schemes, all sorts of communication messages, personal and non-personal communication, communication vehicles and schedules, distribution networks, compensation schemes for intermediaries, exclusiveness arrangements, merchandising schemes, etc. These demand-impinging instruments can theoretically be spread out over time as well as targeted in numerous ways and combined in a myriad of ways. The underlying concept is that of a controllable mixture of demand-impinging elements – or instruments – with divergent potential results depending on the timing and composition of the mixture. This idea received the suggestive and figurative label of 'marketing mix' (concept). It is indissolubly inherent to marketing activity. The reality of a large number and variety of demand-impinging instruments that had to be combined was indeed structurally implied by the new exchange model from its very beginnings. That said, this idea was not clearly identified and described for a long period. It was not only a hardly identified concept; for a long time it also remained a kind of implicit concept without a name (van Waterschoot and De Haes, 2008). The term 'marketing mix' was only coined in 1953 by Neil Borden in his presidential address to the American Marketing Association. He had been inspired by James Culliton (1948), who in the preceding decade had pictured the marketing executive as somebody combining different ingredients (van Waterschoot and van den Bulte, 1992). From that point on, the term 'marketing mix' not only referred to a picture or metaphor of pursuing certain market responses by using mixtures of instruments, but also to the corresponding concept (Borden, 1964) as well as to the included instruments.

The mix metaphor not only suggested the availability of a wide range of possible ingredients as well as numerous ways in which these elements could be combined. It also indicated the fact that different amalgamations might produce different results, with some more preferable than others. The marketing mix expression reminds one of many other types of combination with similar characteristics. Not every mixed grill platter is as delicious as any other platter and not every single drink can be combined successfully with any other type of drink. The metaphor also suggests that the 'mixer' has control over a number of elements which he or she can self-reliantly mix as he or she likes. This is applicable only to some extent since marketing reality is always subject to some constraints. The mix metaphor contains even some more suggestions which cannot be taken literally in all instances, like, for example, the suggestion of a one-time operation versus the reality of interactive operations and a longer term orientation (van Waterschoot and De Haes, 2008).

Formally defined, the concept of the marketing mix refers to the set of 'controllable demand-impinging elements (instruments) that can be combined into a marketing programme used by a firm (or any other organisation) to achieve a certain level and type of response from its target market' (van Waterschoot and van den Bulte, 1992: 88). By definition, instruments are concerned with directly influencing demand to a greater or lesser extent, like the price of a product or the way in which it is advertised.

However, not all marketing instruments are necessarily marketing mix instruments. For example, marketing research – if carried out properly and if its information value exceeds its costs – is often a useful marketing instrument without formally belonging to the marketing mix. The reason is that marketing research, normally speaking – unless the 'research' project is intended as a communications campaign in the first place – does not directly influence demand in any way or to any extent. Customers will not start buying more of brands for the mere reason that their parent company or distributors increase their marketing research budget, employ more competent research personnel, hire a more skilled research agency or start using more appropriate research techniques. Adequate marketing research will normally influence demand only indirectly, for example by helping to (re-)specify product characteristics to better match customer needs and desires and enhance consumers' willingness to adopt a new product, or to communicate the benefits of a product more effectively to consumers (Gourville, 2004; van Waterschoot, 2000).

Next to exerting a more or less direct effect of a variable magnitude sooner or later, the demand-impinging element should also be controllable to be a marketing mix instrument. Fine weather fosters coastal tourism or even makes us appreciate and enjoy a bottle of wine more (Bruwer and Alant, 2009), but is not a marketing mix instrument. However, the distinction between controllable and non-controllable elements is not always obvious and lack of control does not necessarily imply lack of influence. Having control over a variable means being able to establish its value. Influence over a variable means having some but not complete control of it (Ackoff, 1981: 174). A country's birth rate, for example, is an important, but in the short-term uncontrollable demand-impinging element for a manufacturer of baby clothes. If, however, government measures such as birth premiums can significantly raise demand and if government measures are highly dependent on company lobbying, then the birth rate can be called susceptible to influence. As the example suggests, controllable (marketing mix) variables may be used to influence crucial, but uncontrollable environmental elements (van Waterschoot and van den Bulte, 1992).

Marketing arguably applies without any exception to any voluntary exchange situation matching the properties of the new exchange model. Consequently, not just business organizations and their dealings with client publics may be concerned, but possibly also other organizations like, for example, non-profit organizations and possibly also other sorts of publics like, for example, employees or philanthropists and donors. At least, to the extent that and as long as the properties of the new exchange model prevail. This observation fully matches the conclusions of the broadening controversy among academics in the early 1970s and the corresponding, generic definition of marketing by Kotler (1972).

All the applications or situations embraced by Kotler's (1972) generic marketing definition imply the mutual prevalence and use of the earlier mentioned four generic exchange functions, because otherwise exchanges simply cannot be realized. Partial applications in terms of generic exchange functions being used can consequently only be borderline cases. An example of the latter would be when the police try to convince the general public that they are their friend, thereby relying basically on communication only. But in any of these cases – full-fledged or partial – marketing mix instruments are inherently and indissolubly needed. The generic exchange functions are structurally present in any marketing situation, but can at the same time not materialize without the use of concrete demand-impinging instruments. In other words, the mix concept, by definition, applies to any marketing situation without any exception: consumer marketing, B2B marketing, non-profit marketing, service marketing, retail marketing, etc. The mix concept even applies, by definition, also to less traditional sub-fields such as e-marketing (Möller, 2006) and relationship marketing.

Self-evidently, the inevitable logical conclusion that the mix concept applies to any marketing situation without exception, does not counter-argue the fact that major differences exist between the different groups of applications and corresponding schools of thought. Just like there exist lots of differences within these groups, for example as a consequence of different strategic and/or tactical options. Relationship marketing is a case in point. In many instances relationships (in terms of reciprocal personal knowledge, social contacts, emotional ties, etc.) naturally develop between marketers and their customers (or any other relevant public) (Grönroos, 1994). Naturally also, marketers attempt to capitalize on cultivating these relationships as this is an expedient towards gaining control over the exchange process, or, in other words, a means of increasing the likelihood of positive responses from the market (Gruen et al., 2000). As long as relationships do not completely rule the game – that is, as long as the desired responses of the market are not structurally guaranteed – there is still very much a marketing situation at stake. Otherwise, other exchange mechanisms (e.g. social, emotional, financial, ownership, contractual systems) take over and the situation can no longer be considered as possessing a marketing character. The point therefore is, that as long as the upper limits of the relationship have not been reached in terms of magnitude and strength, and as long there is still a marketing exchange framework at hand, the generic exchange functions still largely and unavoidably determine the outcome of the exchange process. These exchange functions in turn cannot do else but materialize by means of demand-impinging instruments under some form or another. Consequently, demand needs to be managed under some form or another. So, also under relationship marketing, prices are charged, product concepts are being conceived, developed, delivered and communicated. The specific mix approach will probably be affected and characterized by the relationship context, resulting, for example, in a relatively great deal of personal and ongoing communication, pricing schemes based on loyalty, etc. The prevalence of these peculiarities, however, does not counter-argue the basic presence of a marketing mix. So, for logical reasons, we fully agree with those authors who are keen on underscoring the peculiarities of their sub-field, as far as they point at genuine differences (Grönroos, 1994). However, also for logical reasons, we do not agree with those who would go as far as denying the undeniable, namely the common generic roots of their sub-field with the overall marketing field, including the marketing mix.

Marketing mix functions, instruments and effects

The generic exchange functions materialize by means of the marketing mix, implying that those functions also represent the generic functions of the marketing mix itself. The most general marketing mix effects are those following from the simultaneous pursuit or execution of all exchange functions by means of the overall mixture of instruments. This will be discussed in the first subsection. The second subsection explores the horizon of possible effects of the mix still further as well as that of individual instruments. The third subsection distinguishes between strategic and tactical effects and instruments, also with an eye on the discussion of mix classifications further on.

Primary versus secondary functions, instruments and effects

In practice, numerous marketing mix instruments exist. Out of a long list of theoretical mix instruments, a specific actual combination or combinations have to be chosen, targeted and timed, taking into consideration their expected effects. A fundamental observation is the fact that any instrument out of that mixture, in itself, predominantly serves one of the four generic functions mentioned previously, but that at the same time it also contributes – albeit to a lesser extent – to the fulfilment of the three other functions.

It should be underscored that all possible individual marketing mix instruments do have primary as well as secondary effects, when looked at from a functional point of view. This distinction follows from the vital observation that any marketing mix instrument serves any generic market-ing mix or exchange function. However, any marketing mix instrument actually serves primarily one of the four generic functions (at the same time it may also primarily serve the so-called 'promotional' function – see **pp. 215–7**). The corresponding effects on demand are the instru-ment's primary effects. At the same time, it is crucial to observe that any marketing mix instrument also contributes, to a lesser extent, to the other generic functions (van Waterschoot, 2000: 189). The corresponding effects on demand are the instrument's secondary effects. The idea is sum-marized in Table 9.1.

Advertising is a classical communication instrument within the marketing mix, meaning that its primary function (and corresponding effect) is one of bringing the offer to the attention of

Table 9.1   The multifunctional effects of marketing mix instruments.

	Marketing mix instruments				
	Product instruments	Price instruments	Communication instruments	Distribution instruments	Promotion instruments
Generic functions					
Need fulfilment function					
Configuration of something valued by the prospective exchange party	xxxxx	x	x	x	x or xxxxx
Pricing function					
Determination of the compensation and sacrifices to be brought by the prospective exchange party	x	xxxxx	x	x	x or xxxxx
Communication function					
Bringing the offer to the attention of the prospective exchange party and influencing its feelings and preferences about it	x	x	xxxxx	x	x or xxxxx
Distribution function					
Placing the offer at the disposal of the prospective exchange party	x	x	x	xxxxx	x or xxxxx
Promotional function					
Inducing immediate, overt behaviour by strengthening the generic functions during relatively short periods of time	x or xxxxx	x or xxxxx	x or xxxxx	x or xxxxx	xxxxx

Notes: xxxxx = primary effects; x = secondary effects.

Source: van Waterschoot and Van den Bulte, 1992: 89

the prospective exchange party and influencing its feelings and preferences about it (van Waterschoot, 2000; van Waterschoot and van den Bulte, 1992). At the same time, however, advertising may add extra need fulfilment to the product – for instance, by providing prestige or the suggestion or belief of power or excellence (Ackerberg, 2001). This is typically the case, for example, with Nike or Adidas advertisements (where wearing certain sneakers or running shoes makes consumers feel like the superstar athlete they admire and want to follow). Conversely, advertising may imply a cost and hence influence the pricing function of the marketing mix. Such could be the case if a highly distinguished, favourite brand of wrist watches was featured in a notorious magazine, like – supposedly – *Playboy*. Advertising also contributes to the availability function of the marketing mix – for instance by informing the public about the available points of sale. Finally, advertising contributes to the promotion function (see **pp. 215–7**) of the marketing mix, even if theme advertising is concerned which, by definition, tries to build a long-term image and to prepare for long-term sales. Coca-Cola theme advertisements, for instance, next to establishing and maintaining this picture of young, smart and joyful people who at crucial moments of their lives never fail to think of Coca-Cola, will also make some people under some circumstances aware of their current thirst, or at least make them search almost on the spot for their favourite thirst quencher.

Each individual marketing mix instrument may in itself foster or hamper any marketing mix function from several points of view. The use of Tetra Briks, for example, fosters large-scale distribution of fruit juice, whereas the use of fragile fantasy bottles would rather hamper this sort of distribution. When the instruments are being mixed, it is logical that any positive or negative primary instrumental and also any secondary effect may – or even will – interact positively or negatively with any other instrument's primary and secondary effects. Tetra Briks would suit sales via hypermarkets and discount establishments, but might sustain less well a quality brand image. The latter would probably be more sustained if the beverages were packed in elegant bottles and sold via upmarket establishments. If the interaction among instruments is harmonious, this will contribute to positive synergy creation within the marketing mix. If the interaction among instruments is negative, though, dis-synergy will follow. The possible mix interactions are manifold and not necessarily easily identifiable and predictable at the level of primary effects. At the level of secondary effects, they are typically even still much less obvious and less easy to predict – a phenomenon adding to the impression of creative genius required to find the magic mix formula.

So, any specific marketing mix instrument affects all four generic marketing mix functions anyhow, but predominantly typically only one of them. On the other hand, any generic marketing mix function is served by any specific marketing mix instrument or hampered by it. Since in actual applications several specific instruments contribute to the fulfilment of all four generic functions, coordination becomes of utmost importance. The instrumental choices should be made in such a way that the different elements do not only reinforce one another's positive effects and neutralize one another's negative effects with regard to one single generic function, but also with regard to all four such functions simultaneously. Moreover, each generic function actually consists of a set of specific sub-functions that require specific instrumental goals. Communication, for example, presumes, among other things, the creation of awareness, knowledge, preference and conviction.

The wide range of marketing mix effects

The range of marketing mix effects is particularly wide and can be looked at from several points of view. Marketing mix effects can be looked at from the point of view of functions, from the stance of the overall mixture, from the stance of specific instruments or from the perspective of interactions among instruments at primary or secondary functional level, etc. Each of these viewpoints, though, can still be differentiated further by looking into, for example, the magnitude and timing of the effect, its desirability, among other things. The effects of marketing mix instruments may, for example, be greater or smaller, may take place sooner or later, and may lead to general demand changes for the whole product category and/or for particular offerings. This section briefly explores some of the most important distinctions (van Waterschoot, 2000: 183–94).

A first distinction is to be made between behavioural and mental responses. Marketing mixes may lead to actual purchases, or else to other forms of visible behaviour such as the visit to trade shows or word-of-mouth communication. They may also lead to non-visible behaviour in the form of mental responses such as increased brand awareness, certain brand associations, increased knowledge of product or service features, strengthening of attitudes, etc. Ultimately, most marketing programmes aim at making people act in a specific way favoured by the marketer. In an economic setting, this is mostly buying. This does not conflict, however, with the fact that other sorts of reactions may also be favoured and somehow fit a marketing programme. The type of response provoked by marketing mix instruments may therefore range all the way from mental changes to visible behaviour. Depending on the case, these changes may (be intended to) take place in a shorter or longer time period. The building of a brand image or preference may take a long time and the development of a strong customer–brand relationship may take longer still. Conversely, when a supermarket chain announces a significant price reduction on a popular brand of soft drinks during one week, its goal is to create store traffic within the course of that particular week. Marketing mix instruments typically provoke both direct and indirect effects or responses. A direct reaction is one that follows from the use of mix instruments without any intermediate reaction. The opposite is the case for indirect effects. The famous Michelin guides, for example, were originally introduced with the intention of encouraging French drivers to travel further, and thus to use more tyres. They did this by informing car owners of the location of attractive towns, hotels, restaurants, etc. Marketing mix effects can range all the way from constructive to destructive ones. For example, as a result of charging a discount price for the products of a prestige brand, massive sales may accrue, but the brand image may become damaged. Furthermore, marketing mix effects can be desirable versus undesirable. For example, a low price strategy may bring about an aspired market share gain, but also cause the undesirable organization of a 'grey' parallel distribution channel supplying neighbouring countries (Cespedes et al., 1988). The use of marketing mix instruments may also lead to major versus minor effects. An advertising campaign, for example by a government organization, may only cause an extremely small effect, probably in spectacular contrast to what had been expected beforehand. Furthermore, immediate effects versus delayed effects may be caused: the immediate effect of a price penetration strategy, for example, may be relatively modest in the short run, but have as a consequence that the corresponding brand can position itself as a mainstream brand in the future (Pauwels et al., 2002).

Last but not least, it should be remarked that most of the typical marketing mix instruments are used to increase demand. Because of possible differences between desirable and undesirable demand, though, other possibilities also prevail. It could be advisable, for example, to limit demand temporarily and/or selectively, and/or to synchronize demand to bring it into harmony with the organization's production capacity (Kotler and Levy, 1971).

Strategic versus tactical marketing mix instruments and effects

With an eye on the discussion of marketing mix classifications in the next sections, some of the distinctions discussed in the previous paragraphs can best be combined already at this point into the crucial distinction between strategic and tactical marketing mix effects and instruments. Strategic instruments are the ones that have their effects essentially spread out over time. They do not have their main effect taking place immediately, but largely in the medium and relatively longer term. Strategic instruments are also the ones of which the effects are not necessarily visible, in the sense of not necessarily leading to overt (visible) behaviour. Tactical instruments, on the other hand, are instruments that predominantly lead to visible, short-term effects.

This distinction results from the fact that the strategic use of the four generic exchange functions does not always suffice to bring about exchanges. There are four typical reasons for this: physical inertia, psychological inertia, typical forms of risks and finally also competitive inertia (Beem and Shaffer, 1981: 16, 18). Direct inducement or provocation is in some situations a necessary condition for the exchange to take place. As a result, an additional 'situational' or 'promotional exchange function' may be needed at times to overcome these forms of inertia or to take extra advantage of favourable market developments, next to the four generic exchange functions. Direct inducement or provocation is indeed in some situations a necessary condition for exchange to take place, or else is called for boosting demand to a still more favourable level. Hence, promotion represents a 'situational' or 'complementary' marketing function (van Waterschoot and van den Bulte, 1992: 88). This non-generic, but oppositely situational marketing mix function specifically provokes immediate, visible reactions.

The instruments which specifically execute this promotional function are tactical or sales promotion (mix) instruments as opposed to strategic marketing mix instruments. Examples are direct-effect advertisements as opposed to indirect-effect advertisements. The latter can often be found when companies try to maintain their image in advertisements with more or less general statements. Direct-effect advertisements focus on price elements and more particularly on temporary price reductions in many cases. Therefore, this type of advertisement typically provokes short-term demand reactions and is thus a promotional instrument. The promotional mix/instruments can more generally be positively defined as follows:

> The subset of demand-impinging instruments that have no power of themselves but can, during relatively short periods of time, complement and sustain the basic instruments of the marketing

mix (namely product, price, distribution, and communication) for the purpose of stimulating pro-spective exchange partners (commonly referred to as target market(s)) to a significant degree of desirable forms of immediate, overt behaviour. (van Waterschoot and van den Bulte, 1992: 89)

In summary, promotional instruments possess the following properties:

1. Their primary effect is visible (overt) behaviour, e.g. purchase or trial use.
2. The instruments are used on a temporary basis, because if they were used for a longer time they would lose their potential effectiveness.
3. They are supplementary instruments.
4. They supplement *any* sort of basic category (see functional marketing mix classification, **see p. 214–5**).
5. They cannot possibly exist on their own.
6. They are used as tactical instruments, depending on the circumstances.
7. Their secondary effect(s) are often not visible (at least not immediately).

It should be emphasized that the multifunctionality of instruments, including the distinction between primary and secondary functionality, also extends to promotional instruments. Promotion or sales promotion instruments (e.g. temporary price discounts), by definition, pri-marily contribute to the promotion function next to their primary generic function (e.g. the pricing function) (van Waterschoot, 2000). Yet, these instruments also affect the (strategic aspects of the) other generic functions, sometimes in a negative way. By their very nature, temporary price reductions, for instance, primarily influence the pricing function next to the promotion function. They could more specifically limit the bracket of pricing possibilities for the future. If customers' price expectations were reshaped by massive price reductions, it may indeed turn out to be difficult to charge a higher price again afterwards. Promotion instruments may, however, also play a secondary, even undeniable, role outside their own strict field of operations. Consumer price discounts may result in, say, retailers spotting massive sales oppor-tunities and therefore granting much more shelf space to the brand than they would have done otherwise. As a result, not only the availability function, but also the communication function may be influenced. More critically, the impression might be created that a very ordinary brand would be involved, available everywhere, with no distinct features except its price. If for that reason the exclusiveness of the product is (becomes) endangered, this loss of exclusiveness touches upon the need fulfilment function of the marketing mix.

Pragmatic, mnemonic and pedagogical mix classifications

In the development of a new body of thought, such as marketing throughout the 20th cen-tury, the making of listings and taxonomies is one of the primary tasks actually carried through. Not surprisingly therefore, early taxonomies were not developed in a deductive way on strictly logical grounds as a derivation from existing theory (Hunt, 1991). Rather, they were made in an inductive way. Known elements, supposedly belonging to the investigated population, were inventoried and grouped into more or less crude, somewhat judgemental or even intuitive classes on the basis of their similarity. In this way, early writers on the marketing mix tried to itemize the large number of controllable demand-impinging instruments. Frey (1956) and Borden (1964) adopted a checklist approach. Other authors developed more succinct and convenient classifications that could be easily memorized (Frey, 1956; Howard, 1957; Lazer and Kelly, 1962; McCarthy, 1960). Of the many developed schemata, only McCarthy's has survived and has even become the 'dominant design' or 'received view', or at least the most popular view.

The McCarthy typology has become known as the '4 Ps classification' of the marketing mix, since it distinguishes four classes of items under four headings beginning with the letter P: 'Product', 'Price', 'Place' and 'Promotion'. Although McCarthy only named these classes without defining them, three of them correspond more or less roughly to the previously mentioned generic marketing mix functions.

The first class contains product-related instruments such as product variety, product quality, design, features, brand name, packaging, sizes, services, warranties and return. The second class comprises price-related instruments like the list price of products, discounts, allowances, the payment period and credit terms. The third class holds place-related instruments like the choice of distribution channels, the coverage of existing outlets or the location of outlets. The fourth class of instruments in the McCarthy typology is a hybrid one. Whereas the three previous classes do roughly correspond to three of the generic exchange functions of the new exchange model, McCarthy's fourth P does not even roughly correspond to the fourth generic function. Indeed this fourth P is typically subdivided into four sub-classes, of which only the first three exclusively encompass instruments that mainly aim to bring the offer to the attention of the prospective exchange party and to influence feelings and preferences about it. These three sub-classes are: mass communication, personal communication and publicity. The fourth P of the McCarthy typology, however, also encompasses a large, residual fourth sub-category, which serves as a catch-all to host all marketing mix instruments that do not find a place in any other category. In contrast with the three previously mentioned typical communication sub-classes, only the fourth sub-category of McCarthy' s fourth P consists of actual promotion instruments in the strict sense of the word, whereas the other three are basically strategic communication instruments. A traditional description representative of this (sales) promotion category of McCarthy's popular split-up is the following: 'Those marketing activities, other than personal selling, advertising and publicity, that stimulate consumer purchasing and dealer effectiveness, such as displays, shows and exhibitions, demonstrations, and various nonrecurring selling efforts not in the ordinary routine' (Alexander, 1960: 20).

In terms of appeal and popularity, the McCarthy typology has been and still is amazingly popular, presumably as a result of the P-mnemonic. From a classificatory point of view, though, it fails to meet most of the basic quality criteria as put forward by Hunt (1991). It has no clearly defined classification dimensions, no positive definition of its classes, it suffers in terms of mutual exclusiveness and implies a major catch-all category.

Since the 1960s, the use and interpretation of the concept of the marketing mix has evolved and developed, not least through the classification of the 4 Ps by McCarthy (1960) in spite of its classificatory shortcomings. This classification, although it quickly became a standard, has not remained static. Later researchers have indeed sought to expand the classification; whereas others still have sought to criticize it.

Throughout the years, a number of alternative marketing mix classifications have been formulated, often to reflect the peculiarities of a specific field of application. Remarkably, in most instances this adaptation was realized by adding one or more Ps to McCarthy's mnemonic 4 Ps list. In instances where an explication of a sub-category of instruments is concerned, such an addition – although conceptually not strictly necessary – is defensible on pedagogical grounds. In instances where an extension outside the boundaries of the marketing mix is concerned, no conceptual justification exists. Despite the indisputable relevance of the managerial issues behind the added Ps, the extension of the mnemonic list mainly serves as a sometimes disputable eye catcher. In further instances, the proposed names of the new categories are indeed not appropriate as a result of the obligatory P. The subsequent paragraphs summarize the main examples of such explications and extensions.

Occasionally, a separate fifth P is added to denote 'People', 'Personnel' or 'Personal selling'. In this way, a collective noun is provided to stress the importance of all types of selling and servicing efforts which are being carried out by any person within the organization. In applications where sales efforts are of a typically high strategic value – as, for example, in the case of service marketing – no fundamental objection can be made to/against this explication, although there is no conceptual necessity since the provision of services belongs to the P of the (service) 'Product', and sales efforts form part of the 'P' of 'Communication'. In retail marketing, aside from the supplementary P of 'People', a further P is often added to denote the 'Presentation' of merchandise as well as the store layout. Again, an explication is involved that is defensible on pedagogical grounds, but which is not necessary from a conceptual or classificatory point of view since the generically rooted 4 Ps also hold these elements.

In service marketing, Ps have also been added to represent 'Participants', 'Physical evidence' and 'Process' (Booms and Bitner, 1981). The participants in a service marketing situation can significantly improve or harm the quality of the execution of service (Eisingerich et al., 2014). However, the activities of the personnel carrying out the service conceptually belong to the first P of 'Product', encompassing all instruments which aim primarily at the fulfilment of needs and wants. Insofar as the clients are meant by 'Participants', the addition becomes conceptually incorrect, since the marketing mix groups demand-impinging elements and not the actual demand-constituting elements. The 'Physical environment' where the service is provided, together with tangible elements which are used to support the service, obviously influences demand. Where these elements are under the control of the marketer, they form part of the instruments 'Product' or 'Place'. If these elements cannot be controlled by the manager, they are, by definition, not marketing mix variables. The same remark also holds for the procedural elements of servicing, meaning that a separate P for 'Process' is not really necessary.

With regard to the persuasion of the public outside the most typical target groups, Kotler (1986) has introduced the concept of 'megamarketing', denoting the art of supplying benefits to parties other than target consumers and intermediaries, like agents, distributors and dealers – parties such as governments, labour unions and other interest groups that can block profitable entry into a market. Specific instruments in this context are 'Public relations' and 'Power'. Public relations try to influence public opinion, mainly by means of mass communication techniques. Power, on the other hand, addresses itself to 'influential industry officials, legislators, and government bureaucrats to enter and operate in the target market, using sophisticated lobbying and negotiating skills in order to achieve the desired response from the other party without giving away the house' (Kotler, 1986: 120). The term 'power' is not at all appropriate, though, in this instance. Power refers to the ability of the marketer to get some other party (consumer, distributor, government, etc.) to do what it would otherwise not have done (buy, search for information, give a permit) (Coughlan et al., 2006: 197). Marketing mix instruments of whatever kind – if properly combined – are capable of developing a certain (smaller or larger) amount of power. Calling one instrument category, applied in a specific context, 'Power' implies both a linguistic and conceptual distortion to make the instrument fit a mnemonic row.

The development of alternative frameworks which led to new discussions of McCarthy's 4 Ps (1960) was further intensified by the rapid growth of the internet – or more concretely, the growth of the World Wide Web (WWW) as the most important information system on the internet. With regard to the e-marketing (or web-marketing) mix of pure-players or click-and-mortars, the 4 C model, the 4 S model and the 4 Ps + $P^2C^2S^3$ model are said to have 'tremendous influence' (Sam and Chatwin, 2012: 14). According to Lauterborn's 4 C model, a successful marketing plan should focus on 'Consumer's wants and needs', '(Consumer's) Cost' (to satisfy that want or need), 'Convenience' (to buy) and 'Communication' (Lauterborn, 1990). The 4 S (or web-marketing mix) model of Constantinides (2002), on the other hand, puts emphasis on strategic elements and interactivity and identifies the 'Scope' (strategic issues), the 'Site' (operational issues), the 'Synergy' (organizational issues) and the 'System' (technical issues) as critical factors. The factor 'Scope' refers to decisions that have to be made with respect to the strategic and operational objectives of the online venture, the market definition, the degree of readiness of the organization for e-commerce and the strategic role of the e-commerce for the organization. These decisions will have consequences, e.g. for the content of the 'Site' – the company–customer interface and 'prime source of customer experience' (Constantinides, 2002: 64). The factor 'Synergy' refers to those integrating processes that are necessary for realizing the organization's objectives, and the term 'System' represents technological and site servicing issues. Unlike the 4 C and the 4 S models, the 4 Ps + $P^2C^2S^3$ framework of Kalyanam and McIntyre (2002) is based on McCarthy's marketing mix, and thus includes the elements 'Product', 'Price', 'Place' and 'Promotion' as well as the factors 'Personalization', 'Privacy', 'Customer service', 'Community', 'Site', 'Security' and 'Sales promotion'.

Undoubtedly, new information and communication technologies have changed the ways that some marketing activities are performed. With regard to the factor 'Product', depending on the industry, personalized products (and services) or even digital products (and services) can be offered, for example. As far as the 'Price' is concerned, organizations can – among others – modify prices in real time. With respect to the 'Place', organizations can sell products online, whereby consumers expect service 24 hours a day, seven days a week, fast distribution, secure ordering and payment systems as well as buyer-friendly return policies. Especially with regard to the factor 'Promotion', the internet offers new possibilities to interact with (potential) customers and improve customer relationship management. As of late, much has been written, for example, on the role of social media and the concept of customer engagement with the advent and growth of the internet and its various applications (Eisingerich et al., 2015; Hennig-Thurau et al., 2010; Verhoef et al., 2010). Thus, the internet can afford economic actors new ways of reaching out to, connecting with and selling to/buying from others in new ways. However, this does not mean that the internet fundamentally changes the role of the marketing mix: the internet is merely a new tool, place of exchange, etc., albeit arguably a critically important one. So, following the conservatives' view, McCarthy's 4 Ps can also be applied to digital environments (Dominici, 2009: 18).

Pragmatic classifications and especially those expressed in particular mnemonics – like a number of Ps – may well be meritorious during the infant stage of a discipline. Intuitive categorizations under the form of mnemonics rightly help in summarizing and memorizing crude key essentials of a new field during its pioneering stage. Over time, however, the drawbacks of this sort of infant classification become more disturbing as the discipline matures and becomes – or should become – more sophisticated. The divisions of the intuitive typologies are not clear cut but arbitrary, and the 'all other' categories become larger and larger, thereby causing increasing confusion (van Waterschoot and De Haes, 2008). The mnemonic form of the early typologies paradoxically risks becoming obligatory, leading to mnemonic extensions which further risk distorting or prohibiting logical reasoning. These disturbing phenomena are very typical for the most well-known of the pragmatic classifications, namely the overly popular 4 Ps classification of McCarthy (1960).

So, in conclusion, sticking to pragmatic mnemonics in a mature discipline is unjustified both from a conceptual and, consequently, also from a managerial point of view. It prohibits the development of logical reasoning as well as the process of scientific fact finding and the formulating of managerial recommendations. Extending mnemonics for eye-catching reasons is tempting, but risky from the point of view of conceptual and terminological distortion.

A functional classification of the marketing mix

In view of the fact that marketing mix instruments make up the central weaponry for influencing demand, commonsense suffices for understanding that it is more than advisable to possess a reliable classification of these instruments. This could be compared with the literal weaponry of an army, where it would matter and make a difference, for instance, to know what sorts of guns make up part of the arsenal in terms of impact, range, etc. (von Clausewitz, 1984). A good classification is one that can host any element of the corresponding – well-defined – population and leaves no room for any outlier. It uses explicit classification criteria clearly informing users about the grounds of the split-ups used. The classification criteria should be independent of each other. Moreover, the resultant classes should be capable of capturing any element belonging to the population, and any element should fit not more than one class at the same time.

This section provides a functional classification of the marketing mix, thereby using two main, explicit criteria (van Waterschoot and van den Bulte, 1992). As a first criterion we will look at the primary generic function of the instruments within the context under study. This enables straightforward classification, since any marketing mix instrument is linked to any exchange function in a secondary fashion. However, depending on the setting, the primary link is unique. In traditional retailing, for example, packaging could be seen as part of the product concept in the first place. In the self-service atmosphere of a hypermarket on the contrary, packaging may be a communication device in the first place.

The second classification criterion is based on the distinction between strategic marketing mix functions versus the tactical, situational or promotional function. In fact, each marketing mix instrument has both strategic and tactical effects. Some marketing mix instruments are primarily strategic instruments, though. Some mix instruments, on the other hand, are primarily tactical (see earlier discussion). The combination of these two explicit classification criteria leads to the fundamental categorization of marketing mix instruments as represented in Table 9.2. The more detailed definitions of the different categories are available in Tables 9.3a and 9.3b.

The columns of Table 9.3 (a and b) represent a classification of the marketing mix instruments on the basis of the generic function they primarily fulfil. Vertically, the marketing mix variables are subdivided according to the criterion of whether the instruments are basic to the consummation of an offer (Table 9.3a) or whether those instruments are more complementary (Table 9.3b). This supplementary mix actually contains the elements fulfilling the previously mentioned 'situational' function that is by definition found in the promotion mix.

Table 9.2 The essence of a functional marketing mix classification.

		Dominant generic marketing mix function			
		Primary instruments of the generic product conception function	**Primary instruments of the generic pricing function**	**Primary instruments of the generic communication function**	**Primary instruments of the generic distribution function**
Situational marketing mix function dominant or not?	Primary strategic instruments				
	Primary tactical instruments				

Adapted from: van Waterschoot and van den Bulte (1992).

Criticism of the marketing mix metaphor and concept

In spite of the immediate and widespread acceptance of the marketing mix concept, especially as put forth by McCarthy (1960), it – or sometimes much more the metaphor – has been criticized in several respects. Based on a literature review (Constantinides, 2002, 2006; Goi, 2009;

Table 9.3a The details of a functional marketing mix classification.

| Marketing mix | Product mix | Price mix | Communication mix | | Distribution mix | |
| | | Mass communication promotion mix | Personal communication mix | | Publicity mix | |
Basic mix	Basic product mix	Basic price mix	Basic mass communication mix	Basic personal communication mix	Basic publicity mix	Basic distribution mix
	Instruments that mainly conceive the way and extent in which the prospective exchange party's needs are satisfied, e.g. product characteristic options, assortment, brand name, packaging, quantity, factory guarantee	Instruments that mainly fix the size and the way of payment exchanged for the goods or services, e.g. list price, usual terms of payment, usual discounts, terms of credit, long-term savings campaigns	Non-personal communication efforts that mainly aim at announcing the offer or maintaining the awareness and knowledge about it: evoking or maintaining favourable feelings and removing barriers to wanting, e.g. theme advertising in various media, permanent exhibitions, certain forms of sponsorship	Personal communication efforts that mainly aim at announcing the offer or maintaining awareness and knowledge about it; evoking or maintaining favourable feelings and removing barriers to wanting, e.g. amount and type of selling, personal remunerations	Efforts that aim at inciting a third party (persons and authorities) to favourable communication about the offer, e.g. press bulletins, press conferences, tours by journalists	Instruments that mainly determine the intensity and manner of how the goods or services will be made available, e.g. different types of distribution channels, density of the distribution system, trade relation mix (policy of margins, terms of delivery, etc.) merchandising advice

Source: van Waterschoot and van den Bulte (1992: 90).

Möller, 2006; O'Malley and Patterson, 1998; van den Bulte, 1991), the most important critical points can be summarized as follows.

① First of all, the marketing mix concept is accused of applying to micro-issues only, because it takes the stance of only one exchange party, namely the seller or the 'cake mixer' or the 'channel captain' rather than the consumer or society at large. Indeed, the channel captain perspective typifies the marketing discipline as a whole, except for those fields where social goals dominate from the outset, as in the case of true charity marketing. The marketing mix concept may not be criticized in this respect, since the usefulness of a known and classified set of demand-impinging instruments – even if suggested by the specific meta-phoric expression – is not by its own nature limited to channel captain applications, but can apply to any exchange situation.

② A second criticism concerns the concept's limited managerial use in an organizational con-text because of its attributed 'lack of attention to the internal tasks of the marketing function, like disseminating information to all people involved in or affected by marketing activities,

Table 9.3b The details of a functional marketing mix classification.

Marketing mix		Price mix	Communication mix			Distribution mix
				Personal	Publicity	Distribution mix
Promotion mix	Product mix	Mass communication promotion mix		communication mix		
	Product promotion mix	Price promotion mix	Mass communication promotion mix	Personal communication promotion mix	Publicity promotion mix	Distribution promotion mix
	Supplementary group of instruments that mainly aim at inducing immediate overt behaviour by strengthening the basic product mix during relatively short periods of time,	Supplementary group of instruments that mainly aim at inducing immediate overt behaviour by strengthening the basic price mix during relatively short periods of time,	Supplementary group of instruments that mainly aim at inducing immediate overt behaviour by strengthening the basic mass communication mix during relatively short periods of time,	Supplementary group of instruments that mainly aim at inducing immediate overt behaviour by strengthening the basic personal communication mix during relatively short periods of time,	Supplementary group of instruments that mainly aim at inducing immediate overt behaviour by strengthening the basic publicity communication mix during relatively short periods of time,	Supplementary group of instruments that mainly aim at inducing immediate overt behaviour by strengthening the basic distribution mix during relatively short periods of time,
	e.g. economy packs, 3-for-the-price-of-2 deals, temporary luxury options on a car at the price of its standard model	e.g. exceptionally favourable price, end-of-season sales, exceptionally favourable terms of payment and credit, short-term savings campaigns, temporary discounts, coupons	e.g. action advertising, contests, sweep-stakes, samples, premiums, trade shows or exhibitions	e.g. temporary demonstrations, salesforce promotions such as salesforce contests	e.g. all measurements to simulate positive publicity about a sales promotion action	e.g. extra point of purchase material, trade promotions such as buying allowances, contests; temporary increase of the number of distribution outlets

Source: van Waterschoot and van den Bulte (1992: 90).

human resources management, and developing incentive and control systems' (van den Bulte, 1991: 11). <u>Another critical point</u> is related to the marketing function: the functional organization has resulted in the creation of marketing departments which are fully responsible for the marketing function although non-marketers, too, often interact with customers, and thus, for example, influence customers' satisfaction. These points of criticism result from unrealistic expectations about a fundamental and powerful, but at the same time limited concept. The marketing mix concept has not been developed to encompass all sorts of direct guidelines for internal organization and communication. On the other hand, a clearly defined and classified set of demand-impinging instruments contributes to a sound demand management. The existence of the mix concept and a sound corresponding classification should be seen as a necessary, but at the same time insufficient condition for theoretical and practical development.

Valuable research has been conducted regarding interactions and interdependencies between mix variables. In this respect, the mix concept is criticized because the hypotheses cannot be derived from the metaphor itself. This criticism can again be countered quite easily. The mere inventory of a set of instruments cannot be supposed to encompass a theory about the interactions among them. The classification of these instruments, however, can to some extent. Empirical investigation and theory building rely heavily on the way such instruments are classified. The classification itself, however, cannot be anything more than a solid tool for theory building and empirical investigation, which it cannot replace.

<u>Furthermore</u>, the mix concept is criticized for its lack of strategic elements. It is said to be 'relatively silent about such questions of which fields and specific markets the firm should be in and how to compete in these markets' (Möller, 2006: 444). Though, answering questions like these was never the primary focus of the mix concept.

A <u>sixth</u> point of criticism notes that the marketing mix concept has a rather mechanistic view of markets. The market is often described in terms of response curves, depending on a certain 'parameter' or 'marketing decision variable' or on the entire mix. In this way, the optimization problem upon which the concept of the marketing mix focuses is solved. Modelling the relationship between demand-impinging instruments and market responses serves analytical and forecasting purposes. Forgetting the limitations and assumptions of the model or technique represents an undeniable risk which cannot be attributed to the marketing mix as a concept, though. Models – whether they are of a stimulus-response or of an interactive type – suppose a sound marketing mix concept and classification, but the characteristics of the former should not be attributed to the latter and vice versa.

A seventh point of criticism is related to the previous one. The concept is accused of having a one-way (stimulus-response) character, which would impede marketing from shifting its focus from exchange as an isolated act towards the richer concept of exchange relationships. However, the marketing mix concept conflicts in no way with an idea of interaction. Indeed, its instruments and their categorization perfectly fit such approaches, as they also fit the idea of an exchange relationship. An exchange relationship supposes, for example, a more pronounced quality and service accent than would a mere one-time exchange (or transaction). Similarly, the concept does not conflict with the idea of personalization, although Constantinides (2006: 417) argues that personalized communication is not supported given the character of the mix as a mass marketing era concept. Against this background and as already outlined in previous sections, the mix concept can also be applied to specific marketing situations, like service marketing, e-marketing and relationship marketing. Though, the concept's applicability to specific marketing areas has often been denied in previous research (Constantinides, 2002, 2006; O'Malley and Patterson, 1998).

The concept's poor market and customer orientation also follows from the suggested view of the customer as someone to whom something is done – by the cake mixer – and not as someone for whom something is done. The stimulus-response approach that is attributed to the marketing mix is at the same time criticized for proposing to lump individuals into a market of homogeneous respondents. Presence or absence, as well as degree of market orientation, depends on factors like market structure, power balance between parties, organizational structures and procedures, personal attitudes as well as corporate culture, mission and goals. However, to blame the mix concept for causing a lack of market orientation is missing the point. This basic, but by its very nature limited, concept is a factual device in numerous market approaches.

The mix concept is also criticized for implying a view of the firm (or any exchange-seeking party in general) – perhaps suggested to some people by the picture of the independent cake mixer – as being a rather self-sufficient social unit having access to a considerable resource base and full control over the mix variables. Except for manufacturer–distributor links, the concept would remove resource dependency between social units. As a result, the different bridging strategies – such as, for example, bargaining contracting, cooption, joint programmes, licensing, integration, trade associations and government action – are issues that would not be taken into consideration. Here the argument can also be turned round. Inter-organizational 'bridges' will influence the specific marketing mix choice. As such, an argument is given not against but in favour of a clear concept and classification.

Another point of criticism concerns the concept's supposed reactive attitude towards the environment:

> Traditionally, marketing mix proponents have myopically considered the transactional environment to be composed of customers and dealers only, putting all other social units into the category 'contextual', hence lumping them together into faceless environmental forces. Thus blinding themselves, they have not taken into consideration the fact that the links with some transaction-environmental units and the activities these deploy can be changed through lobbying, legal action, public relations, issue advertising, strategic partnering and so on. Finding a way to control or influence variables that were previously considered to be beyond discretion, is often the cornerstone of great marketing creativity and the gateway to superior profitability. (van den Bulte, 1991: 18)

This citation contains a major and well-expressed lesson in marketing management. Marketing practice and marketing theory have been putting too much emphasis on their traditional public, but there is no logic in blaming the mix concept for that.

Finally, critics accuse the mix concept of possessing a mechanistic and rational-economic neoclassical view of markets and firms, and stripping out the institutional and social supports to market processes such as attraction, trust, friendship, power and interdependency. As a result, the marketing mix would be 'rendered impotent before many strategic management problems' (van den Bulte, 1991: 20). In this case the criticism also concerns actual marketing practice as well as the conceptual development that has taken place at an instrumental, tactical and strategic level; the criticism does not hit the mix concept itself, though.

Conclusion

The mix concept has been quintessential for marketing, as it links generic exchange functions to demand management. Even if unavoidably implied by the new exchange model, it was formulated – more especially under the form of a metaphor – only several decades after the new discipline's name 'marketing' was mentioned for the first time in 1902 as a course title (Bartels, 1962). Even if the marketing discipline, together with the underlying new exchange model and the implied mix concept originated from the consumer goods field, they generically stretch out to any exchange matching the underlying assumptions, including, for example, B2B marketing, service marketing, e-marketing and relationship marketing. That said, the peculiarities of these sub-fields are well worth being studied and also emphasized. Not to the extent, however, that the undeniably universal mix concept would be denied.

The mix metaphor has gained usage spectacularly quickly as a result of its expressiveness, liveliness, compactness, and thus memorability. Equally imaginative has been McCarthy's pragmatic grouping of the instruments. His 4 Ps classification also received acceptance speedily and easily, presumably as a result of its strong mnemonic appeal. The 4 Ps have even become synonymous with the marketing mix. They are so closely entwined that they could be considered 'Siamese' twin metaphors (van Waterschoot and De Haes, 2008). The mnemonic row, however, has too often been used as a means of explication of sub-mixes (e.g. in the case of service marketing) or in order to draw attention to marketing aspects that were not always mix issues. Over the years, the limitations of the original mnemonic approach have become apparent, among other things, as a result of the increased importance of promotion instruments in marketing practice. Consequently, the 4 Ps classification with its mixing up of strategic and tactical instruments and inherent negatively defined 'Promotion' category within the communication family, has been contested by many authors. Its adaptation, based on modern insight into promotion, significantly improves the original scheme.

The marketing mix concept itself is as elementary, powerful, and at the same time limited in marketing thinking as the alphabet is in the use and development of language. It is therefore unjustifiable to blame the mix concept for the peculiarities of the overall discipline. In the same way, the concept cannot be blamed for the limitations of the metaphor which contributed so significantly to its popularity and understanding during the infancy of the discipline.

The marketing mix concept forms a fundamental building block in theory and practice. A clearly defined, named and classified concept is a necessary, but at the same time insufficient condition for successful theory building and practical implementation. Marketing theory should concentrate its attention on measuring, explaining and predicting the isolated as well as the combined effects of the mix instruments as a solid basis for actual practice in diverse fields and circumstances.

Recommended further reading

Allenby, G.M., Arora, N. and Ginter, J.L. (1998) 'On the heterogeneity of demand', *Journal of Marketing Research* 62: 384–9.

Mason, J.B., Mayer, M.L. and Wilkinson, J.B. (1993) *Modern Retailing: Theory and Practice*, 6th edn. Homewood, IL: Irwin.

O'Malley, L., Patterson, M. and Kelly-Holmes, H. (2008) 'Death of a metaphor: reviewing the "marketing as relationships" frame', *Marketing Theory* 8: 167–87.

Payne, A. (1993) *The Essence of Services Marketing*. London: Prentice-Hall.

Shaw, E.H. and Jones, D.G.B. (2005) 'A history of schools of marketing thought', *Marketing Theory* 5: 239–81.

References

Ackerberg, D.A. (2001) 'Empirically distinguishing informative and prestige effects of advertising', *RAND Journal of Economics* 32: 316–33.

Ackoff, R.L. (1981) *Creating the Corporate Future: Plan or Be Planned For*. New York: John Wiley.

Alexander, R.S. (1960) *Marketing Definitions: A Glossary of Marketing Terms*. Chicago, IL: AMA.

Allenby, G.M., Arora, N. and Ginter, J.L. (1998) 'On the heterogeneity of demand', *Journal of Marketing Research* 62: 384–9.

Bagozzi, R.P. (1975) 'Marketing as exchange', *Journal of Marketing* 39: 32–9.

Bartels, R. (1962) *The Development of Marketing Thought*. Homewood, IL: Irwin.

Beem, E.R. and Shaffer, H.J. (1981) *Triggers to Action – Some Elements in a Theory of Promotional Inducement (Report 81–106)*. Cambridge, MA: Marketing Science Institute.

Bernays, E.L. (1928) *Propaganda*. New York: Liveright Publishing.

Booms, B.H. and Bitner, M.J. (1981) 'Marketing strategies and organization structures for service firms', in J.H. Donnelly and W.R. George (eds) *Marketing of Services*. Chicago, IL: AMA Proceedings.

Borden, N. (1964) 'The concept of the marketing mix', *Journal of Advertising Research* 4: 2–7.

Bruwer, J. and Alant, K. (2009) 'The hedonic nature of wine tourism consumption: an experiential view', *International Journal of Wine Business Research* 21: 235–57.

Bucklin, L.P. (1966) *A Theory of Distribution Channel Structure*. Berkeley, CA: IBER Special Publications.

Bucklin, L.P. (1972) *Competition and Evolution in the Distributive Trades*. Englewood Cliffs, NJ: Prentice-Hall.

Cespedes, F.V., Corey, E.R. and Rangan, V.K. (1988) 'Gray markets: causes and results', *Harvard Business Review* 66: 75–82.

Constantinides, E. (2002) 'The 4S web-marketing mix model', *Electronic Commerce Research and Applications* 1: 57–76.

Constantinides, E. (2006) 'The marketing mix revisited: towards the 21st century marketing', *Journal of Marketing Management* 22: 407–38.

Coughlan, A.T., Anderson, E., Stern, L.W. and El-Ansary, A. (2006) *Marketing Channels*, 7th edn. Upper Saddle River, NJ: Pearson Prentice-Hall.

Culliton, J.W. (1948) *The Management of Marketing Costs*. Boston, MA: Division of Research, Graduate School of Business Administration, Harvard University.

Dominici, G. (2009) 'From marketing mix to e-marketing mix: a literature overview and classification', *International Journal of Business and Management* 4: 17–24.

Eisingerich, A.B., Seigyoung, A. and Merlo, O. (2014) 'Acta non verba? The role of customer participation and word of mouth in the relationship between service firms' customer satisfaction and sales performance', *Journal of Service Research* 17: 40–53.

Eisingerich, A.B., Chun, H.H., Liu, Y., Jia, H. and Bell, S.J. (2015) 'Why recommend a brand face-to-face but not on Facebook? How word-of-mouth on online social sites differs from traditional word-of-mouth', *Journal of Consumer Psychology* 25: 120–8.

Frey, A.W. (1956) *The Effective Marketing Mix: Programming for Optimum Results*. Hanover, NH: The Amos Tuck School of Business Administration, Dartmouth College.

Fullerton, R.A. (1988) 'How modern is modern marketing? Marketing's evolution and the myth of the "production era" ', *Journal of Marketing* 52: 108–25.

Goi, C.L. (2009) 'A review of marketing mix: 4Ps or more?', *International Journal of Marketing Studies* 1: 2–15.

Gourville, J. (2004) 'Why consumers don't buy: the psychology of new product adoption', Harvard Business School Background Note 504-056, Harvard Business School Publishing, Boston, MA.

Grönroos, C. (1994) 'From marketing mix to relationship marketing', *Management Decision* 2: 4–20.

Gruen, T.W., Summers, J.O. and Acito F. (2000) 'Relationship marketing activities, commitment, and membership behaviors in professional associations', *Journal of Marketing* 64: 34–49.

Hennig-Thurau, T., Malthouse, E.C., Friege, C., Gensler, S., Lobschat, L., Rangaswamy, A. and Skiera, B. (2010) 'The impact of new media on customer relationships', *Journal of Service Research* 13: 311–30.

Houston, F.S. and Gassenheimer, J.B. (1987) 'Marketing and exchange', *Journal of Marketing* 51: 3–18.

Howard, J.A. (1957) *Marketing Management: Analysis and Decisions*. Homewood, IL: Irwin.

Hunt, S.D. (1991) *Modern Marketing Theory: Critical Issues in the Philosophy of Marketing Science*. Cincinnati, OH: South-Western Publishing.

Kalyanam, K. and McIntyre, S. (2002) 'The e-marketing mix: a contribution of the e-tailing wars', *Journal of the Academy of Marketing Science* 30: 483–95.

Kotler, P. (1972) 'A generic concept of marketing', *Journal of Marketing* 36: 46–54.

Kotler, P. (1986) 'Megamarketing', *Harvard Business Review* 64: 117–24.

Kotler, P. and Levy, S.L. (1971) 'Demarketing, yes, demarketing', *Harvard Business Review* 49: 71–80.

Lauterborn, B. (1990) 'New marketing litany: four P's passé; C-words take over', *Advertising Age* 61: 26.

Lazer, W. and Kelly, E.J. (1962) *Managerial Marketing: Perspectives and Viewpoints*, revised edn. Homewood, IL: Irwin.

Levitt, T. (1980) 'Marketing success through differentiation of anything', *Harvard Business Review* 58: 83–91.

McCarthy, E.J. (1960) *Basic Marketing: A Managerial Approach*. Homewood, IL: Irwin.

Möller, K. (2006) 'Comment on: The marketing mix revisited: towards the 21st century marketing by E. Constantinides', *Journal of Marketing Management* 22: 439–50.

O'Malley, L. and Patterson, M. (1998) 'Vanishing point: the mix management paradigm re-viewed', *Journal of Marketing Management* 14: 829–51.

Park, C.W., Eisingerich, A.B. and Park, J.W. (2013) 'Attachment-aversion (AA) model of customer–brand relationships', *Journal of Consumer Psychology* 23: 229–48.

Pauwels, K., Hanssens, D.M. and Siddarth, S. (2002) 'The long-term effects of price promotions on category incidence, brand choice, and purchase quantity', *Journal of Marketing Research* 39: 421–39.

Sam, K.M. and Chatwin, C. (2012) 'Measuring e-marketing mix elements for online business', *International Journal of E-Entrepreneurship and Innovation* 3: 13–26.

Schumpeter, J.A. (1942) *Capitalism, Socialism and Democracy*. New York: Harper & Brothers.

Tax, S.S. and Brown, S.W. (1998) 'Recovering and learning from service failure', *Sloan Management Review* 40: 75–88.

van den Bulte, C. (1991) *The Concept of the Marketing Mix Revisited: A Case Analysis of Metaphor in Marketing Theory and Management*. Ghent: The Vlerick School of Management, University of Ghent.

van Waterschoot, W. (2000) 'The marketing mix as a creator of differentiation', in K. Blois (ed.) *The Oxford Textbook of Marketing*. Oxford: Oxford University Press, pp. 183–211.

van Waterschoot, W. and De Haes, J. (2008) 'Marketing mix metaphorosis: the heavy toll of too much popularity', in P.J. Kitchen (ed.) *Marketing Metaphors and Metamorphosis*. Basingstoke: Palgrave Macmillan, pp. 42–61.

van Waterschoot, W. and van den Bulte, C. (1992) 'The 4P classification of the marketing mix revisited', *Journal of Marketing* 56: 83–93.

van Waterschoot, W., Lagasse, L. and Bilsen, R. (2006) *Marketing Beleid: Theorie en Praktijk*, 11th revised edn. Antwerpen: De Boeck.

Verhoef, P.C., Reinartz, W.J. and Krafft, M. (2010) 'Customer engagement as a new perspective in customer management', *Journal of Service Research* 13: 247–52.

von Clausewitz, C. (1984) *On War*. Princeton, NJ: Princeton University Press.

Marketing Strategy

Robin Wensley

Chapter Topics

Introduction	225
Strategy: From formulation to implementation	225
The nature of the competitive market environment	226
Customers, competitors and channels	226
The codification of marketing strategy analysis in terms of three strategies, four boxes and five forces	228
Models of competition: Game theory versus evolutionary ecology	231
Characterizing marketing strategy in terms of evolving differentiation in time and space	233
The nature of research in marketing strategy: fallacies of free lunches and the nature of answerable research questions. Distinguishing between information about means, variances and outliers	237
Getting to management action: The additional problem of economics	239
The recourse to processes, people and purpose in marketing as well as strategy as a whole	240
The new analytics: Resource advantage, co-evolution and agent-based modelling	244
Conclusions: The limits of relevance and the problems of application	245

Introduction

Marketing strategy sometimes claims to provide an answer to one of the most difficult questions in our understanding of competitive markets: how to recognize and achieve an economic advantage which endures. In attempting to do so, marketing strategy, as with the field of strategy itself, has had to address the continual balance between strategy formulation and strategic implementation. At the same time, it has also had to address a perhaps more fundamental question: how far, at least from a demand or market perspective, can we ever develop general rules for achieving enduring economic advantage?

Strategy: From formulation to implementation

From the late 1960s to the mid-1980s at least, management strategy seemed to be inevitably linked to issues of product-market selection and hence to marketing strategy. Perhaps ironically this was not primarily or even mainly as a result of the contribution of marketing scholars or indeed practitioners. The most significant initial contributors, such as Bruce Henderson and Michael Porter, both to be found at or closely linked to the Harvard Business School, were neither located within Marketing. However in various institutions the marketing academics were not slow to recognize what was going on and also to see that the centrality of product-market choice linked well with the importance attached to marketing. This expansion of the teaching domain had a much less significant impact on the research agenda and activity within marketing itself, where the focus continued to underplay the emerging importance of the competitive dimension (Day and Wensley, 1983). Hence the relatively atheoretical development continued into the process of codification of this new area, most obviously in the first key text by Abell and Hammond (1979), which was based on a, by then, well-established second year MBA option at Harvard.

In retrospect, this period was the high point for the uncontested impact of competitive market related analysis on strategic management practice. With the advantage of hindsight, it is clear that a serious alternative perspective was also developing, most obviously signalled by Peters and Waterman (1982), which was to have a very substantial impact on what was taught in strategic management courses and what was marketed by consultancies.

As the decade progressed, it was inevitable that at least to some degree each side recognized the other as a key protagonist. Perhaps one of the most noteworthy cases is that in which Waterman (1988) challenged the value of a Porter-based analysis of competition. Equally, the economists did not take such attacks lying down: Kay (1993) attempted to wrest back the intellectual dominance in matters of corporate strategy and Porter (1990) extended his domain to the nation-state itself. In terms of the disciplinary debate, what was originally broadly a debate between economists and sociologists, now also involved psychologists, social anthropologists, and, if they are a distinct discipline, systems theorists.

However, the key change in emphasis can be summarized as from analysis to process, from formulation to implementation. Perhaps the single most important contributor to this change has been Henry Mintzberg, who has developed over the period an extensive critique of what he calls the 'Design School' in strategic management, culminating in his 1994 book. Since then, he has extended his critique to the domain of management teaching, particularly MBAs, rather than just strategic planning (Mintzberg, 2004). Overall, while his approach and indeed critique of strategy analysis is itself rather polemical and overstated, there is little doubt that the general emphasis in strategic management has shifted significantly towards implementation and away from formulation and planning.

The nature of the competitive market environment

As our analysis of marketing strategy has developed over the last 35 years, so our representation of the marketing context has also changed. In particular there was much less recognition of competitors and distribution was clearly seen as a solely logistical function in the 1970s. On top of this, customers were often very much represented as 'at a distance', with intermediaries such as advertising agencies and market research companies. More recently, marketing has recognized much more explicitly a further range of issues including the key role of competition and the importance of a longer term so-called relationship perspective, particularly in the context of customers. On top of this, various entities in the distribution chain are now clearly seen as very active intermediaries rather than just passive logistics agents.

However, the development of this more complex, dynamic representation of the competitive market, which can be represented broadly in the marketing strategy triangle of the 3 Cs: Customers, Competitors and Channels, also implies a more fluid and complex environment within which to understand the nature of competitive advantage.

Customers, competitors and channels

The early more static model of the nature of the competitive market, which informed many of the still current tools of analysis, was both positional and non-interactive. It was assumed that the market backcloth, often referred to as the product-market space, remained relatively stable and static so that at least in terms of first order effects, strategies could be defined in positional terms. Similarly, the general perspective was that actions by the firm would generally not create equivalent reactions from the relatively passive 'consumers'.

With the adoption of the more interactive and dynamic perspective implied in the 3 Cs approach, the nature of market-based strategy becomes much more complex. We must be wary of the temptation to continue to apply the old tools and concepts without considering critically whether they are appropriate in new situations. They represent in general a special or limiting case which quite often distorts the nature of the environment that we are attempting to characterize. How far this distortion is, as our legal colleagues would say, material, is another but frequently unresolved matter. This notion of materiality is really linked to impact on actions rather than just understanding and the degree to which in practice particular forms of marketing strategy analysis encourage actions which are inappropriate.

This chapter is mainly written around the assumption that we need to recognize in using these simplifying approaches, that: (1) the degree to which they actually explain the competitive performance outcomes of interest will be limited; and (2) the underlying assumptions can cause unintentional biases.

The evolution of analysis, interpretation and modelling in marketing strategy from customers to competitors to channels

Given that the underlying representation of the competitive market environment has changed, so, not surprisingly, have our processes of analysis, interpretation and modelling. Initially the key focus was on customer-based positioning studies in particular product-market space. Such work remains a key component in the analysis of much market research data, but from the marketing strategy perspective we need to recognize that the dimensionality of the analytical space has often been rather low, indeed in some situations little more than a single price dimension which has been seen as highly correlated with an equivalent quality dimension.

The increased emphasis on the analysis of competitors has also required us to make certain compromises. One, of course, relates to the balance between three forms termed public information, legitimate inference and private information. The other to the fact that our colleagues in business strategy now give emphasis to two rather different perspectives on the nature of competitive firms, one essentially based on similarities (strategic groups: McGee and Thomas, 1986) and the other on differences (resource-based view [RBV]: Wernerfeld, 1984, 1995a). Sound competitor analysis should at least enable us to avoid making inconsistent assumptions, particularly in the context of public data, like, for instance, assuming that we will be able to exploit an opportunity which is known to all, without a significant amount of competitive reaction.

Finally there is the question of channels or, in more general terms, supply chains. The issue of retailers in particular as independent and significant economic intermediaries rather than just logistical channels to the final consumer has been an important consideration in consumer marketing at least since the 1970s. Similarly in industrial markets, the issue of the supply chain and the central importance of some form of organization and coordination of the various independent entities within the chain has been seen as an increasingly important strategic issue. Both these developments have meant that any strategic marketing analysis needs to find ways to evaluate the likely impact of such independent strategies pursued by intermediaries, although in many cases our tools and techniques for doing this remain rather limited and often rely on no more than an attempt to speculate on what might be their preferred strategic action.

Beyond this there has been a broader attempt to introduce what has become known as relationship marketing. It is outside the remit of this chapter to provide a full overview but from a strategic viewpoint there are two important issues that need to be emphasized. The first is that a recognition of the relatively stable pattern of transaction relationship within, particularly, most industrial markets, often described as the 'markets as networks' perspective, is not necessarily the same as a more prescriptive notion of the need to manage such relationships. The second is that while the relationship perspective rightly moves our attention away from individual transactions towards patterns of interaction over longer time periods, it often seems to assume that the motivations of each party are symmetric. In both consumer (Fournier et al., 1998) and industrial markets (Faria and Wensley, 2002) this may prove to be a very problematic assumption.

The codification of marketing strategy analysis in terms of three strategies, four boxes and five forces

What can now be regarded as 'traditional' marketing strategy analysis was developed primarily in the 1970s. It was codified in various ways, including the strategic triangle as developed by Ohmae (1982), based on customers, competitors and the corporation. The most significant elements in such analysis can be defined in terms of the three generic strategies, the four boxes (or perhaps more appropriately strategic contexts) and the five forces.

These particular frameworks also represent the substantial debt that marketing strategy owes to economic analysis; the three strategies and the five forces are directly taken from Michael Porter's influential work, which derived from his earlier work in industrial organization (IO) economics. The four contexts was initially popularized by the Boston Consulting Group (BCG) under Bruce Henderson, again strongly influenced by microeconomic analysis. While each of these approaches became a significant component in much marketing strategy teaching (see Morrison and Wensley, 1991), we also need to recognize some of the key considerations and critical assumptions held in any application.

The three strategies

Porter really reintroduced the standard economic notion of scale to the distinction between cost and differentiation to arrive at the three generic strategies of focus, cost and differentiation. Indeed, in his later formulation of the three strategies they really became four in that he suggested, rightly, that the choice between an emphasis on competition via cost or differentiation can be made at various scales of operation.

With further consideration it is clear that both of these dimensions are themselves not only continuous but also likely to be the aggregate of a number of relatively independent elements or dimensions. Hence scale is in many contexts not just a single measure of volume of finished output but also of relative volumes of sub-assemblies and activities which may well be shared. This is even truer in the case of 'differentiation', where we can expect that there are various different ways in which any supplier attempts to differentiate their offerings. On top of this, a number of other commentators, most particularly John Kay (1993), have noted that not only might the cost–differentiation scale be continuous rather than dichotomous but it also might not be seen as a real dimension at all. At some point this could become a semantic squabble but there clearly is an important point that many successful strategies are built around a notion of good value for money rather than a pure emphasis on cost or differentiation at any price. Michael Porter (1980) might describe this as a 'middle' strategy, but he has consistently claimed that there is a severe danger of getting 'caught in the middle'. In fact it might be reasonable to assume that in many cases being in the middle is the best place to be: after all, Porter never presented significant and substantial systematic evidence to support his own assertion (cf. Wensley, 1994).

The four contexts

The four boxes (contexts) relate to the market share/market growth matrix originally developed by the BCG under Bruce Henderson. Although inevitably a whole range of different matrix frameworks have emerged since the early days of the BCG, one remains an outstanding exemplar not only because of its widespread popularity and impact – nowadays even university vice-chancellors have been heard to use terms such as 'cash cow' – but because there was an underlying basic economic logic in its development. Many other similar frameworks just adopted the rather tautologous proposition that one should invest in domains which were both attractive and where one had comparative advantage!

The market growth/market share matrix however still involved a set of key assumptions which were certainly contestable. In particular, alongside the relatively uncontroversial one that in general over time the growth rate in markets tends to decline, there were the assumptions that it was in some sense both easier to gain market share in higher growth rate markets, and also that the returns to such gains were likely to be of longer duration. However, it could be that early investment in market share is inherently more risky so yields, on average, better returns, and that there are other ways of dealing with such risks. Yet companies can benefit from a focus on market share position when it encourages them to place greater emphasis on the marketing fundamentals for a particular business.

More generally, the matrix as an analytical device suffers from some of the problems which we illustrated for the three strategies approach: an analysis which is essentially based on extreme points, when in practice many of the portfolio choices are actually around the centre of the matrix. This implies that any discrimination between business units needs to be on the basis of much more specific analysis rather than broad general characteristics.

Five forces

The five forces analysis was originally introduced by Michael Porter to emphasize the extent to which the overall basis of competition was much wider than just the rivalries between established competitors in a particular market. While not exactly novel as an insight, particularly in suggesting that firms also face competition from new entrants and substitutes, it was presented in a very effective manner and served to emphasize not only the specific and increasing importance of competition, as we discussed, but also the extent to which competition should be seen as a much wider activity within the value chain, as Porter termed it.

Porter used the term value chain when in essence he was concentrating more on the chain of actual costs. While ex post from an economic point of view, there is no difference between value and cost, it is indeed the process of both competition and collaboration between various firms and intermediaries which finally results in the attribution of value throughout the relevant network. In this sense, as others have recognized, a supply chain is an intermediate organization form where there is a higher degree of cooperation between the firms within the chain and a greater degree of competition between the firms within different chains. In this context Porter's analysis has tended to focus much more clearly on the issue of competition rather than cooperation. Indeed, at least in its representational form, it has tended to go further than this and focus attention on the nature of the competitive pressures on the firm itself rather than on the interaction between the firm and other organizations in the marketplace.

The search for generic rules for success amid diversity

As we have suggested above, the codification of marketing strategy was based on three essential schema. This schemata, while it was based on some valid theoretical concepts, did not really provide a systematic approach to the central question, that is, the nature of sustained economic performance in the competitive marketplace. While such an objective was clearly recognized in the so-called search for sustainable competitive advantage (Day and Wensley, 1988), there remained concerns as to whether such a notion was realistic given the dynamic and uncertain nature of the competitive marketplace (Dickinson, 1992).

Indeed, not only is it dynamic and uncertain but it is also diverse: firms are heterogeneous and so is the nature of demand. A useful way of looking at demand-side heterogeneity is from the user perspective directly. Arguably from its relatively early origins, marketing or at least the more functional focused study of marketing management, has been concerned with managerially effective ways of responding to this heterogeneity, particularly in terms of market segmentation. While there remains a substantial debate about the degree to which this market-based heterogeneity is indeed 'manageable' from a marketing perspective (cf. Saunders, 1995; Wensley, 1995), our concern at the moment is to consider the degree to which such diversity on both the supply and demand side facilitates or negates the possibility of developing robust 'rules for success'.

To address this question, we need to consider the most useful way of characterizing the competitive market process. Let us consider the field of ecology, where we observe wide diversity in terms of both species and habitat as well as high interactivity. There are two critical aspects which must inform any attempt to transfer this analogy into the field of strategy. The first is the interactive relationship between any species and its habitat, nicely encapsulated in the title of the book by Levins and Leowontin (1985): *The Dialectical Biologist*. Particularly in the context of strategy, it is important to recognize that the habitat (for which read market domain) evolves and develops at least as fast as the species (for which, rather more problematically, read the individual firm).

The second aspect addresses directly our question of 'rules for success'. How far can we identify, particularly through the historical record, whether there are any reliable rules for success for particular species characteristics? Of course, it is very difficult to address this question without being strongly influenced by hindsight and most observations are seen as contentious.

It would seem that we should at least be very cautious in any search for rules for success amid a world of interactive diversity. Hence we should hardly be surprised that marketing strategy analysis does not provide for consistent and sustainable individual success in the competitive marketplace. However, we do have a set of theoretical frameworks and practical tools which at least allow us to represent some of the key dynamics of both customer and competitive behaviour in a way which ensures we avoid errors of inconsistency or simple naivety.

As we have discussed above, most analysis in marketing strategy is informed by what are essentially economic frameworks and so tend to focus attention on situations in which both the competitive structure of the market and the nature of consumer preferences are relatively well established. As we move our attention to more novel situations these structures tend to be at best indeterminate and therefore the analytical frameworks less appropriate. We encounter the first of many ironies in the nature of marketing strategy analysis. It is often least applicable in the very situations in which there is a real opportunity for a new source of economic advantage based on a restructuring of either or both the competitive environment and consumer preferences.

Models of competition: Game theory versus evolutionary ecology

To develop a formal approach to the modelling of competitive behaviour we need to define:

- The nature of the arena in which the competitive activity takes place;
- The structure or rules which govern the behaviour of the participants;
- The options available in terms of competitor behaviour (when these consist of a sequence of actions through time, or over a number of 'plays', then they are often referred to in game theory as strategies).

In this section, however, we particularly wish to contrast game theory approaches, which in many ways link directly to the economic analysis to which we have already referred, and look in more detail at analogies from evolutionary biology which raise difficult questions about the inherent feasibility of any systematic model building at the level of the individual firm.

Game theory models of competition

A game theory model is characterized by a set of rules which describe: (1) the number of firms competing against each other; (2) the set of actions that each firm can take at each point in time; (3) the profits that each firm will realize for each set of competitive actions; (4) the time pattern of actions – whether they occur simultaneously or one firm moves first; and (5) the nature of information about competitive activity – who knows what, when. The notion of rationality also plays a particularly important role in models of competitive behaviour. Rationality implies a link between actions and intentions but not common intentions between competitors. Models describing competitive activity are designed to understand the behaviour of 'free' economic agents. Thus, these models start with an assumption of 'weak' rationality – the agents will take actions that are consistent with their longer term objectives. The models also assume a stronger form of rationality – the intentions of the agents can be expressed in terms of a number of economic measures of outcome states such as profit, sales, growth, or market share objectives.

Do the results of game theory models indicate how firms should act in competitive situations? Do the models describe the evolution of competitive interactions in the real world? These questions have spawned a lively debate among management scientists concerning the usefulness of game theory models. Kadane and Larkey (1982) suggested that game theory models are conditionally normative and conditionally descriptive. The results do indicate how firms should behave given a set of assumptions about the alternatives, the payoffs and the properties of an 'optimal' solution (the equilibrium). Similarly, game theory results describe the evolution of competitive strategy but only given a very specific set of assumptions.

The seemingly unrealistic and simplistic nature of the competitive reactions incorporated in game theory models and the nature of the equilibrium concept led some marketers to question the managerial relevance of these models (Dolan, 1981). However, all models involve simplifying assumptions, and game theory models, while often highly structured, underpin most attempts to apply economic analysis to issues of competition among a limited number of firms. Indeed, as Goeree and Holt (2001: 1402) observe: 'Game theory has finally gained the central role … in some areas of economics (e.g. industrial organization) virtually all recent developments are applications of game theory.'

Evolutionary ecological analogies

Evolutionary ecology has also emerged as a popular analogy for understanding the types of market-based strategies pursued by companies (Coyle, 1986; Lambkin and Day, 1989). These analogies have been previously used to describe both the nature of the competitive process itself (Henderson, 1983) as well as the notion of 'niche' strategy (Hofer and Schendel, 1977).

Organizational theorists and sociologists have adopted an ecological model, describing the growth of a species in an ecology, to describe the types of firms in an environment. Environments are described by two dimensions: variability and frequency of environmental change. In a highly variable environment, changes are dramatic, and fundamentally different strategic responses are required for survival. In contrast, strategic alterations are not required to cope with an environment of low variability. A specialist strategy in which high performance occurs in a narrow portion of the environment is surprisingly more appropriate when environmental changes are dramatic and frequent. Under these conditions, it is unlikely that a generalist would have sufficient flexibility to cope with the wide range of environmental conditions it would face, while the specialist can at least outperform it in a specific environment. A generalist strategist is most appropriate in an environment characterized by infrequent, minor changes because this environment allows the generalist to exploit its large-scale efficiencies.

Comparing the key elements in different models of competition

The strategic groups and mobility barriers in the industrial organization economics approach recognize the critical asymmetries between competing firms. Three methods are identified by which firms can isolate themselves from competition: (1) differentiation; (2) cost efficiency; and (3) collusion, although the third approach has tended to be ignored. The developments within the IO paradigm have therefore tended to usefully focus on the nature and significance of various mechanisms for isolating the firm from its competition. The evolutionary ecological analogy, on the other hand, focuses on the notion of scope with the general distinction between specialists and generalists. The ecological approach also raises interesting questions about the form, level and type of 'organization' that we are considering. In particular, we need to recognize most markets as forms of organization in their own right, as those who have argued the 'markets as networks' approach have done, and question how far we can justify an exclusive focus on the firm as the key organization unit. Finally, the analogy raises more directly the concern about the interaction between various different units (species) and their evolving habitat. The marketplace, like the habitat, can become relatively unstable and so both affect and be affected by the strategies of individual firms.

As we have suggested, any analogy is far from perfect, as we would expect. The limitations are as critical as the issues that are raised because they give us some sense of the bounds within which the analogy itself is likely to be useful. Extending it outside these bounds is likely to be counter-productive and misleading.

The IO approach in practice tends to neglect the interaction between cost and quality. We have already suggested that while the notion of 'focus' within this analogy is an attempt to recognize this problem; it is only partially successful because it subsumes a characteristic of any successful competitive strategy into one generic category. We must further consider the extent to which we can reasonably, reliably distinguish between the various forms of mixed strategies over time and the extent to which the strategic groups themselves remain stable.

The limitations of analogies from evolutionary ecology are more in terms of the questions that are not answered than those where the answers are misleading. The nature of 'competition' is both unclear and complex, there is confusion as to the level and appropriate unit of analysis, and the notion of 'niche', which has become so current in much strategy writing, overlooks the fact that by definition every species has one anyway.

Characterizing marketing strategy in terms of evolving differentiation in time and space

Central to any notion of competition from a marketing strategy viewpoint is the issue of differentiation in time and space. In a 'real' market: (1) demand is heterogeneous; (2) suppliers are differentiated; and (3) there are processes of feedback and change through time. Clearly these three elements interact significantly, yet in most cases we find that to reduce the overall complexity in our analysis and understanding we treat each item relatively independently. For instance, in most current treatments of these issues in marketing strategy we would use some form of *market segmentation* schema to map heterogeneous demand, some notion of the *resource-based view* of the firm to reflect the differentiation among suppliers and some model of market evolution such as the *product life-cycle* to reflect the nature of the time dynamic.

Such an approach has two major limitations which may act to remove any benefit from the undoubted reduction of analytical complexity by looking at three sub-systems rather than the whole system. First it assumes implicitly that this decomposition is reasonably first order correct: that the impact of the individual elements is more important than their interaction effects. To examine this assumption critically we need some alternative form of analysis and representation such as modelling the phenomena of interest as the co-evolution of firms and customers in a dynamic phase space, which allows for the fact that time and space interact. Second, it assumes that the ways of representing the individual elements that we use – in particular market segmentation and product life-cycle concepts – are in fact robust representations of the underlying phenomena. In terms of the adequacy of each element in its own terms, we need to look more closely at the ways in which individual improvements may be achieved and finally we might wish to consider whether it would be better to model partial interactions, say between two elements only rather than the complete system.

Differentiation in space: Issues of market segmentation

The analysis of spatial competition has of course a long history, stretching back at least to the classical Hotelling model of linear competition such as that faced by the two icecream sellers on the sea-front. In marketing, the competitive space is generally characterized in terms of market segmentation. There is by now a very large body of empirical work in the general field of market segmentation but even so there remain some critical problems. In particular:

- We have evidence that the cross-elasticities with respect to different marketing mix elements are likely to be not only of different orders but actually imply different structures of relationship between individual product offerings.
- Competitive behaviour patterns, which, after all, in a strict sense determine the nature of the experiment from which the elasticities can be derived, seem to be, to use a term coined by Leeflang and Wittick (1993), 'out of balance' with the cross-elasticity data per se.

For the purposes of this chapter we wish to concentrate on the specific question as to how far segmentation provides us with an appropriate definition of the space within which competition evolves. In this sense the key questions are, as we discussed above, about the dimensionality of the space concerned, the stability of the demand function and the degree of mobility for individual firms (or more correctly individual offerings) in terms of repositioning.

These are in practice very difficult questions to deal with for two critical reasons:

1. The nature of the choice process is such that for many offerings, individual consumers choose from a portfolio of items rather than merely make exclusive choices, and, hence, in principle it is difficult to isolate the impact of one offering from the others in the portfolio.

2. The dimensions of the choice space are often inferred from the responses to current offerings and therefore it is difficult to distinguish between the effects of current offerings and some notion of an underlying set of preference structures.

Segmentation and positioning

In principle we can describe the nature of spatial competition in a market either in demand terms or in supply terms. Market segmentation represents the demand perspective on structure while competitive positioning represents the supply perspective. Market segmentation takes as its starting point assumptions about the differing requirements that individual customers have with respect to bundles of benefits in particular use situations. Most obviously in this context it is an 'ideal' approach in that it is effectively assumed that each customer can/does specify their own ideal benefit bundle, and their purchase choice in the relevant use situation is based on proximity to this ideal point. In consumer psychology this is equivalent to an assumption that individuals have strong and stable preferences.

The competitive positioning approach uses consumer judgements, normally on an aggregate basis to the similarities and differences between specific competitive offerings. In principle this provides an analytical output roughly equivalent to the spatial distribution in the Hotelling model. Such an analysis can also be used to provide an estimate of the dimensionality of the discriminant space, but in many situations for ease of presentation the results are presented in a constrained two-dimensional format. Equally, benefit segmentation studies can be used along with techniques such as factor analysis to try and arrive at an estimate of the dimensionality of the demand side.

We can be reasonably certain that the attitude space for customers in any particular market is generally, say, $N>3$: factor analytical studies might suggest at least four or five in general and that of competitive offerings is of at least a similar order. Indeed in the last case if we considered the RBV of the firm very seriously we might go for a dimensionality as high as the number of competitors.

Of more interest from a strategy point of view is how we represent what happens in terms of actual purchase behaviour in a competitive market through time. There have been a number of attempts to apply segmentation analysis to behavioural data with much less information as to attitudes or intention. In one of the more detailed of such studies, Chintagunta (1994) focused on the degree to which the data analysis reveals interesting differences in terms of brand position as shown by individual purchase patterns through time. He suggested that the dimensionality of the revealed competitive space was two-dimensional but even this might be really an overestimate. It would appear that we can rather surprisingly reduce the effective competitive space to a single dimension with the possibility of only some second order anomalies (Wensley, 1996).

A simple model of spatial competition might therefore be one in which a considerable amount of competition can be seen as aligned along a single dimension, in circumstances in which multiple offerings are possible, and where there is no reason to believe a priori that individual offerings will be grouped either by common brand or specification, with a fixed entry cost for each item and a distribution of demand which is multi-modal. To this extent it may actually be true that the very simplifications that many criticize in the Porter 'three generic strategies' approach may be reasonably appropriate in building a first order model of competitive market evolution (see Campbell-Hunt, 2000). In the short run, following the notion of 'clout' and 'vulnerability' (Cooper and Nakanishi, 1988), we might also expect that changes in position in this competitive dimension could be a function of a whole range of what might often be seen as tactical as well as strategic marketing actions.

We must now consider, however, particularly in the context of understanding the time-based nature of market strategies, how we might incorporate in more detail a longer term time dimension with a stronger customer focus.

Differentiation in time: Beyond the PLC. Characterizing the nature of competitive market evolution

> Few management concepts have been so widely accepted or thoroughly criticised as the product life cycle. (Lambkin and Day, 1989: 4)

The product life-cycle has the advantage that it does represent the most simple form of path development for any product (introduction, growth, maturity, decline), but as has been widely recognized, this remains a highly stylized representation of the product sales pattern for most products during their lifetime. While it is reasonably clear that it is difficult, if not impossible, to propose a better single generic time pattern, any such pattern is subject to considerable distortion as a result of interactions with changes in technology as well as both customer and competitor behaviour.

Lambkin and Day (1989) suggested that an understanding of the process of product-market evolution required a more explicit distinction between issues of the demand system, the supply system and the resource environment. However, they chose to emphasize the nature of the demand evolution primarily in terms of diffusion processes. This approach tends to underestimate the extent to which demand-side evolution is as much about the way(s) in which the structure of the demand space is changing as the issue of aggregate demand itself.

Later work on the process of market evolution, partly building on some of the ideas developed by Lambkin and Day (1989), has attempted to incorporate insights from, among other areas, evolutionary ecology. In particular, work on the extensive Disk-drive database, which gives quarterly data on all disk-drive manufacturers, allowed Christensen (1997) to look at the ways in which at the early stages in the market development the existence of competitive offerings seems to encourage market growth, whereas at later stages the likelihood of firm exit increases with firm density. Other computer-related industries have also provided the opportunity for empirical work on some of the issues relating to both the impact of standardization and modularization and the nature of generation effects (Sanchez, 1995), although in the latter case it must be admitted that the effects themselves can sometimes be seen as a result of marketing actions in their own right.

The nature of research in marketing strategy: fallacies of free lunches and the nature of answerable research questions. Distinguishing between information about means, variances and outliers

As we indicated at the start of this chapter, much research in marketing strategy has attempted to address what is in some senses an impossible question: what is the basic and general nature of a successful competitive marketing strategy? This presumes the equivalent of a free lunch. Before we explore this issue further we need to establish a few basic principles. The competitive process is such that:

- Average performance can only produce average results, which in the general nature of a competitive system means that success is related to above average and sometimes even outlier levels of performance.
- We can expect our competitors to be able on average to interpret any public data to reveal profitable opportunities as well as we can. In more direct terms it means that on average competitors are as clever or as stupid as we are. The route to success cannot lie in simply exploiting public information in an effective manner, although such a strategy may enable a firm to improve its own performance.
- As we have discussed above, the basis of individual firm or unit performance is a complex mix of both firm, competitor and market factors. We therefore can expect that any attempt to explain performance will be subject to considerable error given that it is difficult, if not impossible, to identify an adequate range of variables which cover both the specifics of the firm's own situation and the details of the market and competitor behaviour.

For these reasons empirical research in marketing strategy, as in the strategy field as a whole, has almost always tended to be in one of the two categories:

1. Database, quantitative analysis which has relied on statistical and econometric approaches to produce results which indicate certain independent variables which on average correlate with performance. As McCloskey and Ziliak (1996) indicated more generally in econometric work, there is a danger that we often confuse statistical significance with what they term economic significance. This notion of economic significance can be decomposed into two elements: first the extent to which the relationship identified actually relates to a significant proportion of the variation in the dependent variable, and second the extent to which, even if it does, this regularity actually enables one to produce a clear prescription for managerial action.
2. Case-study based research on selected firms, often around outliers such as those that perform particularly well. Here the problems are the extent to which the story which is told about the particular nature of the success concerned can be used to guide action in other organizations. In practice this often results in managerial prescriptions that are at best rather tautological and at worst meaningless.

We will now consider examples of both types of this research.

Market share and return on investment: The 10% rule in practice

One of the most famous results from the PIMS (Profit Implications of Marketing Strategy) database was that first reported by Bob Buzzell, Brad Gale and Ralph Sultan in the *Harvard Business Review* in 1975 under the title 'Market share – a key to profitability'. They reported on the relationship between return on investment (ROI) and market share on a cross-sectional basis within the then current PIMS database. Although over the years estimates of the R^2 of this relationship have varied, it generally shows a value of only around 10% up to a maximum of 15%. In their original article Buzzell et al. 'removed' much of the variation by calculating cohort means.

The cohort mean approach, although now not commonly used in empirical research of this sort, normally shows some deviations from the straight line trend, but as samples get even larger the deviations get, on average, even smaller: indeed some textbook representations of the results go as far as merely illustrating the trend with no deviations at all. Hence in the process of producing a clearer message from the data we have eliminated nearly nine-tenths of the variability in our performance variable.

What does it mean and what about the 'unexplained' 90%?

In developing our understanding of what such a result actually means, the first set of problems relate to the nature of the data themselves and the way in which the axes are measured. In most analysis of this sort, and in the PIMS data as we discussed above, the data are essentially cross-sectional and averaged out over a fixed period. It therefore excludes any lead or lag effects and also compensates for particular one-off effects only to the extent that they are already discounted from the input data which is normally based on management accounts. The nature of the axes in a standard market share/ROI analysis is also a problem in that they are both ratios. There are very considerable advantages that accrue from using ratios in this situation: most obviously the fact that it is possible to plot on the same graph units of very different absolute sizes, but we do then have the problem of measurement errors in both the numerator and denominator for both axes.

Finally, the basic data are also inevitably limited in the extent to which they can measure the specifics of any particular business unit situation. Using basic financial and accounting data we cannot take into account issues such as managerial effectiveness as well as the degree of integration to achieve scale economies and efficiencies in terms of marketing and other functional activities.

However, we must also put this overall critique of 'market share/return' analysis in context. We should not underestimate the original impact of the 'market share' discovery. Even if it only 'explains' around 10% of financial performance, this is still a considerable achievement. The problem is that, as we have seen, even at this level we face difficult interpretation problems. In the end, one perhaps concludes that its greatest impact was merely that it legitimized debate and discussion about key competitive market assumptions in any strategy dialogue.

Getting to management action: The additional problem of economics

Even if we can identify the source of a particular success or indeed the cause of a particular failure, it is a big jump to assuming that suitable action can be taken at no cost or even at a cost which is justified by the subsequent benefits.

We therefore need to overlay our notion of practical significance with one of economic significance: a factor or set of factors which explain a significant proportion of success can also be used as a decision rule for subsequent successful management action. This is a big jump. To return to the market share/ROI relationship, even if we conclude that there is a significant correlation between market share and profitability we have to make two further assumptions to justify an economic rule of 'investing' in market share. First, we have to move from the more general notion of 'correlation' or 'explanation' to the much more specific one of 'causation' and, second, we have to assume that whatever its benefits market share is somehow underpriced. If our first assumption is correct then broadly it can only be underpriced if our competitors, both current and potential, either have a different view, or, for some unspecified reason, happen to value the asset (market share) significantly lower than we do. In fact in specific situations this latter assumption could hold: our competitors will value the benefits given their differing portfolio of assets and market positions but it all depends on the specifics and the details of the individual situation rather than the general picture.

In the end, it is likely that the continued search for general rules for strategic success via statistical analysis and large databases will prove illusory. This does not make the research effort worthless, we merely have to be realistic about what can and cannot be achieved. After all, the in-depth case study narrative approach, which we will consider shortly, often results in another type of economic rule: the truth which is virtually impossible to apply in general. Perhaps the best example is to be found in Peters and Waterman's original work. Among many memorable criteria for success to be found in *In Search of Excellence* (1982) was that undeniable one: the achievement of simultaneous 'loose–tight' linkages. To those who thought that this might seem contradictory Peters and Waterman provided the helpful observation that: 'These are the apparent contradictions that turn out in practice not to be contradictions at all' (1982: 320).

The Honda case: Interpreting success

One of the best known examples of a case history which has been interpreted to generate a number of marketing strategy lessons is the case of Honda and their entry into the American motorcycle market.

In summary, the original consultancy study conducted for the UK government by the BCG interpreted the success that Honda enjoyed in the USA, particularly at the expense of UK imports, as the result of substantial economies of scale for their small bikes based on the Cub model along with a market entry strategy to identify and exploit a new segment and set of customers. Richard Pascale, on the other hand, interviewed a number of the key executives who had worked for American Honda at the time and they told a story which suggested the whole operation was very much working on a shoestring and the final success was down to a number of lucky breaks, including a buyer from Sears persuading them to let him sell their small model bikes when they were really trying, and failing, to break into the big bike market.

In the later debate, Goold, who worked for BCG at the time, focused attention on the 10% that can be explained analytically, while Mintzberg argued that a realization of specific causes of success can be achieved more effectively through processes such as learning (Goold, 1996; Mintzberg, 1996a, 1996b). This is in practice a strong assertion about the efficacy of learning processes in organizations that others might dispute.

Hence the same story can be interpreted in very different ways. One of the underlying dilemmas for Honda, as indeed for any new market entrant, was that if they took the existing market structure as fixed and given, then the possibilities for them were remote; on the other hand, market knowledge could only really hint at possibilities for new market structures.

The recourse to processes, people and purpose in marketing as well as strategy as a whole

More recently in marketing strategy, as in strategy as a whole, there has been a move away from analysis based on real substantive recommendations for management action towards a concern more for processes, people and purposes rather than structure, strategies and systems. This change in emphasis was particularly introduced by Bartlett and Ghoshal (1995) in their influential *Harvard Business Review* article.

While this shift can be seen as a reasonable response to our lack of substantive and generalizable knowledge about the nature of successful marketing strategies in a competitive marketplace, as we have discussed above, it should also be seen as one which itself has rather limited evidence to support it. In marketing strategy in particular, two areas can be identified where this trend has been very evident and we will look critically at both of these: the shift towards a focus on networks and relationship marketing and the increased emphasis on marketing processes within the firm.

Markets as networks

It is clear, as Easton (1990) has indicated, that actual firm relationships must be seen on a spectrum between outright competition at one end and collusion at the other. At the very least, such a self-evident observation raises the issue of the firm (or business unit) as the basic, and often only, unit of analysis: in certain circumstances we might more appropriately consider an informal coalition of such firms as the key unit.

However, the recognition that there is a network of relationships is merely the first step. Approaches need to be developed for the analysis of the network. Håkansson (1987) has, for instance, suggested that the key elements of any network are actors, activities and resources. He also suggests that the overall network is bound together by a number of forces including functional interdependence, as well as power, knowledge and time-related structure.

There is a danger in confusing a detailed descriptive model with a simple but robust predictive one, let alone one which aids the diagnostic process. The basic microeconomic framework which underlies the 'competitive advantage' approach, central to much marketing strategy analysis, should not be seen as an adequate description of the analytical and processual complexities in specific situations. It is a framework for predicting the key impacts of a series of market-mediated transactions: at the very least outcomes are the joint effect of decisions themselves and the selection process. In this sense, the more valid criticisms of the application of such a model is that either the needs of the situation are not met by the inherent nature of the model or that the model fails to perform within its own terms.

Relationship marketing

Equally, we may wonder to what extent the new found concern for relationship marketing is indeed new at all. The recognition that customers faced switching costs and that therefore the retention of existing customers was clearly an effective economic strategy is certainly not new.

Mattsson (1997) has considered much more critically the relationship between the underlying approaches in the 'markets as networks' and relationship marketing perspectives. He rightly observed that much of the problem lies in the various different approaches claiming to represent relationship marketing.

More recently, Vargo and Lusch (2004) developed the argument further on the assumption of a dominant trend from the marketing of goods to the provision of services. They argued that, inter alia, all economies are service economies, that the customer is always a co-producer and that the enterprise can only make value propositions. In a sense, however, to describe, as they do, the trend as being from goods-dominant to service-dominant perspectives over a period of around 100 years is to describe a genuine shift in managerial perspective but a less clear shift in the underlying realities.

The whole development might remind one rather more of M. Jourdain in Moliere's *Le Bourgeois Gentilhomme*, who discovers he has been effortlessly speaking prose all his life. The proposed move towards a more relational and service-based perspective reflects more a changing view of the nature of the customer, from consumer to co-producer, than the fact that those who used to be characterized as consumers are now in some objective way more co-producers. We would do well to remember that memorable expression of Ivan Illich (1981) 'shadow work' to describe real work which we do not see because of the nature of our measurement or value systems. Arnould (2006) notes the clear potential link between the approach advocated by Vargo and Lusch and consumer culture theory but also notes that this aspect is less well developed in their initial presentation. Moreover, Schembri (2006) suggests that the approach adopted still remains somewhat rooted in the more traditional goods-centred logic and needs to engage more with approaches focused around the nature of the customer experience.

It may well be that the relationship marketing movement will in the end have a rather similar impact on marketing as the market share one did in the 1970s and early 1980s. As such the renewed emphasis on the nature of the customer relationship, which is self-evidently important in industrial markets, will encourage retail marketers to take their customers more seriously – even to regard them as intelligent and rational agents. To do so, however, would also mean recognizing severe scepticism about the underlying reality of various developments in relationship marketing such as 'loyalty' cards and one-to-one targeting.

However, it may also be true that the relationship and network perspective will in the longer run change our perception of the critical strategic questions faced by firms as they and their 'markets' evolve and develop. Easton et al. (1993), for instance, suggest that the notion of competition and markets is really only appropriate at specific stages in the life-cycle of the firm or business unit. Indeed, their approach could be taken further to suggest that at a time when there is significant indeterminacy in terms of competitor and customer choice, this way of characterizing strategic choice is, of itself, of limited theoretical or practical value. Almost by definition the product technology and market structure needs to be relatively stable for such strategic choices to be formulated, yet by this stage the feasible choice set itself may be very restricted.

Emergent or enacted environments

The notion of emergent phenomena has itself emerged as a key concept in organizational strategy. Much of the credit for this must go to Mintzberg (1994), but ironically his analysis of the concept itself has been perhaps rather more limited than it could have been. Indeed, in his more recent work, he has tended to define the nature of emergent phenomena in a rather idiosyncratic manner. He implies that emergent phenomena are such that they can ex post be related to the intentions or actions, through time, of the individual actors. However, a more common use of the term emergence incorporates some notion of interpretation at different levels of aggregation. After all, for instance, as a number of authors have previously commented, markets themselves are emergent phenomena. It was originally Adam Smith's insight that each actor in a market following their own interest could, under certain conditions, create an overall situation of welfare maximization: in this sense the invisible hand was much more effective than any attempts at local or even global optimization.

Others have paid much greater attention to the nature of emergent properties, but we also need to recognize a further distinction between what have been termed emergent and enacted environments. In a number of relevant areas, such as information systems, there is no overall agreement on the nature of the differences (see Mingers, 1995) but in the absolute an emergent environment is one in which there are a set of rules but they are generally undetermining of the outcome states – or at least the only way in which an outcome state can be predicted is by a process of simulation, whereas an enacted environment is one in which the nature of the environment is itself defined by the cognitive patterns of the constituents.

This distinction is particularly important when we consider the possibility of 'markets-as-networks' as a perspective to understand the nature of competitive market phenomena. If we recognize the nature of the phenomena we are trying to understand as essentially emergent then there remains considerable value in attempting to model the relevant structure of rules or relationships that characterize the environment. If, on the other hand, we are more inclined to an enactive view of the relationship between organizations and their environment, we need to consider the degree to which the structure of the network is not more than a surface phenomenon resulting itself from other deeper processes. We need to consider the phenomenon that Giddens (1979) identifies in terms of 'structuration', whereby agents and organizations are simultaneously both creators of structures but also have their actions constrained by these structures.

However, even if we are willing to give a relatively privileged ontological status to the detailed network structure in a particular context, we may still face insurmountable problems in developing high-level regularities from a more and more detailed analysis. Cohen and Stewart (1995) warn convincingly about the dangers of drowning in the detail of low-level rules but they give only limited useful advice as to the practical nature of the alternatives.

Despite the fact that some of these general notions have been seen in the mainstream of strategic management thought for some considerable time (see Stacey, 1995), we should remain cautious. Horgan (1997) suggested that we should be wary of the likely advances to be made in the field that he has dubbed 'chaoplexity':

> So far, chaoplexologists have created some potent metaphors, the butterfly effect, fractals, artificial life, the edge of chaos, self-organised criticality. But they have not told us anything about the world that is both concrete and truly surprising, either in a negative, or in a positive sense. They have slightly extended the borders of our knowledge in certain areas, and they have more sharply delineated the boundaries of knowledge elsewhere. (1997: 226)

Marketing processes

Not surprisingly, the 1990s saw a renewed interest in the marketing process and particularly in the nature of the processes which support the development of a marketing orientation. This approach was encouraged by the renewed attempts to model the nature of marketing orientation of both Narver and Slater (1990) and Kohli and Jaworski (1990). In essence the shift is one that Herb Simon (1979) recognized in his original distinction between substantive and procedural rationality. He suggested that it was an appropriate response to the problem of bounded rationality to focus attention more on the process for arriving at a particular choice rather than developing a general analytical approach to make that choice in any particular situation.

Much empirical research, particularly based on key informant surveys, has been undertaken to establish the extent to which various operational measures of marketing orientation are correlated with commercial success. On top of this there has been work to establish some of the possible antecedents for such orientation, including measures related to the accumulation and organizational dispersion of market research data. The results remain somewhat contradictory but it seems likely that some level of association will finally emerge, although whether it will achieve the minimum 10% target which we considered earlier is rather another question.

It is also important to note that the two approaches to measuring market orientation focused on substantially different approaches: one essentially related to a more organizational 'cultural' or attitude measure and the other related to an information processing perspective around market-based data. Hult et al. (2005) reported on a study, still based primarily on survey data, which not only incorporated both of these measures but also attempted to overcome one of the common criticisms of much of the other empirical work in that they used independent and leading performance measures.

On top of this, we need to address more fundamental questions about the underlying logic of procedural rationality in this context. As we have suggested above, it is reasonable to argue that some consideration in any marketing context of each element in the 3 Cs (customers, competitors and channels) must surely be seen as sensible. How far such a process should be routinized within a particular planning or decision-making schema is another matter. Much of the writing in the area of marketing orientation suggests that the appropriate mechanisms and procedures are unproblematic, yet everyday experience in organizations suggests that achieving effective response to the market is difficult and indeed may not be susceptible to programmed responses.

The new analytics: Resource advantage, co-evolution and agent-based modelling

Earlier on in this chapter we identified a number of key characteristics of a competitive market which determine the effectiveness of any specific strategic analysis, in particular: the heterogeneity of demand; the interaction between customer choices and producer offerings; and the degree to which both producers and customers are active agents in this process. More recently various new analytical approaches have given us new and different ways to address these central issues.

First, Hunt (2000a) has argued that the more traditional RBV of the firm is so dominated by a supply-side perspective that a more comprehensive theoretical approach, which he labels 'Resource Advantage' is required.

There are some concerns, however, as to whether Hunt's framework actually provides the most effective way of incorporating heterogeneity of demand (Wensley, 2002), particularly in the context of the evolution of marketing structure. For instance, one of the most established issues in the nature of a market structure is what Wroe Alderson referred to as the sequential processes of 'sorting' between supplier offerings in order to 'match' specific portfolios of customer demands, yet Hunt himself observes that so far he is unclear how this might be incorporated within his framework (Hunt, 2000b).

At best, therefore, it remains an open question as to how far the developments proposed by Hunt will help us to further understand not only a static view of market demand but even more a dynamic and evolving one, although they do provide a very useful perspective on the nature of strategic choices for the individual firm or business unit.

An alternative approach, which resonates with developments in the field of strategic management, is to focus more on the ability of firms to adapt to an evolving and changing market through what are termed 'dynamic capabilities' (Helfat et al., 2007; Teece et al., 1997; Winter, 2003). While previously Day (1994) has suggested that an analogous approach to understanding the nature of market-based firms can prove useful, the overall study of such dynamic capabilities has so far proved to be 'riddled with inconsistencies, overlapping definitions, and outright contradictions' (Zahra et al., 2006: 917).

Second, there have also been interesting developments in empirical studies of co-evolution, but unfortunately most of these so far have focused solely on the competitive and cooperative processes between organizations (Lewin and Volberda, 1999). From a market strategy perspective, however, it is noteworthy that even those few studies which attempt to model the nature of market evolution specifically, rather than treat it more as a backcloth upon which other sociological and economic processes take place, tend to represent the actual process in very limited ways. Only in the resource partitioning approach (Carroll et al., 2002) do we perhaps see the direct opportunities for a more complex model of market development which represents both its continuity, in the sense that one can reasonably expect cycles of competitive imitation followed by the emergence of new forms and market positions for competition, and its indeterminacy, in that various new 'realized niches' could emerge. Even here, however, the implicit emphasis is on the individual firms as the motivating force rather than the collective of customers in the various markets.

Third, advances in agent-based modelling promise new ways of simulating more complex interactive processes of spatial competition (Ishibuchi et al., 2001; Tesfatsion, 2001). Agent-based modelling essentially depends on allowing a simulation to evolve with individual 'agents' making choices within an undetermining but defined rule structure. It may well provide us with a better understanding of the patterns of market-based evolution and the nature of some of the key contingencies. However, again it is proving difficult to adequately reflect the evolving behaviour of customers in the marketplace. Chang and Harrington (2003) did include a process of consumer search in their model but their focus remained on the potential advantages of centralization for what were, in effect, multi-unit retailers.

Conclusions: The limits of relevance and the problems of application

The study and application of marketing strategy therefore reflects a basic dilemma. The key demand in terms of application is to address the causes of individual firm or unit success in the competitive marketplace, yet we can be reasonably confident from a theoretical perspective that such knowledge is not systematically available because of the nature of the competitive process itself. In this way the academic study of marketing strategy remains open to the challenge that it is not relevant to marketing practice. Yet to represent the problem solely in this way is to privilege one particular notion of the nature and use of academic research in marketing as well as the relationship between research and practice. Recognizing the limits to our knowledge in marketing strategy may also help in a constructive way to define what can and cannot be achieved by more investigation and research.

There are a number of areas in which we can both improve our level of knowledge and provide some guidance and assistance in the development of strategy. First, we can identify some of the generic patterns in the process of market evolution which give some guidance as to how we might think about and frame appropriate questions to be asked in the development of marketing strategy. Such questions would be added to those we are used to asking in any marketing management context, such as the nature of the (economic) value added to the customer based on market research evidence and analysis. More recently it has been suggested in strategy that such additional questions are most usefully framed around issues of imitation and sustainability, but, as Dickinson (1992) argues, this really assumes sustainability is a serious option. It may be more appropriate to frame such additional questions around the more general patterns of market evolution – standardization, maturity of technology and stability of current networks – rather than attempt to address the unanswerable question of sustainability directly.

When it comes to the generics of success, we face an even greater problem. By definition, any approach which really depends on analysis of means or averages leaves us with a further dilemma: not only does any relative 'useable' explanation only provide us with a very partial picture where outcomes are more unexplained than explained, but also the very notion of a publicly available set of 'rules for success' in a competitive market is itself contradictory, except in the context of a possible temporary advantage. We can try and resolve the problem by looking at the behaviour of what might be called successful outliers, but here we face a severe issue of interpretation. As we have seen, the sources of such success are themselves ambiguous and often tautological: we often end up really asserting either that to be successful one needs to be successful or that the route to success is some ill-defined combination of innovation, effectiveness and good organization.

It may well be that the best we can do with such analysis is to map the ways in which the variances of performance change in different market contexts: just like our finance colleagues we can do little more than identify the conditions under which variances in performance are likely to be greater and therefore, through economic logic, that the average performance will increase to compensate for the higher risks.

Finally, we may need to recognize that the comfortable distinction between marketing management, which has often been framed in terms of the more tactical side of marketing, and marketing strategy is not really sustainable. At one level all marketing actions are strategic: we have little knowledge as to how specific brand choices at the detailed level impact or not on the broad development of a particular market, so we are hardly in a position to label some choices as strategic in this sense and others as not. On the other hand, the knowledge that we already have and are likely to develop in the context of the longer term evolutionary patterns for competitive markets is unlikely to enable us to engage directly with marketing managerial action choices at the level of the firm: the units of both analysis and description are likely to be different. In our search for a middle way which can inform individual practice it may well be that some of the thinking tools and analogies that we have already developed will prove useful, but very much as means to an end rather than solutions in their own right.

Recommended further reading

Bettis, R.A. and Prahald, C.K. (1995) 'The dominant logic: retrospective and extension', *Strategic Management Journal* 16(1): 5–14.

Bogner, W. and Thomas, H. (1994) 'Core competence and competitive advantage: a model and illustrative evidence from the pharmaceutical industry', in G. Hamel and A. Heene (eds) *Competence Based Competition*. Chichester: John Wiley.

Caves, R.E. and Porter, M.E. (1977) 'From entry barriers to mobility barriers: conjectural decisions and contrived deterrence to new competition', *Quarterly Journal of Economics* 91 (May): 241–62.

Cooke, P. (2002) *Knowledge Economics: Clusters, Learning and Co-operative Advantage*. London: Routledge.

Ehrenberg, A.S.C. (1972) *Repeat Buying: Theory and Applications*. Amsterdam and New York: North-Holland.

Ehrenberg, A.S.C. and Uncles, M. (1995) 'Dirichlet-type markets: a review', Working paper, November.

Hannan, M.T. and Freeman, J. (1977) 'The population ecology of organizations', *American Journal of Sociology* 82(5): 929–63.

Harland, C. and Wensley, R. (1997) 'Strategising networks or playing with power: understanding interdependence in both industrial and academic networks', Working paper, Lancaster/Warwick Conference on 'New Forms of Organization', Warwick, April.

Henderson, B. (1980) 'Strategic and natural competition', *BCG Perspectives*, 231.

Henderson, J.M. and Quant, R.E. (1958) *Microeconomic Theory: A Mathematical Approach*. New York: McGraw-Hill.

Hunt, M.S. (1972) 'Competition in the major home appliance industry, 1960–1970', unpublished doctoral dissertation, Harvard University.

Jones, H.J. (1926) *The Economics of Private Enterprise*. London: Pitman and Sons.

Kaufmann, S. (1995) *At Home in the Universe*. New York: Oxford University Press.

Kotler, P. (1991) 'Philip Kotler explores the new marketing paradigm', *Marketing Science Institute Review* Spring: 1–5.

Moorthy, J.S. (1985) 'Using game theory to model competition', *Journal of Marketing Research* 22 (August): 262–82.

Morrison, A. and Wensley, R. (1991) 'A short history of the growth/share matrix: boxed up or boxed in?', *Journal of Marketing Management* 7(2): 105–29.

Muth, J.F. (1961) 'Rational expectations and the theory of price movements', *Econometrica* 29(3): 315–35.

Peterson, H. (1965) 'The wizard who oversimplified: a fable', *The Quarterly Journal of Economics* 79(2): 209–11.

Porter, M.E. (1979) 'The structure within industries and companies performance', *Review of Economics & Statistics* 61 (May): 214–27.

Porter, M.E. (1985) *Competitive Advantage*. New York: The Free Press.

Prahalad, C.K. and Bettis, R.A. (1989) 'The dominant logic: a new linkage between diversity and performance', *Strategic Management Journal* 10(6): 523–52.

Roberts, K. (1997) 'Explaining success – hard work not illusion', *Business Strategy Review* 8(2): 75–7.

Rumelt, R.P (1996) 'The many faces of Honda', *Californian Management Review* 38(4): 103–11.

Wernerfeld, B. (1995) 'A rational reconstruction of the compromise effect', *Journal of Consumer Research* 21 (March): 627–33.

References

Abell, D. and Hammond, J. (1979) *Strategic Marketing Planning: Problems and Analytical Approaches*. Englewood Cliffs, NJ: Prentice-Hall.

Arnould, E.J. (2006) 'Service-dominant logic and consumer culture theory: natural allies in an emerging paradigm', *Marketing Theory* 6(3): 293–7.

Bartlett, C.A. and Ghoshal, S. (1995) 'Changing the role of top management: beyond systems to people', *Harvard Business Review* 73(3): 132–42.

Buzzell, R.D., Gale, B.T. and Sultan, R.G.M. (1975) 'Market share – a key to profitability', *Harvard Business Review* 53: 97–106.

Campbell-Hunt, C. (2000) 'What have we learned about generic competitive strategy: a meta-analysis', *Strategic Management Journal* 21(2): 127–54.

Carroll, G.R., Dobrev, S.D. and Swaminathan, A. (2002) 'Organizational processes of resource partitioning', *Research in Organizational Behavior* 24: 1–40.

Chang, M.-H. and Harrington, J.E. Jr (2003) 'Multi-market competition, consumer search, and the organizational structure of multi-unit firms', *Management Science* 49(4): 541–52.

Chintagunta, P. (1994) 'Heterogeneous logit model implications for brand positioning', *Journal of Marketing Research* 31 (May): 304–11.

Christensen, C.M. (1997) *The Innovator's Dilemma*. Boston, MA: Harvard Business School Press.

Cohen, J. and Stewart, I. (1995) *The Collapse of Chaos*. New York: Penguin Books.

Cooke, P. (2002) *Knowledge Economics: Clusters, Learning and Co-operative Advantage*. London: Routledge.

Cooper, L. and Nakanishi, M. (1988) *Market Share Analysis: Evaluating Competitive Marketing Effectiveness*. Boston, MA: Kluwer Academic Press.

Coyle, M.L. (1986) 'Competition in developing markets: the impact of order of entry', Faculty of Management Studies Paper, University of Toronto, June.

Day, G.S. (1994) 'The capabilities of market-driven organizations', *Journal of Marketing* 58(4): 37–52.

Day, G.S. and Wensley, R. (1983) 'Marketing theory with a strategic orientation', *Journal of Marketing* 47(4): 79–89.

Day, G.S. and Wensley, R. (1988) 'Assessing advantage: a framework for diagnosing competitive superiority', *Journal of Marketing* 52 (April): 1–20.

Dickinson, P.R. (1992) 'Toward a general theory of competitive rationality', *Journal of Marketing* 56(1): 68–83.

Dolan, R.J. (1981) 'Models of competition: a review of theory and empirical findings', in B.M. Enis and K.J. Roering (eds) *Review of Marketing*. Chicago, IL: AMA, pp. 224–34.

Easton, G. (1990) 'Relationship between competitors', in G.S. Day, B. Weitz and R. Wensley (eds) *The Interface of Marketing and Strategy*. Greenwich, CT: JAI Press.

Easton, G., Burell G., Rothschild, R. and Shearman, C. (1993) *Managers and Competition*. Oxford: Blackwell.

Faria, A. and Wensley, R. (2002) 'In search of "interfirm management" in supply chains: recognizing contradictions of language and power by listening', *Journal of Business Research* 55(7): 603–10.

Fournier, S., Dobscha, S. and Mick, D.G. (1998) 'Preventing the premature death of relationship marketing', *Harvard Business Review* January–February: 42–50.

Giddens, A. (1979) *Central Problems in Social Theory: Action, Structure and Contradiction in Social Analysis*. London: Macmillan.

Goeree, J.K. and Holt, C.A. (2001) 'Ten little treasures of game theory and ten intuitive contradictions', *The American Economic Review* 91(5): 1402–22.

Goold, M. (1996) 'Learning, planning and strategy: extra time', *California Management Review* 38(4): 100–2.

Håkansson, H. (1987) *Industrial Technological Development: A Network Approach*. London: Croom Helm.

Helfat, C.E., Finkelstein, S., Mitchell, W., Peteraf, M., Singh, H., Teece, D. and Winter, S.G. (2007) *Dynamic Capabilities: Understanding Strategic Change in Organizations*. Oxford: Blackwell.

Henderson, B.D. (1983) 'The anatomy of competition', *Journal of Marketing* 47(2): 7–11.

Hofer, C.W. and Schendel, D. (1977) *Strategy Formulation: Analytical Concepts*. St Paul, MN: West Publishing.

Horgan, J. (1997) *The End of Science*. New York: Broadway Books.

Hult, G.T.M., Ketchen, D.R. Jr and Slater, S.F. (2005) 'Market orientation and performance: an integration of disparate approaches', *Strategic Management Journal* 26(12): 1173–81.

Hunt, M.S. (1972) 'Competition in the major home appliance industry, 1960–1970', unpublished doctoral dissertation, Harvard University.

Hunt, S.D. (2000a) *A General Theory of Competition: Resources, Competences, Productivity and Economic Growth*. Thousand Oaks, CA: Sage.

Hunt, S.D. (2000b) 'A general theory of competition: too eclectic or not eclectic enough? Too incremental or not incremental enough? Too neoclassical or not neoclassical enough?', *Journal of Macromarketing* 20(1): 77–81.

Illich, I. (1981) *Shadow Work*. London: Marion Boyars.

Ishibuchi, H., Sakamoto, R. and Nakashima, T. (2001) 'Evolution of unplanned coordination in a market selection game', *IEEE Transactions on Evolutionary Computation* 5(5).

Kadane, J.B. and Larkey, P.D. (1982) 'Subjective probability and the theory of games', *Management Science* 28(2): 113–20.

Kay, J. (1993) *Foundations of Corporate Success*. Oxford: Oxford University Press.

Kohli, A.K. and Jaworski, B.J. (1990) 'Market orientation: the construct, research propositions and managerial implications', *Journal of Marketing* 54(2): 1–18.

Lambkin, M. and Day, G. (1989) 'Evolutionary processes in competitive markets: beyond the product life cycle', *Journal of Marketing* 53(3): 4–20.

Leeflang, P.S.H. and Wittick, D. (1993) 'Diagnosing competition: developments and findings', in G. Laurent, G.L. Lillien and B. Pras (eds) *Research Traditions in Marketing*. Norwell, MA: Kluwer Academic.

Levins, R. and Leowontin, R. (1985) *The Dialectical Biologist*. Cambridge, MA: Harvard University Press.

Lewin, A.Y. and Volberda, H.W. (1999) 'Prolegomena on coevolution: a framework for research on strategy and new organizational forms', *Organizational Science* 10(5): 519–34.

McCloskey, D.N. and Ziliak, S.T. (1996) 'The standard error of regressions', *Journal of Economic Literature* XXXIV (March): 97–114.

McGee, J. and Thomas, H. (1986) 'Strategic groups: theory, research and taxonomy', *Strategic Management Journal* 7(2): 141–60.

Mattsson, L.-G. (1997) ' "Relationship marketing" and the "markets-as-networks approach" – a comparative analysis of two evolving streams of research', *Journal of Marketing Management* 13(5): 447–61.

Mingers, J. (1995) *Self-producing Systems*. New York: Plenum Press.

Mintzberg, H. (1994) *The Rise and Fall of Strategic Planning*. Harlow: Prentice-Hall.

Mintzberg, H. (1996a) 'Reply to Michael Goold', *California Management Review* 38(4): 96–9.

Mintzberg, H. (1996b) 'CMR forum: the Honda effect revisited', *California Management Review* 38(4): 78–9.

Mintzberg, H. (2004) *Managers Not MBAs: A Hard Look at the Soft Practice of Managing and Management Development*. San Francisco, CA: Berrett-Koehler.

Morrison, A. and Wensley, R. (1991) 'A short history of the growth/share matrix: boxed up or boxed in?', *Journal of Marketing Management* 7(2): 105–29.

Narver, J.C. and Slater, S.F. (1990) 'The effect of market orientation on business profitability', *Journal of Marketing* 54(4): 20–35.

Ohmae, K. (1982) *The Mind of the Strategist*. London: McGraw-Hill.

Peters, T.J. and Waterman, R.H. (1982) *In Search of Excellence*. New York: Harper and Row.

Porter, M.E. (1980) *Competitive Strategy*. New York: The Free Press.

Porter, M.E. (1985) *Competitive Advantage*. New York: The Free Press.

Porter, M.E. (1990) *The Competitive Advantage of Nations*. New York: The Free Press.

Sanchez, R. (1995) 'Strategic flexibility in product competition', *Strategic Management Journal* (special issue) 16: 135–59.

Saunders, J. (1995) 'Invited response to Wensley', *British Journal of Management* (special issue) 6.

Schembri, S. (2006) 'Rationalizing service logic, or understanding services as experience?', *Marketing Theory* 6(3): 381–92.

Simon, H.A. (1979) 'Rational decision making in business organizations', *American Economic Review* September.

Stacey, R.D. (1995) 'The science of complexity: an alternative perspective for strategic change processes', *Strategic Management Journal* 16(6): 477–95.

Teece, D.J., Pisano, G. and Shuen, A. (1997) 'Dynamic capabilities and strategic management', *Strategic Management Journal* 18(7): 509–33.

Tesfatsion, L. (2001) 'Guest editorial: Agent-based modelling of evolutionary economic systems', *IEEE Transactions on Evolutionary Computation* 5(5).

Vargo S.L. and Lusch, R.F. (2004) 'Evolving to a new dominant logic for marketing', *Journal of Marketing* 68(1): 1–17.

Waterman, R.H. (1988) *The Renewal Factor*. London: Bantam Books.

Wensley, R. (1994) 'Strategic marketing: a review', in M. Baker (ed.) *The Marketing Book*. London: Butterworth-Heinemann, pp. 33–53.

Wensley, R. (1995) 'A critical review of research in marketing', *British Journal of Management* (special issue) 6: S63–S82.

Wensley, R. (1996) 'Forms of segmentation: definitions and empirical evidence', MEG Conference Proceedings (CD Version) Session G Track 8, Department of Marketing, University of Strathclyde, 9–12 July, pp. 1–11.

Wensley, R. (1997a) 'Explaining success: the rule of ten percent and the example of market share', *Business Strategy Review* 8(1): 63–70.

Wensley, R. (1997b) 'Rejoinder to "Hard work, not Illusions" ', *Business Strategy Review* 8(2): 77.

Wensley, R. (1997c) 'Two marketing cultures in search of the chimera of relevance', keynote address at joint AMA and AM seminar 'Marketing Without Borders', Manchester, 7 July.

Wensley, R. (2002) 'Marketing for the new century', *Journal of Marketing Management* 18(1): 229–38.

Wernerfeld, B. (1984) 'A resource-based view of the firm', *Strategic Management Journal* 5(2): 171–80.

Wernerfeld, B. (1995a) 'The resource-based view of the firm: ten years after', *Strategic Management Journal* 16(3): 171–4.

Wernerfeld, B. (1995b) 'A rational reconstruction of the compromise effect', *Journal of Consumer Research* 21 (March): 627–33.

Winter, S.G. (2003) 'Understanding dynamic capabilities', *Strategic Management Journal* 24(10): 991–5.

Zahra, S.A., Sapienza, H.J. and Davidsson, P. (2006) 'Entrepreneurship and dynamic capabilities: a review, model and research agenda', *Journal of Management Studies* 43(4): 917–55.

Market Segmentation and Segment Strategy

Sally Dibb and Lyndon Simkin

11

Chapter Topics

Introduction	251
Customers' characteristics	252
Market segments	253
The importance of market segmentation	259
The accepted benefits of segmentation	259
Segmentation approaches	261
Segment quality	268
Targeting approaches	269
Operational danger in undertaking segmentation	274
Latest developments in segmentation	276
Summary	279

Introduction

Market segmentation principles are well established in marketing theory and a recognized component of marketing strategy (Boejgaard and Ellegaard, 2010; Webber, 1998; Weinstein, 2004).

As customer needs become increasingly diverse, segmentation provides organizations with the means to handle this complexity by identifying homogeneous groups of customers or target markets (McDonald and Dunbar, 2010). The benefits include more efficient resource allocation, marketing programmes which are a better fit with customer needs, and improved competitiveness (Beane and Ennis, 1987; Wind, 1978). There are many ways in which to undertake segmentation and to decide which to pursue with an organization's marketing resources (Dibb and Simkin, 2008; Sausen et al., 2005; Tonks, 2009). Although segmentation was designed initially to assist with consumer goods, segmentation is appropriate for any product or service, in all markets including business-to-business markets (Clarke and Freytag, 2008; Hassan et al., 2003; Walsh et al., 2010).

This chapter overviews the process of market segmentation and target segment selection. The reasons for undertaking segmentation are first outlined and the resulting benefits are explained. Ways for producing segmentations are described, illustrated with topical examples from the mobile phone, grocery, energy markets and from the health setting. The criteria for judging the qualities of the resulting segments are highlighted, before progressing to examine targeting decisions and segment choice approaches. The latest advances in segmentation in the digital era are summarized, including applications within the rapidly growing field of social marketing. The chapter concludes with a set of warnings for those planning to embark on market segmentation, so as to avoid or minimize the most commonly encountered impediments to undertaking segmentation and operationalizing the resulting target segment strategy.

Customers' characteristics

Are all of an organization's customers the same, sharing common goals, needs, expectations and behaviours? Only very occasionally are there such similarities and circumstances. Does the organization treat every customer individually, with a totally bespoke product/service proposition? While it might prefer to do so, resources rarely permit such tailored servicing, except for a few key accounts in some business markets. Even digitally enabled one-to-one marketing requires decisions about where to focus resources and for priority target market segments to be identified. Are all customers worth the same? Generally this is not the case. Are there resources within the organization to pursue all potential customers? Never! Most organizations – whether in consumer or business markets – must make tradeoff decisions. Segmentation, a core concept of marketing strategy, helps to address these practical constraints facing leadership teams in all types of organizations.

Organizations turn to segmentation for many reasons. Smarter target marketing and effective utilization of resources are the core benefits. A recent resurgence in interest in segmentation (Dibb and Simkin, 2009a; Simkin, 2013; Yankelovich and Meer, 2006) has been helped by the importance of shrewd targeting in times of recession (Venter et al., 2015) and by its use in new applications, such as social marketing. The UK's Chartered Institute of Marketing identified shrewder use of segmentation as one of the most important priorities for marketers striving to tackle the current economic downturn. Scarce marketing resources must be used prudently during periods of difficult trading, and in ways to better engage with customers so as to offer them reassurance and to demonstrate empathy with customers' concerns (Dibb and Simkin, 2012). Social marketing hinges on the effective positioning and communication of anti-smoking, healthy eating, good cause messages, for example, based on a sound appreciation of which stakeholders will/will not respond to specific campaigns (Dibb, 2014). Such targeting strategies require well-crafted segmentations. The growth of global marketing has also encouraged organizations to develop segmentations to help them to manage a complexity of markets (Hassan and Craft, 2012).

Segmentation considers how best to structure the market, selects the most attractive customer groups on which to focus resources, develops a persuasive proposition for these targeted customers or stakeholders, and helps to ensure that an organization 'goes to market' in a far more engaging manner, with clear differentiation and positioning. This chapter explores the nature of market segmentation, segment creation and target segment selection. Other chapters consider the development of a compelling basis for competing and brand positioning.

According to the textbooks, segmentation is the process of grouping customers into markets with some heterogeneity into smaller, more similar or homogeneous groups (segments). In other words, market segmentation is the grouping of like-minded and similarly behaving consumers or business customers together for the purposes of developing products/services, targeting sales and marketing, managing customer service and determining internal resourcing (Wells et al., 2010). A market segment is defined as a group of individual consumers (in B2C markets) or business customers (in B2B markets) sharing one or more similar characteristics that cause them to have relatively similar product needs and buying behaviour. All the individuals allocated to one particular market segment should respond to the same marketing strategy and marketing programme. In layperson's terms, segmentation is understanding what customers want and how they buy, grouping similar or like-minded ones together, choosing which to go after, and then tailoring a proposition accordingly.

However, segmentation goes way beyond the division of consumers or business customers in a market. It is at the heart of creating a target market strategy, deciding which customers to serve and which to ignore, understanding how to attract and retain the most appropriate customers, and knowing through what means to compete successfully. Not only is market segmentation at the heart of a marketing strategy, it is part of an organization's overall strategy.

Market segments

To illustrate what we mean by segments and the identification of groups of like-minded and similarly behaving customers, consider the descriptions below of three of the eight segments used by one mobile phone company:

- *Gaming youths.* 'The game oriented, mobile world addict', rarely using the phone for conversations, but focused instead on games, music and texts. The desired proposition is youth oriented, modern, innovative and games-led and entertainment.

- *Sophisticated careerists.* 'Be successful with mobile technology.' These are career-oriented individualists, with lots of contacts, requiring a mobile phone to organize every aspect of their lives: satnav directions, web searches, address book, diary, communications, networking, work and socializing. Interested in the internet and social media, network reliability and talk-led tariffs, but not TV downloads, games or music.
- *Laggards.* 'Torn between conservative values and the modern world.' These 'late mass consumers' simply do not see the relevance of this technology or how it fits into their lifestyles. Many may have a mobile phone but rarely use it. The mobile world has passed them by. Networks are now trying to entice them and to demystify the mobile world, as potentially these infrequent users present revenue growth.

No doubt you know someone who fits each of these profiles… a sibling, parent, grandparent, colleague or yourself. The games, music and text packages offered to the *Gaming youths* would have no relevance to either the *Sophisticated careerists* or the *Laggards*, while the approaches being taken to entice greater use by the *Laggards* certainly would fail to appeal to *Gaming youths* or *Sophisticated careerists*. Were the mobile phone company to have only one marketing strategy and marketing mix, it would fail to address effectively the requirements and behaviours of each of these groups of consumers – with the added risk being that competitors would target one of these segments with very focused and highly pertinent propositions. Hence, the role of segmentation: to identify such differences between customer groups and then separate them for marketing purposes, deciding which segment or segments on which to focus resources. Case Study 11.1 explains in more detail the approach taken by this mobile phone company.

CASE STUDY 11.1

Teleco segmentation

Background

As the mobile phone market matures and becomes saturated, service operators are seeking new ways to target and serve their customers in order to generate revenue. This particular telecommunications company operates throughout much of Northern and Eastern Europe, regions which are known for their advanced mobile phone usage. Faced with growing competition, the organization sought a more sophisticated customer segmentation approach for four countries in its Eurasian markets. Previously, the company divided its market only into corporate and private users, with a further split between customers on pay-as-you-go and monthly contracts. Such an approach to splitting up the overall mobile phone market was not uncommon until recent years. Growing competition and market saturation have encouraged most players in this sector to produce segmentations and rethink their targeting strategies.

A German marketing research organization was retained by the telecommunications company to conduct the required data collection and segmentation analysis. Initially the focus was a consumer segmentation scheme, quickly followed by a review of the needs, usage and behaviour of corporate users. There were five main phases to the segmentation project (see Figure 11.1):

Phase 1: A preparatory phase exploring the current market structure, involving the organization's senior leadership team, external experts and the research organization. This phase also involved exploratory focus groups, so as to examine consumers' mobile usage and buying behaviour.

Phase 2: 10,000 consumer interviews were conducted (2,500 in four countries: 40% were current users) to allow quantitative analysis of consumers' needs, required benefits, usage, lifestyles and attitudes towards mobile phones. A further 2,000 interviews addressed corporate subscribers in the four countries, examining similar issues, plus buying centre dynamics and decision making, and tariff considerations.

Phase 3: Multivariate techniques, including conjoint, factor, cluster analyses and structural equation modelling, were used to generate customer segments. These were then refined through input from managers and from 'deep-dive' customer focus groups.

Phase 4: The segments were presented throughout the organization, with careful tailoring to each of the specific country markets of the operating brands.

Phase 5: The final stage involved implementing the segmentation. Follow-up qualitative marketing research tested consumer and business customer views of the marketing propositions and competitive standing within each of the targeted segments.

Identifying the market segments

The segmentation solution was developed using a clustering approach. Input variables generated from the earlier interviews included peer group orientation, trend/fashion influences, tradition/family values, communication needs/usage, emotional aspects of usage, technology affinity, demographics/lifestage/lifestyles, media

(Continued)

(Continued)

usage, tariff requirements, purchasing policies, factors influencing buying and buying centre dynamics. A statistically sound and intuitively robust eight-cluster solution was generated, which was also intuitively appealing to managers. The emerging segments reflected the overall set of behaviours in evidence: some were consumer focused, others were business user orientated. The segments were profiled using behavioural and aspirational variables (see Table 11.1). The chosen segment labels closely reflected the allocation of customers to segments using easily remembered language. The clarity aided internal communication, convincing managers that customers could be readily allocated to segments. Existing subscribers were then analysed and allocated to one of the segments.

The analysis produced a statistically sound 14-cluster solution. As the organization had previously operated with just two customer groups (business users and consumers on pay-as-you-go tariffs), managers felt that progressing from two to 14 customer

Phase 1: Preparation
- Internal scoping workshop
- Selection of project partners
- Detailed brief/contract
- Qualitative exploratory research (focus groups)
- Preparation of questionnaire for quantitative phase

Phase 2: Quantitative Study
- Four countries
- $N = 2,500$ interviews per country (including rejecters)
- $N = 1,000$ current/potential users
- Coverage of many issues:
  Needs, benefits, usage, attitudes, lifestyles, etc.

Phase 3: Segmentation Analysis
- Customized solution
- Conjoint tradeoffs
- Factor and cluster analyses
- Workshops for debate and evaluation of emerging solutions

Phase 4: Reporting
- Management presentation of segments
- Management report
- Tailored report for each country
- Tables/cross-tables
- Special analyses:
  Trends, competitors, revenues, etc.

Phase 5: Implementation
- Present segments
- Internal marketing of emerging strategy
- Agree targeting criteria and select target priorities
- Deep-dive focus group research into targeted segments
- Creation and roll-out of marketing programmes for targeted segments
- Ongoing tracking studies

Implementation planning was built-in from the onset.

This project lasted 18 months.

Figure 11.1   The five phases of the segmentation project.

Source: GfK, Germany.

Table 11.1 Analysis input variables.

- Peer group orientation
- Trend/fashion influences
- Tradition/family values
- Communication needs and usage
- Fun and emotional aspects from mobile usage
- Mobile and e-world immersion
- Social media engagement
- Technology affinity
- Interest in Teleco applications and services
- Demographics/lifestage/lifestyles
- Media usage
- Tariff plans and requirements
- Purchasing policies
- Buying centre dynamics
- Influencing factors

groups was too major a transition to handle. The focus shifted instead to the next cut-off point in the clustering, the eight-cluster solution. Tests of the statistical robustness of these eight segments proved satisfactory. Initial reviews suggested the groupings were intuitively robust, with managers readily able to visualize the customers contained within them. The different segments were also mutually exclusive, with each consumer or business user clearly allocated to one of the segments. The segments were then profiled in terms of the behavioural and aspirational variables considered in the analysis and descriptive labels identified (see Table 11.2).

The chosen segment labels were felt to closely reflect the allocation of customers to segments using easy to remember language. The clarity aided internal communication and meant managers were optimistic about the ease with which customers could be allocated to the segments. As part of the project, all of the corporation's existing subscribers in the data warehouse were analysed and each was allocated to one of these segments.

Quality checking the segments

Having statistically and qualitatively identified the segments, the marketing research company applied an agreed set of evaluation criteria to test the quality of the segments. This process took place *prior* to the selection of segments to target with marketing resources. The criteria used were a mix of statistical and qualitative measures, routinely applied by this organization as part of the segmentation projects it undertakes for clients. The rationale is that statistical tests are used to verify the robustness

(Continued)

(Continued)

Table 11.2   The eight segment profiles.

Talk 'n' texters – 'I just have a mobile phone because it is practical'.

- The conservative customer, not immersed in technology but with a few practical needs that can be fulfilled by technical appliances. S/he relies on mobile phones for practical reasons only.
- Interested in basic functions, especially SMS, but not attracted at all by more sophisticated or fun services, be it via mobile phone or the internet.

Talkative trendies – 'Talk around the clock'.

- The modern, fun- and fashion-oriented socializer. This customer needs a mobile phone to keep in constant touch with the social scene and fulfil a strong need for communication.
- Interested in all applications and services.

Aspiring to be accepted – 'Would like to have it but is not really up to it'.

- Wants to be part of the in-crowd, but is not there yet, and possibly never will be! These customers have a mobile phone because they just want to have it (show off) and seek to have trendy handsets and applications they believe are adopted by peer sets they aspire to join.
- Show a special affinity towards social media, photo, video and MP3 applications.

Laggards – 'Torn between conservative values and the modern world'.

- Traditionalist views with low communication needs and basic technical usage.
- The Luddites or those late into the market!
- S/he holds specific aversions against mobile phones (SMS) but also views them as a practical-only device (e.g. for emergency calls only).

Gaming youths – 'Game oriented mobile world addict'.

- Young and very technology-oriented people, belonging to the mobile generation, who need a mobile phone in order to maintain a fast-living fun life.
- Games, games, games! And music.
- These customers search for images and brands that help them keep track with the modern world.

Sophisticated careerists – 'Be successful with mobile technology'.

- Career-oriented individualists with lots of contacts. Highly immersed in technology and very mobile.
- Demanding on value for money. Customer care and respect are very important to these customers.
- They need a mobile phone to organize their life and business, but they are not emotionally attached.
- Self-choosers for work mobiles are included here.

Organization paid – 'No choice – the corporation decides'.

- Demanding on value for money and customer care.
- Network coverage, reliability and volume discounts are the focus.
- Users have little influence in selection, so not particularly fashion or technology-led.

International business users – 'Frequent connected business travellers'.

- Easy quad-band roaming, 4G and smooth data transfer.
- Some similarities with *Sophisticated careerists* but with much greater emphasis on functionality and flexibility of at-destination services.
- Influenced by corporate choice of network and tariff plans.

The first five are consumer segments. The last two are business user segments. The *Sophisticated careerists* are mainly business users who self-select mobile network, handset and tariff option and behave as consumers. These segments have been disguised.

of the segment identification process and its outcomes. The qualitative criteria enable the intuitive managerial logic of the recommendation to be judged. This latter stage is deemed crucial to the satisfactory implementation of any segment solution.

Outcomes

In all four countries, the adopted segmentation strategy resulted in market share and income gains, and significant improvements to brand awareness and customer satisfaction in the targeted segments. The mobile phone company's rivals had not adopted such a focused approach to target marketing or campaign development. In situations where the organization was market leader, challengers' shares were eroded. Where the organization was the challenger brand, there were impressive gains in market share. In all four countries, there were market share gains within targeted segments and aggressive competitors were pre-empted from making any further inroads. Revenues per subscriber in priority segments increased and the more focused marketing programmes improved the company's reputation with targeted consumers and corporate users.

The importance of market segmentation

Market segmentation is part of the strategic marketing process (see Figure 11.2). It is arguably *the* pivotal aspect of this process and one of the most important activities undertaken by marketers. Segmentation creates a more developed understanding of customers' behaviours, differences and similarities, so directing the development of propositions and the use of marketing programmes. In order to make informed decisions about which segments to target, marketers need insights into marketing environment trends and drivers, competitors' capabilities and plans, internal resources and capabilities, and corporate strategy. The process of undertaking market segmentation, therefore, acts as a catalyst to update these insights. The resulting marketing programmes and resource allocation decisions benefit greatly from the understanding that is generated by this process.

The accepted benefits of segmentation

As the following opinions reveal, business practitioners believe that there are a number of benefits associated with segmentation. The CEO of one of the world's largest IT corporations recently stated that, 'Segmentation-based marketing is the essence of sound business strategy and value creation.' A multinational energy company's strategy director expressed the following view, 'Segmentation is about recognising some customers are not worth targeting. Sure, you'll sell to them if they come calling, but you won't invest in chasing them.' For one of the

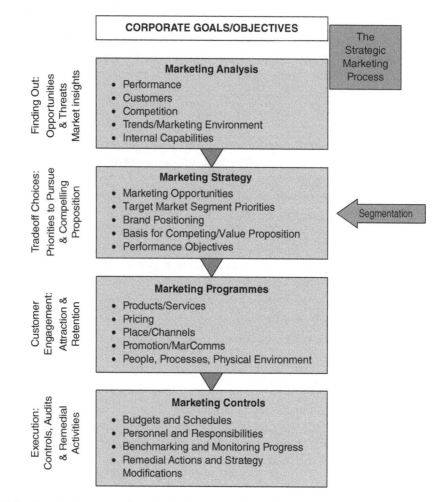

Figure 11.2   The role of target market selection in the strategic marketing process.

largest bankers, 'Segmentation makes handling smaller accounts profitable.' According to a leading global construction equipment manufacturer's CEO, 'Segmentation is just common sense good practice – it gets you closer to the right customers and encourages you to look after them properly.' Even though these executives are not in marketing roles, they still value the important role of segmentation in their strategies and operations.

The key benefits from undertaking segmentation include:

- Improved customer insights: in order to create segments an organization must have up-to-date intelligence, so the process forces a rethink about customers and their current issues. Segmentation focuses on customers' needs, expectations, aspirations and share of wallet, building stronger relationships with customers.

- More focused product and service propositions, differentiated from rivals' propositions: there is every chance that competitive advantage will result from a well-executed segmentation strategy, possibly building barriers to competitors' moves.
- Enhanced awareness of external market trends and competition: an organization cannot decide which segments to target without examining these issues.
- Focused resource allocation and marketing spend on the most worthwhile opportunities: segmentation reveals who *not* to chase and which customer groups on which to focus resources.
- Internal clarity: segmentation invariably aligns the efforts of sales, business development, marketing, proposition development, campaign execution. This is arguably one of the most significant benefits. Segmentation establishes commitment and single-mindedness within the organization: one vision, one voice, harmonized messages.
- Increased revenues from targeted customers: the resulting benefit from the points above should be enhanced performance in the selected target segments.

Segmentation approaches

The reasons for undertaking segmentation are compelling. However, there is no magic formula or standardized off-the-shelf approach that can be used. Figure 11.3 summarizes the many different bases (variables) which can be used to identify market segments. These are the variables which have been used by Experian's analytics team for a multitude of Experian's clients

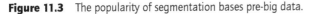

- There are many potential segmentations that can be developed ...

mode usage geography services product

lifestyle lifestage attitudes reasoning functionality

interest technology frequency upgrades affinity

touchpoint customer value loyalty rfv

affluence share of wallet lifecycle advocacy churn

tenure engagement cost service

...and these can be combined and overlaid to address various business needs

Font prominence equates to frequency of their use in
Experian's many segmentation projects.

Figure 11.3   The popularity of segmentation bases pre-big data.

Source: Gareth Mitchell-Jones, Experian; presented at the Chartered Institute of Marketing's Annual Conference, Birmingham, 11 November 2008.

seeking to develop segmentation strategies. In days gone by, demographics, socio-economics, lifestyles, benefits, usage and attitudes were all 'in vogue' as *the* trendy platform for segmentation. In practice, most organizations today seek a wealth of customer insights, including their characteristics, needs, buying behaviour, the influences upon their decisions, perceptions, motives, attitudes, usage and purchasing activity. A decade ago, restricted by data availability, poor computing power and the high costs of acquiring market intelligence, they might have selected only a few of the base variable categories in Figure 11.3. In today's digitally empowered big data era they will strive for a much fuller picture.

The process of conducting segmentation has been revolutionized in recent years owing to data access, reduced costs and time frames, powerful computing, routinized analytics and new heuristics. As in the mobile phone example summarized above, these insights can be modelled together, in order to identify clusters of similarly behaving and like-minded customers, or market segments. The greater the knowledge of customers in a particular market, the stronger the insight for the segmentation solution. A growing body of opinion suggests that the approach that an organization uses needs to reflect their goals and reasons for embarking on segmentation (Dibb and Simkin, 2008; Liu et al., 2010; Palmer and Millier, 2004; Yankelovich and Meer, 2006). Here we summarize some of the more commonly adopted approaches for developing market segments:

1. The survey-based approach, which is very popular. The mobile phone company featured above undertook qualitative research (depth interviews/focus groups), then a quantitative survey of 10,000 consumers, followed by confirmatory qualitative research. The survey findings were statistically analysed and modelled, to produce the eight segment solution, described in Table 11.2. Recent advances have radically altered the time and cost to undertake such a project, reducing both considerably and making such a project far more feasible for many organizations.
2. Often, segments emerge almost by accident, when undertaking customer research for other purposes. For example, when creating a new brand strategy, one leading manufacturer of ready meals conducted qualitative research into consumers' buying behaviour and views of the leading brands. These focus groups identified clusters of consumer behaviour and five segments were suggested as a result. Figure 11.4 provides an overview. Sometimes marketers are researching something other than market segments when groups of like-minded consumers emerge from the data. Although such segments may initially not be statistically validated, the intuitive appeal of these groups of customers may result in them being embraced as the target market strategy. Such segments can be subsequently validated with confirmatory research or data mining.
3. In business-to-business and service markets, the macro-micro approach is very popular, stemming from managerial brainstorming about client types, behaviours, attitudes, their needs and the influences impacting on their choices of brand or service provider. The brainstorming starts by examining the characteristics and buying behaviour of the organization's existing customer groupings, first seeking to disaggregate these into more homogeneous groups, and then reaggregating across the original customer typology to create market segments. This approach was adopted by the energy business described in Case Study 11.2 (see also Simkin and Dibb, 2011).

Figure 11.4   Marketers often stumble upon market segments.

CASE STUDY 11.2

Segmenting the energy market: macro-micro approach

Background

When electricity supplies first spread throughout the UK they were provided by a plethora of local private companies, all using different specifications and power outputs, seeking to capitalize on the surge in demand for this then 'alternative' energy. In order to maximize uptake, harmonize operating standards and ensure the public's safety, government regulation eventually led to state-controlled regional monopolies. Commercial and household customers in a geographic region such as the Midlands or the South East had no choice but to receive both infrastructure and energy from the region's designated regional electricity company (REC). Price and service levels were fixed by regulation and the REC, with customers only able to buy from one supplier. During the 1980s, the UK government privatized or deregulated nearly all remaining state-run enterprises, such as the large airports (BAA), state airline (BA), logistics company (NFC/Excel), defence supply (BAe), car producers (Jaguar, Land Rover and Rover) and telecoms (BT). By the 1990s it was the turn of the

(Continued)

(Continued)

remaining utilities, including gas (British Gas/Transco), and the regional water and electricity companies. For the first time in living memory, consumers and business customers had a choice of electricity supplier.

The newly deregulated market was attractive for other organizations to enter, with many well-known brands such as Tesco, Virgin and Sainsbury's deciding to retail the electricity generated by the major producers. The RECs became acquisition targets, largely for larger energy businesses in France, Germany and the USA. Over the next decade, mergers and acquisitions led to the situation where just six energy firms dominated the supply of electricity and gas in the UK: British Gas, French-based EDF Energy, Npower (owned by Germany's RWE), Scottish and Southern, Scottish Power (owned by Spain's Iberdrola) and Germany's E.on after its purchase of PowerGen.

Initially, consumers were slower to consider switching suppliers than business customers, but now – over two decades since deregulation – many consumers are enticed to switch electricity supplier by the lure of lower prices or a guarantee of no price inflation for a fixed period. Current recession has motivated increasing numbers of consumers to seek better deals, facilitated by online comparison websites and hype in the media. The market has become increasingly price sensitive and few customers exhibit any brand loyalty.

In an increasingly price-led and competitive environment, several of the larger energy suppliers have sought to differentiate themselves on other dimensions, including their green credentials, tariff innovations and customer service capability. As often happens in maturing and highly competitive markets, these companies have also turned to market segmentation in order to identify the most attractive groups of commercial and private customers on which to focus their marketing resources. For example, E.on has identified segments based on the lifetime value for the account, to ensure the resources required to capture a new customer will be recouped before the customer switches to a rival supplier.

One of the main providers of generating capacity, infrastructure and energy distribution decided to adopt the principles of market segmentation in order to energize the efforts of its sales and key account managers, and to help identify the sub-groups of customers on whom the business should focus its sales, marketing and customer support developments. This company had among its leadership team several MBA graduates familiar with the acknowledged benefits of market segmentation and two directors who in other sectors had practised successfully the deployment of market segmentation in their target marketing.

Project objectives and the adopted segmentation process

Despite the acceptance of market segmentation's benefits and the residual knowledge of the necessary techniques for conducting market segmentation, this energy business felt that there would be resistance within the company. This would be for a variety of reasons, not least inertia and a dislike of changing working remits. The strategy director preferred to engender internal support and to foster buy-in by involving throughout the segmentation senior management and those line managers likely to be most affected by the segmentation: notably sales and key account management personnel. It was decreed that the resulting segments must be sizeable enough to warrant serving, markedly unique in their composition and characteristics, easy to populate by sales managers, prioritized in terms of profitability and costs to serve, and based on the characteristics and purchasing behaviour of the customers. A rigorous process was to be deployed that would stand up to external scrutiny and be compliant of regulations governing this sector.

The energy business wanted to:

1. Identify sub-groupings of customers based on a mix of characteristics, including purchasing behaviour and spend, rather than only profitability measures.
2. Generate enthusiasm through the process among those managers engaging directly with customers.
3. Develop a segmentation solution readily transparent, so that staff knew instinctively in which segment a particular customer should be.
4. Seek market leadership in an attractive set of market segments in a differentiated, competitively effective and regulatory compliant way.
5. Facilitate the development of marketing propositions tailored to targeted customer requirements through novel and market-leading sales and marketing programmes.
6. Update its insights into customers, competitors, market trends and associated organizational capabilities.

Initially, the energy company ran an externally facilitated orientation workshop for senior personnel and key line managers responsible for sales, marketing, marketing research, key account management and customer service. This workshop established the requirements for the ongoing segmentation process in terms of actions, resources, personnel, time frames and reporting structures. A cross-functional subgroup of these executives became the core project team. A new marketing manager

(Continued)

(Continued)

was recruited to administer the segmentation project. This team and the marketing manager had the support of external experts.

There are numerous approaches to conducting market segmentation. Many textbooks promote the quantitative survey-based approach, ignoring the company's existing classifications of customer groups and instead analysing the usage and attitude, buying behaviour and characteristics of customers in a quantitative survey. Multivariate analysis then identifies the emerging market segments. So long as internal structures and personnel can be expediently realigned to address these market segments, such an approach has much merit. In practice, many organizations struggle to achieve easy realignment to such a radical redefinition of customer groups and target market priorities. Many business marketers find instead the macro-micro approach easier to operationalize. This approach starts with the company's existing customer groupings and knowledge of these customers, seeking to identify new groupings from within these. There are merits in both approaches, and in the many other possibilities, but it is not the purpose of this chapter to critically assess the different approaches. Rather than commission an extensive quantitative customer survey, the macro-micro approach to market segmentation was preferred by this energy business, owing to cost and time pressures, but also to ensure the direct participation of the organization's personnel in creating the market segments.

Adhering to published best practice, a template was produced which captured the characteristics of customers, buying centre dynamics, energy usage and consumption data, customer needs and expectations, the buying decision-making process and influencing factors. This template was used to acquire these marketing insights for each of the company's existing customer groupings. Cross-functional teams knowledgeable of each customer grouping were assembled for a series of workshops which between them, over a three-week period, examined all of the company's customer types. Each team comprised senior and line managers, sales, marketing, key account and customer service personnel, and the marketing manager as facilitator.

In practice, these teams found it impossible to generalize the customer insights for each customer group: in reality, dissimilar consumers were currently allocated together in each customer group. A variety of reasons explained these allocations: industry 'norms', operational convenience, regulatory compliance and ignorance of customers' behaviour. As a result, while seeking to identify groupings of homogeneous behaviour, during the workshops each existing customer group was split into groups of like-minded and similarly behaving consumers. Typically between five and 12 groups (or separate templates) emerged out of each initial customer group. During a subsequent set of meetings, the project team was able to reaggregate into market segments these many templates, by merging groups identified across the many workshops which exhibited similar characteristics and behaviours.

In parallel to identifying the market segments, the marketing team was updating its competitor intelligence and awareness of market trends, in order to help at the target segment selection stage. The project team, in conjunction with the company's leadership team, adopted the directional policy matrix tool and agreed a set of market attractiveness criteria which would subsequently be weighted and used to rank the emerging market segments in terms of their relative attractiveness and capability fit.

The resulting segmentation solution

Two segmentation schemes emerged: one for consumers (private households) and one for commercial customers (public and private sectors). The details cannot be divulged here for reasons of corporate confidentiality, but there were 10 consumer segments and 14 business segments. The directional policy matrix identified three consumer and two business segments to grow, several to harvest and hold, but interestingly several segments to de-prioritize or ignore. For illustrative purposes, some of the emerging segments are detailed in Table 11.3.

Table 11.3 Examples of the energy provider's segment profiles.

In the business market, segments included two in the public sector:

- *The professionals*. Professional purchasing managers – focused on seeking value for the tax payer and good service levels, while becoming increasingly concerned about carbon footprint and green issues, often with in-house energy specialists.
- *No change traditionalists*. More risk averse public sector traditionalists, committee-led decision making, very influenced by their own networks and similar organizations.

There were several commercial small business segments, including:

- *Independents*. Price conscious owners of small enterprises such as shops, business services or restaurants, very much focused on reducing operating costs to support profitability and influenced by media views.
- *Ego-stroked proprietors*. Deal-seeking localized chains/SMEs, in which the entrepreneur's ego must be massaged.
- *The buyers*. Energy-aware light manufacturing and small industrial firms with energy managers and facilities managers, who want simplified buying and a good deal.

Organizations operating across numerous sites fell into five segments, including:

- *Energy savvy*. Large multi-site energy aware businesses, with an in-house knowledgeable energy team seeking significant cost savings and reliable multi-site billing.
- *Low awareness purchasers*. Multi-site customers requiring cost savings, but not energy savvy or really focused on energy trends.
- *Site churners*. Multi-site operators with quickly changing site portfolios; price is important but not as much as service levels.
- *Frequent switchers*. Multi-site frequent switchers, fully deal-led and quick to change supplier, with no loyalty.

Further details of these three broad options may be found in *Market Segmentation Success: Making it Happen!* by Sally Dibb and Lyndon Simkin (Routledge/The Haworth Press, 2008). Each of the outlined approaches has advantages and disadvantages:

1. The survey-based quantitative approach, adopted by the mobile phone company, is generally effective in creating segments, but is expensive and takes time (18 months in this case), requires expert marketing research that is well specified, and its adoption involves upheaval/disruption to the organization. However, improved analytics and computing power along with digitally-led big data insights have in recent years radically reduced the required time frames and costs. A project previously costing £5 million and taking 12–15 months may be undertaken in 6–8 weeks and cost only £400,000.
2. The qualitative-only 'accidental' approach, as in the grocery example, is certainly quick and easy. A couple of weeks and no more than £60,000 were required. However, this approach is vulnerable to poor scoping and misinterpretation, and is only as good as the up-front thinking in specifying the limited qualitative marketing research. In practice, it must be followed with a quantitative confirmatory study and data mining, otherwise the robustness of the segments is questionable.
3. The macro-micro approach 'evolves' segments, so is much less disruptive and engenders ownership among executives involved in the brainstorming. This approach also requires some subsequent validation and is principally a B2B option (Simkin, 2008). It requires little more than a workshop and the involvement of managers from across the organization, so is quick and inexpensive.

Segment quality

Having created a segmentation, it is necessary to 'sanity-check' the quality of the segments. Segment quality criteria are a set of desirable segment characteristics, for use in consumer and business-to-business contexts. The original version developed by Kotler (1967) refers to segment *measurability*, enabling segment size and potential to be judged; *accessibility*, in order that a segment can be reached and served; *substantiality*, ensuring that a segment is of sufficient size and profit potential; and *actionability*, so that a segment can be reached effectively with a marketing programme. These criteria have been endorsed by other authors (e.g. Bonoma et al., 1983; Wind, 1978), some of whom developed their own checklists for assessing the quality of segmentation output. These criteria are distinct from those variables used when assessing segment attractiveness during targeting (cf. Goller et al., 2002), as discussed in the next section of this chapter.

This distinction is clarified by Hlavacek and Reddy's (1986) view of segmentation comprising (1) segment identification, (2) segment qualification and (3) segment attractiveness. Under this scheme, segment identification relates to the design of the segments, while the qualification phase concerns the extent to which emerging customer groups can be operationalized. Segment attractiveness relates to targeting decisions, resource allocation and segment prioritization. This approach establishes the role of qualifying criteria which appraise the quality of segments, rather than those which are used to judge targeting attractiveness.

Historically, segmentation theory has rested on a basic assumption of market heterogeneity (Beane and Ennis, 1987; Wedel and Kamakura, 2002; Wind, 1978). Once this assumption is satisfied, the role of segment qualification criteria is to assess whether a segment has distinct user characteristics and needs, if the scale of the opportunity is worthwhile, the extent to which these features are measurable and stable over time, whether the competitors can be readily identified, and if a marketing programme can effectively target it. Kotler's (1967) criteria of measurability, accessibility, substantiality and actionability are central to many of the other proposed schemes.

The underlying requirement is that the market to be segmented is heterogeneous. This criterion is implied in Kotler's original list. From the published ideas on this aspect of segmentation, the dominant *segment quality* themes can then be summarized as:

1. *Segments are homogeneous.* Each segment being distinctive in terms of its customer profile and needs. This will impact upon the extent to which the segments are accessible.
2. *Segment size and potential profitability.* This involves two sub-themes: the first is that the size of the segment is sufficient so that resource allocation can be justified and future profitability or revenue stream judged adequate. This fits with Kotler's notion of substantiality, yet more specifically expresses the underlying components. The second sub-theme concerns the ability to predict size and profitability, closely fitting with Kotler's measurability criterion.
3. *Segment stability.* Although not directly included by Kotler, given that profitability could rely upon stability, this is implied by the substantiality criterion.
4. *Segment accessibility.* This theme mirrors one of those originally expressed by Kotler, concerning whether suitable and distinctive marketing programmes can be developed for emerging segments.
5. *Segment compatibility.* Perhaps the most complex theme, this concerns the extent to which the segment output fits the organizational context. This includes synergy with corporate and/or marketing strategy; match to resources and capabilities; and fit with organizational factors such as culture, structure and operational considerations. Although this theme is not the same as Kotler's notion of actionability, it highlights important issues which affect whether a segment can be served.
6. *Segment actionability.* This theme is consistent with Kotler's original interpretation of the term, referring to whether the organization has the resources and capabilities to serve the emerging segments.

The point is that segmentation does not end with the identification of market segments. Certain segments must be selected, they must be worthwhile, and successful engagement must be feasible (Dibb and Simkin, 2010). The segmentation process goes beyond creating the segments.

Targeting approaches

No organization has the resources or capabilities to adequately address all segments in its market with segment-specific sales and marketing programmes. Some tough choices are needed about where to concentrate resources and marketing programmes. Even the largest corporations, such as GM, P&G, IBM, Marriott, Tesco or HSBC, prioritize certain target markets ahead of others, and do not offer all consumers or business customers a proposition. This section considers the available options for selecting target segments. Unless the 'right' segments are targeted, an organization will not enjoy the benefits of adopting the market segmentation concept and the costs of identifying segments will not be repaid.

A few organizations adopt a single-segment targeting strategy and, in effect, become a niche specialist. Most organizations opt to target several segments. In pursuing a multi-segment strategy, organizations spread their risks by trading in several different segments and thereby seek increased sales volumes and revenues. The costs of a multi-segment strategy can be considerable: developing a variety of product offers and marketing programmes requires substantial resources. Nonetheless, a multi-segment strategy is the more commonly adopted approach to target market selection in the vast majority of organizations. For these organizations, the challenge is to ensure that the selection of segments is carefully managed, so that resources are allocated to the 'best' mix of segments. One-to-one marketing may well be practised, but within the segments deemed most important.

The literature examining the targeting stage of the market segmentation process has identified various factors that impact upon an organization's assessment of target market attractiveness, including:

- The organization's existing *market share* and *market homogeneity* – a company's knowledge of an existing market will influence its view as to the relative attractiveness of this market vis-a-vis others.
- Existing *product expertise* – in related applications or adjacent markets on which the organization can build.
- Likelihood of *production and marketing scale economies* – although each segment targeted will require a bespoke marketing programme, there may be certain savings in product development, brand building activity, customer service, logistics, or marcomms (marketing communications) between two or more segments, which are not available if the organization opts to prioritize a different set of segments.
- The nature of the *competitive environment* – one segment may be particularly well served by one or two very strong competitors, whereas there may be the opportunity to establish a competitive advantage in a separate segment.
- The forces of the *marketing environment* and *market trends* – these external developments will present opportunities and threats, impacting on the relative attractiveness of different market segments.
- Capability and ease of matching *customer needs* – the behaviour and expertise of the organization may synergize more strongly with one segment than with the consumers or business customers in another segment.
- Segment attractiveness in terms of *size, structure and growth* – some organizations may deem a segment to be too small or low in spending to be attractive or there may be volatility and instability.

- Available *corporate resources* – no organization has the time, money, people or skills available to address all segments in a market: some segments will be resourced ahead of others.
- Anticipated *profitability, revenue and market share* – ultimately an organization must satisfy its owners, shareholders and investors, who generally equate profitability and ROI with successful business strategies. In certain organizations, notably in Asia Pacific, there is a sensible goal to increase market share, which may be possible in only certain segments.

Best practice suggests that a 'basket' of variables should be considered by managers appraising the attractiveness of segments, including short-term and long-term measures; internal factors such as financial rewards, budgeting costs, operational requirements; along with external factors, including customer satisfaction considerations, competitive intensity, marketing environment factors and so forth. Not all of the factors which are considered will be equally important in determining whether or not a particular segment is attractive to the organization. Some variables will be more important than others, so there needs to be a process for weighting the selected attractiveness criteria. The importance of variables will also vary for separate organizations. Various models – such as the *directional policy matrix* or *segment evaluation matrix* – have been developed to assist managers in choosing which segments to target (Dibb, 1995). Chapter 5 of Dibb and Simkin's book, *Market Segmentation Success: Making it Happen!*, explores all of these options, but for now the focus is on the directional policy matrix (DPM), which is widely used to identify which segments to prioritize.

The market attractiveness–business strength model or directional policy matrix (DPM) employs multiple measurements and observations. Although originally created to examine product and brand portfolios, the tool works well in directing target segment selection. The *market attractiveness* dimension includes all aspects that relate to the market, such as expected profitability or ROI, seasonality, economies of scale, competitive intensity, ability to develop a competitive advantage, industry sales, the overall cost and feasibility of entering the market, or whatever is deemed appropriate for a particular sector and organization in judging the relative merits of segments. By using a set of variables, the technique forces managers to consider attractiveness in terms other than solely short-term profitability. The *business strength* dimension is also a composite of factors, perhaps including relative market share, research and development expertise, price competitiveness, product quality and technical performance, market knowledge, customer handling/service, production and logistical competencies, financial resources, managerial expertise, and so forth. Such strengths or capabilities are internal issues unique to the organization in question and are generally benchmarked against the strongest and most successful competitor. Each organization deploying this tool selects its own market attractiveness and business strength criteria, but uses the same ones over time so as to monitor changes. The DPM grid clearly reveals the attractiveness of segments, providing a numerical value of their relative attractiveness, as depicted in Figure 11.5. The use of the DPM in directing target segment selection is described in Case Study 11.3.

CASE STUDY 11.3

Targeting decisions and outcomes in the mobile phone segmentation case

Following segment quality checks, managers from the four countries considered their targeting options and reviewed the allocation of resources to the emerging segments. Although the eight segments were found in each of the four countries studied, the size and relative attractiveness of each varied between these countries and separate operating companies. Using a jointly agreed set of attractiveness variables (see Table 11.4) within a directional policy matrix (DPM) analysis, the management teams in each country decided which segments should be prioritized. The managers were helped in their task by the provision of a full range of information about each of the segments and the customers contained within them. This included detailed breakdowns of the customers' technology affinity, communication and mobility, mobile phone attitudes and usage behaviour, spending and price sensitivity, internet and mobile office usage, brand awareness, preferences for operator/service providers, current network satisfaction, demographics/lifestage, and lifestyle/leisure activities.

Table 11.4   Illustrative target market attractiveness criteria.

Attractiveness		Business strengths	
Disposable income in the segment	8	Network coverage	11
Willingness to spend on mobiles in the segment	8	Network quality	11
Interest in value-added services in the segment	10	Voice/data roaming	5.5
ARPU/Revenue/Profitability – the financial worth of the segment	8	Attractive tariffs	4
		Fair billing	5.5
Share in prospects in the segment	13.5	Products/services/value added services	17
Loyalty level in the segment	13.5	Distribution (sales) network	5.5
Size of the segment	17.5	Brand awareness (strong)/image	13
Competitive intensity – degree of competition in the segment	4	Innovativeness	5.5
Potential growth of the segment	13.5	Quality of marketing staff and their outputs	11
Our market share in the segment	4	Customer orientation	11

> The numbers relate to the relative weighting of each variable as agreed by the company's leadership team.

These criteria were the variables selected and weighted for use in this mobile phone company's directional policy matrix (DPM) evaluation of market attractiveness versus business capabilities, in order to assist in selecting which market segments were prioritized for marketing programmes.

Each national team had particular market and competitive conditions in which to operate, so each made its own decisions about which segments to target. For one country, marketing resources were focused primarily on three of the consumer segments. One of these had particularly strong growth prospects, while in the other a challenger brand had been stealing market share. A second national team opted to address five of the eight segments. None of the countries focused on all eight segments and no two national teams shared exactly the same selection of target marketing priorities. Figure 11.5 presents an example of one country's DPM.

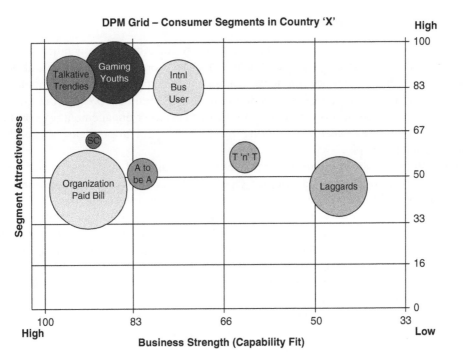

Figure 11.5   The use of the DPM in identifying segments to target.

Once the targeting had been finalized, each country's management team developed a bespoke marketing plan, focusing on each of the selected target segments. These plans were designed to reflect the needs of targeted customers, the competitive and regulatory context, and distribution channel characteristics in each country. The detailed consumer insights obtained from the marketing research were invaluable to this process, particularly when determining the desired positioning strategy for each targeted segment and for the brand.

Whether the DPM is used or less structured assessments of relative attractiveness occur, it must be recognized that the tradeoff choices for which segments to pursue will in effect dictate the success or otherwise of the whole segmentation strategy. This stage inevitably requires further marketing analyses and the inputs from colleagues armed with financial performance data and operational costs. Before making the final selection, it is often necessary to allocate some or all of the organization's existing consumers or business customers to the newly created segments, in order to more fully assess likely revenue streams and profitability levels. Such data mining generally is costly and very demanding in terms of the time and skills required; it should not be viewed as a minor phase of the overall project.

Operational danger in undertaking segmentation

Whichever approach is adopted, it is important to recognize that there is much more to segmentation than merely identifying market segments. Decisions need to be made about which segments to prioritize. For those segments that are chosen, appropriate and compelling brand positions must be developed. A go-to-market plan should then be developed in order to create appropriate marketing programmes and effective customer engagement approaches. This will require rethinking existing marketing programmes and approaches to handling the organization's customers.

Segmentation inevitably requires a reallocation of staff and resources, which generally causes disquiet and organizational stresses. Operationally, a realignment of reporting systems, metrics and performance measurement will be needed to reflect the new target segment strategy. There may well be significant data-mining demands in order to explore the current customer base and to allocate these existing customers to the newly created segments. This will take skills, time and considerable financial resources. Changes like these must be anticipated and carefully managed.

The implementation literature reveals that there are potential problems before segmentation takes place, owing to skill gaps, data deficiencies, internal behaviours, leadership and whether there exists a genuine appreciation of the nature of the journey just starting (cf. Boejgaard and Ellegaard, 2010; Dibb and Simkin, 2001, 2008). A range of resource, skill and behavioural problems can impede progress. These problems, which are summarized in Table 11.5 (see also Dibb and Simkin, 2009b), can continue even after segments have been identified. The following remedial actions can be taken:

- *Auditing*. At the start of any segmentation programme, a period of auditing is warranted. Two main forms are possible: (1) a systematic review of available financial, data, market insight, personnel and other resources matched to the needs of the project; and (2) reflection on the organization's previous record and experiences of change management programmes and strategy implementation.
- *Project teams*. Identifying and empowering an appropriate project team ensures clear allocation of project responsibilities. This team needs to involve managers from a range of different functions, in order to minimize resistance later in the project.

- *Outside experts.* This additional resource can be usefully deployed to fill internal skill gaps, supplement the project team and bring a more objective perspective to the programme. 'Designing-in' such expertise from the outset is possible where shortages of personnel or of particular skills are identified as problematic.
- *Workshops.* Setting up a programme of workshops, to which those involved in the project are invited, helps to set aside the necessary people and time resources for conducting the project. Concentrating these workshops into a relatively short period of time can increase the sense of purpose. Off-site events devoted entirely to the segmentation programme can be especially valuable: as a mechanism for kick-starting the process; to earmark time to conduct some of the required analysis; or to negotiate required implementation changes. Using external facilitators can help defuse political sensitivities.

Table 11.5 Diagnosing and treating key segmentation barriers.

	INFRASTRUCTURE	**SEGMENTATION PROCESS**	**IMPLEMENTATION**
DIAGNOSIS	Problems include data gaps or lack of a marketing information system (MIS); shortfalls in other required resources; low level of marketing or segmentation expertise; lack of customer focus; weak inter/intra-functional communication; organizational resistance to change; insufficient commitment from senior management.	Barriers include a shortfall in required data for identifying segments; insufficient budget; lack of suitably skilled personnel; weak understanding of the segmentation process; poor sharing of data and ideas; inadequate inter-functional buy-in; poor appreciation of the fit with corporate strategic planning.	Problems include inadequate financial resourcing for implementation; insufficient time or suitably skilled employees committed to the segment roll-out; poor internal/external communication of the segment solution and lack of senior management involvement; unclear demarcation of implementation responsibilities; poor fit between tactical marketing programmes and the segment solution; organizational resistance to required changes and/or inflexibility in the distribution system.
TREATMENT	Prior to undertaking segmentation: • Conduct a review of available marketing intelligence. • Identify relevant skills and personnel. • Ensure there is senior management participation. • Plan and facilitate channels of communication. • Earmark required resources. • Instigate internal orientation of segmentation principles and of the programme.	During the segmentation process: • Specify sequential steps for the segmentation process. • Identify skill gaps. Seek external advice and training. • Prioritize information gaps. Collect data. Create/update the MIS. • Instigate regular internal debriefings of data and ideas. • Review the ongoing fit with corporate strategy.	Facilitate implementation: • Identify key internal and external audiences. • Prepare an internal champion-led marketing programme to communicate the segment solution to audiences. • Facilitate necessary changes to organizational culture/structure/distribution. • Reallocate personnel and resources to fit the segmentation solution. • Specify a schedule and responsibilities to roll-out segment solutions. • Instigate a mechanism for monitoring segment and associated marketing plan roll-out.

Adapted from: Dibb and Simkin (2001).

- *Briefings*. The internal marketing of a segmentation project can be even more challenging than the analysis and design of the segments themselves. Agreeing a consistent format for these briefings ensures that all stakeholders are regularly updated about the project's progress and outcomes. In combination with a workshop programme, these briefings provide a mechanism for breaking down internal barriers as the project progresses.
- *Mentoring*. Establishing a system of personal mentoring can be invaluable for projects with wide-ranging strategic and structural implications for the organization. Feelings of insecurity and anxiety among staff are inevitable during such periods of change. Managing these concerns through one-to-one mentoring can reduce the potential for personal interests to threaten project outcomes.

No matter how well the segmentation process is planned, some difficulties are inevitable. These problems may occur during the creation of the segments, when decisions are made about which segments to pursue, or during the implementation of the marketing plans/programmes associated with the segmentation scheme. Anticipating and planning for some of these problems can help to minimize their impact.

Latest developments in segmentation

Times are changing for segmentation. The advent of 'big data', the rise of digital and social media, technological advances and growth in analytics have radically enhanced the segmentation arena. These trends have been accompanied by an increased use of customer insight, a growth in customer relationship and affinity programmes, and changes in how and where segmentation is applied. The expectations of company directors and leadership teams have also been raised, with the anticipation that more extensive and 'in the moment' market intelligence and customer insight will enable faster responses to market changes and trends. In many cases, these developments have implications for segmentation schemes and target market strategy.

Ready access to vast quantities of data enables faster creation and testing of the segments and propositions to take to market. Today's segmentation has greater power and reach than the segmentation of the past (cf. Dolnicar et al., 2012; Hanafizadeh and Mirzazadeh, 2011; Liu et al., 2012). Several years ago, a segmentation solution with between six and 10 segments (we might call them macro-segments) that were generated using cluster analysis was deemed operationally and intellectually appropriate. Today, operational and customer management complexity means that much more granular thinking is generally expected; with markets (or macro-segments) broken down into much smaller and tightly defined micro-segments. Digital marketing and the move to multichannel delivery make it possible to identify and cater for such micro-segments.

Much has happened in the world of marketing in the last few years. Economic turmoil and the financial downsizing of many countries; associated changes in consumer values and behaviours; the emergence of big data, analytics and customer insight programmes; social media and more consumer-to-consumer communication than ever before; the ability to engage with customers one-to-one and on the move; a move towards sustainable living and a growing corporate social responsibility agenda are a few of drivers impacting on marketing. These developments have affected how market segmentation is practised and applied (Simkin, 2013). Segmentation is also increasingly used in new contexts.

Social marketing (not to be confused with social networking and social media), which involves using commercial marketing tools and concepts to tackle the problems of society, is one such emerging context. Thus governments, policy makers and organizations in the third and public sectors are using segmentation alongside behaviour change interventions to solve societal problems and improve well-being. The problems being tackled include debt education, smoking cessation, obesity campaigns, energy saving initiatives and the management of addictive behaviours. Market segmentation is often central to the interventions involved, even though the organizations involved may not always recognize its importance to their outcomes. Table 11.6 refers to the UK government's 'Change4Life' campaign, which is one example of segmentation's use in such a non-commercial setting.

Segmentation is also being used in a more surprising quarter, with the work of governments and security services to identify and pre-empt security threats. The rise in the threat to security from global unrest, terrorism and crime has focused the minds of governments, security chiefs and their advisors, resulting in significant resources, intellectual capability, data and computing power being brought to bear on the problem. The core of this work is mitigating risk by identifying and profiling threats. In practice, much of this security and surveillance work harnesses the tools developed for market segmentation and approaches used to profile different 'consumer' behaviours.

CASE STUDY 11.4

NHS Change4Life

The NHS Change4Life programme offers a range of healthy living advice aimed at adults, young people and families. The intention is to improve the health and well-being of the general public, by encouraging them to take small and simpler steps towards healthier living. The website describes a series of simple approaches to bring about changes, encouraging visitors to *'Try one of our smart tools and make a positive change today!'* (http://www.nhs.uk/Change4Life/)

The smart tools relate to the following healthier living themes:

- Eat well
- Move more
- Drink less

(Continued)

(Continued)

- Be healthier
- Quit smoking
- Parenting.

As the three examples presented in Table 11.6 show, the details for which are taken from the Change4Life website, these tools use segmentation principles and are designed to target specific groups.

Table 11.6   Examples of the Change4Life smart tools and resources.

Change4Life smart tool	Resources available
Sugar Swaps: Targeting FAMILIES It can be surprising just how much sugar there is in everyday food and drinks – and that's sugar you don't even realize you and your family are having. Too much sugar means extra calories, which causes fat to build up inside, that could lead to heart disease, cancer or type 2 diabetes. So it's a good idea to be a Sugar Swapper, and we'll help you with lots of support to help you stick to your swap.	• Free Sugar Swaps Guide, shopping pad, swap idea cards, stickers and money-off vouchers • You can cook up tasty meals with your free Smart Recipes app • You can see how well you're doing with your weekly support emails
Start4Life Parents: Targeting MUMS AND DADS Sign up to get emails and text messages covering all key pregnancy and baby topics. You'll also be able to access reliable information on money, benefits, childcare and early learning. The emails and texts are for mums and dads who are expecting a baby or already have a child up to 18 months old.	• Trusted NHS information • Regular updates straight to your inbox or phone • Info tailored to your stage of pregnancy or the age of your baby
Smokefree: Targeting ADULT SMOKERS With daily support messages throughout the one month period, the Smokefree mobile app provides step-by-step tailored advice to help you through your quit. Daily motivational messages provide you with content according to your personal progress and if you find a craving sneaking up on you there is a 'help' button with tips and distractions to get you through tough times. Making a successful quit attempt is a big achievement which shouldn't go unnoticed. The Smokefree app will reward you with badges that recognize your achievements and progress throughout the duration of the programme.	• A shareable progress indicator so friends can see how you're doing • A savings calculator so you can see how much money you're saving • Success tips – tried and tested ways to help you

Source: https://smarttools.change4life.co.uk/ (accessed on 5 January 2014).

These are exciting and changing times for segmentation. The rapidly evolving economic and technological environment has extended the reasons for its use and expanded its reach into non-commercial areas. In the past it was marketers who took responsibility for the segmentation process, yet today CEOs, COOs, CFOs, market insight managers and analysts are just as likely to sponsor the approach. Those using segmentation have access to far greater market intelligence and customer insight and can apply more advanced analytics than previously were available. Segmentation has become a routine part of the fabric of organizational activity, underpinning other strategic initiatives and guiding business development. This reach extends to new applications and contexts, including the use of segmentation in non-commercial and social marketing settings. Despite many changes in the world of marketing, it is clear that segmentation retains its position as a fundamental concept in marketing and a cornerstone for marketing strategy.

Summary

Segmentation focuses on customers' needs, buying behaviour, expectations and aspirations; and assists in building improved and stronger relationships with customers in the targeted segments. Segmentation also involves the identification of attractive customer segments, on which to focus marketing programmes and resources. Segmentation delivers more highly focused and differentiated product and service propositions, which create barriers for competitors and can lead to increased revenues. Within the organization, there are important benefits associated with segmentation, particularly in terms of deciding where (and where not) to allocate resources and marketing spend. This is why so many segmentation projects are sponsored by CFOs, COOs and CEOs. Above all else, undertaking segmentation establishes commitment and single-mindedness within the organization – one vision, one voice and harmonized messages. As with the *Gaming youths, Sophisticated careerists* and *Laggards* in the mobile phone illustration, segments exist in all markets.

There are various approaches possible for creating market segments. Often they emerge almost accidentally, as a result of marketing research insights attained by an organization for other purposes, such as brand research, testing new products or evaluating fresh marcomms ideas. The macro-micro model – as deployed by the energy company – is popular, particularly in business-to-business markets, but still many organizations opt for a survey-led quantitative approach, as in the mobile phone illustration. Each approach has advantages and disadvantages. Many segmentation bases can be used to identify segment. Today, most segmentation projects seek an array of insights into the consumers' or business customers' characteristics and buying behaviour. The era of big data and digitization, which has been accompanied by a step-change in the availability of analytical tools, has made it much easier to work with big data sets and adopt multiple base variables.

The emerging segments should be assessed for their qualities along several key dimensions, including segment size and potential profitability, segment stability, segment accessibility, segment compatibility and segment actionability. Once deemed to be robust, tradeoff choices must be made to decide which segments to pursue. Most organizations opt to target only some of the emerging segments. Bespoke tools such as the segment evaluation matrix can help in this selection process and the directional policy matrix can assist in prioritizing target segment selection. A balanced set of criteria that goes beyond predicted profitability is needed to judge the attractiveness of the emerging segments. Detailed marketing plans and compelling brand positionings must then be produced for each of the segments selected as the priorities for an organization's marketing programmes and resources.

Many problems are associated with undertaking segmentation and operationalizing the resulting segment strategy. These impediments can be encountered *before* the segmentation commences, *during* the segmentation process, and even *after* segments have been identified when the target segment strategy is implemented. Anticipating and planning for these impediments help to minimize their impact.

Much has changed for segmentation in recent years, with the increase in analytics, better computing power, new heuristics, big data and the more routinized understanding of market segmentation. Segmentation projects have become faster to complete and much cheaper to undertake. Indeed, many consultancies now routinely undertake a segmentation as a prelude to projects for market entry planning, multichannel strategy, customer relation management (CRM), brand strategy, innovation agendas or customer service strategy. Recession led many organizations to rethink their value propositions and target market strategies. The economic crisis also revealed the relevance of market segmentation to CEOs, CFOs, COOs and other colleagues on the leadership team. New applications of segmentation are now common in non-commercial settings. The extension of segmentation into new applications and contexts, including its use in social marketing campaigns to underpin behaviour change, reinforces its fundamental role in marketing and marketing strategy.

Recommended further reading

Dibb, S. and Simkin, L. (2008) *Market Segmentation Success: Making it Happen!* New York: Routledge/The Haworth Press.

References

Beane T.P. and Ennis, D.M. (1987) 'Market segmentation: a review', *European Journal of Marketing* 21 (October): 20–42.

Boejgaard, J. and Ellegaard, C. (2010) 'Unfolding implementation in industrial market segmentation', *Industrial Marketing Management* 39(8): 1291–9.

Bonoma, T.V., Benson, I. and Shapiro, B.P. (1983) *Segmenting Industrial Markets*. New York: Lexington Books.

Clarke, A. and Freytag, P.V. (2008) 'An intra- and inter-organisational perspective on industrial segmentation', *European Journal of Marketing* 42(9/10): 1023–38.

Dibb, S. (1995) 'Developing a decision tool for identifying operational and attractive segments', *Journal of Strategic Marketing* 3(3): 189–203.

Dibb, S. (2014) 'Up, up and away: social marketing breaks free', *Journal of Marketing Management* 30(11/12): 1159–85.

Dibb, S. and Simkin, L. (2001) 'Market segmentation: diagnosing and overcoming the segmentation barriers', *Industrial Marketing Management* 30(8): 609–25.

Dibb, S. and Simkin, L. (2008) *Market Segmentation Success: Making it Happen!* New York: Routledge/The Haworth Press.

Dibb, S. and Simkin, L. (2009a) 'Bridging the segmentation theory/practice divide', guest editorial, special issue, *Journal of Marketing Management* 25(3/4): 219–25.

Dibb, S. and Simkin, L. (2009b) 'Implementation rules to bridge the theory/practice divide in market segmentation', *Journal of Marketing Management* 25(3/4): 375–96.

Dibb, S. and Simkin, L. (2010) 'Judging the quality of customer segments: segmentation effectiveness', *Journal of Strategic Marketing* 18(2): 113–31.

Dibb, S. and Simkin, L. (2012) 'Leadership teams rediscover market analysis in seeking competitive advantage and growth during economic uncertainty', *Journal of Strategic Marketing* 20(1): 45–54.

Dolnicar, S., Kaiser, S., Lazarevski, K. and Leisch, F. (2012) 'Biclustering – overcoming data dimensionality problems in market segmentation', *Journal of Travel Research* 51(1): 41–9.

Goller, S., Hogg, A. and Kalafatis, S. (2002) 'A new research agenda for business segmentation', *European Journal of Marketing* 36(1/2): 252–71.

Hanafizadeh, P. and Mirzazadeh, M. (2011) 'Visualising market segmentation using self-organising maps and fuzzy delphi method – ADSL market of a telecommunication company', *Expert Systems with Applications* 38(1): 198–205.

Hassan, S. and Craft, S. (2012) 'Examining world market segmentation and brand positioning strategies', *Journal of Consumer Marketing* 29(5): 344–56.

Hassan, S., Craft, S. and Kortam, W. (2003) 'Understanding the new bases for global market segmentation', *Journal of Consumer Marketing* 20(5): 446–62.

Hlavacek, J.D. and Reddy, N.M. (1986) 'Identifying and qualifying industrial market segments', *European Journal of Marketing* 20(2): 8–21.

Kotler, P. (1967) *Marketing Management*. Englewood Cliffs, NJ: Prentice-Hall.

Liu, Y., Ram, S., Lusch, R. and Brusco, M. (2010) 'Multicriterion market segmentation: a new model, implementation and evaluation', *Marketing Science* 29(5): 880–94.

Liu, Y., Kiang, M. and Brusco, M. (2012) 'A unified framework for market segmentation and its applications', *Expert Systems with Applications* 39(1): 10292–302.

McDonald, M. and Dunbar, I. (2010) *Market Segmentation*. Basingstoke: Macmillan.

Palmer, R.A. and Millier, P. (2004) 'Segmentation: identification, intuition, and implementation', *Industrial Marketing Management* 33(8): 779–85.

Sausen, K., Tomczak, T. and Herrmann, A. (2005) 'Development of a taxonomy of strategic market segmentation: a framework for bridging the implementation gap between normative segmentation and business practice', *Journal of Strategic Marketing* 13(3): 151–73.

Simkin, L. (2008) 'Achieving market segmentation from B2B sectorisation', *Journal of Business & Industrial Marketing* 23(7): 464–74.

Simkin, L. (2013) 'To boardrooms and sustainability: the changing nature of segmentation', White Paper Series, the Henley Centre for Customer Management, University of Reading, November.

Simkin, L. and Dibb, S. (2011) 'Segmenting the energy market: problems and successes', *Marketing Intelligence & Planning* 29(6): 580–92.

Tonks, D.G. (2009) 'Validity and the design of market segments', *Journal of Marketing Management* 25(3/4): 341–56.

Venter, P., Wright, A. and Dibb, S. (2015) 'Performing market segmentation: a performative perspective', *Journal of Marketing Management* 31(1/2): 62–83.

Walsh, G., Hassan, L.M., Shiu, E., Andrews, J.C. and Hastings, G. (2010) 'Segmentation in social marketing: insights from the European Union's multi-country antismoking campaign', *European Journal of Marketing* 44(7/8): 1140–64.

Webber, H. (1998) *Divide and Conquer: Target your Customer through Market Segmentation*. Hoboken, NJ: John Wiley.

Wedel, M. and Kamakura, W.A. (2002) *Market Segmentation: Conceptual and Methodological Foundations*. Boston, MA: Kluwer.

Weinstein, A. (2004) *Handbook of Market Segmentation*. New York: Routledge/The Haworth Press.

Wells, V., Chang, S., Oliveira-Castro, J. and Pallister, J. (2010) 'Market segmentation from a behavioural perspective', *Journal of Organisational Behaviour Management* 30(2): 176–98.

Wind, Y. (1978) 'Issues and advances in segmentation research', *Journal of Marketing Research* 15 (August): 317–37.

Yankelovich, D. and Meer, D. (2006) 'Rediscovering market segmentation', *Harvard Business Review* 84(6): 141–5.

Part Four

Theoretical Sub-Areas of Marketing

Part IV Contents

12   Consumer Behaviour   285

13   Marketing Communications in a Digital World   318

14   Theories of Value and Brand Equity   344

15   Innovation and New Product Development   361

16   Relationships and Networks   387

17   Theories of Retailing   415

Consumer Behaviour

Margaret K. Hogg and Rob Lawson

Chapter Topics

Introduction   285
Setting the scene   286
Main periods within the field   289
Consumer behaviour as an independent field of research   291
Content analysis of *Journal of Consumer Research* (1974–2008)   292
Developing an integrated approach to consumer behaviour   303
Neuroscience   309
Conclusion   311

Introduction

Consumer behaviour research represents a growing body of work that is seen as increasingly separate from marketing, though its status as an independent academic field rather than as a sub-field of marketing continues to be debated (see MacInnis and Folkes [2010] for an excellent overview of the issues about the academic standing of consumer research as a disciplinary field; and see Figure 12.1). In this chapter we discuss the main arguments, concepts and theories within consumer behaviour research, illustrating both the historical timelines and the varied disciplinary contexts (e.g. psychology, behavioural economics, neuroscience, sociology and anthropology) for studying consumer behaviour. We begin by setting the scene; and then use a rough historical timeline to trace three main periods that can be identified within the evolving field of consumer behaviour. Drawing on one of the key specialist journals, *Journal of Consumer Research*, we then present a content analysis organized into four domains: theoretical focus (see Tables 12.2–12.4 and Figure 12.3); research paradigms and methods (Tables 12.5 and 12.6); study populations (Table 12.7); and marketing applications (Tables 12.8–12.9). In order to offer as current a view as possible, while discussing this analysis of *Journal of Consumer Research*, we also include some qualitatively based observations about the type of publications for the period from 2009 onwards, as well as noting the introduction of *JCR* Curations in 2012, which summarize key articles relating to specific topic areas including self-identity and consumer behaviour (Escalas, 2013); social influences in consumer behaviour (Dahl, 2014); and morality and the marketplace (Grayson, 2015).[1] From here we move to a more thematically based approach and discuss some of the central issues that have been or are currently of major interest within the field, including: models of consumer behaviour and decision making (Figures 12.5 and 12.6); cognitive psychology and experimental approaches to understanding consumer behaviour; consumer culture theory and interpretivist approaches to consumer research (Figures 12.2 and 12.7); transformative consumer research; and finally neuroscience and the potential insights it offers into consumer behaviour.

Setting the scene

While the emergence of a distinctive body of research on consumers clearly becomes evident in the 1950s, a focus on understanding the consumer can be seen in some of the earliest publications in marketing which sought to provide working classifications of goods that could be used as a basis for marketing management and strategy. Of those classifications the most famous and enduring has been Copeland's (1923) *Harvard Business Review* paper suggesting it was possible to classify all products into either convenience, shopping or speciality goods. While these early papers can be seen as motivated by the need to provide necessary typologies for an emerging discipline of marketing, they are clearly based on an analysis of factors in consumer behaviour, such as the extent of information search and levels of perceived risk. Aspinwall's (1958) later classification of red, orange and yellow goods includes other consumer behaviour factors such as replacement, or repeat purchase, rates. Authors such as Copeland (1923) were predicting differences not just in high and low involvement but also in different types of involvement, in line with later theorists' work on involvement. While convenience goods clearly relate to low involvement situations, the difference between shopping and speciality goods in Copeland's (1923) classification primarily relates to changing the focus of involvement from the purchase itself to involvement with the product or brand. Sometimes this is termed the difference between situational involvement around the purchasing decision compared with more enduring involvement with the product or brand, and its use. Looking ahead, consumers' relationships with products and brands have remained an ongoing focus of research up to the present day. Fournier's (1998) qualitative

Table 12.1 A typology of consumer–brand relationship forms.

Relationship form	Definition	Case examples
Arranged marriages	Non-voluntary union imposed by preferences of third party. Intended for long-term, exclusive commitment, although at low levels of affective attachment.	Karen's adoption of her ex-husband's preferred brands (e.g. Mop 'n Glo, Palmolive, Hellman's); Jean's use of Murphy's Oil soap as per manufacturer recommendation.
Casual friends/buddies	Friendship low in affect and intimacy, characterized by infrequent or sporadic engagement, and few expectations for reciprocity or reward.	Karen and her household cleaning brands.
Marriages of convenience	Long-term, committed relationship precipitated by environmental influence versus deliberate choice, and governed by satisficing rules.	Vicki's switch to southern regional Friend's Baked Beans brand from favoured B&M brand left behind in the northeast.
Committed partnerships	Long-term, voluntarily imposed, socially supported union high in love, intimacy, trust and a commitment to stay together despite adverse circumstances. Adherence to exclusivity rules expected.	Jean and virtually all her cooking, cleaning and household appliance brands; Karen and Gatorade.
Best friendships	Voluntary union based on reciprocity principle, the endurance of which is ensured through continued provision of positive rewards. Characterized by revelation of true self, honesty and intimacy. Congruity in partner images and personal interests common.	Karen and Reebok running shoes; Karen and Coke Classic; Vicki and Ivory.
Compartmentalized friendships	Highly specialized, situationally confined, enduring friendships characterized by lower intimacy than other friendship forms but higher socio-emotional rewards and interdependence. Easy entry and exit attained.	Vicki and her stable of perfumes.
Kinships	Non-voluntary union with lineage ties.	Vicki's brand preference for Tetley tea or Karen's for Ban, Joy and Miracle Whip, all of which were inherited from their mothers.
Rebounds/avoidance-driven relationships	Union precipitated by desire to move away from prior or available partner, as opposed to attraction to chosen partner per se.	Karen's use of Comet, Gateway Success Rice.
Childhood friendships	Infrequently engaged, affectively laden relation reminiscent of earlier times. Yields comfort and security of past self.	Vicki's Nestle's Quik and Friendly's ice cream; Jean's use of Esteé Lauder, which evokes memories of her mother.
Courtships	Interim relationship state on the road to committed partnership contract.	Vicki and her Musk scent brands during initial trial period.
Dependencies	Obsessive, highly emotional, selfish attractions cemented by feeling that the other is irreplaceable. Separation from other yields anxiety. High tolerance of other's transgressions results.	Karen and Mary Kay; Vicki and Soft 'n Dry.
Flings	Short-term, time-bounded engagements of high emotional reward, but devoid of commitment and reciprocity demands.	Vicki's trial size shampoo brands.
Enmities	Intensely involving relationship characterized by negative affect and desire to avoid or inflict pain on the other.	Karen and her husband's brands, post-divorce; Karen and Diet Coke; Jean and her other-recommended-but-rejected brands (e.g. Jif peanut butter, Kohler stainless steel sinks).
Secret affairs	Highly emotive, privately held relationship considered risky if exposed to others.	Karen and the Tootsie Pops she sneaks at work.
Enslavements	Non-voluntary union governed entirely by desires of the relationship partner. Involves negative feelings but persists because of circumstances.	Karen uses Southern Bell and Cable Vision because she has no other choice.

Source: Fournier (1998: 362, Table 1).

Reprinted with permission of University of Chicago Press

study of consumer–brand relationships (using three informants' stories) from which she derived 15 metaphors based on relationship theory as a typology of consumer–brand relationships, offered new understandings of how consumers relate to their brands (Table 12.1). Reflecting the ongoing interest in low and high involvement products and brands, there have also been studies of mundane consumption (Kleine et al., 1993; Laverie et al., 2002) and mundane brands (Coupland, 2005) over the last 20 years.

From the earliest days, research in consumer behaviour quickly differentiated itself from the economics frameworks that were used for much managerial marketing by turning to other behavioural disciplines. For a long time, the dominant discipline in consumer research was psychology. Cognitive and social psychology particularly have been used extensively in the search to explain aspects of purchasing and consumption. Psychology still retains its pre-eminent place, but the cultural turn, represented by increasing attention to the social context in which consumption occurs, means that sociology and anthropology have assumed increasing importance from the 1980s onwards – alongside more recent attention to other disciplines such as socio-linguistics and literary criticism from the 1990s onwards. MacInnis and Folkes (2010) mapped consumer behaviour as an academic area of study (Figure 12.1). In their diagram they neatly capture not only the key components of consumer behaviour as a disciplinary field

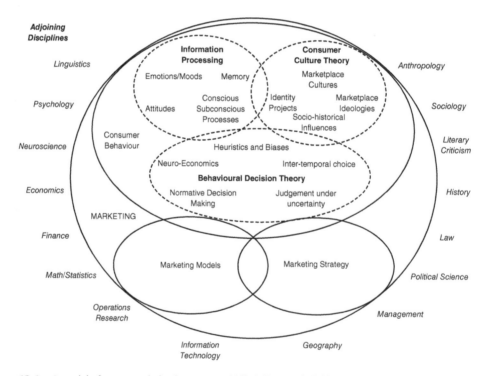

Figure 12.1   A model of consumer behaviour as a multidisciplinary sub-field of marketing.

Source: MacInnis and Folkes (2010: 910, Figure 3).

Reprinted with permission of University of Chicago Press

(e.g. behavioural decision theory, information processing, consumer culture theory), but also identify how adjoining disciplines from across the sciences, social sciences and arts might be usefully aligned with topics in different research areas of consumer behaviour. In our thematic discussion (towards the end of the chapter) we pick up on some of the topics from these key areas of consumer behaviour (see Figure 12.1).

Main periods within the field

Three main periods can be (very roughly) identified where research on consumer behaviour has highlighted different marketing and consumption issues. First, starting in the 1950s there was a 20-year period where research on segmentation and purchasing decision making was prolific. This directly parallels the emergence of the managerial school of thought as identified by Sheth et al. (1988), and buyer behaviour theory was a logical accompaniment to the development of ideas relating to the different aspects of the marketing mix. This period saw classical papers published on the family life-cycle, personality, social class, lifestyles and psychographics all testing the efficacy of these constructs for segmentation, and thus with a clear contribution to marketing management and its understanding of its customer base.

Developing rapidly in the 1960s, and overlapping with the previous research theme, there was a corresponding interest in consumer decision making with key early contributions from authors such as John Howard (1964) and Everett Rogers (see Rogers and Beal, 1957–8). The 1960s saw attempts to develop comprehensive models of consumer decision making by Nicosia (1966), Engel et al. (1968) and Howard and Sheth (1969), and the rapid adoption of developments in attitude theory from psychology, especially the idea of multi-attribute approaches following the work of researchers such as Rosenberg (1960) and Fishbein (1963). Working with Ajzen, Fishbein's early work was developed into more general models of human behaviour (Fishbein and Ajzen, 1974, 1975), which are still used extensively by consumer researchers, especially those working in social marketing areas. A summary of the material on the Theory of Reasoned Action (from the 1970s), later extended to the Theory of Planned Behaviour (Ajzen, 1991) is offered later in the chapter.

Second, by the early 1980s there was something of a switch in the focus within consumer behaviour research. It saw the abandonment of attempts to develop comprehensive decision-making models and a diversification of research interests. There was more research on affect and emotions as opposed to concentration on the cognitive dimensions of consumer decision making and, at the same time, a fresh look at actual consumption as opposed to purchasing. Studies in the latter area started to use more interpretive methods to examine possessions and their meanings, stimulated by work by Hirschman and Holbrook (1982) on the hedonic, emotional and experiential aspects of consumption (see also Holbrook and Hirschman, 1982), and by Belk's (1988) paper on possessions and the extended self, which represented an important contribution to what would become ongoing debates about the interrelationships between self, consumption and the meaning of possessions.

Third, by the 1990s the cultural turn in understanding consumer behaviour and consumption was well established, and this thread developed rapidly alongside the continued focus on experimental approaches (based in cognitive psychology) in seeking to understand consumer behaviour. An important paper in this period was Arnould and Price's (1993) study, which combined both qualitative and quantitative approaches to understanding, first, how consumers consume service experiences, in this case white water rafting; and second, how three experiential themes (harmony with nature; communities; and personal growth and renewal) were linked to consumer satisfaction with their service experiences. Two of the earliest *JCR* papers in this period to employ ethnography were Penaloza's (1994) study of Mexican immigrants into the US; and Schouten and McAlexander's (1995) study of Harley-Davidson bikers. In her work, Penaloza (1994) examined consumer acculturation as a number of processes (movement, translation and adaptation) thus seeking to account for the complexity of Mexican immigrants' encounters with the consumption environment in the US. Schouten and McAlexander (1995) introduced the concept of 'subcultures of consumption', using a study of new bikers to understand how consumption activities, products and brands contribute to social cohesion. Other important interpretivist papers in this period included Holt's (1995) two-year study of baseball spectators in Chicago, in which the author developed a typology of consumption practices. A series of early papers by Thompson including his study of mothers (1996); of the socialized body (Thompson and Hirschman, 1995); and of fashion discourses (Thompson and Haykto, 1997) established his pre-eminence as a consumer researcher. And not to overlook also from this period, Fournier's (1998) paper on brand relationships (discussed above).

From the early 2000s, alongside the well-established experimental work with its roots in cognitive psychology, consumer culture theory and neuroscience emerged as important subfields of consumer research. Studies in both these areas had appeared before 2000, but over the last 15 years the momentum has built behind them both. We discuss some of the important articles on neuroscience below. In the context of the cultural turn, Arnould and Thompson's

Figure 12.2 Four research programmes in consumer culture theory.

Adapted from: Arnould and Thompson (2005).

CCT article (2005) is the standout paper, which identified four programmes of research (see Figure 12.2) and challenged researchers to concentrate on the theoretical contribution of the papers they collated (see their Table 1, Arnould and Thompson, 2005: 872–3) as much as on the empirical context within which the research was undertaken. Transformative consumer research and its concern with social policy issues such as vulnerability and stigmatization of consumers also emerged in this period (see below).

The view that we offer above of the evolution of theory in consumer research is of course a very simplified big picture, and there are important overlaps in trying to offer some periodization of the subject area. Towards the end of the chapter we will look in more detail at the some of the work published in the last 50 years but before that, it is worth reflecting a little more on the early origins of consumer research as an academic field of study.

Consumer behaviour as an independent field of research

Although there is an ongoing debate about the status of consumer behaviour research (is it an independent discipline rather than just a sub-discipline within the field of marketing?), a series of conferences on consumer research in the 1970s marked the emergence of consumer research from under the shadow of mainstream marketing conferences (e.g. American Marketing Association, AMA). These conferences continue today with annual meetings each October of the Association for Consumer Research (ACR) (http://acrwebsite.org) in the US (or Canada), as well as subsequent spin-off conferences in Europe, Asia Pacific and South America. In 2006 a new series of conferences was launched on Consumer Culture Theory (CCT), which reflected the rapid growth of interest over the previous 30 years in the socio-cultural contexts of consumer behaviour. Thinking in terms of Lakatos's 'methodology of scientific research programmes (MSRP)' (Blaug, 1976: 150), we can see that these CCT conferences represented a breaking away, in turn, from the mother disciplinary field, represented by the Association for Consumer Research with its predominant (but not exclusive) focus on the psychological aspects of consumer behaviour. The CCT changes paralleled those witnessed in the 1970s with the establishment of the Association for Consumer Research (ACR) as separate from the American Marketing Association. In 2006 CCT began with an informal, ad hoc set of arrangements, but is now evolving into a more formal organization with an elected chair and officers, subscriptions, a membership register and a website (http://consumerculturetheory.org/), as well as annual conferences, very much on the same lines as the ACR.

Further evidence of the emergence of consumer behaviour as an increasingly independent area of academic study was the development of specialist publications. Over the last 45 years a series of specialist journals have been established including the *Journal of Consumer Research* (1974), *Journal of Consumer Psychology* (1992), *Journal of Consumer Affairs* (1967), *Journal of Consumer Policy* (1977), *Psychology & Marketing* (1984), *Advances in Consumer Research* (1974) (for the link to the conference proceedings: http://www.acrwebsite.org/web/conferences/proceedings.aspx), *Consumption, Markets & Culture* (1997) and *Journal of Consumer Culture* (2001). Proving the continued vibrancy of the field, the *Journal of the Association for Consumer Research* will launch in 2016 with a series of dedicated special issues on such topic areas as: the behavioural science of eating (van Ittersum and Wansink, 2016); consumer ownership and sharing (Belk and Price, 2016); consumer response to regulation (Scammon and Stewart, 2016); and the science of hedonistic consumption (Lee and Vohs, 2016) (https://www7511.ssldomain.com/acrwebsite/assets/PDFs/JACR%20Information.pdf).

As mentioned above there are many journals that deal with consumer behaviour theory and applications. The *Journal of Consumer Research* (*JCR*) remains the leading journal in the subject area. In 2004 *JCR* produced a 30-year cumulative index of their articles, including a classification by subject. Using this classification as the starting point, the next section attempts to give an overview of the subject. Information from keywords and abstracts from 1974 through to 2008 have been coded against the categories below. Closely related categories such as affect and emotion have been collapsed. The results are not claimed to be a comprehensive content analysis of the whole subject of consumer research but they are intended to give some sense of the scope of the subject as published in this leading specialist journal. We also thread in some more qualitatively based evidence to illustrate the ongoing publishing trends within *Journal of Consumer Research* since 2009. The information presented is perhaps best viewed as a description of how researchers in consumer behaviour actually describe their work in the search terms and abstracts they use to promote their papers. For example, it is clear that most if not all papers mention key theoretical constructs or problem areas but far fewer advertise any area of application to any industry sector or particular population. A valuable innovation in the last couple of years has been the inclusion of explicit statements about data collection information at the end of each *JCR* article, which provide useful clues to the epistemological underpinnings of the studies.

Content analysis of *Journal of Consumer Research* (1974–2008)

Theoretical focus

The three tables in this section categorize research papers into broad areas according to whether they deal mainly with actual behaviours, psychological processes, or wider sociological issues. In Table 12.2 there are a range of studies that report some aspect of actual or intended behaviour as a focus of study. Aspects of symbolic consumption are the most comprehensively explored of all these topic areas. These papers reflect both the kinds of meaning that people communicate through consumption and also the behavioural processes that underlie symbolic consumption. The other two major categories in this area are research which deals with time and situational influences. Both these categories are quite diverse and they also cover research that crosses into the psychological area, e.g. dealing with factors and behaviours that influence decision making.

Two areas in particular are central to the subject of consumer research: acquisition patterns and shopping behaviour. Since most decisions and purchases we make as consumers are clearly not independent of other purchases and acquisition patterns, we might have expected that more attention would be paid to these interrelationships. Alderson's (1957) early idea regarding 'potency of assortment', for instance, makes it quite clear that the utility or value

Table 12.2 Research on consumer behaviours (1974–2008).

Consumer behaviours	Number of studies
Acquisition patterns	6
Charity/gift giving	27
Deviant behaviours	12
Possessions	6
Shopping behaviour	10
Situational influences	75
Time	52
Variety seeking	12
Symbolic consumption	74

associated with any particular marketplace exchange is dependent upon its contribution to some total mix, or holding, by the consumer (see also Alderson and Martin, 1965). All the papers that identify themselves as dealing with acquisition patterns were published between 1979 and 1987. It is not at all clear why this should be the case but it could be seen as at least consistent with the start of the third general research phase identified above. In contrast, all the papers that reference or use the term shopping behaviour have been published since 2000. It is possible that this reflects a change in the use of keywords and referencing within the subject since there are earlier papers that reference retailing but this term is not used after the 1990s.

Table 12.3 presents a summary of the types of essentially psychological constructs that have been identified in articles in *JCR*. The most obvious feature of Table 12.3 is the sheer number of papers that deal with these issues compared to those that deal directly with the behavioural aspects of consumption (as outlined in Table 12.2), or indeed the more macro-level and societal issues that are presented in Table 12.4. This concentration of attention on psychological aspects is consistent with William Wells's (1993) critical appraisal of the state of consumer research at *JCR*. Wells (1993) argued that consumer research had been dominated by a concentration of work investigating the pre-purchase aspects of consumer behaviour, mainly brand choices, largely at the expense of both post-purchase issues and also 'higher level' consumer decisions that substantially affect consumers' lives such as choices about higher education, housing or careers. According to Wells's matrix (1993: 491; see Figure 12.3, adapted from Arndt, 1976) studies have concentrated largely on the pre-purchase stages of the buying process, and on the simpler choices between more equivalent options rather than dealing with the complex situations where choices often have to be made between non-comparable alternatives with abstract attributes. In Table 12.3 topics relating to information processing and evaluation tend to dominate. Search for and acquisition of information is a significant part of the information processing group of studies and articles on these topics have appeared consistently throughout the history of *JCR*.

The second major group of studies in Table 12.3 relates to attitude and preference studies which became popular about the same time that *JCR* was founded in 1974. Studies of decision

Table 12.3   Research on consumer psychology (1974–2008).

Consumer psychology	Number of studies
Aesthetics and hedonics	16
Affect, emotion and mood	73
Attention and perception	101
Attitudes and preferences	248
Memory	66
Decision theory and processes	205
Choice and choice models	106
Cognitive processing	110
Expertise and knowledge	57
Satisfaction and dissatisfaction	46
Consumer socialization	28
Learning	38
Self-concept and image	68
Values	17
Inference	35
Information processing	402
Motivation and involvement	130
Perceived risk	30
Personality	55

	Recognition	Search	Purchase	Consumption	Post-consumption
Strategic					
Central					
Genetic					
Variant					

Figure 12.3   Wells's (1993) adaptation of Arndt's (1976) diagram.

Source: Wells (1993: 491), figure adapted from Arndt (1976: 215).

Reprinted with permission of University of Chicago Press

processes and structures have also been a constant feature since the inception of the journal. Other topics, however, do show waves of popularity with peaks of more intensive research followed by lows with much less activity. Satisfaction and dissatisfaction is one example of this with most work undertaken in the 1980s and 1990s, and neatly synthesized in Fournier and Mick's (1999) *Journal of Marketing* article on 'Rediscovering satisfaction'. Similarly, in terms of historical patterning, with the exception of a couple of papers in the early part of this century, all the papers on values were published in the late 1980s and early 1990s, while papers on learning were not classified until the late 1980s but since that date they have appeared at consistent intervals in *JCR*. One recent topic to emerge is that of cognitive processes and processing and these studies have been published regularly since the late 1990s. Another important theme included cognitive processes such as learning and consumer socialization, with one of the stand out papers being John's (1999) *JCR* article with its specific focus on children's experiences of consumer socialization.

Parallel to the evolving research interests in the parent discipline of psychology, consumer behaviour researchers have tended to move away from social psychology to cognitive psychology, on the one hand, and towards neuroscience, on the other hand (where it intersects with psychology and economics). We look at consumer neuroscience in more detail towards the end of the chapter. We should note that we have relied here mainly on research published in one journal, i.e. *JCR*. However, there are two other well-established journals – *Psychology & Marketing* and *Journal of Consumer Psychology* – which also concentrate on the discipline base of psychology in the study of consumers.

The dominance of psychological perspectives on consumer behaviour in the *JCR* becomes very evident when looking at the sociological and macro-studies that have been reported in the journal up until 2008 (Table 12.4).

The ebb and flow of researchers' interests can be seen in such topic areas as class, lifestyles and the family. Four of the papers on social class were published in the first three years of the journal's life. Interest has revived again in this topic area with Holt's (1998: 1) work which re-examined social class, posing the question 'is it true that social class is no longer produced through distinctive patterns of consumption?' Henry's (2005) work also examined the interrelationship between (dis)empowerment and social class within the context of money management and financial planning. While the bulk of the lifestyles papers appeared between 1988 and 1993, Holt's (1997) work, which adopted a poststructuralist approach to lifestyle analysis, revived interest in understanding lifestyles – and more broadly social collectivities such as class, gender, race/ethnicity – through a poststructuralist lens. Holt drew on the sociology of consumption and most notably Bourdieu's work (1977, 1984; Bourdieu and Wacquant, 1992), and stimulated a series of other studies (e.g. Arsel and Thompson, 2011; Coskuner-Balli and

Table 12.4 Societal issues in consumer research (1974–2008).

Macro/sociological issues	Number of studies
Consumer ethics	2
Culture	18
Family	62
Lifestyles	17
Social and reference groups	66
Social class	12
Welfare/well-being	8
Women in workforce	22

Thompson, 2013; Üstüner and Holt, 2007; Üstüner and Thompson, 2012). The family received virtually no attention at all in the 10 years up to 2008, when Epp and Price's (2008) seminal paper on family identity appeared. Epp and Price's (2008) framework of the interplay between identity work and consumption (Figure 12.4) stimulated renewed interest in this area of consumer behaviour and consumer decision making, most noticeably evidenced by the papers at the ACR conferences in the following five years, and available in *Advances in Consumer Research* via the ACR website (http://www.acrwebsite.org). Of all these macro and sociological topics, the one that is clearly receiving most current attention is culture, as illustrated by Arnould and Thompson's summary (see their Table 1, Arnould and Thompson, 2005: 872–3).

However in the last 15 years *Consumption, Markets & Culture* has also established itself as an important outlet for work involving cultural theory. *Journal of Consumer Culture* is another important outlet, with strong links to researchers in sociology, and particularly the sociology of consumption, although there are overlaps with consumer behaviour researchers (e.g. Holt, 1997, 1998). More recently the Consumer Culture Theory conferences (with their associated offshoot publications) have also provided an important vehicle for disseminating consumer research with a particular focus on socio-cultural contexts and issues.

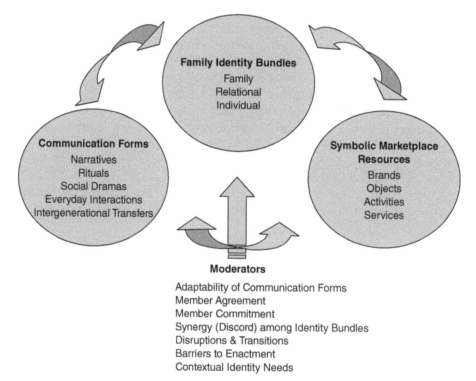

Figure 12.4   Framework of identity interplay in consumption practices.

Source: Epp and Price (2008: 52).

Reprinted with permission of University of Chicago Press

Research paradigms and methods

By no means all papers make reference to the paradigm within which they are based or even explicitly describe aspects of the method within keywords and abstracts. Those papers counted in the listing in Table 12.5 that mention a particular philosophy of science, such as naturalistic enquiry or literary theory, tend to be discursive papers on that topic in consumer research. Those articles that make reference to the more general terms of economic and sociological analysis cover many different methods but include a description of the overall orientation of the research paper or the context in which it was set. For example, the term sociological analysis is often used in the early years of the journal in studies of family decision making or reference group influence. It would seem that the need to describe this overall orientation is less common now than in the earlier years of the journal. In the general categories of both economic and sociological analysis about two-thirds of the papers were published in the first 10 years of the journal's history.

The important role of sociology and anthropology as sources of theories for understanding consumer research, as signalled by attention to Bourdieu (1977, 1984), can be seen in the increasing attention to practice theory and assemblage theory. The importance of the flow of ideas across disciplines, in this case from sociology into consumer research, is also clearly in evidence here. At the ACR conference in October 2014, for instance, a perspectives session was held on assemblage theory, reflecting its increasing contribution to understanding consumer behaviour (e.g. Canniford and Shankar, 2013; Epp and Velagaleti, 2014; Parmentier and Fischer, 2015; Epp et al.'s *Journal of Marketing* paper 2014).

The range of research methods mentioned in the *JCR* index is very extensive but, as with the more general theoretical and philosophical perspectives, it is only a fairly small proportion

Table 12.5 Perspectives in consumer research (1974–2008).

Theory/Philosophical perspectives	Number of studies
Critical theory	13
Economic analysis	78
Feminism	3
Literary theory	5
Marxism	1
Naturalistic enquiry	2
Phenomenology	6
Philosophy of science	35
Positivism	3
Postmodernism and poststructuralism	10
Post-positivism	40
Sociological analysis	73

of papers that explicitly mention methods in their abstracts and keywords. Methods such as causal modelling and choice modelling are referred to consistently throughout the history of the journal. Experimental design has become much more common since the 1980s, and tends to dominate the research designs. Other methods with smaller occurrence levels such as discourse, grounded theory and hermeneutics have also emerged during this same period. This seems to reflect the increasing diversity of research work in consumer theory but the dominant perspective remains cognitive psychology.

Table 12.6   Research methods in consumer research (1974–2008).

Research methods and issues	Number of studies
Bayesian approaches	4
Causal modelling	29
Choice modelling	27
Content analysis	12
Depth interviews	12
Discourse and literary analysis	4
Econometrics	2
Ethnography	18
Experimental design	55
Grounded theory	2
Hermeneutics	2
Historical methods	5
Interpretative methods	5
Mathematical models	3
Measurement and psychometrics	26
Meta-analysis	6
Multi-method approaches	3
Multivariate methods	7
Network analysis	4
Observation	1
Panel data analysis	3
Physiological research	17
Questionnaire design	2
Sampling	3
Semiotics	8
Simulation	3
Structural analysis	1
Survey methods	10
Validity and reliability	78

The largest single grouping of topics in the methods and issues (Table 12.6) are those papers identifying themselves as concerned with either validity or reliability or both. Studies referencing these issues have maintained a steady popularity since the 1980s. It is probable that a similar examination of publications in other areas of marketing would reveal a similar growth in research papers referencing these topics. Although there is some recent revision of thinking regarding measurement in marketing with interest in alternative approaches such as formative measures, COARSE procedures and Rasch methods, it is hard to underestimate the influence of Churchill's (1979) paper on measurement in marketing. This was a paper that raised awareness of these problems and provided a template for aspects of the research process which is still followed.[2] While the early attitude scaling theorists like Guttman and Thurstone have always been acknowledged in marketing (e.g. Richards, 1957; Udell, 1965), what Churchill (1979) did was to tie much research in marketing, especially consumer behaviour, to those scholars particularly reflective of psychological scaling methods as the standard way of approaching our development of theory and knowledge.

Study populations of interest

There are relatively few research papers in *JCR* that mention a particular demographic as the focal point of their research and most of those that do so, concentrate on a particular age group with more research on children and adolescents than on older people (see Table 12.7). This is a slightly surprising finding given the increasing proportion of elderly people within most Western populations combined with the concentration of discretionary expenditure that resides in that part of the population. In terms of changes over time, studies on children and adolescents appear to be more common in the earlier years of the journal than in later decades while the reverse is true for cross-cultural studies. Only five cross-cultural studies appear in the first 10 years of the journal and since 1985 they occur regularly at about two a year.

One other feature remains hidden in the reported study populations that are summarized in Table 12.7. This is the quantity of research in consumer behaviour that uses student samples. It would be a mistake to assume that all, or even the majority, of the remaining papers published in the journal were research studies that investigated consumer behaviour and purchasing among the general population. As noted in Table 12.6 on research methods, experimental formats are the most frequently reported method. A more detailed sampling of one randomly

Table 12.7 Target population (1974–2008).

Sample/population of interest	Number of studies
Adolescents and children	55
Older consumers	20
Sex and sex roles	25
Cross-cultural comparisons	51

chosen issue from each of the 10 years between 2004 and 2014 suggests that for the five years between 2004 and 2009 approximately three-quarters of the papers in those issues were experimental studies using student samples. For example, the February 2009 edition of the journal has 12 full papers. Nine of these are experimental studies, primarily around some aspect of information processing using student samples. The remaining three papers include a qualitative study with a population of 30 gamblers (Cotte and LaTour, 2009), a participant observation study on illicit pleasure (Goulding et al., 2009) and, very unusually for consumer research, a meta-analysis on consumer knowledge (Carlson et al., 2009). For the five years between 2009 and 2014, there was a similar dominance of experimental research. Looking at the October 2014 issue, for instance, there are 18 full papers, of which only three adopt interpretivist approaches to research, with typically small numbers of informants and qualitative data sets. For instance, Dion et al. (2014) used photo-elicitation techniques accompanied by interviews with 25 French informants in order to explore tidiness from the perspective of symbolic pollution. McAlexander et al. (2014) employed 22 interviews along with observation and archive data from publications and online sources such as blogs, posts and discussion boards and adopted Bourdieuian theories of fields and capitals as a lens to examine the role of identity work within the context of religion, ideology and consumption. Giesler and Veresiu (2014: 840) developed an ethnography, drawing on a combination of interviews and archival data collection (e.g. online and print material), to investigate how 'responsible consumption requires the active creation and management of consumers as moral subjects'. All the other papers in this issue were all experimental, using either student samples or Mechanical Turk (MTurk) (which allowed the researchers to generate participants with a wider range of backgrounds via this online data collection facility); or some combination of the two.

It is arguable whether any of the studies using student samples actually investigated a topic specifically relevant to that cohort of the population. Hence, while new relationships are tested and useful insights are contained in all the papers, only the meta-analysis makes any real pretence at producing conclusions that have any generalizability. It would seem that consumer research has really continued to emphasize internal validity at the expense of external validity and once more Wells's (1993) conclusion about the imbalance in consumer research, in at least its leading journal, is supported. Experimental work, using student samples on the pre-purchase aspects of decision making dominates what we know from research about consumer behaviour.

Marketing applications of consumer research

Table 12.8 describes the areas of marketing applications that are referred to in *JCR* papers. The frequencies in this table related to advertising and communication research support the previous conclusion about the overwhelming dominance of enquiries on pre-purchase behaviour. Advertising and communications, together with research on product and brand choice, dominated the first 35 years of *JCR*. Among the other categories, it is interesting to note that the branding literature is more recent, with most papers being published since the mid-1990s, while most of the segmentation work was carried out during the 1980s. The lack of work on market

Table 12.8   Marketing applications of consumer research (1974–2008).

Marketing application	Number of studies
Advertising and advertising effects	222
Bargaining and negotiation	24
Branding	17
Communication and persuasion	180
Innovation and diffusion	36
New products	25
Segmentation	23
Pricing	71
Product/brand choice	144

segmentation is somewhat surprising considering the importance of the concept in marketing and the need to understand heterogeneity among consumers. However, since segmentation work normally requires larger scale survey work with samples drawn from the general population it is clearly not regarded as a priority by consumer researchers, where the major conversations take place around developing and testing theory for different aspects of information processing.

The other interesting facet of Table 12.8 is the lack of research that deals with the distribution element of the marketing mix. While some research relating to this element is perhaps described in Table 12.9, in the few studies that relate to retailing or services, there are no mentions at all of research that deals with issues such as after-sales service, guarantees, dissatisfaction or complaint behaviour. Obviously research has been conducted on all these topics but it is not promoted in an obvious way in the main consumer research journal. Actual purchasing and the continued involvement of consumers in market relationships have generated very little research in consumer behaviour in contrast to organizational and business relationships. While it is now much more common for papers in the *Journal of Consumer Research* to contain the results of several related studies in order to provide depth and reliability to the conclusions, there are very few studies that involve investigation of consumer problems over time. Nearly all knowledge on consumer behaviour is based upon cross-sectional studies which are necessarily limited in the kinds of problems that they can address.

Brands have emerged as an increasingly important topic area (especially as understood in relation to identity projects). One of the most influential papers has been Muniz and O'Guinn's (2001: 412)[3] study of brand community, which is defined as a 'specialized, non-geographically bound community based on a structured set of social relations among admirers of a brand'. They identified three key features of brand communities: 'shared consciousness, rituals and traditions, and a sense of moral responsibility'. Their study was also early evidence of how online-mediated communication, virtual and digital worlds and social media would feature with increasing importance in consumer research studies over the following years (e.g. Arsel and Bean, 2013; Scaraboto and Fischer, 2013). Schau and Gilly's (2003) article deals explicitly with the digital self, and specifically consumers' self-presentation strategies in creating personal webpages.

The spread of contexts covered by Table 12.9 is quite broad but the overall number of papers specifying an industry area is quite small. In Table 12.2 it was noted how few studies in consumer behaviour actually referred to shopping. In a similar way it is surprising how few consumer research papers actually specify any relevance to retailing or retail services, and considering the pervasiveness of the internet, there are also very few that deal with e-consumption. Some research is motivated by particular problems that occur within particular industries or sectors. Table 12.9 provides a summary of where this research is located. It is not surprising to see areas such as alcohol, drugs and health listed since they present particular problems to groups of consumers. Similarly, energy and credit became major issues even before global warming and the current recession became items of general news. Indeed, since credit is such an integral part of many major consumption decisions it is interesting how little investigation has taken place on this topic in the last 30 years. However, a recent *JCR* (2012) Curation on Financial Insecurity and Deprivation (Fischer, 2013), which included Penaloza and Barnhart's (2011) particularly relevant article on 'Living U.S. capitalism: the normalization of credit/debt', points to the growing recognition of the importance of studying consumer financial behaviour. The *JCR* Curation (2012) on Numerosity and Consumer Behavior (Adaval, 2013) also deals with issues around pricing and purchasing behaviour. The Transformative Consumer Research (TCR) initiative launched by David Glen Mick, when he gave the Presidential Address at the ACR conference in October 2005 (published 2006; http://www.acrwebsite.org/search/view-conference-proceedings.aspx?Id=12242), has also directed more research attention to public policy and social marketing issues, e.g. vulnerability and stigmatization of consumers (http://www.acrwebsite.org/web/tcr/transformative-consumer-research.aspx) and we discuss this in more detail towards the end of the chapter.

Table 12.9   Area of economic activity (1974–2008).

Industry or economic sector	Number of studies
Alcohol and drugs	17
Consumer credit	9
Consumer education and information	25
Energy	31
Healthcare and related issues	30
Industrial and organizational buying	8
Leisure and recreation	19
E-consumption	10
Public and not-for-profit	13
Retailing	22
Services	11
Voting behaviour	7

Drawing together the information presented in the previous tables brings to mind Cova's (2005: 205) description of marketing 'that it is an increasingly dispersed sum of constituent parts'.

Thematic threads

In the final part of this chapter we turn attention to a more detailed discussion of some key themes/threads in the research on consumer behaviour in the past 40 years since the ACR was established in 1974. Recognizing that there are a number of different places where the key debates take place about how we understand consumers (e.g. ACR and CCT conferences; special issues of journals with a focus on neuroscience), we try and weave in some of these debates alongside the material from *JCR*. We begin with theory building around models of consumer behaviour (e.g. Figures 12.5 and 12.6) before examining aspects of consumer culture theory and neuroscience.

Developing an integrated approach to consumer behaviour

Theory of Planned Behaviour

One paradigm (or rather disciplinary matrix, to use Kuhn's later and preferred term, 1971) has dominated consumer behaviour research over the last 40 years. However, there have been very few attempts to produce any integrative models that would provide any general theories equivalent to those guiding the earlier approach to the subject such as the Theory of Reasoned Action as it was developed in the 1970s and later extended to the Theory of Planned Behaviour (Ajzen, 1991). The Theory of Planned Behaviour is now infrequently referenced in marketing journals but it does remain a popular framework which is used in consumer research published in areas like health, physical activity and leisure. The theory is based on three central components as predictors of intentions as shown in Figure 12.5.

The principles of the Theory of Planned Behaviour are straightforward and suggest that our behaviour as consumers is goal orientated and determined by three fundamental forces:

1. Our attitude towards the activity or object. This measures the appeal of the item or behaviour under investigation.
2. Our view of social norms around the consumer behaviour under consideration and our desire to comply with those social norms.
3. Our ability to be able to control the situation and act in the way which we desire. Ability to control may be conditioned by outside factors such as prices or internal aspects such as addiction if we were trying to model a behaviour such as cessation of smoking or drinking.

Together these drivers are seen to determine our intentions, while allowing for situational factors, for example a stock out at the store, to predict our final behaviour. Ajzen argues that with

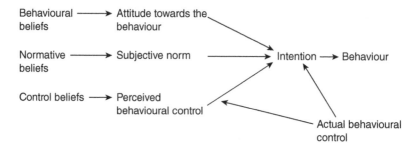

Figure 12.5   The Theory of Planned Behaviour.

Source: Fishbein and Ajzen (2009).

Used with permission

appropriate and precise specification of the behaviour, the Planned Behaviour model will give useful predictions. Examples where it is less successful and where greater discrepancies arise between attitudes and behaviours are usually where there is less precision or more abstraction in the definition of the behaviour. Thus, it may not be a good predictor of how many alcoholic drinks you are likely to have in the next week or month, but it will be more successful in explaining how much wine you are likely to drink at your birthday celebration.

Social cognitive theory

Also widely used in the social marketing arena is an alternative comprehensive approach to considering consumer behaviour known as social cognitive theory. This approach was developed primarily by Bandura in the 1980s and builds on earlier ideas of social learning theory. Social learning theory emphasized that humans learn by imitation; and stresses how we learn to cope with our environment by watching others cope with similar situations. Bandura (1986) developed this idea by introducing personal characteristics, especially motivation and self-efficacy, as mediating effects. As a construct self-efficacy refers to the belief that one can master a particular behaviour and adopt it as a regular practice, so it has a close association with Ajzen's idea regarding perceived behavioural control. Bandura proposed the three elements of the person, the environment and the behaviour interacting in a reciprocal triangle, as captured in Figure 12.6.

Social cognitive theory has many elements that are similar to Planned Behaviour. For example, there are roles for social norms and support, sets of beliefs about the outcomes of the behaviour (e.g. improved health from eating your daily quota of fruit and vegetables), tastes and preferences, and perceptions of the environment which can include factors such as price which determine accessibility. However, there is a fundamental difference in approach between the two models. While Planned Behaviour sees behaviour as more goal orientated and moderated by the environment, social cognitive theory tends to emphasize 'environmental' influences but then allows for them to be mediated by an individual's level of motivation and self-efficacy. In this model the emphasis for encouraging behavioural change lies as much, or more, on

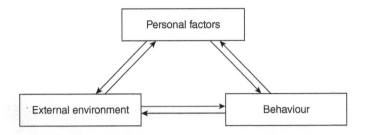

Figure 12.6 A social cognitive model of behaviour.

Source: Bandura (1986).

changing the environment in order to encourage the desired response as it does on persuasive advertising or education in order to try to raise levels of individual motivation.

Although they are not linked in the literature it seems that the principles of social cognitive theory accord well with the work of Bettman et al. (1998), who have tried to provide an integrated framework for understanding decision making. They present a complex view of decision-making processes and strategies that are heavily influenced by the environment. In essence they argue that consumers construct the decision framework they use, including the choice of the appropriate heuristic according to the particular context. Hence environmental factors, such as the number and type of both attributes and alternatives under consideration and the amount of time available, structure how the decision is made as well as do the individual's own goals and abilities.

In some respects then, social cognitive theory can be seen as a step towards the behaviourist tradition in psychology which was not mentioned at all in the earlier discussion of the contents of the *Journal of Consumer Research*. Although cognitive psychology clearly holds the ascendancy, there have been some strong advocates of the behaviourist approach (e.g. Foxall, 1990). Evidence to support basic behaviourist theories as potentially important in explaining consumer behaviour can be found in the work of Andrew Ehrenberg and his colleagues (Ehrenberg et al., 1990). For over 30 years Ehrenberg has been primarily looking at aggregate forms of consumer behaviour with panel data and he has been able to show consistent patterns of consumer responses to things such as repeat purchasing and loyalty irrespective of the precise particulars of the market. For example, his work on double jeopardy shows quite clearly that market share is closely linked to behavioural measures of loyalty, so that the idea of specialist niche products controlling a small but secure part of the market and protected by high levels of loyalty is potentially misleading. The implications of this type of finding in Ehrenberg's work for consumer behaviour are quite simple. It suggests that, as an aggregate body, consumers usually respond quite consistently to simple cues that they receive in the marketplace. If they are more familiar with a market leader, which probably has more shelf space and more promotional support, consumers are also likely to buy it more often than alternatives. It also suggests that in most situations consumers are essentially satisficers as opposed to utility maximizers, and that our behaviour as consumers is not likely to be overcomplicated and too goal orientated.

Overall, the 'mixed' approach suggested by social cognitive theory is appealing. It has the advantage of not reducing humans, who are clearly capable of forethought and planning, to the same level of decision making as their pets, but at the same time it does not turn every decision and behaviour into a complex goal-directed extensive problem. Furthermore, the bi-directional aspects of Bandura's relationships in his social cognitive approach also seem to fit with ideas in marketing such as cocreation. They allow causality to flow from the individual back to the environment in any situation and confirm that the marketing manager may influence, but is never in control in a way that the purely behaviourist approaches might suggest could be the case.

Consumer culture theory

Alongside the dominant cognitive and social psychology research, the other main stream of research published in *JCR* has been the interpretive material focusing on actual consumption and possessions. In this area there has been an attempt by Arnould and Thompson (2005) to generate an integrative framework to bring together much of this research under the banner of Consumer Culture Theory. Even so Arnould and Thompson are absolutely explicit in saying that they are not trying to create any sort of general theory in the area but rather providing an

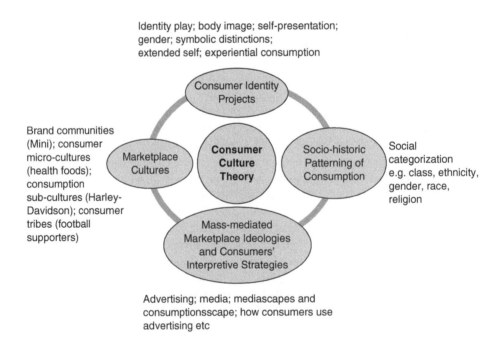

Figure 12.7   Key components within four research programmes in consumer culture theory.

Based on Arnould and Thompson (2005)

evaluation and classification of the research in this area. They draw together a large number of articles into a four-fold classification as follows (see Figure 12.7):

1. Research that develops theory around consumer identity;
2. Studies of marketplace culture where the important role of consumption configures cultural blueprints;
3. Investigations into socio-historic patterns of consumption, involving the institutional and social structures that influence consumption;
4. The examination of mass-mediated marketplace ideologies.

It is accepted that classifications such as these are often the first step towards substantial theory development since they provide both a basis for future integration and assist with the generation of future research questions and propositions. The concerns of researchers working within the socio-cultural domain relate to theory building beyond the immediate empirical context for examining consumer behaviour (e.g. consumption and the meaning of possessions; identity, self and consumption; consumer–brand relationships; and a variety of social collectivities such as sub-cultures of consumption and brand communities) and are summarized by Arnould and Thompson (2005: 872–3, Table 1).

Identity projects and symbolic consumption

A good example of the transition in the focus and approaches to research over the last 40 years – from quantitative studies based on cognitive psychology approaches to more interpretivist studies with qualitative data – can be seen in research on the self. Sirgy's (1982) review paper on the self-concept in the *Journal of Consumer Research* was a culmination of studies from the 1970s and was linked to traditional psychological frameworks around ideas of actual and ideal selves. This approach has continued in mainstream psychology with similar conceptualizations of the self being cited consistently over the past 30 years but it has received almost no attention in the marketing journals. In contrast, in consumer behaviour Belk (1988) and others took work on the self in a different direction and in particular linked it to symbolic communication as they sought to explain how possessions formed part of a person's identity and were used to communicate meaning to others. Hirschman and Holbrook's (1982) work on experiential consumption, as well as Belk's (1988) paper on possessions and the extended self towards the end of the 1980s, sparked a series of *JCR* papers which employed qualitative and interpretive approaches to doing research as well as an associated set of publications in *Advances in Consumer Research*. We can see that US authors like Belk (1988) and Hirschman (1991) were perhaps ahead of influential European sociologists like Giddens (1991) and Chaney (2002), who also later focused their attention on identity and possessions as key indicators of delivering status in a postmodern society. Perhaps the key idea here is that in a modern society people are less constrained by traditional elements that define social class. Constructing an identity through consumption patterns in order to display a particular lifestyle becomes a key means for displaying position and claiming status within society.

Transformative consumer research

Has consumer behaviour research lost touch with important issues facing the marketing system? For example, while some acknowledgement of aspects of sustainability can be found, particularly related to environmental issues, some of the problems associated with the current credit crisis were no surprise to those who had followed credit card or savings behaviours. Similarly, the idea of 'peak oil' has been known for decades, the same with global warming and the need to reduce carbon emissions. For a long time some of these important consumer behaviour issues, together with their consequences for businesses and all the other actors in the marketing system, simply did not figure as issues in building theory and knowledge on consumer behaviour in marketing. Journals in areas such as energy and health are now replete with studies of consumer behaviour arising from the need to deal with issues such as increasing energy efficiency and combating global warming, through to managing the Western obesity crisis.

An early call for consumer researchers to examine the darker sides of consumption was made by Hirschman in 1991. She argued for more research into a range of social problems associated with consumption. She argued then that many such problems were the result of 'consumption gone wrong' and that some of these issues would inevitably rebound as consequences for marketing managers. While there is clearly some evidence of research related to health, addiction and gambling in the consumer journals, they are still a very small proportion of the work carried out. As with Wind et al.'s (1991) list of opportunities from the same time, Hirschman's call looked like another missed opportunity by marketing scholars until it was taken up again by David Mick, during his term as ACR president (2005/6). He launched a challenge to consumer behaviour researchers to make their work relevant to society, in a movement which he termed Transformative Consumer Research with a strong focus on improving well-being, and motivating academic researchers to consider the policy and social marketing implications of their work (see Figure 12.8):

- Improve well-being;
- Emanate from ACR and encourage paradigm diversity;
- Employ rigorous theory and methods;
- Highlight socio-cultural and situational contexts;
- Partner with consumers and their caretakers;
- Disseminate valuable findings to relevant stakeholders.

(See the ACR website http://www.acrwebsite.org/web/tcr/transformative-consumer-research.aspx.)

It is important to note that other specialist journals such as the *Journal of Consumer Affairs* and *Journal of Consumer Policy* deal specifically with consumerism issues, along with the *Journal of Public Policy & Marketing*, which has had a series of special issues linked to the biennial Transformative Consumer Research conferences.

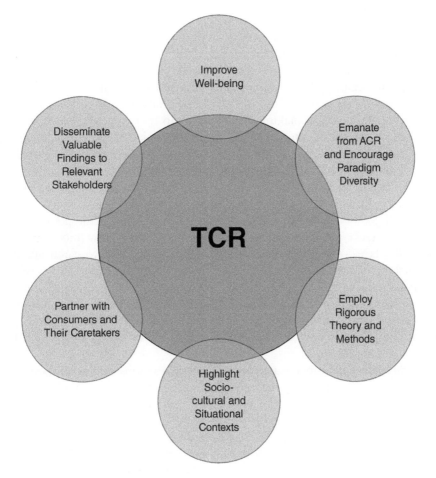

Figure 12.8   Transformative consumer research.

Neuroscience

Over the last 15 years there has been a burgeoning interest in neuroscience, and its potential contribution to understanding consumer behaviour, particularly information processing and consumer decision making. One of the earliest publications which could be linked to the flow of studies from neuroscience approaches was Rothschild et al.'s (1988: 185) *JCR* article. They used EEG ('electroencephalograph ... which aids in the study of brain waves') to explore consumer information processing, and specifically the reaction to verbal and non-verbal components of commercial advertisements. An important early paper on 'Decision neuroscience' appeared in *Marketing Letters* (Shiv et al., 2005) and represented a crucial starting point for moving neuroscience into the centre of debates about how consumers process information and make decisions. Shiv et al. (2005: 376) argued that the drive to integrate neuroscience and decision making was partly 'due to the exponential accumulation of knowledge about brain structures and neurological mechanisms since 1990 (the National Institute of Mental Health and the National Institutes of Health aptly labelled the 90's as the Decade of the Brain) and partly due to the increased availability of neuro-scientific methods to investigate various decision making phenomena'. In their article, Shiv et al. (2005: 375) discussed '(1) how the exponential accumulation of knowledge in neuroscience can potentially enrich research on decision making, (2) the range of techniques in neuroscience that can be used to shed light on various decision-making phenomena, (3) examples of potential research in this emerging area, and (4) some of the challenges readers need to be cognizant of while venturing into this new area of research'.

Ten years later, Smidts et al. (2014: 259) reviewed the progress in the field, identifying that consumer neuroscience now covers all elements of the 'marketing mix – product, price, promotion, and place – [which] have [all] received at least some research attention in the discipline's first decade. Most attention has been given to pricing and products (e.g., Knutson et al. 2007; Plassmann et al. 2008), including branding (for review, see Plassmann et al. 2012). Knutson et al. (2007) demonstrated some of the benefits of using neural methods by having participants engage in a shopping task in the functional MRI (fMRI) scanner. Their work found that adding neural measures to self-report ones led to significantly better predictions of subsequent purchasing decisions.'

More recently there have been a series of special sessions and workshops at the ACR conferences since 2010; and most recently of all, a perspectives session at ACR Baltimore (October 2014) specifically devoted to neuroscience, demonstrating how rapidly neuroscience has been moving towards the mainstream of consumer behaviour research. Introducing the ACR (2014) perspectives session, Yoon (2014) began with a brief historical overview of key publications in the area, pointing to two important special issues, *Journal of Consumer Psychology* (ed. Yoon and Shiv, 2012) and *Journal of Marketing Research* (ed. Yoon and Camerer, 2015, forthcoming), as evidence of the growing academic interest in this area. Yoon (2014) then summarized how tools and theories from neuroscience were currently being used to investigate consumer behaviour and marketing; and discussed at least seven potential contributions from consumer neuroscience. Consumer neuroscience seeks, first, to separate out competing psychological mechanisms in the context of decision making; second, to confirm or refine existing theories about decision making; third, to identify new psychological processes; fourth, to improve predictions of behaviour; fifth, to obtain a better understanding of how the valuation system within the brain works (i.e. reward versus punishment); sixth, to improve predictions of consumer choice; and finally to measure consumers' implicit behaviours and attitudes.

Different conceptions of the consumer emerge from neuro-marketing, as illustrated by Schneider and Woolgar (2012: 1) where they argue that 'certain neuro-marketing technologies simultaneously reveal and enact a particular version of the consumer'. There is some sense that marketing research will follow the move towards the more neurological approaches to the analysis of the brain in order to understand consumer behaviour in the longer term. Early reservations about the sheer scale of costs often involved in these studies, which often kept sample numbers low, and tended to limit the possibilities for generalizability, seem to be receding as the recognition of the potential for wider marketing applications continues to grow. In recent mainstream psychology it would seem that memory research, for example, is now dominated by more clinical studies that analyse chemical changes in the brain. The first tentative steps in this direction have already been made with neuro-marketing, focusing on activation levels in the brain when exposed to stimuli such as products, brands and advertising. The potential contribution from researchers in consumer neuroscience is increasingly recognized as important.

Conclusion

We began this chapter by offering a rough historical timeline which traced the changing areas of research interest within the field of consumer behaviour over the last 40 years (since the Association for Consumer Research and the *Journal of Consumer Research* were established in 1974). We then moved to examining the emergence of consumer research as an increasingly independent academic field, marked most notably by the launch of conferences and specialist journals in the area. From there, we used a content analysis of *JCR*'s (2004) 30-year cumulative index (updated to 2008) combined with some qualitatively based observations to identify where researchers had directed their studies in terms of theoretical focus, research paradigms (or disciplinary matrices) and methods, study populations of interest and marketing applications of consumer research more recently. The final part of the chapter discussed specific topics about the theory of planned action; social cognitive theory; the four programmes of research in consumer culture theory including identity work, the self and symbolic consumption; the new developments around transformative consumer research; and the advances offered by neuroscience in understanding consumer information processing and decision making.

In summary, we have examined consumer behaviour research as a field of endeavour, tracing the flow and interaction of ideas, concepts and disciplinary approaches as researchers have sought to answer the question: how do we best understand consumers? We have not sought to take a position within the debate: should consumer research be closer to marketing? Rather we have sketched out the variety of positions and subjectivities within the field – and sought to show first, how Kuhn's (1970, 1971) idea of a disciplinary matrix (which replaced his early theorization around paradigms) plays out within the field of consumer research as a set of matrices (see MacInnis and Folkes, 2010; Figure 12.1). The main components are: behavioural economics, cognitive psychology, consumer culture theory, neuroscience and transformative consumer research. Each of these approaches is underpinned by its own disciplinary foundation and associated ontological and epistemological assumptions; i.e. what is reality; how do we research the world; and how do we know what we know? And second, returning to Lakatos (1971) we also show how the field of consumer research can be seen as consisting of a series of scientific research programmes – each with its own ontological and epistemological assumptions about what constitutes knowledge about consumer behaviour in order to answer the question: why do consumers do the things they do?

Notes

1. *JCR* 2012 Curations: Block (2013), Fischer (2013), Adaval (2013) and Escalas (2013); *JCR* Curations 2013: Dahl (2014), Ratner (2014), Thompson (2014) and Williams (2014); *JCR* Curations 2014: Hamilton (2015), Grayson (2015) and Aaker (2015): www.ejcr.org/curations.html.
2. A check on Google Scholar on 17 November 2014 reveals 10,732 citations for Churchill's (1979) paper compared with 2,754 for Levitt's classic paper on marketing myopia (1960).
3. 3,015 cites in Google Scholar, accessed 20 November 2014.

Recommended further reading

Arnould, E.J. and Thompson, C.J. (2005) 'Consumer culture theory (CCT): twenty years of research', *Journal of Consumer Research* 31 (March): 868–82.

Belk, R.W. (1988) 'Possessions and the extended self', *Journal of Consumer Research* 15 (September) 139–68.

Carlson, J.P., Vincent, L.H., Hardesty, D.M. and Bearden, W.O. (2009) 'Objective and subjective knowledge relationships: a quantitative analysis of consumer research findings', *Journal of Consumer Research* 39 (February): 864–76.

MacInnis, D.J. and Folkes, V.S. (2010) 'The disciplinary status of consumer behavior: a sociology of science perspective on key controversies', *Journal of Consumer Research* 36(6): 899–914.

Smidts, A., Hsu, M., Sanfey, A.G., Boksem, M.A.S., Ebstein, R.B., Huettel, S.A., Kable, J.W., Karmarkar, U.R., Kitayama, S., Knutson, B., Liberzon, I., Lohrenz, T., Stallen, M. and Yoon, C. (2014) 'Advancing consumer neuroscience', *Marketing Letters* 25: 257–67.

Note also that *Journal of Consumer Research* curations provide valuable overviews (via collections of relevant articles) on a variety of topics (see references below):

Aaker, J. (2015) 'Meaningful choice', *Journal of Consumer Research* Autumn 2014 Research Curation 42 supplement June 2015.

Adaval, R. (2013) 'Numerosity and consumer behavior', *Journal of Consumer Research* Autumn 2012 Research Curation 40 supplement June 2013: S167–S237.

Block, L. (2013) 'Food decision-making', *Journal of Consumer Research* Spring 2012 Research Curation 40 supplement June 2013: S1–S75.

Dahl, D. (2014) 'Social influence and consumer behaviour', *Journal of Consumer Research* Spring 2013 Research Curation 41 supplement June 2014: S1–S76.

Fischer, E. (2013) 'Financial insecurity and deprivation', *Journal of Consumer Research* Summer 2012 curation Vol. 40 supplement June 2013: S76–S166.

Grayson, K. (2015) 'Morality and the marketplace', *Journal of Consumer Research* Summer 2014 Research Curation 40 supplement June 2015.

Hamilton, R. (2015) 'Decision-making at a distance', *Journal of Consumer Research* Spring 2014 Research Curation 40 supplement June 2015.

Thompson, C. (2014) 'The politics of consumer identity work', *Journal of Consumer Research* Autumn 2014 curation.

References

Aaker, J. (2015) 'Meaningful choice', *Journal of Consumer Research* Autumn 2014 Research Curation 42 supplement June 2015.

Adaval, R. (2013) 'Numerosity and consumer behavior', *Journal of Consumer Research* Autumn 2012 Research Curation 40 supplement June 2013: S167–S237.

Ajzen, I. (1991) 'The theory of planned behavior', *Organizational Behavior and Decision Processes* 50: 179–211.

Alderson, W. (1957) *Marketing Behavior and Executive Action.* Homewood, IL: Irwin, pp. 195–217.

Alderson, W. and Martin, M.W. (1965) 'Toward a formal theory of transactions and transvections', *Journal of Marketing Research* 2 (May): 117–27.

Arndt, J. (1976) 'Reflections on research in consumer behavior', in B.B. Anderson (ed.) *Advances in Consumer Research*, Vol. 3. Ann Arbor, MI: Association for Consumer Research, pp. 213–21.

Arnould, E.J. and Price, L.L. (1993) 'River magic: extraordinary experience and the extended service encounter', *Journal of Consumer Research* 20(1): 24–45.

Arnould, E.J. and Thompson, C.G. (2005) 'Consumer culture theory (CCT): twenty years of research', *Journal of Consumer Research* 31(4): 868–82.

Arsel, Z. and Bean, J. (2013) 'Taste regimes and market-mediated practice', *Journal of Consumer Research* 39 (February): 899–917.

Arsel, Z. and Thompson, C.J. (2011) 'Demythologizing consumption practices: how consumers protect their field-dependent identity investments from devaluing marketplace myths', *Journal of Consumer Research* 37 (February): 791–806.

Aspinwall, L.V. (1958) 'The characteristics of goods and parallel systems theories', in J.N. Sheth and D.E. Garrett (eds) *Marketing Theory: Classic and Contemporary Readings.* Cincinnati, OH: South-Western Publishing, pp. 252–70.

Bandura, A. (1986) *Social Foundations of Thought and Action.* Englewood Cliffs, NJ: Prentice-Hall.

Belk, R.W. (1988) 'Possessions and the extended self', *Journal of Consumer Research* 15 (September): 139–68.

Belk, R.W. and Price, L.L. (eds) (2016) 'Consumer ownership and sharing', *Journal of the Association for Consumer Research* 1(2).

Bettman, J.R., Luce, M.J. and Payne, J.W. (1998) 'Constructive consumer choice processes', *Journal of Consumer Research* 25 (December): 187–217.

Blaug, M. (1975) 'Kuhn versus Lakatos, or paradigms versus research programmes in the history of economics', *History of Political Economy* 7(4): 399–433.

Blaug, M. (1976) 'Kuhn versus Lakatos or paradigms versus research programmes in the history of economics', in S. Latsis (ed.) *Method and Appraisal in Economics.* Cambridge and New York: Cambridge University Press, pp. 149–77.

Block, L. (2013) 'Food decision-making', *Journal of Consumer Research* Spring 2012 Research Curation 40 supplement June 2013: S1–S75.

Bourdieu, P. (1977) *Outline of a Theory of Practice.* Cambridge: Cambridge University Press.

Bourdieu, P. (1984) *Distinction: A Social Critique of the Judgement of Taste.* Cambridge, MA: Harvard University Press.

Bourdieu, P. and Wacquant, L. (1992) *An Invitation to Reflexive Sociology.* Chicago, IL: University of Chicago Press.

Canniford, R. and Shankar, A. (2013) 'Purifying practices: how consumers assemble romantic experiences of nature', *Journal of Consumer Research* 39 (February): 1051–69.

Carlson, J.P., Vincent, L.H., Hardesty, D.M. and Bearden, W.O. (2009) 'Objective and subjective knowledge relationships: a quantitative analysis of consumer research findings', *Journal of Consumer Research* 39 (February): 864–76.

Chaney, D. (2002) *Cultural Change and Everyday Life*. London: Palgrave Macmillan.

Churchill, G.A. (1979) 'A paradigm for developing better measures of marketing constructs', *Journal of Marketing Research* 42 (February): 64–73.

Copeland, M.T. (1923) 'Relation of consumer buying habits to marketing methods', *Harvard Business Review* 1(3): 282–9.

Coskuner-Balli, G. and Thompson, C.J. (2013) 'The status costs of subordinate cultural capital: at-home fathers' collective pursuit of cultural legitimacy through capitalizing consumption practices', *Journal of Consumer Research* 40 (June): 19–41.

Cotte, J. and Latour, K. (2009) 'Blackjack in the kitchen: understanding online versus casino gambling', *Journal of Consumer Research* 35 (February): 742–58.

Coupland, J.C. (2005) 'Invisible brands: an ethnography of households and the brands in their kitchen pantries', *Journal of Consumer Research* 32 (June): 106–18.

Cova, B. (2005) 'Thinking of marketing in meridian terms', *Marketing Theory* 5(2): 205–14.

Dahl, D. (2014) 'Social influence and consumer behaviour', *Journal of Consumer Research* Spring 2013 Research Curation 41 supplement June 2014: S1–S76.

Dion, D., Sabri, O. and Guillard, V. (2014) 'Home sweet messy home: managing symbolic pollution', *Journal of Consumer Research* 41(3): 565–89.

Ehrenberg, A.S.C., Goodhardt, G.J. and Barwise, T.P. (1990) 'Double jeopardy revisited', *Journal of Marketing* 54(2): 82–91.

Engel, J.F., Kollat, D.T. and Blackwell, R. (1968) *Consumer Behavior*. New York: Holt, Rinehart and Winston.

Epp, A.M. and Price, L.L. (2008) 'Family identity: a framework of identity interplay in consumption practices', *Journal of Consumer Research* 35 (June): 50–70.

Epp, A.M. and Velagaleti, S.R. (2014) 'Outsourcing parenthood? How families manage care assemblages using paid commercial services', *Journal of Consumer Research* 41(4): 911–35.

Epp, A.M., Schau, H.J. and Price, L.L. (2014) 'The role of brands and mediating technologies in assembling long-distance family practices', *Journal of Marketing* 78 (May): 81–101.

Escalas, J. (2013) 'Self-identity and consumer behaviour', *Journal of Consumer Research* Winter 2012 Research Curation 40 supplement June 2013: S328–S339.

Fischer, E. (2013) 'Financial insecurity and deprivation', *Journal of Consumer Research* Summer 2012 Research Curation 40 supplement June 2013: S76–S166.

Fishbein, M. (1963) 'An investigation of the relationships between beliefs about an object and the attitude toward that object', *Human Relations* 16: 233–40.

Fishbein, M. and Ajzen, I. (1974) 'Attitudes toward objects as predictors of single and multiple behavioral criteria', *Psychological Review* 81: 59–74.

Fishbein, M. and Ajzen, I. (1975) *Belief, Attitude, Intention, and Behavior: An Introduction to Theory and Research*. Reading, MA: Addison-Wesley.

Fishbein, M. and Ajzen, I. (2009) *Predicting and Changing Behaviour: The Reasoned Action Approach*. New York: Psychology Press.

Fournier, S. (1998) 'Consumers and their brands: developing relationship theory in consumer research', *Journal of Consumer Research* 34 (March): 343–73.

Fournier, S. and Mick, D.G. (1999) 'Rediscovering satisfaction', *Journal of Marketing* 63 (October): 5–23.

Foxall, G.R. (1990) *Consumer Psychology in Behavioural Perspective*. London: Routledge.

Giddens, A. (1991) *Modernity and Self-identity*. Cambridge: Polity Press.

Giesler, M. and Veresiu, E. (2014) 'Creating the responsible consumer: moralistic governance regimes and consumer subjectivity', *Journal of Consumer Research* 41(3): 840–57.

Goulding, C., Shankar, A., Elliott, R. and Canniford, R. (2009) 'The marketplace management of illicit pleasure', *Journal of Consumer Research* 35(5): 759–71.

Grayson, K. (2015) 'Morality and the marketplace', *Journal of Consumer Research* Summer 2014 Research Curation 40 supplement June 2015.

Hamilton, R. (2015) 'Decision-making at a distance', *Journal of Consumer Research* Spring 2014 Research Curation 40 supplement June 2015.

Henry, P. (2005) 'Social class, market situation, and consumers' metaphors of (dis)empowerment', *Journal of Consumer Research* 31 (March): 766–78.

Hirschman, E.C. (1991) 'Secular mortality and the dark side of consumer behavior: or how semiotics saved my life', in R.H. Holman and M.R. Solomon (eds) *Advances in Consumer Research*, Vol. 18. Provo, UT: Association for Consumer Research.

Hirschman, E.C. and Holbrook, M. (1982) 'Hedonic consumption: emerging concepts, methods and propositions', *Journal of Marketing* 46 (Summer): 92–101.

Holbrook, M. and Hirschman, E.C. (1982) 'The experiential aspects of consumption: consumer fantasies, feeling and fun', *Journal of Consumer Research* 9 (September): 132–40.

Holt, D.C. (1995) 'How consumers consume: a typology of consumption practices', *Journal of Consumer Research* 22 (June): 1–16.

Holt, D.C. (1997) 'Poststructuralist lifestyle analysis: conceptualizing the social patterning of consumption in postmodernity', *Journal of Consumer Research* 23 (March): 326–50.

Holt, D.C. (1998) 'Does cultural capital structure American consumption', *Journal of Consumer Research* 25(1): 1–25.

Howard, J. (1964) *Buyer Behavior in Marketing Strategy.* Englewood Cliffs, NJ: Prentice-Hall.

Howard, J. and Sheth, J.N. (1969) *Theory of Buyer Behavior.* New York: John Wiley.

John, D.R. (1999) 'Consumer socialization of children: a retrospective look at twenty-five years of research', *Journal of Consumer Research* 26 (December): 183–213.

Kleine, R.E. III, Kleine, S.S. and Kernan, J.B. (1993) 'Mundane consumption and the self: a social-identity perspective', *Journal of Consumer Psychology* 2(3): 209–35.

Knutson, B., Rick, S., Wimmer, G.E., Prelec, D. and Loewenstein, G. (2007) 'Neural predictors of purchases', *Neuron* 53(1): 147–56.

Kuhn, T. (1970) *The Structure of Scientific Revolutions*, 2nd edn. Chicago, IL: Chicago University Press.

Kuhn, T. (1971) 'Second thoughts on paradigms', *The Structure of Scientific Theories*, ed. F. Suppe. Urbana, IL: Illinois University Press.

Lakatos, I. (1971) 'History of science and its rational reconstructions', in R. Buck and R.S. Cohen (eds) *Boston Studies in the Philosophy of Science*, Vol. 8. Dordrecht: D. Reidel.

Laverie, D.A., Kleine, R.E. III and Kleine, S.S. (2002) 'Reexamination and extension of Kleine, Kleine, and Kernan's social identity model of mundane consumption: the mediating role of the appraisal process', *Journal of Consumer Research* 28 (March): 659–69.

Lee, A.Y. and Vohs, K.D. (eds) (2016) 'The science of hedonistic consumption', *Journal of the Association for Consumer Research* 1(4), forthcoming.

Levitt, T. (1960) 'Marketing myopia', *Harvard Business Review* 38: 45–56.

McAlexander, J.H., Dufault, B.L., Martin, D.M. and Schouten, J.W. (2014) 'The marketization of religion: field, capital, and consumer identity', *Journal of Consumer Research* 41(3): 858–75.

MacInnis, D.J. and Folkes, V.S. (2010) 'The disciplinary status of consumer behavior: a sociology of science perspective on key controversies', *Journal of Consumer Research* 36(6): 899–914.

Mick, D.G. (2006) 'Presidential Address: Meaning and mattering through transformative consumer research' 2005, in C. Pechmann and L. Price (eds) *Advances in Consumer Research*, Vol. 33. Duluth, MN: Association for Consumer Research, pp. 1–4.

Mick, D.G., Pettigrew, S., Pechmann, C. and Ozanne, J.L. (2012) 'Origins, qualities, and envisions of transformative consumer research', in D.G. Mick, S. Pettigrew, C. Pechmann and J.L. Ozanne (eds)

Transformative Consumer Research for Personal and Collective Well-Being. New York: Routledge, pp. 3–24.

Muniz, A.M. and O'Guinn, T.C. (2001) 'Brand community', *Journal of Consumer Research* 27(4): 412–32.

Nicosia, F.M. (1966) *Consumer Decision Processes: Marketing and Advertising Implications*. Englewood Cliffs, NJ: Prentice-Hall.

Parmentier, M.-A. and Fischer, W. (2015) 'Things fall apart: the dynamics of brand audience dissipation', *Journal of Consumer Research* 41 (February): 1228–51.

Penaloza, L. (1994) 'Atravesando fronteras/border crossings: a critical ethnographic exploration of the consumer acculturation of Mexican immigrants', *Journal of Consumer Research* 21 (June): 32–54.

Penaloza, L. and Barnhart, M. (2011) 'Living U.S. capitalism: the normalization of credit/debt', *Journal of Consumer Research* 28 (December): 743–62.

Plassmann, H., O'Doherty, J., Shiv, B. and Rangel, A. (2008) 'Marketing actions can modulate neural representations of experienced pleasantness', *Proceedings of the National Academy of Sciences* 105(3): 1050–4.

Plassmann, H., Ramsøy, T.Z. and Milosavljevic, M. (2012) 'Branding the brain: a critical review and outlook', *Journal of Consumer Psychology* 22(1): 18–36.

Ratner, R. (2014) 'Consumer goal pursuit', *Journal of Consumer Research* Summer 2013 Research Curation 41 supplement June 2014: S77–S154.

Richards, E.A. (1957) 'A commercial application of Guttman attitude scaling techniques', *Journal of Marketing* 22 (October): 166-73.

Rogers, E.M and Beal, G.M. (1957–8) 'The importance of personal influence in the adoption of technological changes', *Social Forces* 36: 329–55.

Rosenberg, M.J. (1960) 'A structural theory of attitude dynamics', *Public Opinion Quarterly* 24(2): 319–40.

Rothschild, M.L., Hyun, Y.J., Reeves, B., Thorson, E. and Goldstein, R. (1988) 'Hemispherically lateralized EEG as a response to television commercials', *Journal of Consumer Research* 15(2): 185–98.

Scammon, D.L. and Stewart, D.W. (eds) (2016) 'Consumer response to regulation', *Journal of the Association for Consumer Research* 1(3), forthcoming.

Scaraboto, D. and Fischer, E. (2013) 'Frustrated fatshionistas: an institutional theory perspective on consumer quests for greater choice in mainstream markets', *Journal of Consumer Research* 39 (April): 1234–57.

Schau, H.J. and Gilly, M.C. (2003) 'We are what we post? Self-presentation in personal web space', *Journal of Consumer Research* 30 (December): 385–404.

Schneider, T. and Woolgar, S. (2012) 'Technologies of ironic revelation: enacting consumers in neuromarkets', *Consumption, Markets & Culture* 15(2): 169–89.

Schouten, J.W. and McAlexander, J.H. (1995) 'Subcultures of consumption: an ethnography of the New Bikers', *Journal of Consumer Research* 23(1): 43–61.

Sheth, J.N., Gardner, D.M. and Garrett, D. (1988) *Marketing Theory: Evolution and Evaluation*. New York: John Wiley.

Shiv, B., Bechara, A., Levin, I., Alba, J.W., Bettman, J.R., Dube, L. et al. (2005) 'Decision neuroscience', *Marketing Letters* 16(3–4): 375–86.

Sirgy, J.M. (1982) 'Self concept in consumer behavior: a critical review', *Journal of Consumer Research* 9 (December): 287–92.

Smidts, A., Hsu, M., Sanfey, A.G., Boksem, M.A.S., Ebstein, R.B., Huettel, SA., Kable, J.W., Karmarkar, U.R., Kitayama, S., Knutson, B., Liberzon, I., Lohrenz, T., Stallen, M. and Yoon, C. (2014) 'Advancing consumer neuroscience', *Marketing Letters* 25: 257–67.

Thompson, C.J. (1996) 'Caring consumers: gendered consumption meanings and the juggling lifestyle', *Journal of Consumer Research* 22 (March): 388–407.

Thompson C.J. (2014) 'The politics of consumer identity work', *Journal of Consumer Research* Autumn 2014 Research Curation.

Thompson, C.J. and Haykto, D.L. (1997) 'Speaking of fashion: consumers' uses of fashion discourses and the appropriation of countervailing cultural meanings', *Journal of Consumer Research* 24(1): 15–42.

Thompson, C.J. and Hirschman, E.C. (1995) 'Understanding the socialized body: a poststructuralist analysis of consumers' self-conceptions, body images and self-care practices', *Journal of Consumer Research* 22 (September): 139–53.

Udell, J.G. (1965) 'Can attitude measurement predict consumer behavior?', *Journal of Marketing* 29 (October): 46–50.

Üstüner, T. and Holt, D.B. (2007) 'Dominated consumer acculturation: the social construction of poor migrant women's consumer identity projects in a Turkish squatter', *Journal of Consumer Research* 34(1): 41–56.

Üstüner, T. and Thompson, C.J. (2012) 'How marketplace performances produce interdependent status games and contested forms of symbolic capital', *Journal of Consumer Research* 38 (February): 796–814.

van Ittersum, K. and Wansink, B. (eds) (2016) 'The behavioural science of eating', *Journal of the Association for Consumer Research* 1(1), forthcoming.

Wells, W. (1993) 'Discovery-oriented consumer research', *Journal of Consumer Research* 19(4): 489–504.

Williams, P. (2014) 'Emotions and consumer behaviour', *Journal of Consumer Research* Winter 2013 Research Curation 41 supplement June 2013: S268–S337.

Wind, J., Rao, V.R. and Green, P.E. (1991) 'Behavioral methods', in T.S. Robertson and H.H. Kassarjian (eds) *Handbook of Consumer Behavior*. Englewood Cliffs, NJ: Prentice-Hall.

Yoon, C. (2014) Paper delivered in Perspectives session on Neuroscience, Association for Consumer Research, Baltimore, October.

Yoon, C. and Camerer, C. (eds) (2015) *Journal of Marketing Research* Special issue on Neuroscience, forthcoming.

Yoon, C. and Shiv, B. (eds) (2012) 'Brand insights from psychological and neurophysiological perspectives', *Journal of Consumer Psychology* Special issue on Neuroscience 22(1).

Marketing Communications in a Digital World

Julia Wolny

13

Chapter Topics

Introduction	318
Scope of the chapter	320
Development of thought on marketing communications	320
Evolution of digital and multichannel marketing	324
Emergent themes in digital, multichannel and social media communications	326
Hummel's digital transformation to omnichannel	332
Conclusion: Theorizing in digital marketing	340

Introduction

Marketing communication is an essential component of marketing theory and practice. There is not an aspect of the contemporary world that has not been touched by the power of the marketing message. From outdoor billboards to celebrity endorsement, the promotional power of communications has woven itself into the fabric of everyday life. The discipline has, however, undergone numerous changes since it was first established at the crossroads of commerce, art and science. For one, the primacy of the scientific view has become more acutely evident with the increasing reliance of marketing activities on brand and consumer-generated data. Yet let's not forget that marketing communication is a human-centred discipline, and as such, at its best, should be imbued with empathy, creativity and values.

There is no escaping the fact that technological advances have reshaped the way in which people, as well as companies, communicate. We are in the midst of a transformational shift which is challenging the very basis of marketing. With the advent of the internet and other digital technologies, communication has not only become more instantaneous, routine and trackable, but the very process of communication as illustrated in many established theories has come into question.

This chapter provides an excellent opportunity to pose a greater question than just how communication works in the digital and multichannel marketplace and what theories apply to it. The bigger question implied here is: Can digital innovations with their revolutionary power reinvent marketing communications? So far it seems marketers have been applying digital technologies to the old marketing communication strategies, tactics and structures of yesteryear. Much of what marketing has been doing with new technologies could be likened to building a faster horse, to use Henry Ford's metaphor for what happens when we use limited imagination with revolutionary ideas. Marketing has not changed its paradigm, got out of the box, or reinvented the wheel.

The pressure to reinvent is, however, emanating from multiple sources – the consumer, the media and new models of business. Consumers are visibly switching off from advertising, the media can be anything to anyone, anywhere, and even the most entrenched product companies seem to have an inkling that the ground is shifting underfoot. This is exemplified in the quote from SVP Marketing at Unilever:

> We need to start thinking about marketing in a digital world, a world gone digital. We think too much about digital marketing, which is applying thinking we have learnt to marketing digitally. (Marc Mathieu, SVP Marketing, Unilever, quoted in Parsons, 2014)

The ongoing information revolution provides a transformative opportunity to change the role and mechanics of communication. We can see glimmers of that potential in the Internet of Things (IoT), which promises to enhance the prediction of needs and wants based on real-time information exchange between devices and sensors. Alongside the opportunities, there are new responsibilities and risks that marketers will face in this not-so-distant scenario. In order for marketing to be a responsible practice, it should reflect on the desirability of the direction in which these developments are taking it. It should reflect on the role of human-centred communication in what is increasingly data-driven practice, on design, on creativity and on sustainability, and ask how we can harness and channel those forces for good through the use of technology in marketing.

If we accept that marketing is about maximization of value through cocreation, as suggested by Evert Gummesson (see Chapter 18), then the underlying question becomes *how can digital and the accompanying social transformation support greater value, for whom, and under what conditions?* Addressing this imperative would be a worthwhile guiding focus for the next generation of scholars in this field.

Scope of the chapter

The aim of this chapter is to provide an overview of the key issues and questions inherent in the current ways in which digital marketing is approached. The marketing discipline itself is teeming with dilemmas and identity crises, yet the digital context brings them to the fore, as it clashes the old way of doing things with the new, not yet 'status' quo.

A growing number of books, innumerable blogs, infographics and statistics can be found about digital and multichannel marketing on the Web. If what you are looking for is to bring your understanding up to date and see the latest trends and cases, there is no better place to refer to than the Web itself. *Our focus here is a discussion on the theories of marketing communications and how they might be influenced by the digital transformation.* Communication provides a thread that has enduring relevance, resonates with many readers, and holds yet more potential for revolutionizing marketing and marketplaces.

Starting off with a review of the existing communication models and theories, we trace the development of thought on communications from mass broadcast to individualized and Omni-channel. Alongside we note how those models are affected by, and in turn are shaping, digital and multichannel marketing. A growing scholarly research base helps in this endeavour and signals some emergent research streams which we highlight. The organizational side of digital transformation from single- to omnichannel communication is illustrated by a case study of a top European sports company, Hummel. The chapter concludes by addressing the importance of theorizing within the digital domain and the challenges it brings.

Development of thought on marketing communications

Research on marketing communication has a rich history and provenance from a variety of other disciplines, including psychology, sociology and economics. Mass communication, representing print and broadcast media such as radio and TV, emerged as a research discipline in the early 20th century. The practice of mass communication relies on large, anonymous and often heterogeneous audiences, allowing broadcasters and advertisers to target relatively large groups cost-effectively – but with limited precision – by using basic demographics and consumption criteria such as postcode or magazine circulation. Furthermore, the basic economic function of mass media has been to appeal to and hold the largest audience possible so they can attract revenue from advertisers interested in reaching massive audiences to promote their products or brands.

Mid-20th century, with the rising popularity of advertising, a number of psychologists started addressing the role and influence of marketing communications, particularly in the USA. One of the most often quoted models of communication was developed by Wilbur Schramm (1948), and is known simply as the 'linear model of communication'. The main premise is that the sender and the receiver of communication need to share meaning in order for an effective exchange of information to occur. The primary constructs presented in this model are source, message, medium and receiver, as well as noise and feedback. Theodorson and Theodorson (1969: 13–14) describe the model as representing the 'transmission of information, ideas, attitudes or emotions from one person to another (or others), primarily through symbols'. Thus, the model remains a very useful systematization of actors and actions involved in communication, even though subsequent developments in practice and theory have challenged some of its elements.

Interpersonal influences in communication, stemming from sociological insights, were studied around the same time, and the importance of indirect 'personal influence', in addition to media influence, was already recognized by Katz and Lazarsfeld (1955). In the two-step model of communication, Katz and Lazarsfeld (1955) proposed amendments to the previously held one-step theory of communication that had assumed only direct influence of media on consumers. The recognition of indirect influence has become the principal reason for a move away from the linear communication process model towards the interactive or multi-step influencer model of communications (see Figure 13.1).

The internet and related technologies have continued this transformation and their impact on the above-mentioned process still remains to be fully understood. However some of the traditional dynamics have been visibly altered. For one, the constructs of sender and receiver have not only been redefined, but arguably have disappeared altogether, as each user can play either role at various times. For example, someone can post a video on YouTube while simultaneously being a consumer of content published by other users or brands.

In their oft-quoted article on hypermedia computer-mediated environments, Hoffman and Novak (1996) argued that the model of communication has been changing from one-to-many mass marketing communication, as exemplified by TV, to one-to-one communication,

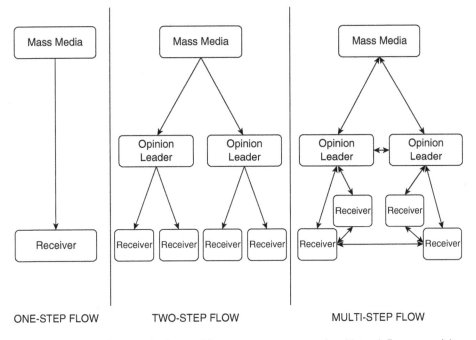

ONE-STEP FLOW   TWO-STEP FLOW   MULTI-STEP FLOW

Figure 13.1   Comparison of communication models – one-step, two-step and multi-step influencer models.

exemplified by direct marketing (including email) and even to many-to-many communications, as exemplified later by the internet and social networks. The many-to-many interactive model has since become one of the most quoted systematizations of digitally mediated communication. It skilfully illustrates that both consumers and firms can interact with the medium and both can generate and consume content. In other words, digital technologies are placing the control of content creation, selection and consumption in the hands of both its creators and users (elsewhere called 'prosumers' or 'cocreators').

To this day much research on marketing communications, and particularly on the effect of advertising, in one way or another uses as a starting point a model known as the Hierarchy of Effects, developed by Lavidge and Steiner (1961). The model proposes that consumers go through discrete stages when responding to marketing stimuli. Cognitive (thinking), emotional (feeling) and conative (acting) responses are said to follow each other in sequence during consumer progression from browsers to buyers of specific products and services. Both the presence and the order of those three stages have been criticized on the basis that during impulse purchase or a considered purchase those stages may be integrated or some elements missed out altogether. Nevertheless, in the absence of reliable measures of early advertising effects, this model has become widely adopted by, and forms a basis of many advertising appeals.

Determining the direct effect of marketing communications, particularly advertising since its conception, has been a very imprecise science. As Hugues (1975: 222) stated, 'It is well known that the relation between exposure and purchase is generally too complex or too weak to be measured. What we can try to measure with some chance of success are the effects of advertising on the aims of the campaign, on the themes of the messages.' Measuring the actual effect on sales is an age-old challenge for marketers. In the 1870s, John Wanamaker (an American merchant and advertising pioneer) was attributed to saying that half of his advertising budgets were wasted, but he did not know which half.

Over a century later, technological advances have drastically improved the accuracy of measuring marketing effectiveness. In the early 1990s the Integrated Marketing Communications programme at Northwestern University (later Kellogg Graduate School of Management) launched a new data-driven, demand-based marketing system – recognizing that the communication's objective was not only one-time exchange, but also ongoing engagement, negotiation, relationships and discussions with customers (Moriarty and Schultz, 2012). Data became the key to the shifting focus on driving long-term loyalty (often referred to as relationship marketing) and engagement between brands and consumers. This development moved the function of communication beyond tactical promotional activities, and into a strategic role where new key performance indicators (KPIs) and ways of measuring marketing effectiveness emerged.

The communications toolbox traditionally consisted of a manageable and predictable number of techniques that brands utilized to appeal, persuade, inform and sell, such as advertising, PR or direct marketing. The decision as to who, when and where to target has never been easy. However, with an increasing variety of channels, media and devices the task of selecting and coordinating branded communications has become more complex. At the same time marketers can benefit from unprecedented opportunities for engaging with users at a time and space and in a manner that suits them, thus potentially increasing effectiveness.

Integrated marketing communication (IMC) has become a notion much promoted among marketing practice and academia. The goal of integrating communication messages and actions on one hand sounds like an obvious necessity, but on the other hand, is an elusive goal for all those dealing with the increasing number of technologies, media, devices and techniques. In fact, in his 2006 article, Don Schultz commented: 'marketing and media communication today are atomistic, driven by specialist media forms, planned, developed and implemented by functional specialists and measured and evaluated by separate specialist research methodologies and firms. It is no wonder integration or alignment of marketing communication activities and programmes by any organisation is, and continues to be, so difficult' (2006: 16). At the same time, he anticipated that usage of more than one medium simultaneously by consumers (what we may now call multi-screening) will force marketers to adopt inter-media planning.

Where once the integration of external communication messages was the goal of IMC, today we speak of organizational integration and the management of brand contacts; in other words, every place and every way in which the organization touches its customers, employees, shareholders and stakeholders. Thus, IMC has moved from being a method of coordinating and aligning external messages towards a more holistic view of communication as the backbone of not just the marketing function but the entire business enterprise as well. Many organizations are adapting to the new reality through *digital transformation* programmes – aligning internal capabilities and structures, skills and resources, in order to take advantage of the new possibilities that digital communication presents.

Finne and Grönroos (2009) conceptualize integration from the consumer perspective, and focus on exploring how users create meaning by integrating a plethora of brand messages that they encounter. This perspective is a particularly useful one to help increase our understanding of the fragmented digital marketplace and how it affects user responses. Schultz et al. (2009) proposed a media consumption model to be used in place of the long-established message distribution model, discussed above. The main concept proposed by Schultz et al. (2009: 6) was that 'marketing communication has an impact based on the number of media messages the consumer accesses and processes, not the number of messages the marketer sends out or distributes through the media form. Further, it is the combination of media forms accessed and consumed by the individual that is important in understanding media effects, not the media plan developed by the marketer.'

The explosion in technologies and the popularization of personal mobile devices have caused an unprecedented multiplicity of media formats and channels for users to engage with and for advertisers to promote their products and services in. Yet not all communications are planned, as one can see by following any brand-owned Twitter stream, where consumers regularly post unprompted messages for the attention of the customer service department, which are visible to other Twitter users. In this regard, Duncan and Moriarty (1997) and Grönroos (2004) differentiated between planned and unplanned communication. In reality, online and on social networks, even when communications are planned, introduced and managed by a brand or their agency, the potential for unplanned consequences (good or bad) in the form of likes, shares, hacks and complaints is the very basis of the Web ecosystem. It is also often encouraged by the design of the message to increase the buzz and hence the reach of the originally designed piece of content.

Along with changes in marketing practice, scholars have been exploring the impact of Web-related technologies on marketing communications since the 1990s. In an early paper on technology-mediated communication, Newhagen and Rafaeli (1996) (later reviewed by Walther et al., 2005) asked 'Why communication researchers should study the internet', and called for research to take into account the following five important defining qualities that differentiate the Web from other media: multimedia, hypertextuality, packet switching, synchronicity and interactivity. This article marked the prevalence of ICT-focused perspective that dominated discourse in this area during the 1990s. However since the 2000s a broader range of business, management and consumer culture discourses started focusing on the societal and commercial consequences of digital communications. With the recent explosion of data-driven marketing and IoT innovations, there is a danger that yet again the emphasis is shifting towards technological efficiencies of big data, to the detriment of the human-centred experience design focus.

Evolution of digital and multichannel marketing

As with many sub-domains of management, the development of terminology, ideas and concepts in digital marketing has been practice-driven. This has resulted in the fragmented and often proprietary nature of digital marketing knowledge. Consolidation is a distant prospect. There are some attempts to bridge this gap by writers such as Dave Chaffey, who has co-authored several editions of books, the titles of which trace the history of the discipline and include such terms as 'e-Marketing', 'Internet Marketing', and more recently, 'Digital Marketing'. This shifting terminology seems to reflect not just changes in nomen-culture but traces the stages of developments in the discipline. Examining the scholarly and practitioner base, three chronological phases can be discerned, with the fourth one being proposed as a current stage of development:

1. The adoption of technology used to facilitate marketing on the web (e-marketing);
2. Focus on the networked nature of internet communications, including social media (internet marketing);
3. The broader integration of digital and social media, channels and devices to achieve marketing objectives (digital marketing and multi-channel);
4. A parallel focus on creating seamless customer experiences through coordination and complementarity of various channels, devices and media, often in real time (omnichannel and Internet of Things).

Many definitions have been provided in the existing literature for these and related terms, and while not addressed here, the reader is referred to Chaffey and Ellis-Chadwick (2013) and Baines and Fill (2014) for a comprehensive comparison of definitions.

Within the digital domain, one of the few journals that aptly reflects the academic and practitioner perspectives (in Europe), and hence traces developments in this field is the *Journal of Direct, Data and Digital Marketing Practice*. In the autumn 2013 edition of the journal, Webber and Stroud (2013) trace the shifting terminologies by text-mining phrases encountered on the journal pages between 1999 and 2012. Apart from the lessening occurrence of 'direct marketing' in favour of 'digital marketing', in this 12-year period, they observed a significant increase in the term 'social media', which reflects the growing popularity of social networks and the increasing impact they are having on marketing communications. Social media marketing has been defined by Tuten and Solomon (2015: 4) as 'Online means of communication, conveyance, collaboration and cultivation among interconnected and interdependent networks of people, communities and organisations enhanced by technological capabilities and mobility.'

Webber and Stroud (2013) highlight a 3,617% increase in the mentions of 'Google' in the same 12-year period. There is also a notable rise in mentions of Googling, i.e. using the world's largest search engine, Tweeting, i.e. sharing 140-character messages accompanied by images, and a plethora of other eponyms, which in themselves denote the key players in the digital marketing ecosystem.

As the semantics of the discipline are constantly fragmenting, finessing and fighting for primacy, it is important not to lose sight of the underlying mechanics and structures of communication in this new ecosystem. Both practitioners and scholars increasingly have attempted to consolidate knowledge about the new digital and multichannel marketplace. Alignment between theory and practice is crucial in this area in order to foster a relevant, rigorous and reflective body of knowledge.

At the 2014 workshop at Google HQ in London, organized by the Academy of Marketing e-Marketing Special Interest Group (SIG) along with the Institute of Direct and Digital Marketing, a set of six research priorities were identified, considered of value to both practitioners and academics. Those priorities emerged from the top seven Digital Marketing Fairs held in London during 2013.

1. Multichannel integration/customer experience;
2. Social and content media strategy;
3. Profitability/return on investment/metrics;
4. Big data/analytics/customer relation management;
5. Mobile and augmented reality;
6. Ethics, privacy and regulation.

A wealth of blog posts and practitioner viewpoints can be found when searching online for any of those terms. Yet performing the same search in academic journals would not have produced a similar result. The main reason for the shortage of academic papers appearing simultaneously to industry articles, is that scholars are traditionally concerned with theory, yet the theories that explain those trends may still need to be shaped or borrowed from other disciplines. With time trends and terms get absorbed in the academic vernacular by being integrated into new or amended models. Therein lies a tremendous opportunity for theoretical developments in technology-driven marketing and consumer behaviour, where some emergent themes can already be discerned.

Emergent themes in digital, multichannel and social media communications

Arguably, one of the most discussed shifts in the nature of communication, precipitated by the interactivity of the internet, is a shift from one-way to multi-way communication. The emphasis on dialogue between brands and consumers, and among consumers themselves, has brought with it not only a renewed focus on the social influences in communication, but has also recognized the permission-based and user-triggered nature of the digital marketplace.

Social networks and blogging platforms have changed the roles of content producers and consumers significantly. Whereas before professional publishers and journalists provided and circulated information, it is now mostly private users (or brand promoters disguised as such) that generate content in digital channels. As users increasingly become content generators, communities form around topics of interest, be they commercial or non-commercial in nature.

Research on online communities

For most brands, engaging with user communities has become an important and necessary marketing activity. Whether it is through explicitly branded fan pages or non-affiliated communities, consumer-to-consumer interaction has the power to affect the fortunes of any company. In fact, some commentators and authors believe that community management should lie at the very core of marketing management activity (e.g. Quinton, 2013).

Preece and Maloney-Krichmar (2005) define an online consumption community as an internet-based group of consumers who interact around a shared consumption purpose, interest or need. Such communities are distinct from social media networks, but are often formed within the realms of a social network such as Facebook that provide a convenient platform for interaction, until such time as a new, more convenient or appropriate network appears. This was the case with visually driven networks such as Pinterest and Instagram, to where much of the fashion chatter has shifted from the traditional, text-based networks. One could in fact chart a history of online communities, from amateur societies which dominated pages of MySpace, virtual worlds such as Second Life, through more professionally managed Facebook fan pages, to brand-driven efforts to create communities by brands such as RedBull, along with its increasingly commercial flavour.

Consequently, one of the growing areas of interest is the shifting characteristics of online communities, and in particular their growing commercialization both overtly, through branding content, and covertly, through gathering intelligence to inform brands' efforts. This trend highlights just how important it is for both scholars and marketers to develop a critical and reflective perspective on the desirability of developments in the digital marketplace. For example, researchers have already started to examine differences between communities focused on a brand's product and those concentrating on a non-commercial activity of interest (e.g. Wiertz and de Ruyter, 2007). In addition to the question of focus, the issue of who controls the community is garnering increasing attention (e.g. Fogel and Nehmad, 2009). Bringing those two perspectives together and building on empirical observations from

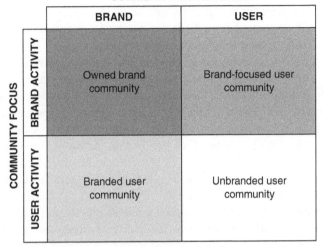

COMMUNITY GOVERNANCE

Figure 13.2   Brand community matrix.

Adapted from: Breitsohl et al. (2013).

Breitsohl et al. (2013), the brand community matrix presented in Figure 13.2 systematizes much of the extensive research conducted over the years and can help to identify the most appropriate community management strategy according to focus and governance criteria.

Unsurprisingly, given the commercial imperative of companies, there is an increasing pressure on them to monetize their social interactions. One of the key challenges facing brand-owned user communities is to implement suitable revenue streams and monetize without decreasing their credibility.

Research on social commerce/social shopping

Originally most of the activities in social networks were not commercial in nature. Studies have shown that sharing opinions, information and photos are the primary reason for being present on social networks (Hennig-Thurau et al., 2004). Such activities, have limited commercial benefit. Even though businesses have entered social media with designated brand pages, it is still challenging for them to measure the exact return on investment of their social media presence. For the most part, their approaches use social media as an acquisition marketing tool rather than as a sales channel.

Social commerce introduces a commercial layer to monetize social interactions while fostering interaction with brands and their products. However, some of the astute commentators caution against this approach: 'There is a very important battle waging between engagement and commercial teams on social platforms. That fight is between teams trying to decide whether the call-to-action for a certain audience or a certain piece of content is "click-to-share" or "click-to-buy". I'm not saying don't sell – I'm just suggesting that we take a step back and remember why we are even on social networks in the first place. We're here to talk to our friends and share cool content. Our intent is not always to purchase' (Jeremy Waite, Head of Strategy at Adobe EMEA, quoted in Lepitak, 2013).

If implemented well, social commerce could enable the discovery of relevant products in this sea of content, while connecting users to peers at the same time. That way, social commerce sites would be addressing the fundamental nature of shopping as a social experience by turning products into conversations by utilizing the elements of social media technologies, community interactions and commercial activities. Much previous research in both offline and online consumer behaviour has shown that purchasing decisions are strongly influenced by people who customers know and trust (e.g. Goldsmith and Horowitz, 2006). A potent research stream of participatory digital consumption is emerging (e.g. Ashman et al., 2015) which also integrates critique of such developments.

Another consideration in consumer shopping behaviour is the extent to which it is directed and goal oriented. Traditional search engine marketing assumes that shoppers are certain of their shopping goal(s) and are seeking a benefit to fulfil a named need or want. Social commerce marketing accepts that shoppers may be uncertain of their shopping goals and gather inspiration and ideas from their peers. Social recommendations can help to discover things that an algorithm will not. This demonstrates that consumers rely on one another as a trusted and credible source for buying decisions, and are less reliant on information from brand advertising. Today, it can be argued, the most important marketing team and, seemingly, the selling department, are each brand's customers.

Research on eWOM

When examining social media communication and its impact through social networks many authors adopt the phrase 'electronic word-of-mouth' (eWOM). eWOM marketing falls under the category of viral marketing. This conceptualization affords a new lease of life to the long-existing concept of word-of-mouth, defined by Arndt (1967: 3) as 'an oral, person-to-person communication between a receiver and a communicator whom the receiver perceives as non-commercial, regarding a brand, product or service'. Clearly, nowadays, that message can be transmitted not just through talking to another person, but by using social networks, sharing images through mobile apps or posting video reviews on YouTube.

By the middle of the last century scholars such as Katz and Lazarsfeld (1955) identified the value of WOM in influencing the consumer decision-making process. According to the authors, WOM was twice as effective as radio advertising, four times as effective as personal selling, and seven times as effective as print advertisements. Had the study been recreated in the 21st century, the results would likely be even more impressive as eWOM can have a direct, undiluted and rapid impact across the Web and hence reach a larger audience than offline WOM ever could. Generally, on the internet, research findings point to non-brand communication – such as blogger editorials or user reviews – as having higher credibility than commercial messages such as traditional advertising.

The major difference between WOM and eWOM is related to the fact that the latter has a physical footprint in the form of comments, blogposts, video reviews, 'likes' and 'follows'. This provides marketers with the ability to measure its effects, understand the network patterns of how it spreads, and potentially influence it in real time. But it also is a (semi-)permanent record of every mention; a record that provides a searchable and value-laden trace of ideas, brands and products in a marketplace. Such transparency can have a positive as well as negative effect on brands and their offering.

With ever-increasing prevalence, social networking sites are being used by consumers to connect with one another in search of information and, increasingly, to connect consumers with brands and vice versa. This means that, on one hand, research is needed to understand consumers' motives for engaging in social media communication, exploring why people write comments and posts on social networks; while on the other hand, it is important to understand the opportunities for brands to engage with users through eWOM communications. Much of the existing research into commercial uses of social networks has focused on understanding the impact of social media usage on brands and their ability to monetize it as well as community formation (e.g. Kozinets et al., 2010).

There is, however, a growing stream of research that aims to understand what motivates consumers to engage with brand-related stories on social networks in the first place, and thus how brands can encourage or discourage these behaviours. One of the most quoted papers in this field is by Hennig-Thurau et al. (2004) outlining key motivations for eWOM engagement as being (1) desire for social interaction, (2) desire for economic incentives, (3) concern for other consumers and (4) the potential to enhance one's own self-worth.

With the expanding universe of what eWOM may signify – from a like to a post, to a recommendation, review, comment or video share – there is still much scope to explore its mechanics, antecedents and consequences.

Research on multichannel decision making

Much of planned marketing communication activity is geared towards influencing decision making. Models of decision making have however been developed in pre-internet days and raise questions about their validity and applicability in the contemporary marketplace.

Traditionally, purchasing was a private act, or at least one that was influenced by close others at a specific stage in the buying process. Nowadays, virtual social structures in which individuals reside have become a growing influence on consumer preference and behaviour throughout the shopping process. This new reality is referred to as participatory digital culture and is a fast-emerging research stream, which brings together cultural theory on the one hand (e.g. Lash, 2007), helping to understand how consumption has evolved, and marketing on the other, analysing the increasing commercialization of social activities and ties (e.g. Zwick and Dholakia, 2008).

A growing stream of research is being conducted to understand how the well-established decision-making models may have changed in the digital marketplace. Much of the discussion

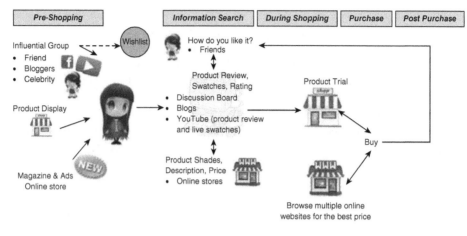

Figure 13.3   Example of a customer journey.

Source: Wolny and Charoensuksai (2014).

thus far has focused on the online versus offline distinction (e.g. Penz and Hogg, 2013) and has contributed greatly to the discourse. With the explosion of mobile technologies and social media, the distinctions between online and offline have blurred, and researchers are turning their attention to multi- and omnichannel decision making. Multichannel shopping has indeed become a journey in which customers choose the route they take and which, arguably, needs to be remapped and reconceptualized to be understood.

Wolny and Charoensuksai (2014) undertook research that inductively illustrated the complex journeys consumers go through in the current multichannel marketplace, and identified three distinct journeys that brands can use to optimize their multichannel strategies: impulsive journeys, balanced journeys and considered journeys.

With the different media, devices and channels available, people are exposed to increasingly complex multichannel shopping journeys (see for example Figure 13.3). That complexity, however, is added only from the marketer's perspective. From a consumer's perspective, new behaviours – such as showrooming and webrooming (shopping cross-channel) – have emerged as a way of simplifying the decision-making processes in the ever-expanding digital universe.

Research on data analytics and ethical considerations

There has been renewed emphasis on accountability of marketing, making it responsible not just for spending money but for accounting on its return on communication investment. Marketing can have both short-term and long-term effects on the bottom-line measures: short-term profits or net cash flow as well as increased marketing assets or brand equity over time. Traditionally brands would attempt to evaluate their marketing efforts through sales and profits tracking, consumer perception studies, panels and ad exposure tests. Increasingly, however, with the pressure to justify expenditure, marketers need to be able to identify the short-term effectiveness of their communication efforts and technology investments, with much discussion taking place around channel attribution.

> Sooner or later, every marketing executive will have to get to grips with demonstrating the contribution of marketing. From deciding whether a major campaign is worth backing, to the immediate and data challenge of managing budgets and measuring activities. (Emerson Inacio, Unilever, foreword to Shaw and Merrick, 2005)

One of the main advantages of digital marketing is the data that are generated from every interaction between a brand and a consumer and between consumers themselves. The data can take the form of conversations, transaction details, site visit statistics, product selection and deselection, click-through on adverts, or even a person's whole social graph. This information is of course very valuable to companies, who can use it for market research purposes, targeting and retargeting, as well as tailoring messages down to individually tailored content, to which any subsequent response can potentially be directly attributable.

Apart from transactional and performance quantitative data, social media analytics can use data-mining techniques to capture social behaviour dynamics – detecting trends, predicting influences and mining for opinions of leaders and followers. Colleoni (2014) identifies three types of qualitative consumer data mining – relational, conversational and emotional – and provides an informed analysis of all three.

With the ease of ongoing testing and dynamic tweaking of communications based on qualitative and quantitative insights from the market itself, marketing messages are becoming ever more targeted and precise. The process is also becoming increasingly automated. Marketing automation software, for example, takes into account a position of prospects in a buying funnel, and targets channel-specific, often personalized (to location, demographics of buying readiness) messages to elicit action. The goal is to create and manage individualized multichannel marketing experiences for their customers, thus ensuring loyalty and return on their marketing investment.

Critics of such individualized targeting of information point to the increasing digital manipulation of consumer responses. With greater behavioural-neurological understanding and ability of technology to target time-specific needs, the fear is that, before long, companies may be targeting sugary-snack messages to our portable devices just at a time when our body trackers identify low sugar levels, triggering a semi-automated response. That is just one instance of many ethical and legal issues surrounding marketing communications. This is still a nascent field lacking overarching ethical frameworks in the digital context, but key considerations are emerging: regulation and compliance, user privacy issues, data and copyright protection, as well as trust and ethics of data-driven marketing itself. What makes this more complex is that each channel and type of device both mutates and further exacerbates the extent to which these issues are impacting business practice. For example, increasing use of mobile devices brings with it new norms related to location-based tracking, while the emergence of the Internet of Things (IoT) will bring challenges related to data access and automated data transfers between devices. The seemingly unstoppable technological progress has a profound impact on organisational strategy and tactics. A case study of Hummel – one of the oldest sports brands in the world – illustrates the stages the company went through at an organisational, departmental and cultural level to achieve successful digital transformation to omni-channel.

CASE STUDY 13.1

Hummel's digital transformation to omnichannel

As the phenomenal growth of mobile and social media continues, many organizations are realizing the need for an online presence to reach out to the digitally savvy customers. Amid such chaotic efforts to jump on the bandwagon, an organization's ability to deliver a seamless customer experience across the various online and offline channels has become increasingly challenging. In this case analysis, we examine how Hummel, a European sport-fashion company, has overcome these challenges and has successfully made the transition towards omnichannel commerce.

The case company

Hummel is one of the oldest sportswear brands in the world. The company was founded in 1923 in Hamburg, Germany, by a young shoemaker. It endured numerous ups and downs for over half a century, including getting burned to the ground. In the late 1990s when the company fell into crisis, a Danish lawyer bought Hummel. Since then, under the new leadership, Hummel has enjoyed approximately 20% growth year after year, and it is one of the fastest growing sport-fashion brands in the industry. Today, Hummel operates in the sport and lifestyle apparel, footwear and accessories market with an annual turnover of US$240 million. The company designs approximately 1,100 product styles per year. Almost 100% of its sales come from wholesale business-to-business (B2B) sales through its own operations, distributors, agents and licensed partners (e.g. large sports retail chains, department stores and boutiques) in over 40 countries.

Problems with digital marketing communication

Before embarking on the omnichannel journey, an audit demonstrated a scattered online presence of Hummel, with many different Hummel websites (launched by partners and distributors in various countries) and inconsistent brand expressions online (Hummel logos, product pack shots, lifestyle images, videos, texts, etc.). Visitors would get a different online brand experience depending on whether they visited a Spanish, Japanese, American or local German website.

> I was shocked when I realized that there were 10-20-30 different brand expressions internationally. All of us should have been telling the same story. I was embarrassed that we hadn't been more caring of our brand. We lacked the McDonald's effect in Hummel. (Hummel's Chief Strategy Officer, 2010)

This chaotic branding threatened to dilute the Hummel brand, obliterating the established heritage image that would speak of its distinctive quality and character.

With the internet, prior dumping practices by some distributors at discounted prices were becoming highly visible online. The need to align the Hummel brand across multiple channels thus became more critical, and the challenge Hummel faced was how to make a successful transition to embrace an omnichannel strategy that would best leverage its brand globally.

Journey to omnichannel – the strategy

Acutely aware of the risk of upsetting the company's traditional wholesale B2B distribution channel, Hummel built its omnichannel strategy around its B2B network of distributors, licensed partners and online and offline retailers. Its primary focus was to strengthen and support the B2B channel partners. Despite various suggestions to grow its B2C e-commerce, however, Hummel repeatedly resisted aggressive direct selling to end-customers.

In mid-2010, a Global Head of Digital, under Marketing, was hired and tasked with the responsibilities of pursuing an omnichannel strategy for Hummel. Supported by her team, IT Department and e-commerce vendors, the Head of Digital led the digital transformation along four key thrusts by (1) aligning the online branding globally, (2) enhancing the e-commerce support for B2B partners, (3) building the omnichannel customer community and (4) complementing the physical store experience (see Figure 13.4).

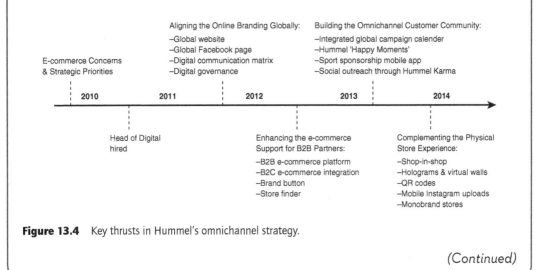

Figure 13.4 Key thrusts in Hummel's omnichannel strategy.

(Continued)

(Continued)

Steps in the journey to omnichannel communications

Taking control of the brand across websites

At the 2010 International Sales Conference, Hummel launched a 'One Brand One Voice' (OBOV) mission to align the online branding globally:

> We need to gather all country websites on one global web and ecommerce platform, so that we don't confuse the consumer, but instead give them the best possible One Brand One Voice experience. (Hummel's Global Head of Digital, 2010)

The move consolidated 22 local (national) Hummel websites to just one global platform with localized sites. Local needs were taken into consideration in developing the global platform; these included a localized view of product categories and collections, and upload of locally licensed products, as well as more content-focused functions such as local news on the homepage. Similarly, Hummel also rationalized its Facebook presence from around 25 different Facebook pages with inconsistent brand expressions (logos, tone of voice, etc.) to a global Facebook page with local pages for local Hummel personnel to engage their customers through social media.

Digital communication matrix

In addition, while Hummel wanted a presence on all relevant social media platforms (mainly to secure the Hummel profile so that it would not be abducted and abused by others), it was careful in considering the customer engagement plan for each platform. A digital communication matrix (see Figure 13.5) was developed to guide the tactical consideration of its purpose, content, communication plan and technical integration requirements. For example, Instagram was primarily intended for brand and product communication (e.g. to support product launches and campaigns), to generate traffic to Hummel's website, to acquire new fans/customers and to forge customer loyalty. It was not intended as a channel to service or interact with customers, to make direct sales to customers, or to crowd-source innovative ideas.

Digital manual

Furthermore, a digital manual was introduced, offering a comprehensive listing of the set of standards and guidelines required for online branding.

For example, all Hummel HQ social media sites were named Hummel International, and those of the countries were named Hummel Germany, Hummel Turkey, etc. and

	Website	Facebook	YouTube	Instagram	Newsletter	Google+	Twitter	LinkedIN	Blogs
Brand & Product Communication	x	x	x	x	x	x	x	x	x
Traffic Generation to Website		x	x	x	x	x	x	x	x
Service/Interaction	x	x	x			x	x	x	
Fan/Customer Acquisition	x	x	x	x	x	x	x	x	x
Loyalty/Retention	x	x	x	x	x	x	x	x	
Direct B2C Sales	x	x							
Crowd Sourcing		x				x		x	x
Feed to hummel.net		x	x	x			x		

Figure 13.5   Hummel's digital communication matrix.

(Continued)

(Continued)

the stores were named Hummel store Berlin, Hummel store Paris, etc. Even the look and feel of profiles, cover photos, newsletters and websites were aligned, as well as the tone of voice, for the different Hummel target groups and the overall brand message. The digital manual also provided guidance on how partners should sell Hummel products across channels such as their own websites, third-party retailers, and market spaces, as well as policies for AdWords, affiliates, retargeting and so on. The manual was regularly updated and reissued every six months.

Building the omnichannel customer community

Recognizing that an omnichannel strategy would change the way the channels worked together, Hummel's next thrust was to revamp its usual channel-specific customer engagement approach by weaving it into a more coordinated enterprise-wide marketing programme. This consisted of a carefully crafted annual campaign calendar which was agreed with and signed off by Hummel's sales and marketing departments in all countries. Specific themes and content for each week of the year were developed and customized for each individual channel. When a new product was launched in retail through either B2B or B2C physical and digital stores, it would be announced on in-store point-of-sale material, in newsletters, banners and blogs. Simultaneously, the launch would also be advertised on local Google sites, Facebook pages, Instagram, YouTube and Twitter, among others, as well as in print magazines with a link or QR code to the website, where the campaign would be fully unfolded on the front page and in more in-depth articles, which again had social media feeds that linked back to the products.

In addition, the unique DNA traits of Hummel as a sportswear brand (e.g. retro, team spirit, playfulness) were continuously reinforced by showcasing real Hummel people in action. This was done, for example, through global competitions such as the 'Hummel Happy Moments' where customers would share their favourite Hummel Moments on Instagram and Facebook, which were broadcast in real-time to webpages or virtual walls at the company HQ (see Figure 13.6).

Hummel even created mobile apps to complement such sponsorships. The Hummel Football Game app, for example, gathered its most prominent teams in one virtual locker room so that fans, customers and even B2B retailers could interact and play with the teams. The app featured the likes of the sunny stadium of Valladolid, the edgy St Pauli field and the dusty Afghanistan desert where players could play and score to win trophies on each field. If they won a bronze trophy on all fields, Hummel would – in the name of the player – send a football to an underprivileged child in Sierra Leone. This

Figure 13.6   Real Hummel people in action – Instagram.

act of 'goodness' was part of another engagement initiative of Hummel called 'Hummel Karma'. The Karma cause was an integral part in the development of Hummel's partnerships. Each sport sponsorship was expected to adopt a Karma cause that would support a social cause by helping the less fortunate in their community through various projects, thus helping to 'change the world through sport'.

Complementing the physical store

A shop-in-shop e-commerce platform was set up where B2B partners could offer all Hummel products for sale in their physical stores without actually carrying the stock. The iPad e-commerce app, for example, offered additional styles, colours and sizes from Hummel's own warehouse as the stores' assortment was typically limited by their physical size. Items ordered would then be delivered to the customers' homes directly or offered for pickup in-store. In addition, lifelike holograms of the latest fashion offerings (e.g. sneakers), virtual walls with life-size models showcasing the season's products on the catwalk and RFID scanners that would bring the products to life on a screen were all digital-in-store innovation experimentations in these Hummel stores (see Figure 13.7).

The most engaging in-store tool was perhaps the customer's own mobile phone. Here, they could upload pictures of themselves or of products via Instagram hashtag

(Continued)

(Continued)

#hummelsport and a style number, which would then be fed to a live screen in-store and also to Hummel's global website. In this way, Hummel allowed for user-generated photos of its products to be showcased almost instantaneously across its various digital channels. Specialty Hummel monobrand stores have also been set up in major European cities, as one of its brand-building initiatives.

Figure 13.7   Hummel's virtual wall, hologram and digital screens.

Effectiveness of omnichannel transformation

Early progress in Hummel's omnichannel strategy could already be seen in its increase in total sales from US$170 million in 2010 to US$240 million in 2013. In particular, sales through online channels grew from 5% of total turnover in 2010 to 21% in 2013 (11% from B2B e-commerce platform and 10% from online retailers). At the same time, there was greater awareness of the Hummel brand. The Hummel community grew from 13,000 people in 2010 to 1.5 million people in 2014. The number of website visitors increased from 216,000 in 2010 to 1.25 million in 2014, and the total number of people reached across all digital channels also increased to 15 million

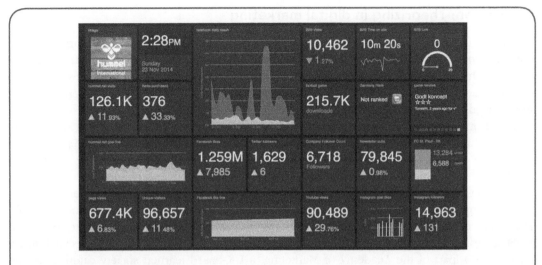

Figure 13.8   Hummel's Dashboard.

people per week in 2014. Comprehensive tracking of these brand indicators was prominently displayed on three large screens at the Hummel HQ. For example, the screens displayed Hummel's Dashboard, a digital board that aggregated real-time data from various sources such as Google analytics on hummel.net, B2C and B2B e-commerce sales, store finder clicks, Facebook, Instagram, YouTube, the Football app downloads and others (see Figure 13.8).

Organizational transformation

Organizations should be clear that going omnichannel is not just about adding e-commerce and social media platforms. From a communication perspective, the process includes the commitment of the CEO to the pursuit of the omnichannel strategy, and the recognition that going omnichannel is not a one-time digital transformation. The success of Hummel's omnichannel commerce, in particular, hinged on the strategic hiring of the Head of Digital and the establishment of the Digital Department.

> The Digital department is very much an integrative function in the company. There is actually not a single department in the company that we are not working with, or that is not influenced by our work. Each of the Digital employees functions as coordinator across many departments, tying together the new and old functions in Hummel. (Head of Digital, 2014)

(With thanks to Dr Rina Hansen, the Head of Digital at Hummel for permission to share Hummel's story. Based on: Hansen and Sia, 2015.)

Conclusion: Theorizing in digital marketing

It is a changeling task to integrate a chapter on digital and multichannel marketing in a book entitled *Marketing Theory*. It may prompt the reader to ask – is there theory specifically developed for this context? If not, what would it look like? Is it even possible or desirable? Are theories developed in other disciplines such as sociology, ICT or information systems perhaps more suited to the digital context than traditional marketing theories?

Those questions are being debated by a growing number of digital marketing researchers and were highlighted in the recently published manifesto (Wolny, 2013). In it, we posit that a 'new wave' of digitally focused marketing academics – similar to the 'new wave' movements in film and art – should be questioning traditional concepts, methodologies and techniques, challenging both marketing theory and marketing practice. Through critical conceptual thinking, contemporary researchers should come up with new insights about what theories still hold true in this digitally mediated world and how best to update the knowledge base to reflect the realities. Some of those 'new wave' scholars congregate in the e-Marketing Special Interest Group (SIG), part of the Academy of Marketing, a UK-based learned society catering for the needs of marketing researchers, educators and professionals. The aim of the e-Marketing SIG, reflecting the desired purpose of digital marketing scholarship altogether, is *building a relevant, rigorous and reflective knowledge base in digital marketing.*

While theorizing may be taking place, theories take a long time to develop and sometimes there is a danger of trying to fossilize what still needs to remain organic. What we need is 'permanent beta' in marketing theory, to allow for ongoing refinements. This term originates in software development, and denotes having a highly functional prototype that is used by a community of 'beta users' to test it out and provide continuous feedback. The virtual nature of concepts, as is the case with software, lends itself to continual tweaking. Against the backdrop of such a fast-shifting landscape, it should be no surprise that any conclusions drawn, while being modelled, need to be periodically reviewed to allow for continuous learning and agility.

There are those, however, who do not believe that digital marketing should have its own theory base: that digital is simply a context for existing marketing theory and practice. For others, digital marketing exists in its own right but it is perceived as a set of skills, and hence not theory-worthy. There are others still who hold that the shifting technologies and tactics of digital and social media marketing preclude theories from being developed. All those perspectives are valid, but if we embrace the philosophy espoused in this chapter that there is a revolutionary transformation taking place, then it is likely to yield new conceptualizations going forward. There is certainly a growing practical base of digital marketing for researchers to draw on for inductive grounded observations to start modelling the practice into theory. Journal editors and reviewers should be encouraged by this and recognize the value of qualitative research in this area. Currently, it seems that development of theory in digital marketing is being thwarted by the pressure placed upon scholars to devote their time to predominantly quantitative studies, which test discrete variables within existing models, thus increasing the likelihood of publication in top journals. While valuable insights can be gained from this approach and existing frameworks need to be reviewed in the light of new realities, such reductionist approach is rarely a source of revolutionary insight; inductive and conceptual thinking is where such insight can more readily be found.

New hybrid disciplines have come to prominence in recent years to assist in understanding the complex techno-cultural as well as organizational implications of the Web, some of those being Web Science, network theory and netnography. Despite the undeniable symbiosis of marketing with commerce, we believe there is much to be gained from applying different lenses to studying the phenomena surrounding the Web – be it cultural, historical, or structural – and hope that this chapter acts as a catalyst for further relevant, rigorous and reflective research into digital marketing communications.

Recommended further reading

Baker, M. and Hart, S. (2008) *The Marketing Book*. Oxford: Butterworth-Heinemann.
Belk, R. and Llamas, R. (eds) (2013) *The Routledge Companion to Digital Consumption*. Abingdon: Routledge.
Dahl, S. (2015) *Social Media Marketing*. London: Sage.
Godin, S. (2007) *Permission Marketing: Turning Strangers into Friends and Friends into Customers*. New York: Pocket Books.
Kozinets, R. (2015) *Netnography: Redefined*. Thousand Oaks, CA: Sage.
Ogilvy (1983) *Ogilvy on Advertising*. New York: Crown.
O'Shaughnessy, J. (2012) *Consumer Behaviour: Perspectives, Findings and Explanations*. London: Palgrave Macmillan.

References

Arndt, J. (1967) 'Role of product-related conversations in the diffusion of a new product', *Journal of Marketing Research* 4 (August): 291–5.
Ashman, R., Solomon, M. and Wolny, J. (2015) 'An old model for a new age: consumer decision-making in participatory digital culture', *Journal of Customer Behaviour* 14(2): 127–46.
Baines, P. and Fill, C. (2014) *Marketing*, 3rd edn. Oxford: Oxford University Press.
Breitsohl, J., Dowell, D.J. and Kunz, W. (2013) 'Community or cuckoo's nest? A taxonomical update on online consumption communities', Academy of Marketing Conference, Bournemouth University.
Chaffey, D. and Ellis-Chadwick, F. (2013) *Digital Marketing, Strategy, Implementation and Practice*. Harlow: Pearson.
Colleoni, E. (2014) 'New forms of digital marketing research', in R.W. Belk and R. Llamas (eds) *The Routledge Companion to Digital Consumption*. Abingdon and New York: Routledge, pp. 124–34.
Duncan, T.R. and Moriarty, S. (1997) *Driving Brand Value*. New York: McGraw-Hill.
Finne, A. and Grönroos, C. (2009) 'Rethinking marketing communication: from integrated marketing communication to relationship communication', *Journal of Marketing Communications* 15(2): 179–95.
Fogel, J. and Nehmad, E. (2009) 'Internet social network communities: risk taking, trust, and privacy concerns', *Computers in Human Behavior* 25(1): 153–60.
Goldsmith, R.E. and Horowitz, D. (2006) 'Measuring motivations for online opinion seeking', *Journal of Interactive Advertising* 6(2): 2–14.

Grönroos, C. (2004) 'The relationship marketing process: communication, interaction, dialogue, value', *Journal of Business & Industrial Marketing* 19(12): 99–113.

Hansen, R. and Sia, S.K. (2015) 'Hummel's digital transformation toward omnichannel retailing: key lessons learned', *MIS Quarterly Executive* 14(2): 51–66.

Hennig-Thurau, T., Gwinner, K.P., Walsh, G. and Gremler, D.D. (2004) 'Electronic word-of-mouth via consumer-opinion platforms: what motivates consumers to articulate themselves on the Internet?', *Journal of Interactive Marketing* 18(1): 38–52.

Hoffman, D.L. and Novak, T.P. (1996) 'Marketing in hypermedia computer mediated environments: conceptual foundations', *The Journal of Marketing* 60: 50–68.

Hugues, M. (1975) 'An empirical study of media comparison', *Journal of Marketing Research* 12(2): 221–3.

Katz, E. and Lazarsfeld, P.E. (1955) *Personal Influence: The Part Played by People in the Flow of Mass Communications*. Glencoe, IL: The Free Press.

Kozinets, R.V., De Valck, K., Wojnicki, A.C. and Wilner, S.J. (2010) 'Networked narratives: understanding word-of-mouth marketing in online communities', *Journal of Marketing* 74(2): 71–89.

Lash, S. (2007) 'Capitalism and metaphysics', *Theory, Culture & Society* 24(5): 1–26.

Lavidge, R.J. and Steiner, G.A. (1961) 'A model for predictive measurements of advertising effectiveness', *The Journal of Marketing* 25(6): 59–62.

Lepitak, S. (2013) 'Debate: What is the future of social commerce? Can you make money from social media?', *The Drum*, 22 March. Available at: http://www.thedrum.com/news/2013/03/22/debate-what-future-social-commerce-can-you-make-money-social-media.

Moriarty, S. and Schultz, D. (2012) 'Four theories of how IMC works', in S. Rodgers and E. Thorson (eds) *Advertising Theory*, 1st edn. Abingdon: Routledge, pp. 491–505.

Newhagen, J.E. and Rafaeli, S. (1996) 'Why communication researchers should study the internet: a dialogue', *Journal of Communication* 46(1): 4–13.

Parsons, R. (2014) 'Unilever's Marc Mathieu: people think too much about digital marketing', *Marketing Week*, 17 June. Available at: http://www.marketingweek.com/2014/06/17/unilevers-marc-mathieu-people-think-too-much-about-digital-marketing/.

Penz, E. and Hogg, M.K. (2013) 'Consumer decision-making in online and offline environments', in R.W. Belk and R. Llamas (eds) *The Routledge Companion to Digital Consumption*. Abingdon and New York: Routledge, pp. 235–48.

Preece, J. and Maloney-Krichmar, D. (2005) 'Online communities: design, theory, and practice', *Journal of Computer-Mediated Communication* 10(4): np.

Quinton, S. (2013) 'The community brand paradigm: a response to brand management's dilemma in the digital era', *Journal of Marketing Management* 29(7/8): 912–32.

Schramm, W. (1948) 'How communication works', in W. Schramm (ed.) *The Process and Effects of Communication*. Urbana, IL: University of Illinois Press, pp. 3–26.

Schultz, D. (2006) 'Media synergy: the next frontier in a multimedia marketplace', *Journal of Direct, Data and Digital Marketing Practice* 8(1): 13–28.

Schultz, D., Block, M. and Raman, K. (2009) 'Media synergy comes of age – Part 1', *Journal of Direct, Data and Digital Marketing Practice* 11(1): 3–16.

Shaw, R. and Merrick, D. (2005) *Marketing Payback: Is Your Marketing Profitable?* Harlow: FT Prentice-Hall.

Theodorson, S. and Theodorson, A. (1969) *A Modern Dictionary of Sociology*. New York: Cassell Education.

Tuten, T. and Solomon, M. (2015) *Social Media Marketing*, 2nd edn. London: Sage.

Walther, J.B., Gay, G. and Hancock, J.T. (2005) 'How do communication and technology researchers study the internet?', *Journal of Communication* 55(3): 632–57.

Webber, R. and Stroud, D. (2013) 'How changes in word frequencies reveal changes in the focus of the JDDDMP', *Journal of Direct, Data and Digital Marketing Practice* 14(4): 310–20.

Wiertz C. and De Ruyter, K. (2007) 'Beyond the call of duty: why customers participate in firm-hosted online communities', *Organization Studies* 28(3): 349–78.

Wolny, J. (2013) 'The E-Marketing SIG beta manifesto – aligning research with practice in digital marketing', *Journal of Direct, Data and Digital Marketing Practice* 14(4): 15, 288–9.

Wolny, J. and Charoensuksai, N. (2014) 'Mapping customer journeys in multichannel decision-making', *Journal of Direct, Data and Digital Marketing Practice* 15(4): 317–26.

Zwick, D. and Dholakia, N. (2008) 'Infotransformation of markets: introduction to the special issue on marketing and information technology', *Journal of Macromarketing* 28(4): 318–25.

Theories of Value and Brand Equity[1]

Mark S. Glynn and Roderick J. Brodie

Chapter Topics

Overview	344
Introduction	345
Equity and branding value	346
Equity and the value of other marketing assets	350
Integrating with financial thinking	352
Towards a theory of brand equity and the value of marketing assets	355

Overview

The term 'equity' has been used in marketing to describe the value of marketing assets such as brands, customers, channels and other marketing relationships. We examine the various uses of the equity concept in relation to brands. The alternative uses of the equity concept and how these link with financial thinking are considered. The chapter then explores issues involved in developing a theory of marketing assets and value that integrates branding, relationship and networks with financial thinking.

Introduction

There is a paradox in how senior management views marketing. While a market-focused strategy may be regarded as an essential component in driving strategic success, at the senior management level marketing executives are often not as strongly represented as executives with a financial background (Webster et al., 2003). Marketing is also seen by some as declining in influence within organizations. One reason for this decline is that marketing's traditional assumptions such as 'creating value for the customer' and 'winning in the product marketplace' do not clearly link with the financial and strategic issues of business. Hence there is a need for new marketing thinking that links marketing activity more directly with the creation of financial value. This led Srivastava et al. (1998: 3) to suggest the purpose of marketing is to 'create and manage market-based assets in order to deliver financial value for the shareholder'. Market-based assets are external focused resources such as brand management, relationships and knowledge. This redefinition of the purpose of marketing implies the marketing–finance interface needs to be better coordinated within firms and one of the central tasks of marketing is resource integration. These market-based assets are most beneficial to firms when linked to complementary internal resources (Lusch and Harvey, 1994). Doyle (2000) refers to this new approach to marketing as 'value-based marketing'. Vargo and Lusch (2004) also develop a new service logic that focuses on resource integration and value creation within networks which provides a broader theoretical foundation for this new approach to marketing.

If ideas about financial value are to be integrated into marketing practice, there is a need for greater linkages between financial terms and marketing concepts to develop a common lexicon. Such a linkage has occurred in the last decade, where marketing academics and practitioners have used the term 'equity' to describe the financial value of brands and other market-based assets. This term is used in accounting and finance to express the value of an organization's financial assets and liabilities. While some marketing academics have used equity in a broader legal and ethical context to indicate fairness, it is the financial use of the term that has been largely adopted.

The concept of brand equity emerged in marketing in the 1980s. Advertising practitioners in the USA used the concept to counter stockmarket emphasis on short-term results and consequent cuts to brand advertising budgets. In order to convince senior managers of the long-term value of brand advertising and other marketing investments, it was argued that marketing needed financial measures of brand value. Thus the term 'brand equity' was coined to refer to the brand's long-term customer franchise which also had a financial value. The marketing community has also used the term equity to refer to the asset value of other marketing investments. Rust et al. (2000) and Blattberg et al. (2001) use the term 'customer equity' to focus on the financial value of customers to an organization, while Anderson et al. (2009) use the term 'marketplace equity' to represent the joint result of investments in brand equity, channel equity and reseller equity. In measuring that customer franchise, what became apparent was the lack of a clear and consistent conceptual framework for brand equity. While marketing academics had devoted considerable attention to understanding the nature of brand equity, less attention had been given to the financial consequences of activities designed to increase brand equity.

Thus the financial costs as indicated by a brand's advertising budget used to build a brand can be measured but not the outcome of such a cost. Furthermore, many practitioners often refer to brand marketing costs as an 'investment' in brand building. Thus attention is needed to focus on measuring the outcomes of brand building.

As a market-based asset, brands need to meet several criteria to be considered as a firm resource of value to the company (Kozlenkova et al., 2014). These criteria include the difficulty of imitation and the extent to which the brand resources may be leveraged to achieve a greater return on investment. The intangibility of brand assets is reflected in the difficulty of imitation as brands have a distinct identity which can be built over the long-term. The brand resource may also be leveraged or extended to complement other firm resources thus creating additional benefits for the firm. For example, a brand can be extended into new product categories for the firm creating additional revenue. In this sense the brand resource is complementary to both the other tangible and intangible assets within the firm.

Aaker (1996: 7) defines brand equity as 'the assets and liabilities linked to a brand, its name and symbol, that add to or subtract from the value provided by a product or service to a firm and/or to that firm's customers'. This asset/liability perspective leads to a broader view about the role of the brand. The Aaker perspective recognizes that the value of brand equity consists of both positive and negative aspects (assets and liabilities) of the brand. Furthermore, these assets and liabilities can enhance or reduce revenues for the firm. The value of a strong brand can be seen when comparing the sales of a national brand with the sales of weaker competitors' brands in the same category or even comparing to sales of a retailer's private label brand (Apelbaum et al., 2003). In addition, brand equity has benefits for the marketer beyond sales revenue performance. Brand equity can improve advertising efficiency, enhance customer loyalty, lead to extension opportunities and create brand licensing opportunities in the future.

The chapter proceeds as follows. First the use of the term equity in branding is considered. The next section examines how equity has been used in relation to other marketing assets such as customers, channels and relationships. We then examine how marketing thinking integrates with financial thinking. Finally the issue of developing a theory of brand equity and the value of marketing assets is considered.

Equity and branding value

Although the exact origins of the term brand equity are unclear, many definitions of the term abound as has research on this subject. This research has been based on four different perspectives: entity-based, financially-based, process-based and network-based. Towards the end of this chapter we integrate these four different perspectives by suggesting a service-based perspective of brand equity.

Entity-based brand equity

Much of the initial research on brand equity was in response to the advertising industry's need to understand the effects of advertising on building brand image and consumer loyalty.

Thus the focus was on mass marketing and the one-way impact of marketing activity (especially advertising) on consumers. This initial research on brand equity was based on concepts from consumer behaviour and marketing communications and emphasizes brand identity (Merz et al., 2009). It follows the traditional view of marketing where the brand functions as an entity. This perspective is consistent with the AMA (2004) definition of the brand (i.e. a name, term, design, symbol, or any other feature that identifies one seller's good or service as distinct from those of other sellers).

Keller (1993) broadens this perspective to include customer behaviour in response to this differentiation. Keller (1993: 2) defines customer-based equity as: 'the differential effect of brand knowledge on consumer response to the marketing of the brand' and describes equity in terms of the strength of consumers' attachment to the brand and their associations and beliefs about the brand. A variety of techniques have been used to measure brand equity. These include consumer awareness, brand associations, perceptions, attachment and consumer-related brand activity. In addition, qualitative research techniques can also highlight the underlying processes that contribute to brand equity development.

Financially-based brand equity

This stream of research considers more direct financial approaches, where the emphasis is less on individual consumers and more on the overall financial value of the brand to the organization. Research by Madden et al. (2006) links branding closely to the creation of shareholder value. Their research showed that well-managed brands provided superior returns in comparison to industry benchmarks. Another finding was that brands reduced risk for firms in terms of volatility and vulnerability of cash flows.

A variety of methods have also been used to develop measures of the financial value of brands to an organization. These methods identify the total asset value of the organization and subtract the tangible assets. The residual value is then used to arrive at a measure of brand equity, an intangible asset. Another approach is to work directly with the organization concerned. For example the consulting firm Interbrand approach to brand valuation first involves a direct analysis of the brand's financial performance to identify the profits attributable to the brand. Second, the role of the brand in the customer purchase process is then assessed. This step is followed by a third step, the assessment of brand strength based on several performance dimensions relative to the brand's competitors. These three measures are then combined to arrive at a single measure of brand value. Each year Interbrand rank and publish a list by value of the top 100 global brands. A feature of the Interbrand list is that the value of individual brands can change from year to year. One example is the Coca-Cola brand, which for many years was the leading brand by value, however more recently its ranking has been displaced by technology brands such as Apple and Google.

Process-based brand equity

This third emerging stream of research focuses on the value of relational and experiential aspects of branding. Research in this area was the result of increased interest about the role of branding in other areas such as services, business-to-business and electronic marketing. In these situations, customers' interactions and relationships with the organization providing the goods and services play a more important role than simply brand identity. In the relational context the organization is the primary determinant of brand equity in contrast to consumer-packaged goods marketing where the product is the determinant of brand equity. This broader perspective goes beyond brand identity and focuses on branding as a process. Thus the customers' relationships and experience with the organization are important determinants of brand meaning. In addition, what is also important is how the reputation and identity of the organization (aspects of the corporate brand) are associated with the product or service brand. Relational and experiential branding can also be important for consumer-packaged goods when the product category is complex and provides considerable choice, and where this choice involves perceived risk and high switching costs between brands.

In contrast to the entity-based branding research, empirical research about brand equity for services, business-to-business and electronic marketing is more limited and has only recently adopted a process approach. The implications for building brand equity by taking this process-based perspective is that interactive communications between buyers and sellers and other stakeholders need to be managed. In the electronic commerce environment information and communication technology (ICT) plays a central role in facilitating interactivity and in these situations the brand becomes a surrogate for trust about the service provision.

Network-based brand equity

This stream of research builds on the process-based approach and includes co-branding, brand alliances and networks. The network perspective of branding recognizes that the equity of the brand comes not only from the end-customer, but also from a range of relationships within the marketing system. Thus the equity is intrinsically linked with a network of associations with people, places, other brands and other entities (Keller, 2003). Some of these associations are based on joint activities between brands and their organizations, while other associations are based on less formal arrangements. Formal arrangements include sponsorship, joint promotions, co-branding, alliances and joint ventures.

The additional value or co-brand equity comes also from the network of other stakeholder relationships. Using more than one brand symbolically builds consumer trust and commitment in these relationships. Thus the corporate reputation and identity of the marketing organization play an important role. The network structure can be seen with business-to-business brands at the corporate, relationship and network levels (Rosenbröijer, 2001). This brand strategy is referred to as 'umbrella branding' where the equity of the umbrella brand augments the equity of the individual brand offerings.

Service-based brand equity

More recently Brodie et al. (2006) drew on the service-dominant logic articulated by Vargo and Lusch (2004) to develop a broader perspective of how the brand functions in the marketplace. Attention is given to integrating the role of the brand in the value-adding processes that create customer experience, dialogue and learning. In this broader theoretical framework the brand is conceptualized as a set of promises. This framework is developed by adapting the frameworks by Bitner (1995) and Grönroos (1996) about the way service value is delivered. The framework, which is outlined in Figure 14.1, allows for customer, employee and organizational perceptions of the service brand. The three types of marketing that influence these perceptions are:

1. External marketing (communication between the organization and its customers and stakeholders *making promises* about the service offer);
2. Interactive marketing (interactions between people working within the organization/network and end-customers that create the service experience associated with *delivering promises* about the service offer);
3. Internal marketing (the resources and processes *enabling and facilitating promises* about the service offer involving the organization and people working in the organization).

The promises framework extends to a network to explicitly take into account the perceptions of other stakeholders (retailers, media, government regulators, etc.). The promises framework suggests a broader context to examine the impact of brand, because the brand is seen to have meaning not only for end-customers but also for the brand-owning company and its responsibilities to employees and a broader network of stakeholders (Jones, 2005). The implications for conventional brand management in this wider, more community-orientated conception of brands and socially constructed notions of meaning are far-reaching.

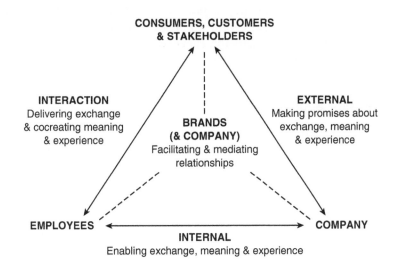

Figure 14.1 The service brand–relationship–value triangle.

Source: Brodie et al. (2006).

Within the promises framework, Brodie et al. (2006: 373) provides a definition of the service brand where it functions as both an entity and a process:

> Service brands facilitate and mediate the marketing processes used to realize the experiences that drive co-creation of value. They provide sign systems that symbolize meaning in the marketing network, and hence are a fundamental asset or resource that a marketing organisation uses in developing service-based competency and hence competitive advantage.

Thus the service brand equity can be defined as 'the differential effect of brand in the co-creation of value between the organisation, its customers and network of stakeholders'.

Brodie et al. (2009) provide empirical support for the service brand theoretical framework showing the importance of both the 'making of promises' (brand image with company image) and the 'delivery of promises' (employee trust and company trust) in creating customer value and customer loyalty. Further theory development and empirical research on the service brand has been undertaken by Fyrberg and Juriado (2009). Their research on service brands highlights the importance of networks and how these networks encourage interaction between customers and providers which produces customer value. The service brand relationship triangle underscores the function of a brand both as an entity and a process.

Equity and the value of other marketing assets

In the last decade, the term equity has been used to express the value of other marketing assets, such as channels, resellers and customers. These assets include relationships with other stakeholders such as retailers who form part of the value creation processes for brands. Srivastava et al. (1999) identify three business processes which are important in creating shareholder value: supply chain management, new product development and customer relationship management. In this section we examine the effects of brand equity on other types of equity in the channels of distribution and also discuss the customer equity concept.

Channel and reseller equity

While it is recognized that channel members as well as the end-customers have a role in creating marketplace equity, there has been a lack of research about how this occurs (Glynn et al., 2007). However, more general research about channels provides sound foundations to develop research in this area.

Anderson et al. (2009) propose the concept of marketplace equity, which is the value the customer receives through a reseller of branded goods. Marketplace equity is the joint result of brand equity, channel equity and reseller equity, but provides little further conceptual development. Reseller equity is the value of purchasing a particular brand though a reseller such as a distributor or retailer. Arnett et al.'s (2003) measurement of reseller equity shows that loyalty, awareness, product quality, value and service quality are important components. Srivastava et al. (1998) describe channel equity as the outcome of partner relationships between the selling firm and resellers in the channel. Channel relationships have strategic value because strong channel relationships can reduce financial commitment by channel members and this relationship dependence has benefits that enhance performance throughout the value chain. These long-term inter-firm relationships can increase return on investment so these types of relationships are often the firm's most important assets.

Channel equity is based on different attributes than those for brand equity. While brand equity is associated directly with consumer demand, channel equity is associated with derived demand and the network processes that supply goods in response to end-consumer demand. In research conducted with retailers of national brands, Davis and Mentzer (2008) showed that trade equity, which measured aspects of channel equity, had different effects on retailer dependence and commitment to the manufacturer compared to brand equity. Thus aspects of inter-organizational relationships such as experience and knowledge play a central role in conceptualizing channel equity.

Influence of brands on channel equity

Building strong manufacturers' brands has become more difficult due to increased brand competition and the emphasis on retail price promotions. There has also been an increase in the concentration of ownership of retail outlets that has resulted in shifts in power and control within the channels of distribution. Thus the 'trade leverage' provided by manufacturers' brands has been eroded and manufacturers have become more dependent on retailers. Understanding how to influence power and control within channels is thus an important issue.

The equity of the manufacturer's brand provides channel members several benefits, such as pre-established demand, lower selling costs, image and relationship enhancement of retailers with consumers, higher margins and better inventory management. However, retailers are also powerful within the channel and retailer costs such as cooperative advertising and slotting allowances can reduce the marketing funds available for manufacturers to build the brand–consumer relationship. Research by Glynn et al. (2012) shows that the brand benefits within the channel consists of four dimensions, including supplier support, customer expectations, financial benefits as well as brand equity. Of these four dimensions, brand equity had the least effect on reseller satisfaction.

To ensure that the equity of the brand is maximized, manufacturers' brands have focused on the inter-organizational requirements with retailers within the channels of distribution. Aspects of this relationship management approach with retailers (resellers) include: category management, efficient consumer response, promotions and pricing management. Conversely, manufacturer actions such as developing other channels and reducing supply chain costs can increase costs for the retailer. Thus the individual actions of both manufacturers and retailers can impact on the supply chain, leading to worsened channel relations and weakened channel equity.

Manufacturers' marketing strategies for a brand usually involve both activities with channel members and direct interactions with the end-customer. Thus implementing both these strategies means that channel, reseller and brand equity are interrelated. Examples of this interrelationship include the negative effect on brand equity of retailer price reductions, and the positive effect of a retailer's store image and distribution intensity (which reflects the brand's availability in the marketplace) on brand equity.

Customer equity

The customer-oriented view has been central in the managerial approach to marketing for a long time. However, there has been a shift from thinking about customer orientation to a focus on the nature and profitability of specific customers. This change in focus means issues about relationship building and customer retention have become more important. As a result metrics have been developed that measure the asset value of customers to the organization. The overall asset value of customers has been referred to as 'customer equity'.

Rust et al. (2000: 4) define customer equity as 'the total of the discounted lifetime values over all of the firm's customers' and identify three important components:

1. Value equity (the end-customer's perception of value);
2. Brand equity (the end-customer's emotional and subjective assessment of the brand above the perception of value); and
3. Relationship equity (elements that link the end-customer to the brand).

Vogel et al. (2008) in their investigation of customer equity show that value equity and brand equity are stronger drivers of loyalty intentions than relationship equity. Blattberg et al. (2001) provide a similar framework of customer equity that focuses on the associations between customer preference, image and customer retention and affinity for the brand. The measure of brand equity used in the customer equity framework differs from the traditional brand equity measures. These models also differ from the process and network models of brand equity because they are restricted to just considering end-customers. Thus these frameworks do not explicitly focus on the interactions and relationships between buyers and sellers or the network of interactions between brands.

Integrating with financial thinking

In this section we examine how these perspectives about brands can be integrated with financial concepts. The financial perspective is introduced and then ideas about relationships and governance mechanisms are examined.

A financial asset perspective of brand equity

The approaches to conceptualizing brand equity reviewed in this chapter provide initial thinking about brands as assets. Srivastava et al. (1998) have advanced this thinking by providing a more comprehensive theoretical framework. At a general level, the framework views market-based assets as consisting of external relationships such as customer relationships (brands and the installed customer base) and partner relationships (channels, co-branding and the network). To understand how these marketing assets create value, the first step is to examine how they influence market performance. Indicators of market performance include faster market penetration, price premiums, share premiums, extensions, reducing sales service costs and increased loyalty and retention.

The next step is to link market performance with financial value. This is achieved by using Rappaport's (1986) financial value planning approach. The approach uses four measures of cash flow that are assumed to determine financial value. These are increasing cash flows, enhancing cash flows, reducing volatility and vulnerability of cash flows, and enhancing the residual value of cash flows. It is recognized that there is considerable debate about which are the most appropriate financial valuation methods. Other valuation methods include: price/earnings multiples, market-to-book value ratio, economic value added (EVA), or cash flow return.

The specific types of market activities and types of market performance that influence the first three cash flow measures are summarized in Table 14.1. A fourth measure, 'enhancing the residual value of cash flows', is defined as 'the residual value of a business attributable to a business beyond a reasonable forecast period' (Srivastava et al., 1998). This measure is based on expectations about the ability of the organization to increase the size, the loyalty and the quality of the customer base.

Srivastava et al. (1999) extend their framework to include what they consider are the three core business processes that create financial value. These processes are product development management, supply chain management and customer relationship management. These authors then explore how marketing activities are embedded in these processes. In the case of brands, the dominant interactions and relationships are between the organization that supplies the goods and services and the end-customers. However there are also relationships between the organization and other internal and external stakeholders that

Table 14.1 Linking marketing activity and performance with cash flow and financial value.

Accelerating cash flow	Enhancing cash flow	Reducing volatility and vulnerability of cash flows
Achieving faster response to marketing efforts	Differentiation that leads to price/market share premiums	Enhancing loyalty and raising switching costs
Achieving earlier brand trials	Cross-selling products/services	Differentiation from shifting to services and consumables
Faster time to market acceptance	Developing new uses	Integrating operations to reduce capital requirements
Developing strategic alliances and cross-promotions	Reducing sales service costs Reducing working capital Developing brand extensions Developing co-branding and co-marketing	

Adapted from: Srivastava et al. (1998).

need to be considered. These include employees, distributors, retailers, other strategic partners, community groups, and even government agencies.

Srivastava et al.'s framework provides a useful starting point to conceptualize the nature of the relational and network activities that are associated with the core business processes. To extend the framework it is useful to draw on other literatures to help develop a more comprehensive description. These include the IMP[2] research, relationship marketing research and more general research on marketing strategy and strategic management relating to governance.

Integrating relationship and network thinking

IMP research focuses on the nature of the relationships and the resources between buyers and sellers. These relationships are built from interaction processes in which technical, social and economic issues are dealt with. Brands are resource ties that link these actors within the network. Relationships are developed to cope with increasing heterogeneity in supply and demand, coordinate sophisticated delivery mechanisms and provide innovation. The economic, social and technical interactions between buyers and sellers require trust and mutual commitment beyond legal control mechanisms. Thus markets are seen as institutions for coordination, cooperation and governance. Within these markets the economic content of the relationships is seen as an asset or market investment in a similar way to Srivastava et al.'s (1998) study. Thus the IMP research provides a richer contextual understanding about the nature of relational assets (Håkansson and Snehota, 2000).

The historical review of the value literature by Payne and Holt (2001) describes how the value chain, customer value and relationship value have been linked to financial value. They conclude that the relationship marketing perspective provides a more comprehensive long-term view of how financial value is created. This is because relationship marketing integrates other aspects of management. However, the division between what is 'relationship marketing' and what is 'relationship management' is somewhat arbitrary. For example Morgan and Hunt (1994: 22) define relationship marketing as: 'all marketing activities directed towards establishing and maintaining successful relational exchanges'. Morgan and Hunt's perspective is also important because it integrates the resource-based theory of the firm, thus providing a strong theoretical foundation across functional boundaries. As with the IMP perspective, it is recognized that it is not only the relationships between sellers and buyers that are important but also a network of other relationships and interactions both within the organization and external to the organization.

Gummesson (2008) develops a more elaborate classification of relationship types. After two decades of studying marketing organizations, he identifies 30 generic types of relationships that he categorizes into five groups. These are: mega-relationships (relationships on levels above the market proper, e.g. political and economic alliances between countries), inter-organizational relationships (such as alliances between companies), mass relationships (such as communications with different segments of a market), individual relationships and nano ('dwarf') relationships (such as relationships within an organization). In order to understand and manage these relationships, it is important to not focus on simple dyads alone (e.g. buyer and seller interactions), but to understand and manage *all* the networks of relationships and interactions around the dyad. This classification provides a framework to understand how networks of relationships create value for an organization. Similarly, Grönroos (2007) provides detail about how relationship value is created and managed by incorporating the service processes associated with relationships including brands

Integrating governance thinking

The notion of governance extends the understanding about coordination and cooperation in relationships. Governance refers to the formal and informal rules of exchange and the initiation, maintenance and termination of relationships between two parties. Heide (1994) outlines a typology of governance forms consisting of market, hierarchical and relational approaches. Market governance is associated with discrete types of exchange. Hierarchical or unilateral governance gives the right of one party to impose conditions on another. Relational or bilateral governance means a more open-ended relationship.

Ghosh and John (1999) extend the traditional transaction cost analysis framework using Heide's (1994) typology of governance mechanisms in channels. Transaction costs are costs such as search costs that are incurred in exchanges between buyers and sellers. Their framework addresses marketing strategy decisions, especially with regard to strategies grounded in cooperative relationships and investments with supply chain partners. End-customers can also make specific investments in the relationship. The investment by the end-customer is important in determining whether an organization decides to adopt an open or closed (proprietary) standard. They suggest that partners in a relationship devise governance forms to safeguard the value of their assets in order to maximize joint value creation. Thus stronger brands are in a better position to use market governance forms to build customer demand for the brand. However relational governance is better for weaker brands that benefit more from closer relationship with resellers. Many brands, especially high-priced brands, have product attributes that are not easy to assess, so brand expenditures as well as price premiums act as market governance forms and offer the buyer a safeguard against potential quality problems.

Towards a theory of brand equity and the value of marketing assets

This chapter has examined how the terms equity and value have been used in the various marketing discourses and the extent to which these terms have integrated financial thinking with marketing thinking. It has been shown that the term equity has been used extensively in the marketing literature and applied to a range of concepts. The initial focus was on entity-based brand equity for packaged consumer goods and the long-term financial value of advertising expenditure. More recently, the focus on brand equity has been extended to include all consumer goods, services and business-to-business brands where the brand functions as a process among stakeholders as well as an entity. The term has also been used to express the value of investments in channel relationships and other business relationships. In these situations the equity that is generated by marketing activity is much more than the end-customer's awareness and image of the brand and includes the value generated from customer and organizational relationships. This leads to the concept of the service brand equity where the brand functions as both an entity and a process. Service brand equity can be defined as the differential effect of brand in the cocreation of value between the organization, its customers and network of stakeholders.

Value has been used and defined in multiple ways in marketing, so it has taken on a number of meanings. In contrast, equity is a more neutral term than value and one that naturally integrates financial thinking with marketing thinking. Equity is also a financial term that can be easily understood and is meaningful across organizations and at all levels of management. It is also superior to the term 'goodwill' that has traditionally been used to describe the value of intangible assets and liabilities of a business. Thus it is suggested a theory of marketing assets should be centred on the term equity rather than value.

It is tempting to use brand equity as a vehicle to represent the value of everything associated with marketing, but the review in this chapter suggests its use needs to be restricted. Building on the ideas of Anderson et al. (2009), it is suggested that the term marketplace equity is a more useful concept that represents the value of all market-based assets. The marketplace equity for an organization comes from the broader network of relationships with channels, brands and other marketing entities and can be linked to the core business processes that create financial value. Thus brand equity is an important subset of marketplace equity.

When defining marketplace equity it is important to distinguish between the roles that marketing and other organizational activities play in the creation of value for an organization. Complications occur when distinguishing between what is relationship marketing and what is relationship management. A further problem occurs in defining market-based assets. For example, Srivastava et al. (1998) distinguish between relational and intellectual market-based assets. They define relational market-based assets as the outcomes of the relationships between the firm and its stakeholders, while intellectual market-based assets are defined as the types of knowledge and intelligence the organization has about its environment. However the development and evolution of relational and intellectual market-based assets are highly interrelated, to the point that they become difficult to separate.

It is suggested that Srivastava et al.'s (1998) market-based assets framework provides a useful starting point to develop a theory of marketplace equity. However the framework needs to be extended to link relational marketing and network thinking with the three core business processes that Srivastava et al. (1999) suggest are the drivers of financial value. In this framework, networks, relationships and interactions are the building blocks. Hence the IMP, relationship marketing and network literatures provide the necessary background. In addition, the ideas associated with inter-organizational governance provide a useful way to understand how coordination and cooperation occurs within networks and relationships.

Perhaps one of the biggest benefits in developing a theory of marketplace equity is that it focuses on the core business processes that deliver financial value in a way that incorporates the intellectual or knowledge aspects of marketing with other aspects of business. It also leads to the integration of the traditional entity-based consumer-based branding literature with the more recent process-based branding literature.

Another important consideration is to identify the underlying theories that a theory of marketplace equity should be based on. As shown by Hunt and Morgan (1995), relationship marketing theory is to a large extent derived from the resource-based view of the firm. Thus it is suggested that the resource-advantage-based view of the firm provides a natural starting point to develop this middle-range theory. However as discussed in the previous section, there are important links between governance thinking, transaction cost analysis theory and relationship thinking. In addition, consumer-based branding modelling that has closer links to traditional microeconomic and psychological theories needs to be integrated. Thus further research is needed to resolve exactly where the foundations of a theory of marketplace equity lie, and how these theories contribute to this more applied or middle-range theory.

Of particular importance is how a theory of marketplace equity relates to what is an emerging general theory of markets and marketing based on the service logic. Vargo and Lusch's (2004) initial eight fundamental premises have now been modified and extended to 10 (Vargo and Lusch, 2008). Of these, they suggest four premises are core to developing a general theory of markets. These are:

FP1: Service is the fundamental basis of exchange.

FP6: The customer is always a cocreator of value.

FP9: All economic and social actors are resource integrators.

FP10: Value is always uniquely determined by the beneficiary.

FP1 highlights the need to focus on the application of knowledge and skills; FP6 emphasizes the interactional nature of value creation; FP9 emphasizes the context of value creation is within networks; and FP10 recognizes that value is idiosyncratic. These and the other six fundamental premises provide a foundation to inform a middle-range theory of marketplace equity.

Further consideration also needs to be given to how a theory of marketplace equity links with more general financial theory about assets and market equity. Srivastava et al.'s (1998) framework uses a planning approach and focuses on cash flow as the determinant of shareholder value. However there is a choice of other valuation methods including price/earnings multiples, market-to-book value ratios, economic value added (EVA), cash flow return on investment (CFROI) and market value added (MVA) that could be used. Thus the choice of valuation method and the more general issue of how a theory of marketplace equity links with general financial theory require further consideration.

Finally, the development of a theory of marketplace equity provides a number of important managerial implications. As Doyle (2000) has emphasized, this 'new' marketing thinking leads to a better understanding about the role marketing plays in value creation in an organization. Rather than just focusing on brand or customer equity, the theory leads to a more comprehensive framework about the core business processes that create financial value. This framework can be used to explore tradeoffs in the way marketing resources can be allocated within a marketing system. The theory provides a better way to understand the extent an organization's marketing strategy should focus on end-customers versus investments in channels and other business processes. It also leads to better understanding about how to manage alliance activities with other organizations and relationships with key stakeholders within the organization's network.

Notes

1. This chapter is based on the authors' article 'Towards a theory of marketplace equity: integrating branding and relationship thinking with financial thinking', *Marketing Theory* 2(1): 5–28, 2002.
2. IMP stands for the International/Industrial Marketing and Purchasing project and involves a group of international researchers who have undertaken collaborative research into business organizations since the mid-1970s. Håkansson and Snehota (2000) provide a good overview of the nature of its research and its history.

Recommended further reading

Ghosh, M. and John, G. (2005) 'Strategic fit in industrial alliances: an empirical test of governance value analysis', *Journal of Marketing Research* 42(3): 346–57.

Glynn, M.S. (2009a) 'Integrating brand, retailer and end-customer perspectives', *Marketing Theory* 9(1): 133–6.

Kirk, C.P., Ray, I. and Wilson, B. (2013) 'The impact of brand value on firm valuation: the moderating influence of firm type', *Journal of Brand Management* 20(6): 488–500.

Leone, R.P., Rao, V.R., Keller, K.L., Luo, A.M., McAlister, L. and Srivastava, R. (2006) 'Linking brand equity to customer equity', *Journal of Service Research* 9(2): 125–38.

Merz, M.A., He, Y. and Vargo, S.L. (2009) 'The evolving brand logic: a service-dominant logic perspective', *Journal of the Academy of Marketing Science* 37(3): 328–44.

References

Aaker, D.A. (1996) *Building Strong Brands*. New York: The Free Press.

AMA (American Marketing Association) (2004) Available at: http://www.marketingpower.com/_layouts/dictionary.aspx?dLetter=B.

Anderson, J.C., Narus, J.A. and Narayandas, D. (2009) *Business Market Management: Understanding, Creating and Delivering Value*, 3rd edn. Upper Saddle River, NJ: Prentice-Hall.

Apelbaum, E., Gerstner, E. and Naik, P.A. (2003) 'The effects of expert quality evaluations versus brand name on price premiums', *Journal of Product & Brand Management* 12(3): 154–65.

Arnett, D.B., Laverie, D.A. and Meiers, A. (2003) 'Developing parsimonious retailer equity indexes using partial least squares analysis: a method and applications', *Journal of Retailing* 79(3): 161–70.

Bitner, M.J. (1995) 'Building service relationships: it's all about promises', *Journal of Academy of Marketing Science* 23(4): 246–51.

Blattberg, R.C., Getz, G. and Thomas, J.S. (2001) *Customer Equity: Building and Managing Relationships as Valuable Assets*. Boston, MA: Harvard Business School Press.

Brodie, R.J., Glynn, M.S. and Van Durme, J. (2002) 'Towards a theory of marketplace equity integrating branding and relationship thinking with financial thinking', *Marketing Theory* 2(1): 5–28.

Brodie R.J., Glynn, M.S. and Little, V. (2006) 'The service brand and the service dominant logic: missing fundamental premise or the need for stronger theory', *Marketing Theory* 6(3): 363–79.

Brodie, R.J., Whittome, J.R.M. and Brush, G.J. (2009) 'Investigating the elements of the service brand: a customer value perspective', *Journal of Business Research* 62(3): 345–55.

Davis, D.F. and Mentzer, J.T. (2008) 'Relational resources in interorganizational exchange: the effects of trade equity and brand equity', *Journal of Retailing* 84(4): 435–48.

Doyle, P. (2000) 'Value-based marketing', *Journal of Strategic Marketing* 8(4): 299–311.

Fyrberg, A. and Juriado, R. (2009) 'What about interaction? Networks and brands as integrators within service-dominant logic', *Journal of Service Management* 20(4): 420–32.

Ghosh, M. and John, G. (1999) 'Governance value analysis and marketing strategy', *Journal of Marketing* (special issue) 63: 131–45.

Glynn, M.S., Motion, J.M. and Brodie, R.J. (2007) 'Sources of brand benefits in manufacturer–reseller B2B relationships', *Journal of Business & Industrial Marketing* 22(6): 400–9.

Glynn, M., Brodie, R.J. and Motion, J. (2012) 'The benefits of manufacturer brands to retailers', *European Journal of Marketing* 46(9): 1127–49.

Grönroos, C. (1996) 'Relationship marketing logic', *Asia-Australian Marketing Journal* 4(1): 7–18.

Grönroos, C. (2007) *Service Management and Marketing: A Customer Relationship Management Approach*, 3rd edn. Chichester: John Wiley.

Gummesson, E. (2008) *Total Relationship Marketing*, 3rd edn. Oxford: Butterworth-Heinemann.

Håkansson, H. and Snehota, I.J. (2000) 'The IMP perspective of assets and liabilities of business relationships', in J.N Sheth and A. Parvatiyar (eds) *Handbook of Relationship Marketing*. Thousand Oaks, CA: Sage.

Heide, J.B. (1994) 'Interorganizational governance in marketing channels', *Journal of Marketing* 58 (January): 71–85.

Hunt, S.D. and Morgan, R.M. (1995) 'The comparative advantage theory of competition', *Journal of Marketing* 54 (April): 1–18.

Jones, R. (2005) 'Finding sources of brand value: developing a stakeholder model of brand equity', *Journal of Brand Management* 13(1): 10–32.

Keller, K.L. (1993) 'Conceptualizing, measuring, and managing customer-based brand equity', *Journal of Marketing* 57(1): 1–22.

Keller, K.L. (2003) 'Brand synthesis: the multidimensionality of brand knowledge', *Journal of Consumer Research* 29(4): 595–600.

Kozlenkova, I.V., Samaha, S.A. and Palmatier, R.W. (2014) 'Resource-based theory in marketing', *Journal of the Academy of Marketing Science* 42(1): 1–21.

Lusch, R. and Harvey, M. (1994) 'The case for the off-balance sheet controller', *Sloan Management Review* 35: 101–5.

Madden, T.J., Fehle, F. and Fournier, S. (2006) 'Brands matter: an empirical demonstration of the creation of shareholder value through branding', *Journal of the Academy of Marketing Science* 34(2): 224–35.

Merz, M.A., He, Y. and Vargo, S.L. (2009) 'The evolving brand logic: a service-dominant logic perspective', *Journal of the Academy of Marketing Science* 37(3): 328–44.

Morgan, R.M. and Hunt, S.D. (1994) 'The commitment–trust theory of relationship marketing', *Journal of Marketing* 58(3): 20–38.

Payne, A.F.T. and Holt, S. (2001) 'Diagnosing customer value: integrating the value process and relationship marketing', *British Journal of Management* 12(2): 159–82.

Rappaport, A. (1986) *Creating Shareholder Value*. New York: The Free Press.

Rosenbröijer, C.-J. (2001) 'Industrial brand management: a distributor's perspective in the UK fine-paper industry', *Journal of Product & Brand Management* 10(1): 7–25.

Rust, R.T., Zeithaml, V.A. and Lemon, K.N. (2000) *Driving Customer Equity: How Customer Lifetime Value is Reshaping Corporate Strategy*. New York: The Free Press.

Srivastava, R.K., Shervani, T.A. and Fahey, L. (1998) 'Market-based assets and shareholder value: a framework for analysis', *Journal of Marketing* 62(1): 2–18.

Srivastava, R.K., Shervani, T.A. and Fahey, L. (1999) 'Marketing, business processes and shareholder value: an organizationally embedded view of marketing activities and the discipline of marketing', *Journal of Marketing* (special issue) 63: 168–79.

Vargo, S.L. and Lusch, R.F. (2004) 'Evolving to a new dominant logic for marketing', *Journal of Marketing* 68 (January): 1–17.

Vargo, S.L. and Lusch, R.F. (2008) 'Service dominant logic: continuing the evolution', *Journal of the Academy of Marketing Science* 36(1): 1–10.

Vogel, V., Evanschitzky, H. and Ramaseshan, B. (2008) 'Customer equity drivers and future sales', *Journal of Marketing* 72(6): 98–108.

Webster, F.E.J., Malter, A.J. and Ganesan, S. (2003) 'Can marketing regain its seat at the table?', Working Paper Series, Marketing Science Institute. Cambridge, MA. Available at: http://www.msi.org/publications/publication.cfm?pub=659.

Innovation and New Product Development

Susan Hart

Chapter Topics

Overview	361
Introduction	362
New product development models	363
A critique of new product development process models	370
Factors affecting success and failure of new product development	373
Summary	382

Overview

The subject of new product development, much like marketing, according to Baker (1973), is 'synthetic', drawing on multiple disciplinary and domain bases of literature. Yet the synthesis is rarely realized, as, in the nature of much scientific enquiry, the concepts, frameworks and vocabularies used remain locked in separate traditions, journals, conferences and networks, which tend, at best, to reference only a few of the overlapping and interconnected threads of discussion. Based on literature(s) spanning some 40 years, the premise of this chapter is that while new product development (NPD) is fundamentally cross-disciplinary, both in terms of a field of study underpinned by multiple theories and as a business function, both markets and customers as well as technology management form twin focal points around which theoretical and practical perspectives are examined. The primary objectives of the chapter are:

1. To present the multidisciplinary nature of NPD;
2. To identify the centrality of the process in NPD and distinguish other factors leading to the successful development of new products, including inter- and intra-organizational structures, people and information;
3. To describe the core activities (models) commonly used to guide new product success;
4. To calibrate the utility of process models for theory and practice.

Introduction

The purpose of this chapter is to synthesize the major theoretical perspectives on the issues involved in developing successful new products and services. In early writings the term 'new products' was largely confined to physical products and much of the traditional research into NPD was implicitly concerned with *consumer* physical products. Alternative terminology, reflected in the major organ of dissemination of NPD research – the *Journal of Product Innovation Management* – is the term 'product innovation', which is more expansive in its array of topics, including radical, technological and service perspectives on innovation. Across the journal spectrum, wider attention given to the dominance of service as the focus of exchange has resulted in more attention being given to new service development – also known as service innovation (e.g. Ottenbacher et al., 2006; Storey and Hughes, 2013; Syson and Perks, 2004). The terminology of new product development and product innovation theory is connected to the context of physical products, since it is based on research whose major focus is, at least implicitly, concerned with physical products. The author, however, having conducted studies specifically focusing on service innovation, would contend that many of the ideas relating to product innovation are equally applicable to service innovation (Hart et al., 2008). A further area of interest in product innovation is concerned with 'discontinuous innovation', which the Marketing Science Institute identified as a significant research topic tied to the issue of economic growth. Yet, the traditional research on product innovation does not foreground the specifics of 'radical' or 'discontinuous' innovation, which is surprising, given that Michel et al. (2008: 54–66) demonstrate how discontinuous innovations 'significantly change how customers co-create value' and 'significantly affect market size, prices, revenues, or market shares'. Disruptive environments may require processes and organizational patterns quite different from those designated as appropriate for the more incremental, progressive type of product innovation, where the management of markets, competitors and organizations benefits from established norms and expectations. The chapter will therefore draw on perspectives from various technological contexts.

Central to an understanding of NPD theory is that contributions to theoretical understanding come from a number of broad journal domains, including management, marketing, strategy and research and development. Sub-fields within these broad domains include organizational behaviour, finance, psychology and technology management. In addition to theory development being located within these domains, and the existence of journals such as the *Journal of Product Innovation Management*, *Research Policy* and *European Journal of Innovation*

Management, two more specific 'domains' can be identified: one named simply New Product Development, and the other NPD and exploratory/atheoretic approaches (Page and Schirr, 2008). Further research domains which feature studies of NPD include operations research, design management, engineering and creativity/aesthetic studies. These bases give rise to a wide array of 'topics of study' in NPD, including:

- Organization for innovation
- Product development
- Entrepreneurship
- New product planning
- Technology innovation
- Supply chain
- Networks
- Organizational learning
- International comparisons.

Given this diversity of NPD research and theory themes, any attempt to produce 'new product development theory' in the confines of one chapter would be misguided. What is possible, however, is the identification of a number of themes forming the foundations of the development of knowledge in NPD. These are:

- The basic activities required to develop new products;
- The knowledge of what separates success and failure in NPD;
- The necessary considerations for NPD activities to be managed effectively, both inside and outside the organization.

The chapter, therefore, is split into three sections. The first gives an overview of various models of NPD in order to identify the tasks required to bring new products and services to market; next, a summary of research into the factors associated with success and failure in NPD is given; and the final section presents methods for developing the models with insights from studies of success and failure, including considerations of organizational structure, people and information management.

New product development models

Process models of NPD enumerate and organize the activities needed to complete a project and they are therefore general in their orientation and often criticized for not being applicable to individual contexts. For example, does the development of new services require different stages in the models? Will high-tech product development follow the same steps as fast-moving consumer goods? In a reflection on debunking the myths of his Stage-Gate™ model, Cooper (2008a) pointed out that models take numerous forms and have evolved in their level of prescription over the years. Early representations of new product development models were confining, often describing the NPD process by focusing on the departments or functions that were presumed to carry out various tasks. Over the last three decades these early representations evolved, becoming increasingly based on activities, which were recognized to be fluid, overlapping, open systems, which retain a reference process, widely known examples being the Booz Allen Hamilton model of new product development (1968) and Cooper's Stage-Gate™ system for major new product developments (Cooper, 2001).

These commonly comprise periods of development activity, followed by points of evaluation (gates), where the decision to continue (or not) with the development is made. Both the existence and importance of feedback loops are implicit in these models, but in the work of Hart et al. (2003) each stage is viewed in terms of its potential output into the next stage of the development, as shown in the further refinement of the process in Figure 15.1.

The key stages are briefly summarized below.

Idea generation

There are a number of terms used to describe the stage – or indeed stages – involved in bringing new ideas to the fore for development consideration, including 'idea generation', ideation and 'the fuzzy front end' (of the development process). In many instances, the term idea *generation* might be perceived as inappropriate because ideas abound in organizations and often do not have to be 'generated'. They must, however, be managed. It is tempting when thinking of successful new products that the basic idea behind them was so good, they were bound to succeed. For example, mobile music gadgets, from the Walkman through MP3 and 4, to music systems such as iTunes or Spotify seem, once established in the market, inevitable successes. But could they have failed with a different execution? The basic idea is that portable, personal audio entertainment might have been realized by means of: a bulkier headset which contains the tape-playing mechanism and earphones; a small hand-held player, complete with carrying handle, attached to earphones via a cord; a 'backpack' style player with earphones, player device attached to spectacles, sunglasses or forms of head gear. All of these ideas would have delivered to the idea of 'portable, personal audio entertainment', but could they have enjoyed the same success as the Walkman, Discman, Flashdrives, iPod, Spotify, to name but a few? Then there is the issue of an idea whose time has (or has not) come. Take, for example, the lightweight, low-pollution, low-cost, easily-parked town car. One realization of the idea took place 30 years ago – a three wheeler, battery-run (with 80 km worth of charge), and an optional roof. This realization is, of course, the widely quoted failure, the C5. Yet the basic idea remains a good one. It is, however, important to work out how to translate ideas into realities that will work, to turn failed ideas into successes, such as, for example, the Smart car, which enjoys sales in 36 countries – a total of 770,256 units sold between the launch in 1997 and 2006 – or Renault's Twizy, another electric small, single-seater car, which has sold over 12,000 units since its launch in 2012. The point here is that the 'idea generation' by itself is no guarantee of success; ideas which form the output of this first stage must fall within the mission of the organization and what it seeks to achieve with its NPD efforts, and be amenable to further development, evaluation and management. New product idea sources exist in and outside the firm. Internal sources include technical areas such as R&D, design, engineering – all of which work on translating applications and technologies

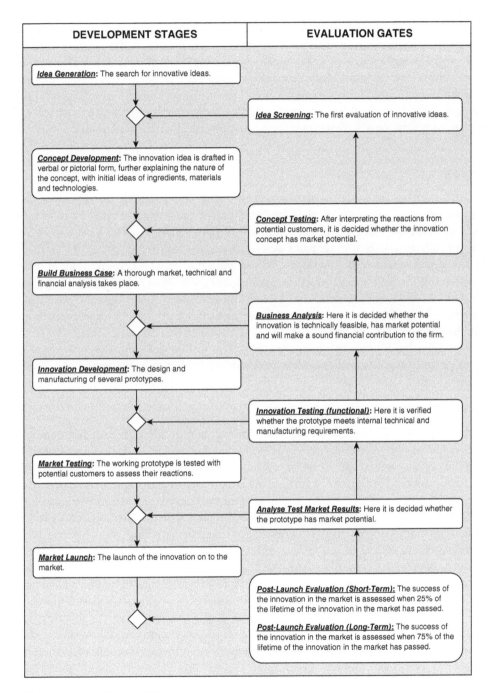

Figure 15.1   Evaluation Gates in NPD Models.

into new product ideas. Customer-facing functions such as sales and marketing can provide ideas and many company employees may have actionable ideas. Outside the company, distributors, inventors and universities as well as competitors and customers provide rich sources of information from which new product ideas may flow, if organized in such a way as to extract ideas. Much of the theory in NPD deals explicitly with how fertile repositories of information might be activated, using a battery of techniques, including simple brainstorming or one of its many derivatives, morphological analysis, perceptual mapping and scenario planning.

Screening

The second stage in the NPD process is a preliminary evaluation of the extent of the likely demand for the ideas generated and of the capability of the company. As the first of a number of stages of evaluation (see Figure 15.1), only a rough estimation of an idea can be made as it is not yet fully expounded in terms of design, materials, features or price. The primary locus for the initial judgement of the viability of ideas will be internal company opinion from R&D, sales, marketing, finance and production, against criteria such as whether the idea would fit a market demand and could be produced by existing plant, and to estimate the payback period. Recent research by Markham and Lee (2013) suggests that firms linking these evaluations more formally to the budget have higher performance profiles. The output of this stage in the process is typically a bank of ideas which are suitable for further development. Much research has served to produce toolkits and checklists designed to guide this early appraisal of ideas.

Concept development and evaluation

The initial screening of ideas allows the development team to identify a smaller number which are assessed as having potential to be translated into more clearly specified propositions – new product concepts – which are fit to be evaluated for their fit with company capability and market expectations. This phase of further selection, specification and testing is part of what Koen et al. (2014) have studied as part of the 'front end development process', also known as the 'fuzzy front end'. It involves the task of transforming a new product idea into a fully elaborated new product concept and is more than semantic labelling. As Montoya-Weiss and O'Driscoll (2000: 145) explain, 'an idea is defined as the initial, most embryonic form of a new product or service idea – typically a one-line description accompanied by a high-level technical diagram. A concept, on the other hand, is defined as a form, technology plus a clear statement of customer benefit.' Essentially, there are two sub-phases concerned, the first requires that the idea be more fully elaborated, to include drafting of product or service features, levels of specification, materials, design, aesthetic values and so on. This in turn allows for a more careful presentation of the concept to potential customers, to allow assessment of market fit, done through direct customer research. In addition, the development team needs to assess which configurations are most compatible with current production plant, which require plant acquisition and which require new supplies. This step in the process is important to collect data that are also central to the full economic analysis to come (see below) but in addition, the iterations within the process allow for adjustment of the eventual product realization at significantly lower cost than after development begins. There are, in addition, many digital tools to facilitate the process, such as CAD packages, rapid prototyping, technology and web-based visualization, which can involve customers and other stakeholders to assist getting the product fit for market. The outcome of this step in the process is the information required to carry out the analysis of the full business case.

Business analysis

A pivotal stage, it is at this juncture that the major 'go vs. kill' decision will be made. There needs to be conviction at this point in time that the venture is potentially viable, because once physical development resources have been committed, expenditure will increase exponentially after this stage. The analysis of the business case, therefore, has to be thorough and comprises:

1. Estimation of potential total market, market share within specific time span, evaluation of competing products, likely price bracket, break-even volume, identification of early adopters and specific market segments;
2. Specification of technical aspects: production methods and implications, supplier identification and management, any further R&D required, or investment in plant, equipment or other know-how;
3. Justification of the project's fit with corporate strategy.

The sources of information for this stage are both internal and external, incorporating any market or technical research carried out thus far. Where the result of the business analysis is the decision to 'go' with the development, further stage output will be the development plan with budget and with an initial marketing plan.

Product development and testing

In the case of physical products, at this stage prototypes are physically made, involving several tasks. First, the prototype will be tested for its level of functional performance, sometimes called 'alpha testing'. Until this point, the product has only taken theoretical form – a description, drawing or model. Now that component parts are brought together in a functioning product, the viability of the theoretical product can be established. Second, although manufacturing considerations have entered into previous deliberations, only when the prototype is developed, can adjustments to the design or to manufacturing specifications be drafted and implemented. Third, potential customers now have the opportunity to assess their reactions to the product in its real, rather than depicted form. Some kinds of product are more easily tested by customers than others. Services and capital equipment are difficult to 'test', the former due to inseparability, and the latter due to logistics and cost implications. In the case of the latter, however, in situ testing of new equipment, called 'beta testing', is practised widely. In consumer markets, numerous market research techniques are commonly used to test new products.

Product testing has been much aided by the use of the internet for a number of reasons. The cost of 'building' and 'testing' prototypes virtually is small compared to that required by physical prototypes. Consequently, market research costs are lower, and more concepts can be tested by potential customers than is the case with physical products, resulting in a final design which is more attuned to the voice of the customer. In addition, more end-customers can be sampled more efficiently via the internet, although the risk of population deterioration is increased as is the likelihood of bias, since not all potential customers selected will be willing to 'test' the product virtually. The output of this stage in the process is the final specification of the product, which will then be produced for the whole market, including the segment or geographical variations.

Test marketing

Test marketing consists of small-scale tests with customers. Until now, the idea, the concept and even the product have been 'tested' or 'evaluated' in contexts other than a 'real' purchase situation. Other elements of the marketing mix have not been tested, nor has the likely marketing reaction by competitors, nor the attractiveness of the product once offered alongside competing products. For test marketing, the total product appeal is evaluated among the mix of activities comprising the market launch: salesmanship, advertising, sales promotion, distributor incentives and public relations.

As an expensive stage, developers must decide whether the costs of test marketing can be justified by the additional information that will be gathered. Moreover, some new offerings are unsuitable for a small-scale test launch: cars have market testing complete before the launch, while services such as personal insurance cannot be withdrawn once launched on a small scale. The delay caused by a test market to the 'real' launch of the new product to market may benefit competitors, who, appraised of a new product launch in the offing, can use the delay to be 'first-to-market'. Alternatively, competitors may profit from the results of a test market as input to their own launch. Further, for some new services, a direct market entry (perhaps on a limited scale) is a viable strategy because new product launch has fewer tangible elements in which to invest, so costs (and therefore risks) are lower.

Test market simulations use basic models of consumer buying as inputs. Elements such as consumer awareness, trial and repeat purchases, collected via limited surveys or store data, are used to predict adoption of the new product. The most recent comparative performance study carried out for the Product Management Development Association (PDMA), by Markham and Lee (2013), has grouped the tools and techniques used across the concept design and product development phases, reporting that most frequently used across these phases are 'voice of the customer', customer site visits and beta testing, especially in the case of the more radical and innovative products. The better performing innovators used significantly more market research tools, including those mentioned above as well as online communities, lead users, concept tests and online focus groups/surveys, to name but a few. The most used engineering, R&D and design tools employed during these phases included critical path, PERT and GANNT, and these again were used more by the higher performing innovators. The output of this stage in the process is the final marketing mix and plan for the market launch.

Commercialization or launch

The last stage of the NPD process comprises decisions such as when to launch the product, where to launch it, how and to whom to launch, and is very costly. These decisions are based on information collected throughout the development process and will be moderated by the resources available. In recent years, there has been a surge in research interest on what makes up the dynamic of the stage of product launch, perhaps as a response to the relatively sparse attention given to launch in the early product development research literature, despite the large resource commitment required at this stage (Roberts and Candi, 2014). Decisions such as when to launch the product, where to launch it, how and to whom to launch it are based on tacit and experiential knowledge, as well as information collected throughout the development process. With regard to timing, important considerations include:

- Seasonality of the product;
- Whether the launch should fit any trade or commercial event;
- Whether the new product is a replacement for the old one;
- Whether it is advantageous to be first to market (much debate exists regarding this decision).

The factors upon which such decisions will be based depend upon the required lead-times for the product to reach all the distributive outlets and the relative power and influence of channel members. While the possibilities of the internet make instant, international product launch possible in terms of the announcement of market entry, fulfilment still requires consideration being given to lead-times, distribution negotiations and market and supply chain familiarization where the product is new to the market.

Launch strategy encompasses any advertising and trade promotions necessary. Space must be booked, copy and visual material prepared, both for the launch proper and for the pre-sales into the distribution pipeline. The salesforce may require extra training in order to sell the new product effectively.

Attention has been given recently to those activities that are internally directed to support the new product – or particularly service – launch. For example, the research by Kuester et al. (2012) observed that across a sample of over 700 companies in both B2B and B2C industries the internally directed launch activities had a direct effect on the success of the external product launch. These activities are directed at management and employees involved in organizing the launch and contribute to fast market penetration of the new product by highlighting the complexities and proper incentivization of the whole launch cycle and its intended outcome.

The final target segments should not be, at this stage, a major decision for companies who have developed a product with the market in mind and who have executed the various testing stages. Attention should be more focused on identifying the likely early adopters of the product and on focusing communications on them. In industrial markets, early adopters tend to be innovators in their own markets. A recent study by Talke and Snelders (2013) studied the different types of messages and their response in the adoption of new high-tech products. They found that adoption behaviour of consumers is positively affected by the inclusion of information on the personal and social consequences of using the new product, especially when such information is presented by using examples and figurative descriptions. Additionally, they found that when technical and financial information is conveyed using fact-based descriptions and specifications, there is also a positive and strong impact on adoption of the new product. This research and others in the same field underline the importance of using market research throughout the development and evaluation process to ensure that the right information will be presented in the right form to the intended market segment(s). The central concerns of the launch should be the development of a strong, unified message to promote to the market and to ensure that supply and delivery chains are stocked and equipped to fulfil demand and orders. Once accepted by the market, the company will elicit feedback to continue the improvement and redevelopment of the product.

A critique of new product development process models

One of the keys to the usefulness of the staged process models is the indication they provide regarding the magnitude of the project required to develop and launch a new product. A study in the UK by Hart, Tagg and Ozdemir (2008) reported 'variable recognition' of the different stage gates in the NPD process, more recently Markham and Lee (2013) report that 49.1% of the 383 firms responding to the PDMA comparative performance study claimed to have a formal, cross-functional process for NPD. This contrasts with previous PDMA surveys which showed that in 1994, 69% of firms reported such a process. Despite the decrease in the overall reported usage of such models, Markham and Lee (2013) observed in their study that significantly more of the higher performing product developers (labelled *The Best*) used cross-functional models, whereas the remainder of the survey respondents (labelled *The Rest*) used the relay approach (department to department as each task is completed) to a greater extent. Despite the fact that the foundations of these models were laid down over two decades ago, researchers and practitioners alike tend to base their discussions and practices on a framework which attempts to capture the really important capabilities concerned with directing and controlling the NPD process to ensure the efficient use of scarce resources. In other words, the development of capabilities is often embedded within the frameworks of NPD models, although both their iterative nature and cross-functional and multidisciplinary input 'disrupt' a simple view of these frameworks.

Iteration and cross-functional development

As noted above, the topic of NPD is multidisciplinary, mirroring the multifunctional tasks required to identify and develop a new product that is fit for purpose in the market. The single-strand linear representation ignores these multifunctional inputs, which include marketing, technical (design) and production tasks or decisions that occur as the process unwinds. Each of these strands of development creates both problems and opportunities within the other two. For example, if, at the product development stage, production has difficulties which push costs up, this could affect market potential through increased pricing rendering the product less attractive to potential buyers. In this case, the new information requires reworking of the market and technical assumptions. New courses of action might include a new design, alternative distribution, acceptance of longer payback horizons, none of which are represented by the single-strand view of NPD. Whatever the nature of the final solution, it has to be based on the interplay of technical, marketing and manufacturing development issues, meaning that product development activity is iterative, not only between stages, but also within stages.

It is also worth noting that the NPD process is idiosyncratic to each individual firm and to the new product project in question. Its shape and sequence depend on the type of new product being developed and its relationship with the firm's current activities (Cooper, 1988; Hart et al., 2008; Markham and Lee, 2013). In addition to the need to adapt the process to individual instances, it should be stated that in real situations there is no clear beginning, middle and end to the NPD process.

For example, from one idea, several product concept variants may be developed, each of which might be pursued. Also, as an idea crystallizes, the developers may assess the nature of the market need more easily and the technical and production costs become more readily identified and evaluated.

The iterative nature of the NPD process results from the fact that each stage or phase of development can produce numerous outputs which implicate both previous development work and future development progress. Using the model provided by Booz Allen and Hamilton, if a new product concept fails the concept test, then there is no guidance as to what might happen next. In reality, a number of outcomes may result from a failed concept test, and these are described below and depicted in Figure 15.2.

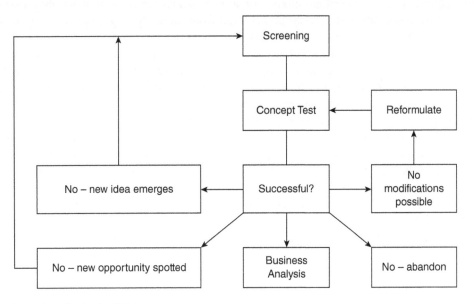

Figure 15.2   Iteration in the NPD Process.

- *A new idea/opportunity.*
  It is possible that although the original concept is faulty, a better one is found through the concept tests; it would then re-enter the development process at the screening stage.

- *A new customer.*
  Alternatively, a new customer may be identified through the concept testing stage, since the objective of concept testing is to be alert to customer needs when formulating a new product. Any new customers would then feed into the idea generation and screening process.

Related strands of development

A further point in relation to the sequencing of product development tasks is the existence of related strands of development. These related strands of development refer to marketing, technical (design) and production tasks or decisions that occur as the process unwinds. Each strand of development gives rise to problems and opportunities within the other two. For example, if, at the product development stage, production people have a problem which pushes production costs up, this could affect market potential. The marketing and technical assumptions need to be reworked in the light of this new information. A new design may be considered, or a new approach to the marketplace may be attempted. The crucial issue here is that the activity- and decision-stage models do not adequately communicate the horizontal dimensions of the NPD process.

This shortcoming resulted first in the advancement of the idea of 'parallel processing', later 'process concurrency' which acknowledges the iterations between and within stages, categorizing them along functional configurations. The idea of parallel processing is highly prescriptive: it advises that major functions should be involved from the early stages of the NPD process to its conclusion. This, it is claimed, allows problems to be detected and solved much earlier than in the classic task-by-task, function-by-function models. In turn, the entire process is much speedier, which is now recognized to be an important element in new product success. It should be mentioned that a substantial amount of what has been written about the concept of parallel processing is in the engineering domain.

Although greater integration through parallel processing has been attempted by various technical disciplines, for example manufacturing and engineering, the market perspective still appears to be 'tacked on' in the technical and engineering literature. True multidisciplinary integration, embracing technical and commercial functions, is seen as crucial to the outcome of new products and will be considered later in the chapter. Examination of different projects at Hewlett Packard led Rivas and Gobeli (2005) to conclude that freely distributed information, across multifunctional teams where there were clearly identified roles, is a crucial lesson for success. Recent research by Drechsler et al. (2013) showed that marketing as a distinct function contributing to the NPD processes was important for driving innovation success and that distinct marketing capabilities, together with an influential status of marketing in the NPD process, forge higher levels of marketing performance. So, there remains a strong case for multifunctional involvement in NPD to integrate technical and market knowledge to bring a successful innovation to market. While there is significant face validity in the view that successful NPD needs multifunctional perspectives to enhance success, there is also a large body of evidence, reviewed by Gerwin, Sprott and Barrowman in 2002, to suggest that process concurrency enhances NPD performance; however, a more recent study by Ahmad et al. (2013) did not find evidence of an association between process concurrency and NPD performance.

The inclusion of third parties in the process

Another criticism of the 'traditional' process models is that they fail to show the importance of parties external to the firm, who can have a decided impact on the success of new product development. Several studies have shown the importance of involving users in the NPD process to increase success rates (Hillebrand and Biemans, 2004; Thomke and von Hippel, 2002; von Hippel, 1978). Equally, there is growing interest in the need for greater supplier involvement, in order to benefit from the advantages of supplier innovation and just-in-time (JIT) policies.

These observations bring into focus the way the NPD process is organized, to account for multifunctional inputs, to allow for iteration and to involve third parties. These issues are picked up at the end of this chapter in discussing the management of NPD across, as well as within, organizational boundaries.

The next section of the chapter looks at the wider body of literature which informs theory by identifying factors beyond the process activities which have an impact on new product success and failure.

Factors affecting success and failure of new product development

There have been several 'stages' of product development research associated with optimizing product innovation outcomes. Prior to the early 'success/failure' (S/F) comparisons (Cooper, 1979), seminal work by Carter and Williams (1957) compared processes associated with different levels of outcome success. A meta-analytic study in 1994 by Montoya-Weiss and Calantone consolidated findings, as have Page and Schirr (2008), who suggested that the proportion of published articles analysing factors which differentiate successful and unsuccessful NPD is somewhat low (at about 4% of the total the authors consulted), while Guo (2008) estimated that 16% of the articles published in the *Journal of Product Innovation Management* between 1984 and 2005 were concerned with NPD performance measures and drivers. The PDMA has been active in promoting understanding of 'what works' in product innovation and has undertaken several best practices studies as well as the more recent comparative performance study (Markham and Lee, 2013). It is fair to say that the 'performance' studies have had a large and enduring impact on theory development in the field. In the PDMA best practices research, for example, 59% of products in development made it to market and of these, 60% are commercially successful. For decades, success (or failure) rates for NPD, reported in aggregate, tend to give varying results. Cooper (2001) gives a market success rate of 15%, while Hultink et al. (2000) reported an average 60% successful launch rate in the US, the UK and the Netherlands and in 2004, Cooper et al. report success rates of 60% on average. Over the years, much research has reported success rates for product innovation as between 35% and 75%, with a recent study reporting a more consistent average of 40% (Castellion and Markham, 2013). Although lower than some of the commonly cited failure rate figures of 80% plus (Friedman, 2011), there is ample impetus to find ways to improve the success rate in new product development, given its resource implications for organizations. Despite this variation, it is clear that a sizeable proportion of NPD effort goes to waste, encouraging researchers to continue to research factors that make a difference in bringing new products to market successfully. The next section gives a brief overview of the consistent themes in the findings.

The themes can be grouped at two levels: strategic and operational. The former is comprised of those factors that describe how an organization is managed as a whole, its strategic orientation, strategy for NPD, or top managers' styles. These have a vital contribution in setting the scene for new product development and can and do have a profound effect on the outcomes of development programmes. The latter refers to a number of task-specific factors, which although influenced by the strategic issues, exert their own influence on the outcome of *a particular* NPD project. This brief review, therefore, summarizes findings on success and failure across these two levels.

Strategic level success factors

Innovation strategy

The strategy of a company contextualizes its internal operation as well as its interfaces with the outside world. To be successful, theory advocates that NPD should be derived from the corporate strategy of the company, which in turn sets clearly defined objectives for its NPD endeavours. Beerens et al.'s (2004) report for Booz Allen Hamilton found that most companies have difficulty in controlling their product development activities. Symptoms included ignorance of the NPD roles and responsibilities, frequent reprioritizing of projects and the discovery of projects by top management previously unknown to them, and lack of robustness in the process and its management. In other words, a lack of a strategic focus on product innovation. Setting a clear strategy for new product development, on the other hand, not only provides guidelines for resource allocation, but also sets up the key criteria against which all projects can be managed through to the market launch. The approach Komatsu took to compete with Caterpillar throughout the 1970s and 1980s consisted of numerous strategies, among which feature the frequent launch of new products developed to extend the product lines, future new products based on envisioning programmes and a period of matching increased product variety with efficiency gains. The NPD benchmarking study by Cooper et al. (2004) found that more of the best performing companies defined the strategic areas for NPD, clearly identified NPD goals, took a long-term view of NPD and strategically allocated resources to portfolios of NPD projects. While it is often argued that new product development should be guided by a new product strategy, the strategy should not be so prescriptive as to restrict, or stifle, the creativity necessary for NPD. The history of Cannon's success is described by Hamel and Prahalad (2005) as one where their strategic intent ('beat Xerox') was broken down into a series of product (and market) development tasks, including competitive study and technology licensing to gain experience, developing technology in-house and selective market entry to exploit the weakness of the competition, before going on to develop completely new technological solutions in the form of disposable cartridges.

A recent discussion paper placed by Booz Allen Hamilton on their website by Dehoff and Neely (www.boozallen.com) noted that due to competing internal resources and priorities, the need to set priorities, clear barriers and instil focus was a distinguishing feature of good leadership that determined product innovation success. In the comparative performance assessment study, Markham and Lee (2013) report that senior managers in the best performing firms support innovation significantly more than in the rest of the firms surveyed. This comes as no surprise given that senior management is responsible for the articulation and delivery of how an organization will operate internally, and how it will approach the outside world. To be successful, NPD must be guided by, that is be derived from, the corporate goals of the company, and therefore there is a need to set clearly defined objectives for new product development projects. A new product strategy ensures that product innovations become a central facet of corporate strategies, that objectives are set and that the 'right' areas of business are developed. Thus, a critical success factor for NPD is the extent to which a specific strategy is set for guiding NPD efforts. The recent benchmarking study by Markham and Lee (2013) reported that there has been a drop in the proportion of firms overall that claim to deploy a specific new product strategy. In 2004, the benchmark study had reported 74% of firms having a new product strategy whereas in 2012, the figure had dropped to 60%. Within this broad statistic, however, a significantly higher proportion (76%) of the highest performing innovators still reported development of a new product strategy in comparison to only 54% of the rest of the sample of firms reported having new product strategies. These findings suggest that it is still important to have a new product strategy to articulate the direction and magnitude of the deployment of resources, but the drop in overall articulation of a new product strategy is still perplexing and raises the question as to whether this one study might be out of line with the general trends. A different perspective is taken by a recent meta-analytic review of new product success literature covering research studies spanning a 12-year period (1999–2011), which reported that among the most important predictors of success were new product strategy characteristics, such as market and technological synergy (familiarity with markets and technologies) and dedicated human and company resources (Evanschitzky et al., 2012).

While it is often argued that new product development should be guided by a new product strategy, it is important that the strategy is not so prescriptive as to restrict, or stifle, the creativity necessary for NPD. The historic assault by Komatsu on Caterpillar though the 1970s and 1980s was comprised of numerous strategies, among which feature the frequent launch of new products developed to extend the product lines, future new products based on envisioning programmes and a period of matching increased product variety with efficiency gains. New product strategy is an effective 'stage' because it helps provide the standard against which a development project might be judged, particularly in the early phases.

The way in which the strategic focus or intent of product development is formed can be seen as a function of four interrelated aspects: technology and marketing inputs, product differentiation, synergy and risk acceptance.

Technology and marketing.

There is in the literature, a broad acceptance that there should be a *fusion* between technology-led and market-led innovations at the strategic level, which is echoed throughout the studies reviewed by Evanschitzky et al. (2012). The examples of both Komatsu and Cannon, above, show how, at various times in their pursuits to topple the market leaders, both market and technology orientations have played their part. Similarly, problems can be found if one approach is allowed to dominate, despite competitive market and technological conditions. Classic examples include companies such as Kodak, which although dominant in analogue photography was less able when making the change to digital camera technology, or Nokia, where there are sequential examples of reluctance to change from current to new design forms, such as the flip phone in the mid-2000s to the later delay to invest in touchscreen technology.

In recent findings, Drechsler et al. (2013) report that the quality of marketing research and the capability to translate customer needs into technical product specifications positively contribute to the influence of marketing and to innovation performance.

Product differentiation and advantage.

New product literature has consistently referred to new product strategies which emphasize the search for a differential advantage, through the product itself. Once again, the most recent meta-review of the literature confirms product as one of only two product-related factors consistently associated with superior in-market performance (Evanschitzky et al., 2012). Product advantage is of course a subjective and multifaceted term, but may be seen as comprising the following elements: technical superiority, product quality, product uniqueness and novelty, product attractiveness and high performance to cost ratio (Hultink and Hart, 1998). In their attempt to rise to the competitive challenge of IT-based play products, the makers of iconic board games such as Scrabble and Monopoly, Hasbro, launched Hasbro Interactive. This new format began by converting Hasbro products to an interactive format and went on to develop video games bought on licence from TV shows before finally investing in a new internet platform, games.com (Govindarajan and Trimble, 2005).

Synergy.

A further consideration for those developing new product strategies, identified in the literature, is the relationship between the NPD and existing activities, known as the synergy with existing activities. High levels of synergy are typically less risky because a company will have more experience and expertise, although perhaps this contradicts the notion of pursuing product differentiation. With Hasbro, for example, the switch to interactive technology at first kept some synergies by sticking to the traditional games for which the company was known. Once the new interactive versions were successful, the company could then move to unfamiliar (less synergistic) games, before combining the completely new games with a new technological platform. Even then, there was a need for learning, as the corollary of less synergy is lack of knowledge. The Hasbro management team did not know whether it could turn other companies' video games into successes as it had done with its own games, nor did the team have any knowledge of how quickly video game players might switch to the internet (Govindarajan and Trimble, 2005).

Risk acceptance.

Finally, the creation of an internal orientation or climate which accepts risk is highlighted as major for the new product strategy. Although synergy might help avoid risk associated with lack of knowledge, the pursuit of product differentiation and advantage must entail acceptance that some projects will fail. An atmosphere that refuses to recognize this tends to stifle activity and the willingness to pursue something new. Again, the Hasbro example reveals some insights here. The original switch to an interactive platform took place back in 1997, and results for 1997/8 were strong. On the basis of early successes, the investment in the new platform was initiated but results in both 1999 and 2000 were disappointing. Risk was accepted, but almost blindly, since according to Govindarajan and Trimble (2005), there was a reluctance to make predictions, or plan, based on the idea that both would be wrong anyway, and that first to market was the key to success. There was therefore a lack of planning, a lack of learning, which meant that little attempt was made to ditch the initiatives that were not succeeding and to focus more resources on those that were doing well. A further example of the negative effects of not taking risks is the development of Nokia, where there was an admitted reluctance to take the risks necessary to keep up with, let alone lead, the new directions required to remain at the top of the mobile phone market internationally (Cheng, M., 2014, accessed at www.CNET.com).

Top management influence

Early research into success and failure examined the role of top management in the eventual success of NPD. The classic Stanford Innovation Project (Maidique and Zirger, 1984) found new product successes underpinned by a high level of top management support, as did the work of Hart and Service (1988), while Cooper and Kleinschmidt (1987) found less proof of top management influence, discovering that new product failures often do have the support of top management. In the comparative performance assessment study, Markham and Lee (2013) report that senior managers in the best performing firms support innovation significantly more than in the rest of the firms surveyed. This comes as no surprise given that senior management is responsible for the articulation and delivery of how an organization will operate internally, and how it will approach the outside world.

Top management plays a crucial role in setting the climate for innovation by signalling the nature of the corporate innovation culture (Goltz, 1986; Gupta and Wilemon, 1988; Gupta et al., 1986; McDonough, 1986). In some cases it is necessary for the firm to change its philosophy on NPD, in turn causing a change in the whole culture. Nike's NPD process changed dramatically during the 1990s, from a belief that every new product started in the lab to the view that it is the consumer who leads innovation. Research by Wei and Morgan (2004) in China has shown that the relationship between organizational climate and new product performance is in fact increased as climate affects market orientation. In other words, the climate of the firm affects how those responsible for NPD respond to the changing market conditions, which in turn affects the performance of NPD. Much of this resonates with the importance of top management involvement in product innovation strategy, a trend echoed in the comparative performance assessment study, which reports a decrease in the proportion of companies with an executive responsible for NPD at the business unit from 75.6% in 2004 to 62.6% in 2012, with a slight decrease in the participation of corporate level NPD responsibility, from 66.8% to 64.2% in the same time frame. That said, the study also reports an increasing trend towards greater seniority in the mix of managers engaged in NPD strategy. Setting a clear direction for new product development not only provides guidelines for resource allocation, but also sets up the key criteria against which all projects can be managed through to the market launch.

Operational level success factors

The previous paragraphs have reviewed the major *strategic* themes of theory development in NPD. Much of the research and theory base of product innovation, however, has been derived from examination of the way in which *specific* processes, the people involved and the role of information are instrumental in its outcome.

NPD process activities

Over the past 30 years, much research has examined what steps comprise the efficient and effective execution of the development process, an example of which was described earlier in this chapter. Companies including ExxonMobil, Bausch and Lomb, Air Products and Chemicals have specific processes guiding the development of new products in the belief that the payback from following these guidelines has improved their success rates (Cooper et al., 2004).

Although a fulsome completion of the NPD process may be desirable, each additional activity extends the overall development time and may lead to late market introduction, for which there can be penalties in terms of competitive advantage. Therefore a tradeoff has to be made between completing all the suggested activities in the NPD process and the time which these activities take.

Cooper et al.'s (2004) benchmarking report highlights that, in general, marketing tasks were more poorly carried out than the technical activities and that in particular, many firms do not have adequate go/no go decision points. A study of the Korean telecommunications market also highlights that in new service development, factors such as 'poor demand forecasting' and 'ineffective marketing strategies' are often associated with failure (Ahn et al., 2005). The importance of the market research activities in the NPD process has been often highlighted yet there is still a valid argument to suggest that any notion of formal market research may well be redundant, particularly if the customers' technical knowledge is inferior to that of the developer.

Despite the decrease in the overall reported usage of such models, Markham and Lee (2013) observed in their study that significantly more of the higher performing product developers (labelled *The Best*) used cross-functional models whereas the remainder of the survey respondents (labelled *The Rest*) used the relay approach (department to department as each task is completed) to a greater extent. Despite the fact that the foundations of these models were laid down over two decades ago, researchers and practitioners alike tend to base their discussions and practices on a framework which attempts to capture the really important capabilities concerned with directing and controlling the NPD process to ensure the efficient use of scarce resources.

Speed in the process

Eling et al. (2013) reported that new product strategy should articulate the desired 'time to market' to ensure optimum profit impact of speed, echoing many earlier studies which surfaced speed in the NPD process as an important factor, although various terms have been used, including: product development time (Lilien and Yoon, 1990), lead time (Ulrich et al., 1993), project completion time (Terwiesch and Loch, 1999), as well as time to market (Tatikonda and Montoya-Weiss, 2001). Relatedly, Cankurtaran et al. (2013) undertook a meta-analysis of the impact of speed on NPD outcomes, concluding that development speed is associated, overall, with new product success. With greater granularity in their findings which examined 52 independent samples' results, however, this study found that speed in process is more associated with customer and financial success than, for example, technical product quality. Theories relating to the nature of speed in process as a correlate of success, therefore, need to be more finely tuned, in order to reflect the tradeoffs that may be required with respect to the nature of the product innovation outcomes sought – market, technical, financial and so on.

Accommodation of third parties and networks

Several classic studies have shown the importance of involving users in the NPD process to increase success rates (Hillebrand and Biemans, 2004; Thompke and von Hippel, 2002; von Hippel, 1978). Equally, there is growing interest in the need for greater supplier involvement, in order to benefit from the advantages of supplier innovation and just-in-time (JIT) policies. For example, Dell shifted much of its component design work – laptop screens, optical drives – to supplier partners Dolan (2005). Recent research has emphasized the benefits of leveraging networks through the NPD process (Story et al., 2008), again requiring a flexible approach to modelling these processes.

This brief review of research into the correlates of success and failure in NPD does not claim to be exhaustive, but it does give a flavour of the variety of issues and disciplines central to furthering our understanding of the processes of product and service. Nearly all contributions to the literature on NPD, irrespective of the 'base discipline' of the author, will touch on aspects of either the process of development, or the people responsible for carrying out the process. The interrelationships between the two, however, are rarely given explicit attention, yet the development of theory requires acknowledgement of their interdependence and how they might be integrated from a theoretical perspective. The next section reviews these interdependencies and concludes with recent trends in thinking about how to manage the process and structure the people involved.

Interrelationships in process, people and management of NPD

The processes involved in developing new products and the people who carry them out are related to three of the most commonly cited critical success factors in NPD:

- *The need for interdisciplinary inputs.* In order to combine technical and marketing expertise, a number of company functions have to be involved: R&D, manufacturing, engineering, marketing, finance and sales. Linked to these is also the need for the voice of the suppliers, where changes to supply may be required or advantageous and other third parties, such as venture capitalists, brokers, and, increasingly, sources of intellectual property.
- *The need to develop product advantage.* Technical and market information, which are building blocks of NPD, have to be both accurate and timely, and must be constantly reworked in the light of changing circumstances during the course of the development, to ensure that the product under development has competitive advantage in the eyes of the customer. Therefore the *people* must deliver the appropriate expert information to inform the *process.*
- *The need for speed in the process.* As discussed above, the NPD process has to be managed in such a way as to be quick enough to capitalize on the new product opportunity before competitors do. The extent to which *people* work together enhances the speed of the *process.*

These three recurrent factors underline the importance of finding mechanisms and processes to encourage information sharing and decision taking across multiple boundaries both within one organization and across organizations. Research has covered a variety of aspects concerning these, for example, the R&D–marketing interface (Gupta and Wilemon, 1988); the marketing–design interface (see the *Journal of Product Innovation Management* Vol. 22, Nos. 1 & 2, 2005 for several articles in this area; in addition to Rubera and Droge, 2013); marketing and engineering (Michalek et al., 2005; Shaw and Shaw, 1998); marketing, R&D and finance (Hempelmann and Engelen, 2015). Whatever the precise focus of the integration, companies need to institute processes and design structures which promote integration and coordination, at the same time as preserving the efficiencies and, importantly, the expertise within functional speciality. Many alternatives have been described over the years, from bureaucratic control mechanisms towards more organic and participative structures, where the structural complexity of the mechanisms increases. Generally accepted principles agree that the more organic and participative approaches are more likely to share information across functional boundaries and to undertake interdependent tasks concurrently rather than sequentially (Olsen et al., 1995), echoing the classic theoretical contribution of Burns and Stalker (1961). Relatively organic mechanisms such as 'design teams' or 'new venture groups' have some important potential advantages for coordinating product development. Such participative structures can also create an atmosphere where innovative ideas are proposed, criticized and refined with a minimum of financial and social risk, while participative decision making, consensual conflict resolution and open communication processes of such a structure can help reduce barriers between individuals and functional groups.

More participative structures also carry potential disadvantages, especially in terms of costs and temporal efficiency. Creating and supporting several development teams can lead to an overabundance in staff and facilities. The main reason for this is that employees have less relevant experience when developing innovative product concepts and then depend more heavily on other functional specialists for the expertise, information and other resources needed to achieve a creative and successful product. Thus, there is potential for stagnation in the process if the focus of control is unclear. O'Reilly and Tushman (2004) describe what they call 'the ambidextrous organisation', to describe the challenges facing many organizations where they have to be able to exploit current products at the same time as exploring the future.

There is, however, a final set of issues which impact upon the management of product and service innovation projects, namely, the extent to which this now takes place in networks that cross firms' traditional boundaries.

Managing networks for NPD

In developing product innovations, it is recognized that firms tap into networks of external actors (Howells, 2006; Koschatzky et al., 2001; Pyka and Kueppers, 2002), although much of the research to date focuses on incremental or ongoing product innovation. This largely occurs within stable partnerships (Perez and Sanchez, 2003; Sivadas and Dwyer, 2000), and it has proven difficult to translate these insights to radical innovation (Birkinshaw et al., 2007), which relies upon more fluid, emergent and ambiguous networks (Håkansson and Waluszewski, 2002; Story et al., 2009; Tushman and Anderson, 1990). Möller (2010) specifically articulates that 'we lack frameworks that allow us to understand how firms can make sense of and navigate in radical innovation networks' (2010: 361–71). The difficulties associated with understanding how to facilitate radical innovation are further exacerbated by difficulties associated with identifying and defining radical innovations in the marketplace.

Although there has been an implicit within-firm perspective on much of the research into NPD and innovation, attention in specific quarters – for example, radical innovation and 'open' innovation, the importance of 'inter-organizational collaboration' and 'innovation networks' – has also been highlighted (Powell et al., 2005; Pyka, 2002). The fortunes of companies such as Wal-Mart and Microsoft have been attributed to their system of networks (Iansiti and Levien, 2004). Powell (1998) argues that in order to reduce the inherent uncertainties associated with new products or markets, inter-organizational learning in firm's networks plays a crucial role in creating a firm's competitive advantages. Eisenhardt and Martin (2000: 1107) define 'dynamic capability' as 'the firm's processes that use resources to integrate, reconfigure, gain and release resources – to match and even create market change ... by which firms achieve new resource configurations'. Dynamic capabilities consist of processes such as alliancing in product development, by which managers combine varied skills and functional backgrounds through inter-firm collaboration. Moreover, 'dynamic capabilities', by achieving new resource configurations, turn the inter-organizational relationships in new product development networks into another important topic: 'the changing dynamics of competition and cooperation' (Wind and Mahajan, 1997), which has resulted in a stream of emergent theory into 'co-opetition' (Cassiman et al., 2009; Ritala and Hurmelinna-Laukkanen, 2013).

Dittrich and Duysters (2007) have examined how innovation networks can be used to deal with a changing technological environment, concluding that innovation networks offer flexibility and speed in innovation together with the ability to adjust more smoothly to changing market conditions. Although there are some adjacent topics such as knowledge creation and transference in studying inter-firm learning in new product development networks, it is far from developed enough to be able to propose normative theory in this context. Of course, the broader topic of relationship marketing has not been widely studied in relation to innovation and product development, but as relationships are conceptualized as the means by which companies cope with their increasing interdependence, and build themselves into a network of interactions that are linked by economic, technical and social dimensions (Ford et al., 2003), this is a promising field for future theory development in NPD. In particular, the theoretical perspectives of transaction cost economics (Williamson, 1985), resource dependency theory (Pfeffer and Salancik, 1978), relational exchange theory (Dwyer et al., 1987) and models of business networks (Håkansson and Snehota, 1995) present fertile furrows for the NPD researcher to plough.

Summary

This chapter has outlined the evolution of NPD models and described the main tasks involved in the process of developing new products, including the importance of both strategic and tactical processes. Research on success and failure in new product development were then reviewed in order to point out those critical issues which developers of new products must manage actively if their efforts are to be successful. Finally, the chapter discussed some of the key structures used to organize NPD activities and considered emergent research which will develop further theory into the management of product innovation and development across networks, alliances and partnerships.

Recommended further reading

Baker, M. and Hart, S. (2007) *Product Strategy and Management*. Upper Saddle River, NJ: Prentice-Hall.
Cooper, R. (2011) *Winning at New Products: Creating Value Through Innovation*. New York: Basic Books.
Trott, P. (2011) *Innovation Management and New Product Development*. Upper Saddle River, NJ: Prentice-Hall.

Useful websites

http://www.boozallen.com
http://www.pdma.org/

References

Ahmad, S., Debasish, N.M. and Schroeder, R.G. (2013) 'New product development: impact of project characteristics', *Journal of Product Innovation Management* 30(2): 331–48.
Ahn, J.-H., Kim, M.-S. and Lee, D.-J. (2005) 'Learning from the failure: experiences in the Korean telecommunications market', *Technovation* 25: 69–82.

Baker, M.J. (1973) *Marketing: An Introductory Text*. London: Macmillan.

Beerens, J., Van Boetzelaer, A. et al. (2004) *The Road Towards More Effective Product/Service Development*. Chicago, IL: Booz Allen Hamilton.

Birkinshaw, J., Bessant, J. and Delbridge, R. (2007) 'Finding, forming, and performing: creating networks for discontinuous innovation', *California Management Review* 49: 67–85.

Booz Allen and Hamilton (1968) *Management of New Products*. Chicago, IL: Booz Allen Hamilton.

Burns, T. and Stalker, G.M. (1961) *The Management of Innovation*. London: Tavistock.

Cankurtaran, P., Langerak, F. and Griffin, A. (2013) 'Consequences of new product development speed: a meta analysis', *Journal of Product Innovation Management* 30(3): 465–86.

Carter, C.F. and Williams, B.R. (1957) 'The characteristics of technically progressive firms', *The Journal of Industrial Economics* 7(2): 87–104.

Cassiman, B., Di Guardi, M.C. and Valentini, G. (2009) 'Organizing R&D projects to profits from innovation: insights from co-opetition', *Long Range Planning* 42(2): 216–33.

Castellion, G. and Markham, S.K. (2013) 'Perspective: new product failure rates: influence of argumentum ad populum and self-interest', *Journal of Product Innovation Management* 30(5): 976–9.

Cooper, R.G. (1979) 'The dimensions of industrial new product success and failure', *Journal of Marketing* 43(3): 93–103.

Cooper, R.G. (2001) *Winning at New Products: Accelerating the Process from Idea to Launch*, 3rd edn. New York: Perseus Books.

Cooper, R.G. (2008a) 'Perspective: The Stage-Gate® idea-to-launch process – update, what's new, and nexgen systems', *Journal of Product Innovation Management* 25(3): 213–32.

Cooper, R.G. (2008b) 'Predevelopment activities determine new product success', *Industrial Marketing Management* 17, pp. 237–47.

Cooper, R.G. and Kleinschmidt, E.J. (1987) 'New products: what separates winners from losers?', *Journal of Product Innovation Management* 4(3): 169–84.

Cooper, R., Edgett, S. and Kleinschmidt, E. (2004) 'Benchmarking best NPD practices-I', *Research Technology Management* 47(1): 31–43.

Dehoff, K. and Neely, D. (2004) 'Innovation and product development: clearing the new performance bar', Discussion paper, Booz Allen Hamilton.

Dittrich, K. and Duysters, G. (2007) 'Networking as a means to strategy change: the case of open innovation in mobile telephony', *Journal of Product Innovation Management* 24: 510–21.

Dolan, K. (2005) 'Speed, the new X factor', *Forbes* 176(13): 74.

Drechsler, W., Natter, P. and Leeflang, P.S.G. (2013) 'Improving marketing's contribution to new product development', *Journal of Product Innovation Management* 30(3): 298–315.

Dwyer, F.R., Schurr, P.H. and Oh, S. (1987) 'Developing buyer–seller relationships', *Journal of Marketing* 51(2): 11–27.

Eisenhardt, K. and Martin, J. (2000) 'Dynamic capability: what are they?', *Strategic Management Journal* 21(10/11): 1105–21.

Eling, K., Langerak, F., Griffin, A. et al. (2013) 'A stage-wise approach to exploring performance effects of cycle time reduction', *Journal of Product Innovation Management* 30(4): 626–41.

Evanschitzky, H., Eisend, M., Calantone, R.J. and Jiang, Y. (2012) 'Success factors of product innovation: an updated meta analysis', *Journal of Product Innovation Management* 29 S1 (December): 21–37.

Ford, D., Gadde L.E., Håkansson H. and Snehota, I. (2003) *Managing Business Relationships*, 2nd edn. Chichester: John Wiley.

Friedman, H.H. (2011) 'Product policy; product development'. Available at: http://academic.brooklyn. cuny.edu/economic/friedman/mmproductpolicy.htm.

Gerwin, D., Sprott, E. and Barrowman, N.J. (2002) 'An evaluation of research on integrated product development', *Journal of Management Science* 48(7): 938–53.

Goltz, G.E. (1986) 'A guide to development', *R&D Management* 16: 243–9.

Govindarajan, V. and Trimble, C. (2005) 'Building breakthrough businesses within established organization', *Harvard Business Review* May: 58–68.

Guo, L. (2008) 'Perspective: an analysis of 22 years of research in JPIM', *Journal of Product Innovation Management* 25(3): 249–60.

Gupta, A.K. and Wilemon, D. (1988) 'The credibility–co-operation connection at the R&D marketing interface', *Journal of Product Innovation Management* 5(1): 20–31.

Gupta, A., Raj, S.P. and Wilemon, D. (1986) 'A model for studying R&D–marketing interface in the product innovation process', *Journal of Marketing* 50(2): 7–17.

Håkansson, H. and Snehota, I. (1995) *Developing Relationship in Business Networks*. London: Routledge.

Håkansson, H. and Waluszewski, A. (2002) *Managing Technological Development: Ikea, the Environment and Technology*. London: Routledge.

Hamel, G. and Prahalad, C.K. (2005) 'Strategic intent', *Harvard Business Review* July–August: 148–61.

Hart, S. and Service, L. (1988) 'Cross-functional integration in the new product introduction process: an application of action science in services', *International Journal of Service Industry Management* 4(3): 50.

Hart, S.J., Hultink, E., Tzokas, N. and Commandeur, H. (2003) 'Industrial companies' evaluation criteria in new product development gates', *Journal of Product Innovation Management* 20(1): 22–36.

Hart, S., Tagg, S. and Ozdemir, S. (2008) 'NSD vs. NPD dominant logic? An analysis of similarities and differences between the anatomy of the innovation processes in services and products: processes, stages and evaluation gates', Product Development Management Association Research Conference, Orlando, Florida, October.

Hempelmann, F. and Engelen, A. (2015) 'Integration of finance with marketing and R&D in new product development: the role of project stage', *Journal of Product Innovation Management* 32: 636–54.

Hillebrand, B. and Biemans, W. (2004) 'Links between internal and external cooperation in product development: an exploratory study', *Journal of Product Innovation Management* 21(2): 110–22.

Howells, J. (2006) 'Intermediation and the role of intermediaries in innovation', *Research Policy* 35(5): 715–28.

Hultink, E.J. and Hart, S. (1998) 'The world's path to the better mousetrap: myth or reality? An empirical investigation into the launch strategies of high and low advantage new products', *European Journal of Innovation Management* 1(3): 106–22.

Hultink, E.J., Hart, S., Robben, S.J. and Griffin, A. (2000) 'Launch decisions and new product success: an empirical comparison of consumer and industrial products', *Journal of Product Innovation Management* 17(1): 5–23.

Iansiti, M. and Levien, R. (2004) 'Strategy as ecology', *Harvard Business Review* 82(3): 68.

Koen, P.A., Bertels, H.M.J. and Kleinschmidt, E.J. (2014) 'Managing the front end of innovation – Part I: results from a three-year study: Senior management commitment, vision, strategy, resource commitment, and culture are the keys to front-end success', *Research-Technology Management* March–April.

Koschatzky, K., Kulicke, M. and Zenker, A. (eds) (2001) *Innovation Networks: Concepts and Challenges in the European Perspective*. Heidelberg: Physica.

Kuester, S., Homburg, C. and Hess, S.C. (2012) 'Externally directed and internally directed market launch management: the role of organizational factors in influencing new product success', *Journal of Product Innovation Management* 29 S1 (December): 38–52.

Lilien, G.L. and Yoon, E. (1990) 'The timing of competitive market entry: an exploratory study of new industrial products', *Management Science* 36(5).

McDonough, E.F. III (1986) 'Matching management control systems to product strategies', *R&D Management* 16: 141–9.

Maidique, M.A. and Zirger, B.J. (1984) 'A study of success and failure in product innovation: the case of the US electronics industry', *IEEE Transactions on Engineering Management* 31: 192–203.

Markham, S.K. and Lee, H. (2013) 'Product development management association's 2012 comparative performance assessment study', *Journal of Product Innovation Management* 30(3): 408–29.

Michalek, J.J., Feinberg, F.M. and Papalambros, P.Y. (2005) 'Linking marketing and engineering product design decisions via analytical target cascading', *Journal of Product Innovation Management* 22(1): 42–62.

Michel, S., Brown, S.W. and Gallan, A.S. (2008) 'An expanded and strategic view of discontinuous innovations: deploying a service-dominant logic', *Journal of the Academy of Marketing Science* 36(1): 54–66.

Möller, K. (2010) 'Sense-making and agenda construction in emerging business networks – how to direct radical innovation', *Industrial Marketing Management* 39(3): 361–71.

Montoya-Weiss, M.M. and Calantone, R.J. (1994) 'Determinants of new product performance: a review and meta-analysis', *Journal of Product Innovation Management* 11(5): 397–417.

Montoya-Weiss, M. and O'Driscoll, T. (2000) 'Applying performance support technology in the fuzzy front end', *Journal of Product Innovation Management* 17(2): 143–61.

Olsen, E.M., Walker, O.C. Jr and Ruekert, R.W. (1995) 'Organising for effective new product development: the moderating influence of product innovativeness', *Journal of Marketing* 59(1): 48–62.

Olsen, E.M., Walker, O.C. Jr, Ruekert, R.W. and Bonner, J.M. (2001) 'Patterns of cooperation during new product development among marketing, operations and R&D: implications for project performance', *Journal of Product Innovation Management* 18(4): 258–71.

O'Reilly, C.A. and Tushman, M.L. (2004) 'The ambidextrous organization', *Harvard Business Review* April: 74–83.

Ottenbacher, M., Gnoth, J. and Jones, P. (2006) 'Identifying determinants of success in development of new high contact services', *International Journal of Services Industry Management* 17(4): 433–63.

Page, A. and Schirr, G.R. (2008) 'Growth and development of a body of knowledge : 16 years of new product development research 1989–2004', *Journal of Product Innovation Management* 25(3): 233–48.

Perez, P.M. and Sanchez, A. (2003) 'Cooperation and the ability to minimize the time and cost of new product development within the Spanish automotive supplier industry', *Journal of Product Innovation Management* 20(1): 57–69.

Pfeffer, J. and Salancik, G.R. (1978) *The External Control of Organizations: A Resource Dependence Perspective*. New York: Harper & Row.

Powell, W. (1998) 'Learning from collaboration: knowledge and networks in the biotechnology and pharmaceutical industries', *California Management Review* 40(3): 228–40.

Powell, W., White, D.R., Koput, K.W. and Owen-Smith, J. (2005) 'Network dynamics and field evolution: the growth of interorganizational collaboration in the life sciences', *The American Journal of Sociology* 110(4): 1132–207.

Pyka, A. (2002) 'Innovation networks in economics: from the incentive-based to the knowledge-based approaches', *European Journal of Innovation Management* 5(3): 152–63.

Pyka, A. and Kueppers, G. (eds) (2002) *Innovation Networks: Theory and Practice*. Cheltenham: Edward Elgar.

Ritala, P. and Hurmelinna-Laukkanen, P. (2013) 'Incremental and radical innovation in co-opetition – the role of absorptive capacity', *Journal of Product Innovation Management* 30(1): 154–69.

Rivas, R. and Gobeli, D.H. (2005) 'Accelerating innovation at Hewlett-Packard: a case study identifies significant enablers as well as barriers to innovation, along with management lessons for speeding the process', *Research-Technology Management* 48(1): 32–9.

Roberts, D.L. and Candi, M. (2014) 'Leveraging social network sites in new product development: opportunity or hype?', *Journal of Product Innovation Management* 31: 105–17.

Rubera, G. and Droge, C. (2013) 'Technology versus design innovation's effects on sales and Tobin's Q: the moderating role of branding strategy', *Journal of Product Innovation Management* 30(3): 448–64.

Shaw, V. and Shaw, C.T. (1998) 'Conflict between engineers and marketers: the engineer's perspective', *Industrial Marketing Management* 27(4): 279–91.

Sivadas, E. and Dwyer, F.R. (2000) 'An examination of organizational factors influencing new product success in internal and alliance-based processes', *Journal of Marketing* 64(1): 31–49.

Storey, C. and Hughes, M. (2013) 'The relative impact of culture, strategic orientation and capability on new service development performance', *European Journal of Marketing* 47(5/6): 833–56.

Story, V., O'Malley, L. and Hart, S. (2008) 'The development of relationships and networks for successful radical innovation', *Journal of Customer Behavior* 7(3): 187–200.

Story, V., Hart, S. and O'Malley, L. (2009) 'Relational resources and competences for radical product innovation', *Journal of Marketing Management* 25(5–6): 461–81.

Syson, S. and Perks, H. (2004) 'New service development: a network perspective', *Journal of Services Marketing* 18(4): 255–66.

Talke, K. and Snelders, D. (2013) 'Information in launch messages: stimulating the adoption of new high-tech consumer products', *Journal of Product Innovation Management* 30(4): 732–49.

Tatikonda, M.V. and Montoya-Weiss, M. (2001) 'Integrating operations and marketing perspectives of product innovation: the influence of organizational process factors and capabilities on development performance', *Management Science* 47(1): 151–72.

Terwiesch, C. and Loch, C.H. (1999) 'Measuring the effectiveness of overlapping development activities', *Management Science* 45(4): 455–65.

Thomke, S. and von Hippel, E. (2002) 'Customers as innovators: a new way to create value', *Harvard Business Review* 80(4): 74.

Tushman, M.L. and Anderson, P. (1990) 'Technological discontinuities and dominant designs: a cyclical model of technological change', *Administrative Science Quarterly* 35(4): 604–33.

Ulrich, K.T., Sartorius, D., Pearson, S. and Jakiela, M. (1993) 'Including the value of time in design-for-manufacturing decision-making', *Management Science* 39 (April): 429–47.

von Hippel, E (1978) 'Successful industrial products from customer ideas – presentation of a new customer-active paradigm with evidence and implications', *Journal of Marketing* January: 39–49.

Wei, Y. and Morgan, N.A. (2004) 'Supportiveness of organizational climate, market orientation, and new product performance in Chinese firms', *Journal of Product Innovation Management* 21: 375–88.

Williamson, O.E. (1985) *The Economic Institutions of Capitalism*. New York: The Free Press.

Wind, J. and Mahajan, V. (1997) 'Issues and opportunities in new product development: an introduction to the special issue', *Journal of Marketing Research* 34: 1–12.

Relationships and Networks[1]

Kristian Möller

16

Chapter Topics

Overview	387
Relationship marketing and business networks research – roots and principles of meta-theoretical analysis	388
Theoretical mapping of relationship marketing and business networks	390
Conclusions and research agenda	402

Overview

This chapter takes a critical look at relationship marketing (RM) and business or industrial networks (BN) as sub-fields of the business marketing discipline. Some scholars see these as nested and use relationship marketing as a generic term to cover the research on both business relationships and inter-organizational networks. For example, Gummesson and Mele (2010), and Vargo and Lusch (2011) advocate the integration of these interrelated domains in the pursuit of a new general theory of marketing under the guidance of the service-dominant logic principles (Vargo and Lusch, 2010). However, several authors have emphasized the dispersed origin of relationship marketing and suggest a need to explore the differences between business-to-business marketing relationships and business networks

(Egan, 2008; Eiriz and Wilson, 2006; Möller, 2013). Möller and Halinen (2000) claim that relationship marketing consists of two theoretically different and distinctive approaches: market-based RM and network-based RM. This view is supported by Mattsson (1997) and Möller (2013), who make a clear distinction between the theoretical assumptions that provide the foundations for relationship marketing research and network research.

In fact, both of these domains can be seen as relatively broad and fragmented research traditions in which the founding researchers have, by utilizing concepts and theories from a variety of social science disciplines, tried to cover and synthesize phenomena. These range from the behaviours of marketers and customers and the processes that constitute relationships, to business networks, their structures and their dynamics. In addressing this complexity and diversity, this chapter seeks to:

- Examine and articulate the origins of the different views underlying current relationship marketing thought and the business networks approach;
- Provide a theoretical comparison of the disciplinary foundation of RM and BN;
- Articulate two distinctive theoretical views covering the marketing phenomena captured by the RM and BN terms: the market-based relationship marketing and the network-based relationships and business networks;
- Provide a 'theory map' of the research streams constituting the current RM and BN;
- Discuss the theoretical and managerial consequences of the advocated multi-theory approach.

The outlined conceptual analysis, while also describing the structure of this chapter, is helpful in revealing the differences and similarities in the key approaches to the RM and BN, and this is indispensable for any business marketing scholar. Without a proper understanding of the fundamental disciplinary approaches, it is difficult to navigate through the assortment of research and literature that constitutes the widespread relationship marketing and business networks domains. Thus, in order to utilize different traditions efficiently or to challenge them, it is essential to understand their theoretical positions and core assumptions. By providing an articulated theory map, this chapter contributes not only to the current marketing knowledge but to its future development as well.

Relationship marketing and business networks research – roots and principles of meta-theoretical analysis

Extant research suggests that several intertwined research streams in marketing since the 1970s have influenced the emergence of relationship marketing and business networks as important schools of business marketing thought (Egan, 2008; Eiriz and Wilson, 2006; Möller and Halinen, 2000; Pels et al., 2009). These streams include services research, customer–supplier relationships and interaction in business marketing research concerning marketing channel relationships, and more pragmatic knowledge concerning the emerging practices of database and direct marketing (subsequently termed interactive marketing). The industrial network approach, which emerged in the early 1990s, is the last piece in the relationship marketing puzzle.

The role of these streams in understanding the current RM and BN is crucial. They are not only the roots or sources of current relationship marketing, but actually the streams of research that constitute RM and BN. The fact that these research streams are not monolithic makes matters even more complicated. Their researchers draw from a variety of disciplines and theories, ranging from economics and the organizational sciences to political science and social psychology. This disciplinary multiplicity is depicted in Figure 16.1 and builds primarily on the work of Möller (2013), Möller and Halinen (2000) and Eiriz and Wilson (2006).

This framework can be used to explicate a number of theoretical questions raised in the introduction. Do the current RM and BN research traditions form coherent middle-range theories of business marketing or are they too fragmented for that (Merton, 1967)? More optimistically, can the RM and BN research traditions be merged into a single overarching

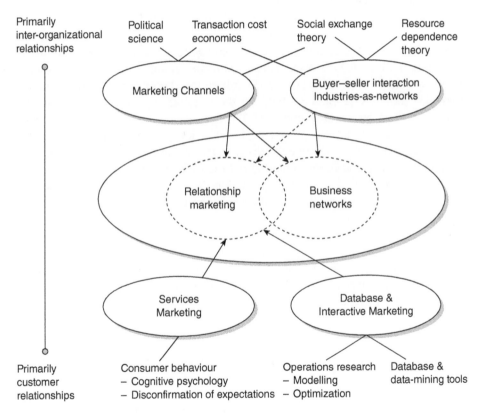

- The solid arrows indicate strong influence, dashed arrows minor influence.
- The overlap of the relationship marketing and business networks ellipses indicates that these traditions share a number of common concepts and address some of the same empirical domains.

Figure 16.1   Roots of relationship marketing and business networks research.

Adapted from: Möller (2013).

lens to explain business marketing phenomena as recommended by Gummesson and Mele (2010) and Vargo and Lusch (2011)?

These questions can be approached using the two dimensions Okhuysen and Bonardi (2011) proposed to evaluate and construct theoretical lenses: (1) the proximity of the empirical domain the theories or research traditions under investigation address; and (2) the congruence or compatibility of their underlying assumptions. If the empirical domains of two theories are relatively close – say customer and service provider relationships and industrial salesperson and organizational buyer relationships – and the assumptions of the theories covering them are reasonably congruent, it is safe to integrate the theories into a more comprehensive research approach. This congruence or compatibility is similar to what Gioia and Pitre (1990), in their examination of research traditions in management, call the permeability of paradigmatic boundaries. One should note that two theories can address the same domain and yet have incongruent underlying assumptions.

In order to carry out this kind of theory comparison, also called meta-theoretical analysis, we need a set of criteria or indicators to assess the domain proximity and degree of theoretical compatibility. The criteria the extant analyses employ generally cluster around the two aspects Okhuysen and Bonardi (2011) endorsed: (1) indicators describing the domain, goals and content of the theory or school, and (2) indicators describing the theory's underlying meta-theoretical assumptions, i.e. the view researchers hold on the ontology, epistemology and methodology (see e.g. Arndt, 1985; Möller and Halinen, 2000; Pels et al., 2009; Vargo and Lusch, 2004).

The domain and goal indicators are relatively self-evident. In assessing the meta-theoretical assumptions, it is useful to first describe the disciplinary background of a theory and then examine the views researchers and theories hold about the focal phenomena (business relationships and networks), the context of the focal phenomena (markets, channel environment, network environment) and the actors carrying out the exchange and value-creating behaviours. These assumptions describe the ontological core of the theory. By complementing this procedure with an examination of the kind of research procedures and empirical analyses the tradition uses to produce knowledge, one can identify its epistemological views and primary methodology. In sum, an examination of these standpoints should reveal the integration potential or incongruence of the theories constructing the RM and BN approaches in business marketing as well as provide us suggestions of how to carry out theoretically anchored research and thus sound research in these domains.

Theoretical mapping of relationship marketing and business networks

As illustrated in Figure 16.1, the extant research on relationship marketing indicates that RM has been constructed primarily utilizing four root theories or research traditions: services research, customer–supplier relationships in business marketing, marketing channel research and interactive marketing. Moreover, based on a careful meta-theoretical analysis of these root traditions, Möller and Halinen (2000) argue that we should distinguish between two fundamental types of RM theories: market-based and network-based. The former deals with fairly simple exchange relationships and assumes a market context, whereas the latter examines complex relationships and presumes a network-like business environment (see Möller and Halinen, 2000). Their view is supported by the work of Mattsson (1997) and Eiriz and Wilson (2006), both of whom have compared the relationship and network views in business marketing studies. This chapter uses the market- and network-based RM propositions as a starting platform for developing a less abstract, but more complex, view of current research schools focused on marketing relationships and business networks.

Based on an updated analysis of the current research in RM (primarily business marketing applications) and BN, a theory map (portrayed in Figure 16.2) is proposed. It extends the work by Möller and Halinen (2000) and draws primarily on Möller (2013). The theory map provides a grounded meta-theoretical classification and discussion of the RM research and especially the rapidly developing business networks domain. In this respect, the theory map enables drawing new conclusions about potentially combining specific streams of relationship marketing and networks research, as well as about whether RM and BN research can form the basis of a unified theory of business marketing. In the analysis the following review articles, in addition to the material provided by Möller and Halinen (2000), were especially helpful: Brodie et al. (2008), Chandler and Vargo (2011), Eiriz and Wilson (2006), Gummesson and Mele (2010), Möller and Rajala (2007), Möller et al. (2005, 2009), Parmigiani and Rivera-Santos (2011), Pels et al. (2009), Ritter et al. (2004) and Vargo and Lusch (2004, 2008a, 2008b).

Exchange continuum – key for understanding research approaches

Before discussing the proposed constituents of the RM and BN approaches, the key construct of the theory map, the continuum outlining the exchange and value-creating relationships, is briefly described. The original version of the continuum, developed by Möller and Halinen (2000), depicted the degree of relational complexity. Complexity, as used here, is a multidimensional construct that refers to the number of actors involved in exchange, their interdependence, the intensity and nature of business interaction and the potential temporal contingencies (short-term versus enduring) in the relationship. Complexity is closely related to the kind of task exchanged, administered or created through the relationship, how standardized the task is, and how complex and novel it is (Möller, 2006a). For example, are we trying to understand the development of a new electronic banking system, involving multiple parties with different competencies, or is the focus on analyzing the exchange of standardized production components or maintenance, repair and operative services?

Moreover, one can argue that complex exchange or value cocreation tasks demand a high level of mutual understanding between the companies involved. This kind of mutuality is generally not fostered by market-governed relationships but involves deep and often multiple, relationships (Håkansson and Ford, 2002), and so-called network governance (Powell, 1990). Through increased mutual learning and relationship-specific investments, actors become interdependent, and this makes switching difficult (Wathne and Heide, 2004). When these conditions characterize exchange behaviour, the exchange context also tends to become network-like. Similar conclusions have been suggested for value cocreation situations (Gummesson and Mele, 2010) and service systems (Vargo and Lusch, 2011). On the other hand, because of the relative simplicity of the offerings, there are generally several acceptable alternatives for customers at the low complexity end of the exchange continuum. This makes switching possible and leads to relationships that are less interdependent. These kinds of relationships tend to be more efficiently governed by markets (Möller and Törrönen, 2003; Powell, 1990).

The notions presented here concern the characteristics of exchange and value creation relationships and their contexts. The reasoning lends additional support to the theoretical usefulness of distinguishing market-based relationship marketing theories from networks-based business marketing theories, or more briefly networks, as proposed by Möller and Halinen (2000) and Möller (2013) and depicted at the top of the theory map. This distinction provides a strong sense-making tool for understanding the various research streams in current business marketing but does not offer much guidance for more detailed theoretical and managerial propositions which are needed from a good middle-range theory (Brodie et al., 2011). To fill this gap, the research approaches positioned in the theory map will be analysed next. The positioning is

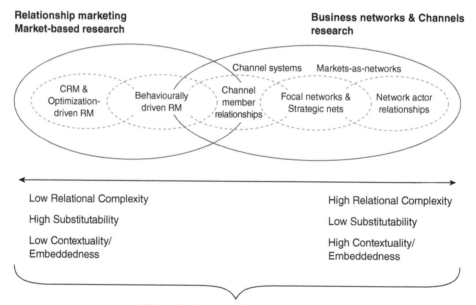

- The ellipses drawn with solid lines represent the clusters of research traditions. The overlap of the two clusters (market-based RM and network-based RM) indicates an area where the paradigms share certain assumptions and are theoretically permeable.
- The ellipses drawn with dashed lines indicate the borders of particular research traditions or theories. Their overlap indicates theoretical congruence.
- The continuum underlying the theory space summarizes the views that the RM and BN theories have about the exchange and its context.

Figure 16.2   Theory map of relationship marketing and business networks research approaches.

Adapted from: Möller (2013).

based on the ontological assumptions that the approaches make about the focal exchange, the actors carrying out the exchange and about the exchange context.

This kind of meta-theoretical analysis involves broad generalizations. In trying to capture the basic themes of each constituent theory one has to gloss over many details. There are probably individual studies that do not match current interpretations, and authors who disagree with them.

The theory map: Part 1 – Market-based relationship marketing

The theory map contains five interrelated research traditions addressing business relationships and networks and their contexts: customer relationship management (CRM), behaviourally driven RM, channel system and channel member relationships, markets-as-networks and network actor relationships, and focal networks and strategic nets. The positioning of these constituents on the map reflects their view of relational exchange, what kind of role the context plays or fails to play, and whether constituents' theorizing is reductionist or embedded, i.e. considering the context and history of the focal behaviour. The analysis proceeds from left to right. Note, however, that the 'markets-as-networks' approach, including 'network actor relationships', is addressed before the 'focal networks and strategic nets' although it is positioned at the far right. The reason for this is that the approach provides a theory of network context for examining all types of networks and network relationships.

Customer relationship management-driven RM

Primary goals and empirical domain.

Customer relationship management originated in the mid-1980s, and was driven by rapidly developing information technology. It was originally formed primarily by practice-based and consultant-driven activities and tools for managing customer relationships through databases and direct-marketing activities (see e.g. Jenkinson, 1995; Peppers and Rogers, 1997). Enhanced by the internet and mobile technology, marketers gained additional opportunities to customize their offerings and messages for individual customers (Blattberg and Deighton, 1991; Malthouse and Blattberg, 2005). CRM utilizes the tools offered by customer databases and data-mining techniques to optimize a firm's customer equity and the customer's lifetime value through customer relationships and customer portfolio management (Malthouse and Blattberg, 2005). The goals of CRM are primarily managerial or normative. The approach aims to enhance marketing efficiency by better targeting of marketing activities, especially marketing communications, and to achieve a high level of customer retention and share of customer (Boulding et al., 2005; Rust et al., 2004). The applications cover both consumer and business customer products and services, which are prominent in the internet and mobile marketing fields (Kumar, 2008).

Disciplinary background.

Although the CRM approach aims to increase customer loyalty by tailoring marketing communications and offerings to customers, it is not deeply interested in the psychological and behavioural aspects of customer relationships. In this respect, it does not have a clear disciplinary basis, but has a pragmatist problem-solving orientation. The emphasis on optimization in CRM relies implicitly on the marginal utility principle of microeconomics underlying the marketing mix approach (Möller, 2006b).

Ontological assumptions – view of relationships, actors and context.

Perhaps because of its pragmatist nature CRM does not have clear assumptions or theories about the context of exchange relationships. Competitive markets seem to be implicitly presumed. Although interactivity is emphasized, the marketer–customer relationship perspective is fairly superficial, portraying a relatively loose and distant connection. The focus is on interactive communication, where the seller is the active partner who plans offers and communication on the basis of customer profiles and feedback.

Although customer relationships are seen as long-term in nature, conceptual or other efforts to tackle the dynamism of these relationships have been limited. The main focus is on how to efficiently keep customers loyal and profitable. This managerialism incorporates a rational view of the marketer, generally observed from the perspective of a single firm (unit), and a mechanistic view of the organization. Individual customer(s) are defined by preferences and response profiles. Customer types (segments) are also used as a unit of analysis.

Epistemological view and methodology.

The goals and analytical tools mainstream CRM researchers employ have led to relatively reductionist research with emphasis on customer objectivist profiles and response measures. This implies low contextuality and a stimulus–organism–response view of theory development.

Behaviourally driven RM

Primary goals and empirical domain.

The behaviourally driven RM label covers a broad collection of research and represents much about what is generally regarded as 'relationship marketing'. The key theoretical interest lies in understanding relational exchange, especially supplier–customer relationships, their elements and development, and the factors influencing them. The application areas cover all possible marketer–customer relationships, from services and consumer products to inter-organizational or business relationships. Sometimes RM propositions are also claimed to cover all focal firm–stakeholder relationships (Christopher et al., 1991; Gummesson, 2008).

The core theoretical goals of behaviourally driven RM are to identify the antecedent factors that shape customer–supplier relationships and to identify and explain how relationship characteristics influence relational outcomes. This logic is well illustrated by Morgan and Hunt's (1994) influential 'commitment–trust theory of relationship marketing' where the relationship benefits, termination costs, shared values, communication and potential opportunistic behaviours are seen to influence perceived trust and commitment towards the relationship (forming the key characteristics of the relationship). These are then driving the relational outcomes constituted by the propensity to cooperate in or leave the relationship, perceived uncertainty and functional problem solving (see also Anderson and Narus, 1990). The managerial aims of the tradition emphasize the creation and management of effective stakeholder relationships, especially customer relationships, in an enduring and mutually beneficial manner, and the development of the capabilities involved in these processes. This has led to emphasis on understanding and assessing customer/supplier perceived value; the relationships are examined from the value creation process perspective (Grönroos, 2011; Ulaga, 2003; Ulaga and Eggert, 2006).

Disciplinary background.

In addition to utilizing the service marketing research (see Figure 16.1), behaviourally driven RM has been significantly influenced by social exchange theory (SET) (Cropanzano and Mitchell, 2005; Emerson, 1976) and its applications within channels research. Since the seminal publication by Dwyer et al. (1987), key SET concepts, such as actor reciprocity, attraction, trust, shared values and commitment, have played central roles in examining business buyer–seller and marketer–consumer relationships. Other, less significant sources of influence are the relational contracts approach by Macneil (1980) and aspects of transaction cost economics and its applications in channels research, especially the concept of power and opportunistic behaviour (Anderson and Narus, 1990; Heide and John, 1992).

Ontological assumptions – view of relationships, actors and context.

Deeply influenced by social psychology-driven social exchange theory, behaviourally driven RM is principally interested in reciprocal relationships in which both parties play active roles. It also sees relationships emerging or being constructed through an evolutionary process in which perceived satisfaction over each exchange episode is important. Actors seek mutual benefits and avoid potential relational costs and risks (Dwyer et al., 1987). In contrast to CRM, behaviourally driven RM offers theory-based tools for rigorous modelling of the relationships and their evolutionary dynamics. By focusing keenly on dyadic relationships, it has, however, little to say about the context in which these relationships are embedded. The approach is not interested in how exchange contexts might influence parties to the relationship and the relationship itself. Generally, an implicit assumption of a market context involving several customers and buyers can be detected. Another limitation is the scant use of other social exchange theory concepts such as power, dependency or interdependency, and comparison between available alternatives (Kelley and Thibaut, 1978), which are more prominent in channels research (Anderson and Narus, 1990; Heide and John, 1992).

Epistemological view and methodology.

Despite the social exchange theory-driven emphasis on the activity of the actors and the reciprocal character of relationships and their formation dynamics, the majority of academic research in behaviourally driven RM follows the 'antecedents-relationship profile-relational outcomes' research format strongly influenced by Morgan and Hunt's (1994) study and the dominant position of the structural equation modelling methods in marketing. Although elegant and theory driven, this approach does not provide adequate tools for understanding the dynamic process aspects of relationships development or their connections to the context of relationships. It primarily explains relationships and their outcomes only in terms of relationship-specific factors.

The theory map: Part 2 – Channel systems and networks-based relationship marketing

Research in business networks has been expanding rapidly since the turn of the millennium. In order to provide an in-depth understanding of the broad research in the networks and channel domains it is discussed via three interrelated research streams (the ellipses in the right side cluster in Figure 16.2). These are categorized into channel system-related and networks-related research.

Channel systems and channel member relationships

Primary goals and empirical domain.

One can distinguish two interrelated layers in the studies of marketing channels and their members. Channel systems are studies that examine channel structures, their characteristics and evolution, and the factors that influence specific structures and change (Robicheaux and Coleman, 1994). The channel system forms the context for dyadic research concerning relationships among channel members, manufacturers, channel intermediaries and business customers (Stern and Reve, 1980). This layered character of channel studies is also reflected in their theoretical goals. At the system level, the aim is to understand and explain how channel structures evolve and how they influence dyadic channel relationships. On the relational level, the goal is to understand how the channel context influences channel member relationships and to identify efficient governance structures for various relationships. The normative aim is to provide the basis for the design of efficient governance norms and mechanisms for channel relationships.

Disciplinary background.

Channel studies have a dualistic disciplinary background, reflected in the seminal political economy framework introduced by Stern and Reve (1980), suggesting that channel structures and relationships should be studied by combining the economic perspective and the behavioural or political perspective. The economic perspective is influenced predominantly by transaction cost economics, which defines the efficient governance structure in dyadic exchange relationships through the use of a set of transaction and market characteristics (Rindfleisch and Heide, 1997; Williamson, 1985). Its core concepts include asset specificity, uncertainty and transaction frequency; under specific combinations of these contingency factors, matching governance structures and safeguarding mechanisms can be postulated (see e.g. Kumar et al., 2011; Wathne and Heide, 2004).

The behavioural perspective draws from social exchange theory and organizational sociology; it employs political economy concepts, such as power and dependency, and social aspects, such as expectations, cooperation, trust, commitment, communication and conflict behaviour to analyse channel relationships. As such, it has long roots in the bases of power (French and Raven, 1959) and conflict behaviour (Pondy, 1967) perspectives (cf. Anderson and Narus, 1990; Dwyer et al., 1987; Gaski, 1984; Heide, 1994).

Ontological assumptions – view of relationships, actors and context.

An essential aspect of channels research is its strong programmatic and systemic nature. Driven by the political economy framework and utilizing the rich social exchange theory base, the tradition offers three essential points: both economic and political aspects and their interactions must be considered in examining channel behaviour; a focal channel and a dyadic relationship form the recommended unit(s) of analysis; and complex relationships cannot be understood outside their context or environment, as 'dyadic behaviour' and 'channel' are reciprocally interrelated (Heide, 1994; Rindfleisch and Heide, 1997; Wathne and Heide, 2004).

As such, the approach stresses the collective nature of distribution channels. The relationships are seen as multidimensional and interactive. Both parties are assumed to be active and are seen to simultaneously pursue selfish and collective goals. Efficiency can be evaluated at the individual member and system levels. Actors are seen to be boundedly rational (minimizing their transaction costs), yet they remain very much like black boxes in most of the empirical research.

Epistemological view and methodology.

Channels research is relatively heterogeneous in its theoretical bases. Research on manufacturer–channel member relationships, particularly on governance, draws primarily on transaction cost economics (e.g. Heide, 1994; Wathne and Heide, 2004); as such this research holds a rational and mechanistic outlook of companies. Research driven by the political economy framework (Stern and Reve, 1980) also focuses on channel structure and company (and dyad) interaction, perceiving – at least implicitly – organizations as adaptive agents. They are described mainly through their roles (in the channel system) and goals. Both approaches primarily use forms of causal modelling in their empirical analysis, which precludes the analysis of complex contingencies posed by the channel system–dyadic relationships framework. Research on the channel system level is scarce, which is unfortunate as it could answer fundamental questions, such as why we have different channel structures, how they evolve and whether different evolutionary patterns exist and why. Another shortcoming is the insufficient empirical research into the development processes of channel relationships and the channel structure–channel relationship interaction; see, however, Grewal and Dharwadkar (2002). These limitations are connected to the constraints posed by structural equation modelling; focus on channel system evolution and relationship processes would entail long-term processual research methods (van de Ven, 2007).

It is interesting to compare channel-driven relations research with behaviourally driven RM as both have social exchange theory as an important disciplinary background. The major theoretical difference is that, in the channels tradition, channel relationships, especially their form and governance, are assumed to depend on a larger channel system. Another aspect is the combining of behavioural concepts from the social exchange theory and the transaction cost framework to study efficient forms of governance for manufacturer–channel member relationships, and examine the influence of governance norms on relational performance. A further theme exclusive to channels research is the investigation of how one party develops safeguards against becoming overly dependent on the other party. Advanced studies also examine the influence the channel system exerts on relationship-level behaviour. In sum, the channel research tradition assumes more context-dependent business relationships compared to behavioural RM, and enables empirical analysis of the complex interplay between social norms and economic incentives in driving relational performance outcomes (Kumar et al., 2011).

Markets-as-networks and network actor relationships

Primary goals and empirical domain.

In the business networks domain, the markets-as-networks label refers to similar macro-level research as channel systems in the channels tradition. It provides a theory of network context for examining actor relationships and the management of an individual firm in a network context, as well as for understanding the evolution of focal networks and so-called strategic nets or value nets (Möller and Halinen, 1999; Möller et al., 2005). As such, markets-as-networks explore complex questions: how networks emerge, why we have different network structures, what their key drivers are and through what kinds of processes networks evolve. The approach challenges the market-based view of industries and business fields and contends that networks provide a more realistic descriptive theory. Understanding macro-networks and their dynamics is also fundamental in managing in the more restricted focal networks and dyadic network relationships.

Relatively few empirical macro-network studies exist, however. The approach has been employed primarily to examine how new business or technological networks evolve (Håkansson and Waluszewski, 2002a; Lundgren, 1995; Möller and Svahn, 2009). The issue of network structures has also been addressed in economic sociology, where Powell and colleagues (Powell et al., 1996, 2005) address the new field's emergence and structure (biotechnology and life sciences), and in organization science and strategy studies, where Rosenkopf and colleagues (Rosenkopf and Padula, 2008; Rosenkopf and Schilling, 2007) examine network formation through strategic alliances.

Research on the network actor level investigates issues that have more immediate managerial implications. Compared to channel research in business relationships, the network approach is more interested in issues pertaining to which kinds of resource ties, activity links and social and organizational bonds connect network actors and through which kinds of interactive processes – resource exchange, social exchange and adaptations – the relationships evolve and the parties try to achieve relational benefits (Håkansson and Ford, 2002). The economic aspect is included in terms of the parties' investments in the relationship and in the costs of adaptation (Hallen et al., 1991). The application of industrial network theory covers practically all business fields with an emphasis on complex technological relationships (Håkansson and Snehota, 1995). The managerial goal is to gain a more realistic view of the creation and management of complex interactive business relationships in a network context.

Disciplinary background.

The industrial network approach is the result of a disciplinary amalgamation. It has been influenced by resource dependency theory (Pfeffer and Salancick, 1978), social exchange theory and transaction cost economics. Moreover, channels research, business marketing research and international business studies have contributed to its formation (Turnbull et al., 1996). Like the channels school, it utilizes economic aspects (i.e. investments in relationships) and behavioural aspects (i.e. expectations, relationship atmosphere, mutuality) to analyse relationships. Since the 1990s, the approach has concentrated on understanding business networks and organizational action in a network context manifested in the actors–resources–activities (ARA) framework (Håkansson and Snehota, 1995). This perspective draws primarily on the resource dependence view between organizations, showing how firms and other organizations rely on each other's resources for their performance and survival (Aldrich, 1979; Pfeffer and Salancick, 1978). The core ARA framework has been augmented by the '4R' model focusing on the resource interdependencies and interaction. The 4R studies show that actors' resource constellations effectively constrain their joint business relationships and potential (Baraldi, 2008; Håkansson and Waluszewski, 2002b). In addition, aspects of institutional studies, evolutionary economics and organizational theory are being applied. As a broad research approach, the IMP-based network approach has also influenced and been influenced by research in the resource-based view of the firm, strategy, market construction and service-dominant logic (Baraldi et al., 2007; Golfetto et al., 2007).

Ontological assumptions – view of relationships, actors and context.

The market-as-networks approach is interested in all kinds of actor relationships involving not only firms, but government and research agencies, individual actors and collective actors. Actors are fundamentally linked through resource dependency, and this linkage is characterized by the exchange and cocreation of resources. Consequently, relationships are seen as vehicles to access and control resources, as well as to create new resources, generally through cocreation (Håkansson and Ford, 2002; Möller and Svahn, 2006). This view involves a combined interest in competition and cooperation; actors can simultaneously compete on one level and collaborate on another. It also includes the idea of actors as resource integrators, an idea that is becoming prominent in the development of value-based general theory (Gummesson and Mele, 2010; Vargo and Lusch, 2011).

The network approach contains several departures from mainstream relationship marketing and channel studies. Both relationships and networks form the unit of analysis, focusing on their structures and dynamics. More importantly, the worldview of network studies emphasizes contextuality and time. Actor behaviour is highly embedded in a layered manner. Singular events or actor relationships cannot be understood without knowledge of their context and evolution in the particular dyadic relationship which is embedded in the macro-network (Alajoutsijärvi et al., 1999). Moreover, the environment is not transparent; actors are seen as perceiving its structure and meanings and learning about them through enactment (Weick, 1985). The ambiguity produced by the non-transparence or opaqueness of the network environment forms another major distinction to the channel systems research and to behavioural relationship marketing. Compared to channel studies, there is also a clear difference in how the network approach emphasizes the processual character of relationships and describes them through resource and social exchange processes and adaptations. Another departure is the interest in the creation of new resources through exchange relationships, not just the exchange of resources, and the strong emphasis on contextual and historical embeddedness.

Epistemological view and methodology.

The ontological assumptions of the network approach have significant consequences for its methodological orientation. Studies primarily use qualitative case analyses that often involve features of historical research. Firms and other actors are seen as 'organic' and adaptive. The historical explanation view and the non-transparence perspective have important consequences for the normative and managerial applications of the network approach, which can provide only relatively broad guidelines regarding how to manage in a network environment. More specific normative suggestions require an historical understanding of the particular network situation and must always remain context dependent. This is a significant difference from market-based relationship marketing studies and also differs clearly from the more structured contextual view of channels relationship research using primarily causal modelling frameworks and techniques. In more meta-theoretical terms, the network approach relies on critical or transcendental realism and seeks to achieve understanding of the layered causal powers and mechanisms influencing particular historical network relationships and their events (cf. Easton, 2002).

Focal networks and strategic nets

Primary goals and empirical domain.

The previous section discussed macro-level research in business networks and network actors and their relationship, which form the micro-layer of business network theory. It is useful to distinguish this research from the study of focal networks and the so-called strategic nets, forming the meso-level of network studies; see Eiriz and Wilson (2006) and Möller and Halinen (1999) for a discussion on the levels of analysis in network research. These closely related streams of network research have greatly similar theoretical bases with an important distinction concerning the assumptions of learning in the networks and the manageability of a business network.

The term *focal network* refers to the view that, although networks are borderless, the cognitive capacity of the actors, as well as their limited resources, constrains their ability to make sense of and use these borderless networks. Thus, the actors are dealing primarily with actors forming their focal network – namely, the actors they are able to perceive and regard as relevant (Alajoutsijärvi et al., 1999). Objectives of the focal network approach are to understand how these networks evolve and how companies are trying to take advantage of them. An essential aspect is the roles and network positions that an actor can try to achieve in the focal network. This process is influenced by an actor's learning capacity. Each actor is assumed to form his or her network view, which is influenced by the actor's accumulated network experience, based on the actor's network position and the number and variety of relationships the position enables as well as the actor's learning capacity (Möller, 2010). The resulting view, also called the network picture, is actually an actor's theory of the network. This network theory influences the actor's network perceptions, interpretations and actions (Henneberg et al., 2006; Ramos and Ford, 2011).

Besides network roles and the cognitive view, focal networks are also studied from the learning organization perspective. This involves such questions as through what kind of processes do networks learn and what capabilities are essential in network learning (Knight, 2002; Möller and Svahn, 2006; Peters et al., 2010).

If focal networks form the network actors' 'playground', what are the *strategic nets* or *value nets*? These terms refer to intentionally planned and mobilized network organizations (Möller et al., 2005; Raab and Kenis, 2009). Many scholars representing the strategic management perspective suggest that more intentionally created strategic networks or value nets exist that contain a specific set of organizations with agreed-upon roles and distributed tasks (see e.g. Jarillo, 1993; Möller and Rajala, 2007; Parolini, 1999). This observation is in contrast to the ontological view of networks as emerging and 'non-manageable' entities (Ford, 2011; Håkansson and Ford, 2002). This distinction is an essential element in the debate over the extent to which networks can be managed. While sharing the view that open, borderless networks are not manageable, Möller and colleagues have developed a theory of value nets. Their work explores basic net types and management requirements (Möller and Rajala, 2007; Möller and Svahn, 2003; Möller et al., 2005). A key suggestion is that the structure and management of specific nets are influenced by the value creation logic of those nets. The extent to which this logic can be specified shapes the role of knowledge exploitation and exploration in value creation. For example, Möller and colleagues (Möller and Rajala, 2007; Möller and Svahn, 2006) have shown that vertical demand–supply nets, horizontal customer service nets and various innovation nets differ significantly in their management solutions. This contingency theory – the manageability and mode of management is dependent on the value creation logic of the net – provides a significant opening for the creation and management of specific strategic nets.

Disciplinary background.

Focal networks and strategic nets share a disciplinary background of the studies on macro-networks and network relationships. The most notable difference is the inclusion of the cognitive approach and the organization learning view for achieving a deeper understanding of the actors' sense making of their focal networks and for studying how focal networks can create new resources and practices through network learning. These are, again, clear departures from market-based RM and from channel relationship studies.

Ontological assumptions, epistemological view and methodology.

There are only a few major distinctions to be added here. The key new aspect is the point that specific networks can be seen as partially closed systems, with a definite set of members with jointly agreed-upon roles and responsibilities. This strategic or value net perspective enables firms to collectively create and manage specific types of network organizations (Gulati et al., 2012; Möller and Rajala, 2007). The new theory formation of value nets relies on the contingency principle by postulating that the goals of strategic nets and the characteristics of their underlying value creation system influence effective organizational forms, governance structures and managerial capabilities required by the specific nets. This discovery provides the basis for the formation of more advanced normative theory for network management. It also encourages the adoption of theory-testing types of case study research designs.

Conclusions and research agenda

The meta-theoretical analysis and resulting theory map have several significant consequences for theory development in business marketing. Because of the richness of the outcomes, they are discussed in terms of three themes: (1) understanding the current relationship marketing theory and network approach; (2) opportunities offered for the construction of middle-range theories in business marketing; and (3) the prospect of a general theory for marketing. Discussion on themes 2 and 3 forms a research agenda.

Relationship marketing and business networks – understanding the current research

The analysis indicates that current theoretical aspirations (e.g. by Gummesson and Mele, 2010) for combining relationship marketing and business networks in a unified theory of business marketing are highly idealistic because of the diverse disciplinary bases of the research in market-based relationship marketing and business networks. The key distinctions between these approaches are summarized in Table 16.1 (the channel systems have been omitted for the sake of clarity; the approach is well established and documented). The summary provides the necessary material for applying the criteria that Okhuysen and Bonardi (2011) offer for evaluating the possible combination of theoretical 'lenses': the proximity of the empirical domain, the focused theories and the congruence or compatibility of their underlying assumptions.

As can be noted, market-based RM research and network perspective-driven research have their interrelated, yet distinct empirical domains and research goals and are based on very different ontological and epistemological assumptions. They also utilize dissimilar research methods.

Table 16.1 Core differences between market-based relationship marketing and business network approach.

Approach characteristics	Market-based relationship marketing	Business networks approach
Domain & goals	Focus on supplier–customer relationships. *Theoretical goals*: describe and explain primarily dyadic relationships by identifying their key antecedents, elements and outcomes. *Managerial goals*: management of supplier–customer relationships and portfolios. Enhance marketing efficiency through better targeting of marketing activities, especially marketing communications; optimization of the value of customer portfolio.	Focus on inter-organizational relationships, network structures and network types. *Theoretical goals*: describe and understand inter-organizational relationships, networks and strategic nets and their evolution in network context, understand how markets function and evolve from a network perspective. *Managerial goals*: gain descriptively valid views of networks of actor relationships for managing in a network context; mobilizing and managing strategic nets.
Disciplinary background	*CRM* – No disciplinary background; driven by the evolution of information technology, pragmatic problem solving and consultants. Underlying link to optimization and the marginal utility principle of microeconomics. *Behaviourally driven RM* – Social exchange theory (attraction, trust, shared values, commitment and relational norms) with some attention to transaction cost economics (power, opportunistic behaviour, governance norms).	An eclectic tradition; earlier influenced by resource interdependence theory, social exchange theory and transaction cost economics; later by evolutionary economics and strategic research, especially the dynamic capability and cognitive management literatures.
Ontology, view of: – Relationships – Actors – Context	View on relationships ranges from relatively independent and loose (CRM) to interdependent and with active participants. The focus is on dyadic relationships and their explanation with social exchange theory constructs (attraction, trust, shared values, commitment and relational norms). Primarily silent about relationship context; implicit assumption of the market as the dominant environmental context.	Focus on reciprocal relationships amid different types of actors (firms, government and research agencies, individuals); all kinds of resources are exchanged through relationships. Relationships are seen as vehicles to access and control resources and to co-creation of new resources. Environment is seen as networks of actor relationships. Actor behaviour is embedded, i.e. specific actions cannot be understood out of their historical context. Actors learn and construct their environment through enactment; the actor–environment relationship is reciprocal and environment is non-transparent. Actors are seen as organic and adaptive.
Epistemology & methodology	The majority of research follows the antecedents-relationship profile-outcomes research format generally applying structural equation modelling on cross-sectional data.	The emphasis is on the embeddedness of relationships in nets and networks. Time and history are essential, the present cannot be understood without the past. Dynamic perspective, focus on both structure (content) and processes (how dyads, nets and networks evolve). Emphasis on historical case analysis.

Adapted from: Möller (2013).

Due to this difference, one cannot speak meaningfully of a single relationship marketing theory. CRM-driven RM, behaviourally driven RM and the way relationships are conceptualized and studied in channels research and in business networks research are all distinctive approaches to business marketing.

Because of their significant theoretical relevance, the key differences between the ontological assumptions of the market- and network-based approaches are briefly highlighted. By assuming a working market context, the former approach considers exchange relationships as mutually independent. This may be an acceptable assumption in the marketing of mass type products and services for both consumer and business customers, but it is not reasonable in the exchange of more complex offerings, where exchange relationships are more directly influenced by their context. In such domains, researchers have to develop theories that inform us about how the context and exchange relationships are interrelated. Channels research and the business networks approach are good examples. The market- versus network-based distinction also involves clear differences in the epistemology and methodology of the research approaches, ranging from reductionist models under assumptions of low relational complexity to historical analysis seeking causal mechanisms influencing the formation of complex business networks.

A critical question in this connection is whether the meta-theoretical distinctions among these approaches are so deep or paradigmatic that they form a clear barrier to 'paradigm crossing' (see e.g. Arndt, 1985; Burrell and Morgan, 1979; Kuhn, 1962). Although Kuhn's early ideas of the strong paradigmatic incommensurability of research traditions have received well-articulated criticism and have been reformulated into a weaker form by Kuhn himself (1987) – see the discussion by Tadajewski (2008) – the differences between the ontological and epistemological premises of the market-based research and the networked-based research are so distinctive that they make blending or combining these approaches untenable or at least useless in any pragmatic sense.

The majority of the CRM and behaviourally driven RM research follows primarily a positivistic orientation in terms of its ontological assumptions and epistemological practices. Researchers tend to use objectivist measures of their focal phenomena and employ logical empiricism informed methodological orientation involving hypothesis testing frameworks. These practices presume a strong realist position. This is in sharp contrast with the network-based approaches in assuming a critical realist position and involving also constructionist research reflected in the emphasis on interpretative and historical research methods (Easton, 1995, 2002; Morgan and Smircich, 1980; Peters et al., 2013; Welch et al., 2011). However, as indicated in Figure 16.2, the channel systems research shares aspects of market-based RM and network-based RM suggesting that its results and ideas can more easily be utilized across these paradigmatic borders. This is important for the theory-combining discussion in the next section.

One should note that all the research traditions identified in the theory map are reasonably logical configurations; their research foci and practices follow the goals and underlying theoretical assumptions. Another relevant point is that the traditions are results of historical social construction. They are by no means predestined by their disciplinary origins or focal empirical domains. Yet, in their current configuration they form relatively programmatic middle-range theories of business marketing, combining empirical aspects with an articulated theoretical base and specific research goals. As such, each provides a partial theory of the complex domain of business marketing and its embeddedness in our social and economic environment. Each has a defined role in understanding and explaining relationships. This is the strength of the multi-theory or multi-lens approach recommended by Gioia and Pitre (1990), Möller et al. (2009) and Okhuysen and Bonardi (2011). However, researchers working within a given school do not necessarily recognize the assumptions and their consequences, as these have not been explicitly described often. If we want to master these traditions, we must learn their conceptual languages and underlying assumptions to transcend their semantic incommensurability (Tadajewski, 2008). By becoming fluent in many theoretical languages we can achieve a better understanding of the various forms of business marketing and how to conduct research on them.

How to advance business marketing theory: Theory map-driven research agenda

The meta-theoretical analysis also offers a basis for developing a research agenda for advancing business marketing theory. Instead of looking at individual partial theories, the agenda focuses first on the opportunities offered by combining aspects of interrelated theories and concludes with broader suggestions concerning the construction of a general theory of marketing.

Theory combining: Development of stronger middle-range theories

The meta-theoretical analysis contains a number of heuristics for research agenda construction: limitations and white spaces of the key research traditions, and the potential combination of the positive aspects of traditions sharing permeable borders. In addition, the recognition that all the partial theories are strongly guided by their ontological assumptions suggests that a conscious utilization of the contingency perspective offers a valuable guideline for theory development.

Research agenda for the market-based approaches

The analysis revealed a number of significant limitations within CRM research and behaviourally driven relationship marketing. Because of their non-contextual nature and focus on the efficiency and functioning of customer–supplier relationships, these approaches have not been interested in such questions as:

- What kind of CRM programmes and modes of customer–supplier relationships do companies have in various kinds of business contexts?
- Through what kind of organizational arrangements are these relationships being created and maintained?
- If specific principal forms can be identified, why do they exist, and what aspects and factors are driving them and their diversity?

These basic 'what' and 'why' questions are significant for achieving a more comprehensive understanding of the various forms of business marketing and the underlying reasons for the development and existence of these forms (Terho and Halinen, 2012). In a similar fashion, deeper comprehension is required of the following processual issues (although the literature contains a few models addressing the process aspects of business relationships, e.g. Dwyer et al., 1987; Halinen, 1997; Wilson, 1995; proper empirical coverage is still missing):

- Through what kind of processes are customer–supplier relationships created, maintained and terminated?
- Can one identify systematic patterns across different relationship types and business contexts?
- If specific principal patterns can be identified, why do they exist, and what aspects and factors are driving them and the differences among them?

Rigorous answers to these sets of content and process questions would offer us a stronger evidence-based foundation for creating context-specific guidelines for business marketing and relationship management. How can a researcher meet these ambitious research goals? We need a well-specified theory of business markets which, in combination with our knowledge of relationship-specific factors, could be used to examine the existence of different modes of relationships. Transaction cost theory and resource dependence theory, both prominent in channels research, offer additional lenses for enriching the primarily behaviourally driven and dyadic relationship marketing. Although proper treatment of the potential contingency combinations covered by these theories would require a paper of its own, a few sample postulations are ventured:

- In exchange settings dominated by relatively established product and service offerings requiring low relationship-specific investments (indicating low technological uncertainty), and with the availability of several suppliers and buyers (indicating low interdependence and market uncertainty), one expects primarily market-driven business relationships governed by relatively simple contractual forms.
- In exchange settings dominated by novel and complex product and service offerings requiring considerable relationship-specific investments (indicating high technological uncertainty and interdependence) and characterized by relatively few and less known suppliers and customers (indicating high market uncertainty), one expects gradually developing, relational governance-driven relationships with relatively complex relational norms.

Both examples contain relatively simple contingency postulations. They can be made more realistic but also more complex by adding more factors to complement the initial contingency dimensions. For example:

- The negotiation power of buyers and sellers predicts which party will be more active in the relationship; parties' resource profiles and the resulting dependence determine their relative power positions.

- The cultural climate – competitive orientation versus collaborative orientation – of the exchange context moderates the effect of the transaction cost analysis (TCA) and resource-dependence factors.
- Company orientation and experience – positive/negative experiences from competitive versus collaborative relationships – moderate the effect of the TCA and resource-dependence factors.

In sum, these examples demonstrate the usefulness of extending the behaviourally driven relationship marketing research to incorporate theories of exchange context. The propositions were derived by combining the behaviourally driven RM with notions from the TCA and resource dependency theory and illustrate possibilities offered for combining the permeable aspects of the channel system and market-based relationship marketing (see Figure 16.2) into a more extensive middle-range theory. The rapidly developing configurational analysis, based on fuzzy set comparative analysis (Fiss, 2011; Ragin, 2008; Woodside and Baxter, 2013), offers tools for addressing the influence of complex contingencies on the chosen focal phenomenon.

Research agenda for the network-based approaches

Because of its primary interest in historically oriented analytical description and understanding, the network approach suffers from two main limitations. First, because of the relatively idiosyncratic case-based tradition, we have only little representative knowledge of the following fundamental 'what' and 'why' questions:

- What kinds of network forms exist in various business contexts?
- Through what kind of organizational arrangements are these network relationships being created and maintained?
- If specific principal forms can be identified, why do these exist, and what aspects and factors are driving them and their diversity?

These questions mirror the issues identified in the market-based approaches. Again, we seem to need a specified theory indicating which environmental or institutional factors influence the formation of various types of business networks. This is a paradoxical point since the entire network approach incorporates the environment through network relationships. Researchers have, however, not been interested in developing such an axiomatic contextual view required for network classification, and some of them see the classification of networks problematic in itself (Håkansson and Ford, 2002).

One way to approach this dilemma is to apply the proposition that the level of determination of a value-producing system has a significant influence on relative stability versus flexibility, and exploitation versus exploration characteristics of value creation networks (Möller and Svahn, 2006). From the theory construction perspective, this means using ideas from the strategic net approach to contribute to the more traditional network theory. In mature business fields, with less uncertainty and slower change, one can expect to find more intentionally created strategic nets (Möller and Rajala, 2007), whereas emerging business fields, characterized by high market and technological uncertainty, are populated by more loose innovation networks and R&D coalitions (Möller and Svahn, 2009). It would be useful to have programmatic cross-field comparative case studies to examine this broad proposition and to develop a more advanced theory of the range of network forms and the macro-forces that influence their emergence.

The second limitation of the network approach is its weakness in producing specific managerial recommendations. This issue is related to the ontological orientation of traditional network research; networks are seen as unique and complex historical phenomena with little predictability. This strong view is being challenged by the strategic net approach, as pointed out above and in the section 'Focal networks and strategic nets'. The new theory suggests that the goals of the strategic nets and the underlying characteristics of the value creation system influence the effective organizational forms, governance structures and managerial capabilities required by the specific nets. The critical examination of these propositions calls for theory-testing type comparative case research. Programmatic studies supported by the emerging analytical methods for addressing complex social systems (Ragin, 2008; Ragin and Amoroso, 2010) would allow us to construct a much-needed theory of network management.

Theory map and the prospect of a general theory of marketing

Can the theory map be useful in developing a general theory of marketing? The notion of cocreation of value by actors integrating, exchanging and cocreating resources through networks of relationships is central to the provision of a new lexicon for marketing (Gummesson and Mele, 2010). Other important aspects are the expressed need to develop a more realistic theory of markets and their evolution than economic theory provides, and the emphasis on the contextual and layered character of value creation and the involved actor relationships. To this end, Vargo and colleagues have proposed an ecosystem perspective for capturing these themes (Chandler and Vargo, 2011; Vargo and Lusch, 2011). These aspects are remarkably similar to the conceptual lexicon and theory the business networks approach provides, but do not resonate with the ontological and epistemological groundings of market-based relationship marketing.

Because of these strong paradigmatic differences between the market-based research traditions and the network approach, it does not seem tenable to pursue one general theory of marketing covering all its domains and layers. Based on the theory map results and discussion we should consider developing at least two general theories of marketing. One would cover market-based exchange practices, the other would cover the value creation aspect and the emergence and construction of new business fields.

Both general theories would benefit from a clearly specified contextual aspect. They should be able to answer the essential questions of 'what specific forms of marketing exist' and 'why specific forms of marketing emerge and exist'. For example, if there are differences in exchange relationships and their organization, and in the business networks and strategic nets, or in value-creating systems, why do these differences exist? In addition, we should be able to answer the question, 'what are efficient forms of organizing and managing value production in different contexts?' It is hoped that the meta-theoretical analysis carried out in this chapter paves the way for this kind of systemic development of marketing theory and advances our understanding of marketing as a complex and layered social phenomenon.

Note

1. This endeavour, although independent, draws heavily on Möller (2013) and owes to Möller and Halinen (2000) and Möller et al. (2009). The author wishes to thank all the colleagues involved in these publications. The work goes on.

Recommended further reading

Aarikka-Stenroos, L., Sandberg, B. and Lehtimäki, T. (2014) 'Networks for the commercialization of innovations: a review of how divergent network actors contribute', *Industrial Marketing Management* 43: 365–81.

Dwyer, F.R., Schurr, P.H. and Oh, S. (1987) 'Developing buyer–seller relationships', *Journal of Marketing* 51 (April): 11–27.

Håkansson, H. and Snehota, I. (eds) (1995) *Developing Relationships in Business Networks*. London: Routledge.

Heide, J.B. (1994) 'Interorganizational governance in marketing channels', *Journal of Marketing* 58 (January): 71–85.

Kumar, V. (2008) *Managing Customers for Profit: Strategies to Increase Profits and Build Loyalty*. Upper Saddle River, NJ: Wharton School Publishing.

Morgan, R.M. and Hunt, S.D. (1994) 'The commitment–trust theory of relationship marketing', *Journal of Marketing* 58 (July): 20–38.

Möller, K. and Halinen, A. (1999) 'Business relationships and networks: managerial challenge of a network era', *Industrial Marketing Management* 28(5): 413–27.

Möller, K. and Halinen, A. (2000) 'Relationship marketing theory: its roots and direction', *Journal of Marketing Management* 16(1–3): 29–54.

Möller, K. and Rajala, A. (2007) 'Rise of strategic nets – new modes of value creation', *Industrial Marketing Management* 36(7): 895–908.

Möller, K., Rajala, A. and Svahn, S. (2005) 'Strategic business nets – their type and management', *Journal of Business Research* 58: 1274–84.

Palmatier, R.W., Dant, R.P., Grewal, D. and Evans, K.R. (2006) 'Factors influencing the effectiveness of relationship marketing: a meta-analysis', *Journal of Marketing* 70(4): 136–53.

Stern, L.W. and Reve, T. (1980) 'Distribution channels as political economies: a framework for comparative analysis', *Journal of Marketing* 44 (Summer): 52–64.

References

Aldrich, H.E. (1979) *Organizations and Environments*. Englewood Cliffs, NJ: Prentice-Hall.

Alajoutsijärvi, K., Möller, K. and Rosenbröijer, C.J. (1999) 'Relevance of focal nets in understanding the dynamics of business relationships', *Journal of Business-to-Business Marketing* 6(1): 3–35.

Anderson, J.C. and Narus, J.A. (1990) 'A model of the distributor's perspective of distributor–manufacturer working partnerships', *Journal of Marketing* 54(1): 42–58.

Arndt, J. (1985) 'On making marketing science more scientific: role of orientations, paradigms, metaphors, and puzzle solving', *Journal of Marketing* 49(1): 11–23.

Baraldi, E. (2008) 'Strategy in industrial networks: experiences from IKEA', *California Management Review* 50(4): 99–126.

Baraldi, E., Brennan, R., Harrison, D., Tunisini, A. and Zolkiewski, J. (2007) 'Strategic thinking and the IMP approach: a comparative analysis', *Industrial Marketing Management* 36(7): 879–94.

Blattberg, R. and Deighton, J. (1991) 'Interactive marketing: exploiting the age of addressability', *Sloan Management Review* 33: 5–14.

Boulding, W., Staelin, R., Ehret, M. and Johnston, W.J. (2005) 'A customer relationship management roadmap: what is known, potential pitfalls, and where to go', *Journal of Marketing* 69(4): 155–66.

Brodie, R., Coviello, N.E. and Winklhofer, H. (2008) 'Contemporary marketing practices research program: a review of the first decade', *Journal of Business & Industrial Marketing* 23(1): 84–94.

Brodie, R., Saren, M. and Pels, J. (2011) 'Theorizing about the service dominant logic: the bridging role of middle range theory', *Marketing Theory* 11(1): 75–91.

Burrell, G. and Morgan, G. (1979) *Sociological Paradigms and Organisational Analysis.* Aldershot: Ashgate.

Chandler, J.D. and Vargo, S.L. (2011) 'Contextualization and value-in-context: how context frames exchange', *Marketing Theory* 11(1): 35–49.

Christopher, M., Payne, A. and Ballantyne, D. (1991) *Relationship Marketing: Bringing Quality, Customer Service and Marketing Together.* London: Butterworth.

Cropanzano, S. and Mitchell, M.S. (2005) 'Social exchange theory: an interdisciplinary review', *Journal of Management* 31(6): 874–900.

Dwyer, F.R., Schurr, P.H. and Oh, S. (1987) 'Developing buyer seller relationships', *Journal of Marketing* 51(2): 11–27.

Easton, G. (1995) 'Methodology and industrial networks', in K. Möller and D. Wilson (eds) *Business Marketing: An Interaction and Network Perspective.* Boston, MA: Kluwer, pp. 411–92.

Easton, G. (2002) 'Marketing: a critical realist approach', *Journal of Business Research* 55(2): 103–9.

Egan, J. (2008) 'A century of marketing', *The Marketing Review* 8(1): 3–23.

Eiriz, V. and Wilson, D. (2006) 'Research in relationship marketing: antecedents, traditions and integration', *European Journal of Marketing* 40(3/4): 275–91.

Emerson, R.M. (1976) 'Social exchange theory', *Annual Review of Sociology* 2: 335–62.

Fiss, P.C. (2011) 'Building better causal theories: a fuzzy set approach to typologies in organizational research', *Academy of Management Journal* 54(2): 393–420.

Ford, D. (2011) 'IMP and service dominant logic: divergence, convergence and development', *Industrial Marketing Management* 40(2): 231–9.

French, J. and Raven, B.H. (1959) 'The bases of social power', in D. Cartwright (ed.) *Studies in Social Power.* Ann Arbor, MI: Institute for Social Research, pp. 150–67.

Gaski, J.F. (1984) 'The theory of power and conflict in channels of distribution', *The Journal of Marketing* 48(3): 9–29.

Gioia, D. and Pitre, E. (1990) 'Multiparadigm perspectives on theory building', *Academy of Management Review* 15(4): 584–602.

Golfetto, F., Salle, R., Borghini, S. and Rinallo, D. (2007) 'Opening the network: bridging the IMP tradition and other research perspectives', *Industrial Marketing Management* 36(7): 844–8.

Grewal, R. and Dharwadkar, R. (2002) 'The role of the institutional environment in marketing channels', *Journal of Marketing* 66(1): 82–97.

Grönroos, C. (2011) 'A service perspective on business relationships: the value creation, interaction and marketing interface', *Industrial Marketing Management* 40(2): 240–7.

Gulati, R., Puranam, P. and Tushman, M. (2012) 'Meta-organization design: rethinking design in interorganizational and community contexts', *Strategic Management Journal* 33(6): 571–86.

Gummesson, E. (2008) 'Extending the service-dominant logic: from customer centricity to balanced centricity', *Journal of the Academy of Marketing Science* 36(1): 15–17.

Gummesson, E. and Mele, C. (2010) 'Marketing as value co-creation through network interaction and resource integration', *Journal of Business Market Management* 4: 181–98.

Håkansson, H. and Ford, D. (2002) 'How should companies interact in business networks?', *Journal of Business Research* 55(2): 133–9.

Håkansson, H. and Snehota, I. (eds) (1995) *Developing Relationships in Business Networks*. London: Routledge.

Håkansson, H. and Waluszewski, A. (2002a) 'Path dependence: restricting or facilitating technical development?', *Journal of Business Research* 55(7): 561–70.

Håkansson, H. and Waluszewski, A. (eds) (2002b) *Managing Technological Development: IKEA, the Environment and Technology*. London: Routledge.

Halinen, A. (1997) *Relationship Marketing in Professional Services: A Study of Agency–Client Dynamics in the Advertising Sector*. London: Routledge.

Hallen, L., Johanson, J. and Seyed-Mohamed, N. (1991) 'Interfirm adaptation in business relationships', *Journal of Marketing* 55(2): 29–37.

Heide, J.B. (1994) 'Inter-organizational governance in marketing channels', *Journal of Marketing* 58(1): 71–98.

Heide, J.B. and John, G. (1992) 'Do norms matter in marketing relationships?', *Journal of Marketing* 56(2): 32–44.

Henneberg, S.C., Mouzas, S. and Naudé, P. (2006) 'Network pictures: concepts and representations', *European Journal of Marketing* 40(3/4): 408–29.

Jarillo, J.C. (1993) *Strategic Networks: Creating the Borderless Organization*. Oxford: Butterworth-Heinemann.

Jenkinson, A. (1995) *Valuing Your Customers: From Quality Information to Quality Relationships Through Database Marketing*. London: McGraw-Hill.

Kelley, H.H. and Thibaut, J.W. (1978) *Interpersonal Relations: A Theory of Interdependence*. New York: John Wiley.

Knight, L. (2002) 'Network learning: exploring learning by interorganizational networks', *Human Relations* 55(4): 427–53.

Kuhn, T.S. (1962) *The Structure of Scientific Revolutions*. Chicago, IL: University of Chicago Press.

Kuhn, T.S. (1987) 'What are scientific revolutions?', in L. Kruger, L.J. Daston and M. Heidelberger (eds) *The Probabilistic Revolution*. Cambridge, MA: MIT Press, pp. 7–22.

Kumar, A., Heide, J.B. and Wathne, K.H. (2011) 'Performance implications of mismatched governance regimes across external and internal relationships', *Journal of Marketing* 75(2): 1–17.

Kumar, V. (2008) *Managing Customers for Profit: Strategies to Increase Profits and Build Loyalty*. Upper Saddle River, NJ: Wharton School Publishing.

Lundgren, A. (1995) *Technological Innovation and Network Evolution*. London: Routledge.

Macneil, I.R. (1980) *The New Social Contract: An Inquiry into Modern Contractual Relations*. New Haven, CT: Yale University Press.

Malthouse, E. and Blattberg, R. (2005) 'Can we predict customer lifetime value?', *Journal of Interactive Marketing* 19(1): 2–16.

Mattsson, L.G. (1997) 'Relationship marketing and the markets-as-networks approach: a comparative analysis of two evolving streams of research', *Journal of Marketing Management* 13(7): 447–62.

Merton, R.K. (1967) *On Theoretical Sociology: Five Essays, Old and New*. New York: The Free Press.

Möller, K. (2006a) 'Role of competences in creating customer value: a value-creation logic approach', *Industrial Marketing Management* 35: 913–24.

Möller, K. (2006b) 'Marketing mix discussion – is the mix misleading us or are we misreading the mix? Comment on: The Marketing Mix Revisited: Towards the 21st Century Marketing by E. Constantinides', *Journal of Marketing Management* 22: 439–50.

Möller, K. (2010) 'Sense-making and agenda construction in emerging business networks – how to direct radical innovation', *Industrial Marketing Management* 39(5): 361–71.

Möller, K. (2013) 'Theory map of business marketing: relationships and networks perspectives', *Industrial Marketing Management* 43(3): 324–35.

Möller, K. and Halinen, A. (1999) 'Business relationships and networks: managerial challenge of a network era', *Industrial Marketing Management* 28(5): 413–27.

Möller, K. and Halinen, A. (2000) 'Relationship marketing theory: its roots and directions', *Journal of Marketing Management* 16(1–3): 29–54.

Möller, K. and Rajala, A. (2007) 'Rise of strategic nets: new modes of value creation', *Industrial Marketing Management* 36(7): 895–908.

Möller, K. and Svahn, S. (2003) 'Managing strategic nets: a capability perspective', *Marketing Theory* 3(2): 201–26.

Möller, K. and Svahn, S. (2006) 'Role of knowledge in value creation in business nets', *Journal of Management Studies* 43(5): 985–1007.

Möller, K. and Svahn, S. (2009) 'How to influence the birth of new business fields', *Industrial Marketing Management* 38: 450–8.

Möller, K. and Törrönen, P. (2003) 'Business suppliers value creation potential: a capability-based analysis', *Industrial Marketing Management* 32: 109–18.

Möller, K., Rajala, A. and Svahn, S. (2005) 'Strategic business nets: their type and management', *Journal of Business Research* 58: 1274–84.

Möller, K., Pels, J. and Saren, M. (2009) 'The marketing theory or theories into marketing? Plurality of research traditions and paradigms', in P. Maclaran et al. (eds) *The Sage Handbook of Marketing Theory*. London: Sage.

Morgan, G. and Smircich, L. (1980) 'The case for qualitative research', *Academy of Management Review* 5(4): 491–500.

Morgan, R.M. and Hunt, S.D. (1994) 'The commitment–trust theory of relationship marketing', *Journal of Marketing* 58: 20–38.

Okhuysen, G. and Bonardi, J. (2011) 'The challenges of building theory by combining lenses', *Academy of Management Review* 36(1): 6–11.

Parmigiani, A. and Rivera-Santos, M. (2011) 'Clearing the path through the forest: a meta-review of inter-organizational relationships', *Journal of Management* 37: 1108–36.

Parolini, C. (1999) *The Value Net: A Tool for Competitive Strategy*. Chichester: John Wiley.

Pels, J., Möller, K.E. and Saren, M. (2009) 'Do we really understand business marketing? Getting beyond RM–BM matrimony', *Journal of Business & Industrial Marketing* 24(5/6): 322–36.

Peppers, D. and Rogers, M. (1997) *Enterprise One to One: Tools for Comparing in the Interactive Age*. New York: Currency/Doubleday.

Peters, L., Johnston, W., Pressey, A. and Kendrick, T. (2010) 'Collaboration and collective learning: networks as learning organisations', *Journal of Business & Industrial Marketing* 26(6): 478–84.

Peters, L., Pressey, A., Vanharanta, M. and Johnston, W. (2013) 'Constructivism and critical realism as alternative approaches to the study of business networks: convergences and divergences in theory and in research practice', *Industrial Marketing Management* 42(3): 336–46.

Pfeffer, J. and Salancick, G.R. (1978) *The External Control of Organisations: A Resource-dependence Perspective*. New York: Harper & Row.

Pondy, L.R. (1967) 'Organizational conflict: concepts and models', *Administrative Science Quarterly* 12: 296–320.

Powell, W.W. (1990) 'Neither market nor hierarchy: network forms of organization', *Research in Organizational Behavior* 12: 295–336.

Powell, W.W., Kogut, K. and Smith-Doerr, L. (1996) 'Interorganizational collaboration and the locus of innovation: networks of learning in biotechnology', *Administrative Science Quarterly* 41(1): 116–45.

Powell, W.W., White, D.R., Koput, K.W. and Owen-Smith, J. (2005) 'Network dynamics and field evolution: the growth of interorganizational collaboration in the life sciences', *The American Journal of Sociology* 110(4): 1132–206.

Raab, J. and Kenis, P. (2009) 'Heading toward a society of networks: empirical developments and theoretical challenges', *Journal of Management Inquiry* 18(3): 198–210.

Ragin, C.C. (2008) *Redesigning Social Inquiry: Fuzzy Sets and Beyond.* Chicago, IL: University of Chicago Press.

Ragin, C.C. and Amoroso, L.M. (2010) *Constructing Social Research: The Unity and Diversity of Method*, 2nd edn. Thousand Oaks, CA: Sage.

Ramos, C. and Ford, D. (2011) 'Network pictures as a research device: developing a tool to capture actors' perceptions in organizational networks', *Industrial Marketing Management* 40(3): 447–64.

Rindfleisch, A. and Heide, J.B. (1997) 'Transaction cost analysis: past, present and future', *Journal of Marketing* 61(4): 30–54.

Ritter, T., Wilkinson, I. and Johnston, W.J. (2004) 'Managing in complex business networks', *Industrial Marketing Management* 33: 175–83.

Robicheaux, R.A. and Coleman, J. (1994) 'The structure of marketing relationships', *Journal of the Academy of Marketing Science* 22: 38–51.

Rosenkopf, L. and Padula, G. (2008) 'Investigating the microstructure of network evolution: alliance formation in the mobile communications industry', *Organization Science* 19(5): 1–19.

Rosenkopf, L. and Schilling, M. (2007) 'Comparing alliance network structure across industries: observations and explanations', *Strategic Entrepreneurship Journal* 1: 191–209.

Rust, R.T., Lemon, K.N. and Zeithaml, V.A. (2004) 'Return on marketing: using customer equity to focus marketing strategy', *Journal of Marketing* 68(1): 109–27.

Stern, L.W. and Reve, T. (1980) 'Distribution channels as political economies: a framework for comparative analysis', *Journal of Marketing* 44: 52–64.

Tadejewski, M. (2008) 'Incommensurable paradigms, cognitive bias and the politics of marketing theory', *Marketing Theory* 8(3): 273–97.

Terho, H. and Halinen, A. (2012) 'The nature of customer portfolios: towards new understanding of firms' exchange contexts', *Journal of Business-to-Business Marketing* 19(4): 335–66.

Turnbull, P.W., Ford, D. and Cunningham, M. (1996) 'Interaction, relationships and networks in business markets: an evolving perspective', *Journal of Business & Industrial Marketing* 11(3/4): 44–62.

Ulaga, W. (2003) 'Capturing value creation in business relationships: a customer perspective', *Industrial Marketing Management* 32(8): 677–93.

Ulaga, W. and Eggert, A. (2006) 'Value-based differentiation in business relationships: gaining and sustaining key supplier status', *Journal of Marketing* 70(1): 119–36.

van de Ven, A.H. (2007) *Engaged Scholarship: A Guide for Organizational and Social Research.* Oxford: Oxford University Press.

Vargo, S.L. and Lusch, R.F. (2004) 'Evolving to a new dominant logic for marketing', *Journal of Marketing* 68(1): 1–17.

Vargo, S.L. and Lusch, R.F. (2008a) 'From goods to service(s): divergences and convergences of logics', *Industrial Marketing Management* 37: 254–9.

Vargo, S.L. and Lusch, R.F. (2008b) 'Service-dominant logic: continuing the evolution', *Journal of the Academy of Marketing Science* 36(1): 1–10.

Vargo, S.L. and Lusch, R.F. (2010) 'From repeat patronage to value-co-creation in service ecosystems: a transcending conceptualization of relationship', *Journal of Business Marketing Management* 37: 169–79.

Vargo, S.L. and Lusch, R.F. (2011) 'It's all B2B... and beyond: toward a systems perspective of the market', *Industrial Marketing Management* 40: 181–7.

Wathne, K.H. and Heide, J.B. (2004) 'Relationship governance in a supply chain network', *Journal of Marketing* 68: 73–89.

Weick, K.E. (1985) *Sensemaking in Organizations*. Thousand Oaks, CA: Sage.

Welch, C., Piekkari, R., Plakoyiannaki, E. and Paavilainen-Mäntymäki, E. (2011) 'Theorizing from case studies: Towards a pluralist future for international business research', *Journal of International Business Studies* 42: 740–62.

Williamson, O.E. (1985) *The Economic Institutions of Capitalism*. New York: The Free Press.

Wilson, D.T. (1995) 'An integrated model of buyer–seller relationships', *Journal of the Academy of Marketing Science* 23(4): 335–45.

Woodside, A.G. and Baxter, R. (2013) 'Achieving accuracy, generalization-to-contexts, and complexity in theories of business-to-business decision processes', *Industrial Marketing Management* 42(3): 382–93.

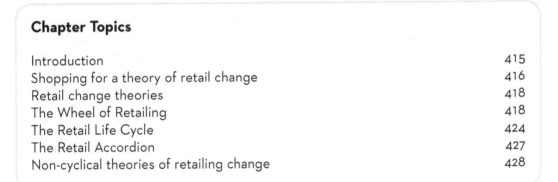

Theories of Retailing

Christopher Moore and Stephen Doyle

17

Chapter Topics

Introduction   415
Shopping for a theory of retail change   416
Retail change theories   418
The Wheel of Retailing   418
The Retail Life Cycle   424
The Retail Accordion   427
Non-cyclical theories of retailing change   428

Introduction

What we readily identify and understand to be the purpose, nature and scope of retailing has changed markedly as a result of the digital revolution in the past decade. In the pre-digital age (and other than for catalogue distributors), retailing was synonymous with a specific place – the shop space – which served as the location for the exchange of goods and services from retailer to end-consumer. Now, those companies that still self-identify as retailers can secure the sale of their goods and services through the use of applications downloaded onto mobile devices. They have no need for a shop place. The new version of the retail sales floor is the coordinated outfit display presented as an Instagram image, from which a consumer can purchase directly through a sequence of screen taps. Increasingly and commonly, space within the retailer's store (which was previously designated as their most and only economically productive selling space) is now being converted into non-productive 'Click and Collect' storage areas for goods bought not in store, but through digital distribution channels, which await customer collection.

Within this context of swift and deep structural upheaval in retail markets, there is a very clear need for theories and concepts to help us make better and fuller sense of what has happened, and what is likely to happen, within the retailing sector. Yet, while there would be a clear benefit in having relevant theories of retailing to assist in the analysis and interpretation of the recent and ongoing revolution that is happening in retailing, it is certainly the case that retailing theories are much less developed than theories relevant to consumption in general and specifically to shopping. This can be partly explained by the fact that retailing has long been perceived as a marginal, low-skill, low-status sector and has, as a result, struggled to find deep recognition within the mainstream of business and management academic research.

Yet, despite the comparative underdevelopment, it would be misleading to suggest that there is no credible theoretical basis for the study of retailing. Thanks to the perseverance of a cluster of high calibre researchers within the US, the UK and Scandinavia over the past 40 years, a credible, if narrow, theory of retailing has been established. In truth, the most important of the theories were established before the mid-1980s, but that does not mean that there have not been recent theoretical advances. With the emergence of major global retailers, such as Zara, H&M, Louis Vuitton and Wal-Mart, these firms now are recognized as among the world's largest and most successful companies. As a consequence, the status, scope and pace of research within retailing have improved significantly, and perhaps in recognition of the global reach of retailers, theories of retailer globalization have been the most prevalent in the past decade.

Notwithstanding these recent developments, one area of retail theory dominates the field – that which relates to retail change. Before discussing these aspects of retailing theory in the remainder of this chapter, the next section will consider and locate this strand of theory within the wider context of shopping and consumer behaviour research.

Shopping for a theory of retail change

Invariably, retailing and shopping are used as interchangeable terms within the mainstream media (and in some areas of the academic literature) and little or no attempt has been made to locate their differences, similarities or functions. Clearly, both are interdependent but distinct: shopping is a consumer act, retailing is a business system. Retailing and shopping are inextricably linked through a shared process. Shopping is the often repetitive, demonstrable act of acquiring goods and services for personal use by a consumer. Its counterpart is retailing. Retailing is the formalized business system that emerges, establishes and evolves as a means of facilitating, enabling and stimulating the consumer's shopping act.

Arguably, the study of how and why consumers shop is more theoretically advanced than that of retailing. Drawing contributions from a variety of fields and disciplines (particularly psychology, social anthropology and human geography), the study of shopping is used to provide insights into how products, brands and shopping are adopted by consumers to create, augment and enhance their personal identities, and define their role and status within society, and to explain how individuals find their place within sub-groups and other social forms.

In the past generation, in particular, the case for the study of shopping has advanced as a result of a number of significant drivers. The first is the emergence of consumer behaviour as a critical component of marketing education. The study of shopping provides an accessible and inclusive platform for researchers to explore and understand a variety of behavioural dimensions, including the dynamics that influence and affect patterns of consumption, the dynamics of group interaction upon brand selection, and the impact of product aesthetics and environmental cues upon product choice within discrete consumption settings.

Second, consideration of the motives, methods and developments in shopping, from the perspective of both consumer and retailer, has shifted into the realm of mainstream culture. There is an appetite – in many instances, taking the form of entertainment – for a lighter-touch analysis of how people shop and the factors that influence and affect what, how and where they purchase. As a result, new strands of research outputs have emerged which seek to provide explanations for trends in shopping and in particular the extremes in shopping behaviour.

Third, the transformational impact of digital technologies upon shopping has resulted in a deluge of new research. The digital era means that retailers can communicate and sell to consumers on an individualized basis. The process of product selection no longer begins in store, but instead begins from viewing a mobile device in the palm of the customer's hand. Opening hours are no longer restricted but are perpetual and consumer access to retailers and their goods is no longer local but global. The impact of digital upon the form and function of shopping has been enormous and in many instances academic research trails significantly behind the many and complex advances that have affected shopping in the digital age.

While there may be no definitive and/or universal theory of shopping, there does exist an advanced understanding of the characteristics of shopping behaviour, of the impact of shopping within society and its contribution to the creation and maintenance of individual identity.

Within the context of retailing theory, the appetite for the development of theories of retailing appears now to be very limited. From an historical perspective, the 'golden age' of retail theory building was from the mid-20th century until the early 1990s. Since then, there has been no significant advancement of theory in the area. This may be due to a number of reasons. First, the initial theory building was well developed and efficient and the attendant debates have been fought and won. Perhaps there is a view that there is not much more to meaningfully say. Second, the study of retailing has declined drastically in many territories, including the UK, the USA and Europe. At best, the study of retailing exists as a marginal option in many universities and is no longer viewed as a vibrant and growing area for academic teaching and learning. Consequently, there are far fewer academics actively engaged in the study of retailing in general and as a result, the interest in the development of contemporary theories of retailing is very low.

The decline in interest and engagement with theories of retailing is perhaps peculiar given the degree of turbulence and change that the sector currently faces as a result of the advances in digital technology. But on the other hand, as Fernie et al. (2015) propose, retailing markets have continually faced disruption and change and so the change precipitated by the digital revolution is just a new form of an established pattern. Furthermore, they recognize that the theories that seek to explain retail change are as relevant today as they were when they were formulated 30–40 years ago.

Retail change theories

Expressed simply, the purpose of retail change theories has been to provide some explanation of the structure of retail markets, the dominant business strategies and the trading activities of retail firms. These theories share a common view that change within retailing is cyclical – and is deterministic and predictable. In the main, these theories suggest that retailers largely follow a sequential pattern of evolvement and development that provides little or no opportunity for deviation. Consequently, the theories infer that retailers have little or no scope for strategic choice. Their advancement is premeditated and inevitable.

Perhaps the most extensive and challenging critique of the various theories of retail change was provided by Brown (1987, 1995) and he questions the extent to which these rigid expectations of retail evolvement reflect an environment that is by its very nature unpredictable, unstable, fragmented and constantly varying. Brown rightly questioned the appropriateness of the theories in general terms and his reservations will be used to critique the core perspectives of these theories later in this chapter. However, while mindful of these potential limitations, it is important to note that other researchers see some value in reviewing longitudinal patterns of retail development in order to gain some insight into trends and opportunities within the sector. Fernie at al. (2015) noted Hollander's (1986) observation that taking a longer term view is advantageous and while history may not perfectly repeat itself, it will suggest both questions and useful answers with respect to the nature of retail change.

There are three principal cyclical theories of retail change: the Wheel of Retailing; the Retail Life Cycle; and the Retail Accordion. Each will be considered in more detail below.

The Wheel of Retailing

First proposed by Professor Malcolm P. McNair in 1958, the priority of the Wheel of Retailing was to suggest a cyclical pattern for retail business development. The essence of McNair's hypothesis is that new types of retailers begin life at the lowest end of the retail price, status and margin spectrum. From their initial low price positioning, retailers then advance their business models to become more sophisticated in their activities and complex in their organization. Their cost structure inflates as they begin to 'trade-up' in terms of their pricing policy, selling

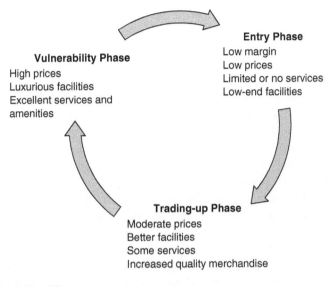

Vulnerability Phase

High prices
Luxurious facilities
Excellent services and
amenities

Entry Phase

Low margin
Low prices
Limited or no services
Low-end facilities

Trading-up Phase

Moderate prices
Better facilities
Some services
Increased quality merchandise

Figure 17.1   The Wheel of Retailing.

Source: Brown (1988).

methods and service provision. They achieve this shift upmarket through investments in store environments and by selecting bigger and better locations and through the diverse scrambling of their product and service provision. As a result of these significant investments, these retailers shift from low to high operating cost businesses. The final stage of their evolvement (as predicted by the theory) is that these retailers mature to become high-cost, high-price, and ultimately inefficient businesses. At this stage, and perhaps even before, these once flexible and efficient businesses become vulnerable to the innovations and cost-efficiencies of newer, more agile low-price entrants.

Brown (1988) provides a clear representation of the Wheel of Retailing as consisting of three distinct change phases – entry, trading-up, vulnerability. Further, as Figure 17.1 illustrates, Brown proposes that each phase is characterized by distinct management activities and priorities.

In his analysis of McNair's theory, Hollander (1960) acknowledged many examples which conform to this pattern of retailer development. In particular, he noted that department store merchants, who originally emerged as strong low-price competitors to specialist retailers, themselves through trading-up over time became vulnerable to discount houses and supermarket competition. However, as a caveat to the supporting evidence, Hollander also questioned whether the expectation of an increase in operating expenses and a decrease in profitability was indeed inevitable and possible to demonstrate from external evidence. He noted the difficulties associated with the verification methodology – particularly with respect to accessing historical retail expense information due to the scarce and fragmented nature of data sources. Furthermore, such data are usually published on an aggregate basis and as such may mask significant divergent tendencies and underlying patterns of change.

Yet, setting aside the difficulties associated with verifying the theory, Hollander did identify six dimensions that may precipitate the cyclical forms of retail developments as espoused by the Wheel of Retailing. These were as follows:

- *Retail personalities.* New types of retail businesses are founded by aggressive, highly cost-conscious entrepreneurs who make every penny count and who have no interest in providing unprofitable frills. However, as these entrepreneurs increase in age and wealth, their cost control vigilance deteriorates. Further, their successors may be less competent and they (or their successors) may be less able to manage costs effectively and less dexterous as their businesses increase in scale and complexity. This change and deterioration in management results in a movement along the wheel.
- *Misguidance.* Retailers are seduced by the power of supplier advertising and marketing persuasion to install overly elaborate facilities and undertake unnecessary modernizations. This results in a shift towards a higher, more expensive market positioning.
- *Imperfect competition.* Based upon the premise that most retailers would prefer to avoid direct price competition – principally to avoid damaging retaliation from competitors – they instead seek to compete for differentiation through service improvements, particularly in terms of selecting better locations. Through what Hollander described as 'a ratchet process', retailers – across all sectors – appear almost predisposed to provide more elaborate services at increasingly higher margins.
- *Excess capacity.* Linked to the above, as more retailers enter the market, available consumer demand is spread thinly. As McGoldrick (2002) suggests, in order to avoid suicidal price cutting, retailers opt instead for non-price competition that typically involves the development of additional higher cost service provision.
- *Secular trend.* As markets become more affluent, opportunities emerge for retailers to trade-up their offer in response to the aspirations of their customers. This results in a shift of the wheel through the provision of additional services and higher margin goods.
- *Illusion.* Rather than supporting the premise of the Wheel of Retailing, Hollander suggests that the trend towards the extension of ranges through merchandise scrambling may in fact create an incorrect illusion of trading-up – when the reality is that the margins on the original merchandise may remain unchanged.

A further dimension in support of the 'Wheel Hypothesis' is provided by Goworek and McGoldrick (2015), who suggested that the personal preferences and tastes of retail owners/senior management may result in their creating enhanced store environments and adding services which they themselves may expect but which are in reality beyond the financial capabilities and interests of their less affluent customers.

Marks & Spencer – a perfect Wheel?

The corporate development of leading British retailer Marks & Spencer reflects – in broad terms – the various phases included in the Wheel of Retailing. In 1884 Michael Marks, a

Russian-born Polish refugee opened a stall in Leeds' Kirkgate Market. All items – ranging from nails and spoons, to soap and luggage labels – were sold for a penny. Within 10 years, the firm had extended to 12 stores and a partner found – Thomas Spencer – who developed the company's skills in organizational structure development and supplier contract management. By 1901 the company had built a stock-holding warehouse to its own specification. After a period of acquisition of other smaller 'penny bazaars' before the First World War, the company then began to move up-scale with the launch of their own branded merchandise range, the opening of a flagship store in London's Oxford Street and the establishment of an impressive headquarters in a prime district within central London. Furthermore, throughout the inter-war years, the company extended the scope and complexity of their business to include premium grocery departments, a scientific research lab for garment testing and product development, and went on to provide enhanced customer services in the form of coffee bars and self-service forms of product merchandising.

Internally, from the 1930s onwards, the company became a leading provider of staff welfare programmes, through the development of a generous pension scheme, subsidized canteens, health and dental services, hair dressing and a generous staff clothing allowance.

As the company grew in scale and success in the years after the Second World War, it became more complicated as a business (in 1954 an internal initiative, Operation Simplification removed 26 million paper forms from internal processes), while the products and services offered by the company became more extensive and elaborate. Marks & Spencer was the first UK chain to offer a no quibble refund and exchange policy and the company also pioneered new product categories – such as petite clothing ranges for smaller women – and introduced new food technologies – such as 'boil-in-the-bag' cooking in 1973, followed by sell-by dates marked on all food products and ready-made Chinese and Indian meals in 1975.

Selling space is arguably a retailer's most expensive asset and any attempt to use it for service provision is clearly an indication of business trade-up. In 1979 Marks & Spencer introduced their first fitting rooms – thereby sacrificing valuable selling place to augment and enhance the customer experience.

Buoyed by the successes that emerged as a result of these developments, further trading-up in the form of international store openings, acquisition of premium foreign retailers (such as the American Brooks Brothers and Kings supermarket chains in 1988), premium-priced furniture goods selling and the launch of a financial services company, became an essential element of the firm's trading strategy. By 1997, company pre-tax profits exceeded £1 billion, making Marks & Spencer Europe's most profitable retailer. The following year, pre-tax profits grew a further 6% to £1.17 billion. The chairman, Sir Richard Greenbury, in his statement in their Annual Report for 1998 stated that: 'Our business [Marks & Spencer] has become increasingly complex, both operationally and in terms of product.' Further, he noted that:

> ... there is no longer a typical Marks & Spencer store. Outlets vary enormously in size and each is laid out and merchandised for a specific purpose – from a departmental store of 150,000 square feet serving a wide area such as Newcastle to a sandwich shop in the City of London. The extra

space we are acquiring also enables us to create a more comfortable and convenient shopping environment – with improved facilities for elderly people and parents with young children, more and better fitting rooms and toilets and, in larger stores, coffee bars and restaurants. (*Marks & Spencer Annual Report*, 1998: 5)

The chairman's final observations were that the company had 'entered a period of bold investment – however, we have always prudently managed our cash resources, and, more important, taken the long-term view when growing your business. I am therefore confident that we will remain as we are today; the most profitable retailer in Europe' (*Marks & Spencer Annual Report*, 1998: 7).

As the old adage goes: pride comes before a fall. This was certainly the case for Marks & Spencer. The next year, 1999, Sir Richard Greenbury, in his last statement as company chairman, adopted a very different tone. His statement read:

In the year just ended, the Group suffered a major setback, interrupting our record of consistent and profitable progress over many previous years. Pre-tax profits were £665.7m compared with last year's record breaking figure of £1,114.8m. … Unfortunately, and notably over the all-important Christmas trading period, clothing sales fell away very badly and significant quantities of fashionable merchandise needed to be reduced in the post Christmas sale. The demand for food was also flat with extremely competitive prices, whilst our Home Furnishings Group suffered from the cyclical downturn in demand for such products. As I forewarned, the ambitious expansion programme in prime selling footage, infrastructure developments, property acquisitions and the Catalogue, has significantly cut into our operating profits. (*Marks & Spencer Annual Report*, 1999: 4–5)

Since their profit peak of 1998, the company has faced formidable competition from domestic and international competitors. In some instances, as predicted by the Wheel of Retailing, competition has come from low price alternatives such as H&M and New Look. But in the main, the nature of the competitive challenge for Marks & Spencer in the past 15 years has been far more connected to the superior ability of competitors, such as Zara, to respond to the latest fashion trends through the creation at speed of contemporary fashion collections that are presented in store environments that are more sophisticated and engaging. While not as fashion-led as Zara, Next has outpaced Marks & Spencer through their development of an efficient and effective digital offer that has eliminated the long delivery wait time and secured their market superiority through their combination of an extensive store network with fast online delivery of products that are competitively priced and sufficiently fashion-forward.

In response to the significant competitor challenge that Marks & Spencer face from more agile, fashion-led competitors, the company identified a number of approaches to improving their performance in the women's wear market. The Annual Report for 2015 stated:

When we see a trend coming, we work quickly to interpret it for our customers. As the UK market leader in Womenswear denim, we knew that the recent denim catwalk trend would resonate with our shoppers. With strong editorial backing on M&S.com, a feature in Vogue, bold in-store visual merchandising and joined-up marketing, our range was a hit. We sold 4.3m pairs of women's jeans, up 7% on the year. Customers love newness, so we've made sure that we send more to more stores, with new lines landing in store every 2–3 weeks. Our Limited Edition range is now in all stores and our Rosie for Autograph lingerie and sleepwear is in the majority of stores, giving more choice to more of our customers, no matter where they live.

Over 70% of our female customers deem the fit of a garment to be the number one determining factor of quality. Our Fit Development team, which is unique to M&S, undertook a major project to ensure a consistent, good fit across all our brands. It has resulted in a 20% reduction in customer complaints about fit. We want our customers to feel confident about finding stylish clothes that fit and flatter, whatever they buy. (*Marks & Spencer Annual Report*, 2015: 12)

Unquestionably, Marks & Spencer's current strategic approach is in direct response to the actions and successes of their competitors. Reflecting upon their origins as a one penny market-stall trading business and tracking their development to become, at one point, Europe's most profitable retailer, the subsequent decline in their success and their recent attempt to emulate the business actions of their newer entrant rivals, does indicate that Marks & Spencer's business history fits well with the schema suggested by the Wheel of Retailing.

Non-conforming retailing formats

While it is possible to find some broad applications for the Wheel of Retailing, many commentators have noted there is a paucity of hard empirical evidence to support its claims. Indeed, there are sufficient examples of retailer formats that do not conform to the Wheel's stages. Three particular formats can be readily identified.

The first is the specialist, luxury goods retailer. Firms such as Louis Vuitton, Chanel and Hermes were each founded by expert craftspersons who established their businesses in order to serve the needs of affluent customers. The salons that they established were immediately prestigious and impressive – designed and organized principally to match the expectations and requirements of demanding, rich clients. Their service levels were high to match their prices and margins. Consequently, these luxury retailers avoided the low-price, low-service entry level phase as dictated by the linear progression of the Wheel and instead acquired a top positioning from their earliest days. This does not mean however that these luxury brands do not engage with the mass market. Through the creation of pyramid business models that enable engagement with the lower end of the market through the sale of sunglasses, make-up and fragrances, these retailers have instead taken the reverse route that is proposed by the Wheel of Retailing by engaging initially at the top end of the market and then have progressed to engage downwards but without compromising their premium brand positioning.

The advent of digital business has provided an opportunity for the online-only retailer to provide an impressive 'brand experience', complete with a deep and wide merchandise range and an array of relevant and compelling customer service dimensions. Online businesses like Amazon, Net-a-Porter and Zalando have been able to avoid the elementary stages of business development as expected by the Wheel, due to the very nature of their trading medium. This is because digital businesses have low barriers to entry. In comparison to the establishment of a physical retail property portfolio, market entry and development by digital-only retailers is much less expensive, significantly less risky and can be done at much greater speed. It is also acknowledged that the management of a digital retail store is far less problematic but just as effective as that of a multinational chain of retail stores (Fernie et al., 2015).

Furthermore, these firms have created businesses where none previously existed and have in so doing, secured a dominant market positioning. As such, digital/online retailers are a second non-conforming format.

The third are those retail formats that are created by previously successful entrepreneurs or by established, cash-rich conglomerates that create upscale businesses from scratch from their significant investment capability. These firms are created with a specific target segment in mind and their trading dimensions are precisely defined in order to match the segment's requirements. The Swedish apparel retailer H&M has extended the company's retail format portfolio to include other brands such as And Other Stories and COS. Each brand, respectively, is geared towards a progressively older age segment. The product assortment, store environment, pricing strategy and communications plan for each brand is customized to match the aspirations and expectations of each discrete target group.

Each of H&M group's new brands has been created to be format-precise and ready. None has evolved in the manner predicted by the Wheel of Retailing, since the positioning plan, investment resources and trading support were immediately available from the outset to establish each brand as premium within their respective markets. None entered the market and evolved in the staged and predicted route as suggested by the Wheel.

Consequently, as Hollander (1960) noted, the number of non-conforming examples clearly indicates that the Wheel of Retailing theory does not universally define the evolution of all forms of retailing. However, there is sufficient evidence that the Wheel does reflect at least a general pattern of progression for certain retailing forms. Perhaps most importantly, the Wheel of Retailing connects the development of retailing formats with the increasing affluence and prosperity of consumers. As such, this theory of retailing certainly hints that format evolvement is linked to external environmental influences.

The Retail Life Cycle

Fernie et al. (2015) have identified two important failings with respect to the Wheel of Retailing. First, as has been previously noted, the Wheel does not recognize the possibility of premium/luxury retailers that enter the market, from the outset, with a high-cost and high-margin position. Consequently, the model does not recognize that these retailers will retain their high-profit, high-cost and high-price positioning indefinitely. Second, they maintain that the sequential nature of the Wheel of Retailing framework is unable to accommodate and allow for the possibilities that arise from the speed, diversity and complexity of new retailing developments.

Davidson et al. (1976) proposed in an article in the *Harvard Business Review* an alternative theory of retail development in the form of the Retail Life Cycle. Paralleling the phases and strands of Levitt's (1965) product life cycle, this version for retailing proposes that businesses follow a four-stage pattern of development: introduction, growth, maturity and decline.

A number of business and trading characteristics are particular to each stage. As retailers enter the introductory stage – motivated by the desire to bring some innovation or novelty to the market – they operate with few competitors. At this first stage, they enjoy a rapid sales growth but gain only low or moderate levels of profitability. The next is the growth stage – where rapid sales increases not only generate uplifts in profitability, they also attract the interest of competitors who likewise will seek to make gains in the new area/sector. The maturity stage follows, and this is when the sector is populated with the largest number of competitors and as a result, price competition increases and profitability levels reach a plateau. Finally, the decline stage sees the emergence of agile, often indirect, competitors in the market – and with the onslaught of such high levels of competitor challenge, the retailer faces the double difficulty of declining sales and reduced profitability.

As McGoldrick (2002) noted, the Retail Life Cycle theory has been applied to both specific retail business and to general retail formats. In terms of the latter, Davidson et al. (1976) provide some interesting observations with respect to the life cycle gestations of a range of retail formats in the USA. Noting the time taken for each format to reach its peak and then to fall into decline, American department stores were found to have reached their maturity stage after 80 years, while variety stores peaked after 45 and discount department stores within 20 years. Other than identifying the gestation of each of the formats, these observations also highlight the fairly rapid contraction in the sustainability and viability of retail formats in recent years.

Looking specifically at examples of the Retail Life Cycle at the retailer level, the decline of the variety retailer Woolworths in the UK provides a clear application of the Retail Life Cycle theory. Established in Liverpool in 1909, as a subsidiary of the American retailer F.W. Woolworth that had been founded 30 years earlier in Pennsylvania, Woolworths entered the UK with an innovative trading, product and pricing formula. With most items costing three pence, and none over sixpence, the product assortment was large and included children's clothes, haberdashery, stationery, toys and of course, pic'n'mix sweets. The business gained a significant cost advantage from the scale economies obtained from its American parent and this enabled Woolworths to sell china and glassware basics at far cheaper prices than their British competitors. Significantly, Woolworths was the first variety store retailer to adopt a self-service layout plan. Rather than every product being 'sold' to a customer by an assistant, the Woolworths approach was to allow customers to browse, self-select, purchase and leave.

Woolworths in the UK really accelerated in terms of growth in the mid-1920s – with a new store opening every month across the country. Their British success led the parent company to float a 15% stake in their British subsidiary on the London Stock Exchange in 1931. The floatation was so successful that the company was able to pay 90 cents for every dollar invested as an exceptional dividend to all of its shareholders. The emergence of the postwar baby boomers provided a new consumer category – the teenager – and this brought new and important spending power into the company. With their interest in music, magazines and fashions, the company extended their offer to become the leading entertainment/leisure retailer in the country.

Having been acquired from its American owners in 1982 by Paternoster stores (a forerunner of the Kingfisher Group), a variety of strategies was deployed in order to resuscitate growth after a sharp decline in the late 1980s. However, by the early 1990s, the company faced formidable competition from specialist firms, such as HMV and Superdrug who offered a more authoritative brand and product offering within Woolworths' core product areas. Further, the rise and expansion of food retailers, particularly Tesco and Asda, into non-food areas meant that Woolworths was further undermined by the huge scale, competitive pricing and convenience offered by these important retailers. New ventures, such as Big W, were launched by the company. This large store format sought to compete head-on with the major food retailers on edge and out-of-town locations. However, without a food offer, these stores failed as destination centres for the more affluent, car-travelling customer and their non-high-street location meant that these stores were inaccessible for the traditionally older and poorer Woolworths customer.

The company was demerged from Kingfisher to become Woolworths Group plc on the London Stock Market in 2001. With an opening (modest) share price of 32p, the shares peaked at 55p in April 2005. However, with relentless price, brand and product competition, company performance withered and their shares fell into constant decline from January 2008. Share dealing was eventually suspended on 26 November 2008. A Woolworths ordinary share was then worth 1.2p. Unable to secure a buyer in December 2008, all 800 stores were closed just short of the company's 100th anniversary of UK trading.

Woolworths provides a competent example of Davidson et al.'s (1976) Retail Life Cycle. A once innovative business that pioneered new retail formats, helped create and shape new customer segments and which became part of the very fabric of the British high street landscape, it eventually fell foul of the twin pressures of the changing consumer and more efficient and enticing competitors.

It is perhaps to oversimplify the history and situation of all failed retailers to explain their demise simply by relying upon the Retail Life Cycle. But the theory does provide at least some indication of how retailers typically evolve and develop. However, as was identified previously with respect to the Wheel of Retailing, the Retail Life Cycle theory does not accommodate those retailers that are able to sustain demand and increase profitability over protracted periods of time. In particular, luxury retailers like Louis Vuitton, Hermes, Cartier and Chanel have been able to achieve consistently strong growth and profit performance. Nor does the Life Cycle theory recognize that a retailer may, through brand repositioning and business re-engineering, enhance the long-term sustainability of their business. The theory assumes that retailers are passive victims of the vagaries of market change and competitor action. There are a sufficient number of examples of retailers who have successfully reinvented, repositioned and re-engineered their organizations to significantly grow their businesses to prove that the inevitable decline predicted by the Retail Life Cycle is not necessarily the case.

Perhaps the more significant value of the Retail Life Cycle theory is its application to the evolvement of retail formats in general. Davidson et al. (1976) emphasize the shortening of the life cycle for retailing formats. More recent work by Burns et al. (1997) suggested that earnings for new formats/concepts would be likely to stagnate within a decade after launch. The truncation of retail life cycles has important implications for retailers and McGoldrick (2002) suggested that retailers must carefully consider the implications of long-term investments in expensive, inflexible and confining property assets. Further, the life cycle encourages retailers to adopt a portfolio approach to brand management and so provide for a coherent balance of risk, cost and opportunity. Perhaps, most importantly, contemporary applications of the Retail Life Cycle indicate that in the future retailers must recognize that an acceptable return on investment must be secured within an ever-decreasing timescale.

The Retail Accordion

The third of the three important theories of retail change is the Retail Accordion. Established by Hollander (1970) as a means of understanding the oscillations of prominent retailing formats, it proposes that the domination by wide-assortment retailers is inevitably and subsequently followed by superiority of narrow-line specialist sellers. McGoldrick (2002) argued that this theory is clearly evident in the evolution of retailing within the USA. He noted that in the early settlements, the general stores offered comprehensive assortments to locals, but as settlements grew in scale and sophistication, more specialist and sophisticated retailers emerged. These specialists subsequently lost ground to department store operators that offered a wide merchandise assortment to a new urbanized customer base. But these wide assortment sellers in turn lost market share to specialized chains who responded better to the particular needs of a more demanding customer. These specialist retailers, in an attempt to retain customer loyalty through the provision of convenience and choice, extended their offering and so retailers, such as supermarkets and drug store operators, began to sell merchandise categories that were not typically associated with their particular format type. However, as these specialist retailers became more general in their offer, they became susceptible to the impact of other retailers with a particular focus within a product category.

While the Retail Accordion theory recognizes the wide–narrow–wide pattern of the dominant retailing forms within a market, it has little or no value for the purposes of predicting or explaining future retailing developments. The theory does not offer any insights as to why one form inevitably gives way to another – nor does it explain why that format should return to dominate at some future point. Instead it serves only to illustrate the predominance of particular formats at specific points in time.

What the model fails to recognize, if applied to the experience of a particular business, is the capability of certain firms to operate wide and narrow formats concurrently. Leading retailers such as Boots the Chemist, The Gap, Tesco and Marks & Spencer have developed a variety of formats and brands that each cover a range of different narrow and wide segments. For example, Boots has more than 2,500 stores in the UK and operates five different retail formats. Each of the five formats is described below:

- *Local pharmacy stores.* These are healthcare-focused community stores, with a resident pharmacy and a limited range of essential medical and health/beauty products. Typically these are based in high street locations.
- *Boots Opticians.* These stores focus upon the provision of optician services and the supply of reading-aid products.

- *Boots travel and airport stores.* Located in train and bus stations, as well as airports, these stores offer a focused range of products that meet the last minute needs of customers before they travel.
- *Health and beauty stores.* These are on edge of town, convenience and high street locations. Pharmacy-led, these stores offer a wide range of products including all Boots' leading brand items.
- *Flagship stores.* These are located in large city centre and important shopping centre locations. The flagships offer the widest healthcare offering as well as pharmacy services, Boots Optician practices and Boots Hearingcare centres and the biggest range of premium beauty and exclusive brands. (Source: http://www.boots-uk.com/about-boots-uk/about-boots/boots-in-numbers/)

In an era where retailers have the resources and management expertise to cover what would appear to be all market eventualities, the usefulness of the Retail Accordion theory to provide any new and relevant insights with respect to retail developments at the macro or the corporate business unit level is at best limited and at worst irrelevant.

Non-cyclical theories of retailing change

The cyclical theories of change – while offering some broad insights – are largely inadequate in that their linearity reflects a deterministic, prescriptive and inflexible perspective on the nature of retailer development. These models speculate that businesses are powerless to resist the force of the change cycle and, as such, are predestined to follow a non-negotiable path. Further, as Brown (1991) noted, the models fail to allow for the influence of the economic environment or for the strategic plans and interventions of management. Consequently, he proposed that non-cyclical, environmental theories are more flexible and efficient in providing an explanation for the patterns of change within the sector.

Likewise, Goworek and McGoldrick (2015) proposed that changes in retail formats are better explained as an outcome of economic and socio-cultural developments within a market. Meloche et al. (1988) identified that the failure of retail businesses and the demise of particular formats were invariably linked to some negative environmental change or market alteration. Failure was not always an inevitable stage in the history of an organization. Nor are retailers passive participants in some grand market lottery. Instead, traders may deploy strategies that either circumnavigate difficult market trends or which exploit opportunities that arise from changed market conditions. Environmental theories therefore provide an alternative explanation for retail change and also provide frameworks which recognize that retailers can proactively respond to market challenges. Corporate fate is not therefore viewed as predestination, nor is the survival of a particular trading format destined to be active for a prescribed and finite period as suggested by the cyclical theories.

Environmental change – such as economic downturns – provides some explanation as to why market demand may shift away from premium retailers to those that operate on a value/discount basis. The recent, significant growth in the popularity and profitability of value retailers – such as Aldi, Lidl and Primark – is inextricably linked to the deep economic recession that began in 2008 and which has affected consumer confidence in the UK and Europe for almost a decade since. Survival in periods of change and challenge depends upon a retailer's ability to respond positively to challenging market conditions. Etgar (1984) and McGoldrick (2002) have suggested that the environmental perspective on retail change recognizes that an 'economic ecology' exists within retailing where the principle is that only the fittest survive. It is the level of retailer fitness that determines their continuance and also explains their decline and failure.

A second non-cyclical change theory exists. Pioch and Schmidt (2000) noted that conflict theory attributes retail change not to the impact of environmental challenge, but instead to the trading rivalry that exists between new and established retail businesses. A pattern of conflict emerges which contains three stages: thesis, antithesis and synthesis. When an established retailer is threatened by the differential advantage of a new entrant, it will seek to respond to that challenge by imitating the core features of the competitor's advantage. In response, the new entrant will modify its strategy to regain the momentum. Pioch and Schmidt (2000) predict that the adaptations undertaken by both sides result in their adopting strategies that are largely similar in terms of scope and impact. As such, a position of synthesis is reached and in the end there is much less to differentiate the two businesses that initially appeared to be so different.

Examples exist within both the food and clothing sectors of this form of inter-firm rivalry. The emergence of Asda as the leading innovator and challenger within the British grocery market in the 1970s, prompted Sainsbury's and Tesco, the market leaders, to rapidly adopt the large format, edge and out-of-town locations pioneered by their new up-start competitor. Likewise, through time, Asda adopted many of the trading features of its competitors in such areas as own-brand development, premium food ranges and customer service provision. Within a generation, these initially very disparate operators soon began to merge in terms of their core business and soon there was little to differentiate the top three in terms of their competitive strategies.

More recently, significant turbulence has occurred within the UK retail grocery sector as a result of the significant market share gains achieved by discount retailers Lidl and Aldi. Initially both retailers entered the UK market using a low-cost operating model of a relatively limited number of stores, in marginal locations and with a narrow product assortment range. Marketing communications were initially confined to the distribution of leaflets promoting weekly offers delivered to local households. In recent years, the business operating models of both retailers have changed significantly. Each has sharply increased the pace of new store openings and their new outlets are in more prosperous neighbourhoods. Marketing communications activity has switched from low-grade print door-to-door distribution to high-quality television advertising. Perhaps the most significant indicator of a migration towards the business approaches of their well-established rivals became apparent in September 2015, when Aldi announced that it would begin an online shopping service in the UK in order to attract more affluent consumers that do not have ready access to an Aldi store (Armstrong, 2015).

Yet, while it is possible to find evidence to support the general principles contained within the conflict theories, Pioch and Schmidt (2000) also recognized that these fail to take into account the importance and impact of environmental drivers related to economic and social change on a retailer's success. To assume that retail change depends only upon inter-firm rivalries is narrow and incomplete. Therefore, in this regard, the conflict theories are not so different from the limited perspectives contained within the cyclical theories of retail change.

A combination of theories?

While each of the theories of retail change may incorporate dimensions that offer some insight and value in terms of explaining developments within the sector, none provides a comprehensive and complete account of the dynamics of that change. As a means of assimilating all that is good from the theories and models, as well as addressing their areas of weakness, a number of combination models have been proposed. Bringing together dimensions of the cyclical with the environmental and conflict theories, new hybrid-form models have been proposed by researchers, such as Brown (1991) and Sampson and Tigert (1994). These models, which bring together dimensions from all three model formats, serve, in particular, to highlight the complexity and diversity of change within the retailing sector. In so doing, they provide a comprehensive system for explaining both the manner and the reasons for change within retailing.

What is perhaps most interesting is the fact that many of the theories of retail change were developed some time ago during a period when retailers were less advanced in their strategic thinking and less efficient in their ability to understand and respond to environmental challenges. As retailers have become more professional, strategic and robust in the planning and execution of their strategies, their capabilities and resources now often exceed the limitations that are implicit in the theories of retail change. As such, the emergence and acceptance of combination models of change – which incorporate more complex systems of influence – is perhaps inevitable and necessary. This reflects the trend towards pluralism of theories and theorizing in the wider marketing domain (Maclaran et al., 2009). The multidimensionality of these new models better reflects the realities of retailing markets that are both complex and turbulent and which require, by necessity, strategic responses that are complex, agile and robust.

But rather than dismiss these various theories of retailing as inadequate, anachronistic and/ or overly simplistic, Fernie et al. (2015) indicate that these do have merit and value – not least in terms of their ability to identify and remind us of the factors and influences that have resulted in the demise and failure of individual firms, or trading formats and/or even whole sectors of retailing. The digital age of now, and of the future, may appear to predict the demise of the great business names of retailing and the ultimate failure of formats that have been long cherished by retailers and consumers alike. However, reflecting upon the indications and dimensions inherent to the theories of retail change, there is value in the recognition that sometimes history does repeat itself – regardless of the why and the how. Consequently, that which may appear lost to us now is very likely to reappear at some point in the future.

Recommended further reading

Brown, J.R. and Dant, R.P. (2009) 'The theoretical domains of retailing research: a retrospective', *Journal of Retailing* 85(2): 113–28.

Fernie, J., Fernie, S. and Moore, C.M. (2015) *Principles of Retailing*, 2nd edn. Abingdon: Routledge.

Markin, R.J. and Duncan, C.P. (1981) 'The transformation of retailing institutions: beyond the Wheel of Retailing and Life Cycle Theories', *Journal of Macromarketing* 1 (March): 58–66.

Peterson, R.A. (2002) 'Retailing in the 21st century: reflections and prologue to research', *Journal of Retailing* 78(1): 9–16.

Roth, V.J. and Klein, S (1993) 'A theory of retail change', *International Review of Retail, Distribution and Consumer Research* 3(2): 167–83.

References

Armstrong, A. (2015) 'Aldi steps up supermarket war by launching online shopping', *The Telegraph*, 28 September. Available at: www.telegraph.co.uk/finance/newsbysector/retailandconsumer/11895559/Aldi-steps-up-supermarket-war-by-launching-online-shopping.html.

Brown, S. (1987) 'Institutional change in retailing: a review and synthesis', *European Journal of Marketing* 21(6): 5–36.

Brown, S. (1988) 'The wheel of the wheel of retailing', *International Journal of Retailing* 3(1): 16–37.

Brown, S. (1991) 'Variations on a marketing enigma: the wheel of retailing theory', *Journal of Marketing Management* 7(2): 131–55.

Brown, S. (1995) 'Postmodernism, the wheel of retailing and the will to power', *International Review of Retail, Distribution and Consumer Research* 5(3): 387–414.

Burns, K.B., Enright, H., Hayes, J.F., McLaughlin, K. and Shi, C. (1997) 'The art and science of renewal', *McKinsey Quarterly* 2: 100–13.

Davidson, W.R., Bates, A.D. and Bass, S.J. (1976) 'The retail life cycle', *Harvard Business Review* 54(6): 89–96.

Etgar, M. (1984) 'The retail ecology model: a comprehensive model of retail change', in J. Sheth (ed.) *Research in Marketing*, Vol. 7. Greenwich, CT: JAI Press, pp. 41–62.

Fernie, J., Fernie, S. and Moore, C.M. (2015) *Principles of Retailing*, 2nd edn. Abingdon: Routledge.

Goworek, H. and McGoldrick, P. (2015) *Retail Marketing Management: Principles and Practice*. London: Pearson.

Hollander, S.C. (1960) 'The wheel of retailing', *Journal of Marketing* 24(3): 37–42.

Hollander, S.C. (1970) *Multinational Retailing*. East Lansing, MI: Michigan State University Press.

Hollander, S.C. (1986) 'A rear-view mirror might help us drive forward: a call for more historical studies in retailing', *Journal of Retailing* 62(1): 7–10.

Levitt, T. (1965) 'Exploit the product life cycle', *Harvard Business Review* 43: 81–94.

McGoldrick, P.J. (2002) *Retail Marketing*. Maidenhead: McGraw-Hill Education.

Maclaran, P., Saren, M., Stevens, L. and Goulding, C. (2009) 'Rethinking theory building and theorizing in marketing', Proceedings of the 38th European Marketing Academy Conference, University of Nantes, France, 23–26 May.

McNair, M.P. (1958) 'Significant trends and developments in the post war period', in A.B. Smith (ed.) *Competitive Distribution in a Free High Level Economy and its Implications for the University*. Pittsburgh, PA: University of Pittsburgh Press, pp. 1–25.

Marks & Spencer Annual Report and Accounts (1998, 1999, 2015) London: Marks & Spencer plc.

Meloche, M.S., di Benedetto, C.A. and Yudelson, J.E. (1988) 'A framework for the analysis of the growth and development of retail institutions', in R.L. King (ed.) *Retailing: Its Present and Future*. Charleston, IL: American Collegiate Retailing Association.

Pioch, E.A. and Schmidt, R.A. (2000) 'Consumption and the retail change process: a comparative analysis of top retailing in Italy and France', *International Review of Retail, Distribution and Consumer Research* 10(2): 183–203.

Sampson, S.D. and Tigert, D.J. (1994) 'The impact of warehouse membership clubs: the wheel of retailing turns one more time', *International Review of Retail, Distribution and Consumer Research* 4(1): 33–59.

Part Five

Theories of Service in Marketing

Part V Contents

18 The New Service Marketing   435

19 Service-Dominant Logic   458

The New Service Marketing

Evert Gummesson

Chapter Topics

Overview   435
From the marketing of services to the new service marketing   436
The service sector: From garbage can to universal sector   437
Alleged differences between goods and services   439
Quality, satisfaction, excellence, value and productivity   441
Marketing mix and relational approaches   444
Organizing for service marketing   445
Drivers of the new service marketing   446
The future   455

Overview

A decade ago it would have been much easier to write this chapter. Marketing of services had established itself and become mainstream. It built on differences between goods and services and their consequences for marketing. This was productive for a period and contributed to a deepened understanding of marketing. The problem was that goods and services and other products such as software, information and knowledge – it has never been agreed if these are goods or services or something very different – always appear together. This has now come to a point where goods and services merge and their interdependency is acknowledged.

This means that we have entered a transition phase in marketing thought and the student may easily feel lost in contradictions. The transition will take time, some adopting it quickly, with others still attached to the services marketing from the 1980s and 1990s. To facilitate the student's understanding of the differences between mainstream services marketing and the new service marketing, this chapter will explain both and compare them. The chapter therefore starts with a background to the ongoing changes in the perception of service and services and proceeds with a review of the contributions of mainstream services marketing. The last part of the chapter is assigned to the drivers of a new service logic and how it opens up the new service marketing. The chapter wraps up with views on the future.

From the marketing of services to the new service marketing

The 1970s was a milestone in marketing. The hegemony of the 1960s marketing management began to crack when conceptualization of services marketing gathered a critical mass of researchers from Europe and the US. It happened in conflict with mainstream marketing management where consumer goods were the focal point of interest. Official statistics showed that the service sector, including private and government providers, accounted for the larger part of economic activity. Despite this, services were absent in marketing textbooks even if some individual researchers had noted it. Service practitioners had found limited inspiration in marketing theory with the exception of retailers as the marketing theory was about consumer goods. Hotels, airlines, insurance companies, consultants and others developed their own practices.

Gradually the way was paved for a new tradition in marketing theory, referred to as services marketing or service management and marketing. The latter expression emphasized interfunctional dependency and the avoidance of organizational silos; contributions from strategic management, human resources, organization, operations management, quality management and other areas were needed to put services marketing in context.

This was further supported by recognizing that service consumption often (but not always) takes place simultaneously with the customer's active participation in production and delivery. It led to an innovation, *the service encounter*, as a platform for service providers and customers to build interactive relationships. At the same time, a school of thought in business-to-business (B2B) marketing began to stress networks between organizational sellers and buyers as the key to efficient marketing, purchasing and resource utilization. Through these contributions *relationships*, *networks* and *interaction* gradually stood out as overriding concepts in marketing. This conclusion has been further reinforced by the internet, email, social media and other information technology (IT) applications.

Inspired by these developments, *relationship marketing, CRM (customer relationship management)* and *one-to-one marketing* had their breakthrough in the 1990s. With some differences in emphasis, all three concern the creation and maintenance of long-term relationships with individual customers. These dimensions of marketing were missing in research and education. Successful practitioners, on the other hand, have always known that relationships with customers and the interaction in networks are fundamental in business. Again, marketing theory and education showed a blind spot.

The new millennium started with a gradual change in our perception of what suppliers deliver and where and when service, value, quality, excellence, customer satisfaction and productivity are brought into being. From an initial focus on goods marketing, the focus went to services marketing and now the two have merged on a higher level of understanding, the new service marketing. It prepares the ground for more general, valid and relevant marketing theory.

Several current developments are turning the tide. These will be explained later in the chapter but a brief introduction of them will facilitate the reading. *Service-dominant (S-D) logic* offers more integrated theory. It merges goods and services into value propositions and the outcome of economic activity is defined as service and value, no matter if it is based on what is traditionally called services or goods. S-D logic acknowledges the crucial role of the customer in cocreating service. *Service science* merges theory with practice aiming to develop our ability to design and maintain efficient and innovative service systems. Third, contributions from relational thinking help to address the *complexity* of the service world.

In the next sections the characteristics of services marketing as it developed from the 1970s and through the 1990s will be reviewed. The vantage point for services marketing was the alleged existence of a service sector. Services were claimed to have certain unique traits that made them different from goods. I refer to this as the *Paradigm 2* era. It was preceded by *Paradigm 1*, the pre-1970s era when American marketing management dominated the scene with marketing mix models emanating from empirical studies and experiences from consumer goods marketing. Paradigm 2 stressed differences between goods and service marketing and between B2B and B2C (business-to-consumer) marketing. With the spotlight on differences, we learnt new lessons but also established certain service myths that must now be weeded out of the minds of researchers, educators, textbook writers and practitioners.

Paradigm 3 (2000s–) is the era of recognizing commonalities, redefining categories and concepts, and letting lingering myths go. It represents the new service marketing, a new logic or theory of marketing with a holistic and systemic perspective, better theory and better implementation. To stimulate the development and understanding of Paradigm 3, the biennial, international conference series the Naples Forum on Service was established in Italy in 2009, and is to be held for the fourth time in 2015. Its website offers more details and references on the new service marketing (www.naplesforumonservice.it).

The service sector: From garbage can to universal sector

Official statistics report changes in three overriding economic sectors: the manufacturing (or industrial) sector, the service sector and the agricultural sector. Once everything was agriculture (including fishing, hunting and forestry). The Industrial Revolution swung the economy towards manufacturing and the industrial sector grew. What was not allocated to these two sectors was labelled miscellaneous, intangibles, invisibles, the tertiary sector and later the service sector. Numerous efforts to define the service sector have been made, with limited success. Its statistics include trade, hotels and restaurants, transport (including tourism, travel agencies, tour operators), storage and communication, financial services, real estate and dwellings, business services (e.g. accounting, software development, management consultancy, technical consultancy), public administration, defence, education, health services, religious and other community services, legal services, recreation, entertainment and personal services. But what for example is meant by 'communication' and 'personal services' and what does transport have in common with financial service and brain surgery? The service sector has become a garbage can (Gummesson, 2005).

Today official statistics report that the service sector in developed economies is growing while the manufacturing and agricultural sectors are shrinking. Then consider that we:

- Have never had so many goods and so much product waste;
- Have never had so much food and were never so fat – but at the same time undernourished;
- Lack basic services such as healthcare for everyone, affordable care for the elderly, good schools, security in the streets and working legal systems.

The sector definitions are diffuse and arbitrary compromises. For example, a restaurant offers agricultural and manufactured products, and has its own in-house manufacturing plant, the kitchen. Waiters take orders and bring the food and drink to the table. The food cannot be excluded – then it is no restaurant – but the service can be cut down to a minimum. The guests can pick the food themselves at lavish buffets in high-class restaurants or at the counter in cheap fast-food outlets. All the same the restaurant is referred to the service sector.

Scales are presented that range from pure goods to pure services. They may sound compelling but what marketing strategies and action can they inspire? One continuum puts clothing as the pure goods extreme and a visit to the psychiatrist as the pure services extreme. However, retailing offers conveniently located stores surrounding clothing with different types of service, from the availability of cheap ready-to-wear and self-service in special fitting rooms to expensive made-to-measure with assistance in selecting suitable designs. Huge resources are put into clothes brands to fit lifestyle, luxury, romance and sex. The service of the shrink is more often than not a prescription for manufactured pills. It is not possible to 'purify' goods and services.

As the service sector is now officially presented, 80–90% of all people employed work in services and all new jobs (net) come from services. Keeping in mind how arbitrary the definitions of the economic sectors are and that they do not acknowledge the interdependence between goods, services and other phenomena, the sector division is meaningless for marketers. It has no ability to discriminate, which is the meaning of categorization.

The former special case of the service sector has now become the universal case. The way service is being reconceptualized in the new service marketing – to signify value to customers and complex networks of stakeholders – moves the focus to users without losing sight of suppliers.

What should replace the three economic categories then? Nothing, really. These overriding categories do not serve any purpose. We should talk about healthcare as healthcare and not mix it into a service sector with hamburger restaurants, lawyers and sports events. But even healthcare is so diverse that the category has little meaning. It could be divided into private and government hospitals, physicians' offices, nursing facilities, health insurers and diagnostic labs. It could be divided by type of illness and type of therapy as it is experienced by patients. Performing eye surgery is very different from cosmetic surgery, the treatment of gastric disorders, stopping global epidemics, or offering pain relief. Consider another example, the housing sector. It consists of the sub-sectors and professions of building and construction, building supplies, real estate and mortgage brokers, furniture and appliance manufacturing and distribution, home-supply stores, architects and interior designers. If we build or repair a house we may need all or part of this. The sub-sectors and professionals are each operating in their special market contexts requiring partially different marketing skills and strategies.

An addition to the service sector during recent decades is administrative routines and internal services that have progressively been incorporated to form subsidiaries or are outsourced to independent providers. Examples are computer support, property maintenance, security and cleaning. It means re-registration in the official statistics, augmenting the service sector and reducing the manufacturing sector. The same or similar service is still performed but the hidden services have become visible in the market.

Service sector classifications are based on overgeneralized macro-level criteria whereas in marketing practice micro-level criteria must be considered. Several such efforts were made, for example pinpointing the difference in marketing high versus low contact services, or frequently versus infrequently bought services. It is evident that the diversity within services requires specific marketing solutions for each instance and context. Knowledge of the conditions of a particular service, its provision and markets, is necessary in order to design a proper marketing plan and marketing organization.

Alleged differences between goods and services

In the Paradigm 2 services marketing literature and education, the big issue was differences between goods and services and what effect these might have on marketing strategies and customer behaviour. Unfortunately, the 'differences' are seldom well grounded in empirical data and experience. They are generalized far beyond their capacity to discriminate between goods and services and they appear together with a plethora of other marketing dimensions. Still the 'differences' form the introduction to almost every textbook and chapter on services marketing. They are listed below with examples, and their usefulness or inadequacy is exemplified (Lovelock and Gummesson, 2004):

- Services are characterized by *intangibility*; goods by *tangibility*. The idea is that services are activities and processes that cannot be touched – for example, the service of getting a meal to your table or an opera performance. A surgeon is in a healthcare service, but it seems odd that the service of cutting your belly open, messing around with your physical organs and then suturing your belly together again could be perceived by either the provider or the patient as intangible. Could it be more tangible? Further, it has often been claimed that services do not need investment in tangible goods to the same degree as manufacturing; services are performed by people and service firms are thus people-intensive while manufacturing is capital-intensive. Then just consider the enormous investment in tangible goods of an airport and an airline in order to make the flying service possible, and the high-tech hardware necessary to make internet and mobile service possible.

- Services are characterized by *heterogeneity, variability* or *non-standardization*; goods by *homogeneity* and *standardization*. This is based on the observation that services are often performed by people and goods are primarily produced by machines. People are individuals who tend to do it their way based on differences in competence, willingness to serve, mood swings and so on. Thanks to IT, service can increasingly be performed in a strictly standardized mode. This is often called 'mass customization', which seems like a paradox. By, for example, withdrawing money from a cash machine, millions of standardized services are performed every day. Although it is standardized mass production, the service is adapted to each customer by considering the sum to be withdrawn, the customer's personal account and its balance, and the time and place for withdrawal.

- Services are characterized by *inseparability* between production, delivery and consumption, also expressed as *simultaneity*; goods by *separability* as goods are produced without the presence of the customer. This service encounter is characterized by interaction between: (1) the supplier's contact personnel (the front line) and the customer; (2) those customers who are present at a specific place and point of time and interact customer-to-customer, C2C, for example in a retail store or on a ferry; (3) the customer and the supplier's products and physical environment, the servicescape, which is recognition that physical objects play a role in services marketing; and (4) the customer and the supplier's service system which consists of the logic through which all the bits and pieces of a service have been put together to form a coherent network. In many businesses the service encounter constitutes the essence of its marketing but it is not limited to services in the mainstream sense.

- Services are characterized by *perishability*, meaning that they cannot be stored; goods by *non-perishability*. The rationale behind this claim is that a service expires if not used immediately, for example a hair stylist who has no customers at a particular time cannot just style a few heads and store them on a shelf, waiting for buyers to come. On the other hand, service can be stored in systems and equipment and a provider's preparedness to perform the service when a customer enters. Although many manufactured goods can be stored, some goods are highly perishable like fresh fish, not to mention oysters. Furthermore, long storage can cause damage; fashion clothes become unfashionable after the season is over and can then only be put on sale at 50% or more discount; and it is costly to store because it ties up capital and physical space. A recent example is the market for passenger cars that went down by 50% in 2008–9. Where will the unsold cars be stored, what damage will they be exposed to during the storage, what is the cost of storing them, and will they become obsolete?

- An additional dimension that was noted early on but then somehow got lost claims that services are characterized by *non-ownership* and goods by *ownership*. Services are often borrowed or rented, like you pay for a day in a theme park, a night in a hotel room or two hours in a cinema seat. A car can be rented and is then referred to the service sector, while if you buy the car it is a deal with the manufacturing sector. In both cases it is about the same core service, transportation. And how many of the goods we have are owned? A car may be leased or bought with money from a bank loan and most homes are mortgaged. In legal terms they are not owned by the customers although they talk about 'my car' and 'my house'. But again, goods and services are there to provide service in some kind of functional combination, and it is the combination that is marketed and bought.

The first four are the top listed differences between goods and service that built a foundation for services marketing in the Paradigm 2 era. Intangibility, heterogeneity and perishability will not be brought forward in the new service marketing except as possible sub-dimensions in contingent marketing situations. Inseparability and the service encounter, on the other hand, bring out the customer's interactive role in all business and not least in marketing, and are reinforced by IT applications. The ownership issue deserves increased attention in the new service marketing. It is a pricing and financial aspect with a huge impact on customer behaviour. For example, the irresponsible generosity with which mortgages were granted in the US, the subprime loans, was one of the major triggers of the global financial crisis that broke out in 2008.

Quality, satisfaction, excellence, value and productivity

Under the label of total quality management *quality* went through a revival in the 1980s. In marketing, quality had been used in a loose sense; it was primarily a technical issue for manufacturing. Service quality had not been dealt with in an organized way and was a constant cause for complaints from customers and citizens.

Defining quality is not so easy; it is multifaceted and fuzzy concept. One distinction is between *quality-in-fact*, which is technical, measurable and objective, and *quality-in-perception*, which is relational, perceptual and subjective. These two are in interaction, though. For example, the delay of a flight can be objectively measured in minutes but the delay is perceived differently if the cabin crew is helpful or indifferent. In everyday language we say that the quality of the food in the restaurant was good, so-so, or bad; that we are dissatisfied with our hotel room; or that our house has an excellent heating system.

Services marketing defined quality by means of the *disconfirmation paradigm*. It meant that customers have *expectations* which they compare with their *experiences* of a service and then determine whether their expectations are confirmed or disconfirmed. Ideally there is no gap between the two or the experiences exceed expectations. Marketing can influence customer expectations through, for example promises in the promotion of the service, and by handling customer relationships well during the service performance. A common problem is the tendency of marketing to overpromise, leaving the customer dissatisfied and thus jeopardizing long-term relationships. Another is that expectations and experiences are both fuzzy concepts.

As service quality was claimed to be different from goods quality, special service quality dimensions were established. The survey technique Servqual first listed 10 'general' dimensions and later reduced them to five. One was 'tangibles', a modest recognition of the goods part of an offering. It always ranked lowest in the surveys, a fact that should make one suspicious. Consider this: is the technical quality of an aircraft – the engine, the seats, leg space and food – low-ranking, even negligible? Of course not. Service quality focused on quality-in-perception and treated the technical aspects and quality-in-fact lightly. Among the specific service quality dimensions were reliability, sensitivity, competence, availability, pleasant behaviour, communication, credibility, security and recovery (compensation for bad service). In contrast, the manufacturing quality tradition listed performance, features, conformance to specification, durability and aesthetics as central. IT quality did not enter the service agenda with the breakthrough of the internet in the 1990s. For services delivered through the web, email and mobile phones, quick response, assistance, flexibility, ease of navigation, efficiency, security, clearly stated prices and adaptation for individual customer use were found to be important. Caution should be exerted in ranking quality dimensions as they are interdependent. They can all contribute to the quality of the total value proposition and appear in a huge variety of combinations.

Several claims about service quality from Paradigm 2 have not stood the test of time. Their departure from courses and textbooks is already long overdue. Among them are the following:

- *Service quality is difficult to determine while goods quality is easy.* This is built on the obsolete idea that goods are manufactured in standardized components by easily controlled machines whereas services are 'handmade' by erratic human beings.
- *Service quality cannot be assessed before consumption while goods quality can.* This builds on the misunderstanding that it is easy to assess the quality of a product 'as it is tangible'. More realistically, consumers understand very little about the technical quality of a car and therefore buy on trust for the brand and under considerable stress and insecurity. Among the few quality properties we can assess are size and colour. Not even the fuel consumption can be checked until the car has been used for some time as it also depends on driving style. In light of the definition of service where the customer is cocreator, the quality of a car is variable and dependent on the way the customer creates value for himself or herself.

Customer satisfaction has long been a buzz word in the Paradigm 1 marketing management. It has mainly been defined by means of standardized and randomized surveys and focus groups. This is a rather crude and shallow way of getting to know customers as masses but not as individuals. For too long services marketing became preoccupied with customer satisfaction measured through statistical surveys and scales. This drew the attention away from more intricate and fundamental issues. Among them are the *design and engineering of service systems,* the very topic of service science. Service systems are often launched without sufficient design and testing of their workability in practical situations. The goods part of a service is usually much better engineered and tested, based on a long tradition in manufacturing. Efforts were made with service flowcharts or blueprints where service activities and customer interaction were defined and analysed for more efficient ways of performing a service. They were excellent contributions but required technical and specific knowledge and hard empirical and analytical work. Such studies became too complex and demanding for academic service researchers and remained in the background. It is only now that the customer becomes a cocreator of service development and innovation (Edvardsson et al., 2012).

Gradually *value* has taken over from satisfaction and excellence. But value in the terms of the traditional value chain is the same as cost. When cost is added it is deceptively called value-added. Value-added tax, VAT, should therefore be called cost-added tax, CAT. For companies there are also values other than money, such as enjoying a great reputation, being popular among job applicants, feeling that you contribute to society and being the pride of the owners.

The traditional value chain stops when the customer enters but we can tie in with a customer value chain or rather a stakeholder network. B2B firms buy in order to produce or distribute value for themselves and for consumers and citizens. For consumers and citizens, value should match their needs and wants. The financial side – the price and the costs associated with a purchase – becomes a substantial part of the consumer's sacrifice in using and enjoying a value proposition and the service it renders.

In the new service marketing, value has taken over as the key concept. Value is dependent on the circumstances; it is *value-in-context* (Vargo et al., 2008). For a business, value is when customers buy what it sells at a price that leaves a profit. For a consumer, value is actualized when you use what you bought.

This is influenced by the new service logic but influences also come from other directions. One is the Malcolm Baldrige National Quality Award which was first handed out in the US in 1988. It approached quality in a holistic way, embracing not only traditional technical dimensions but also quality of leadership, employee training, marketing and other functions. It further puts emphasis on productivity and profitability. The Baldrige inspired a global upsurge in quality awards but the broadened quality concept caused some misunderstandings and they went over to performance excellence and so did the European Quality Award.

In earlier publications on the marketing of services I have talked about 'service quality, productivity and profitability' as triplets, 'separating one from the other makes an unhappy family'. But quality became the pet of services marketing and productivity and profitability were kept at arm's length. *Productivity* had little tradition in services but a long tradition in manufacturing. It is defined as the ratio between output and input; the less input of resources (cost) for manufacturing a unit of a product, the higher the productivity. Eventually a business firm has to make a profit to survive and therefore quality and productivity must be linked to *profitability*. In similar vein, government operations and NGOs without a profit motive have to make ends meet, which is controlled through budgeting. The linking of quality, productivity and profitability has turned out to be hard work and is not yet successfully managed. For marketing, service quality and productivity affect the price level, margins, sales volume and competitiveness in general.

Two myths about service cost and productivity have to be abandoned:

- *Better quality costs more.* This taken-for-granted assumption has persisted around quality and may still be around. If true, quality improvements lead to rising prices with a negative effect on sales volume and competitiveness. The good news is that it is not true. Better quality sometimes costs more, sometimes the same and sometimes less; there are only specific instances. Quality in the form of a bigger hotel room can be more expensive for obvious reasons. A smarter service system reduces the cost of breakdowns, complaints from dissatisfied customers and rework. By improving the technical quality a supplier may save money without lowering the price, which adds to profit.
- *Service productivity does not improve whereas goods productivity keeps improving at a rapid rate.* This is often presented as a shortcoming of the service sector. Productivity indicators have to be adapted to service in the new sense to be meaningful. Productivity is easiest to measure and control when something can be broken down in detail and linked together in one single best sequence. This works well in a factory but is not applicable to the same extent in the less controllable situations of service where the customer is a cocreator. Further, when a manual service like washing was packaged in a machine, the gains were not credited to the service sector. In the new service marketing, part of the value cocreation is in interaction within a network of customers, intermediaries, computers, transport companies, factories and so on. Although mainstream services marketing defined the service encounter and recognized the customer's role, quality and productivity measurements did not include the customer's contribution, thus making them less valid.

Simply put, all these concepts – quality, satisfaction, excellence, value and productivity – try to pinpoint whether something is good or bad. They do it from slightly different but overlapping angles.

Marketing mix and relational approaches

In the core of the traditional marketing management of Paradigm 1 is the marketing mix, mostly described as a combination of the 4 P strategies: *product, price, promotion* and *place.* It was partly taken over by service research and 'product' was made to include services.

The marketing mix has been criticized for being incomplete and manipulative, not properly considering the needs of the customer. *The marketing concept* states that once you know your customers, you can design, price, promote and distribute a product that matches these needs and then become a success in the marketplace. The seller is the active party and the customer is persuaded to buy. The empirical basis of the marketing mix is mass manufacturing and standardized consumer goods. It was never wholly embraced by service firms, who found it difficult to apply in practice.

To overcome some of their limitations, the 4 Ps were expanded into the 7 Ps by adding *participants* (or *people*), *physical evidence* (later referred to as *servicescape*) and *processes*.

Although adding Ps has a certain pedagogical appeal it should not form a strategy for theory development; other avenues have to be explored. Such alternatives are found within the relational approaches which had a breakthrough in the 1990s. As an alternative to the marketing mix, the core of marketing can now be perceived as *relationships*, *networks* and *interaction*. In Paradigm 3 special attention is given to interaction in S-D logic and to networks.

To some extent the service Ps incorporate relationships and interaction through 'participants' and 'processes' (customers participating in a service process). In addition, relationship marketing emphasizes a long-term interactive relationship between the service provider and the customer and long-term profitability. Relationships need not be restricted to the customer/supplier dyad. Many-to-many marketing adds the more realistic network aspect, recognizing that in today's complex economies we are embedded in networks of stakeholders. In these networks customers are exposed to a bundle of service systems, an issue that is at the core of service science.

The relational approach recognizes that both the customer and the seller are active parties. Furthermore, consumers and suppliers should be treated as equal partners, albeit with different objectives. Both should find a relationship rewarding; it should be a win–win relationship. In this spirit, the Ritz-Carlton hotel chain created the now classic but highly relevant catch-phrase: 'We are ladies and gentlemen serving ladies and gentlemen'.

Organizing for service marketing

Mainstream services marketing did not offer general guidelines for the services marketing organization nor prescribed in what way it should be different from a goods marketing organization. There is considerable practical knowledge about how to organize, for example, the marketing of hotels, cleaning services or professional services. The difficulty is that it is not possible to give general advice and that the difference is not between goods and services marketing but between other specific properties such as company size, target groups, market conditions and kind of value proposition.

An organization is traditionally built around functions but can also be built around service systems and be perceived as a set of networks. For example, major full-service airlines ran into hard competition from small, no-frills airlines with limited service and low fares. Ryanair was one of the first companies to concentrate on their website for information and ticket sales, thus controlling the fares and being able to instantly adjust them according to supply and demand. They organized themselves around this marketing system and the core service of transportation. The big full-service airlines were organized to inform and sell through travel agencies and serve numerous destinations. Several years ago Ryanair surpassed British Airways in number of passengers and it has kept up its profitability.

Organizations are complex networks of relationships, systems, processes and functions that gradually transcend into the market and society and the boundary between a company and its environment becomes diffuse. Three organizational strategies which have developed over a number of years are applicable to the new service marketing and in line with network theory:

- *Decentralization and multiplication of a global business concept to local markets.* Large companies are decentralized because of the need for local presence, for example a retail chain or a firm of accountants. For them growth is a matter of multiplying a well-defined business concept to more sites. Franchising, like 7-Eleven and the Body Shop, has proved to be a viable concept as it unites the marketing muscle of a large-scale operation with the agility of small scale and closeness to customers. Direct selling through door-to-door and home parties is a smaller but expanding way of multiplying a business concept, with special significance in new economies where entrepreneurship and small business must be encouraged with little financial investment. Even if IT is partially independent of physical presence, it will never make the need for physical proximity between suppliers and customers redundant.

- *Part-time marketers (PTMs) and full-time marketers (FTMs).* The marketing and sales departments, which are populated by FTMs, are unable to handle more than a limited portion of the marketing. They cannot always be in the right place at the right time with the right customer contact. As a consequence of the embeddedness of marketing in the network organization everyone else becomes a PTM, one who is not hired specifically for marketing and sales tasks but in the cocreative processes with customers interacts with them and thus influences their buying behaviour. Although the PTMs were hired for other tasks they have to be aware of their part-time role and be recruited, trained and motivated accordingly, whatever their main job is.

- *Internal marketing.* Services marketing came up with the idea of applying marketing techniques to internal markets, the employees. If a company has 50,000 employees spread in 50 countries it has a huge problem to communicate with the organization. Internal marketing can be used to empower and enable employees. They should understand the company mission, the organization, the service that can be provided, the value it has to customers, and how to interact with customers. They should behave in a way that creates positive rapport with customers and a long-term relationship.

Drivers of the new service marketing

As outlined initially, several contributions are driving the reinvention of service marketing. They have been brewing for decades, not least within the Nordic School (Grönroos, 2015; Gummesson and Grönroos, 2012), but the time has not been ripe for them to assume a lead role – until now. The drivers are supportive of each other but emphasize different fundamental facets of service and marketing. Three topic areas, S-D logic, service science and relational contributions, will be briefly explained in the next sections. To emphasize the compatibility between the drivers a concluding section deals with the contributions in a joint context.

Service-dominant logic: Theory generation

S-D logic was first proposed in a 2004 *Journal of Marketing* article by Steve Vargo and Bob Lusch. It took the authors five years to get the article accepted for publication but it had an overnight impact on readers. It is now the journal's most cited article since it was established in 1936, but today it is history. S-D logic is being continually developed through an open code and in co-authorship with people all around the world. I therefore prefer to see later publications cited, among them Vargo and Lusch (2008) and Ballantyne and Varey (2008); the book by Lusch and Vargo (2014), which in 225 pages gives a coherent state-of-the-art account of S-D logic; and Chapter 19 in this book written by Vargo, Lusch and Koskela-Huotari.

S-D logic is a theoretical synthesis of service knowledge and conceptual developments. A brief review is given here of what is directly pertinent to my interpretation of S-D logic and its place in new service theory and marketing. Its emerging grand theory has been received in two ways. The majority, including me, has hailed it as a constructive effort to create coherent theory out of fragmented contributions and welcomed the open code where everybody is invited to improve the theory. Others have missed this and complain about various things, one is that it silently discards several of the earlier contributions and that its concepts are not unambiguously defined, another is that there is a lack of empirical testing of the theory, and that it is hard to get it accepted by practitioners. That may be so but the originators do not sell S-D logic as the final answer but invite anyone to join the theory-generating journey. Much of the fragmented research from Paradigm 2 was sold as a ready-made package, the ultimate truth. It opened up for a win–lose debate but not for a win–win dialogue. Unfortunately, international textbooks used in education are still primarily Paradigm 2 books.

S-D logic is based on a set of axioms, assumptions, foundational premises and a lexicon, together constituting its paradigm. According to S-D logic, service is the basis for exchange and goods are distribution mechanisms for service. There is no need for the Paradigm 1 *goods-dominant (G-D) logic* as all economies are seen as service economies. This is an important change of focus, moving from the traditional marketing management perspective to a broadened stakeholders approach. Among the stakeholders are not only the supplier/customer dyad but intermediaries, other manufacturers, shareholders, etc. who contribute to the service. The stakeholders are generalized to *actors* and their behaviour to *actor-to-actor interaction, A2A*.

The network aspect is implicit through the statement that all social and economic actors are resource integrators implying that value creation takes place through interaction in complex networks. From a marketing perspective the end user has a focal role in such a network. This is a move from product and supplier orientation to customer orientation and broadened to all those involved; I use the term *balanced centricity*.

Some current service research pursues the ideas of *servitization* and *service-infusion in goods*. They are however based on G-D logic and the goods/services divide from Paradigm 2. B2B suppliers can concentrate on manufacturing parts with reliable quality and at low cost. This is a perfectly rational business mission asked for by large companies outsourcing manufacturing and focusing on one or several of design and engineering, assembly and marketing. When I worked for Ericsson in the 1980s their complex telephone systems were based on customized solutions to each individual buyer, installation on the customer's site, testing, continued maintenance, education of buyer personnel, financial solutions, and Ericsson outsourcing part of the order to firms in the buyer's country to help them keep down unemployment. This was the value proposition which was outlined in the tender and finally in the contract.

It was neither servitized manufacturing nor service infusion. For a supplier of complex equipment it was not unique; it was rather the rule and a necessity to get the order.

To recall the basic message of S-D logic: it is 'service' and not 'services versus goods'; the outcome is service, the input can appear as goods, services, knowledge, software or whatever. I did not buy my Toyota Prius to acquire a piece of goods but for the core service it could render me, transportation. For each individual, customer value is created in his or her interaction with the car and rarely with the Toyota Motor Corporation or its repair and maintenance outlets. Toyota is the engineering and car assembly resource while the customer is the resource driving and taking care of the car. The customer keeps interacting with the car when driving it to a desired destination and doing it well or badly; praising its convenience and cursing traffic jams, absence of parking space or rising petrol prices; enjoying music and the privacy of the sheltered and private space; or getting bored by long, lonely hours on straight highways. A car obviously contributes a large variety of value-in-use.

Traditionally businesses are the *operant* (active) resources while customers are *operand* (passive) resources. In S-D logic all actors are active resources to a varying degree. Within this spirit a supplier can offer value propositions to the market; the value actualization is the *value-in-use*. The fact that goods and services appear together had disturbed many over the years but it was not until conceptualized in the S-D logic that the many scattered thoughts and observations fell into place. For example, efforts had been made to get *product* accepted as a joint term for goods and services and to use *offering, package* or *solution* as all-inclusive concepts for what the customer buys.

The division into B2C and B2B is immaterial in S-D logic. B2C and B2B are only two of many sub-dimensions of marketing and should not be used as overriding categories. If you try to understand service under the B2B and B2C headings you will be led astray.

In S-D logic the concept of *ecosystem* is promoted as the best way of creating a full picture which handles both parts and the whole. I have above all used modern network theory, and been more inspired by its use in natural sciences than in social sciences. 'Eco' may lead our thinking to ecology and environmental issues but here it is about 'economic systems'. I see network theory (in its modern sense in natural sciences) and systems theory as supplementary, offering somewhat different traditions and a difference in languages, nodes and links in network theory and systems, sub-systems and what is outside (the environment) in systems theory.

Service science: Merging theory with practice

While S-D logic arose from the scholarly world, *service science, management and engineering (SSME)*, usually just referred to as *service science*, emanated from a practitioner, IBM. For decades IBM was the world's largest manufacturer of computer hardware. After a crisis it turned to software and management consultancy. With its 400,000 employees it is now the global leader in developing and improving service systems. But IBM is a for-profit business meaning that it works with practitioners to learn about the hazards of implementing new service theory.

The goal of service science is to design, innovate and implement better service systems. Service science and its approach to service systems is best described by IBM's service research programme director, Jim Spohrer, and his colleague Paul Maglio:

> Service systems are value cocreation configurations of people, technology, value propositions connecting internal and external service systems, and shared information (e.g. language, laws, measures, and methods). Service science is the study of service systems, aiming to create a basis for systematic service innovation. Service science combines organization and human understanding with business and technological understanding to categorize and explain the many types of service systems that exist as well as how service systems interact and evolve to cocreate value. The goal is to apply scientific understanding to advance our ability to design, improve, and scale service systems. (Maglio and Spohrer, 2008: 18)

Many years ago IBM was instrumental in introducing the concept of computer science, today an established discipline in the academic world. By introducing service science, IBM is changing from product centricity – the computer in focus – to customer centricity and value-in-use in focus by designing better service systems. The vision is expressed in the slogan 'Create a smarter planet!' In the service science programme it has so far been found that the most complex and densest networks of service systems are cities and universities.

The service science programme works globally and engages academic researchers and educators in 500 universities and technical institutes to add service to the research agenda and curriculum. IBM is cocreating value with the academic world. It is a call for academia, industry and governments to become more systematic about service performance and innovation. It is a proposed academic discipline and research area that would complement – rather than replace – the many disciplines that contribute to knowledge about service. Service science has adopted S-D logic as its theory and philosophy.

Service science is needed to master seamless and reliable service systems at a time when systems are becoming increasingly complex and global, making us increasingly vulnerable to system sluggishness and failure. It is a godsend for implementing S-D logic and relational approaches in marketing. The road is bumpy though; marketing theory and education have too long been insensitive to the signals from society and business practice.

Relational approaches to service complexity

Seminal contributions to service marketing are based on *relationships, networks* and *interaction.* They are found in relationship marketing, CRM (customer relationship management), one-to-one marketing, many-to-many marketing and B2B marketing, the last two especially drawing on network theory.

Relationship marketing and CRM usually focus on the two-party relationship between a customer and a supplier. Many-to-many marketing broadens the context to multi-party relationships and is defined in the following way: 'Many-to-many marketing describes, analyses and utilizes the network properties of marketing' (Gummesson, 2016a). It is a further development of relationship marketing, going from the two-party relationship of a single supplier and a single buyer, one-to-one, to the multi-party realism of today's marketing, many-to-many. It applies *network theory* to marketing in general. It has long been used in B2B marketing (Håkansson et al., 2009) but not in B2C. Now the application of networks embraces all marketing and the new service marketing. It is a head-on approach to the complexity, context, systems, relationships and interactions of business and consumption.

For example, in a B2B relationship two companies in a selling and buying negotiating stage are backed by many people and influences. They each represent their own many-headed organization, membership of alliances, commitment to other suppliers and intermediaries, and so on. It is not just one-to-one; it is many meeting many. In B2C shopping consumers can represent a family, buy for their children and pets, and are influenced by advice from friends and the lifestyle groups to which they belong. A consumer network cocreates value with a retailer network.

As marketing and value creation through service systems is complex, *complexity* should be an overriding issue for the new service marketing. To handle real-world complexity and scientific requirements *case study research* together with *network theory* and *systems theory* could be used (Gummesson, 2016b). Many universities accept case study research in marketing while others consider statistical techniques, such as surveys, to be more scientific. A weakness with the statistical techniques is that they cannot handle the complexity of service systems and the new service marketing.

Network theory offers a way of thinking in relationships and interaction but also techniques for addressing complexity, context and change. It can be used with different degrees of sophistication: a verbal treatise (discussion or text), graphics (from sketches of nodes and links to computer-generated diagrams), mathematical processing and computer simulations.

Marketing is part of or a perspective on management and to become efficient marketing should be seen in a management context; it is marketing-oriented management rather than marketing management. Combining case study research with network theory can resolve much of this conflict. In practical marketing complexity has to be handled whether it fits our preconceived ideas or not. It is about survival.

Service systems quickly become complex. Even the simple micro-service system of buying a ticket consists of many parts that must work smoothly together. Service delivered through machines is often very simple and can be performed by unskilled labour. All the same it took 50 or more years to design the service system that makes up a washing machine. It required herds of engineers, high-tech and low-tech, electro-mechanics and IT to eventually assemble this household appliance into a reliable and efficient service provider. But the service is cocreated with the consumer who has to feed and instruct the machine and then has to continue the service process after the washing and perhaps drying; the machine cannot handle the whole process.

There are also supportive macro-service systems – *infrastructure* – making it possible for people and companies to function. The national and global financial systems are part of an infrastructure which is ridden with problems, the major one being that it is complex, dynamic through transactions every split second 24/7, and that it is non-transparent and can be tampered with by insiders. In 2008 the world economic system started to break down and the fragility of the financial infrastructure became visible to everyone. More stability is found in the almost 200-year-old railway infrastructure that is constantly being upgraded to fit new customer demands of comfort, speed and environmental considerations. The European Union is an economic and political infrastructure. Through the implementation of its 'four freedoms' – free movement of goods, services, people and money across the national borders of member states – gradually new opportunities open up for marketers.

New infrastructures do not emerge often but they have a major impact on society, business and marketing. The newest is of course IT. Its interactive C2C part, the social media, is currently growing rapidly offering a new social and market order. As stated in a newsletter from the service science programme (*SSME*, 15 May 2009):

> Social media refers to a conversational, distributed mode of content generation, dissemination, and communication among communities. Recent years have witnessed tremendous growth of social media through platforms and applications enabled by the Web and mobile technologies (for example, weblogs, microblogs, online forums, wiki, podcasts, lifestreams, social bookmarks, Web communities, social networking, and avatar-based virtual reality). Social media is a tremendous asset for understanding various social phenomena and has found applications in a wide spectrum of problem domains, including business computing, entertainment, politics and public policy, and homeland security.

Social sciences, including marketing, management and economics, dodge complexity by straightening out the road they travel. Research and practice in marketing can be compared to driving a wreck on a dirt road; it is an instance of complexity and non-linearity. But marketing theory and academic research behave as if they were driving a new Lexus hybrid on a straight and empty highway under perfect weather conditions; the world is pretended to be simple and linear. Curves, loose gravel, holes in the road, wet or icy spots, crossing animals, imperfections of the car, and not least the behaviour of other cars, are largely disregarded. Practitioners have to take the consequences while marketing theorists do not. Book-smarts are not enough. Driving a car requires street-smarts to handle unforeseen situations by using *tacit knowledge* such as experience, commonsense, intuition, hunches, gut feelings, reflexes, wisdom, insight and judgement calls. Book-smarts and street-smarts should not be too far apart; better book-smarts could help avoid the pitfalls of spur of the moment street-smarts.

Network thinking and many-to-many marketing have ramifications for organizing marketing. In American terminology a company is led by a Chief Executive Officer, CEO, and the former Marketing Director is now called Chief Marketing Officer, CMO. It does not fit the view of the new service marketing. My suggestion is instead that they be renamed *Network Executive Officer, NEO*, and *Network Marketing Officer, NMO,* thus establishing that interacting in networks of complex relationships is their main task. That is what they do in practice anyway.

Connecting the drivers

S-D logic, service science and relation-based marketing are viable syntheses and additions on the way to marketing theory on a higher level of generalization and abstraction – grand theory.

The drivers are interdependent and should be treated in an integrative spirit. S-D logic dissolves the divides between goods/services and supplier/customer into cocreated service and value. It offers a philosophy for service science and its application in education, research and practice in its effort to create hassle-free, innovative service systems. Network and systems theory offer holistic ways of thinking, offer methodology to go beyond fragmented research in management and marketing, and to address complexity and context for application on service systems.

The following case study gives a flavour of how a service situation can appear in a real-life situation (based on Gummesson, 2010).

CASE STUDY 18.1

The reality of being a patient: The case of Anna, 82

Eighty-two-year-old Anna has 23 age-related disorders including fatigue, pain, memory loss and reduced eyesight and hearing. She has been through 11 different therapies encompassing 41 components. During one year she was exposed to seven types of therapies performed by 55 specialists. From five doctors she has been prescribed nine types of medication to be consumed daily, and two to be used on demand. She regularly goes to massage and physical exercise, and twice a week a social assistant comes to her home to help. Assistants stay for only short periods on the job and new ones appear constantly. Anna is also dependent on social insurance people – who also come and go. Apart from all these contacts with people, Anna is exposed to an endless amount of capital goods (huge hospital buildings, x-ray equipment, operating theatres) and disposable products (pills, food, syringes). During a year she is perhaps in contact with 100 different health-care representatives. To get 23 disorders, 11 therapies, 9 + 2 pills and other products, and 100 people together to cocreate value and service requires advanced systems and network management.

Anna is a customer of the healthcare sector, a sub-category of what is conventionally called the service sector. But healthcare is not about sectors; it is about thousands of health-related value propositions of excessively diverse kinds. She is exposed to value propositions from a large number of people, and these are only loosely and haphazardly coordinated into a service system. Each may be an efficient system within the supplier value chain, but they do not concur with Anna's value network; they are not customer-centric. In healthcare, the necessity of cocreation is obvious. The patient must do her part and be active within her ability: communicate with the therapists, take her pills, eat well, rest, exercise and so on. Each therapy and other activity is a system in itself and somebody has to manage the network of systems.

Would you hire Anna as network manager? No, you would say – but that is what you have already done.

Figure 18.1 shows the network of people, therapies, products and systems in which Anna is supposed to cocreate value and get service. Although the figure is simplified, a little fantasy and empathy will enable you to visualize the complex context and the many-to-many relationships within which Anna lives. If there is one thing that Anna needs in her situation it is certainly not complexity. She needs simplicity. Each therapeutic system by itself may have the good intention to provide just that, but first, each system is too provider-centric, and second, it is operating within the logic of its speciality, career system, organization, budget, locations and so on, with sparse cocreation between the systems.

Where does marketing enter this network? Anna's service is a combination of government service (which can be a free citizen's right paid through taxes), private insurance, and service and value propositions from enterprises. Healthcare offers opportunities to sell to government organizations like hospitals and laboratories, and

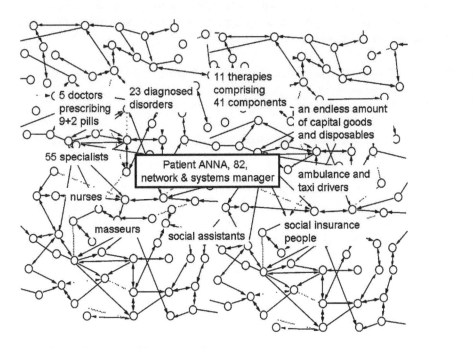

Figure 18.1   A sketch of Anna's healthcare network.

Source: Gummesson (2010).

(Continued)

(Continued)

to private doctors and other therapists. Anna herself may be in the market for health food, vitamins, minerals, medication, eyeglasses and so on. She may listen to family and friends, television and radio programmes and read, all of this forming an information network affecting her behaviour as a consumer. Among the providers to hospitals are pharmaceutical companies, suppliers of equipment and disposable goods, computer and software consultants, building and construction firms, catering firms and cleaning firms. So the healthcare systems for the elderly are replete with marketing opportunities. It is a many-to-many marketing situation where networks meet networks and where the simple supplier–customer relationship is too limited to explain what happens.

In conclusion, S-D logic, service science and relation-based marketing have broadened the service encounter to cocreation of value and value propositions. It is important to note that cocreation is not just interaction in a service encounter. In designing value propositions the following questions therefore must be answered:

- Who are the customers and who are the suppliers?
- What do suppliers do best?
- What do customers do best?
- What do third parties do best?
- What should be one-party (individual) action?
- What should be two-party (dyadic) interaction?
- What should be multi-party (network) interaction?
- What should be C2C interaction?
- What should be face-to-face interaction, ear-to-ear interaction, email interaction, internet interaction, text messaging and interaction with automatic machines?
- What do human beings do best?
- What does technology do best?
- Is there a no-man's land where service is neglected?

In the new service marketing the customer and supplier roles have merged, although they perform different tasks. The following categories of suppliers are found in the market:

- Business enterprises;
- Governments on a national, regional and local level and increasingly on a mega, supranational level, such as the EU;
- NGOs which arise where the first two have failed, or act as supplementary to them.

In B2B, suppliers are also customers. In B2C we find:

- Consumers
- Citizens.

These are traditionally referred to as end-users. In many-to-many marketing the roles have broadened from a single individual consumer to social networks of family, friends, neighbours and others. Being a citizen goes beyond the commercial consumer role; a citizen has certain rights and should primarily be served by the government sector. In the new service marketing with cocreation as a foundational premise, consumers are also suppliers of value. Therefore, consumers and citizens assume both the role of customer and supplier.

The future

In the early 1990s I concluded that all organizations produce and sell both goods and services but in varying proportions, that customers buy utility and need satisfaction and not goods and services as such, that we know no more about services today than people knew about iron in the Iron Age, that we now have to understand the atoms and molecules and genes, and that we need a general theory of value-creating offerings. This is taken seriously within Paradigm 3 but there is still a long way to go. It got a kick start in 2004 through S-D logic and service science. My own line of thinking, complex networks actualized in many-to-many marketing, had taken me part of the way towards more comprehensive service theory but now there was a quantum leap.

Instead of making predictions that will probably prove wrong anyway, I will express preferences. We should continue to work along the lines expressed by the new service marketing theory. It will take us places that we did not know existed. Some of the contributions will be viable and others will be less so, and may even lead us astray. There is no certainty in basic research and new discoveries. There will be discontinuities when something new and unexpected takes the lead and changes the world forever. Just think of a recent discontinuity, the internet. In the same sense as Columbus thought he was eastbound to India but instead went west and discovered America, IT applications have taken unexpected turns. This is called *serendipity*; you search for one thing and discover another – which also turns out to be useful.

Some years ago I concluded that 'marketing theory must reinvent itself and be refined, redefined, generated, and regenerated – or it will degenerate' (Gummesson, 2005: 317). There is now a call for basic research and theory on higher levels of abstraction, both better mid-range theory and grand theory. We need to take further steps up the marketing theory ladder. Marketing of services over the past decades offered mid-range theory. The new service marketing is taking us to the next rung of the marketing ladder towards grand theory, but I do not know how many rungs there are before we reach the top. Contributions from scholarly research should be the generation of theory, both grand theory for deeper understanding of the complexity of marketing and of its inner core and soul, and of how complexity can be condensed into simplification and mid-range theory for practical implementation. Michael Baker has pointed to the necessity of *currently useful generalizations*, simplifications that can be used by practitioners until something better comes up. They are examples of *pragmatism* formulated in checklists, models and heuristics. We need them temporarily; they are better than nothing. The problem is that if they become popular and are sold through textbooks and consultants they may become permanent and hard to get rid of even when better knowledge becomes available.

It is further imperative that *explicit knowledge* is coupled with *tacit knowledge* that lacks words and can only be validated in action including experience, commonsense and intuition – to arrive at *pragmatic wisdom*. A researcher always has to make a series of *judgement calls* based on his/her combined explicit and tacit knowledge. This is so in quantitative research as well but statisticians do not seem to be aware of it; they refer to their research as rigorous and following approved standards.

Finally, 'general' marketing textbooks are still dominated by Paradigm 1 theory and service marketing textbooks by Paradigm 2 theory. The development of Paradigm 3, now in progress for over 10 years, is not yet found in the marketing textbooks except for a short paragraph, a note or a single reference. For the future I wish that the *textbook theory* should more rapidly catch up with seminal theory developments, not least because new graduates are important agents for the dissemination of new knowledge to marketing practice.

Recommended further reading

Badinell, R., Barile, S., Ng, I., Polese, F., Saviano, M. and Di Nauta, P. (2012) 'Viable service systems and decision making in service management', *Journal of Service Management* 23(4): 498–526.

Gummerus, J. and von Koskull, C. (eds) (2015) *The Nordic School – Service Marketing and Management for the Future*. Helsinki: Hanken School of Economics. E-book to be downloaded for free on: https://www.hanken.fi/en/about-hanken/organisation/departments-and-subjects/department-marketing/cers/nordic-school-book

Gummesson, E. (2007) 'Exit services marketing – enter service marketing', *Journal of Customer Behaviour* 6(2): 113–41. (Also in Baker, M.J. and Hart, S.J. (eds) (2008) *The Marketing Book*, 6th edn. Oxford: Butterworth/Heinemann/Elsevier, pp. 451–71.)

Lusch, R.F. and Vargo, S.L. (2014) *Service-Dominant Logic*. Cambridge: Cambridge University Press.

Mele, C., Colurcio, M. and Russo-Spena, T. (2014) 'Research traditions of innovation: goods-dominant logic, the resource-based approach, and service-dominant logic', *Managing Service Quality* 24(6): 612–42.

Närvänen, E., Gummesson, E. and Kuusela, H. (2014) 'The collective consumption network', *Managing Service Quality* 24(6): 545–64.

References

Readers are advised not to consult earlier editions than those referred to below.

Ballantyne, D. and Varey, R.J. (2008) 'The service-dominant logic and the future of marketing', *Journal of the Academy of Marketing Science* 36(1): 11–13.

Edvardsson, B., Kristensson, P., Magnusson, P. and Sundström, E. (2012) 'Customer integration in service development and innovation – methods and a new framework', *Technovation* 32(7): 419–29.

Grönroos, C. (2015) *Service Management and Marketing*, 4th edn. Chichester: John Wiley.

Gummesson, E. (2005) 'Qualitative research in marketing: roadmap for a wilderness of complexity and unpredictability', *European Journal of Marketing* 39(3/4): 309–27.

Gummesson, E. (2010) 'The future of service is long overdue', in P.P. Maglio, C.A. Kieliszewski and J. Spohrer (eds) *Handbook of Service Science*. New York: Springer, pp. 625–42.

Gummesson, E. (2016a) *Total Relationship Marketing*, 4th edn. Abingdon: Routledge.

Gummesson, E. (2016b) *From Case Study Research to Case Theory*. London: Sage.

Gummesson, E. and Grönroos, C. (2012) 'The emergence of the new service marketing: Nordic School perspectives', *Journal of Service Management* 23(4): 479–97.

Håkansson, H., Ford D., Gadde, L.-E., Snehota, I. and Waluszewski, A. (2009) *Business in Networks*. Chichester: John Wiley.

Lovelock, C. and Gummesson, E. (2004) 'Whither services marketing? In search of a paradigm and fresh perspectives', *Journal of Service Research* 7(1): 20–41.

Lusch, R.F. and Vargo, S.L. (2014) *Service-Dominant Logic*. Cambridge: Cambridge University Press.

Maglio, P.P. and Spohrer, J. (2008) 'Fundamentals of service science', *Journal of the Academy of Marketing Science* 36(1): 18–20.

Vargo, S.L. and Lusch, R.F. (2008) 'Service-dominant logic: continuing the evolution', *Journal of the Academy of Marketing Science* 36(1): 1–10.

Vargo, S.L., Maglio, P. and Akaka, M.A. (2008) 'On value and value cocreation: a service systems and service logic perspective', *European Management Journal* 26(3): 145–52.

Service–Dominant Logic

Stephen L. Vargo,
Robert F. Lusch and
Kaisa Koskela-Huotari

19

Chapter Topics

Introduction	458
Complexity of markets and society	459
Challenging the goods-dominant logic worldview	460
The transcending nature of service-dominant logic	464
The systemic and institutional nature of value	470
Service-dominant logic possibilities for marketing and innovation	471
Conclusion	473

Introduction

Marketing, like every other discipline, has an underlying dominant logic consisting of the foundational assumptions that guide scholars' and practitioners' worldview, interests and attention (cf. Kuhn, 1970). Institutionalized logics, like these, provide a lens for viewing the complex world and separating noise from signal. They are often inherited from related disciplines and gradually evolve as new ideas are introduced and combined with existing ones. The logics are, therefore, enabling as they contribute to comfort and understanding of the world, but also constraining as they simultaneously restrict perceptions and thinking (Thornton et al., 2012).

In 2004 Vargo and Lusch published an article called 'Evolving to a new dominant logic for marketing'. The article aimed at identifying and re-evaluating the underlying assumptions behind traditional marketing theory, which they called 'goods-dominant (G-D) logic', as well as highlighting some of the more recent developments that were challenging and reframing the assumptions of this dominant worldview. Many of these transitions and alternative reformulations in the way markets and marketing are understood have been developed in the sub-disciplines of marketing (Vargo and Lusch, 2008a), most notably services marketing and business marketing, and are only slowly seeping into mainstream marketing. It is these transformations, together with others taking place outside of marketing, that are converging into a potentially transcending perspective now known as 'service-dominant (S-D) logic' (e.g. Vargo and Lusch, 2004, 2008a, 2011; see also Lusch and Vargo, 2006a, 2014).

The starting point of S-D logic is the idea that *service is exchanged for service* (Vargo and Lusch, 2004). It is this simple, underlying idea of S-D logic arguing that humans apply their competences to benefit others (i.e. *service*) and reciprocally benefit from others' applied competences, which has, over the past decade, found increasing resonance among theorists in business and economics, as well as others studying social collaboration. Hence, S-D logic has become a cocreated effort of numerous scholars across disciplines, who share the common goal of contributing to the understanding of human value cocreation, by developing an alternative to traditional logics of exchange. In this chapter, the evolution and premises of S-D logic are highlighted. Special attention is focused on how S-D logic overcomes several dichotomies prevailing in G-D logic that constrain the way markets and marketing are seen and thought about, and how the transcending nature of the S-D logical mindset opens up new possibilities for thinking about marketing, markets and innovation.

Complexity of markets and society

Complexity characterizes human society and solutions (Simon, 1996). It is interesting to consider how humankind has evolved from scattered small groups of individuals using hand axes to the connected and information-driven modern day society filled with a vast range of continually changing technologies (see e.g. Ridley, 2011). Complexity has arisen, in part, from human specialization or the development of specific skills and competences for different individuals and the exchange of these specialized skills with others (Lusch and Vargo, 2014; Vargo and Lusch, 2004).

Consider the example of a fisherman and a farmer. Some of the necessary resources for life are protein, for example in the form of fish, and carbohydrates, for example in the form of wheat. These resources are unevenly distributed, as are the skills and abilities necessary to obtain them. The fisherman has become very proficient at harvesting fish from the sea, by developing her/his physical skills as well as her/his mental skills – the know-how concerning when and where to fish. S/he has also innovatively developed tools and technology to assist her/him, such as nets, hooks and spears. Similarly, the farmer has developed both the physical and mental skills necessary to grow and harvest grain and innovatively develop tools to assist her/him in these tasks. In order for the fisherman and farmer to specialize in their respective skills, they need to exchange and benefit from each other's specialized skills – the fisherman benefits from the farmers' skills by exchanging her/his competences to fish with farmers' competences to grow wheat and vice versa. Thus, specialization and exchange become the dual and reinforcing sources of advantage for actors as the exchange of specialized competences frees up time and resources, which enables learning and further specialization and so forth.

Hence, by specializing humans enhance their advantageous individual abilities but in turn need to exchange with other actors (Ridley, 2011; Vargo and Lusch, 2004). This results in systemic dependencies and interdependencies among individuals and groups resulting in complex exchange systems (Chandler and Vargo, 2011; Vargo and Lusch, 2011). Consider a local grocery store. How many people's specialized knowledge and skills are available in the grocery store in the form of various kinds of protein and carbohydrate sources?

Society and, along with it, many institutions, such as language, norms, economic currency and payment mechanisms, industries, markets and organizations (e.g. firms, or enterprises), are created from this exchange system for efficiency and governance purposes (Lusch and Vargo, 2014). In other words, the better humans can communicate with each other and predict each other's behaviour, the better they can collaborate and benefit from each other's specialized skills and competences, which in turn leads to more specialization and new knowledge and skills.

To unlock the complexity of the society and the exchange system(s), S-D logic uses the notions of service ecosystems and institutions when studying markets and marketing among other things. Both of these concepts will be covered in more detail later on in this chapter. First, however, it is important to examine the causes for the oversimplistic views on markets and marketing dominating the current academic discussion and how S-D logic is challenging and transcending these issues.

Challenging the goods-dominant logic worldview

While exchange systems are complex, theories of marketing, business and society that deal with them need to be appropriately simple if they are to be broadly generalizable. At the same time, these theories need to be sufficiently isomorphic with the complexity of the world of exchange to serve as the basis of useful, normative applications that they are intended to facilitate. Problems and obstacles emerge immediately when constructing simple theories of exchange, business and society. Arguably, the most difficult of these problems is the dominance of a logic developed in a previous context for a different purpose but that has become deeply rooted and institutionalized, therefore monopolizing scholars' and practitioners' conceptualization processes. One such logic that has monopolized academic marketing thought since its beginning is 'goods-dominant (G-D) logic'.

G-D logic frames the world of exchange in terms of units of output (primarily goods) and views the production and exchange of goods as the central elements of business and economics (Vargo and Lusch, 2004; Vargo et al., 2008). That is, it frames the purpose of the firm and the function of economic exchange in terms of making and distributing products – usually tangible units of output. This logic is closely aligned with neoclassical economics, which views actors as rational, firms as profit maximizing, customers as utility maximizing, information and resources flowing easily among economic actors and markets as equilibrium seeking. Others, before us, have referred to the G-D logic as 'manufacturing logic' (e.g. Normann, 2001), 'old enterprise logic' (Zuboff and Maxmin, 2002), 'marketing management' (Webster, 1992), or 'company-centric, efficiency-driven view of value creation' (Prahalad and Ramaswamy, 2002).

There are several problems with G-D logic, but some of the most important challenges to this worldview relate to where it focuses attention. As the name describes, G-D logic fosters goods-centricity and sees the firm as the central and (the only) active actor of exchange. G-D logic is also preoccupied with emphasizing the importance of *value-in-exchange* – what something is worth when exchanged. It focuses on maximizing the difference between what a firm pays for the cost of production and distribution and at what price the firm's output can be sold – that is, maximizing economic value-added or profit. Ignored is *value-in-use* – the extent to which the use of something contributes to the well-being of some actor(s). Thus, before offering a more useful and robust framework for understanding economic (and, more generally, social) exchange, a brief review of these problematic 'centricities' of G-D logic is useful in order to understand how they misguide academic and practical thought and action. These focal areas of G-D logic are illustrated in Figure 19.1.

G-D logic's overemphasis on goods, firms and value-in-exchange has led to several deeply ingrained dichotomies that are used in marketing to make sense of exchange in human society. We argue that these dichotomies constrain the development of a broader, more general view on economic and social exchange.

Goods-centricity and goods versus services dichotomy

As the term G-D logic implies, the major problem with this worldview is that it fosters goods-centricity. According to G-D logic economic exchange is fundamentally concerned with units

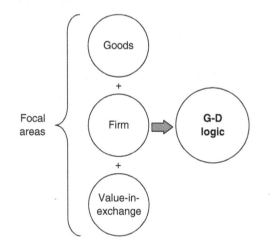

Figure 19.1 Focal areas of G-D logic.

of output (products) that are embedded with value during the manufacturing (or agricultural, or extraction) process (see Vargo and Lusch, 2004). These products can be sold in the market in which firms aim to increase the quantity of units sold, in order to maximize profits. In short, the purpose of the firm is to produce and sell value-laden units of output and the role of the customer, on the other hand, is to purchase and consume these units and then buy more.

It is this goods-centric thinking that Theodore Levitt (1960) over 50 years ago labelled 'marketing myopia'. He argued that firms often see themselves producing and selling products – railroad and theatre seats – and act accordingly, while that is not what customers buy. Instead, what the customers actually want or need are the transportation and entertainment services. Hence, customers seek to buy solutions and experiences, rather than products per se. To this day Levitt's marketing myopia continues in the form of the highly institutionalized G-D logic worldview that dominates the world of business research and practice.

As a response to the narrow focus of G-D logic on goods that characterized mainstream marketing thought, services marketing (e.g. Berry and Parasuraman, 1991; Fisk et al., 1993; Grönroos, 1984; Zeithaml et al., 1985) as a sub-discipline of marketing emerged to highlight the importance of this other 'form' of offering that had largely been ignored. Given the dominance of G-D logic, at least for the last several hundred years, definitions of 'services' have been couched in terms of what goods are not, or creating a dichotomy in which goods and services are seen very different from each other (Gummesson, 1993; Shostack, 1977; Vargo and Lusch, 2008b, 2008c). In other words, services were conceptualized as anything that was not defined in terms of being manufactured, extracted, or grown. Services were either seen as an add-on to goods (e.g. after-sale services) or a special type of (intangible) good. It has been argued that service is more than what goods are not or a type of intangible good (Vargo and Morgan, 2005). In S-D logic, the notion of 'service' – the application of operant resources (e.g. knowledge and skills) for the benefit of another actor – represents activities that provide benefits for another party and is therefore the basis of all exchange (Vargo and Lusch, 2004).

Part of the problem is revealed in the use of the word 'services', which implies units of output – intangible goods. Hence, the term 'services' (plural) is still a term grounded in goods-dominant logic (see e.g. Vargo and Lusch, 2008b). It suggests that an airline produces seat miles, rather than provides transportation service, a bank sells quantities of loans, rather than provides financial service, a hotel produces units of lodging (bed nights), rather than provides lodging services, as we will argue later in this chapter.

Firm-centricity and producers versus consumers dichotomy

In the G-D model, the firm is seen as the only proactive actor and, hence, is central to economic exchange (Vargo and Lusch, 2004) and wealth creation. The firm is seen as the innovator, developer, producer, distributer and promoter of goods, and thus seen as representing the heart of markets and exchange. Markets, on the other hand, are seen as almost passively waiting, with unfilled demand and as something pre-existing 'out there' (Lusch and Vargo, 2014). They are described as comprising 'consumers' from whom the firm profits by producing, distributing and selling goods. Hence, a G-D logical worldview implies that some actors (mainly firms) produce and create value, whereas other actors (such as customers) consume and destroy that value (Vargo et al., 2008).

The producer versus consumer dichotomy has at least some of its roots in the development of indirect exchange (Vargo and Lusch, 2011). That is, initially, when exchange was direct through barter, the producer–consumer distinction was trivial, if not non-existent, since each party was clearly doing something for the other and benefiting from having something done for them. However, once a monetary system was created and economic organization (i.e. 'business firm') separated from households, more and more exchange began to take place indirectly (e.g. through intermediaries, such as merchants) and, as a result, the symmetry of the roles became blurred. Now one party ('producer') did something for another party ('consumer') relatively directly, while the latter provided indirect benefit (money) obtained by providing direct benefit to a third party. As the economy became 'industrialized' this usually meant that this direct benefit to a third party was provided through an individual household member opting to work exogenously to the home, for a firm, in return for monetary wages which then were used to participate in the market. Thus, the parties appeared to be playing different roles, though each was providing and receiving benefit, albeit not necessarily directly.

In the same way that goods are not the central purpose of exchange, firms and organizations are not the central actors of exchange. Organizations and firms are vehicles that humans have invented to help them solve the problems associated with the exchange of their individual advantageous abilities (Lusch and Vargo, 2014). It is always the human actors that are centre stage in the creation of their own well-being by combining resources from various sources including market-facing (e.g. other organizations and actors), private (themselves, friends, family, etc.) and public (public infrastructure, public institutions, etc.) sources (Vargo and Lusch, 2011), to continually resolve issues in the context of their own lives. Additionally, all human actors, in turn, contribute to the well-being of other actors as well through the ongoing market-facing, public and private exchange. We will come back to this more generic actor conceptualization later in this chapter.

Exchange-value centricity and firm-created versus customer-created value dichotomy

G-D logic is also problematic because it promotes exchange-value centricity (Lusch and Vargo, 2014). Scholars have been debating the primacy of 'exchange-value' – what something is worth in exchange – and 'use-value' – the extent to which something contributes to the well-being of some actor – at least since the time of Aristotle, who discussed and distinguished between them. Generally, the debates have highlighted the primacy and centrality of use-value. However, with the development of a more formal economic philosophy, beginning with the work of Adam Smith (1937 [1776]), and, later extended in the development of economic science, the focus on use-value largely diminished, at least temporarily. Although Adam Smith acknowledged value-in-use as 'real value', he used 'exchange-value' as a surrogate, because he felt it was both easier to understand and provided a standardized measurement of wealth for considering the issue of national wealth creation in the context of the early part of the Industrial Revolution.

Since Adam Smith, the meaning of exchange-value was amplified and institutionalized as economic thought transformed from philosophy to science at a time that 'science' meant Newtonian Mechanics – a model that viewed matter as embedded with properties – and thus provided for an easy translation to the concept of a product, or 'good', embedded with 'utilities' (exchange-value). This, in turn, paved the way for marginal utility theory, which became the basis of the neoclassical model of economics that, in time, was adopted by other business disciplines.

The exchange-value centricity in G-D logic paved the way for a firm-centric view on value creation in which firms are seen as the value creators and customers as value destroyers. The customer was slowly brought into focus by first examining quality and customer satisfaction and later the customer perspective on value (Khalifa, 2004; Woodruff, 1997). The lack of inclusion of the customer role in value creation has also sometimes resulted in a counter, overreaction that considers the customer as the sole value creator (see e.g. Heinonen et al., 2010) and firms only as value *facilitators* (Grönroos, 2011). Though the early scholars, including Smith in his original analysis of economic exchange, had it right all along – value is created at the point of what we have been calling 'consumption', rather than during production – the S-D logic view on value does not privilege the role of a beneficiary (e.g. a customer) over the role of service provider in the process of value creation. The role of both (all) actors in value cocreation is recognized as important, as the direct and/or indirect reciprocity of service exchange makes all actors simultaneously to be both beneficiaries and service providers in value cocreation.

The transcending nature of service-dominant logic

The products-versus-services, producers-versus-consumers, firm-created versus customer-created value dichotomies caused by the G-D logic's emphasis on goods, firm and exchange-value are important to understand, because they represent the core assumptions that direct attention away from both the nature of value and the way it is created, interactively, in concert with a whole host of actors, singly and collectively (e.g. through organizations, firms), contributing resources that are eventually integrated by other actors to provide service – that is, value is cocreated. They also direct attention away from the most important integrating and integrated resources – human actors with their skills, knowledge and innovative and entrepreneurial abilities. What is needed is a logic that focuses on these central, benefit-providing (i.e. service providing) resources, not by abandoning goods logic but rather by transcending it.

S-D logic responds to the general calls for a new paradigm, as well as more specific calls for reformulating thought in specific areas of academic interest in business and marketing, such as services and relationship marketing (e.g. Grönroos, 1994; Gummesson, 1995), resource-advantage theory (e.g. Hunt, 2000), resource-based view of the firm and core competency theory (e.g. Barney, 1991; Day, 1994; Prahalad and Hamel, 1990), network theory (e.g. Achrol and Kotler, 1999; Håkansson and Snehota, 1995; Normann and Ramirez, 1993), consumer culture theory (e.g. Arnould and Thompson, 2005) and others, which collectively point towards an alternative logic of the market (for detailed evolution see Vargo and Lusch, 2004). It is a logic that implies moving the understanding of markets and marketing from a product or output-centric focus to a service or process-centric focus.

Four axioms of service-dominant logic

The first few years in the development of S-D logic focused on the historical unfolding of the events and contexts that led to the development of the foundations of economic science, which are now referred to in terms of G-D logic. It was found that many of the assumptions on which the standard, G-D logic-based model of economic thought was based were being questioned, and that an alternative, service-based model seemed to be emerging. To capture the essence of this emerging model, eight foundational premises (FPs) of S-D logic were identified (Vargo and Lusch, 2004) and later, slightly revised and expanded to 10 (Lusch and Vargo, 2006b; Vargo and Lusch, 2008a). It should be noted that in the FPs, many of the concepts are neither exclusive to nor invented by S-D logic itself. Rather, S-D logic captures a shift in contemporary marketing thought, in which marketing is seen as a facilitator of ongoing processes of voluntary exchange through collaborative, value-creating relationships among actors. Of the 10 FPs, there are four that particularly capture the essence and from which the other FPs could arguably be derived. Thus, these four FPs are considered as the axioms of S-D logic (Table 19.1)

The first axiom, '*Service is the fundamental basis of exchange*', is based on the previously introduced definition of service: the application of operant resources (knowledge and skill) for the benefit of another actor. S-D logic argues that it is always fundamentally service, rather than goods, per se, that actors exchange as they strive to become better off. In other words, service is exchanged for service and, as noted and discussed later in more detail, this implies that (1) goods are appliances for service provision, (2) all businesses are service businesses and (3) all economies are service economies. It follows that money, when it is involved in exchanges, represents rights to future service, or money can be viewed as a placeholder for future service.

The second axiom, '*The customer is always a cocreator of value*', contradicts G-D logic, which views the firm as the producer, the creator, of value; rather, it suggests that value is

Table 19.1 The axioms of S-D logic.

Axioms	Explanation
1. Service is the fundamental basis of exchange (FP1)	The application of operant resources (knowledge and skills), 'service', is the basis for all exchange. Service is exchanged for service.
2. The customer is always a cocreator of value (FP6)	Implies value creation is interactional.
3. All economic and social actors are resource integrators (FP9)	Implies the context of value creation is networks of networks (resource integrators).
4. Value is always uniquely and phenomenologically determined by the beneficiary (FP10)	Value is idiosyncratic, experiential, contextual and meaning laden.

something that is always cocreated through the interaction of actors, either directly or through goods. This axiom also enables one to see more clearly that the service-oriented view is inherently relational, because value does not arise prior to the exchange transaction but following it, in the use of the offering in a particular context, in conjunction with resources provided by other service providers, and this unfolding value extends over time with a consequence of continuing social and economic exchange, implicit contracts and relational norms.

The third axiom, '*All social and economic actors are resource integrators*', highlights that all actors are fundamentally doing the same thing, that is, integrating resources, and that the integrated resources come from a variety of sources. It is in the integration of these resources in its many possible explicit and implicit combinations, facets and intricacies that value is cocreated. This resource integration not only occurs with the resources directly available to actors involved in an exchange, but also with the resources and actors that provide these resources – or, simply value is created through a network of other resource integrating actors.

In the fourth axiom of S-D logic, '*Value is always uniquely and phenomenologically determined by the beneficiary*', the term 'beneficiary' reflects the generic nature of actors. This axiom reinforces that value is experiential. The key message of this axiom is that all market offerings, all service provisioning, all goods and all value propositions are perceived and integrated differently by each unique actor and thus, value is also uniquely experienced and determined. Together these four axioms of S-D logic provide the basis for transcending the dichotomies caused by G-D logic's overemphasis on goods, firms and exchange-value and offer the opportunity to take marketing thought forward, as shown below.

From goods versus services to service

The most distinguishing difference between G-D logic and S-D logic is the conceptualization of service. In S-D logic service is defined as the application of competences (knowledge and skills) for the benefit of another party (Lusch and Vargo, 2006b; Vargo and Lusch, 2008a). The use of the singular 'service', as opposed to the plural 'services', is subtle but critical. It signals a shift from thinking about value creation in terms of operand resources – usually tangible, static resources (e.g. natural resources) that require some action to make them valuable – to operant resources – usually intangible, dynamic resources (e.g. human knowledge and skills) that are capable of acting on other resources to create value (Vargo and Lusch, 2004, 2011). This means that whereas G-D logic sees services as units of output that are somewhat inferior to goods, S-D logic sees 'service' as the process of applying one's knowledge and skills for and with another actor, and thus always dynamic and collaborative.

It is important to note that S-D logic represents a shift in the logic of exchange, rather than a shift in the type of product that is under investigation. That is, S-D logic is not about making services more important than goods, but is about transcending both goods and what have been referred to as 'services' with the common denominator, service – a process of doing something for and with another party (Figure 19.2).

Consider the fisherman and the farmer again. When the fisherman and farmer exchange, what are they exchanging? The answer might seem obvious: they are exchanging fish for grain.

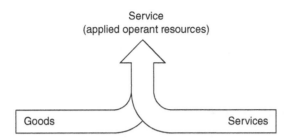

Figure 19.2 Transcending goods and services with service.

This 'obvious answer', however, is grounded in goods-dominant logic and reflects a view that the world is primarily about the outputs produced and exchanged by actors. We argue this answer is wrong, or at least not the whole story. We suggest that, more accurately, or at least more generally, what the two actors are exchanging is the application of protein-provisioning competences for the application of carbohydrate-provisioning competences. That is, they are exchanging fishing service for farming service. Why is this distinction between outputs and the application of competences important? First, the service interpretation focuses attention on the only resource the actors really possess to take to market: their own knowledge and skills, rather than the by-products of their application (fish and wheat). Thus, the service (application of competences) focus is more general and transcending, since it applies equally to exchange situations, involving different types of goods, and also in situations where there are no inter-mediate products (i.e. direct service provision).

In short, service is the transcending, and thus the unifying, concept for understanding exchange in all economies (and all businesses) as it overcomes the goods/products versus services dichotomy. Perhaps more subtly, but arguably more important, is that, extrapolating from fishing and farming to business in general, there is a fundamental difference in how the business process is informed between understanding the purpose as selling things to people and understanding it to be serving the exchange partner's needs. Hence, we suggest that 'service' implies a process of one actor doing something for another – a beneficiary. The process of serving requires the application of knowledge and skills – competences, as discussed.

From this definition of service, it follows that goods can be seen as distribution mechanism for service. Goods began with some individual(s) applying their competences (knowledge and skills) to invent and/or manufacture the good. The good is then used by other individual(s) and in this sense goods are appliances, which act as intermediaries in service delivery. At this very moment, this book – a tangible product – is being used as an appliance in the learning process of its reader. Another way to provide information about S-D logic would have been to give a face-to-face lecture, something that could be considered a service also in traditional terms. Instead, the authors tried to embed their knowledge in this book so that the reader could get these ideas in use for his/her learning process by reading about them. The same underlying service still applies in both cases, which is the authors applying their knowledge and skills for the learner's benefit. This idea is maybe more obvious in some settings, such as this book or the kitchen, where appliances clearly assist cooks in the process of meal service. However, it is just as true in the factory, in which equipment and machinery function as appliances for manufacturing services, when combined with labour (another resource) and materials (another resource), or in everyday life, where automobiles serve as transportation appliances.

From producers versus consumers to resource integrating actors

Just as it is helpful to refocus on what is being exchanged, it is also essential to refocus on the nature of the actors doing the exchanging. Though we can see social and economic actors exchanging in many different contexts and roles, we will argue that they are fundamentally always doing three common things: (1) integrating resources from various sources, (2) exchanging service for service and (3) cocreating value. However, to see this clearly and to fully understand and appreciate the significance and power of this requires refocusing away from firms and customers to a transcending actor-to-actor (A2A) framework (Figure 19.3).

In other words, S-D logic suggests that, to the extent that 'production' and 'consumption' are appropriately descriptive, they apply to all actors (Vargo and Lusch, 2011). Consider a professor who uses a car, gas, etc. to go to the university to teach students; is s/he a producer or a consumer? Likewise, consider the students, who take notes so that the professor's insights can be used in their jobs; are they producers or consumers? How about one of the students who is an employee of the car company that makes the car driven by the professor, which in turn, pays tuition which provides the university with the resources to pay the professor? Are they producers or consumers? The answer to all of these is 'both' and 'neither'. On the one hand, all economic actors both 'produce and consume'; on the other hand, these characterizations do not inform us about anything useful concerning the actors, at best, and at worst, mislead us about their role in economic exchange in ways that misinform attempts to engage them economically.

For this reason, it is important to think about and refer to economic (and social) actors as just that, generic 'actors', at least to the extent possible, without introducing confusion. As noted, fundamentally, all actors (e.g. business firms, non-profit and government organizations, individuals, households) have a common purpose: value cocreation through resource integration and service-for-service exchange. Therefore, in S-D logic the terms 'consumers' and

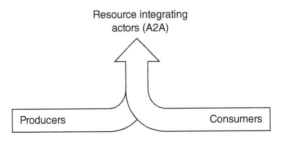

Figure 19.3   Transcending producers and consumers with resource integrating actors.

'producers' are generally avoided (except in citations of others). The terms 'firm' and 'customer' are however sometimes used when there is a need to distinguish between actors, with the firm referring to the provider of direct service or indirect service through a good and the customer referring to the provider of service indirectly, through money.

Due to the generic actor notion, S-D logic often uses an 'actor-to-actor' (A2A) notation, rather than the conventional 'business-to-business' (B2B), 'business-to-consumer' (B2C) and 'consumer-to-consumer' (C2C) notations. In other words, S-D logic suggests that economic and social exchange, viewed from a perspective of actors interacting with other actors, as opposed to business exchanging with other businesses or consumers or any combination of these differentiated actors, opens the investigator to a more revealing and transcending view of the world (Vargo and Lusch, 2011). An actor-centric, versus a firm-, producer-, household-, customer- or any other role-centric labelling is also less restrictive and less biasing because it does not predispose differential, single activities, such as 'production' and 'consumption'.

From firm-created versus customer-created value to cocreated value

As stated, G-D logic emphasizes the role of the firm in value creation. In other words, G-D logic sees the firm as the primary actor, which, in its production process, embeds value in (usually tangible) output. This output is distributed to 'consumers', who consume the value and then return to the firm for more value-embedded outputs. S-D logic, on the other hand, argues that value creation occurs at the intersection of activities of providers, beneficiaries and other actors and that it is the beneficiary who cocreates and determines the value. Alternatively stated, value is created through use (i.e. integration of resources) in a specific context, rather than manufactured and then delivered. This use implies the application of the beneficiary's (e.g. customer) operant resources to those applied by the provider. All of this, in turn, implies that the beneficiary is always an active participant of the value-creation process – that is, a cocreator of value. However, it is important to note that the A2A view makes all economic and social actors simultaneously providers and beneficiaries through direct and indirect service-for-service exchange. This means that though the beneficiary's role in value determination is highlighted in S-D logic, it does not diminish the importance of other actors (such as service providers) in the process of value cocreation. Stated differently, S-D logic provides a conceptualization of value as cocreated that transcends both the firm-created and customer-created views on value (Figure 19.4).

Lately, it has become increasingly apparent that even the term 'value-in-use' might not adequately reflect the contextual nature of value creation. It is for this reason that S-D logic scholars have more recently been referring to 'value-in-context'. *Value-in-context* (Chandler and Vargo, 2011; Vargo et al., 2008) suggests that value is not only always cocreated, it is contingent on the integration of other resources and thus is contextually specific. It also resonates with the notion that all social and economic actors are resource integrators and that the value perception is always uniquely and phenomenologically determined by the beneficiary. Thus, value creation needs to be viewed in the context of social networks in which value is created and evaluated, idiosyncratically.

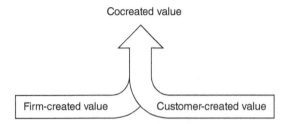

Figure 19.4   Transcending firm-created value and customer-created value with cocreated value.

This idiosyncrasy however should not be confused with randomness. Rather, social network structures (and the actors they comprise) display apparently purposeful, systemic, autopoietic behaviours driven not only by connections between (potential) resources but also by rules that govern their exchange, combination and, to some extent, the determination of the value of some kinds of resource integration (i.e. values). The systemic and institutional nature of value creation is discussed in more detail next.

The systemic and institutional nature of value

To fully unlock the complex nature of value cocreation in society, S-D logic introduces the notions of service ecosystems (Vargo and Lusch, 2011) and institutions (Edvardsson et al., 2011; Vargo and Akaka, 2012). S-D logic argues that all economic and social actors cocreating value are part of nested service ecosystems (Vargo and Lusch, 2011) that are conceptualized as 'relatively self-contained, self-adjusting system[s] of resource-integrating actors connected by shared institutional logics and mutual value creation through service exchange' (Lusch and Vargo, 2014: 161). In service ecosystems, institutions provide the enabling and constraining structure that shapes the ways in which the actors cocreate value by integrating resources, such as competences and skills, for the benefit of others and themselves (Edvardsson et al., 2011; Lusch and Vargo, 2014; Vargo and Akaka, 2012). Hence, the service ecosystems view emphasizes two aspects: the cocreation of value through dynamic integration of resources and the importance of institutions in interrelated systems of service-for-service exchange (Vargo et al., 2014).

Institutions in this context are the glue that hold service ecosystems together (Lusch and Vargo, 2014). In other words, institutions can be seen as 'the rules of the game' (North, 1990; Williamson, 2000) as they provide the structure for value cocreation and resource integration in service ecosystems. Within service ecosystems, social contexts are composed of networks of actors as well as the institutional arrangements (i.e. sets of institutions that are nested in multiple levels of social systems) that guide their actions and interactions (Vargo et al., 2014). That is, institutions shape the ways in which actors apply their competences and other available resources for the benefit of others (Lusch and Vargo, 2014; Vargo and Akaka, 2012). Institutions, in particular, are seen as guiding forces of value determination (Lusch and Vargo, 2014). However, within service ecosystems, institutional arrangements intersect and overlap and often create conflicting views on value and how value is derived (Vargo et al., 2014). This is because value cocreation is driven through resource integration and service exchange among multiple stakeholders, with varying views on value (institutional arrangements), which determine what works and what does not work (i.e. what is valuable and what is not) (Lusch et al., 2007).

It is through this iterative and dynamic process, involving firms, customers and other actors, that institutionalization (i.e. maintenance, disruption and change) of integrative, normative and representational practices, and ultimately, innovation, occurs (Vargo et al., 2014). In other words, a service ecosystem's view highlights the actions and interactions that collaboratively contribute to value creation, including those that help to maintain and change institutions. Furthermore, this perspective emphasizes the social forces that govern those actions and guide the development, integration and use of new technologies, as well as the formation of markets.

Service-dominant logic possibilities for marketing and innovation

With an understanding of the four axioms of S-D logic and the recent developments emphasizing the systemic nature of value cocreation and the role of institutions, it is possible to provide a brief glimpse of what marketing is like with S-D logic and how it differs from a G-D logic perspective.

Marketing 'with'

Some of the transitions in S-D logic can also be seen in the way that marketing seems to have transitioned to thinking in terms of marketing 'with', rather than 'to' customers. The shift in primacy of resources, from operand to operant, the systemic nature of value cocreation, the A2A perspective and the importance of institutions have implications for how markets and customers are perceived and, thus, how they are approached. S-D logic considers customers to be operant, dynamic, knowledge-generating and value-creating resources (Vargo and Lusch, 2004). This is a fundamental transition away from G-D logic, which views customers as passive operand resources that the firm acts upon. From a G-D logic perspective, customers are considered exogenous to the firm and are 'segmented' and 'targeted', and often considered to be 'manipulated' in the process of value creation. Hence, the primary focus of marketing within G-D logic is to identify customers, and market and sell to them. Alternatively, S-D logic views all exchange partners (customers and 'suppliers') as operant resources that through direct and indirect exchange are always collaborators in the value creation process. From this perspective, employees, customers and other network partners become the source, rather than the object, of a firm's innovation, competence, value and ultimately, equity.

Like other concepts and transitions that characterize S-D logic, we do not claim that we invented the idea of customers as value (co)creating resources but rather see it as the logical extension of more isolated and focused concepts and transitions found in the S-D logic pedigree.

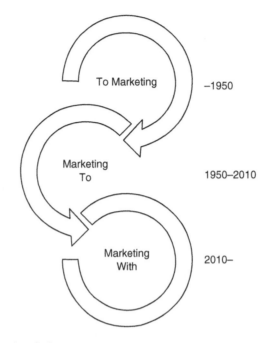

Figure 19.5   The evolution of marketing.

Source: Lusch et al. (2007: 7).

Figure 19.5 (Lusch et al., 2007: 7) depicts this shift of marketing philosophies and the evolution from a goods- towards a service-dominant logic.

In addition to changing the fundamental approach behind marketing, S-D logic also broadens the scope of innovation in several ways.

Innovation as institutional change in value cocreation

The service ecosystem perspective in S-D logic has several fundamental implications on how innovation is viewed. First, by emphasizing the cocreated nature of value and offering a transcending notion of 'service' as the basis of exchange, the service ecosystem perspective offers a unifying basis for framing all innovation, whether traditionally seen as 'economic' or 'social', as aiming towards value cocreation through direct and indirect service exchange. Second, it portrays innovation not as a novel firm-produced output, but as an institutional change in how value is cocreated by integrating resources through service exchange in a service ecosystem (Vargo et al., 2014). Third, it blurs the distinction between 'innovators' and 'adopters'. By reframing innovation as an ongoing and systemic process of institutional work, that is the creation, maintenance and disruptions of the institutions that enable and constrain market practices, S-D logic highlights that innovation processes are not limited to innovating firms or entrepreneurs, but include the active engagement of a broad range of actors, including users and those traditionally referred as 'non-adopters', as all these actors are part of the process that influences the practices, identities and meanings associated to specific solutions and, therefore, their use as resources in value cocreation.

Conclusion

For the last several decades, marketing practitioners have been calling for more relevance from marketing academics and marketing academics have been calling for a paradigm shift. More generally, there has been a call for more meaningful and informed approaches to common human needs and social issues. Not only does the dominant, G-D logic model of economics not lend itself fully to this need for more relevance, it is arguably part of the problem. This should not be entirely surprising. How could a model based solely on the exchange of goods in which one actor creates value and another consumes or destroys value and from which the derivative normative purpose is to sell increasingly more (preferably tangible) products, inform issues of mutual well-being? We argue that responding to these calls requires perspectives and ideas that challenge the G-D logic centricities and transcend the resulting dichotomies currently narrowing the academic discussion on markets and marketing.

Fortunately, many of these perspectives and reconceptualizations can be found in sub-disciplines and research initiatives of marketing thought, as well as similar divergences outside of marketing. S-D logic is not so much an attempt to create a paradigmatic shift as it is to discover one convergence of these ongoing divergences and then to accelerate its extension. Rather than the creation of a top-down, definitive position, it represents a collaborative work in process. Although our initial focus is on perspective and the underlying logic of the market, we also recognize the considerable work that needs to be done in theory building and its empirical testing and, ultimately, in establishing and reframing practice, both in marketing and other social institutions. As such we continue to invite and encourage others to participate with us to cocreate S-D logic and to use it to create a unifying theory of the market and, from this theory, a more meaningful and relevant theory of marketing, among other applications.

Recommended further reading

Lusch, R.F. and Vargo, S.L. (2006) *The Service-Dominant Logic of Marketing: Dialog, Debate and Direction*. Armonk, NY: M.E. Sharpe.

Lusch, R.F. and Vargo, S.L. (2014) *Service-Dominant Logic: Premises, Perspectives, Possibilities*. New York: Cambridge University Press.

Vargo, S.L. and Lusch, R.F. (2004) 'Evolving to a new dominant logic for marketing', *Journal of Marketing* 68(1): 1–17.

Vargo, S.L. and Lusch, R.F. (2008) 'Service-dominant logic: continuing the evolution', *Journal of the Academy of Marketing Science* 36(1): 1–10.

Vargo, S.L. and Lusch, R.F. (2011) 'It's all B2B...and beyond: toward a systems perspective of the market', *Industrial Marketing Management* 40(2): 181–7.

Vargo, S.L. and Lusch, R.F. (2016) 'Institutions and axioms: an extension and update of service-dominant logic', *Journal of the Academy of Marketing Science* 44(1): 5–23.

Vargo, S.L., Maglio P.P. and Akaka, M.A. (2008) 'On value and value co-creation: a service systems and service logic perspective', *European Management Journal* 26(3): 145–52.

References

Achrol, R. and Kotler, P. (1999) 'Marketing in the network economy', *Journal of Marketing* (special issue) 63: 146–63.

Arnould, E.J. and Thompson, C.J. (2005) 'Consumer culture theory (CCT): twenty years of research', *Journal of Consumer Research* 31 (March): 868–83.

Barney, J. (1991) 'Firm resources and sustained competitive advantage', *Journal of Management* 17(1): 99–120.

Berry, L.L. and Parasuraman, A. (1991) *Marketing Services. Competing through Quality.* Lexington, MA: The Free Press/Lexington Books.

Chandler, J.D. and Vargo, S.L. (2011) 'Contextualization and value-in-context: how context frames exchange', *Marketing Theory* 11(1): 35–49.

Day, G.S. (1994) 'The capabilities of market-driven organization', *Journal of Marketing* 58 (October): 37–52.

Edvardsson, B., Tronvoll, B. and Gruber, T. (2011) 'Expanding understanding of service exchange and value co-creation: a social construction approach', *Journal of the Academy of Marketing Science* 39(2): 327–39.

Fisk, R.P., Brown, S.W. and Bitner, M.J. (1993) 'Tracking the evolution of the services marketing literature', *Journal of Retailing* 69 (Spring): 61–103.

Grönroos, C. (1984) 'A service quality model and its marketing implications', *European Journal of Marketing* 18(4): 36–44.

Grönroos, C. (1994) 'From marketing mix to relationship marketing: towards a paradigm shift in marketing', *Asia-Australia Marketing Journal* 2 (August): 9–29.

Grönroos, C. (2011) 'Value co-creation in service logic: a critical analysis', *Marketing Theory* 11(3): 279–301.

Gummesson, E. (1993) *Quality Management in Service Organization.* New York: International Service Quality Association.

Gummesson, E. (1995) 'Relationship marketing: its role in the service economy', in W.J. Glynn and J.G. Barnes (eds) *Understanding Services Management.* New York: John Wiley.

Håkansson, H. and Snehota, I. (1995) *Developing Relationships in Business Networks.* London: Routledge.

Heinonen, K., Strandvik, T., Mickelsson, K.J., Edvardsson, B., Sundström, E. and Andersson, P. (2010) 'Rethinking service companies' business logic: do we need a customer-dominant logic as a guideline?', *Journal of Service Management* 21(4): 531–48.

Hunt, S. (2000) *A General Theory of Competition: Resources, Competences, Productivity, Economic Growth.* Thousand Oaks, CA: Sage.

Khalifa, A.S. (2004) 'Customer value: a review of recent literature and an integrative configuration', *Management Decision* 42(5): 645–66.

Kuhn, T.S. (1970) *The Structure of Scientific Revolutions.* Chicago, IL: University of Chicago Press.

Levitt, T. (1960) 'Marketing myopia', *Harvard Business Review* 38 (July–August): 44–56.

Lusch, R.F. and Vargo, S.L. (eds) (2006a) *The Service-Dominant Logic of Marketing: Dialog, Debate, and Directions.* Armonk, NY: M.E. Sharpe.

Lusch, R.F. and Vargo, S.L. (2006b) 'Service-dominant logic: reactions, reflections and refinements', *Marketing Theory* 6(3): 281–8.

Lusch, R.F. and Vargo, S.L. (2014) *Service-Dominant Logic: Premises, Perspectives, Possibilities.* New York: Cambridge University Press.

Lusch, R.F., Vargo, S.L. and O'Brien, M. (2007) 'Competing through service: insights from service-dominant logic', *Journal of Retailing* 83(1): 5–18.

Normann, R. (2001) *Reframing Business: When the Map Changes the Landscape.* New York: John Wiley.

Normann, R. and Ramirez, R. (1993) 'From value chain to value constellation: designing interactive strategy', *Harvard Business Review* 71 (July–August): 65–77.

North, D.C. (1990) *Institutions, Institutional Change and Economic Performance*. New York: Cambridge University Press.

Prahalad, C.K. and Hamel, G. (1990) 'The core competence of the corporation', *Harvard Business Review* 68 (May–June): 79–91.

Prahalad, C.K. and Ramaswamy, V. (2002) 'The co-creation connection', *Strategy and Business* 27 (Second Quarter): 50–61.

Ridley, M. (2011) *The Rational Optimist*. New York: Harper Perennial.

Shostack, G.L. (1977) 'Breaking free from product marketing', *Journal of Marketing* 41 (April): 73–80.

Simon, H.A. (1996) *The Sciences of the Artificial*, 3rd edn. Cambridge, MA: MIT Press.

Smith, A. (1937 [1776]) *An Inquiry into the Nature and Causes of the Wealth of Nations*. London: W. Strahan and T. Cadell.

Thornton, P.H., Ocasio, W. and Lounsbury, M. (2012) *The Institutional Logics Perspective: A New Approach to Culture, Structure and Process*. Oxford: Oxford University Press.

Vargo, S.L. and Akaka, M.A. (2012) 'Value cocreation and service systems (re)formation: a service ecosystems view', *Service Science* 4(3): 207–17.

Vargo, S.L. and Lusch, R.F. (2004) 'Evolving to a new dominant logic for marketing', *Journal of Marketing* 68(1): 1–17.

Vargo, S.L. and Lusch, R.F. (2008a) 'Service-dominant logic: continuing the evolution', *Journal of the Academy of Marketing Science* 36(1): 1–10.

Vargo, S.L. and Lusch, R.F. (2008b) 'Why "service"?', *Journal of the Academy of Marketing Science* 36(1): 25–38.

Vargo, S.L. and Lusch, R.F. (2008c) 'From goods to service(s): divergences and convergences of logics', *Industrial Marketing Management* 37 (May): 254–9.

Vargo, S.L. and Lusch, R.F. (2011) 'It's all B2B… and beyond: toward a systems perspective of the market', *Industrial Marketing Management* 40(2): 181–7.

Vargo, S.L. and Morgan, F.W. (2005) 'Services in society and academic thought: an historical analysis', *Journal of Macromarketing* 25(1): 42–53.

Vargo, S.L., Maglio P.P. and Akaka, M.A. (2008) 'On value and value co-creation: a service systems and service logic perspective', *European Management Journal* 26(3): 145–52.

Vargo, S.L., Wieland, H. and Akaka, M.A. (2014) 'Innovation through institutionalization: a service ecosystems perspective', *Industrial Marketing Management*. Published online ahead of print. DOI: 10.1016/j.indmarman.2014.10.008.

Webster, F.E. Jr (1992) 'The changing role of marketing in the corporation', *Journal of Marketing* 56 (October): 1–17.

Williamson, O.E. (2000) 'The new institutional economics: taking stock, looking ahead', *Journal of Economic Literature* 38: 595–613.

Woodruff, R.B. (1997) 'Customer value: the next source for competitive advantage', *Journal of the Academy of Marketing Science* 25(2): 139–53.

Zeithaml, V.A., Parasuraman, A. and Berry, L.L. (1985) 'Problems and strategies in services marketing', *Journal of Marketing* 49 (Spring): 33–46.

Zuboff, S. and Maxmin, J. (2002) *The Support Economy*. New York: Penguin.

Part Six

Marketing Theory, Society and The Environment

Part VI Contents

20 Social Marketing Theory   479

21 Sustainable Marketing   492

Social Marketing Theory

Sharyn Rundle-Thiele

20

Chapter Topics

What is theory?	479
Social marketing: A science in itself?	485

Science is facts, just as houses are made of stone. ... But a pile of stones is not a house, and a collection of facts is not necessarily science. (Poincarre, 1983, cited in Whetton, 1989: 493)

In order to understand social marketing theory and the current state of knowledge in social marketing it is important to first delve into an understanding of theory.

What is theory?

Definitions of theory are not straightforward. Moreover the notion of theory is not unanimously understood. According to Hammersley (2004), there are few terms in the social sciences whose usage is more diverse, and often vague, in meaning than 'theory'. In a similar vein, Joas and Knobl (2009), in their introduction to a series of lectures on social theory, note there is no agreed understanding of what constitutes theory, and hence what does not.

To put it simply, different people have a different understanding of what constitutes theory. Consider the following definitions:

1. A statement or group of statements about how some part of the world works – frequently explaining relations among phenomena (Vogt, 1993: 232);
2. A systematic explanation for the observed facts and laws that relate to a particular aspect of life (Babbie, 1992: 55); or
3. A systematic explanation for a diverse range of social phenomena (Schwandt, 1997: 154); and
4. A theory is a hypothesis of a correspondence between definitional systems for a universe of observations and an aspect of the empirical structure of these observations, together with a rationale for such a hypothesis (Guttman, 1971: 333);
5. A theory is a systematically related set of statements, including some law-like generalizations, that is empirically testable. The purpose of theory is to increase scientific understanding through a systematized structure capable of both explaining and predicting phenomena (Hunt, 2002: 193).

The first four definitions of theory are general and highlight the explanatory role of theory while the final definition emphasizes empiricism. The notion of empiricism is evident in Guttman's (1971) definition, which formed the basis of 'facet theory' but can be applied to any area of investigation, including social marketing. In this definition, theory as science seeks to give an organized account of phenomena, thus the necessity for a systematically related set of statements. Law-like generalizations are what give theories predictive and explanatory powers. Theories need to be empirically testable as they must be intersubjectively certifiable, capable of explaining and predicting real-world phenomena and differentiated from purely analytic schemata (which are not in themselves testable). A theory is empirically testable when it is possible to derive from them hypotheses that are amenable to direct confrontation with data. Evidence, which can be discovered in causal research, via experiments or reviews of the evidence base, is what is needed to support (or deny) hypotheses.

According to Sutton and Staw (1995), good theory 'explains, predicts and delights'. Taken together, theory encapsulates what we know about the way things are, the way they work, and the way they interact or fit together. Notwithstanding, variation in the definition of theory (or theories) has a central role in the social sciences. This is captured in the famous quote from Kurt Lewin (a pioneer in social psychology, and founder of the equation: $B = f(P + E)$ – behaviour is a function of the person and their environment): 'There is nothing so practical as a good theory' (in Vogt, 2005: 324).

Going back to the introductory quote, each hypothesis that is supported can be considered as a stone. Ideally, a hypothesis underpinned via a strong causal design and valid measurement tools needs to be supported across a wide range of different contexts that extend beyond laboratory settings into real-world settings in order to develop law-like generalizations. For social marketing science a series of law-like generalizable hypotheses then in turn can be considered as a series of stones which together make up a house. In social marketing, as in any other social science, theory is 'an ordered set of assertions about a generic behaviour or structure assumed to hold throughout a significantly broad range of specific instances' (Sunderland, 1976: 9, in Wacker, 1998: 364).

Theory in social marketing

According to Whetton (1989), a theory seeks to answer questions of how, when (if longitudinal data are available), where or why, which is distinct from description, which simply answers the questions of what or who. In other words, theories consist of a set of factors which should be considered to explain a social phenomenon and outlines how the factors are related. These can be illustrated graphically to visually represent the authors' thinking. If all links have been empirically identified then the model is ready for the classroom to teach future social marketing practitioners (Whetton, 1989). The mission for a social marketing researcher is to challenge and extend existing knowledge, not to simply rewrite it. To do this, social marketing scientists (researchers) have to be able to answer why. Why did social marketing form? How did the social marketing journey start? Why are we collectively working in this field? The goal of a good theory is to provide a clear explanation of how specific relationships lead to specific events and why we should expect these relationships. Without theory to explain or predict phenomena, social marketers risk the potential of failing to translate their work in a way that can be easily taught to future generations of social marketers (Walsh et al., 1993).

When considering theory and definitions of social marketing, it is easy to see that there currently appears to be a consensus that social marketing is more an area of application for findings from the sciences or a process and not a science in itself. For example, Luca and Suggs (2013: 21) state:

> Social marketing is an approach to developing health, environment, and social change campaigns that aim to influence target audiences to voluntarily accept, reject, modify, or abandon a behavior for the benefit of individuals, groups, or society.

While Truong (2014: 24) states:

> Social marketing is not a theory in itself. Instead, it draws upon different theories and models to identify determinants of behavior change and thereby develop appropriate intervention strategies.

The consensus definition of social marketing (iSMA, 2013) which emerged following extensive consultation with social marketing researchers and practitioners also highlights that social marketing is more an area of application for findings from the sciences or a process. The consensus definition of social marketing states:

> Social marketing seeks to develop and integrate marketing concepts with other approaches to influence behaviors that benefit individuals and communities for the greater social good.

> Social Marketing practice is guided by ethical principles. It seeks to integrate research, best practice, theory, audience and partnership insight, to inform the delivery of competition sensitive and segmented social change programmes that are effective, efficient, equitable and sustainable.

Table 20.1 outlines the factors that were deemed to be essential or important by the 167 social marketing experts from across the globe who completed the survey in 2012.

Table 20.1   Summary of social marketing activities deemed to be important or essential.

Description	Essential + Important (% total responses)	Rank
Set and measure behavioural objectives	83	1
Use audience insight and research	81	2
Focus on the production of social good	79	3
Use audience segmentation to understand and target interventions	76	4
Apply data, research, evidence and behavioural theory in developing programmes	73	5
Rigorous evaluation and reporting of short-term impacts, ROI and longer term outcomes	73	6
Use systematic planning and marketing management methodology	68	7
Undertake competition analysis and develop competitor intervention strategies	67	8
Apply and be guided by an ethical analysis and standards	66	9
Apply commercial marketing theory and practice to social challenges	61	10
Focus on upstream, mid-stream and downstream audiences	58	11
Analyse communication channels and other forms of influence	57	12
Inform and shape the total social policy intervention mix	54	13
Focus on creating value for citizens and civil society through valued negative exchanges	51	14
Focus on creating value for citizens and civil society through valued voluntary exchange	50	15
Undertake stakeholder analysis and apply relationship management strategies	49	16
Consider applying the 4 marketing Cs tool box (Lauterborn)	43	17
Understand and use forms of influences that draw on rational choice and rapid cognition	42	18
Design programmes that aim to increase social equity	42	19
Analyse the potential costs and benefits of supporting and/or partnering with private sector organizations	42	20
Consider applying the 4 Ps tool box defined by McCarthy in the intervention	41	21
Understand and make known the social consequences of commercial sector marketing	37	22

If we consider social marketing as an area of application for findings from the sciences or a process and not a science in itself we quickly agree that social marketing practice is guided by ethical principles and that social marketing should integrate research, best practice, audience and partnership insight, to inform the delivery of competition-sensitive and segmented social change programmes that are effective, efficient, equitable and sustainable. Theory use in social marketing was considered to be important for 61% of social marketing experts across the globe. The role of theory in social marketing practice is also recognized in the third Social Marketing Benchmark criterion offered by the UK's National Social Marketing Centre (see http://www.snh.org.uk/pdfs/sgp/A328466.pdf), which states:

Social Marketing uses behavioural theories to understand behaviour and inform the intervention:

The theory, or theories used, are identified after conducting the customer orientation research

Appropriate behavioural theory is clearly used to inform and guide the methods mix (Benchmark 8)

Theoretical assumptions are tested as part of the intervention developed by pre-testing.

Theories used by social marketers

Although theory is recognized as central for social marketing practice, research suggests that the application of theory in social marketing interventions has been inconsistently reported. Extending on previous work that examined social marketing interventions, Truong (2014) concludes that only a minority of studies published between 1998 and 2012 in peer-reviewed journals explicitly reported theory and models used in interventions. Truong's (2014) systematic literature review indicates that downstream interventions aimed at changing individual health behaviours constituted the largest number of social marketing studies.

In a systematic literature review of social marketing interventions, Luca and Suggs (2013) identified:

- A total of eight out of 17 papers reported theory use with seven papers reporting how theory was used.
- The transtheoretical or stages of change model was used most often ($n = 4$) in social marketing papers in the Luca and Suggs (2013) review.
- Theories such as the theory of planned behaviour ($n = 3$), theory of reasoned action ($n = 2$), health belief model ($n = 2$), social network theory ($n = 2$) and social learning theory ($n = 2$) were all reported to be used on more than one occasion in the Luca and Suggs (2013) review.

The Luca and Suggs (2013) systematic literature review suggests that social marketers borrow ideas from psychology and sociology. For example, extending upon Fishbein and Ajzen's (1975) Theory of Reasoned Action (attitudes influence behaviour through behavioural intentions), the Theory of Planned Behaviour (see Ajzen and Madden, 1986) links beliefs held by an individual to planned future behaviour. The Health Belief model first proposed by Rosenstock (1966), also originating from psychology, suggests that your belief in a personal threat together with your belief in the effectiveness of the proposed behaviour will predict the likelihood of that behaviour. The Transtheoretical or Stages of Change (see Prochaska and DiClemente, 1983) model assesses an individual's readiness to act on a healthier behaviour while Social Learning theory (see Bandura, 1977, 1986) explains how people learn within a social context. All are theories that originate in psychology. These models all assume behaviour is under the control of the individual, and once behavioural intention is formed, facilitators and inhibitors then determine whether that intention is transformed into behaviour. Using this structure, there are a number of potential avenues of influence. Increasing knowledge, changing beliefs or attitudes, emphasizing benefits and removing barriers, are all mechanisms used by social marketers (and others) to facilitate behaviour change.

The dominant theories that are used in social marketing practice are focused on the individual, that is, they all inspire downstream interventions which seek to change individual factors like knowledge, attitude or intention. Only the social ecological models (Bronfenbrenner, 1977, 1979) recognize the influence of factors beyond the individual, and support intervention at one or many of the levels of intrapersonal, interpersonal, organizational, community, physical environmental and policy (Sallis et al., 2008). While there is support for social marketing to intervene further upstream (Gordon, 2013; Hoek and Jones, 2011; Wymer, 2011), at this point in time the social marketing evidence base remains dominated by a downstream approach (Truong, 2014).

Extending social marketing's theoretical base

The pervasiveness of theories such as Social Cognitive theory and the Transtheoretical model of change reinforce social marketers' need to step out of their comfort zones. Alternative thinking is required for social marketers seeking to change behaviours. Consider Ehrenberg's (2005) Dirichlet theory of repeat buying and brand choice, a commercial marketing theory that has been tested in a wide variety of commercial marketing contexts. Dirichlet theory is a law-like generalization that has been empirically supported across a diverse range of contexts. Dirichlet theory asserts that rather than changing what people think about your brand, which is hard to achieve, you need to have more people think about your brand on more occasions than competing brand alternatives. The key assertion in Dirichlet theory is to remind people rather than informing them. Think about Page and Sharp (2012), who employed marketing metrics that have been used in commercial settings to examine market penetration to assess the effectiveness of an intervention targeting schools. Their study identified the programme had penetrated approximately 30% of schools targeted, suggesting considerable room for improvement in terms of programme efficacy. While an unknown alternative presents more ambiguity for researchers, it also represents a shift that can contribute meaningfully to the body of knowledge.

Let us now consider a social marketing context, namely eating, which is an important issue to consider in light of the global obesity epidemic. Social marketing is a field that addresses real social problems such as eating. Eating is influenced by a multitude of variables. For example, eating behaviour is influenced by previous food intake, genetic predispositions, socio-economic status, health status, access to transport, living arrangements, physiological aspects (e.g. cravings, hunger), demographic characteristics, situation-specific factors such as mood, body image, habit, cost, price promotions, beliefs, culture, religion, taste preferences, parental influence, peer influence, benefits of food (e.g. health), availability, convenience, package size, package appeal, food advertising and food environments. For social marketers to be effective in changing eating behaviour thought needs to be given about exactly where to turn – the individual, environment, family homes, schools, restaurants, supermarkets and the list goes on.

Social marketing needs to emerge as a science that encourages researchers to delve into theories to develop frameworks for describing and enhancing social marketing practice.

A broad reconceptualization of theory use in social marketing needs to occur. For example, Holdershaw et al. (2011) challenged the Theory of Planned Behaviour by considering blood donation behaviour (the desired outcome for a social marketer) and intentions to donate blood as asserted in the Theory of Planned Behaviour. Their findings identified that consistent with the theory's assertions the Theory of Planned Behaviour predicted intentions to donate ($R^2 = 0.52$) but was less effective in predicting blood donation behaviour, which yields medical supplies ($R^2 = 0.19$), suggesting that other factors were explaining 81% of the variance in blood donation factors. The Holdershaw et al. (2011) study is not alone in low levels of variance explained for the desired behaviour the social marketer is aiming to change. This raises the question of whether the reliance by social marketers on psychological theories is limiting our ability to achieve social change.

Taken together, social marketing researchers need to use theory exercising care to report how theory was used in empirical studies. Further, to extend beyond current boundaries in social marketing thinking, which are largely relying on psychological and sociology theories, social marketers need to expand the theoretical base of social marketing.

If social marketing scholars (scientists) can develop good theory we can ensure that other social change disciplines will turn to social marketing in time to understand how they can achieve behaviour change. Theories that can compete with Kurt Lewin's equation (B = f (P + E) – behaviour is a function of the person and their environment) are needed to provide essential building blocks to encapsulate what we know about social marketing practice, the way social marketing practice works, and the way different aspects of social marketing practice interact or fit together.

Social marketing: A science in itself?

Initial definitions of social marketing were focused on the notion that ideas could be promoted (e.g. Kotler and Zaltman, 1971). Today our understanding of social marketing has expanded and we now understand the main focus of social marketing is on the broad application of a wide range of well-known marketing tools and techniques (i.e. delivery of a full marketing mix) to foster social change (Wymer, 2011). Social marketing is now widely recognized as a credible behaviour change discipline with governments across the globe acknowledging the importance of social marketing as a discipline that can change behaviours for the better.

Over the past 40 years as the discipline of social marketing has grown and evolved, a range of frameworks outlining the series of activities that constitute social marketing have been put forward (examples include Andreasen, 2002; French and Blair-Stevens, 2005; Lefebvre and Flora, 1988; Robinson-Maynard et al., 2013; Walsh et al., 1993; as depicted in Figure 20.1).

The characteristics of social marketing have been defined most notably by Andreasen (2002) when he set down six benchmark criteria, stating that social marketing must have:

1. *Behaviour change* as the objective;
2. *Audience research* to understand audiences during design, pre-testing and monitoring;
3. *Audience segmentation* to ensure maximum efficiency and effectiveness;

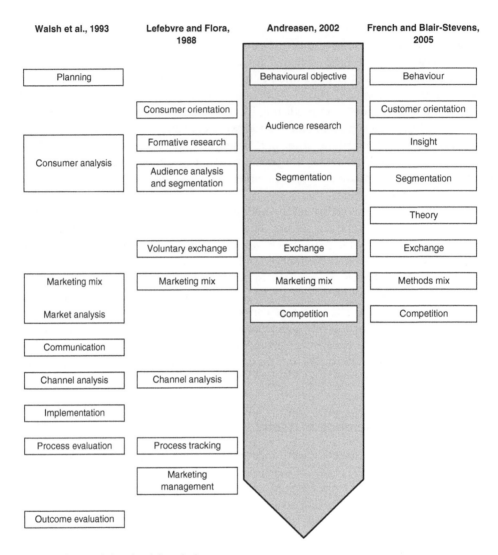

Figure 20.1   Characteristics of social marketing.

4.   The creation of attractive and motivational *exchanges* with target audiences;
5.   A *marketing mix* (not just advertising or communications);
6.   An awareness of the *competition* faced by the desired behaviour.

None of the social marketing frameworks proposed has been empirically validated. Recent systematic literature evidence of social marketing interventions indicates the majority of such interventions do not adopt social marketing to its full extent (see e.g. Carins and Rundle-Thiele, 2014; Kubacki et al., 2015a, 2015b). Empirical evidence arising from a recent systematic review of healthy eating interventions (see Carins and Rundle-Thiele, 2014) suggests that social marketing interventions employing more of the six social marketing benchmark criteria proposed by Andreasen (2002) are more likely to change the targeted behaviour. Taken together, previous studies indicate there is a possibility that social marketing may be operating under false assumptions and perhaps, more importantly, by empirically examining the assumptions underlying social marketing there may be room to increase the efficacy of social marketing interventions by understanding what works (and what does not).

If we are to consider social marketing as a science then an organized account of social marketing is required. A systematically related set of statements, similar to social marketing benchmark criteria, could be offered that provide a clear predictive and explanatory power for social marketing practice. For example, after extensive empirical testing a law-like generalization may be that the inclusion of the 'segmentation' benchmark criterion can enhance intervention effectiveness by Y%. Law-like generalizations are what give theories predictive and explanatory power. Theories need to be empirically testable and therefore they need to be derived from hypotheses that are amenable to direct confrontation with data. Evidence, which can be discovered in causal research, via experiments or reviews of the evidence base, is what is needed for social marketing science.

Consider the following examples of how evidence can be discovered in causal research via field experiments to test hypotheses to challenge social marketing assumptions that are currently held.

One of the six benchmark criteria, namely segmentation, will first be used to outline how social marketing assumptions can be empirically examined. A key social marketing benchmark criterion (Andreasen, 2002; French and Blair-Stevens, 2005), segmentation is proposed as a means to ensure maximum efficiency and effectiveness for social marketing programmes (Donovan and Henley, 2010; Lefebvre, 2013). Market segmentation techniques help decision makers strategically define target consumer groups and subsequently direct the available resources to the most promising segments (Elliot et al., 2014). According to the segmentation assumption, theoretically social marketers should deliver tailored interventions to different segments thereby catering to different audience needs and wants. Taken together, this would generally mean that different segments (as identified in segmentation studies) will require different intervention designs (target marketing). A rigorous segmentation study process identifies homogeneous sub-groups within a target audience and it provides insights for the different strategies and approaches to reach and motivate each target group (Kotler, 1980).

Consider programmes targeting alcohol delivered in school settings, where the notion of segmentation remains largely untested and unexplored (Mathijssen et al., 2012; Moss et al., 2009). Alcohol programmes delivered in schools are either delivered as a one-size-fits-all approach (one programme to all students) or one programme is developed that aims to change the behaviour of the group most at risk (Botvin and Griffin, 2007). Alcohol programmes in school settings are not alone. A recent literature review (Kubacki et al., 2015a) indicates that only two out of 23 interventions targeting children aged 12 years and under adopted segmentation. Segmentation studies based on multiple segmentation factors, namely psychographics, demographics, geography and behaviour, could identify homogeneous sub-groups in the target population. If different segments differing in motivations, needs, wants and behaviours are identified, social marketing theory states that a different intervention design tailored to each segment may enhance effectiveness of the intervention (Donovan and Henley, 2010). This assumption needs to be empirically tested and validated in a broad range of contexts. An important first step involves understanding whether segments respond differently to social marketing programmes (see Dietrich et al. [2015a, 2015b], who examine differential responses to one-size-fits-all programmes in school settings). The next step involves empirically examining the assumption that use of segmentation to identify unique groups and subsequent catering to group differences can deliver better outcomes using an experimental design. An experimental design would examine whether targeted programmes that are differentially designed to meet the needs and wants of identified segments deliver more change than one programme delivered to a matched group.

Many commercial marketing concepts may not clearly translate to social marketing and this needs to be examined by social marketing scholars (scientists). Commercial marketers are typically charged with the responsibility of selling a better, faster, stronger, new and improved product, service or idea to a target audience. In contrast, social marketers are seeking to make the least desirable alternative (e.g. vigorous physical activity) appealing for a target market that has little or no interest in performing the desired behaviour, e.g. vigorous activity. Further differences exist which may prevent commercial marketing theories from being extended into a social context. In commercial marketing the competition is typically different product or service alternatives (Apple versus PC or Samsung Galaxy versus Apple's iPhone) each of whom differ subtly. Social marketing can be thought of more easily as category replacement. In many cases social marketers are seeking to swap behaviours – give up sitting on the couch to watch TV at night to being more physically active. The differences between the two fields may limit transferability of some commercial marketing ideas that currently underpin social marketing practice.

For example, in the social marketing literature there is a lot of debate around the 4 Ps of marketing. Many social marketing scholars (researchers) believe the 4 Ps of commercial marketing cannot be applied in social marketing. Note how the 4 Ps of marketing was ranked as number 21 by the 167 social marketing experts in Table 20.1. Some believe the 4 Cs (convenience, cost, communication, consumer) of marketing proposed by Lauterborn (1990) may be more applicable in social marketing as it offers a clearer framework for application when compared to the 4 marketing Ps (product, price, place and promotion) originally proposed by Jerome McCarthy (1964). The hypothesis that social marketing programmes designed to deliver a full marketing mix (a clear example of full marketing mix is outlined in Rothschild et al., 2006) are more effective than information only or social advertising programmes (examples of programmes that deliver one marketing P only, include Atlantis et al., 2008; Croker et al., 2012) can also be empirically examined in a field experiment. An understanding of whether competing alternatives should be offered to change behaviour is needed to inform social marketing practice, which remains dominated by practice not involving a complete marketing mix (see reviews by Kubacki et al. [2015a, 2015b] for a summary of the extent of 4 P use in contemporary social marketing studies).

The incomplete and inconsistent reporting of theory use in social marketing (see Luca and Suggs, 2013; Truong, 2014), the lack of shared understanding of theory and the importance of empiricism to underpin development in the field make it difficult to identify whether theory enhances (or not) effectiveness. As the goal of social marketing is to change behaviour, this reported gap in the social marketing literature may need to be addressed with reference to the contrasts highlighted by Hammersley (2004) between theory and practice, evidence and fact. If we are to consider social marketing as a science then an organized account of social marketing is required. Following extensive empirical testing arising from longitudinal causal and experimental empirical research designs, meta-analyses and systematic reviews of the social marketing evidence base, a series of related statements could be offered that provide a clear predictive and explanatory power for social marketing practice. For example, after extensive empirical testing a law-like generalization may be the use of XYZ theory which can accurately deliver intervention effectiveness improvements of Y%. As stated earlier, theories need to be empirically testable and therefore they need to be derived from hypotheses that are amenable to direct confrontation with data. Social marketing practice offers an evidence base, which can be discovered in causal research, via experiments or reviews of the evidence base. Social marketing scholars must consider themselves scientists who deal only in facts and not theoretical assumptions because without theory to explain or predict, social marketing risks the potential of failing to translate work in a way that can be easily taught to future generations (Walsh et al., 1993).

Recommended further reading

Donovan, R. (2011) 'Social marketing's mythunderstandings', *Journal of Social Marketing* 1(1): 8–16.
French, J. and Gordon, R. (2015) *Strategic Social Marketing*. London: Sage.
Hastings, G. and Domegan, C. (2013) *Social Marketing: From Tunes to Symphonies*, 2nd edn. Abingdon: Routledge.
Kubacki, K. and Rundle-Thiele, S. (eds) (2013) *Contemporary Issues in Social Marketing*. Newcastle upon Tyne: Cambridge Scholars Publishing.
Lefebvre, C. (2013) *Social Marketing and Social Change: Strategies and Tools for Improving Health, Wellbeing and the Environment*. New York: John Wiley.

References

Ajzen, I. and Madden, T.J. (1986) 'Prediction of goal-directed behavior: attitudes, intentions, and perceived behavioral control', *Journal of Experimental Social Psychology* 22(5): 453–74.
Andreasen, A.R. (2002) 'Marketing social marketing in the social change marketplace', *Journal of Public Policy & Marketing* 21(1): 3–13.
Atlantis, E., Salmon, J. and Bauman, A. (2008) 'Acute effects of advertisements on children's choices, preferences, and ratings of liking for physical activities and sedentary behaviours: a randomised controlled pilot study', *Journal of Science and Medicine in Sport* 11(6): 553–7.
Babbie, E. (1992) *The Practice of Social Research*. Belmont, CA: Wadsworth.
Bandura, A. (1977) *Social Learning Theory*. Englewoods Cliffs, NJ: Prentice-Hall.
Bandura, A. (1986) *Social Foundations of Thought and Action: A Social Cognitive Theory*. Englewood Cliffs: NJ: Prentice-Hall.

Botvin, G.J. and Griffin, K.W. (2007) 'School-based programmes to prevent alcohol, tobacco and other drug use', *International Review of Psychiatry* 19(6): 607–15.

Bronfenbrenner, U. (1977) 'Toward an experimental ecology of human development', *American Psychologist* 32(7): 513–31.

Bronfenbrenner, U. (1979) *The Ecology of Human Development*. Cambridge, MA: Harvard University Press.

Carins, J. and Rundle-Thiele, S.R. (2014) 'Eating for the better: a social marketing review (2000–2012)', *Public Health Nutrition* 17(7): 1628–39.

Croker, H., Lucas, R. and Wardle, J. (2012) 'Cluster-randomised trial to evaluate the "Change for Life" mass media/social marketing campaign in the UK', *BMC Public Health* 12(1): 404–54.

Dietrich, T., Rundle-Thiele, S.R., Leo, C. and Connor, J. (2015a) 'One size never fits all: cluster responses to a school based social marketing alcohol program', *Journal of School Health* 85(4): 251–9.

Dietrich, T., Rundle-Thiele, S.R., Schuster, L., Drennan, J., Russell-Bennett, R., Leo, C., Gullo, M. and Connor, J. (2015b) 'Differential segmentation responses to an alcohol social marketing program', *Addiction* 49: 68–77.

Donovan, R. and Henley, N. (2010) *Principles and Practice of Social Marketing: An International Perspective*. Cambridge: Cambridge University Press.

Ehrenberg, A. (2005) 'Repeat buying', *Journal of Empirical Generalisations in Marketing Science* 5(2): 1–21

Elliot, G., Rundle-Thiele, S.R. and Waller, D. (2014) *Marketing*. Milton, Australia: John Wiley.

Fishbein, M. and Ajzen, I. (1975) *Belief, Attitude, Intention, and Behavior: An Introduction to Theory and Research*. London: Addison-Wesley.

French, J. and Blair-Stevens, C. (2005) *The Big Pocket Guide to Using Social Marketing for Behaviour Change*. London: National Social Marketing Centre. Available at: www.thensmc.com/sites/default/files/Big_pocket_guide_2011.pdf (accessed 21 February 2015).

Gordon, R. (2013) 'Unlocking the potential of upstream social marketing', *European Journal of Marketing* 47(9): 1525–47.

Guttman, L. (1971) 'Measurement as structural theory', *Psychometrika* 3(4): 329–47.

Hammersley, M. (2004) 'Theory', in M.S. Lewis-Beck, A. Bryman and T.F. Liao (eds) *The Sage Encyclopedia of Social Science Research Methods*. Thousand Oaks, CA: Sage, pp. 1124–5.

Hoek, J. and Jones, S.C. (2011) 'Regulation, public health and social marketing: a behaviour change trinity', *Journal of Social Marketing* 1(1): 32–44.

Holdershaw, J., Gendall, P. and Wright, M. (2011) 'Predicting blood donation behaviour: further application of the theory of planned behaviour', *Journal of Social Marketing* 1(2): 120–32.

Hunt, S.D. (2002) *Foundations of Marketing Theory: Toward a General Theory of Marketing*. London: M.E. Sharpe.

iSMA (International Social Marketing Association) (2013) 'Consensus definition of social marketing'. Available at: http://www.i-socialmarketing.org/assets/social_marketing_definition.pdf (accessed 15 January 2016).

Joas, H. and Knobl, W. (2009) *Social Theory: Twenty Introductory Lectures*. Cambridge: Cambridge University Press.

Kotler, P. (1980) *Principles of Marketing*. Englewood Cliffs, NJ: Prentice-Hall.

Kotler, P. and Zaltman, G. (1971) 'Social marketing: an approach to planned social change', *Journal of Marketing* 35(3): 3–12.

Kubacki, K., Rundle-Thiele, S., Lahtinen, V. and Parkinson, J. (2015a) 'A systematic review assessing the extent of social marketing principle use in interventions targeting children (2000–2014)', *Young Consumers* 16(2): 141–58.

Kubacki, K., Rundle-Thiele, S.R., Pang, B. and Buyucek, N. (2015b) 'Minimising alcohol harm: a systematic social marketing review (2000–2014)', *Journal of Business Research* 68(10): 2214–22.

Lauterborn, B. (1990) 'New marketing litany: four Ps passé: C-words take over', *Advertising Age* 61(41): 26.

Lefebvre R.C. (2013) *Social Marketing and Social Change: Strategies and Tools for Health, Well-Being, and the Environment*. San Francisco, CA: Jossey-Bass.

Lefebvre, R.C. and Flora, J.A. (1988) 'Social marketing and public health intervention', *Health Education Quarterly* 15: 299–315.

Luca, R.N. and Suggs, L.S. (2013) 'Theory and model use in social marketing health interventions', *Journal of Health Communication: International Perspectives* 18(1): 20–40.

McCarthy, J.E. (1964) *Basic Marketing: A Managerial Approach*. Homewood, IL: Irwin.

Mathijssen, J., Janssen, M., van Bon-Martens, M. and van de Goor, I. (2012) 'Adolescents and alcohol: an explorative audience segmentation analysis', *BMC Public Health* 12(742): 1–10.

Moss, H.B., Kirby, S.D. and Donodeo, F. (2009) 'Characterizing and reaching high-risk drinkers using audience segmentation', *Alcoholism: Clinical and Experimental Research* 33(8): 1336–45.

Page, B. and Sharp, A. (2012) 'The contribution of marketing to school-based program evaluation', *Journal of Social Marketing* 2(3): 176–86.

Prochaska, J.O. and DiClemente, C.C. (1983) 'Stages and processes of self-change of smoking: toward an integrative model of change', *Journal of Consulting and Clinical Psychology* 51(3): 390–5.

Robinson-Maynard, A., Meaton, J. and Lowry, R. (2013) 'Identifying key criteria as predictors of success in social marketing: establishing an evaluation template and grid', in K. Kubacki and S. Rundle-Thiele (eds) *Contemporary Issues in Social Marketing*. Newcastle upon Tyne: Cambridge Scholars Publishing.

Rosenstock, I.M. (1966) 'Why people use health services', *Milbank Memorial Fund Quarterly* 4(4): 94–124.

Rothschild, M.L., Mastin, B. and Miller, T.W. (2006) 'Reducing alcohol-impaired driving crashes through the use of social marketing', *Accident Analysis and Prevention* 38: 1218–30.

Sallis, J.F., Owen, N. and Fisher, E.B. (2008) 'Ecological models of health behavior', in K. Glanz, B. Rimer and K. Viswanath (eds) *Health Behavior and Health Education: Theory, Research, and Practice*, Vol. 4. San Francisco, CA: Jossey-Bass, pp. 465–86.

Schwandt, T.A. (1997) *Qualitative Inquiry: A Dictionary of Terms*. Thousand Oaks, CA: Sage.

Sutton, R.I. and Staw, B.M. (1995) 'What theory is not', *Administrative Science Quarterly* 40(3): 371–84.

Truong, V.D. (2014) 'Social marketing: a systematic review of research 1998–2012', *Social Marketing Quarterly* 20(1): 15–34.

Vogt, W.P. (1993) *Dictionary of Statistics and Methodology: A Nontechnical Guide for the Social Sciences*. Newbury Park, CA: Sage.

Vogt, W.P. (2005) *Dictionary of Statistics and Methodology*, 3rd edn. Thousand Oaks, CA: Sage.

Wacker, J.G. (1998) 'A definition of theory: research guidelines for different theory-building research methods in operations management', *Journal of Operations Management* 16(4): 361–85.

Walsh, D.C., Rudd, R.E., Moeykens, B.A. and Moloney, T.W. (1993) 'Social marketing for public health', *Health Affairs* 12(2): 104–19.

Whetton, D.A. (1989) 'What constitutes a theoretical contribution?', *Academy of Management Review* 14(4): 490–5.

Wymer, W. (2011) 'Developing more effective social marketing strategies', *Journal of Social Marketing* 1(1): 17–31.

Sustainable Marketing

William E. Kilbourne and Anastasia Thyroff

Chapter Topics

Philosophical antecedents	493
Marketing today	496
Marketing in transition?	498
IPAT revisited	502
Summary and conclusion	505

'Consumption is the sole end and purpose of all production; and the interest of the producer ought to be attended to only so far as it may be necessary for promoting that of the consumer' (Smith, 1993 [1776]: 376). Smith argued that, while this proposition was self-evident, actual practice at the time indicated that the opposite was more the case. To the astute student of marketing, this statement ought to sound vaguely familiar. It is, of course, paraphrased in the first chapter of every introductory marketing textbook, and it has, since about 1955, been labelled 'the marketing concept'. Look to the consumers first to see what they desire, and then produce and sell that at a profit. An interesting take away here is that, like the mercantilists of Smith's time, few marketing professionals seem to follow this self-evident proposition even today.

While the marketing concept may seem self-evident, there are a number of philosophical issues that are incorporated into it that are themselves not self-evident. They should be examined to better understand the ramifications, both social and ecological, that are neatly hidden within this seemingly simple concept. It actually carries with it substantial excess baggage for which globalizing societies are now beginning to pay. To get even a rudimentary understanding of the ramifications of a marketing process driven by the marketing concept, we must look both backward to understand the antecedents of market philosophy and forward to better understand the long-run consequences.

While Adam Smith is clearly implicit in the process through which contemporary marketing evolved, he would have been incapable of arriving at his economic theory had he not been preceded by two other giants upon whose shoulders he stood. They were Francis Bacon in the early 17th century and John Locke in the late 17th century. The contribution of these two is absolutely essential in the development of neoclassical economics out of which grew both the idea of formalized, but abstract markets and the contemporary marketing process used in serving them. While a complete survey of their contributions is beyond the scope of this chapter, the reader is referred to Leiss (1972) and Macpherson (1962) for both accessible and interesting studies of Bacon and Locke respectively. Magdoff and Foster (2011) suggest the need for examining the past directly when they state, 'Instead, we must look to the fundamental workings of the economic (and political/social) system for explanations' (2011: 7). To get to the fundamental workings, we must understand the historical assumptions that underlie the process.

Philosophical antecedents

Science and technology

In Bacon's (1944 [1620]) classic work, *Novum Organum*, he outlines the methods for a new science that became what we now consider to be science. It was predicated on the experimental method which he explained in the book. In addition to the method itself, he argued that the purpose of science was to make life easier and more hospitable for human existence. This is what he referred to as the 'betterment of man's estate' and made a direct link between science and its technical application. The essence of good science was that which resulted in improving life as it was then known. He also suggested that within a few short years his method would lead to complete understanding of the physical nature of the world by 'hounding' nature to reveal her secrets (Leiss, 1972). He was also certain that the same methods used to discover the workings of nature would be equally effective in discovering the inner workings of the individual and society. It is hard to overestimate the contributions his new science made to understanding mechanics and their later role in precipitating and advancing the Industrial Revolution.

But Bacon's most important contribution in the context of ecology and marketing was probably the attitude that it engendered towards both nature and human beings' inconveniences.

Bacon clearly argues that the confluence of science, industry and technology would lead inexorably to the satisfaction of human desires. With the recognition of the power to enlist nature in the services of humankind, the remedy for inconveniences was at hand. It becomes clear in Bacon that with the mastery of nature the future of human desires is open because the impediments to their satisfaction will be removed. As Leiss (1972: 37–8) argues, mastery will lead to 'the unimpeded growth of technology and industry' which in turn can 'maximize the supply of goods available for the satisfaction of wants'. The implications are also that human desires 'ought' to be satisfied and that nature serves the instrumental purpose of providing the material to do that.

So within the philosophy of Bacon, humankind takes a decisive turn towards the material and away from the spiritual view of nature. It is also consistent with the Hobbesian (1950 [1651]) view that human desires are both insatiable and worthy of being satisfied. This view has been argued by ecologists and historians such as Merchant (1980) to have resulted in the 'death of nature'.

Political philosophy

The development of science and technology by itself was not enough to have created the state of affairs that we seek to explain however. While the confluence of science, technology and industry was a necessary condition, it was not sufficient. Shortly after the *Novum Organum* was received, the political climate in England was transforming from the Hobbesian *Leviathan* with absolute power in the hands of the monarch, to the more noble principle of the individual in control of his own political destiny. It was at the end of the 17th century that Locke appeared on the scene with the second of the major treatises that would push English society 75 years later into the waiting hands of Adam Smith. But first, we must digress into two other factors that had been percolating for several centuries: private property and individualism.

It is important to include historical factors that have contributed to the beliefs that industrial societies now hold so that we may better understand how to modify prevailing institutions. One of these institutions is private property. The common belief is that property has always existed, or at least since, as Ullmann (1963) argued, people could distinguish between mine and thine. But here a clear distinction needs to be recognized separating that which we refer to as possessions from that which is private property. There have always been, as most believe, possessions that I may take, use, sell, trade, etc. However, possessions were little more than a Barmecide feast as they could be taken by someone more physically or politically powerful without recourse to the victim. *Private* property came into being with the *Magna Carta* precisely because King John had been systematically dispossessing both the lords and the Church, thus managing to shoot himself in both his secular and ecclesiastic feet. The result was the imposition of the rule of law in protecting one's possessions. This means that private property is the product of possessions and the rules surrounding them. But it is more the rules than the material itself. This transforms mere possessions into private property (Hodgson, 2001).

To this must be added another dimension that is important in today's conception of private property. That is exclusivity. In the original conception, the rights to property were not as strict as they are today. In Aquinas' *Summa Theologica* for example, he argues that if some individuals have more possessions than they need, say in food for example, and others have less than they need, those in need should be allowed to use the property of others and it not be considered theft:

> Since man has a natural need to procure, to dispense, and to use material goods, it is lawful for him to possess such goods as his own. But in the use of such goods, man must be willing to give or share, according to reason and justice, to a neighbor in need. (*Summa Theologica*, question 66 article 2)

Thus, even private property was not 'exclusively' one's own. The current conception of private property includes the principle of exclusivity which adds to the rules that it is simultaneously mine and 'not yours'. Locke's Labour Theory of Property was also instrumental in legitimizing the means by which property is acquired so as to attain its legal status in both ownership and exclusivity.

The second factor that was percolating throughout the Middle Ages was incipient individualism. Another of the myths persisting in contemporary industrial societies is that of the individual. Most people fail to appreciate both the importance of the concept of the individual and the relative recency of its development.

From the standpoint of its development, Ullmann (1963) argues that it arose out of the benign neglect of the peasantry during the Middle Ages. His conjecture is that because the monarch and his agents were occupied with the greater affairs of the state, the small villages and towns were left to fend for themselves in such things as handling village affairs and government. As a result, they began to, in a sense, think for themselves in their affairs. In doing so over considerable time, they began to think of themselves individually. He argues that the emergent individual was one of the most ingenious and monumental creations of the human mind. For purposes here, it was a necessary condition for the emergence of the concept of a market.

The atomized individual, one who is free from the dictates of an absolute monarch and emersion in the society, class, or legal position, is the fundamental requirement for the existence of modern markets. The market was defined as free and independent individuals seeking their own interests in mutual beneficial relationships with other similarly situated individuals. This is the *sine qua non* of markets and its importance cannot be overestimated. It was again Locke who legitimized this conception of the individual who is the primary element in Macpherson's (1962) political theory of possessive individualism.

Economic philosophy

It was the possessive individual who was passed on to Smith half a century later and became the basis for the modern conception of a market. This, in turn, transformed the intellectual hierarchy of Western society, and economics ascended from a distant third behind ethics and politics as proper intellectual pursuits and created the space for a new science of economics. This was a major contribution of Adam Smith (Hirschman, 1977).

A third necessary condition for the development of the market construct was that atomistic individuals were allowed to choose their own course in navigating markets. This contributed the concept of powerlessness within market actions. No entity within the market or external to it could exert direct or indirect influence on the choices of market actors. While internal influence was and is a deficiency in markets, Locke proffered a condition of limited government, the sole function of which was to enforce contracts and protect private property. Thus producers and consumers in the market had no direct control over each other and neither was controlled by government actions. A casual observer of today's market system can detect these elements in political and economic debates over policy on an almost daily basis. Since the era of Reagan and Thatcher, this set of conditions has been referred to as neoliberalism.

To summarize the conditions briefly, from Bacon we receive the new science of experimentation which is applied, through technological development, to the enhancement of the material conditions of life. This translates into the goods and services used to make life easier and more enjoyable that have become coterminous with the contemporary meaning of progress. Locke legitimizes private property with exclusivity, the possessive individual and limited government (also related to procedural neutrality [Sandel, 1996]). Smith melds these constructs together to conceptualize the perfectly competitive market forming the basis for modern economics. Because contemporary marketing practice evolved through neoclassical economics, it carries with it the same set of core values. Foremost among these is the imperative of growth (more on this later) that pervades all of neoclassical economics (and through it, marketing) with a few minor exceptions such as Mill (1872 [1848]), who made a reasoned argument for 'steady-state' economics.

Marketing today

If we are to fully understand the theory and practice of marketing, it is necessary that we first understand the values and institutions that underlie it. This is particularly the case if it becomes necessary to transform marketing practice in any way. This is critical because failing to recognize the essence of marketing will limit change to within the narrow framework of the assumptions that form it in the first place. Thus, the only changes that will be possible are those that fit within the prevailing institutions, and this simply perpetuates the status quo which may require transformation in the first place. Change will result in more of the same, but with different clothes yielding the illusion of change. We will now examine this process within the context of sustainability and pose the question, 'Under what conditions is sustainable marketing possible?' The obvious point of departure for this question is with marketing as it is now practised. Is contemporary marketing sustainable?

The question has been addressed for decades under different rubrics such as socially responsible consumption (Fisk, 1973), the societal marketing concept (Kotler, 2002), green marketing, and several others. Despite the obvious institutional concerns of marketing brought up earlier in this chapter, research on the topic of marketing sustainability is limited. To help explore the strengths and weaknesses of research in this area, McDonagh and Prothero (2014) conducted a literature review on sustainable marketing from the past 40 years. In their comprehensive reflection, they found that marketing sustainability literature has historically focused on five areas: consumer concerns and desires, environmental policy, literature reviews, organizational strategy and redefining sustainability.

The first and perhaps most common marketing sustainability research area focuses on consumer concerns and desires. For instance, researchers have explored what makes a green consumer and what individual characteristics tend to make consumers environmentally conscious (Cho et al., 2013; Follows and Jobber, 2000; Kilbourne and Beckmann, 1998; Kidwell et al., 2013; Meneses, 2010). Marketers have also voluntarily studied simplicity, green consumption and anti-consumption (Cherrier, 2009, 2010; Iyer and Muncy, 2009). In this stream of consumer research, there is also discussion around how to target products for the sustainable consumer demographic (Lin and Chang, 2012). McDonagh and Prothero (2014) suggest that, in the future, sustainable consumer research should take what we have learned about sustainable consumers and begin to apply this knowledge to society as a whole.

A second large area of marketing sustainability research revolves around environmental policy and law making – specifically, discussion on how policy can be used to help marketing conservation efforts is examined. Further, environmental labelling and taxation are explored (Aasness and Larsen, 2003; Bickart and Ruth, 2012). A third area of marketing sustainability research includes literature reviews on the topic (Kilbourne and Beckmann, 1998; Leonidou, 2011; McDonagh and Prothero, 2014).

A fourth area of marketing sustainability research is on sustainable organizational strategy. However, despite the large demand for research in this area, not much has been done on the topic since the 1990s when the concept of organizational 'green washing' was first introduced. That is, not much research has examined how companies incorporate sustainability into their business strategy. Recent theoretical research has suggested that the lack of progress in this area may be a result of the neoliberal basis for business that makes it difficult to incorporate sustainable business practices (Fisk, 1973; McDonagh and Prothero, 2014). Specifically, marketing business practices must move away from a continuous pursuit of growth and consumption and instead incorporate ideas of ecology into business models to see significant advances in sustainable marketing strategy.

Lastly, the fifth area of sustainable marketing research explores the theoretical framing of marketing sustainability. Research in this area takes a more macro or broad approach to all of the marketing sustainability research. That is, rather than examining marketing sustainability through micro-trends or a consumer viewpoint, this research critically examines marketing's relationship with the natural environment (Kilbourne, 2006; Kilbourne and Beckman, 1998; McDonagh and Prothero, 2014; Press and Arnould, 2009; Prothero et al., 2011). This research has theoretically challenged the neoliberal paradigm (referred to as the dominant social paradigm, or DSP) that currently pervades the marketing field. However, despite the strong theoretical arguments to challenge marketing within the DSP, a macromarketing analysis on how to shift this paradigm has been lacking. To summarize the most recent literature review on marketing sustainability, McDonagh and Prothero (2014) suggest that marketing sustainability must move away from being a small 's' – micro-managerial sustainability – and move towards sustainability with a big 'S' – macro-level critical Sustainability.

What most of these views had in common was that they proposed solutions within the parameters of existing practice, that is within the prevailing institutions of the DSP. In effect, they proposed reform within the system rather than radical change of the system. It was not the system with its underlying institutions that was deficient, and what was necessary was to 'tweak' the prevailing practices with technological improvements in production (greener products) and recycling or reverse channels (Zikmund and Stanton, 1971). The prevailing institutions were never challenged in these proposals. During the nearly 30-year period of such proposals, the ecological impact of consumption and production accelerated rather than diminished (Dowie, 1995).

Toby Smith (1999) argued that this result was inevitable because of what he referred to as the myth of green marketing. His analysis argued that green marketing was little more than a diversion that allowed the prevailing institutions underlying the market to remain unchanged. Here again was an early, but disregarded, call for radical transformation in the institutional structure of markets and marketing, not for the reform of the market system itself. We must consume less, not more efficiently. The imperative of growth in modern economics won out in the contest for ideas. The focus of marketing practice and theory remained on the mandate to produce more and sell more in accordance with this economic imperative.

Marketing in transition?

In the ensuing 15 years, very little changed regarding sustainability except, unfortunately, that the term became almost synonymous with green marketing. This further exacerbated the problem as practitioners and theorists alike began to use the term sustainability while talking about greening the marketing mix. The problem here is that the two are hardly even kindred spirits, and this serves to diminish the discourse on sustainability. It essentially allows one to engage in green marketing (not a bad thing, of course) and falsely claim victory on the field of sustainability (the illusion of success). Magdoff and Foster (2011) argue that this is a potentially dangerous stance to take in marketing because it proffers the problem as the solution, and in doing this, practitioners get the false impression that things are getting better when, in fact, they are getting worse. Rational economic goals and, through them, marketing goals require fulfilling basic human needs now and ensuring that such needs are met for future generations. This is the essence of sustainable marketing, and it is easy to see that such conditions cannot be met through greening the marketing process. After 40 years of limited green marketing practice, it appears that mainstream marketing scholars are beginning to see the nature of the problem and, while not yet fully integrated, are turning in the right direction.

Calls for sustainable marketing

As stated earlier, the relationship between marketing and the environment was established decades ago. But it has assumed many guises during that period. Kilbourne and Beckmann (1998) summarized the relationship and concluded that the notion of sustainability and the larger issues in the relationship have not been well examined. Most research fell in the green marketing, green consumer and green product categories. In more recent years, the situation appears to have changed little. The volume of research has increased, but the focus has remained fairly narrow, eschewing the more macro-dimensions. There have been some exceptions however. As an example, Sheth and Parvatiyar (1995) discussed 'ecological imperatives' and approached the topic from a sustainability perspective. They argued that consumption must be redirected in less harmful ways including reduction, the 4 Ps must be reoriented towards sustainable strategies, industry should be reorganized translating strategies into plans, and reconsumption should be initiated focusing on product longevity and consumer reuse. Kilbourne et al. (1997) also argued that sustainable consumption would require fundamental shifts in the practice of marketing going beyond green initiatives. Beyond these calls for a sustainable marketing, few true sustainability initiatives have been evident until very recently.

More recently, the calls for sustainable marketing have reappeared from major mainstream marketers such as Kotler (2002), Huang and Rust (2011) and Sheth et al. (2011). Huang and Rust (2011) argue that sustainability requires, above all, a systems perspective integrating the environment, the economy and social justice. Kotler argues that marketing must be reinvented to respond effectively to the environmental imperative. Sheth et al. argue that marketers must inculcate in consumers a new perspective they refer to as *mindful consumption*. Each of these perspectives will be examined briefly to determine their relationship to sustainability as it is normally used, i.e. not synonymous with green marketing.

Kotler (2011) argues that the sustainability imperative has begun and is being adopted by many firms. He proposes a number of changes in the 4 Ps to facilitate the sustainability agenda in more firms. Briefly, he suggests that products and packages should be designed to reduce their carbon footprint. Greener products, in turn, might command higher prices from committed green consumers, and prices might reflect the potential to cover externalities. Distribution chains should be considered for their commitment to sustainability practices, and companies should consider more online marketing to reduce transportation costs to consumers. Finally, he argues that consideration should be given to shifting from print to online promotion because it is less resource intensive, and that labels should provide information about ingredients and their carbon footprints. He then suggests that companies seek more sustainable paths to growth.

Sheth et al. (2011) are not in agreement with Kotler's assessment of sustainability within large companies. They argue that a very small percentage of companies have sustainability strategies, and when they do engage, it is for reactive and opportunistic reasons. These types of initiatives are seldom integrated into normal responsibilities of management. While they do highlight some exceptions to this, they state that they really are exceptions and not the norm. Sheth et al. also argue that the benefits of green production are probably overstated because the gains in efficiency are easily offset by increased consumption. Their perspective shifts to the consumer rather than the producer, and they suggest that while the idea of green consumption is expanding, its growth rate is insufficient to sustain gains to the environment. While all would agree that the small gains and expanding awareness are in the right direction, they have not received support from corporate leaders. Whereas Kotler mentions reduced consumption as part of the solution, Sheth et al. focus on it arguing that overconsumption can be addressed through the inculcation of mindful consumption that entails caring for the self, for community and for nature. To initiate mindful consumption, firms can use the 4 Ps in encouraging lower consumption in addition to Kotler's more efficient production. This approach marks a major shift in thinking for scholars in mainstream marketing who have thus far viewed the consumption–environment relationship as one type of consumption and not quantity of consumption.

Assessment of changes

While these three papers signal a potential for growing interest in sustainability, they do not represent the call to arms that is necessary to begin the transformation of marketing that will be required for sustainability. To see this, we will provide a brief assessment of their deficiencies, which actually lie in the DSP of Western societies. The essential elements of the paradigm were provided in the first section of this chapter.

Kotler's position falls into the general area referred to as ecological modernization (EM). This position is based primarily in the capacity for technological development and concludes that economic development and growth are not incompatible with sustainability. In fact, the suggestion is that through more eco-efficient development the environment will actually benefit from further economic growth and development. The basis for this position rests on what is known as the Environmental Kuznets Curve (EKC). This is an inverted U curve that suggests environmental integrity decreases in the early stages of economic development and market growth, but when GDP per capita reaches a high enough level, then environmental integrity will begin to increase and environmental problems will begin to diminish. Kotler's position seems to be that if we develop more eco-efficient products, price them right, spend less on distribution and advertise eco-benefits and carbon footprints, the condition of the environment will improve. We must point out that this is an interpretation of his approach from EM and EKC perspectives.

The Sheth et al. approach is more comprehensive and does address some paradigm issues albeit in a very indirect and incomplete way. One instance of this is the assumption regarding positive freedom (Berlin, 2013; Sen, 1999) through which individuals have the freedom to enact the life they choose to live including their consumption choices. It is also suggested that mindful consumption is characterized by caring for community and the environment. These two together seem to violate two aspects of the DSP, possessive individualism and self-interest both reinforced by limitations on government. These are the essence of consumer sovereignty and are integrated into procedural neutrality (Sandel, 1996) that pervades the market system. Procedural neutrality specifies that the government and external forces must remain neutral regarding the choices people make or the lives they choose to enact. Because of this, Sheth, et al. are correct in questioning the efficacy of government intervention in consumption choices including quantity. This is the reason they choose market-driven alternatives. But another problem remains for the market-based solution to be effective, and that is its internal contradictions.

Contradictions in the system

There have been many allusions to the contradictions within the system of capitalism in which modern marketing is embedded. They are most prominent in Marx and neo-Marxists such as Harvey (2006) and O'Connor (1994), but others such as Bell (1976) have addressed the issue as well. It is not the purpose of this chapter to examine all the contradictions that have been discussed in the past, and, as a result, only the contradiction related directly to sustainability will be discussed, and that briefly. O'Connor (1994) explains what he refers to as the second contradiction of capitalism, which relates directly to the issue of sustainable marketing. The issue is the availability of resources (sources) and waste disposal (sinks).

The first basic assumption in what follows is that the law of conservation of matter and energy and the entropy law will continue indefinitely. From a marketing/economic perspective these laws mean respectively that nothing ever comes from nothing and that everything goes somewhere. Production and consumption require matter and energy and always produce waste. This condition is what justifies Daly's (1972) conception of the impossibility theorem, which states that infinite growth in a finite system is *prima facie* impossible.

These assumptions combined, with the many critiques of the nature and logic of capitalism (e.g. Heilbroner, 1985; Magdoff and Foster, 2011; O'Connor, 1994), lead to a seemingly impossible task. That is creating a vision of sustainable marketing within the context of capitalism as practised in the West and, increasingly, Asia as well. While the complexities of this type of analysis are formidable to say the least, a brief explanation of their conclusions will be attempted here as they are critical in the development of sustainable marketing. Every analysis from Marx to the present concedes one basic principle about the capitalist form of economic organization, and that is that its driving force is the accumulation of capital effected through profits. Profits are achieved by competing successfully with similarly situated firms all having the same inner logic. This leads to the ubiquitous conclusion that economic growth is the desired effect of competition. Firms must grow or die (Heilbroner, 1985), making growth an imperative rather than strategy. This leads to a clear contradiction between marketing as the means through which continuous growth is achieved and sustainability. The goal of contemporary marketing is to serve the needs of the system of which it is a part by selling in ever-increasing volumes. Can this continue indefinitely, and, if not, why not? An additional concern for engendering sustainable marketing is the time frame within which real and effective change needs to occur.

Under the assumptions made previously, the answer to the first question is an emphatic no. This simply violates the conservation and entropy laws and, because of that, the impossibility theorem. A system with finite resources (as we currently define resources) cannot grow indefinitely. It is limited by both sources and sinks. Ironically, while these limits are ignored to a large extent in Western business practices, they were not ignored by the original authors who defined the modern economic world. We discussed how their principles became the underlying principles of capitalism in the beginning. It seems, however, that neoclassical economics is adept at bowdlerizing principles. Possessive individualism, private property, limited government, self-interest, etc. suited the development of economics centred on growth very well and it would scarcely have been possible without them. At the same time, Locke imposed limitations on his conceptions. For sustainability purposes he included what is known as the 'as much and as good' limitation, which put restrictions on what individuals could exclude others from. Western society has long passed this limitation. Smith (1993 [1776]) seemed at first to contradict himself in the 'Adam Smith problem' in that he seemed to be one person in the *Wealth of Nations* and another in the *Theory of Moral Sentiments* (Smith, 1976 [1759]). This related directly to the construct self-interest, which he seems to argue for in one book and against in the other. Sen (1999) argues that there is really no contradiction, in that Smith's use of self-interest in the *Wealth of Nations* referred only to the narrow confines of individual exchanges and not to the whole of society. Again, neoclassical economics and marketing treat self-interest as the primary motivation of all behaviour and treat it as a universal motive. Finally, Mill (1872 [1848]) argued that the growth model of economics could not endure forever and, at some point in the future, it would have to give way to what he referred to as 'steady-state' economics: economics without growth. These warnings have clearly not been heeded by modern marketing and economics in which growth is still the *summum bonum* of market performance.

This leads ultimately to a fundamental contradiction between sustainability and marketing as practised within Western industrial societies. As we argued earlier, the assumptions underlying traditional marketing practices are aligned with the assumptions of neoclassical economics. They are the fundamental elements of the DSP of Western societies. That is atomistic possessive individualism motivated by self-interest to accumulate private property through powerless impersonal market mechanisms with strict limitations on the power of government in the market. This is the perfect storm of cultural conditions to achieve unlimited growth in GDP which becomes synonymous with progress. The fundamental contradiction is that this must be carried out within the context of finite resources (both sources and sinks).

Marketing has been characterized by Fisk (1974) as the provisioning technology of society. As such it is the direct link between production and consumption. Its primary function is to match the capabilities of production with consumer demand to achieve market equilibrium. Because industry must incessantly expand for the accumulation of capital to continue, marketing must continuously increase consumption in current markets and pursue larger markets to absorb greater production that yields economies of scale. This is a ceaseless cycle of growth.

The question must be asked again. Is marketing sustainable under these conditions? The mounting ecological evidence suggests it is not unless there are major transformations in the nature and logic of capitalism in which marketing practice is embedded. While there is still no real call for such changes within the marketing academy, Sheth et al. (2011) have alluded to some contradictions and at least intimate that fundamental change may be necessary in the not too distant future. This is a positive step to be sure. But the second question posed earlier queries as to the time frame within which such transformations in the underlying conditions of marketing must change. This leads to another dimension of the sustainable marketing problem.

IPAT revisited

Up until recently there has been no really effective way to assess the level of or path to sustainability. While the theory regarding the elements of sustainability has been examined, there was no way to incorporate this into a model that would offer insight into the current state or trajectory of sustainability. This has begun to change in the last 15 years or so. Empirical measures related to sustainability are improving annually and are becoming available for about 150 countries around the world thanks to the development and refinement of the 'ecological footprint' construct. This has opened up the possibility for better understanding the ecological consequences of continuous economic growth through unsustainable marketing practices, and it can provide guides to more effective policy relating to sustainability. We begin with a discussion of the original IPAT equation and trace it to its current conception, which is far more useful.

The IPAT was developed in the 1970s to measure human impact on the environment (Ehrlich and Holdren, 1971). Specifically, the IPAT (I = PAT) examines the total environmental impact (I) as a multiplicative function of population (P), affluence (A) and technology (T). Affluence in this form is defined as GDP/P, or per capita GDP, and T is defined as I/GDP, or ecological impact per unit of GDP produced. This provides the identity:

$$I = P \times GDP/P \times I/GDP$$

This provided a convenient way to think about the relationship between ecological impact and its contributors. However, it did not provide more than a way of thinking about the problem because it is not an equation. Rather, it is an identity which is, by definition, always true. It did give pause to reflect on the nature of the sustainability problem in that it demonstrated what had to happen in one variable to achieve sustainability under different scenarios for the other variables. For example, if P = 1.03 and A = 1.03 for the next 50 years, by how much would T have to decrease to maintain ecological impact (I) at its present level. The result suggests that under this scenario, T would have to be reduced to approximately 5.2% of its current level. But this only provides a series of 'what if' scenarios that catch our attention but do not provide policy input. To rectify this, a number of improvements to the IPAT formulation have been made.

The IPAT was originally developed for use in the natural sciences (specifically, biology and physics). However, since its original development it has been used in many other fields including economics, environmental biology, engineering, finance, public policy and sociology (Guang-ming and Qiang, 2008; Soule and DeHart, 1998; York et al., 2003a; Zhongwu and Jiansu, 2003). However, the IPAT/STIRPAT has yet to be used in marketing.

In the IPAT's original format, the effects of P, A and T are considered proportional to each other. Therefore, more recent literature has reformatted the equation into a stochastic form so that each parameter can be estimated individually. Hence the STIRPAT equation was developed: the stochastic (ST) estimation of impacts (I) by regression (R) on population (P), affluence (A) and technology (T) (Rosa and Dietz, 1998; York et al., 2003a). The formula for the STIRPAT equation is as follows:

$$I_i = aP_i^b A_i^c T_i^d e_i$$

In this equation, a is the constant term, b, c and d are exponents of the independent variables and e is the error term. Typical variables used to measure environmental impacts (I) include carbon dioxide emissions and ecological footprint (York et al., 2003a, 2003b). Further, population (P) is measured using different country's total population, and affluence (A) is measured using GDP per capita. Because there has been no agreed measurement for technology (T), it has traditionally been measured through the error term (York et al., 2003b).

As mentioned, in the original IPAT each variable in the equation is assumed to be proportional (i.e. a = b = c = d = e = 1). However, in stochastic form, both sides of the equation are converted into their (natural) logarithmic form so that the individual elasticity of each variable can be measured. The advantage of using data in a logarithmic form is that it changes linear data to an order of magnitude. That is, rather than having a scale based on sequential numbering, each number on the scale is based on the previous mark, multiplied by a value. The main advantage of logarithmic scaling is that it allows variables with different measurements or highly variable data to vary similarly. Therefore, it ultimately makes data much easier to interpret. The resulting model is as follows:

$$\ln(I) = a + b[\ln(P)] + c[\ln(A)] + e$$

In this equation, a and e stay the same as the first model, but b and c are in logarithmic scale form. The b and c parameters can be interpreted as elasticities. This means that parameter values are the percentage change in I for every 1% change in P or A with all else held constant. Therefore, values of b and c that are greater than 1.0 indicate that P and A are elastic and every increase of 1% in the independent variable results in an increase of greater than 1% in I. Values of b and c less than 1.0 but greater than 0 indicate that changes of 1% in P and A have a less than 1% increase in environmental impact. Essentially, the higher the coefficients of P and A, the more of an impact they are having on the environment.

We expect there are many benefits to be derived in marketing from applying the STIRPAT. First, sustainability research can begin to shift from analysing sustainability-related attitudes in individuals to analysing sustainability in society. Macro-level sustainability research has been primarily theoretical in nature (e.g. Kilbourne and Beckmann, 1998) and has yet to be analytically tested. Further, the move to macro-sustainability research has been called for in the marketing literature: 'it is imperative to consider the (im)possibility of both sustainable consumption and consumption practices ... at a broader societal level' (McDonagh and Prothero, 2014: 1198).

Second, studying the STIRPAT can give marketing researchers a starting point to analyse and explain the need to move away from the growth-oriented imperative of capitalism. When applying the IPAT or STIRPAT, researchers may add other variables to the model to address other theoretical questions, so long as the new variables follow the same logarithmic modelling as the original variables (York et al., 2003a). Therefore, marketing researchers can begin to add marketing variables to the STIRPAT formula to see which marketing variables have the largest impact on the environment. This gives marketing researchers a starting point to bring change and to incorporate the environment in future marketing strategy, and perhaps change marketing ontology. This has already been called for in the marketing literature: 'we need research which fundamentally explores marketing's raison d'etre and considers how we change the consumption ideology (Kilbourne, McDonagh and Prothero 1997; Prothero and Fitchett 2000)' (McDonagh and Prothero, 2014: 1201).

Future research may also consider adding dimensions of the DSP to the STIRPAT formula. As mentioned earlier in this chapter, the DSP has been used in marketing to understand large patterns of social thought within cultures (Pirages and Ehrlich, 1974). Within Western industrial societies the DSP is generally classified in two domains. The first domain is comprised of three micro-level dimensions of the DSP: economic, technological and political. The second domain is comprised of three cosmological dimensions: structure, competition and organization (Kilbourne and Beckmann, 1998). Measures for these dimensions have been established in the literature (see e.g. Kilbourne and Carlson, 2008) and can be added to the STIRPAT model to contribute more analytical understanding to the DSP body of research. Since an element of the DSP is technology, it can also remove the need to capture technology (T) in the STIRPAT equation with an error term.

While the STIRPAT equation has not been used in marketing, it has been successfully used in assessing some macromarketing type variables. Earlier we briefly examined the EKC and EM, two prevailing theories regarding economic development and market expansion. They both are frequently alluded to in economic research on sustainability and argue that continuous economic growth is possible and desirable despite ecological arguments to the contrary. York et al. (2003a) examined both of these theories using STIRPAT. In a study of 142 nations, they examined, among other variables, estimates for ecological modernization theory and the environmental Kuznets curve. In the study they concluded that there is little support for either theory. As population becomes more modernized and affluence increases, the ecological footprint continues to increase. While much more needs to be done in this area, it raises serious questions about traditional marketing practice, the purpose of which is to continuously increase levels of consumption worldwide in support of the neoliberal agenda.

Summary and conclusion

What we have attempted to show here is that sustainable marketing is very frequently misinterpreted within the marketing literature. It is most often used almost synonymously with green marketing. However, the two are very different from each other. Green marketing is predicated on the notion that true sustainability can be achieved following a 'business as usual' philosophy, and we have attempted to demonstrate that this is simply not the case. Only recently in the marketing literature has the difference begun to come to light. Kotler (2011), Huang and Rust (2011) and Sheth et al. (2011) are among the first mainstream marketing scholars to call for transformation in how marketing is done. Most importantly, they argue that the business as usual approach will probably be insufficient.

The purpose of this chapter is to expand on the traditional concept of marketing showing that if we are to carry out these calls for transformation, then we must better understand how the underlying philosophy that directs marketing practice must be changed first. The DSP of Western industrial societies represents the confluence of technological, political and economic theory developing since before the industrial revolution. This DSP both informs and motivates marketing practice in the modern world and it is aligned with the resulting neoliberal philosophy underlying neoclassical economics. In the relationship, marketing is the provisioning technology that links production to consumption, and it assumes the same character under which increasing consumption is virtually the definition of progress. Until this relationship is understood, there is little hope that any major transformations in marketing will occur.

The requisite changes will not occur spontaneously through consumer action because consumers are, for the most part, wrapped in the ideology of neoliberalism without knowing it. In addition, producers are a part of the same ideology. Consumers still believe that if some is good, more is better, spawning such books as *Is the American Dream Killing You?* (Stiles, 2005). Producers believe that the key to a better life for all is to invest in producing more, and as the GDP rises, so does human well-being. The rising tide lifts all boats. In the short run under specific circumstances (prevalent in the past), both beliefs may have been true. But they are no longer true, and we must stop pretending, as suggested by Keynes (1931), that 'fair is foul and foul is fair'. He suggested that foul is fair because it produced needed growth at the time. We now think fair (social justice) is foul because it could limit growth, condemning the already poor to an even worse fate. But it is becoming widely accepted that growth without justice leads to crippling inequality (Stiglitz, 2013), which further deteriorates the environment. It seems in these critiques that marketing is serving a world turned upside down. But because we are still ideologically driven, it is necessary to show how these philosophical underpinnings are driving marketing in the wrong direction.

To do this, new analytical techniques are necessary. Ehrlich and Holdren (1971) began to do this, and their original work has now been updated to be more informative. In addition, new data on environmental conditions are being developed and provide more information for modelling the ecological footprint of the globe. This modelling can lead to better understanding of the factors shaping the environment and provide information on developing policy initiatives for ameliorating ecological degradation. In particular, it is becoming possible to model the effects of growth, affluence, technology, politics, social structure, and a variety of other contributing factors. Doing this successfully could be the impetus for transformation of a market system that may have outlived its usefulness.

Recommended further reading

Best, Steven and Douglas Kellner (2001), *The Postmodern Adventure: Science, Technology, and Cultural Studies at the Third Millennium*. Guilford Publications, Inc: New York, NY.

Dobson, Andrew (2004), Green Political Thought. London, UK: Routledge Press.

Dryzek, John (1996), Democracy in Capitalist Times. Oxford, UK: Oxford University Press.

Eckersley, Robyn (2004), The Green State. Cambridge, MA: The MIT Press.

Kilbourne, William E. (1998), "Green marketing: A theoretical perspective," *Journal of Marketing Management*, 14 (6), 641–55.

Kilbourne, William E., Michael J. Dorsch, Pierre McDonagh, Bertrand Urien, Andrea Prothero, Marko Grünhagen, Michael Jay Polonsky, David Marshall, Janice Foley, and Alan Bradshaw (2009), "The Institutional Foundations of Materialism in Western Societies A Conceptualization and Empirical Test," *Journal of macromarketing*, 29 (3), 259–78.

Peterson, Mark (2013), Sustainable Enterprise: A Macromarketing Approach. Los Angeles, CA: Sage.

References

Aasness, J. and Larsen, E.R. (2003) 'Distributional effects of environmental taxes on transportation', *Journal of Consumer Policy* 26(3): 279–300.

Bacon, F. (1944 [1620]) *Advancement of Learning and Novum Organum*. New York: John Wiley.

Bell, D. (1976) *The Cultural Contradictions of Capitalism*. New York: Basic Books.

Berlin, I. (2013) *Three Critics of the Enlightenment*. Princeton, NJ: Princeton University Press.

Bickart, B.A. and Ruth, J.A. (2012) 'Green eco-seals and advertising persuasion', *Journal of Advertising* 41(4): 51–67.

Cherrier, H. (2009) 'Anti-consumption discourses and consumer-resistant identities', *Journal of Business Research* 62(2): 181–90.

Cherrier, H. (2010) 'Custodian behavior: a material expression of anti-consumerism', *Consumption, Markets & Culture* 13(3): 259–72.

Cho, Y.-N., Thyroff, A., Rapert, M., Park, S.-Y. and Lee, H.J. (2013) 'To be or not to be green: exploring individualism and collectivism as antecedents of environmental behavior', *Journal of Business Research* 66(8): 1052–9.

Daly, H.E. (1972) *Toward a Steady-State Economy*. San Francisco, CA: W.H. Freeman.

Dowie, M. (1995) *Losing Ground: American Environmentalism at the Close of the Twentieth Century*. Cambridge, MA: MIT Press.

Ehrlich, P.R. and Holdren, J.P. (1971) 'Impact of population growth', *Science* 171(3977): 1212–17.

Fisk, G. (1973) 'Criteria for a theory of responsible consumption', *Journal of Marketing* 37(1): 24–31.

Fisk, G. (1974) *Marketing and the Ecological Crisis*. New York: Harper and Row.

Follows, S.B. and Jobber, D. (2000) 'Environmentally responsible purchase behaviour: a test of a consumer model', *European Journal of Marketing* 34(5/6): 723–46.

Guang-ming, H.E. and Qiang, L.V. (2008) 'Analysis of ecological environmental impact based on IPAT model – a case study of Beijing', *Journal of Central University of Finance & Economics* 12: 016.

Harvey, D. (2006) *Limits to Capital*. London: Verso.

Heilbroner, R.L. (1985) *The Nature and Logic of Capitalism*. New York: W.W. Norton.

Hirschman, A.O. (1977) *The Passions and the Interests: Political Arguments for Capitalism before its Triumph*. Princeton, NJ: Princeton University Press.

Hobbes, T. (1950 [1651]) *Leviathan*. New York: E.P. Dutton and Sons.

Hodgson, G.M. (2001) *How Economics Forgot History*. London: Routledge.

Huang, M.-H. and Rust, R. (2011) 'Sustainability and consumption', *Journal of the Academy of Marketing Science* 39: 40–54.

Iyer, R. and Muncy, J.A. (2009) 'Purpose and object of anti-consumption', *Journal of Business Research* 62(2): 160–8.

Keynes, J.M. (1931) *Essays in Persuasion*. London: PAIS International.

Kidwell, B., Farmer, A. and Hardesty, D.M. (2013) 'Getting liberals and conservatives to go green: political ideology and congruent appeals', *Journal of Consumer Research* 40(2): 350–67.

Kilbourne, W. (2006) 'The role of the dominant social paradigm in the quality of life/environmental interface', *Applied Research in Quality of Life* 1(1): 39–61.

Kilbourne, W.E. and Beckmann, S.C. (1998) 'Review and critical assessment of research on marketing and the environment', *Journal of Marketing Management* 14(6): 513–32.

Kilbourne, W. and Carlson, L. (2008) 'Dominant social paradigm, consumption, and environmental attitudes: can macromarketing education help?', *Journal of Macromarketing* 28(2): 106–21.

Kilbourne, W., McDonagh, P. and Prothero, A. (1997) 'Sustainable consumption and the quality of life: a macromarketing challenge to the dominant social paradigm', *Journal of Macromarketing* 17(1): 4–24.

Kotler, P. (2002) *Marketing Management*, 11th edn. Upper Saddle River, NJ: Prentice-Hall.

Kotler, P. (2011) 'Reinventing marketing to manage the environmental imperative', *Journal of Marketing* 75 (July): 132–5.

Leiss, W. (1972) *The Domination of Nature*. New York: George Braziller.

Leonidou, C. (2011) 'Research into environmental marketing/management: a bibliographic analysis', *European Journal of Marketing* 45(1/2): 68–103.

Lin, Y.-C. and Chang, C.-C.A. (2012) 'Double standard: the role of environmental consciousness in green product usage', *Journal of Marketing* 76(5): 125–34.

McDonagh, P. and Prothero, A. (2014) 'Sustainability marketing research: past, present, and future', *Journal of Marketing Management* 30(11/12): 1186–219.

Macpherson, C.B. (1962) *The Political Theory of Possessive Individualism*. Oxford: The Clarendon Press.

Magdoff, F. and Foster, J.B. (2011) *What Every Environmentalist Needs to Know About Capitalism*. New York: Monthly Review Press.

Meneses, G.D. (2010) 'Refuting fear in heuristics and in recycling promotion', *Journal of Business Research, Advances in Spreadsheet and Database Training* 63(2): 104–10.

Merchant, C. (1980) *The Death of Nature: Women, Ecology and the Scientific Revolution*. London: Wildwood House.

Mill, J.S. (1872 [1848]) *Principles of Political Economy: With Some of Their Applications to Social Philosophy*. New York: D. Appleton.

O'Connor, M. (ed.) (1994) *Is Capitalism Sustainable? Political Economy and the Politics of Ecology*. New York: The Guilford Press.

Pirages, D.C. and Ehrlich, P.R. (1974) *Ark II: Social Response to Environmental Imperatives*. San Francisco, CA: Freeman.

Press, M. and Arnould, E.J. (2009) 'Constraints on sustainable energy consumption: market system and public policy challenges and opportunities', *Journal of Public Policy & Marketing* 28(1): 102–13.

Prothero, A. and Fitchett, J.A. (2000) 'Greening capitalism: opportunities for a green commodity', *Journal of Macromarketing* 20(1): 46–55.

Prothero, A., Dobscha, S., Freund, J., Kilbourne, W.E., Luchs, M., Ozanne, L. and Thørgersen, J. (2011) 'Sustainable consumption: opportunities for sustainable consumption: opportunities for consumer research and public policy', *Journal of Public Policy & Marketing* 30(1): 31–8.

Rosa, E.A. and Dietz, T. (1998) 'Climate change and society: speculation, construction, and scientific investigation', *International Sociology* 13(4): 421–55.

Sandel, M.J. (1996) *Democracy's Discontent*. Cambridge, MA: Belknap Press of Harvard University.

Sen, A.K. (1999) *Development as Freedom*. New York: Knopf.

Sheth, J.N. and Parvatiyar, A. (1995) 'Ecological imperatives and the role of marketing', in M.J. Polonsky and A.T. Mintu-Wimsatt (eds) *Environmental Marketing Strategies, Practice, Theory and Research*. Binghamton, NY: Haworth Press, pp. 3–20.

Sheth, J.N., Nirmal K.S. and Srinivas, S. (2011) 'Mindful consumption: a customer-centric approach to sustainability', *Journal of the Academy of Marketing Science* 39(1): 21–39.

Smith, A. (1976 [1759]) *The Theory of Moral Sentiments*. Oxford: Oxford University Press.

Smith, A. (1993 [1776]) *An Inquiry into the Nature and Causes of the Wealth of Nations*. Oxford: Oxford University Press.

Smith, T.M. (1999) *The Myth of Green Marketing: Tending Our Goats at the Edge of Apocalypse*. Toronto: University of Toronto Press.

Soule, P.T. and DeHart, J.L. (1998) 'Assessing IPAT using production and consumption based measures of I', *Social Science Quarterly* 79(4): 754–65.

Stiglitz, J.E. (2013) *The Price of Inequality*. New York: W.W. Norton.

Stiles, P. (2005) *Is the American Dream Killing You?* New York: Collins.

Ullmann, W. (1963) *The Individual and Society in the Middle Ages*. Baltimore, MD: The Johns Hopkins Press.

York, R., Rosa, E.A. and Dietz, T. (2003a) 'Footprints on the earth: the environmental consequences of modernity', *American Sociological Review* 68(2): 279–300.

York, R., Rosa, E.A. and Dietz, T. (2003b) 'Stirpat, Ipat and impact: analytical tools for unpacking the driving forces of environmental impacts', *Ecological Economics* 46: 351–65.

Zhongwu, L. and Jiansu, M. (2003) 'Crossing "environmental mountain" on the increase and decrease of environment impact in the process of economic growth', *Engineering* 12: 005.

Zikmund, W.G. and Stanton, W.J. (1971) 'Recycling solid wastes: a channels of distribution problem', *Journal of Marketing* 35 (July): 34–9.

Index

Page numbers in *italics* refer to figures and tables.

Aaker, D.A. 346
Achrol, R.S. and Kotler, P. 23–4, 25
actor–resources–activities (RCA) framework 399
actor-to-actor interactions (A2A) 447, 469
adoption behaviour categories 253–4, *258*, 369, 472–3
advertising
    brand equity 345, 346
    and cognition 139
    cross-cultural issues 185, 190, 191–2
    in marketing mix 206–7, 209–10
    problem of measurement 322
    see also psychology
agent-based modelling 245
Ajzen, I. 303–4
    and Fishbein, M./Fishbein, M. and Ajzen, I. 152–3,
        289, 483
Alderson, W. 35, 36, 40, 72–3, 163, 165, 244, 292–3
    and Cox, R. 33–4, 35, 40
Alexander, R.S. 211
'alpha testing' 367
American Marketing Association (AMA) 26, 40–1, 63,
    203, 347
American Psychology Association 138
Anderson, J.C. et al. 345, 350, 356
Anderson, J.M. 44

Anderson, P.F. 36, 37, 38
Andreasen, A.R. 485–7
anthropology 116
Aquinas, T. 495
Araujo, L. 50, 124
    et al. 50
Arndt, J. 39–40, 164, 293
Arnould, E.J. and Thompson, C.J. 51, 290–1, 296, 306–7
Association for Consumer Research (ACR), 291, 297
attention-seeking approaches 44–5
attitudes 149–54
auditing 274

B2B markets *see* business to business (B2B) markets
Bacharach, S.B. 32
Bacon, F. 493–4, 496
Bagozzi, R.P. 34, 43, 49, 122, 201
    and Dholakia, U.M. 189
Baker, M.J. 6, 9, 13, 34, 41–2, 53, 75, 456
balanced centricity 447
Bandura, A. 304, 306
Barger, H. 64, 71
Bartels, R. 63–4, 65, 66, 72, 74, 117, 200, 220
Becker, G.S. 122, 123, 128
behavioural economics 121–2

behavioural intentions model 152–4
behaviourally driven relationship marketing (RM)
     394–6, 398
'beta testing' 367
biographical research 72–3, 75
'black economy' 176
Boots: retail formats 427–8
Booz Allen Hamilton 374
     model of new product development 364, 371
Borden, N. 13–14, 203, 211
Boston Consulting Group (BCG) 228, 229, 239–40
bounded rationality 121, 243
Bourdieu, P. 170, 297
brand
     consumer–brand relationships typology 286–8
     image and marketing mix instruments 207, 208–9
     loyalty 150–2
brand community 169–70, 189, 301
     matrix 327
brand equity
     concept of 345
     definition of 346
     integrating with financial concepts 352–5
          financial asset perspective 352–4
          governance 355
          relationships and networks 354–5
     perspectives 346–50   ·
          entity-based 346–7
          financially-based 347
          network-based 348
          process-based 347–8
          service-based 348–50
     and theory of marketplace equity 355–8
     and value of other marketing assets 350–2
          channel and reseller equity 350–1
          customer equity 352
          influence of brands on channel equity 351–2
'brand journalism' 191–2
brand research 262, 263
     historical 77–8
bridging theories 45
briefings 276
Brodie, R.J. et al. 26, 45, 49, 350
Brookes, R.W. and Little, V.J. 26
Brown, S. 42, 45, 46, 72, 73, 418, 419, 428, 430
     et al. 68
Brownlie, D.
     et al. 52
     and Saren, M. 47–8
business analysis in new product development (NPD)
     366–7
business to business (B2B) markets
     as A2A interaction 469
     and B2C markets 52, 253, 437, 448, 455

business to business (B2B) markets cont.
     Hummel: digital transformation to omnichannel
          (case study) 332–9
     market segmentation 253, 262, 268
     networks and relationships 49, 52, 436,
          449–50
buyers and sellers, numbers of 165–6
Buzzell, R. 35, 36
     et al. 238

Cacioppo, J.T. and Petty, R.E./Petty, R.E. and
     Cacioppo, J.T. 139, 154, 155
capitalism
     contradictions in 501–2
     models of 17–18
     and neoclassical economics 119–20
     new 125–6
     provisioning system 114, 502
     see also neoliberalism
case study research 237, 239–40
     Honda 239–40
     and network theory 450
cash flow measures 353
Centre for the History of Retailing and Distribution
     (CHORD) 67
channel(s)
     3 Cs approach 226–8
     and brand equity 350–2
     member relationships research 396–8
     and network-based research 398–402
'chaoplexity' 243
CHARM see Conference on Historical Analysis and
     Research in Marketing
China
     Coca-Cola marketing 190
     Hong Kong: Vitasoy marketing 193–4
     and US 183, 185, 190, 192–3
     Zhangjiajie National Park 186–7
choice, as essence of economy 119–20
Churchill, G.A. 139, 299
citizen-consumers 26–7
co-branding 348
co-creation of value 22, 470–1
     citizen-consumers 26–7
     exchange continuum 391–3
     role of customers 465–6, 471
     role of institutions 472–3
co-evolution in marketing strategy analysis 245
co-evolution studies 245
Coca-Cola 190, 347
cognition
     and advertising 139
     social cognition theory 304–6
combination models of retail change 430

commercialization: new product development (NPD) 368–9

'commitment–trust theory of relationship marketing' 394–5

communication
in marketing mix 201–2, 206–7
see also information and communication technology (ICT)

community, concept of 169–70

competition models 231–3

complex flux model 12–13

complexity of markets and society 459–60

concept development and evaluation in new product development (NPD) 366

Conference on Historical Analysis and Research in Marketing (CHARM) 62–3, 67, 69

conflict theories 173–4, 429–30

conglomerates and entrepreneurs: retailing format 424

conspicuous consumption 141–2

Constantinides, E. 213, 215–16, 218–19

consumer behaviour research 285–6, 311–12
content analysis of *Journal of Consumer Research (JCR)* 292–303
marketing applications 300–3
research paradigms and methods 297–9
study populations of interest 299–300
theoretical focus 292–8
deductive and inductive approaches 121–2
development and scope of 286–9
identity and symbolic consumption 296, 307
as independent field 291–2
main periods 289–91
neuroscience 309–11
new theories and integrated approach 50–2, 303–11
social cognition theory 304–6
Theory of Planned Behaviour 303–4
transformative 308, *309*

Consumer Culture Theory (CCT) 51, 103, 290–1, 296, 306–7

consumer data mining 331

consumer sovereignty 120, 122, 185, 500

consumer–brand relationships typology 286–8

consumers
4 C model 213
citizen-consumers 26–7
ethical treatment of 101–2
Hierarchy of Effects model 322
sustainability concerns 98–9, 497
use of term 129
see also psychology; sociology

consumers and producers
capitalist provisioning system 114
Service-Dominant (S-D) logic 462–3, 468–9

Contemporary Marketing Practice (CMP) group 49

contracts 172

Converse, P.D. 64–5

Coolsen, F. 65

Cooper, R. 364, *371*, 373
et al. 373, 374, 378

cooperation 173

Copeland, M.T. 286

corporate social responsibility 99

cost–differentiation scale 228–9

cross-functional development 370–1

culture 180–1, 194–5
balancing localization and standardization 191–2
Consumer Culture Theory (CCT) 51, 103, 290–1, 296, 306–7
dynamics 193–4
globalization 189–90, 195
learning from 192–3
potential marketing problems and solutions 182–5
respecting 185–7
and sub-culture 170–1
utilizing 187–9

Cunningham, W. and Sheth, J.N. 42

Customer Relationship Management (CRM) 21, 393–4, 449–50

customer surveys 262, 268
Teleco (mobile phone company) 254–9

customer-based equity 347, 352

customer(s)
characteristics 252–3
as co-creator of value 465–6, 471
competitors and channels (3 Cs approach) 226–8
expectations and experiences 441–2
insight 260, 262, 276–7
satisfaction 442–3

cyclical theories of retail change 418–28

data
'big data' 276–7
mining 331

database analysis 237
market share and return on investment (ROI) 238, 239

Davidson, W.R. et al. 424, 425, 426

decentralization 446

decision making
marketing theory and practice 34, 45–6
multichannel 329–30
neuroscience 309–10
psychology 145–9
see also marketing ethics

deductive and inductive approaches to consumer behaviour 121–2

'demand enhancing marketing' 11

demand-impinging instruments 203–4, 209–10

development economics 126

diffusion of innovations 174–5

digital marketing *see* information and communication technology (ICT)
directional policy matrix (DPM) 271
  mobile phone company (case study) 272–3
Dirichlet theory 484
disconfirmation paradigm 441–2
'discontinuous innovation' 362
distribution function in marketing mix 202, 207
division of labour 7–8, 9
dominant social paradigm (DSP) 497–8, 500, 502, 505–6
Drucker, P. 13–14, 17

e-Marketing Special Interest Group (SIG) 325, 340
Eagly, A.H.
  and Chaiken, S. 149
  Johnson, B.T. and 146
ecological modernization (EM) 500, 505
ecology 116, 230, 233
  evolutionary ecological analogies 232
  social ecology models 484
  see also ecosystems; sustainable marketing
'economic choice making' 119–20
economic growth, exchange and 5–9
economic recession 428–9
economics 113–17
  behavioural 121–2
  development 126
  feminization of 128
  political economy/classical school 117, 119, 397
  recent challenges and implications 124–30
  reflection 130–2
  and sustainability 500, 502
  transaction cost 124, 395, 396–7, 398, 399
  welfare 124
  see also neoclassical economics
'economistic fallacy' 121
ecosystems
  concept of 448
  and institutions 460, 470–1
ecotourism 186–7
Ehrenberg, A. 484
  et al. 305
Eisingerich, A.B. et al. 212, 214
elaboration likelihood model (ELM) 154–6
emergent/enacted environments 242–3
employees: internal marketing 446
energy market (case study) 263–7
entity-based brand equity 346–7
entrepreneurs and conglomerates: retailing format 424
entropy law 501
environmental Kuznets curve (EKC) 500, 505
environmental policy and law 497
Epp, A.M. and Price, L.L. 296

'equity', definition of 344
ethics *see* marketing ethics
European perspective 14–18
European Quality Award 443
European Union (EU) 451
evolutionary ecological analogies 232
eWOM ('electronic word-of-mouth') research 328–9
excessive consumption 25
exchange
  continuum 391–3
  and economic growth 5–9
  illegal 175–6
  marketing as 162–3
  new model 200–2
  service as 459, 465
  social exchange theory (SET) 395, 397, 398, 399
  value-in-exchange 461, 463–4
explicit and tacit knowledge 451, 456

family 169
  identity 296
  life-cycle 169
fashion, theory as slave to 42–3
fast-moving current generalization 41–2
feminization of economics 128
financial asset perspective of brand equity 352–4
financial value planning approach 353
financially-based brand equity 347
firms
  behaviour 122–3
  dependence on markets 165, 166
  performance and ethical marketing 99
  Service-Dominant (S-D) vs Goods-Dominant (G-D) logic 462–4
  see also marketing strategy; organizations; retail change theories
Fishbein, M. *see* Ajzen, I.
focal networks and strategic nets 400–2
Ford, H. 10
4 C classification 213
4 Ps classification 211–14, 220
  development 13–14, 15–16, 17
  and relational approach 444–5
  and social marketing 488
  and sustainable marketing 499, 500
  see also marketing mix
4 S classification 213
Fourcade, M. et al. 127
Fournier, S. 286–8
  and Mick, D.G. 294
franchising 446
'front end development process' 366
full-time marketers (FTMs)/part-time marketers (PTMs) 446

Fullerton, R.A. 37, 68, 69, 77, 199–200
  evolution of modern marketing 10–13
  and Nevett, T.R. 70

Galbraith, J.K. 8–9, 112, 124
  and Salinger, N. 116, 117
game theory 231–2
gaming youths 253, 254
Gestalt principles 144–5
Gibson, H. et al. 18–21
Giddens, A. 163, 243, 307
Gilman, Charlotte Perkins 128
global financial crisis 142
globalization 189–90, 195
goal-directed behaviour 140–1
goods
  classification of 286
  and services, alleged differences between 439–41,
    442–3
  servitization and service-infusion 447–8
goods-dominant (G-D) logic 447, 459
  vs service-dominated (S-D) logic 21–3, 460–4,
    471–2, 473
Google 325, 347
governance 355
green marketing and sustainable marketing, difference
  between 505
'green washing' 497
Greenbury, Sir Richard 421–2
Grönroos, C. 15–16, 17, 26, 201, 204, 205, 323, 349,
  355, 464
groups, concept of 168–9
Gummesson, E. 14–15, 22, 25, 354–5, 438, 449, 450,
  455, 462
  LovelocK, C. and 439–41
Guttman, L. 480

Hahn, F.H. 124
Haire, M. 168
Halbert, M. 34, 47
Harley-Davidson study 187–9, 290
Hatch, E. 180–1
Health Belief model 483
health care (case studies,) 277–8, 452–4
health and safety issues 100–1
  infant formula marketing 185–6
Heide, J.B. 355
Henderson, B.D. 225, 228, 229
Hennig-Thurau, T. et al. 327, 329
heuristics 148
Hierarchy of Effects model 322
Hierarchy of Needs model 5–6, 9, 142
Hill, R.P. and Martin, K.D. 99

Hirschman, A.O. 120, 495
Hirschman, E.C. 308
  and Holbrook, M. 289, 307
historical evolution of marketing theory 33–5
  see also philosophy vs function of marketing
historical research 10–11, 60–3, 77–8
  1930-59 63–6
  1960-79 65–6
  1980-2009 66–75
  emerging discipline 75–7
  methods 67–9
Hodgson, G.M. 124, 494
Hoffman, D.L. and Novak, T.P. 321–2
Hollander, S.C. 66, 74–5, 76, 418, 419–20, 424, 427
  et al. 69
  and Rassuli, K. 67, 74–5
Honda study 239–40
Hong Kong
  McDonald's advertising campaign 192
  Vitasoy marketing 193–4
Horgan, J. 243
Hotchkiss, G.B. 64
household see family
Hovland, C.I. 154
Hugues, M. 322
Hunt, S. 32, 36, 37–9, 40, 44, 97–8, 114, 162, 210, 211,
  244, 480
  and Vitell, S. 94, 97–8, 103
Hunt, S.D. and Morgan, R.M./Morgan, R.M. and Hunt,
  S.D. 354, 357, 394–6
hybrid models of retail change 430
hypermedia computer-mediated environments
  321–2

IBM 448–9
idea generation in new product development (NPD)
  364–5
identity and symbolic consumption 296, 307
illegal exchange 175–6
Inacio, Emerson 331
individualism 495–6
  possessive 495, 500, 502
  self-interest 119–20, 502
  and socio-centrism 126–7
inductive realist model of theory generation 97–8
industrial marketing see business to business (B2B)
  markets
Industrial Marketing and Purchasing (IMP) study 49
industrial network approach 399
industrial organization (IO) approach 233
Industrial Revolution 8, 12, 437–8, 463, 493
  and Scientific Revolution 115
infant formula marketing 185–6

information and communication technology (ICT) 318–19
  adoption behaviour categories 253–4, *258*, 369
  and consumer power 174
  development of thought on marketing
      communications 320–4
  digital, multichannel and social media 326–31
    brand communities 301
    'electronic word-of-mouth' (eWOM) research 328–9
    Hummel (case study) 332–9
    impact of 417, 451
    multichannel decision making research 329–30
    online communities research 326–7
    return on investment, metrics and measurement
        research 330–1
    social commerce/social shopping research 327–8
    stage of development 324–5
  extension of 4 Ps classification 213–14
  network thinking 172–3
  new product development (NPD) 375
  online retailing 423–4
  theorizing 340–1
  see also data; database analysis; service science
information search in decision making 146, 147–8
infrastructure 450–1
innovation networks 381–2
innovation strategy 374–5
innovators 369, 472–3
institutionalist approach 121, 124
institutions
  and ecosystems 460, 470–1
  emergence of marketing institutions 11, 13
  primacy of 126
  private property 494–5
  role in value co-creation 472–3
  social 169
integrated marketing communication (IMC) 323
inter-cultural negotiations 183
inter-firm rivalry 429–30
internal marketing 446
International/Industrial Marketing and Purchasing (IMP)
    project 354
internet
  extension of 4Ps classification 213–14
  see also information and communication technology
      (ICT)
intersubjectivity/objectivity 37–8, 39–40
involvement: construct, types and processes 146–8
IPAT/STIRPAT equations 502–5
iteration in new product development (NPD) 370–1

Japan
  motorcycle industry 187–8, 239–40
  Proctor & Gamble (P&G) 183–5

Johnson, B.T. and Eagly, A.H. 146
Jones, D.G.B. 68, 69
  et al. 62–3, 67
  and Monieson, D.D. 74
  and Richardson, A. 73
  and Shaw, E./Shaw, E. and Jones, D.G.B. 62–3, 67,
      72, 74
  Tadajewski, M. and 75, 77
journals
  consumer research 286, 290, 291–2, 310
    content analysis *see under* consumer behaviour
        research
  digital marketing 325
  ethical marketing 91, 92–8, 100, 101
  historical research reviews 62–4, 67–8, 69, 72,
      77–8
  Journal of Marketing (JM) 36, 38, 46, 62, 63–4, 68,
      72, 94, 99, 446–7
  new product development 362, 363
'just noticeable difference' (JND) 145

Keith, R.J. 10, 73–4
Keller, K.L. 347, 348
Kerin, R. 36, 38, 47, 72
Keynes, J.M. 506
Kick it Over campaign 126
knowledge
  and future of marketing theory 47–8
  tacit and explicit 451, 456
Knox, S. and Walker, D. 150–1
Korten, D. 125
Kotler, P. 13–14, 25–6, 200–1, 204, 212–13, 268, 269,
    499–500, 505
Kuhn, T. 33–7, 38–9, 404

Laczniak, G.R. 94, 100
  and Murphy, P.E. 91–2, 94–5, 97
  Santos, N.J.C. and 95, 96, 101, 102
laggards 254
Lambkin, M. and Day, G. 236
Laswell, H. 154
launch: new product development (NPD) 368–9
Lauterborn, B. 213
Lavidge, R.J. and Steiner, G.A. 322
Lehman, D.R. and Jocz, K.E. 33–4
Leiss, W. 493, 494
Lepitak, S. 328
Levitt, T. 13–14, 189–90, 195, 201, 424
  'marketing myopia' 9–10, 27, 462
Lewin, K. 32, 139–40, 480, 485
lexicographic rule 148
liberating paradigm 40
lifestyles 170, 295

localization 446
  and standardization, balance between 191–2
Locke, J. 494, 495, 496, 501–2
logical empiricist paradigm 39, 40
Lovelock, C. and Gummesson, E. 439–41
Lowrey, T.M. et al. 144
Luca, R.N. and Suggs, L.S. 481, 483
Lusch, R.F. *see* Vargo, S.L.; Webster, F.E. Jr.
luxury goods retailing 423, 424

McAlexander, J.H.
  et al. 300
  Shouten, J.W. and 171, 290
McCarthy, E.J. 13–14, 211–12, 220
McDonagh, P. and Prothero, A. 496–7, 504
McDonalds 191–2
McGoldrick, P.J. 420, 425, 426, 427, 429
McInnes, W. 114
MacInnis, D.J. and Folkes, V.S. 288–9
Maclaran, P. et al. 33, 54
McNair, M.P. 418–19
macro-micro approach 262, 268
  energy market (case study) 263–7
Maglio, P. and Spohrer, J. 449
Malcolm Baldridge National Quality Award, US 443
management role in new product development (NPD) 377
managerial marketing 25
managerial technology 116, 117
Marion, G. 14–15
market attractiveness–business strength model *see*
  directional policy matrix (DPM)
market growth/market share matrix 299
market segmentation
  approaches 261–8
  benefits of 259–61
  case studies
    energy market 263–7
    NHS Change4Life 277–8
    Teleco (mobile phone company) 254–9, 272–3
  customers' characteristics 252–3
  definitions of 253
  importance of 259
  latest developments in 276–9
  operational danger in undertaking 274–6
  and positioning 234–6
  segment characteristics 268–9
  segment profiles 253–4, *258*
  social marketing 277–8, 487–8
  summary 279–80
  targeting approaches 269–74
market share
  market growth matrix 299
  and return on investment (ROI) analysis 238, 239

market-based relationship marketing (RM) 393–6
market-oriented organization 20–1
marketing, definitions of 18–20
marketing communications *see* information and
  communication technology (ICT)
marketing ethics 90–2
  base of pyramid 101–2
  definition of 91
  digital marketing 331
  health and safety issues 100–1
  research 98–9
    future directions 99
    suggestions for conducting 102–3
  sustainable marketing 100
  theoretical focus 92–8
marketing institutions, emergence of 11, 13
marketing management school 10, 13–14
  European perspective 14–18
marketing mix
  classifications
    functional 214–15, *216, 217*
    mnemonic 210–14
  functions, instruments and effects 205–10
    primary vs secondary 205–7
    strategic vs tactical instruments and effects
      209–10
    wide range of effects 208–9
  metaphor and concept
    criticism of 215–20
    nature and scope of 202–5
  and neuroscience 310
  origin and background 199–202
  and relational approaches 444–5
  summary 220–1
  see also 4 Ps classification
'marketing as practice' 50
marketing processes/orientation 243–4
Marketing Science Institute (MSI) 33–4, 362
marketing strategy
  codification of analysis 228–31
    five forces 229–30
    four contexts 229
    rules for success amid diversity 230–1
    three strategies 228–9
  competition models 231–3
    comparison 233
    evolutionary ecological analogies 232
    game theory 231–2
  customers, competitors and channels (3 Cs approach)
    226–8
  evolving differentiation 233–6
    in space 234–6
    in time 236

marketing strategy *cont.*
  formulation to implementation 225–6
  nature of competitive market environment 226
  processes, people and purpose 240–4
    emergent/enacted environments 242–3
    marketing processes/orientation 243–4
    markets as networks 240–1, 242–3
    relationship marketing (RM) 227–8, 241–2
  research
    case study-based 237, 239–40
    database 237, 238, 239
    key informant surveys 243–4
    limits and problems of application 245–6
    principles of competitive process 237
  resource advantage, co-evolution and agent-based
      modelling 244–5
marketing theory
  future of 47–54
    alternative approaches 52–4
    'marketing as practice' 50
    networks and relationships 49
    new consumer theories 50–2
    service-dominant logic 48
  historical evolution of 33–5
  problems with 41–7
    attention-seeking and memorable approaches 44–5
    fast-moving current generalization 41–2
    impact on practice 45–7
    influence of fashion 42–3
    quantitative measures 43–4
  role of 31–3
  as science 35–41
marketplace equity, theory of 355–8
Marketplace Literacy Project 102
markets-as-networks 240–1, 242–3, 398–400
Markham, S.K. and Lee, H. (PDMA) 368, 370, 373,
    374–5, 377, 378
Marks & Spencer 420–3
Marx, K. 501
Maslow, A. 5–6, 9, 142
mass assembly 10
mass consumption 8–9
mass marketing 165
Mathieu, Marc 319
measurement
  in advertising 322
  brand equity 347, 352
  communication technology investments 330–1
  financial valuation 353, 357
  in research 43–4
'megamarketing', concept of 212–13
memorable approaches 44–5

mentoring 276
Michel, S. et al. 362
Mick, D.G. 37, 302, 308
  et al. 27
Mickwitz, G. 16
'mid-life crisis' of marketing 20–3
Mintzberg, H. 225–6, 240, 242
mobile devices 323–4, 331, 415–16, 417
mobile phone company 253–4
  case study 254–9, 272–3
Möller, K. 218, 388, 389, 391, 392, 394, 398, 401
  et al. 53
  and Halinen, A. 388, 389, 390–1, 392
Montoya-Weiss, M.
  and Calantone, R.J. 373
  and O'Driscoll, T. 366
Moore, E. 101
moral commitments 123
Morgan, G. 39, 47
Morgan, R.M. and Hunt, S.D./Hunt, S.D. and Morgan,
    R.M. 354, 357, 394–6
motivation 140–2
multi-segment strategy 270
multi-theory perspective 49
multichannel marketing *see* information and
    communication technology (ICT)
multidisciplinary research
  consumer 288–9
  and multifunctional product development 370, 371,
    379, 380
multiplication of global business concept 446
Muniz, A.M. and O'Guinn, T.C. 169–70, 301
Murphy, P.E. 91, 99, 100, 102
  et al. 91–2, 95–6, 97, 102, 103
Myers, J.G. et al. 41, 45
'myopia' 9–10, 26, 27, 462

National Social Marketing Centre, UK 482–3
'needs' and 'wants', distinction between 5–6
neoclassical economics 112, 113–14, 117–18
  critique of 118–24, 502
neoclassical synthesis approach 121
neoliberalism 127
  as dominant social paradigm (DSP) 497–8, 500, 502,
    505–6
  globalized 125
network actor relationships 398–400
network management in new product development
    (NPD) 381–2
network model/paradigm 16, 17, 25
network theory 445–6, 450, 452
network-based brand equity 348

networks
  markets as 240–1, 242–3, 398–400
  and relationships 49, 52, 166, 172–3, 354–5, 436,
    449–50
  see also entries beginning relational; relationship
neuroscience 309–11
Nevett, T.R. 42, 69–70
  Fullerton, R.A. and 70
new consumer theories 50–2
new marketing paradigm 23–6
new product development (NPD) 361–2
  critique of process models 269–73
    inclusion of third parties 372–3
    iteration and cross-functional development 370–1
    related strands of development 371–2
  models 363–9
    business analysis 366–7
    commercialization or launch 368–9
    concept development and evaluation 366
    idea generation 364–5
    product development and testing 367
    screening 365–6
    test marketing 367–8
  network management 381–2
  process, people and management interrelationships
    379–80
  success/failure factors 373–82
    operational level 377–9
    strategic level 374–7
new service marketing 435–6
  development of 436–7
  drivers of 446–51
    connecting 451–5
  future of 455–6
  goods and services, alleged differences between
    439–41, 442–3
  marketing mix and relational approaches 444–5
  organizational issues 445–6
  patient care (case study) 452–4
  quality, satisfaction, excellence, value and
    productivity 441–4
  service sector growth and categories 437–9
NHS Change4Life (case study) 277–8
niche marketing 188
non-cyclical theories of retail change 428–30
norms, concept of 167–8

obesity
  and consumer perception 145
  and marketing ethics 100–1
  and social marketing 484
objectivity/intersubjectivity 37–8, 39–40

Okhuysen, G. and Bonardi, J. 390, 402
online communities research 326–7
online retailing 423–4
operand and operant resources 21–2, 448, 471
opinion-leaders 175
organizations
  industrial organization (IO) approach 233
  market-oriented 20–1
  new service marketing 445–6
  sustainable strategy 497
'organized behaviour system' 163
outside experts 275
ownership/non-ownership of services and goods 441

'parallel processing' 372
parameter theory 16
Parsons, R. 319
part-time marketers (PTMs)/full-time marketers
  (FTMs) 446
perception 143–5
performativity/performative approach 50, 51
perishability/non-perishability in services and
  goods 440
persuasion 154–6
  'megamarketing' concept 212–13
Peters, T.J. and Waterman, R.H. 225, 239
Petty, R.E. and Cacioppo, J.T./Cacioppo, J.T. and
  Petty, R.E. 139, 154, 155
philosophy vs function of marketing 3–4, 28
  definitions of marketing 18–20
  exchange and economic growth 5–9
  marketing management school 10, 13–14
    European perspective 14–18
  'mid-life crisis' 20–3
  new marketing paradigm 23–6
  rediscovery of marketing 9–13, 26–7
PIMS (Profit Implications of Marketing Strategy)
  database 238
Pioch, E.A. and Schmidt, R.A. 429, 430
pluralism 40
Polanyi, K. 162–3
political economy/classical school 117, 119, 397
political philosophy 494–5
political science 116
Pollay, R.W. 70
Porter, M.E. 225, 228–9
possessive individualism 495, 500, 502
power 173–4, 213
practice 50, 51
  lack of impact of marketing theory 45–7
'practice theory' 47
pragmatism 456

Prahalad, C.K. 101–2
Preece, J. and Maloney-Krichmar, D. 326
private property 494–5, 496, 502
problem recognition in decision making 146
'process concurrency' 372
process-based brand equity 347–8
Proctor & Gamble (P&G) 182, 183–5
product advantage 376, 380
product conception function 201
product development and testing 367
product differentiation 376
product life cycle (PLC) 236, 424
Product Development and Management Association *see* Markham, S.K. and Lee, H. (PDMA)
production-sales-marketing eras 10–12, 13
productivity and profitability 443–4
project teams 274
promises framework: service-based brand equity 349–50
promotional mix/instruments 209–10
protection motivation theory 142
psychology 116, 137–8
    attitudes 149–54
    behavioural economics 121–2
    and consumer research 288, 289–91, 293–5
    decision making 145–9
    as discipline 138–40
    future applications 156
    motivation 140–2
    perception 143–5
    persuasion 154–6
    and social marketing 483–4

qualitative-only 'accident' approach 262, *263*, 268
quality, service 441–2
quantitative and qualitative evaluation 43–4

Rapaport, A. 353
realism/relativism debate 37–8, 40
rediscovery of marketing 9–13, 26–7
reference groups 168–9
reformation of market model 124
Reibstein, D.J. et al. et al. 43, 46
relational approaches in new service marketing 444–5, 449–55
relational and experiential context of brand equity 347–8
relational and intellectual market-based assets 356
relationship marketing (RM) 17, 20, 28
    and marketing ethics 95–7
    and marketing mix 204–5
    and marketing strategy 227–8, 241–2
    and services marketing 436–7

relationship marketing (RM) and business networks (BN) research
    core differences *403*
    roots and principles of meta-theoretical analysis 388–90
    summary 402–5
    theoretical mapping 390–1
        channel systems and networks-based RM 396–402
        developing future agenda 405–9
        exchange continuum 391–3
        market-based relationship marketing 393–6
relationships
    power and conflict 172–4
    see also entries beginning network
research
    definitions of marketing 18–21
    importance of theory for 31–2, 33–4, 37–8, 45
    measurement in 43–4
    myopic focus 26, 27
    see also specific topics
reseller equity 350–1
resource advantage 244
resource allocation 261, 269–70
resource dependency theory 399
resource integrating actors 466, 468–9
resource and staff reallocation 274–6
resources, operand and operant 21–2, 448, 471
Retail Accordion 427–8
retail change theories 418
    combination models 430
    cyclical 418–28
    non-cyclical 428–30
    shopping for 416–18
Retail Life Cycle 424–7
'Rethinking Economics' group 128–9
return on investment (ROI)
    brand resource 346
    and market share analysis 238, 239
    metrics and measurement research 330–1
Richardson, A. 76–7
    Jones, D.G.B. and 73
risk acceptance 376–7
Robinson, Joan 128
Rogers, R.W. 142
role, concept of 166–7
Rostow, W.W. 6–7, 8–9
Routh, G. 121
Rust, R.T. et al. 352

Sachs, W. 131
Samuelson, P.A. 23, 118
Santos, N.J.C. and Laczniak, G.R. 95, 96, 101, 102
satisficing strategy 148

Savitt, R. 42, 67–8
schools of marketing thought 74, 75
Schramm, W. 320
Schulz, D. 323
    et al. 323
Schumacher, E.F. 129, 200
Schwartz, G. 65–6
science
    marketing theory as 35–41
    neuroscience 309–11
    social marketing as 485–9
    and technology 493–4
Scientific Revolution 115
screening of ideas 365–6
self-concept 150–1
self-interest 119–20, 502
sensory information/stimulation 143–5
separability/inseparability of services and goods 440
service brand–relationship–value triangle 349
service encounter 436
service market segmentation 262
service marketing see new service marketing
service science 448–9, 451–5
service-based brand equity 348–50, 355–6
service-dominant (S-D) logic 22, 48, 437, 458–9, 473
    complexity of markets and society 459–60
    four axioms of 465–6
    in new service marketing 446–8, 451–5
    possibilities for marketing and innovation 471–3
    systemic and institutional nature of value 470–1
    transcending nature of 464–70
    vs goods-dominant (G-D) logic 21–3, 460–4,
        471–2, 473
Shapiro, S. and Doody, A.F. 66
Shaw, E. 73
    and Jones, D.G.B./Jones, D.G.B and Shaw, E. 62–3,
        67, 72, 74
Shaw, R. and Merrick, D. 331
Sheth, J.N.
    Cunningham, W. and 42
    et al. 74, 116, 118, 289, 499–500, 502, 505
    and Parvatiyar, A. 499
Shiv, B. et al. 309–10
Shouten, J.W. and McAlexander, J.H. 171, 290
Simon, H.A. 121, 243
single- and multi-segment strategy 270
Smith, A. 7–8, 23, 113, 117, 120, 121–2, 124, 463–4, 492,
        493, 494, 495, 496, 502
'social business' 27
social capital 173
social change 174–5
social class 170, 295

social cognition theory 304–6
social commerce/social shopping research 327–8
social ecology models 484
social exchange theory (SET) 395, 397, 398, 399
social marketing 252–3, 277, 289
    characteristics of 485–7
    and commercial marketing concepts 488
    definitions of theory 479–81
    extending theoretical base 484–5
    NHS Change4Life (case study) 277–8
    and psychological theories 483–4
    as scientific discipline 485–9
    theory and definitions of 481–3
social media see information and communication
        technology (ICT)
social nature of marketing 117
social organization 164
social psychology 116
socialization 174
socio-political paradigm 39
sociology 116, 160–2, 163, 295–6
    borrowing and influence 164–6, 175–6
    individuals, groups and larger society 166–71
    learning and change 174–5
    marketing as exchange 162–3
        illegal 175–6
    relationships, power and conflict 172–4
    social organization 164
    two-step model of communication 321
sophisticated careerists 254
speed of NPD process 378–9, 380
Srivastava, R.K. et al. 345, 350–1, 352–4, 356, 357
Stage-Gate model of NPD 364, 371
Stages of Economic Growth model 6–7, 8–9
stakeholder theory 97
standardization and localization, balance between
        191–2
status, concept of 167
Steffen, A. 125
Stiglitz, J.E. 128, 506
STIRPAT equation 503–5
Strasser, S. 70–1
strategic nets 398
    focal networks and 400–2
'structuration' 243
sub-culture, concept of 171
subjective world paradigm 39
Subsistence Marketplaces movement 102
supermarkets: inter-firm rivalry 429
supply chains see channel(s)
sustainability of globalized neoliberal capitalism 125–6
sustainable development of ecotourism 186–7

sustainable marketing 100, 492–3
  contemporary research 496–8
  philosophical antecedents 493–6
    economic philosophy 495–6
    political philosophy 494–5
    science and technology 493–4
  possible transition 498–505
    assessment of changes 500
    calls for sustainability 498–9
    contradictions in capitalist system 501–2
    IPAT/STIRPAT equations 502–5
  summary and conclusion 505–6
symbolic consumption, identity and 296, 307
synergy in new product development (NPD) 376
systems theory 450

tacit and explicit knowledge 451, 456
Tadajewski, M. 73–4
  and Jones, D.G.B. 75, 77
tangibility/intangibility of services and goods 439–40
target population studies 299–300
targeting approaches 269–74
task specialization and division of labour 6–8, 9
technology *see* information and communication
    technology (ICT)
Tedlow, R. 70–1
Teleco (case study) 254–9, 272–3
test marketing 367–8
Theodorson, S. and Theodorson, A. 320–1
Theory of Planned Behaviour 303–4, 483, 485
third parties in new product development (NPD)
    372–3, 379
3 Cs approach 226–8
three-tiered marketing model 23–5
top management role 377
trading up 418–19, 420
transaction cost economics 124, 395, 396–7, 398, 399
transformative consumer research 308, *309*
tricomponent theory of attitudes 149
Truong, V.D. 481, 484
Tuten, T. and Solomon, M. 325
two-step model of communication 321

UNESCO 186–7

Vaile, R. 35
value
  determined by beneficiary 466
  nature of 22, 23
  new services marketing 443
value and brand equity 345–6
value chain 229–30

value nets *see* strategic nets
value-in-context 443, 469
value-in-exchange 461, 463–4
value-in-use 461, 469
van den Bulte, C. 216–18, 219–20
  see also van Waterschoot, W.
van Waterschoot, W. 206–7, 210
  and De Haes, J. 199, 200, 201, 202–3, 214, 220
  and van den Bulte, C. 202, 203, 204, 207, 209–10,
    214–15
Vargo, S.L.
  et al. 443, 463, 470, 471
  and Lusch, R.F. 4, 21–2, 48, 95, 241, 345, 348–9, 357,
    387, 446–7, 458–75
  Lusch, R.F. and 48, 462–3, 465, 466, 470
Veblen, T. 124, 128, 141
Venkatesh, A. 44, 46
Viswanathan, M. et al. 102
Vitell, S.
  et al. 98
  Hunt, S. and 94, 97–8, 103
Vogt, W.P. 480

Waite, Jeremy 328
Wales, H. 64, 66
'wants' and 'needs', distinction between 5–6
web-marketing mix (4 S classification) 213
Webber, R. and Stroud, D. 325
Weber, M. 173
Weber's law 145
Webster, F.E. Jr. 14, 49
  et al. 345
  and Lusch, R.F. 26–7
welfare economics 124
Wells, W. 293, 300
Wensley, R. 47, 235, 244
Wheel of Retailing 418–20
  Marks & Spencer 420–3
  and non-conforming formats 423–4
Whetton, D.A. 479, 481
Wind, J.
  et al. 308
  and Mahajan, V. 381
Wind, Y. 51–2
Witkowski, T.H. 78
Woolworths 425–6
word-of-mouth and eWOM 328–9
workshops 275

Zaltman, G.
  et al. 50
  and Wallendorf, M. 176